Lecture Notes in Artificial Intelligence   12468

Subseries of Lecture Notes in Computer Science

More information about this series at http://www.springer.com/series/1244

Lourdes Martínez-Villaseñor ·
Oscar Herrera-Alcántara ·
Hiram Ponce · Félix A. Castro-Espinoza (Eds.)

Advances in Soft Computing

19th Mexican International Conference
on Artificial Intelligence, MICAI 2020
Mexico City, Mexico, October 12–17, 2020
Proceedings, Part I

 Springer

Editors
Lourdes Martínez-Villaseñor (iD)
Facultad de Ingeniería
Universidad Panamericana
Mexico City, Mexico

Hiram Ponce (iD)
Facultad de Ingeniería
Universidad Panamericana
Mexico City, Mexico

Oscar Herrera-Alcántara (iD)
Universidad Autónoma Metropolitana
Mexico City, Mexico

Félix A. Castro-Espinoza (iD)
Universidad Autónoma del Estado
de Hidalgo
Hidalgo, Mexico

ISSN 0302-9743 ISSN 1611-3349 (electronic)
Lecture Notes in Artificial Intelligence
ISBN 978-3-030-60883-5 ISBN 978-3-030-60884-2 (eBook)
https://doi.org/10.1007/978-3-030-60884-2

LNCS Sublibrary: SL7 – Artificial Intelligence

This Springer imprint is published by the registered company Springer Nature Switzerland AG
The registered company address is: Gewerbestrasse 11, 6330 Cham, Switzerland

Preface

The Mexican International Conference on Artificial Intelligence (MICAI) is a yearly international conference series that has been organized by the Mexican Society for Artificial Intelligence (SMIA) since 2000. MICAI is a major international artificial intelligence (AI) forum and the main event in the academic life of the country's growing AI community.

MICAI conferences publish high-quality papers in all areas of AI and its applications. The proceedings of the previous MICAI events have been published by Springer in its *Lecture Notes in Artificial Intelligence* (LNAI) series, vol. 1793, 2313, 2972, 3789, 4293, 4827, 5317, 5845, 6437, 6438, 7094, 7095, 7629, 7630, 8265, 8266, 8856, 8857, 9413, 9414, 10061, 10062, 10632, 10633, 11288, 11289, and 11835. Since its foundation in 2000, the conference has been growing in popularity and improving in quality.

The proceedings of MICAI 2020 are published in two volumes. The first volume, *Advances in Soft Computing*, contains 37 papers structured into three sections:

- Machine and Deep Learning
- Evolutionary and Metaheuristic Algorithms
- Soft Computing

The second volume, *Advances in Computational Intelligence*, contains 40 papers structured into three sections:

- Natural Language Processing
- Image Processing and Pattern Recognition
- Intelligent Applications and Robotics

The two-volume set will be of interest for researchers in all fields of AI, students specializing in related topics, and for the public in general interested in recent developments in AI.

The conference received for evaluation 186 submissions from 26 countries: Argentina, Armenia, Austria, Belgium, Brazil, Colombia, Cuba, Czech Republic, Ecuador, Finland, France, India, Ireland, Kazakhstan, Mexico, Nepal, Nigeria, Pakistan, Peru, Portugal, Russia, South Africa, Spain, Switzerland, Ukraine, and USA. From these submissions, 77 papers were selected for publication in these two volumes after a peer-reviewing process carried out by the International Program Committee. The acceptance rate was 41%.

The International Program Committee consisted of 152 experts from 16 countries: Australia, Brazil, Colombia, France, Greece, Ireland, Japan, Kazakhstan, Malaysia, Mexico, Philippines, Portugal, Russia, Spain, the UK, and the USA.

MICAI 2020 was honored by the presence of renowned experts who gave excellent keynote lectures:

- Ljiljana Trajkovic, Simon Fraser University, Canada
- Pedro Larrañaga, Technical University of Madrid, Spain

- Manuel Morales, University of Montreal, Canada
- Soujanya Poria, Singapore University of Technology and Design, Singapore
- Francisco Hiram Calvo Castro, CIC-IPN, Mexico

Four workshops were held jointly with the conference:

- The 13th Workshop on Intelligent Learning Environments (WILE 2020)
- The 13th Workshop of Hybrid Intelligent Systems (HIS 2020)
- The Second Workshop on New Trends in Computational Intelligence and Applications (CIAPP 2020)
- The 6th Workshop on Intelligent Decision Support Systems for Industry (WIDSSI 2020)

The authors of the following papers received the Best Paper Awards based on the paper's overall quality, significance, and originality of the reported results:

- First place: "An NSGA-III-based Multi-Objective Intelligent Autoscaler for Executing Engineering Applications in Cloud Infrastructures," by Virginia Yannibelli, Elina Pacini, David Monge, Cristian Mateos, and Guillermo Rodriguez (Argentina)
- Second place: "Speaker Identification using Entropygrams and Convolutional Neural Networks," by Antonio Camarena-Ibarrola, Karina Figueroa, and Jonathan García (Mexico)
- Third place: "Dissimilarity-Based Correlation of Movements and Events on Circular Scales of Space and Time," by Ildar Batyrshin, Nailya Kubysheva, and Valery Tarassov (Mexico/Russia)

We want to thank all the people involved in the organization of this conference: to the authors of the papers published in these two volumes – it is their research work that gives value proceedings – and to the organizers for their work. We thank to the reviewers for their great effort spent on reviewing the submissions, to the track chairs for their hard work, and to the Program and Organizing Committee members.

We are deeply grateful to the Universidad Panamericana for their warm hospitality of MICAI 2020. We would like to express our gratitude to Dr. Santiago García Álvarez, Rector of the Universidad Panamericana, Campus Mexico, Dr. Alejandro Ordoñez Torres, Director of the School of Engineering of the Universidad Panamericana, Campus Mexico, and Dr. Roberto González Ojeda, Secretary of Research at the School of Engineering.

The entire submission, reviewing, and selection process, as well as preparation of the proceedings, was supported by the EasyChair system (www.easychair.org). Last but not least, we are grateful to Springer for their patience and help in the preparation of these volumes.

October 2020   Lourdes Martínez-Villaseñor
                                                                 Oscar Herrera-Alcántara
                                                                            Hiram Ponce
                                                                 Félix A. Castro-Espinoza

Organization

MICAI 2020 was organized by the Mexican Society of Artificial Intelligence (SMIA, Sociedad Mexicana de Inteligencia Artificial) in collaboration with the Universidad Panamericana, the Universidad Autónoma del Estado de Hidalgo, and the Universidad Autónoma Metropolitana.

The MICAI series website is www.MICAI.org. The website of SMIA, is www.SMIA.mx. Contact options and additional information can be found on these websites.

Conference Committee

General Chair

Félix A. Castro Espinoza	Universidad Autónoma del Estado de Hidalgo, Mexico

Program Chairs

Lourdes Martínez-Villaseñor	Universidad Panamericana, Mexico
Oscar Herrera-Alcántara	Universidad Autónoma Metropolitana, Mexico

Workshop Chair

Noé Alejandro Castro Sánchez	Centro Nacional de Investigación y Desarrollo Tecnológico, Mexico

Tutorials Chair

Roberto Antonio Vózquez Espinoza de los Monteros	Universidad La Salle, Mexico

Doctoral Consortium Chairs

Miguel González Mendoza	Tecnolóogico de Monterrey, Mexico
Juan Martínez Miranda	CICESE Research Center, Mexico

Keynote Talks Chair

Sabino Miranda Jiménez	INFOTEC, Mexico

Publication Chair

Hiram Ponce	Universidad Panamericana, Mexico

Financial Chair

Oscar Herrera-Alcántara	Universidad Autónoma Metropolitana, Mexico

Grant Chair

Félix A. Castro Espinoza   Universidad Autónoma del Estado de Hidalgo, Mexico

Local Organizing Committee

Local Chair

Hiram Ponce   Universidad Panamericana, Mexico

Local Logistics Chairs

Lourdes   Universidad Panamericana, Mexico
   Martínez-Villaseñor
Karina Pérez Daniel   Universidad Panamericana, Mexico
León Palafox   Universidad Panamericana, Mexico

Finance Chairs

Hiram Ponce   Universidad Panamericana, Mexico
Lourdes   Universidad Panamericana, Mexico
   Martínez-Villaseñor

Publicity Chairs

Hiram Ponce   Universidad Panamericana, Mexico
Monserrat Rosas Libreros   Universidad Panamericana, Mexico

Track Chairs

Natural Language Processing

Grigori Sidorov   CIC-IPN, Mexico
Obdulia Pichardo Lagunas   CIC-IPN, Mexico

Machine Learning

Alexander Gelbukh   CIC-IPN, Mexico
Navonil Majumder   CIC-IPN, Mexico

Deep Learning

Pierre Baldi   University of California, Irvine, USA
Francisco Viveros Jiménez   Eficiencia Informativa, Mexico

Evolutionary and Metaheuristic Algorithms

Laura Cruz Reyes   Instituto Tecnológico de Ciudad Madero, Mexico
Roberto Antonio Vázquez   Universidad La Salle, Mexico
   Espinoza de los
   Monteros

Soft Computing

Ildar Batyrshin	CIC-IPN, Mexico
Miguel González Mendoza	Tecnológico de Monterrey, Mexico
Gilberto Ochoa Ruiz	Tecnológico de Monterrey, Mexico

Image Processing and Pattern Recognition

Heydy Castillejos	Universidad Autónoma del Estado de Hidalgo, Mexico
Francisco Hiram Calvo Castro	CIC-IPN, Mexico

Robotics

Luis Martín Torres Treviño	Universidad Autónoma de Nuevo León, Mexico
Eloísa García Canseco	Universidad Autónoma de Baja California, Mexico

Intelligent Applications and Social Network Analysis

Helena Gomez Adorno	IIMAS-UNAM, Mexico
Iris Iddaly Méndez Gurrola	Universidad Autónoma de Ciudad Juárez, Mexico

Other Artificial Intelligence Approaches

Nestor Velasco Bermeo	University College Dublin, Ireland
Gustavo Arroyo Figueroa	Instituto Nacional de Electricidad y Energías Limpias, Mexico

Program Committee

Antonio Marín Hernández	Universidad Veracruzana, Mexico
Juan Martínez Miranda	CICESE, Mexico
Iskander Akhmetov	IICT, Kazakhstan
José David Alanís Urquieta	Universidad Tecnológica de Puebla, Mexico
Miguel Ángel Alonso Arévalo	CICESE, Mexico
Giner Alor Hernandez	Instituto Tecnológico de Orizaba, Mexico
Maaz Amjad	CIC-IPN, Mexico
Erikssen Aquino	ITSSMT, Mexico
Segun Aroyehun	CIC-IPN, Mexico
Gustavo Arroyo Figueroa	Instituto Nacional de Electricidad y Energías Limpias, Mexico
Ignacio Arroyo-Fernández	Universidad Tecnológica de la Mixteca, Mexico
Pierre Baldi	University of California, Irvine, USA
Alejandro Israel Barranco Gutiérrez	Cátedras CONACYT, Instituto Tecnológico de Celaya, Mexico
Ramon Barraza	Universidad Autónoma de Ciudad Juárez, Mexico
Ari Yair Barrera-Animas	Tecnológico de Monterrey, Mexico
Rafael Batres	Tecnológico de Monterrey, Mexico
Ildar Batyrshin	CIC-IPN, Mexico

Gemma Bel-Enguix	UNAM, Mexico
Igor Bolshakov	Russian State University for the Humanities, Russia
Vadim Borisov	National Research University, MPEI, Russia
Alexander Bozhenyuk	Southern Federal University, Russia
Ramon F. Brena	Tecnológico de Monterrey, Mexico
Davide Buscaldi	LIPN, Université Sorbonne Paris Nord, France
Alan Calderón Velderrain	CICESE, Mexico
Francisco Hiram Calvo Castro	CIC-IPN, Mexico
Ruben Cariño Escobar	INR, Mexico
J. Víctor Carrera-Trejo	Instituto Nacional de Astrofísica, Óptica y Electrónica, Mexico
Heydy Castillejos	Universidad Autónoma del Estado de Hildago, Mexico
Norberto Castillo García	Instituto Tecnológico de Ciudad Madero, Mexico
Félix A. Castro Espinoza	Universidad Autónoma del Estado de Hildago, Mexico
Noé Alejandro Castro Sánchez	Centro Nacional de Investigación y Desarrollo Tecnológico, Mexico
Ofelia Cervantes	Universidad de las Américas Puebla, Mexico
Haruna Chiroma	Federal College of Education (Technical) Gombe, Nigeria
Nareli Cruz Cortés	CIC-IPN, Mexico
Laura Cruz-Reyes	Instituto Tecnologico de Ciudad Madero, Mexico
Andre de Carvalho	University of São Paulo, Brazil
Andrés Espinal	Universidad de Guanajuato, Mexico
Edgardo Manuel Felipe Riverón	Centro de Investigación en Computación, Instituto Politécnico Nacional, Mexico
Denis Filatov	Sceptica Scientific Ltd., UK
Dora-Luz Flores	Universidad Autónoma de Baja California, Mexico
Juan José Flores	Universidad Michoacana, Mexico
Leticia Flores-Pulido	Universidad Autónoma de Tlaxcala, Mexico
Roilhi Frajo Ibarra Hernández	CICESE, Mexico
Anilu Franco-Arcega	Instituto Nacional de Astrofísica, Óptica y Electrónica, Mexico
Gibrán Fuentes-Pineda	UNAM, Mexico
Sofía N. Galicia-Haro	UNAM, Mexico
Eloisa García	UABC, Mexico
Vicente García	Universidad Autónoma de Ciudad Juárez, Mexico
Alexander Gelbukh	CIC-IPN, Mexico
Salvador Godoy-Calderón	CIC-IPN, Mexico
Claudia Gómez	Instituto Tecnológico de Ciudad Madero, Mexico
Helena Gómez	UNAM, Mexico
Eduardo Gómez-Ramírez	Universidad La Salle, Mexico
Gabriel González	TecNM, CENIDET, Mexico
Pedro Pablo González	Universidad Autónoma Metropolitana, Mexico
José Ángel González Fraga	UABC, Mexico

Alicia Morales-Reyes	Instituto Nacional de Astrofísica, Óptica y Electrónica, Mexico
Ernesto Moya-Albor	Universidad Panamericana, Mexico
Dante Mújica-Vargas	CENIDET, Mexico
Masaki Murata	Tottori University, Japan
Antonio Neme	UNAM, Mexico
Cesar Núñez-Prado	IPN, Mexico
Gilberto Ochoa Ruiz	Tecnológico de Monterrey, Mexico
C. Alberto Ochoa-Zezatti	Universidad Autónoma de Ciudad Juárez, Mexico
José Carlos Ortiz-Bayliss	Tecnológico de Monterrey, Mexico
Ismael Osuna-Galán	Universidad Politécnica de Chiapas, Mexico
Sergio Padilla	UNAM, Mexico
Ivandré Paraboni	University of São Paulo, Brazil
Karina Ruby Pérez Daniel	Universidad Panamericana, Mexico
Obdulia Pichardo	UPIITA-IPN, Mexico
Garibaldi Pineda García	University of Sussex, UK
Hiram Ponce	Universidad Panamericana, Mexico
Mukesh Prasad	University of Technology Sydney, Australia
Tania Aglaé Ramírez Del Real	Universidad Politécnica de Aguascalientes, Mexico
Jorge Reyes	Universidad Autónoma de Yucatán, Mexico
José A. Reyes-Ortiz	Universidad Autónoma Metropolitana, Mexico
Elva Lilia Reynoso Jardón	Universidad Autónoma de Ciudad Juárez, Mexico
Gilberto Rivera-Zarate	Universidad Autónoma de Ciudad Juárez, Mexico
Ángel Rodríguez Liñan	Universidad Autónoma de Nuevo León, Mexico
Noel Enrique Rodríguez Maya	Instituto Tecnológico de Zitácuaro, Mexico
Katya Rodríguez-Vazquez	IIMAS-UNAM, Mexico
Alejandro Rosales	Tecnológico de Monterrey, Mexico
Horacio Rostro	Universidad de Guanajuato, Mexico
Ángel Sánchez	Universidad Veracruzana, Mexico
Antonio Sánchez	Texas Christian University, USA
Luis Humberto Sánchez Medel	ITO, Mexico
Romeo Sánchez Nigenda	Universidad Autónoma de Nuevo León, Mexico
Eddy Sánchez-De la Cruz	Instituto Tecnológico Superior de Misantla, Mexico
Christian Sánchez-Sánchez	Universidad Autónoma Metropolitana, Mexico
Guillermo Santamaría	CONACYT-INEEL, Mexico
Aurelio Alejandro Santiago Pineda	Universidad Politécnica de Altamira, Mexico
Gabriel Sepúlveda Cervantes	IPN, Mexico
Grigori Sidorov	CIC-IPN, Mexico
Rafaela Silva	Universidad Autónoma Metropolitana, Mexico
Efraín Solares Lachica	Autonomous University of Sinaloa, Mexico
Valery Solovyev	Kazan University, Russia

Merlin Teodosia Suárez	Center for Empathic Human-Computer Interactions, Philippines
Israel Tabárez	Tecnológico de Monterrey, Mexico
Eric S. Téllez	CONACYT-INFOTEC, Mexico
David Tinoco	UNAM, Mexico
Aurora Torres	Universidad Autónoma de Aguascalientes, Mexico
Luis Torres Treviño	Universidad Autónoma de Nuevo León, Mexico
Diego Uribe	Instituto Tecnológico de la Laguna, Mexico
José Valdez	CIC-IPN, Mexico
Genoveva Vargas Solar	CNRS-LIG-LAFMIA, France
Roberto Antonio Vázquez Espinoza de los Monteros	Universidad La Salle, Mexico
Nestor Velasco Bermeo	University College Dublin, Ireland
Yenny Villuendas Rey	CIDETEC, Mexico
Francisco Viveros Jiménez	Eficiencia Informativa, Mexico
Fernando Von Borstel	Cibnor, Mexico
Saúl Zapotecas Martínez	Universidad Autónoma Metropolitana, Mexico
Alisa Zhila	NTENT, USA
Miguel Ángel Zúñiga García	Instituto Nacional de Electricidad y Energías Limpias, Mexico

Additional Reviewers

Alan Arturo Calderó-Velderrain	José Eduardo Valdez Rodríguez
Alberto Iturbe	Kazuhiro Takeuchi
Ángel Rodríguez	Marco Sotelo-Figueroa
Erick Ordaz	María Dolores Torres
Erik Ricardo Palacios Garza	Mario Aguilera
Fernando Von Borstel	Miguel Alonso
Gabriel Sepúlveda-Cervantes	Roilhi Frajo Ibarra Hernández
Hector-Gabriel Acosta-Mesa	Romeo Sanchez Nigenda
Joaquín Gutiérrez	Saúl Domínguez-Isidro
Jorge Alberto Soria-Alcaraz	Teodoro Macías-Escobar
José A. González-Fraga	Yasushi Tsubota

Contents – Part I

Evolutionary and Metaheuristic Algorithms

Best Paper Award, First Place

Soft Computing

Contents – Part II

Natural Language Processing

Best Paper Award, Third Place

Image Processing and Pattern Recognition

Intelligent Applications and Robotics

Machine and Deep Learning

LSTM Classification under Changes in Sequences Order

Edgar Ek-Chacón[1]([✉]) [iD] and Erik Molino-Minero-Re[2]([✉]) [iD]

[1] Postgraduate Program in Computer Science and Engineering, IIMAS-Merida,
Universidad Nacional Autonoma de Mexico, Merida, Yuc., Mexico
ekchacon89@gmail.com

[2] IIMAS-Merida, Universidad Nacional Autonoma de Mexico, Merida, Yuc., Mexico
erik.molino@iimas.unam.mx

Abstract. Recurrent Neural Networks (RNNs) have been widely used for sequences analysis and classification. Generally, the sequences are a set of samples following a specific order, like a time-based process or a structured dataset. This type of neural network is very efficient for exploring sequences patterns and other relevant features highlighting temporal behavior and dependencies. This is accomplished because the information loops within the different stages of the network, and in this process, it remembers and tracks features at different segments of the data. In this work, we are interested in exploring how an RNN based on Long-Short Term Memory (LSTM) units behaves in a classification problem when the dataset of sequences are organized in different order and lengths. That is, the same information is presented to the network, but the order of the samples within the sequences and the length of the sequences are different in each experiment. In order to evaluate this effect, we used five datasets of grayscale images of 28×28 pixels (MNIST, MNIST-C, notMNIST, FashionMNIST, and Sign Language MNIST). For every experiment, we segmented the images in different sizes and orders and built a set of sequences consisting of vectors of pixels organized following three different rules, and on each case, we set the sequences to a specifically fixed length. The results bring to light that good accuracies can be achieved for different sequences configurations. We considered the 28×28 configuration as the baseline for reference. We found that this baseline generally leads to high accuracies, but for some datasets it is not the best one. We believe that this study may be useful for video tagging and for general image description.

Keywords: Recurrent Neural Network · LSTM network · Sequences order

1 Introduction

Recurrent Neural Networks are commonly used to analyze sequential data, as time-series, language, genomes, etc., but many other engineering problems can

© Springer Nature Switzerland AG 2020
L. Martínez-Villaseñor et al. (Eds.): MICAI 2020, LNAI 12468, pp. 3–20, 2020.
https://doi.org/10.1007/978-3-030-60884-2_1

be formulated as sequential data [7, 22]. For example, in classification tasks, images are normally treated as two or more dimensional data [8], but they can be re-organized as sequences by vectorizing the images to build vectors of pixels of certain length and order, and the RNNs have shown good results classifying grayscale images [1, 2, 21, 27].

We are interested in understanding if the order within the sequences, and their length, have an effect on the overall performance of the RNNs, particularly when they are based on LSTM units. This question maybe relevant for data setup procedures, and it may be useful for video tagging and for general image description.

There are different reports in the literature that use RNNs and related architectures for analysing images as sequences, as shown in Table 1, where accuracies of several neural networks are presented, as the LSTMs, the Gated Recurrent Units (GRU), the Temporal Convolutional Network (TCN), and the Skip-Connected LSTM Identity (SC-LSTM-I). The TCN is a kind of Convolutional Network with a temporal approach that treat sequences as the RNNs does. The SC-LSTM-I enhances the information flow between two time steps with a wide range distance in an LSTM unit. Also, they have shown good performances for grayscale images classification. The architectures SC-LSTM-I, GRU, and TCN were tested with sequences of 784 samples only; in [2] and [21], both used LSTM networks but with different architectures, the former was tested with sequences of 28 samples only, and the latter tested sequences with ranges between 140 and 420 samples.

These reports explore different ways to improve the performance of recurrent neural networks (mostly LSTM-based). The SC-LSTM-I approach works by adding more connections between the time steps for modeling long sequences (P-MNIST's 784 length sequences). On [2], another approach is reported for exploring the effect on performance of different architectures and hyper-parameters, and the networks were trained on fixed lengths of 28 pixels from the MNIST's dataset. On the other hand, the work of Schak [21] they explored the effect of catastrophic forgetting (especially with high-dimensional sequences length), that is, when a deep recurrent LSTM losses its knowledge of a previous training by retraining it with new samples. Likewise, on [1] another proposal for dealing with sequence modeling tasks, such as convolutional network architecture with temporal approach (TCN), is explored.

Table 1. State of the art of LSTMs with grayscale image datasets.

Method	Dataset	Accuracy
SC-LSTM-I [27]	P-MNIST	94.80%
LSTM [2]	MNIST	99.27%
LSTM [21]	Devanagari	99.40%
GRU [1]	Seq. MNIST	96.20%
TCN [1]	Seq. MNIST	99.00%

In this work, we present a procedure to evaluate the classification accuracy of LSTM networks when trained with different image datasets, where images are organized as sequences. In order to build these sequences, we follow three different rules to establish the order of the pixels and the lengths of the vectors. The datasets are the handwritten digits MNIST [12], the MNIST-Corrupted [14], notMNIST [3], FashionMNIST [28], and Sign Language MNIST [23]. The combination of different lengths, order of pixels within the sequences and the datasets yield a total of 180 experiments.

This work is organized as follows. Section 2 describes how sequential data was built from grayscale images, and the theory behind RNN and LSTM networks. In Sect. 3, the methodology for training and assessing the accuracy is described. The experiments setup is detailed in Sect. 4, and the results and discussion are in Sect. 5. Final Section corresponds to the conclusions.

2   RNN and LSTM Framework

Sequential data is a type of data where the order of the samples or bits of information has significance. A common place where this can be seen is in log data produced by servers or sensors, which generate what is known as time-series data. Time-series data may be defined as any data that has a set of samples each coupled with a time-stamp. These samples, ordered chronologically, track a process activity over time [17]. Examples of sequential data can be found in many fields science and engineering, as natural language processing, music analysis, weather forecasting, or genome characterization.

RNNs are a type of machine learning algorithms designed to handle sequenced data (signals or time series) [9], and are able to process samples or symbols taking into account the order in which they appear [16,18].

A typical recurrent neural network receives sequences as shown in Fig. 1a, where the diagram at the left shows the iterative flow of data, here the RNN processes the input x to yield an output o at time step t. The right diagram shows the unfolded structure of the same network, which highlights how data is processed through time, that is, first an input is processed at time step $t - 1$, then another at time step t and finally, another at time step $t + 1$. Each input is a sequence or vector, whose length represent the number of features.

2.1   Long Short-Term Memory

Long Short-Term Memory (LSTM) architecture is essentially a recurrent neural network model and designed to deal with vanishing gradient problem [10]. Its ability to successfully learn on data with long range temporal dependencies makes it a natural choice for sequential data problems due to the considerable time lag between the inputs and their corresponding outputs [25].

The learning ability is due its internal component cell state c^t that behaves like a memory. Its reading or modifying is controlled by three internal sigmoidal gates, the input gate i^t, the output gate o^t and the forget gate f^t, Fig. 1b.

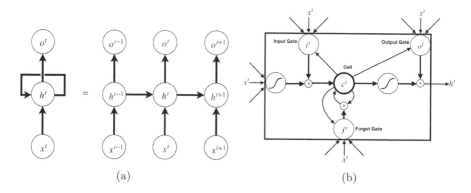

Fig. 1. (a) Basic diagram of a Recurrent Neural Network. At left, a compact representation of a RNN which processes the input x through state h, and yields the output o at time step t. At right, the same network with an unfolded view through time, it shows the flow from input at h^{t-1} to h^t. (b) LSTM unit.

At each time step t the LSTM unit receives the input x^t and the output h^{t-1} from the previous time step and the cell state c^t is updated and we have the output h^t as follows:

$$i^t = \sigma(W^{xi}x^t + W^{hi}h^{t-1} + W^{ci}c^{t-1} + b^i), \tag{1}$$

$$f^t = \sigma(W^{xf}x^t + W^{hf}h^{t-1} + W^{cf}c^{t-1} + b^f), \tag{2}$$

$$c^t = f^t c^{t-1} + i^t \tanh(W^{xc}x^t + W^{hc}h^{t-1}), \tag{3}$$

$$o^t = \sigma(W^{xo}x^t + W^{ho}h^{t-1} + W^{co}c^t + b^o), \tag{4}$$

$$h^t = o^t \tanh(c^t), \tag{5}$$

where σ and $\tanh$ are the logistic sigmoid and the hyperbolic tangent functions, respectively. The weight matrices are self-descriptive, for example, W^{hi} is the hidden-input gate matrix, W^{xo} is the input-output gate matrix, etc. All the matrices are dense, except the weight matrices $W^{c\bullet}$ from the cell state, which are diagonal. And b with subscripts i, f, c and o, are the bias for input gate, forget gate, cell state and output gate.

After all, from the LSTM unit we can have a final output

$$y^t = \phi(W^{hy}h^t + b^y), \tag{6}$$

where W^{hy} is the hidden-output matrix and b^y the bias term. And the output y can be one or more units, whose values are computed with a function activation ϕ at time step t. Also, the output y can be returned at each time step t or till the last time step [10,18,24].

An LSTM architecture can be trained by a supervised or unsupervised learning. In this work, we use supervised learning, once we have the output y of the model with a softmax activation function, we use cross-entropy [17] to calculate the error between the predicted label and the target label. And to minimize this error, we use Adam method for stochastic optimization [11].

2.2 Conditional Independence Test

Two random variables X and Y are conditionally independent given a third variable Z if and only if $P(X, Y|Z) = P(X|Z)P(Y|Z)$. We denote this relationship by $X \perp\!\!\!\perp Y|Z$, and its negation, the case of conditional dependence, by $X \not\!\perp\!\!\!\perp Y|Z$.

Conditional Independence Test (CIT) consists of testing or measuring for independence between X and Y given Z, or more generally, given the values of set of further variables [4]. CIT is the most challenging task for causal discovery. In time series causal discovery's goal is to statistically reliably estimate causal links between variables, including their time lags.

PCMCI is a causal discovery method that allows accommodating a large variety of conditional independence tests. It consists of a Markov discovery algorithm, the PC algorithm, and the momentary conditional independence (MCI) [20].

2.3 Entropy

In information theory, entropy (or Shannon Entropy) is a measure of unpredictability or chaos [13]. An example can be when a woman is pregnant and the baby's gender is wanted to know. There is a probability of 50% to guess the gender correctly. However, during the pregnancy an ultrasound analysis can help to determine the gender with a better accuracy, over time the accuracy can improve because the fetus development. This accuracy gain, or information gain, is there because uncertainty or entropy drops [5].

The entropy of a random variable X with a probability mass function $p(x)$ is defined by

$$H(X) = -\sum_{x} p(x) log_2 p(x), \tag{7}$$

where we use base 2 logarithms. The entropy will then be measured in bits. The entropy is a measure of the average uncertainty in the random variable. It is the number of bits on average required to describe the random variable [6].

2.4 Adam Optimizer Method

Adam optimizer method consists of two important parts, the adaptive learning rate (from AdaGrad optimizer) and the momentum method, these parts are used by RMSProp optimizer too. The momentum method help to converge faster, it accelerates the travel towards local minima avoiding many oscillations even it helps learning process to escape local minima and finding better solutions. The adaptive learning rate depends on the momentum part, which are the first moment and the second moment term, for this, the learning rate value can adapt up and down.

The update parameters θ for Adam method is as follows:

$$g_t = \nabla_\theta f_t(\theta_{t-1}) \tag{8}$$

$$m_t = \beta_1 \cdot m_{t-1} + (1 - \beta_1) \cdot g_t \tag{9}$$

$$v_t = \beta_2 \cdot v_{t-1} + (1 - \beta_2) \cdot g_t^2 \tag{10}$$

$$\widehat{m}_t = \frac{m_t}{1 - \beta_1^t} \tag{11}$$

$$\widehat{v}_t = \frac{v_t}{1 - \beta_2^t} \tag{12}$$

$$\theta_t = \theta_{t-1} - \frac{\alpha \cdot \widehat{m}_t}{\sqrt{\widehat{v}_t} + \epsilon} \tag{13}$$

where $f(\theta)$ is the stochastic objective function with parameters θ, the gradient g, the first β_1 and second β_2 moment term. The first m and second v moment vector, first $\widehat{m}$ and second raw $\widehat{v}$ moment estimation. The learning rate α and the epsilon ϵ term to prevent division by zero [11,17].

2.5 Cross-entropy

Cross-entropy, the term "Cross" refers to the comparison between two distributions. "Entropy" is a term from information theory that refers to uncertainty. The cross-entropy of two distributions is expressed as

$$H(p,q) = - \sum_x p(x) log q(x), \tag{14}$$

the value of $H(p,q)$ represents how wrong or far away are the two distributions p and q. So minimizing this value is equivalent to bring closer these distributions. In other words, if q is the probability distribution of a neural network prediction and p is the true distribution of the labeled dataset then minimizing the cross-entropy $H(p,q)$ (loss function) is similar to decrease the error between these two distributions [9,17].

3 Methodology

In this work, we use an LSTM for testing different sequential data extracted from grayscale images. Our LSTM model has various outputs units, which are in o output at the time step $t-1$, and then another at time step t, and another at time step $t+1$. The number of outputs units depends on the number of class labels of a dataset. Here, we use three hidden layers and a supervised training.

With the purpose of selecting the appropriate LSTM architecture and parameter, to classify each image-datasets under the same conditions, first we tested different configurations. The best performance was achieved using the following parameters: three layers, 512 LSTM units per layer, a learning rate of 0.001 with exponential decay, and 256 images per batch size. Also, an early stopping condition has been implemented, consisting on training until there are no changes in the loss function. The model is compiled with Adam optimizer [11], the cross-entropy [17] loss function and metric accuracy.

In order to explain how an image is processed by the LSTM network, lets consider the matrix A in Eq. (15) represents a 2D grayscale image with $M \times N$ pixels, and $a_{i,j}$ is a specific pixel with coordinates (i, j) [8]. The LSTM may process this image as sequences of rows for each time step. That is, the first row is processed at time step $t - 1$, the second row at time step t, and so on, up to the last row M, processed at time step $t + M$, as detailed in Eq. (16). A set of these images is a batch size to be processed by the neural network and a set of these batch sizes is the whole training dataset.

$$A = \begin{bmatrix} a_{0,0} & a_{0,1} & \cdots & a_{0,N-1} \\ a_{1,0} & a_{1,1} & \cdots & a_{1,N-1} \\ \vdots & \vdots & \ddots & \vdots \\ a_{M-1,0} & a_{M-1,1} & \cdots & a_{M-1,N-1} \end{bmatrix} \tag{15}$$

$$x^{t-1} = \begin{bmatrix} a_{0,0} \\ a_{0,1} \\ \vdots \\ a_{0,N-1} \end{bmatrix}, \quad x^t = \begin{bmatrix} a_{1,0} \\ a_{1,1} \\ \vdots \\ a_{1,N-1} \end{bmatrix} \ldots, and \quad x^{t+M} = \begin{bmatrix} a_{M-1,0} \\ a_{M-1,1} \\ \vdots \\ a_{M-1,N-1} \end{bmatrix} \tag{16}$$

Various training datasets were built for each image dataset, following three different rules. The first rule considers to build the sequences from the rows of the images, which we call horizontal order (H); the second rule consists of building the sequences using the columns of the images, which we call vertical order (V); and the third rule, that we call spiral order (S), consists of building the sequences by collecting the pixels from the center and going out from the center in circular ways till the border of the image.

A grayscale image in X commonly comes with a $M \times N$ pixels, in this work all raw images are 28×28 pixels. From the model's point of view, varying the shape $M \times N$ of an image is equivalent to varying the sequences length and using the sorts of order (H, V and S) is equivalent to varying the order in each sequence. M defines the number of sequences and N defines the length of a sequence that can be got in an image.

Table 2. Experiments showing specific setting of $M \times N$ and sequences order for each dataset.

Shape	Dataset1		
$M \times N$	E	E	E
Order sorts	H	V	S

An experiment E is carried on with a specific combination of $M \times N$ shape of the image and a sort order H, V or S as shown in Table 2. Each experiment yields an accuracy.

The $M \times N$ combinations considered in this work are as follow: (2,392), (4,196), (7,112), (8,98), (14,56), (16,49), (28,28), (49,16), (56,14), (98,8), (112,7) and (196,4). These shapes were chosen mainly because they have an integer value for M and N. As previously mentioned, the datasets used in this work are the well known MNIST, MNIST-C, notMNIST, FashionMNIST and Sign Language MNIST. The combinations of datasets, image shapes and order sorts yield a total of 180 experiments.

3.1 Conditional Independence Test with Grayscale Images

The PCMCI causal discovery method can work with many conditional independence tests but the linear partial correlation (ParCorr) is used for grayscale images conditional independence test. The source code is implemented in the Tigramite open-source software package for Python [19].

PCMCI receives a dataset with N variables with a sample size. In the terms of images of $M \times N$ shape, N is the number of variables and M the sample size for an image. A total of 500 images are taken uniformly from a specific training dataset for conditional independence testing, therefore the whole sample size is $500 \times M$.

The three free parameters of this method is used as default except the maximum time lags τ parameter, which is set to 2.

After analyzing the dataset with PCMCI we can get the significant links (dependence or independence) between one variable and the others, or get the links graph of the variables. Those are not necessarily the best ways for comparing the conditional independence of variables from one dataset with variables of another dataset.

In order to have a better way of comparison, we observe on one of the two arrays the PCMCI return, the independence and dependence arrays. Generally, the former has zero values most of the time, which means no independence between variables, but the latter, the one we have chosen, has always significant values in the range of $[0,1]$.

The dependence array shape is $(N, N, \tau + 1)$, the value $d_{i,j,k}$ is the measure of dependence between the variables N_i and N_j at time lag τ_k.

To get a value of dependence for all the variables in a dataset, we sum all the elements $d_{i,j,k}$ of the dependence array as follows,

$$\sum_{k=0}^{\tau} \sum_{j=0}^{N-1} \sum_{i=0}^{N-1} d_{i,j,k}, \tag{17}$$

we call the result of the sum operation as *dependence index* (DI) per dataset and $M \times N$ shape, as Table 3 shows.

Table 3. Dependence index per dataset and $M \times N$.

Shape	Dataset1		
$M \times N$	DI	DI	DI
Order sorts	H	V	S

3.2 Entropy of Grayscale Images

The entropy of an image dataset is calculated in two ways, these are entropy by image and entropy by image row.

The entropy by image of a dataset consists of calculating the entropy of each 2D grayscale image with shape $M \times N$ and then get the mean entropy on all the images. To calculate the entropy of an image the probability distribution of the pixels is required then the image entropy is computed with the Eq. (14).

The entropy by image row of a dataset is calculated by getting the entropy of each row of a 2D grayscale image with shape $M \times N$ and the same for all images in a dataset and then get the mean entropy on all the rows of the images. To calculate the entropy of an image row the probability distribution of the row pixels is required then the image row entropy is computed with the Eq. (14), which is implemented in the open-source image processing library scikit-image for Python [26].

4 Experiments Setup

We used five grayscale image datasets, all of them with images of 28×28 pixels: (a) The MNIST is a dataset of handwritten digits (0–9), that has 10 classes, with 60,000 images for training and 10,000 for testing. (b) The MNIST-C dataset is a comprehensive suite of 15 corruptions applied to the MNIST dataset. We choosed the MNIST-C glass blur corruption from 15 corruptions sorts as our second dataset. It has 60,000 images for training, 10,000 for testing, and 10 classes as the MNIST. (c) The notMNIST dataset contains images of the English letters from A to J, thus it consists 10 classes. The original training set contains 500,000 images and the test part 19,000, from these we selected randomly [15] 60,000 for training and 10,000 for testing. (d) The FashionMNIST dataset has 10 classes as well, and consist on images of Zalando's articles from T-Shirt, Trouser till Bag, and Ankle boots. It has 60,000 and 10,000 images for training and testing, respectively. (e) The Sign Language MNIST (SLMNIST) dataset contains all the alphabet, except J and Z, of the standard American Sign Language (ASL). It consists of 27,455 and 7,172 images for training and testing, respectively, with 24 classes.

All the datasets are normalized with the standardization method to have a zero mean and a unit variance, producing values in the range of $[-1, 1]$. Data normalization can help making the training process easier [17]. Our model is built with TensorFlow (v2.2), Keras API and Python (v3.7) and run on an NVIDIA GeForce RTX 2080Ti GPU accelerator.

5   Results and Discussion

To choose our current architecture, 3 layers and 512 units, we evaluated several LSTM configurations, using as a reference to the SLMNIST dataset and the sequences lengths $M \times N$, described in Sect. 3. The architectures that were studied encompasses combinations of 1 to 6 layers, and 32, 64, 128, 256 and 512 units. All these, a set of 30 architectures, were evaluated for each $M \times N$ shape and only for the horizontal order. The 3 layers and 512 units architecture got the best accuracy (90.53%) for shape (28,28). The number of units were increased up to 1024 units, but it did not improve the accuracy significantly. Furthermore, we increased the number of layers to 10 for these 1024 units but the accuracy dropped considerably.

After choosing our best architecture, we evaluated our experiments on it with the five datasets, organized in different shapes and order of pixels (H, V and S). Our main results are shown in Table 4, from which we observe the following:

– Doubtless, the shape (28,28) or sequences with 28 features obtained the maximum accuracies within six experiments, equally distributed between the vertical and horizontal order.
– The shape (2,392) is the second with four maximum accuracies, mostly distributed in the spiral order.
– Generally, the horizontal and vertical order accuracies are slightly above the spiral order accuracies.
– Overall, we observe the maximum accuracies tend to stay above (28,28), where the sequences are longer than those below.

We analyze the accuracies shown in the Table 4 with the help of a boxplot chart, as shown in Fig. 2a. In according to the median and maximum values of the boxplots, we can see the two first datasets (MNIST and MNIST-C) in the H order has better accuracies than the V and S orders. Also, the S order gets the lower accuracies in general. The same pattern appears in the FASHION dataset, though it has a smaller accuracy than MNIST and MNIST-C.
The notMNIST and SLMNIST datasets, Fig. 2a, have different results, the V order has a slightly better median accuracy than the H order median accuracy. Although one dataset is around 95% and the other around 85%, they both follow the same pattern. And the S order has the worst median accuracy in both cases.

On the other hand, we can observe from the Fig. 2a, accuracies in the H order are in general less disperse, and the S order has more dispersed accuracies. It means that working with horizontal order is more reliable than the others and it has better median accuracies and are less spread.

Comparing the results from Table 1 with accuracies per sequence length in Fig. 3, we can observe that for SC-LSTM-I [27] and GRU [1], which were trained with 784 sequence length, they both have accuracies of 94.80% and 96.20%, respectively, which can be improved if the sequence's length changes to 28. It is interesting that the convolutional network TCN [1] reached 99%, though it was trained with a 784 length sequence. The LSTMs in [2] and in [21] reached accuracies of 99.27% and 99.40%, respectively; both were trained with a length

Table 4. Experiments results showing accuracies for specific setting of $M \times N$ (rows), and datasets (columns). Maximum accuracies shown in bold.

Shape	MNIST			MNIST-C			notMNIST		
(2,392)	98.16	98.19	**98.16**	97.45	97.36	97.19	94.74	94.55	**94.52**
(4,196)	97.41	98.50	97.94	97.33	97.01	**97.40**	94.81	94.59	94.08
(7,112)	98.52	98.43	**98.16**	97.96	**97.89**	97.05	95.38	95.43	93.81
(8,98)	98.52	98.04	97.63	96.84	97.09	97.20	94.24	94.58	94.12
(14,56)	98.83	98.34	97.89	**98.14**	97.74	96.53	95.37	**95.86**	93.17
(16,49)	98.30	98.09	97.76	97.28	96.96	96.81	93.91	94.09	93.13
(28,28)	**98.95**	**98.71**	97.55	98.10	**97.89**	96.43	**95.54**	95.60	92.40
(49,16)	98.56	97.43	96.69	97.80	95.85	95.67	93.17	93.00	91.60
(56,14)	98.86	98.08	96.90	97.83	97.34	95.33	93.98	94.29	90.95
(98,8)	98.32	97.36	95.07	97.46	96.72	94.00	93.04	92.57	90.63
(112,7)	98.35	96.97	94.36	97.77	95.84	92.84	93.10	92.66	89.53
(196,4)	98.23	97.59	94.79	97.42	95.65	93.40	90.89	93.56	90.56
Order sorts	H	V	S	H	V	S	H	V	S

Continued: for the two last datasets.

Shape	FashionMNIST			SLMNIST		
(2,392)	90.02	**89.58**	89.72	79.94	79.38	**79.45**
(4,196)	**90.20**	89.43	**89.94**	82.57	82.65	76.05
(7,112)	89.26	88.56	88.80	85.57	87.55	71.42
(8,98)	89.35	89.27	88.69	77.24	71.53	71.57
(14,56)	90.09	88.43	88.38	84.66	89.46	72.64
(16,49)	88.75	88.06	87.63	65.96	70.30	74.58
(28,28)	89.65	88.88	87.71	**90.53**	**92.28**	68.38
(49,16)	88.57	87.20	87.05	85.30	83.81	63.23
(56,14)	89.36	88.71	87.09	80.83	85.46	61.89
(98,8)	88.25	87.07	86.23	88.39	78.08	66.47
(112,7)	88.85	88.51	85.92	73.58	84.68	52.30
(196,4)	88.87	88.06	84.16	73.93	77.76	57.82
Order sorts	H	V	S	H	V	S

of 28 features, although in [21] it says the sequence length varied in order to gather between 5 and 15 images of 28×28 pixels.

The mean amount of epochs required to get the accuracies in the Table 4 is shown in the Fig. 2b. The dataset SLMNIST required significant more epochs than the others, between 200 and 250 epochs. The MNIST-C dataset, in the horizontal and vertical order, required up to 100 epochs, in contrast with the spiral order which required no more than 25 epochs. The MNIST, notMNIST and FASHION datasets took around 25 epochs.

Another perspective of epochs is from the variation of sequence length, rows in Table 4. Taking a sight across the accuracies of all datasets, in a row way, and the epochs they took to learn, it turns out the Fig. 3, in which, there are normalized mean values with min-max scaling method, the epochs are normalized in the range of 45 and 177, and the accuracies in the range of 88 and 92.5. Epochs and accuracies are per sequence length. The Fig. 3 is a comparison of epochs

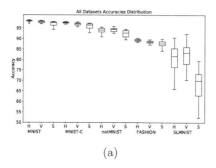
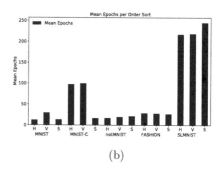

(a)   (b)

Fig. 2. (a) Accuracy distribution of the datasets under H, V and S order. (b) The mean amount of epochs required to get the accuracies in the Table 4.

and accuracy by which can be observed the sequence length (14,56) takes the minimum epochs to reach 90%, though it has not the better accuracy; and the sequence length (196,4) takes the maximum epochs and the minimum accuracy.

The sequence length, or image shape, with faster and slower learning cycles are shown in Table 5. The image class "5" from the MNIST dataset shows clearly how the shape (14×56) duplicate the features of this class (with lower resolution) when it is ordered in a horizontal and vertical way, but it is not clearly visualized in the spiral order. When this image class has the shape (196,4), the classes features are less clear from a visual and spatial perspective, while showing high similarity in the three representations, the horizontal, vertical and spiral order.

5.1 Conditional Independence Test Results

In accordance with the dependence index results in Table 6, the following points are observed. First, the smaller the number of variables N or the smaller the sequences length is, the smaller the dependence index becomes, this happen in all the datasets. But there is no link with the accuracies in the Table 4 because they have not changes in the same proportions as dependence index does. Second, the information in Table 6 is also represented in Fig. 4 in a boxplot chart, which shows the median line of the boxplots are similar in H, V and S order for each dataset. In the accuracy chart, Fig. 2a, the boxplots' median lines are not similar in H, V and S order for each dataset because they lie outside of the box of the neighbor boxplot. From the boxplots' point of view, between the accuracy and the dependence index chart, the changes of boxplots' median lines are not connected. And finally, most of the boxplots in Fig. 4 show outliers that become visible with large changes in the dependence index, but these are not reflected in the accuracies on Fig. 2a, in which there are fewer outlier.

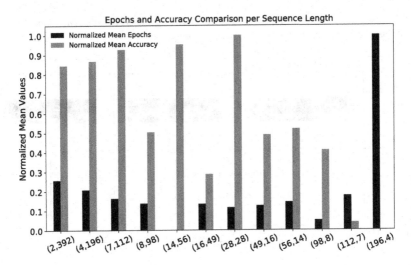

Fig. 3. Epochs and accuracy comparison per sequence length across all datasets.

5.2 Entropy of Grayscale Images Results

The entropy by image of each dataset is shown in Table 7, which is the mean entropy of the whole training dataset.

Comparing the Table 7 and the Fig. 2a of accuracies of the datasets, there is a connection between them. For example, the MNIST's entropy is smaller than the SLMNIST's and the MNIST's accuracies are better than the SLMNIST's. The smaller the entropy is, the better the accuracy becomes.

On Fig. 5 it is shown the entropy by image row of the datasets in the form of boxplot chart. From the comparison between the accuracy chart (Fig. 2a) and the entropy chart (Fig. 5) the following is observed: (A) In the accuracy figure, the H order for the datasets MNIST, MNIST-C and FASHION, it appears that data is less spread than the H order on the entropy chart, for the same datasets. (B) The entropy is similar between the V and the S order, in contrast with the accuracies, which are not similar within datasets. Therefore, it may be possible that the entropy and the accuracy are not completed related with the order of the datasets. (C) As the entropy increases the accuracy drops, per dataset.

Finally, on Fig. 6a and Fig. 6b it is shown the dependence index, the entropy and the accuracy analysis. On these charts data has being normalized with the min-max scaling method. The former shows the normalized mean values of the dependence index (in the range of 649 to 6,160.4), the entropy (in the range of 0.89 to 4.33) and the accuracy (in the range of 88.3% to 91.2%The latter shows the normalized mean values of the dependence index (between 9 and 21,526.2), the entropy (between 1 and 3.6) and the accuracy (between 88.1% and 92.5%).

On Fig. 6a we observed the following: (A) when the accuracy decreases across the datasets (MNIST, MNIST-C, and so on) the opposite pattern is observed in the values of the dependence index, while there is also an increase in the

Table 5. Visual examples of faster and lower learning based on sequence lengths. The (14×56) is the faster and the (196×4) the lower.

Shape	MNIST(for example)		
14×56			
196×4			
Order Sorts	H	V	S

Table 6. Dependence index results for a specific setting of $M \times N$ (rows), and datasets (columns).

Shape	MNIST			MNIST-C			notMNIST		
(2,392)	2588.57	2284.74	9104.79	4763.58	4377.89	14221.11	23084.16	25730.64	29847.78
(4,196)	2441.18	2592.74	5010.51	3410.92	4687.81	6682.01	7193.16	8321.07	6925.10
(7,112)	1003.30	1192.69	1825.33	1079.35	1886.42	2378.47	2736.26	3009.62	2128.19
(8,98)	947.29	1009.38	1628.29	882.62	1304.18	2085.20	1954.37	2164.55	1554.87
(14,56)	290.88	307.38	534.44	214.47	436.37	686.80	800.04	695.20	515.75
(16,49)	296.72	282.90	443.09	195.84	342.96	597.21	523.20	488.31	443.21
(28,28)	68.16	66.59	147.50	44.88	117.78	186.04	218.75	151.69	195.28
(49,16)	57.48	58.61	70.20	50.54	59.87	81.78	74.65	66.09	92.13
(56,14)	43.51	49.25	57.91	40.97	49.47	65.73	55.96	63.75	74.41
(98,8)	23.34	24.52	26.90	25.38	30.43	29.08	26.56	31.24	32.67
(112,7)	19.09	20.53	21.99	20.91	25.07	23.16	22.55	27.61	25.79
(196,4)	8.40	8.55	8.98	7.96	9.31	8.61	8.83	9.71	9.53
Order sorts	H	V	S	H	V	S	H	V	S

Continued: for the two last datasets.

Shape	FashionMNIST			SLMNIST		
(2,392)	24446.24	23584.04	24448.73	44546.30	49307.73	40557.46
(4,196)	8820.22	10268.31	8063.70	11890.63	14382.26	9533.88
(7,112)	3244.85	3847.89	4320.24	3881.56	4652.22	2411.29
(8,98)	2333.17	2742.65	3203.95	2839.19	3312.38	1718.03
(14,56)	776.37	925.88	953.90	918.86	1042.19	583.16
(16,49)	552.54	709.64	748.42	662.50	751.61	484.34
(28,28)	199.34	224.79	250.89	202.58	229.18	261.73
(49,16)	84.97	100.68	121.51	76.29	90.66	114.91
(56,14)	74.49	96.26	93.12	71.98	83.92	90.93
(98,8)	32.41	33.39	35.47	29.86	33.63	35.22
(112,7)	24.61	28.22	27.31	26.10	29.33	26.98
(196,4)	9.10	9.59	9.54	9.36	10.28	9.62
Order sorts	H	V	S	H	V	S

Table 7. Mean entropy by image of the whole training dataset.

Dataset	Entropy
MNIST	1.60
MNIST-C	3.52
notMNIST	3.68
FASHION	4.12
SLMNIST	6.72

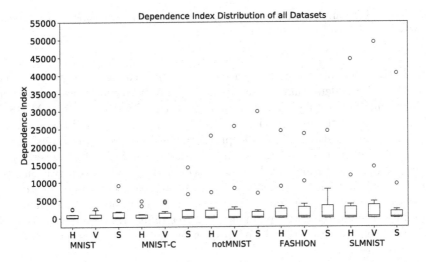

Fig. 4. Dependence index distribution under H, V and S order of all the datasets.

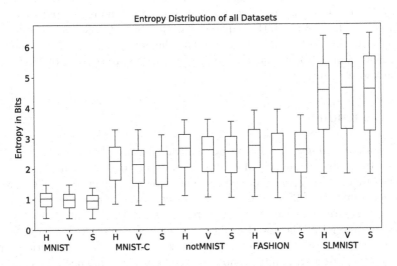

Fig. 5. Entropy distribution of the datasets under H, V and S order.

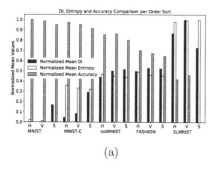
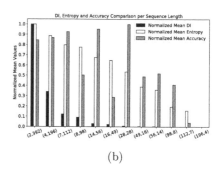

Fig. 6. (a) and (b) are dependence index, entropy and accuracy comparison per order sort and per sequence length, respectively.

entropy. (B) The entropy and the accuracies values changes are proportional on the V and S orders, that is, they behave similarly in most cases, except in two cases only where they are not proportional, the V order in the notMNIST, and the S order in the SLMNIST. (C) The dependence index and the accuracy on cases V and S order are inversely proportional, except in three cases, the V order in the notMNIST, and the V and S order in the SLMNIST, where they are proportional. (D) Finally, taking into account the previous observations, we have observed that the dependence index is always inversely proportional with respect to the accuracy, except in the three cases mentioned. Also, there are small differences in the entropy among the three different orders (H, V and S), and it is in general proportional with respect to the accuracy, except in the two cases mentioned.

From Fig. 6b it is possible to observed that for each sequence length, the dependence index and the entropy are proportional, but the accuracy does not follow the same pattern. The accuracies behavior are more related to specific sequences lengths. That is, if the sequence length (28,28) is taken as the reference, to the left we found the longest sequences and the better accuracies (though there are small accuracies too), and to the right part there are the shortest sequences and the lowest accuracies.

6 Conclusion

In this work we presented a procedure to evaluate the accuracy of a recurrent neural network based on LSTM units, for datasets organized in sequences of different order and lengths. The experiments where conducted on five datasets of grayscale images of 28×28 pixels, where sequences were extracted from the images using three different rules. The results show that in most of the cases the best accuracies are achieved when the sequences are extracted from images following a horizontal order, but there are some cases where a vertical order can be better. We found there is no link between a dependence index and the accuracies of the evaluated datasets as well as the entropy and the accuracy are not connected when the sequences order and lengths are changed. However, the smaller the entropy is, the better the accuracy becomes per dataset (MNIST, MNIST-C and so on). As a future work, for the sequence length (14,56) gets the faster learning, it would be interesting to tune the model to reach or overcome the accuracy of the sequence length (28,28).

Acknowledgements. This work was supported by UNAM-PAPIIT IA103420. EJEC thanks the support of CONACyT.

References

1. Bai, S., Kolter, J.Z., Koltun, V.: An empirical evaluation of generic convolutional and recurrent networks for sequence modeling (2018). http://arxiv.org/abs/1803.01271. Accessed 29 June 2020
2. Breuel, T.M.: Benchmarking of LSTM Networks (2015). https://arxiv.org/abs/1508.02774. Accessed 01 June 2020
3. Bulatov, Y.: The notMNIST dataset (2011). http://yaroslavvb.blogspot.com/2011/09/notmnist-dataset.html. Accessed 03 July 2020
4. Chalupka, K., Perona, P., Eberhardt, F.: Fast conditional independence test for vector variables with large sample sizes (2018). http://arxiv.org/abs/1804.02747. Accessed 25 June 2020
5. Cielen, D., Meysman, A.D.B., Ali, M.: Introducing Data Science, 1st edn. Manning Publications Co., Shelter Island (2016)
6. Cover, T.M., Thomas, J.A.: Elements of Information Theory, 2nd edn. Wiley-Interscience, Hoboken (2006)
7. Dieterich, T.G.: Machine learning for sequential data: a review. In: Caelli, T., Amin, A., Duin, R.P.W., de Ridder, D., Kamel, M. (eds.) SSPR /SPR 2002. LNCS, vol. 2396, pp. 15–30. Springer, Heidelberg (2002). https://doi.org/10.1007/3-540-70659-3_2
8. Gonzales, R.G., Woods, R.E.: Digital Image Processing, 4th edn. Pearson, New York (2018)
9. Goodfellow, I., Bengio, Y., Courville, A.: Deep Learning, Final edn. The MIT Press, Cambridge (2016)
10. Graves, A.: Generating sequences with recurrent neural networks (2013). http://arxiv.org/abs/1308.0850. Accessed 17 June 2020
11. Kingma, D.P., Ba, J.L.: Adam: a method for stochastic optimization (2014). https://arxiv.org/abs/1412.6980. Accessed 09 July 2020
12. LeCun, Y.: The MNIST database of handwritten digits (1998). http://yann.lecun.com/exdb/mnist/index.html. Accessed 15 June 2020
13. McMillan, B., Slepian, D.: Information theory. In: Encyclopedia of Cognitive Science, pp. 1151–1157 (2006)
14. Mu, N., Gilmer, J.: MNIST-C: a robustness benchmark for computer vision (2019). https://zenodo.org/record/3239543#.X0UgJC2ZO00. Accessed 21 June 2020
15. Ng, R.: Exploring notMNIST with TensorFlow (2018). https://www.ritchieng.com/machine-learning/deep-learning/tensorflow/notmnist/. Accessed 04 July 2020
16. Ostmeyer, J., Cowell, L.: Machine learning on sequential data using a recurrent weighted average. Neurocomputing **331**, 281–288 (2019)

17. Patterson, J., Gibson, A.: Deep Learning, a Practitioner's Approach, 1st edn. O'Reilly Media, Sebastopol (2017)

18. Raschka, S., Mirjalili, V.: Python Machine Learning, 3rd edn. Packt Publishing Ltd., Birmingham (2019)

19. Runge, J.: TIGRAMITE - Causal discovery for time series datasets (2019). https://github.com/jakobrunge/tigramite#tigramite-causal-discovery-for-time-series-datasets. Accessed 17 June 2020

20. Runge, J., Nowack, P., Kretschmer, M., Flaxman, S., Sejdinovic, D.: Detecting and quantifying causal associations in large nonlinear time series datasets. Sci. Adv. **5**(11), eaau4996 (2019)

21. Schak, M., Gepperth, A.: A study on catastrophic forgetting in deep LSTM networks. In: Tetko, I.V., Kůrková, V., Karpov, P., Theis, F. (eds.) ICANN 2019. LNCS, vol. 11728, pp. 714–728. Springer, Cham (2019). https://doi.org/10.1007/978-3-030-30484-3_56

22. Schuster, M.: Better generative models for sequential data problems: bidirectional recurrent mixture density networks. In: Leen, T.K., Dietterich, T.G., Tresp, V. (eds.) Advances in Neural Information Processing Systems 13 - Proceedings of the 2000 Conference, NIPS 2000, Denver, CO, United States, pp. 589–594. Neural Information Processing System Foundation (2000)

23. Sreehari: The Sign Language MNIST (2016). https://www.kaggle.com/datamunge/sign-language-mnist. Accessed 03 July 2020

24. Srivastava, N., Mansimov, E., Salakhutdinov, R.: Unsupervised learning of video representations using LSTMs. In: Bach, F., Blei, D. (eds.) 32nd International Conference on Machine Learning, ICML 2015, Lile, France, vol. 1, pp. 843–852. International Machine Learning Society (IMLS) (2015)

25. Sutskever, I., Vinyals, O., Le, Q.V.: Sequence to sequence learning with neural networks. In: Ghahramani, Z., Welling, M., Cortes, C., Lawrence, N., Weinberger, K. (eds.) Advances in Neural Information Processing Systems 27–28th Annual Conference on Neural Information Processing Systems 2014, NIPS 2014, Montreal, QC, Canada, vol. 4, pp. 3104–3112. Neural Information Processing Systems Foundation (2014)

26. van der Walt, S., Schönberger, J.: Scikit-Image: Image Processing in Python (2019). https://scikit-image.org/. Accessed 11 June 2020

27. Wang, Y., Tian, F.: Recurrent residual learning for sequence classification. In: Su, J., Duh, K., Carreras, X. (eds.) 2016 Conference on Empirical Methods in Natural Language Processing, EMNLP 2016, Austin, TX, United States, pp. 938–943. Association for Computational Linguistics (ACL) (2016)

28. Xiao, H., Rasul, K., Vollgraf, R.: Fashion-MNIST (2017). https://github.com/zalandoresearch/fashion-mnist. Accessed 01 June 2020

Best Paper Award, Second Place

Speaker Identification Using Entropygrams and Convolutional Neural Networks

Antonio Camarena-Ibarrola[1]([✉])[ID], Karina Figueroa[2][ID], and Jonathan García[2]

[1] Facultad de Ingeniería Eléctrica, División de Estudios de Postgrado, Universidad Michoacana de San Nicolás de Hidalgo, 58000 Morelia, Michoacán, Mexico
camarena@umich.mx
[2] Facultad de Ciencias Fisico-Matemáticas, Universidad Michoacana de San Nicolás de Hidalgo, 58000 Morelia, Michoacán, Mexico
karina@fismat.umich.mx
http://dep.fie.umich.mx/~camarena
http://fismat.umich.mx/~karina

Abstract. Speaker Identification is a problem that consists in discovering the identity of an individual from the captured speech signal and it is still an open problem. Recent advances in deep learning in combination with spectrograms encouraged us to propose the use of entropygrams in combination with convolutional neural networks. We extract the entropygrams of specific words uttered by the individual whose identity needs to be found among those known to the system. An entropygram is an image that shows how the information contentained in the speech signal distributes along with frequency and how such distribution evolves in time. By extracting the entropygram from the speech signal we effectively transform the problem into an image recognition issue, and Convolutional Neural Networks (CNN) are known to be very useful for image recognition. In our experiments we used a collection of 21 young mexican speakers from both genders and confirmed our hypothesis that entropygrams can successfully be used instead of spectrograms for speaker identification using CNN. We also experimented with noisy speech and found that entropygrams outperform spectrograms as images that better represent speakers to be identified using CNN.

Keywords: Speaker identification · Spectral entropy · Convolutional Neural Network

1 Introduction

Automatic Speaker Recognition is a general term for both Automatic Speaker Identification (ASI) and Automatic Speaker Verification (ASV). In ASV, the speaker claims to be a specific individual and the system has to corroborate if what the speaker claims is true. ASV systems only compare the features

© Springer Nature Switzerland AG 2020
L. Martínez-Villaseñor et al. (Eds.): MICAI 2020, LNAI 12468, pp. 23–34, 2020.
https://doi.org/10.1007/978-3-030-60884-2_2

extracted from the speech signal that has just been captured from the individual whose identity is being verified with the stored features that belong to the individual he/she claims to be. ASI systems on the other hand have to check the whole database of individuals known to the system in search for clues that would allow guessing with high probability that the individual is one of them. ASI systems are more complicated than ASV systems as the number of speakers known to the system grows. When the database of speakers known to the systems is large, the classical way to avoid a sequential search of the individual most similar to that whose identity is required (i.e. the nearest neighbor) is building a proximity index. Proximity indexes are able to retrieve the nearest neighbor to a query without sequentially comparing the query to each of the members of the database, however proximity indexes suffer from the curse of the dimensionality, which means that if the intrinsic dimension of the database is high, the index would have to compute too many distances, and could even result worse than sequential search. Also proximity indexes in metric spaces require a way to compare any two objects of the database in order to build the index, the preferred way to compare two objects is with a distance measure which is frequently expensive in terms of time complexity. That is exactly the case when the features from one speaker are compared to the features of another speaker, the comparison is time consuming. The neural network approach does not perform such a search, instead of building an index, the parameters of the neural network are determined in training time using an optimization method normally through a gradient descent algorithm known as back-propagation. After the neural network has been trained it is able to identify the speaker very quickly, which is great because it is precisely when time matters the most (querying time). The only problem is we do not know a priory the topology of the network (number and kind of layers, neurons per layer, connectivity, etc.) that would work. Convolutional Neural Networks (CNN) are known to be very effective for classifying images, in order to use them we need to change from classic feature extraction techniques of speech signals, such as sequences of Mel Frequency Cepstral Coefficients to ways for converting the audio signals into images such as spectrograms which depict how the amount of the energy content distribute along frequency and evolve in time. We decided to use entropygrams which depict the way entropy (i.e. the amount of information content in the signal) distribute in frequency and evolve in time, if they do work, we expect them to be more robust when the audio signals are noisy.

2   Previous Work

Speaker recognition has been studied since 1978 where the PARtial CORrelation (PARCOR) coefficients were used for identification of speakers [11]. The PARCOR coefficients are determined by the Levinson-Durbin algorithm, they are the negative of the reflection coefficients of the concatenated lossless tubes model of the vocal tract. In 1988 physiology studies about the sensibility of the human auditory system were published by Lieberman *et al.* [6], it turns out that humans perceive low frequencies much better than high frequencies. From then on, most works in speaker recognition use logarithmic scales of frequency such as the Mel or the Bark scales. In 1995, [13] the error signal obtained after computing the difference between the original speech signal and the synthesized speech signal using the Linear Prediction Coding (LPC) coefficients was used for speaker identification by Plumpe et al.. Assuming the envelope of this error signal resembles a train of glottal pulses, and it is a known fact that the shape of the glottal pulse is different for each individual. In 1999, also use the glottal flow for speaker identification but estimating it in a much better way, by inverse filtering the speech signal using the LPC coefficients was used also by Plumbe et al.[10]. In 2000, subband coding was used as a way to efficiently determine the amount of energy per band in a base two logarithm scale for speaker identification by Besacier et al. [2]. Hermansky [5] used Perceptual Linear Prediction (PLP) coefficients since according to his experiments they worked better than LPC coefficients for the purpose of speaker identification. Furthermore, since Linear Prediction Cepstral Coefficients (LPCC) are less correlated than LPC coefficients they were supposed to work even better. However, in 2009 MFCCs were as being more robust than LPCCs for speaker recognition by Yu et al. [16]. MFCCs are determined using a filter-bank made of triangular filters followed by logarithmic compression and the Cosine transform. MFCCs are now extensively used for speaker identification [15]. In [4], Spectral Entropy determined for critical bands according to the Bark Scale was reported as being more robust than MFCC for Text-dependent speaker identification. In 2019, Supaporn et al. extracted the spectrogram from every 2 s of the speaker's voice, the spectrogram is an image that depicts how energy distributes in frequency and how this distribution changes with time, this image is the input to a convolutional neural network for text-independent speaker recognition [3].

3   Description of Our Speaker Identification System

We will now describe our proposed speaker identification system, first of all we have to describe the signal processing behind our system. The purpose of signal processing is transforming a signal to a most convenient form.

3.1   Pre-processing

The speech signal is first pre-processed by normalization, pre-emphasization, framing, and windowing. Normalization prevents changes in the amplitude of the signal due to variation in transmission channels. We normalize the signal so the samples are within interval $[-1, 1]$. Pre-emphasization aims to boost the higher frequency components of the signal since it has been noted that higher frequencies are more important for signal disambiguation than lower frequencies. A pre-emphasis filter is really a Finite Impulse Response Filter whose output y is obtained from its input x as:

$$y(n) = x(n) - ax(n-1) \tag{1}$$

we use $a = 0.98$

Framing is the process of dividing the speech signal in segments short enough for them to be stationary but long enough for them to capture the dynamics of the lowest frequency components. We use segments of 30 ms, and each frame has an overlap of two thirds with the next frame. Windowing is the process of applying a window to a frame for the purpose of avoiding leakage of the spectrum which occurs because the short-time Fourier transform (STFT) assumes the signal is periodic and the period is the length of the frame. When the signal at the beginning of the frame would require a sudden change to connect it to the signal at the end of the frame, then the STFT introduces phony frequencies. A window's purpose is to force the signal to vanish both at the beginning and at the end of the frame. We use the Hamming window which is defined as:

$$hamming(n) = 0.54 + 0.46cos(2\pi n/N) \tag{2}$$

where N is the size of the frame in samples

3.2 Segmentation

The beginning and the end of a utterance inside an audio signal have to be found, the standard way of combining short time energy and zero crossing rate to segment a utterance is not really useful for noisy signals because both energy and ZCR increase not because of the presence of speech but of noise. That is why we prefer to use entropy for segmentation purposes, after all the presence of speech in the signal increase the amount of information content in it.

Let $v_1, v_2, ..., v_n$ be the possible values of the samples of the audio signal, with a precision of 8 bits per sample this values would be all the integers in the interval $[-128, 127]$. Now each v_i has probability p_i and $p_1, p_2, ..., p_n$ is the Probability Distribution Function (PDF) of the audio signal.

The information content I in a value v_i also called "self information", depends only on its probability p_i to occur, so it is denoted $I(p_i)$. The less likely a sample value is, the more information brings with itself if it does show up. Equivalently, if a value is expected, it brings very little self information when it arrives. Therefore, the self information must be a monotonically decreasing function of the probability. In addition to this, $I(p_i)$ has to be computed in a way that if v_i depends on two or more independent events with probabilities $p_{i1}, p_{i2}, ...,$ then the contribution to the information content of each event must be added to be taken into consideration and the total sum must equal $I(p_i)$ to be handled has information, so if $p_i = p_{i1}p_{i2}...$ then $I(p_i) = I(p_{i1}) + I(p_{i2}) + ...$ The one function to accomplish this is the logarithm, that is why the self information is computed using (3) [12],

$$I(p_i) = ln\left(\frac{1}{p_i}\right) = -ln(p_i) \tag{3}$$

Entropy H is the expected information content in a sequence, so it is the average of all the information contents weighted by their probabilities to occur as in (4), its continuous version as in (5) is called "differential entropy".

$$H = E[I(p)] = \sum_{i=1}^{n} p_i I(p_i) = - \sum_{i=1}^{n} p_i ln(p_i) \tag{4}$$

$$H(X) = - \int_{-\infty}^{+\infty} p(x) log[p(x)] dx \tag{5}$$

For each frame, we estimate the PDF of the sample values of the signal inside the frame using a histogram according to Eqs. (6) and (7)

$$p_i = \frac{f_i}{N} \tag{6}$$

where N is the number of samples in the signal and f_i is the number of times value v_i occurs in the signal x as in (7).

$$f_i = \sum_{j=1}^{N} \varphi(x_j, v_i) \tag{7}$$

where $\varphi(x, y) = 1$ if $x = y$ and $\varphi(x, y) = 0$ otherwise

A frame is considered to be part of the speech signal if its entropy H as computed with Eq. (4) is above some threshold. After the utterance has been segmented we can extract the entropygram as explained below.

3.3   Entropygram Extraction

The entropygrams that we extract are images that show how spectral entropy distributes in frequency and how this distribution evolves in time. Spectral entropy is the entropy of the Fourier coefficients after the Discrete Fourier Transform has been used to determine the spectrum of the signal. The spectral entropy as defined in [14] computes a single value per frame, and it was used only for voice activity detection. It makes sense to see how much espectral entropy there is in the low frequencies, the middle, or the high ones, in [8] Misra *et al.* proposed the use of spectral entropy in this way for robust speech recognition. The entropygrams that we extract from the speech signal are based on this idea but we also take advantage of psychoacoustics studies, specifically the Bark scale [17].

The Bark Scale. It is always a good idea to reproduce the natural way how people identify sounds. We should measure the information content in audio signals but in the perspective of the human ear. Not all frequencies can be heard with the same sensitivity, the human ear perceives better the lower frequencies than the higher ones, the bark scale models how the human ear perceives sound. Equation (8) is used to convert Hertz to Barks. There are 25 critical bands, the bandwidth of each critical band is one bark, the 25th band corresponds to the frequencies between 15.5 to 20 khz. However, since the maximum frequency found in speech is about 4 KHz, we only use the first 16 critical bands in this work.

$$z = 13 \arctan(0.76 f/1000) + 3.5 \arctan(f/7500) \tag{8}$$

Estimating Entropy per Critical Band. We cannot determine entropy per band in the same way that we estimated entropy in time domain since specially in the lower bands we simply do not have enough Fourier coefficients to build a histogram, instead we use a parametric method to estimate the probability density function. In parametric methods, first a kind of distribution is chosen and then its parameters are determined [1]. If a variable $X \sim N(0, \sigma^2)$ (distributes normally with zero mean and variance σ^2), then the probability density function $p(x)$ is as Eq. (9)

$$p(x) = \frac{e^{-x^2/2\sigma^2}}{\sqrt{2\pi} \; \sigma} \tag{9}$$

Replacing $p(x)$ into (5) we get this known formula for determining the entropy of a random variable with a gaussian distribution (10):

$$
\begin{aligned}
H &= -\int_{-\infty}^{\infty} \frac{e^{-x^2/2\sigma^2}}{\sqrt{2\pi} \; \sigma} ln\left[\frac{e^{-x^2/2\sigma^2}}{\sqrt{2\pi} \; \sigma}\right] dx \\
&= \frac{ln(\sqrt{2\pi} \; \sigma)}{\sqrt{2\pi} \; \sigma} \int_{-\infty}^{\infty} e^{-x^2/2\sigma^2} dx \\
&\quad + \frac{1}{\sqrt{2\pi} \; 2\sigma^3} \int_{-\infty}^{\infty} x^2 e^{-x^2/2\sigma^2} dx \\
&= \frac{ln(\sqrt{2\pi} \; \sigma)}{\sqrt{2\pi} \; \sigma} \sqrt{2\sigma^2\pi} + \frac{4\sqrt{\pi}(\sqrt{2}\sigma/2)^3}{\sqrt{2\pi} \; 2\sigma^3} \\
&= \frac{1}{2} ln(2\pi) + ln(\sigma) + \frac{1}{2} \\
&= \frac{1}{2} ln(2\pi e) + \frac{1}{2} ln(\sigma^2)
\end{aligned}
\tag{10}
$$

Similarly, for the multivariate (i.e. n-dimensional) case it is not difficult to demonstrate that the entropy of a random variable with distribution $N(\mathbf{0}, \mathbf{R})$ is computed with (11), where $\mathbf{R}$ is the co-variance matrix [9].

$$H = \frac{n}{2} ln(2\pi e) + \frac{1}{2} ln[\det(\mathbf{R})] \tag{11}$$

Since the real and imaginary part of the Fourier Transform can be modeled as zero mean Gaussian random variables according to [7], the spectral entropy for any band is determined with Eq. (11) as a bivariate case of (12).

$$H = ln(2\pi e) + \frac{1}{2} ln(\sigma_x^2 \sigma_y^2 - \sigma_{xy}^2) \tag{12}$$

where σ_x^2 and σ_y^2 are the variances of the real and the imaginary parts of the spectrum respectively and σ_{xy} is the covariance between the real and the imaginary parts of the spectrum.

In a few words, for each frame with speech content, the Hamming window is applied, then its discrete Fourier transform produce the Fourier coefficients which are grouped into the first 16 critical bands according to the Bark scale, and for each band entropy is determined. The result is a matrix of entropy values, this matrix has a fixed number of rows (sixteen) and a number of columns that depend on the duration of the utterance (i.e. the number of frames with speech content). The matrix values are depicted in the entropygram as gray-level or color values.

Figures 1(a) and (b) show two entropygrams for the word "cero" uttered by the same individual (Aaron). Figures 1(c) and (d) show two entropygrams for the word "cero" uttered by another individual (Erendira), observe that entropygrams Fig. 1(a) and (b) look very similar, while entropygrams Fig. 1(c) and (d) also look very similar, but the two entropygrams on top of figure of Fig. 1 look different from the two entropygrams at the bottom of the same figure, based on this we can hypothesize that there is a long distance between classes (i.e. interclass distance), and a short distance between objects of the same class (i.e. intraclass distance), that is exactly what we need to implement a speaker identification system.

Since entropygrams are images produced from a speaker that uttered some word or phrase, we may label entropygrams with the speaker id and use them to discover the identity of the speaker, this way we have effectively turned the problem into an image recognition problem, and we know convolutional neural networks are very effective in recognizing images.

3.4 Convolutional Neural Network (CNN)

Convolution is the basic operation for manipulating images, a filter may be designed to smooth an image, or to increase contrast, or to emphasize edges, it all depends on the coefficients (i.e. parameters) of the filter. A window of a predefined size is moved across the whole image, and for every position of the window, the pixel of at the center is modified so that the new value is the result of the convolution of the values of the image inside the window and the coefficients of the filter. Convolutional neural networks have convolutional layers that do just what filters do, but the parameters or coefficients for the convolution need not to be known a-priori, they are learned during training by an algorithm such as back-propagation. For every possible position of the window there is a neuron in the convolutional layer, that neuron corresponds to the pixel at the center of the window, all the pixels inside the window are used as inputs to that neuron, then there are many connections between the input layer and the first convolutional layer, one may believe that there is a huge number of parameters (i.e. weights) to be learned, however, convolutional layers use the same parameters for all the windows in the image, then the number of parameters to be learned does not depend on the size of the image but on the size of the window used.

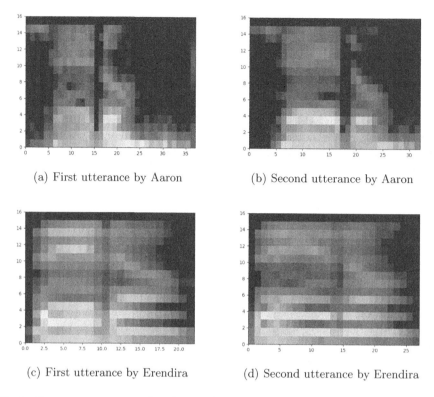

(a) First utterance by Aaron   (b) Second utterance by Aaron

(c) First utterance by Erendira   (d) Second utterance by Erendira

Fig. 1. Four entropygramas for the word "cero" uttered by two different speakers (Aaron and Erendira)

For a convolutional layer the learned parameters will make it to work as a filter that discover primitive shapes, but there are many possible primitive shapes, the solution is to add parallel convolutional layers so each one ends up working as a filter that find different primitive shapes. Normally the next layer after these filters are pooling layers which have the purpose of reducing the size of the image to reduce the computational effort of subsequent convolutional layers. These subsequent convolutional layers that follow find forms that are more and more complex because they are formed with the more simple forms discovered in the first convolutional layers.

The Convolutional Neural Network Used in Our Speaker Recognition System. Our CNN has two convolutional layers, both using the $ReLU$ (Rectified Linear Unit) activation function and each followed by maxPooling layers, then a flattener layer which converts 3D tensors to 1D tensors, followed by a dense layer of 64 neurons that use the $ReLU$ activation function and finally a dense layer of 21 output neurons with the *softmax* activation function. Table 1 shows the specifics of the CNN. The images (entropygrams) are standardized to a size of 24×32 pixels, the window's size used is 3×3, and the number of filters

Table 1. Specifics for the CNN used

Layer	Shape	Parameters
Conv2d_1	22,30,16	592
Maxpooling2d_1	11,15,16	0
Conv2d_2	9,13,32	4,640
Maxpooling2d_2	4,6,32	0
Flatten_1	768	0
Dense_1	64	49,216
Dropout(0.2)	64	0
Dense_2	21	1,365
		Total 55,813

is 16, so the first convolutional layer requires $(3 \times 3 \times 4) \times 16 + 16 = 592$ parameters (i.e. weights) to be learned. The maxpooling layers use 2×2 windows so the second convolutional layer receives images of size 11×15 pixels and adds $3 \times 3 \times 16 \times 32 + 32 = 4,640$ parameters because it uses 32 filters. After the *flatten* layer there are $4 \times 6 \times 32 = 768$ neurons fully connected to the first dense layer of 64 neurons which requires $768 \times 64 + 64 = 49,216$ parameters. Finally the last dense layer fully connect 64 neurons to 21 neurons of the output layer, and so requires $(64 \times 21 + 21 = 1,365$ additional parameters. The total number of parameters that the *adam* learning algorithm had to optimize was 55,813. This number of parameters is relatively low in deep learning, thanks to the fact that our entropygrams are small images. We also decided to add a Dropout layer as an attempt to reduce overfitting when it became an issue, this is not really a layer but an indication for the training algorithm that at every training step, with some given probability, each neuron of the preceding layer can be left out, or *dropped out* of the collated contribution from connected neurons, we adjusted that probability of dropping out to 0.2 since it seemed to work best with that value.

4 Experiments

We used a collection of the recordings from 21 Mexican speakers from both genders, ages between 18 and 30, in Spanish. Each speaker uttered 34 words four times, so there are $21 \times 34 \times 4 = 2,856$ recordings, this dataset can be downloaded from http://dep.fie.umich.mx/~camarena/dsp/elocuciones21.tar.gz. Since each speaker uttered each word four times, we used the first three utterances for the training set, so we extracted $21 \times 34 \times 3 = 2,142$ entropygrams, and for the test set, we extracted $21 \times 34 = 714$ entropygrams. This way 75% of the utterances conform the training set and 25% of them conform the test set. Since the speakers did not sorted the utterances in any special way we considered that taking the first three was the same as choosing them randomly.

We implemented the CNN in Python with the Keras library, which is built over TensorFlow. We used Google's Colab environment which made it easier for us to work and share results. For training we started with random weights, and used the *adam* optimizer which is a gradient descent algorithm for training the CNN. The number of epochs was 100 and the batch size was 32. We obtained an accuracy of 91% with the training set and 80% with the test set using entropygrams. Then using the same collection of utterances, we extracted spectrograms with the same resolution as our entropygrams, we simply determined energy instead of entropy for the same first 16 critical bands according to the Bark scale, the same bands used when we determined entropy for building entropygrams; after that we used another CNN with exactly the same parameters we used for recognizing speakers with entropygrams, except using spectrograms instead; we obtained an accuracy of 82% with the training set and 63% with the test set. So, at this point we confirmed not only that spectrograms are useful as a tool to transform the speaker identification problem into an image identification problem in the same way that spectrograms are used but that entropygrams outperform spectrograms in that issue when they are both at the same low resolution. Out next hypothesis was that in the presence of white noise, entropygrams would still work while spectrograms might not. So we mixed with gaussian white noise all the recorded utterances from both the training set and the test set up to a Signal to Noise Ratio (SNR) of 0dB, this means that the amount of energy is the original speech signal and the amount of energy in the noise is about the same. By listening to some of this noisy audio signals it is sometimes hard to hear the speech in those recordings. We turned each wav sound file with a noisy utterance into a low resolution png image with the corresponding entropygram and another one with the espectrogram. Again we used a convolutional neural network with the same topology and parameters as we used before and obtained an accuracy of 90% with the training set and 79% with the test set for the entropygrams and an accuracy of 62% with the training set and 55% with the test set for spectrograms. Table 2 shows the results of our experiments, it is worth saying that because the CNN had random weights before training, all the experiments were run five times and Table 2 shows the means of the accuracies, the variances are not shown in the table but they are all below 0.5, which mean the distributions of the accuracies are very narrow. For example, when entropygrams were used with noisy speech, the minimum

Table 2. Results

Experiment	Training set accuracy	Test set accuracy
Entropygrams/Clean speech	91%	80%
Spectrograms/Clean speech	82%	63%
Entropygrams/Noisy speech	90%	79%
Spectrograms/Noisy speech	62%	55%

accuracy obtained with the test set was 77% and the maximum was 81%, the mean (79%) is shown in the table.

5   Conclusions and Future Work

We hypothesized that entropygrams could be used as a tool for turning the speaker identification problem into an image recognition problem where convolutional neural networks are known to work very well. Our experiments confirmed our hypothesis, it is worth remarking that entropygrams have not been used before for this purpose. Furthermore, we found that entropygrams outperform spectrograms with clean audio for low resolution images. Finally we confirmed our hypothesis that when the speech signal is very noisy, spectrograms are not very useful but entropygrams are almost unaffected and can still be used to represent speakers for a CNN based speaker identification system. We can see that there is overfitting in our experiments, which was reduced by the use of a dropout layer, but we should try with alternative ways of reducing overfitting, for example data augmentation is a technique for reducing overfitting that consists in increasing the number of images present in the training. Some popular image augmentation techniques are flipping, translation, rotation, scaling, changing brightness, adding noise, etc. In our case, since we are dealing with entrpygrams and spectrograms, rotations and scaling make no sense but what do make sense are horizontal translations which can be interpreted as variations in segmentation (discovering the beginning and the end of the utterance) and perhaps vertical translations, change of brightness and noise adding.

References

1. Bercher, J., Vignat, C.: Estimating the entropy of a signal with applications. IEEE Trans. Signal Process. **48**(6), 1687–1694 (2000)
2. Besacier, L., Bonastre, J.F.: Subband architecture for automatic speaker recognition. Sig. Process. **80**(7), 1245–1259 (2000)
3. Bunrit, S., Inkian, T., Kerdprasop, N., Kerdprasop, K.: Text-independent speaker identification using deep learning model of convolution neural network. Int. J. Mach. Learn. Comput. **9**, 143–148 (2019). https://doi.org/10.18178/ijmlc.2019.9. 2.778
4. Camarena-Ibarrola, A., Luque, F., Chavez, E.: Speaker identification through spectral entropy analysis. In: 2017 IEEE International Autumn Meeting on Power, Electronics and Computing (ROPEC), pp. 1–6 (2017). https://doi.org/10.1109/ ROPEC.2017.8261607
5. Hermansky, H.: Perceptual linear predictive (PLP) analysis of speech. J. Acoust. Soc. Am. **87**(4), 1738–1752 (1990)
6. Lieberman, P., Blumstein, S.E.: Speech Physiology, Speech Perception, and Acoustic Phonetics. Cambridge University Press, Cambridge (1988)
7. Martin, R.: Noise power spectral density estimation based on optimal smoothing and minimum statistics. IEEE Trans. Speech Audio Process. **9**(5), 504–512 (2001)

8. Misra, H., Ikbal, S., Bourlard, H., Hermansky, H.: Spectral entropy based feature for robust ASR. In: 2004 IEEE International Conference on Proceedings of Acoustics, Speech, and Signal Processing (ICASSP 2004), vol. 1, pp. I–193. IEEE (2004)
9. Mohammad-Djafari, A.: Entropy in signal processing. Traitement du signal, pp. 87–116 (1994)
10. Plumpe, M.D., Quatieri, T.F., Reynolds, D.A.: Modeling of the glottal flow derivative waveform with application to speaker identification. IEEE Trans. Speech Audio Process. **7**(5), 569–586 (1999)
11. Rabiner, L.R., Schafer, R.W.: Digital Processing of Speech Signals. Prentice Hall, Upper Saddle River (1978)
12. Shannon, C., Weaver, W.: The Mathematical Theory of Communication. University of Illinois Press, Champaign (1949)
13. Thévenaz, P., Hügli, H.: Usefulness of the LPC-residue in text-independent speaker verification. Speech Commun. **17**(1–2), 145–157 (1995)
14. Toh, A., Togneri, R., Nordholm, S.: Spectral entropy as speech features for speech recognition. In: Proceedings of PEECS, January 2005
15. Wang, J.C., Wang, C.Y., Chin, Y.H., Liu, Y.T., Chen, E.T., Chang, P.C.: Spectral-temporal receptive fields and MFCC balanced feature extraction for robust speaker recognition. Multimed. Tools Appl. **76**, 4055–4068 (2016). https://doi.org/10.1007/s11042-016-3335-0
16. Yu, J.C., Zhang, R.l.: Speaker recognition method using MFCC and LPCC features. Comput. Eng. Des. **5**, 050 (2009)
17. Zwicker, E.: Subdivision of the audible frequency range into critical bands. J. Acoust. Soc. Am. **33**(2), 248 (1961)

Convolutional Neural Networks with Hebbian-Based Rules in Online Transfer Learning

Fernando Javier Aguilar Canto[✉]

Facultad de Matemáticas, Universidad Autónoma de Yucatán, Anillo Periférico Norte, Tablaje Cat. 13615, Colonia Chuburná Hidalgo Inn, Mérida, Yucatán, Mexico
pherjev@gmail.com

Abstract. In 1949, Donald Hebb proposed its Neurophysiologic Principle, which models the weight change of connected neurons. Although similar mechanisms have been experimentally proven to exists in several brain areas, traditional Deep Learning methods do not implement it, generally using Gradient-based algorithms instead. On the other hand, Convolutional Neural Networks (CNNs) has slight inspiration on the structure of Visual Cortex, particularly on the Hierarchical model of Hubel-Wiesel. Using convolutional layers it is possible to perform feature extraction and a final classification with dense layers. In this paper, we propose a combined technique of using pre-trained convolutional layers and a final classification using Hebbian-based rules (Basic Hebb, Covariance, Oja, and BCM). Once the feature extraction is done, Hebbian rules can discriminate the classes with high accuracy. These theoretical ideas were tested using this MNIST database, reaching 99.43% of test accuracy training CNNs layers with a final Hebb layer. Similar results were found using Hebbian-based rules in other datasets with RGB images and Transfer Learning. Even when these results are slightly lower than Gradient-based methods, Hebbian learning can perform online learning, which suggests that this combined strategy might be useful to design Online Machine Learning Algorithms for Image Classification.

Keywords: Hebb rule · Oja rule · Convolutional Neural Networks · Transfer learning · Online machine learning · Biological models of neural networks

1 Introduction

Since the discovery of Long-Term Potentiation (LTP) in the hippocampus of mammals [32], Hebbian learning has been verified as a valid model of associative learning in real neurons [7,36] and has also been detected in neurons located in Neocortex and Cerebellum [8,46]. However, despite the amount of evidence, Hebbian-based rules have not received enough attention in current fields of Machine Learning [50] and, instead, parameters of recent models of

© Springer Nature Switzerland AG 2020
L. Martínez-Villaseñor et al. (Eds.): MICAI 2020, LNAI 12468, pp. 35–49, 2020.
https://doi.org/10.1007/978-3-030-60884-2_3

Artificial Neural Networks are usually optimized by using gradient-based learning algorithms such as Adam [23].

As we will discuss later, Hebbian learning is not an appropriate model to minimize cost functions such as Sum of Square Errors (SSE) in Neural Networks. Experimental results show that a direct application of Hebbian learning in problems such as Image Classification does not yield better results than current algorithms [1]. Why does a more natural approach to Neural Networks perform worse than gradient-based optimizers? Is there a computational advantage of using biologically inspired methods such as Hebbian learning? One possible answer can be found in Mathematics. Gradient descent converges at least to a local minimum given some conditions (see [37] for further details), whereas this statement does not necessary hold in Hebbian learning for any cost functions[1]. As a corollary, we cannot expect a better performance using the Hebb rule, which can be incompletely described.

Nevertheless, as a model of natural learning, Hebbian learning provides some interesting advantages, including the possibility of being applied in contexts of Online Machine Learning, since it satisfies the conditions proposed by [30]. Traditional formulation of Gradient-based algorithms cannot perform Online Machine Learning tasks, because several loss functions (for instant, SSE or Cross Entropy) are a sum of functions of the data, such as $J_{\mathbf{w}}(x, y) = \sum_{i=1}^{n} j(NN_{\mathbf{w}}(x_i), y_i)$, where j measures error between $NN_{\mathbf{w}}(x_i)$ (output of the neural network with weights $\mathbf{w}$) and y_i, and therefore the gradient is given by $\sum_{i=1}^{n} \nabla j_{\mathbf{w}}(NN_{\mathbf{w}}(x_i), y_i)$. In this case, it is required to compute n data points or a sample of the dataset. It is possible to use only one data point, but this situation yields the Perceptron Learning Rule (see Methodology). However, there exist some attempts to implement Gradient-based rules in Online Deep Learning contexts, such as [42].

On the other hand, more biologically-inspired neural networks have achieved important results. Perhaps the clearest example is the case of Convolutional Neural Networks. Since its formulation (see [28]), Convolutional Networks (CNNs) are slightly based on the Hierarchical Model [43] (proposed by Hubel and Wiesel in [21]), but according to some authors [45], CNNs are not exactly a model of Visual Cortex. Nevertheless, its success in large image classification [24,47] problems provide some evidence of its validity.

Therefore, the combined usage of Hebbian learning with Convolutional Neural Networks might be a better computational model of Visual Recognition and can be useful to perform real-time learning in image classification tasks. Previously we had discussed that Gradient-based implementations of Neural Networks are more common than Hebbian algorithms. For that reason, a hybrid optimization algorithm could be ideal to improve the general performance of Hebbian learning and the efficiency of Gradient-based algorithms. Transfer learning with conventional methods and deep convolutional architectures do not need to retrain weights, and it is possible to extract image features by using a pre-trained model. Thus, our proposal consists of applying Hebbian rule as a

---

[1] Hebbian Learning optimizes specific functions, see [9].

classifier of a feature vector extracted using pre-trained convolutional layers. This idea provides a more natural approach for Deep Learning, enable the possibility of real-time learning and a provisional solution of an effective Hebbian-based optimization algorithm.

2 Related Work

As mentioned previously, Hebbian learning has not been extensively applied in contexts of Neural Networks, in particular, Feedforward Neural Networks and CNNs for image classification. However, there are some recent implementations of Hebbian-based learning using CNNs. Most related works have focused on how to train convolutional layers using Hebbian principles. In 2016, [50] developed a convolutional neural network with three layers, trained with an unsupervised algorithm called Adaptive Hebbian Learning for lower layers and Discriminative Hebbian Learning for higher layers, making possible feature extraction, which is tested using a final Support Vector Machine (SVM) classification. A deeper network was proposed in [2], using Competitive Hebbian Learning. Its results showed just a slightly lower accuracy in comparison with Stochastic Gradient Descent (SGD) in the classification layer and also suggests that Hebbian rule might be used in lower and higher convolutional layers but not in the intermediate layers.

An application of Transfer Learning with Hebbian optimization can be found in [34], where the authors pre-trained a convolutional neural network in the Cifar10 dataset and proposed the usage of backpropagation of plastic layer network. However, Online learning is not considered in that context. This aspect has been considered in [3,4], where the authors introduced the Deep Hebbian Network, a similar approach to Convolutional Neural Networks to develop feature extraction and using an SVM classification layer.

Our approach consists of using a pre-trained convolutional network but with a final classification layer using Hebbian/Perceptron learning rules in order to be used in Online Learning tasks. MNIST dataset of handwritten digits was used to test our proposal. Most of the mentioned related papers test its algorithms by using Cifar-10 or Cifar-100 datasets [2–4,34,50]. However, [50] was able to reach 99.35% of test accuracy using Adaptive Hebbian Learning. Other Hebbian-based algorithms but using shallow networks have also been tested with the MNIST. For instance, [22] reached 92. $\pm$ 0.2% of test accuracy using lateral inhibition and a logarithmic activation function. An improvement of this result was done by [20] using Acetylcholine and Dopamine models, which yields 97.12$\pm$ 0.05% of test accuracy.

Spiking Neural Networks (SNNs) have also been used. For example, [31] implemented a version of the Hierarchical Model with SNNs, reaching 82 $\pm$ 2% of MNIST test accuracy. Since we are using pre-trained convolutional neural networks (which are very effective in the MNIST dataset, [28]), we only made a brief mention of its existence.

3 Methodology

In this section, we detailed the structure of the idea presented previously. The general sketch of that idea is provided in Fig. 1. Two relevant components require a deeper description: the convolutional network involved and the Hebbian-based algorithms selected. Convolutional Neural Network yield a *feature vector* $\mathbf{x}$, which is used as the input of the Hebbian network (without using hidden layers). Although our approach is related to Online Learning, in order to test our model we used finite datasets: MNIST [29], Cats-vs-Dogs Tensorflow's dataset [15] and we finally proposed a dataset with free-commercial usage videos taken from Pexels with ten categories: airplane, ship, cat, horse, computer, desert, fish, flower, dog, and fire.

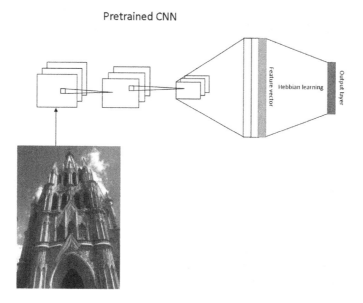

Fig. 1. General model of Hebbian-based algorithms with Convolutional pretrained layers

This Pexels dataset[2] consists in 13 videos of 200 frames from each category in the training set and 2 in the testing set. This dataset was included in order to provide a more natural learning context where our algorithms might be applied. Finally we included two principal Gradient-based algorithms to compare the Hebbian-based learning rules, which are Adam as optimizer of the Categorical Cross Entropy loss function, and RMSProp as optimizer of the Binary Cross Entropy function. The last loss function was only implemented in the Cats-vs-Dogs dataset.

---

[2] Links of the videos and full code can be found in https://github.com/Pherjev/Hebbian-CNN.

3.1 Convolutional Layers

We selected two convolutional architectures to perform MNIST classification, principally inspired in VGG convolutional structure [47]. These models, called $VGGS_1$ and $VGGS_2$ are provided in Table 1.

Table 1. Convolutional architectures of $VGGS_1$ and $VGGS_2$.

$VGGS_1$	$VGGS_2$
64 filters of 3×3	64 filters of 3×3 with same padding
Batch Normalization	Batch Normalization
64 filters of 3×3	64 filters of 3×3 with same padding
Batch Normalization	Batch Normalization
Max Pooling of 2×2	Max Pooling of 2×2
Dropout of 0.25%	Dropout of 0.25%
128 filters of 3×3	128 filters of 3×3 with same padding
Batch Normalization	Batch Normalization
128 filters of 3×3	128 filters of 3×3 with same padding
Batch Normalization	Batch Normalization
Max Pooling of 2×2	Max Pooling of 2×2 with strides of 2×2
Dropout of 0.25%	Dropout of 0.25%
	256 filters of 3×3 with same padding
	Batch Normalization
	Dropout of 0.25%
Fully connected layer of 256 neurons	Fully connected layer of 512 neurons
Classification layer of 10 neurons	Classification layer of 10 neurons

All layers of the first model were activated with ReLU [17], but the output layer, which uses the softmax activation function. This first model was compiled using Adam [23] and the Categorical Crossentropy loss function (see [14,35]). This second model was trained with 30 fixed epochs and using RMSprop with initial $\alpha = 0.01$ and $\rho = 0.9$. Reduction of learning rate was performed by using a factor of 0.5 with a patient of 3. No hyperparametric optimization was included.

On the other hand, we used pre-trained architectures in the case of datasets with RGB images. All the selected convolutional networks have been trained with the Imagenet [41] dataset with successful results. These architectures are:

- VGG19 [47]
- InceptionV3 [49]
- ResNet50 [18]
- Xception [10]
- InceptionResNetV2 [48]

3.2 Hebbian Learning

Hebbian-based learning rules can be written in the form

$$\tau_{\mathbf{w}} \frac{d\mathbf{w}}{dt} = H(\mathbf{x}, y) \tag{1}$$

where H is a *Hebbian function* that describes the learning process, $\mathbf{x} = (x_1, \ldots, x_m)$ is the vector of presynaptic activities (firing rate) of input neurons, y is the firing rate of the postsynaptic neuron whereas $\mathbf{w} = (w_1, \ldots, w_m)$ represents the weights. $\tau_{\mathbf{w}} > 0$ is a time constant which is the inverse of the learning rate.

In addition, this function can include other parameters such as the weight vector itself ($\mathbf{w}$) and a third factor, which can be the effect of biological instances such as neuromodulators (Dopamine, Acetylcholine, Noradrenaline, Serotonin, see [39]), neurotransmitters, glial factors, and retrograde axonal signal [25]. In this case, $\frac{d\mathbf{w}}{dt} = H(\mathbf{x}, y, g, \mathbf{w})$, where g is the called third factor. Numerically, Hebbian rules can be computed using Euler's Method

$$\mathbf{w} \leftarrow \mathbf{w} + H(\mathbf{x}, y, g, \mathbf{w}) \tag{2}$$

Hebbian rule was first proposed in 1949 in [19], and basically states that simultaneous activity of presynaptic and postsynaptic neurons yields an increment of the weight between both neurons. In terms of Computational Neuroscience (see [13]), a simplified model of the firing rate y is given by the dot product $y = \mathbf{w} \cdot \mathbf{x}$, but models usually add an activation function. In this paper we included common formulations of Hebbian functions, following [13], which are the Basic Hebb Rule, Covariance Rule, BCM Rule and the Perceptron Learning Rule.

Basic Hebb Rule. The Basic Hebb Rule is given by the differential equation

$$\tau_{\mathbf{w}} \frac{d\mathbf{w}}{dt} = y\mathbf{x} \tag{3}$$

This rule is the simplest learning rule that follows the original ideas of Donald Hebb and, as commented in [13], is a computational model of LTP.

Covariance Rule. Experimental results showed the existence of a similar process of depression of synaptic response given some particular condition. This process is called *Long-Term Depression* (LTD) and was not considered in the original Hebbian model and in the Basic Hebb Rule. Both LTP and LTD occur in biological neural networks: induction of LTP is done when presynaptic and postsynaptic neurons have strong activity in the same moment, whereas LTD occurs when the presynaptic neuron has a high firing rate but the postsynaptic neuron shows a low activity [33]. A simple model of LTP-LTD response is given by:

$$\tau_{\mathbf{w}} \frac{d\mathbf{w}}{dt} = (y - \theta_y)\mathbf{x} \tag{4}$$

where θ_y is called *postsynaptic threshold* because if $\theta_y > y$, the response will be depression and otherwise, if $\theta_y < y$, LTP will happen [13]. The last formulation was proposed by [44] and it was named as *Covariance Learning Rule*.

Oja Rule. One referred problem of the previous learning rules is the unbounded growth of the weights, which contradicts experimental evidence [13]. Oja [38] proposed a synaptic normalization using the equation

$$\tau_\mathbf{w} \frac{d\mathbf{w}}{dt} = y\mathbf{x} - \beta y^2 \mathbf{w} \tag{5}$$

which is a weight normalization that helps to prevent the described problem.

BCM Rule. Another solution to the unbounded growth of the weights is the addition of a sliding threshold. This idea was proposed by Bienenstock, Cooper and Munro in 1982 [6] and has received empirical evidence (see [12,27]). The BCM learning rule is given by the following system

$$\tau_w \frac{d\mathbf{w}}{dt} = y\mathbf{x}(y - \theta_y) \tag{6}$$

$$\tau_\theta \frac{d\theta_y}{dt} = y^2 - \theta_y \tag{7}$$

where τ_θ is the time scale of the rate of change of the threshold.

Peceptron Learning Rule. Finally, we considered the Perceptron Learning Rule [40], which can be understood as an intermediate rule between gradient-based rules and Hebbian-based rules with the advantage of performing gradient descent with one data point and does not require to use more data. This rule is given by the expression

$$\tau_\mathbf{w} \frac{d\mathbf{w}}{dt} = (y - \mathbf{w} \cdot \mathbf{x})y \tag{8}$$

In the context of MNIST, a three-layered perceptron has been tested reaching 99.2% [26]. A direct application of Basic Hebbian rule in this dataset was attempted and yielded 68% of test accuracy, very low in contrast with Gradient-based algorithms. For that reason, the improvement of architecture might be a possible solution, but we can not expect to surpass the accuracy of Gradient-based methods.

Input Integration. Additionally, [20,22] suggest the usage of a linearised logarithm function reduces the growth of the weight vector. This function is

$$S(w) = \begin{cases} w & w < 1 \\ \log(w) + 1 & w \geq 1 \end{cases} \tag{9}$$

Thus, the output of the neural network is $y = \sum_{i=1}^{m} S(w_i)x_i$.

4   Results

4.1   MNIST

We trained $VGGS_1$, $VGGS_2$ with the MNIST dataset to optimally develop the appropriate convolutional kernels for feature extraction. The last classification layer was truncated to use the feature vector, which was retrained using some variations of the discussed learning rules. These variants are

- *Basic Hebb*: Consists in using the update rule $\mathbf{w} \leftarrow \mathbf{w} + y\mathbf{x}$.
- *L-Hebbian*: Adds function $S(w)$ to the weights, using Basic Hebb Rule.
- *Covariance*: Consists in Covariance Rule: $\mathbf{w} \leftarrow \mathbf{w} + (y - \theta)\mathbf{x}$, where $\theta = 1$. Logarithmic control was included.
- *Oja*: Implements Oja Rule with $\beta = 0.01$: $\mathbf{w} \leftarrow \mathbf{w} + y\mathbf{x} - \beta y^2 \mathbf{w}$.
- *L-Oja*: Oja Rule using $S(w)$: $\mathbf{w} \leftarrow \mathbf{w} + v\mathbf{x} - \beta y^2 S(\mathbf{w})$.
- *BCM*: Implements the BCM Learning Rule using $S(w)$ and $\mathbf{w} \leftarrow \mathbf{w} + y\mathbf{x}(y - \theta_y)$ and $\theta_y \leftarrow \theta_y + \tau(y^2 - \theta_y)$. $\tau = 0.5$ and initial $\theta_y = 1$.
- *PLR*: Implements the Perceptron Learning Rule using $\mathbf{w} \leftarrow \mathbf{w} + (y - \mathbf{w} \cdot \mathbf{x})\mathbf{x}$.
- *SPLR*: Implements the Perceptron Learning Rule using a sigmoid function σ: $\mathbf{w} \leftarrow \mathbf{w} + (y - S(\mathbf{w}) \cdot \mathbf{x})\mathbf{x}$.
- *LSPLR*: Implements the Perceptron Learning Rule using a sigmoid function σ and $S(w)$: $\mathbf{w} \leftarrow \mathbf{w} + (y - \sigma(S(\mathbf{w}) \cdot \mathbf{x}))\mathbf{x}$

$VGGS_1$ was trained in the MNIST dataset and EMNIST letters dataset to perform Transfer Learning with different images. EMNIST [11] letters dataset consists of 124800 training images and 20800 testing images of letters, thus, it can be considered as a slightly similar dataset. Training $VGGS_1$ yielded 94.74% of accuracy in 20 epochs, which, according to the benchmark done in [5], is not far from the state-of-art.

Once the CNNs were trained, we eliminated the final layer using convolutional layers as a feature extractor. Finally, Hebbian-based algorithms were trained using the feature vector. The results are summarized in Table 2. In general, most algorithms achieve an acceptable rate and Perceptron Learning Rule yielded the best results. Logarithmic Hebbian and Logarithmic Oja also performed well and in general, L-Oja was just slightly better. However, the combined usage of Oja and Perceptron rules did not perform better (95% in Transfer Learning). The addition of logarithmic control of the weights and sigmoid activation function in Perceptron significantly improved the results in almost all cases.

A summary of related works about Hebbian learning applied in MNIST dataset is provided in Table 3, in comparison with out best results. This hybrid approach yielded higher accuracy than other applications of Hebbian-based rules in the MNIST classification, which means that usage of pretrained convolutional layers might be ideal to reach higher accuracy. However, this implementation is not an appropriate Transfer Learning since it is not trained with another dataset. For that reason, we applied additional testings with different datasets.

Table 2. Test accuracy using different models. CNN accuracy is given by its respectively test accuracy of baseline model. Better results with Hebbian-based rules are highlighted

Model	$VGGS_1$	$VGGS_2$	Transfer learning
Basic Hebb	98.44	99.43	70.86
L-Hebbian	99.14	99.43	94.56
Covariance	98.4	98.94	70.86
Oja	98.36	99.25	70.06
L-Oja	99.14	99.42	94.72
BCM	99.17	99.42	94.57
PLR	9.80	9.80	9.80
SPLR	9.40	9.40	10.37
LSPLR	**99.30**	**99.60**	**96.40**
CNN	99.32	99.66	94.74

Table 3. Summary of related works about Hebbian learning in MNIST dataset in comparison with the results exposed in this paper (last two rows)

Method	Year	Learning rule	Accuracy
Two-layered network [26]	2001	Perceptron	99.2%
Two-layered network [22]	2012	Hebb (variant)	$92 \pm 0.2\%$
Spiking Network [31]	2016	Hebb (variant)	$82 \pm 2\%$
Hebbian CNN [50]	2016	Adaptative Hebbian	99.35%
Acetylcholine + Dopamine models [20]	2017	Hebb (variant)	$97.12 \pm 0.05\%$
$VGGS_2$	2020	L-Hebb + RMSprop	99.43%
$VGGS_2$	2020	LSPLR + RMSprop	**99.6%**

4.2   Pexels Dataset

In the last subsection we showed the possibility of incorporate some of the proposed Hebbian-based methods, including Basic Hebb Rule, Oja Rule, Covariance Rule (with $\theta = 1$), BCM Rule and Perceptron Learning Rule, all of them with logarithmic control. Gradient-based algorithms, however, performed better in all experiments.

In this case, architectures VGG-19. ResNet50, InceptionResNetV2 and Xception were used to extract image features and a final neural network classification layer was added to perform Transfer Learning. All algorithms were compared with Adam, which as trained with 10 epochs. Principal results are summarized in Table 4. Unexpectedly Perceptron Learning and BCM rules were unable to generalize the data in all cases. Adam, on the other hand, performed well and it reached the maximum accuracy. The other rules (Hebb, Covariance, Oja) showed more consistent results, and in some cases (especially using Xception) they were very close to the maximum accuracy.

Table 4. Test accuracy of the Pexels' dataset

CNN	Adam	LSPLR	L-Hebb	Covariance	L-Oja	BCM
VGG19	0.9057	0.335	0.8893	0.8673	0.8933	0.5345
ResNet50	0.9433	0.36175	0.84325	0.8705	0.82925	0.46975
InceptionResNetV2	0.9998	0.1502	0.8382	0.889	0.849	0.535
Xception	0.9995	0.16325	0.996	0.99625	0.9785	0.55225

4.3 Dogs vs Cats Dataset

Finally we include a comparison of Hebbian-based using different convolutional neural networks. This dataset consists in 18610 images in the training set of cats and dogs, and 2326 in the testing set. Main results are provided in the Table 5.

Table 5. Main results of the Dogs-vs-Cats dataset

CNN	RMSprop	LSPLR	L-Hebb	Covariance	L-Oja	BCM
VGG19	0.9858	0.9845	0.9699	0.9398	0.9742	0.9733
InceptionV3	0.9905	0.9901	0.9828	0.8422	0.9837	0.9832
ResNet50	0.9927	0.9914	0.9746	0.9424	0.9776	0.9802
InceptionResNetV2	0.9931	0.9931	0.9767	0.9871	0.9746	0.9751
Xception	0.9897	0.9897	0.9879	0.9622	0.9841	0.985

In general we can observe that RMSprop was always better, as expected, but in several cases Perceptron Learning Rule reached its accuracy. The usage of Xception yielded the more balanced results. Oja and BCM Rules performed slightly better than Basic Hebb Rule in most cases, but this rule with 98.79% reached the best accuracy using the Xception. Figures 2 provides an example of convergence graphs of the Hebbian and Gradient-based methods. In this specific case, Covariance rule failed to converge and more data do not represent and improvement. In the other cases, convergence is reached using $n = 5000$. In contrast with RMSprop, Hebbian-based rules do not seem to maximizes accuracy almost monotonically. On the contrary, these rules seem to reduce the probability of making mistakes over the time.

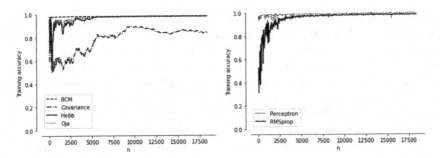

Fig. 2. Convergence graphs of Hebbian-based methods (left) and Gradient-based methods using InceptionV3, where n represents the number of datapoints used in the training.

5   Conclusions

In this paper, we proposed an Online Transfer Learning technique by using Hebbian-based rules with pre-trained convolutional layers. This approach attempts to introduce more biologically inspired retraining of Convolutional Neural Networks with further applications in robotics and other systems that receive real-time information from sensors or other sources, using deeper networks with kernels trained with the Imagenet dataset. However, empirical testings of Hebbian-based rules have yielded lower accuracy in comparison with Gradient-based rules. With the addition of Convolutional layers, we expected to reduce the distances between Hebbian and Gradient approaches, without sacrificing the advantages of Hebbian-based rules. Rather than performing Unsupervised Learning (as followed in most related works), this paper aims to allow Online Transfer Learning by using Hebbian principles.

In the MNIST dataset, it was found that Perceptron Learning Rule yields better results than other Hebbian-based, and performed very similar to the baseline CNN, optimized with Adam or RMSprop. Usage of $VGGS_2$ was able to yield better comparative results than other Hebbian-based algorithms described previously, even in the case of Logarithmic Hebbian and Logarithmic Oja. This means that an increment of the power of the convolutional network results in an increment of the potential of Hebbian based methods. Also, it is worth mentioning that the inclusion of control functions was considered useful.

Transfer learning tests, however, yielded less effective results. Convolutional layers were trained using a dataset of handwritten letters. As shown in [16], first kernels are very similar to Garbor filters which mean that capture universal features of images, but deeper filters are more complex and recognize proper features of the images of the training set. It is possible that a final tunning in final convolutional layers, done with the techniques suggested by related works in Hebbian convolutional layers, is required to improve the performance of this Hebbian networks.

Although it was expected to see a lower performance in the Basic Hebb Rule, followed by Covariance, Oja, BCM, and finally the Perceptron Learning Rule, the situation was more complex. Oja and Hebb Rule performed well in all tests and can be proposed as valid models of Transfer Learning. Covariance was lower than Hebbian in some cases (but it reached the maximum accuracy of Hebbian-based rules in the Pexels' dataset), and BCM performed very badly in specific cases, but in others, it yielded the maximum accuracy of Hebbian rules. In general, some Hebbian-based rules (Basic Hebb, Oja, and Covariance) performed almost as well as Gradient-based rules in almost all cases, which achieves the main objective of this research.

Both RGB considered datasets yielded more balanced results using Xception. Why does this Convolutional Neural Network tend to produce better comparative results in Hebbian learning than other recent deep neural networks such as InceptionResNetV2? Why does a more biologically inspired learning rule such as BCM rule failed in specific cases whereas Basic Hebb Rule did not show a similar behavior? Perhaps a full implementation of these rules depends on other factors and requires more comprehension about the nature of Biological Neural Networks. Some other questions might also remain unanswered. Do our neurons perform any similar Gradient-based algorithm, or they just use well-known Hebbian rules? A review of the literature (see [25]) indicates that some mechanisms involved in neural learning are not completely functionally understood, and just a few models exist about other factors that amplified or reduce the potentiation/depression. A future research line might be incorporate the neuromodulators models suggested in [20].

Acknowledgments. I would like to thank Carlos Francisco Brito-Loeza for his comments and support.

References

1. Aguilar Canto, F.J.: Eficacia de diferentes reglas hebbianas en el aprendizaje supervisado. Tecnología Educativa Revista CONAIC **7**(1), 92–97 (2020)
2. Amato, G., Carrara, F., Falchi, F., Gennaro, C., Lagani, G.: Hebbian learning meets deep convolutional neural networks. In: Ricci, E., Rota Bulò, S., Snoek, C., Lanz, O., Messelodi, S., Sebe, N. (eds.) ICIAP 2019. LNCS, vol. 11751, pp. 324–334. Springer, Cham (2019). https://doi.org/10.1007/978-3-030-30642-7_29
3. Bahroun, Y., Hunsicker, E., Soltoggio, A.: Building efficient deep Hebbian networks for image classification tasks. In: Lintas, A., Rovetta, S., Verschure, P.F.M.J., Villa, A.E.P. (eds.) ICANN 2017. LNCS, vol. 10613, pp. 364–372. Springer, Cham (2017). https://doi.org/10.1007/978-3-319-68600-4_42
4. Bahroun, Y., Soltoggio, A.: Online representation learning with single and multi-layer Hebbian networks for image classification. In: Lintas, A., Rovetta, S., Verschure, P.F.M.J., Villa, A.E.P. (eds.) ICANN 2017. LNCS, vol. 10613, pp. 354–363. Springer, Cham (2017). https://doi.org/10.1007/978-3-319-68600-4_41
5. Baldominos, A., Saez, Y., Isasi, P.: A survey of handwritten character recognition with MNIST and EMNIST. Appl. Sci. **9**(15), 3169 (2019)

6. Bienenstock, E.L., Cooper, L.N., Munro, P.W.: Theory for the development of neuron selectivity: orientation specificity and binocular interaction in visual cortex. J. Neurosci. **2**(1), 32–48 (1982)
7. Bliss, T.V., Cooke, S.F.: Long-term potentiation and long-term depression: a clinical perspective. Clinics **66**, 3–17 (2011)
8. Bromer, C., et al.: Long-term potentiation expands information content of hippocampal dentate gyrus synapses. Proc. Natl. Acad. Sci. **115**(10), E2410–E2418 (2018)
9. Choe, Y.: Hebbian Learning. Springer, Incorporated (2015)
10. Chollet, F.: Xception: deep learning with depthwise separable convolutions. In: Proceedings of the IEEE conference on Computer Vision and Pattern Recognition, pp. 1251–1258 (2017)
11. Cohen, G., Afshar, S., Tapson, J., Van Schaik, A.: EMNIST: extending MNIST to handwritten letters. In: 2017 International Joint Conference on Neural Networks (IJCNN), pp. 2921–2926. IEEE (2017)
12. Cooper, L.N., Bear, M.F.: The BCM theory of synapse modification at 30: interaction of theory with experiment. Nat. Rev. Neurosci. **13**(11), 798–810 (2012)
13. Dayan, P., Abbott, L.: Computational neuroscience (2002)
14. Dorfer, M., Kelz, R., Widmer, G.: Deep linear discriminant analysis. arXiv preprint arXiv:1511.04707 (2015)
15. Elson, J., Douceur, J.J., Howell, J., Saul, J.: Asirra: a CAPTCHA that exploits interest-aligned manual image categorization. In: Proceedings of 14th ACM Conference on Computer and Communications Security (CCS). Association for Computing Machinery, Inc., October 2007
16. Erhan, D., Bengio, Y., Courville, A., Vincent, P.: Visualizing higher-layer features of a deep network. Univ. Montreal **1341**(3), 1 (2009)
17. Hahnloser, R.H., Sarpeshkar, R., Mahowald, M.A., Douglas, R.J., Seung, H.S.: Digital selection and analogue amplification coexist in a cortex-inspired silicon circuit. Nature **405**(6789), 947–951 (2000)
18. He, K., Zhang, X., Ren, S., Sun, J.: Deep residual learning for image recognition. In: Proceedings of the IEEE Conference on Computer Vision and Pattern Recognition, pp. 770–778 (2016)
19. Hebb, D.O.: The Organization of Behavior: A Neuropsychological Theory. Wiley, Chapman & Hall, New York (1949)
20. Holca-Lamarre, R., Lücke, J., Obermayer, K.: Models of acetylcholine and dopamine signals differentially improve neural representations. Front. Comput. Neurosci. **11**, 54 (2017)
21. Hubel, D.H., Wiesel, T.N.: Receptive fields, binocular interaction and functional architecture in the cat's visual cortex. J. Physiol. **160**(1), 106 (1962)
22. Keck, C., Savin, C., Lücke, J.: Feedforward inhibition and synaptic scaling-two sides of the same coin? PLoS Comput. Biol. **8**(3), e1002432 (2012)
23. Kingma, D.P., Ba, J.: Adam: a method for stochastic optimization. arXiv preprint arXiv:1412.6980 (2014)
24. Krizhevsky, A., Sutskever, I., Hinton, G.E.: ImageNet classification with deep convolutional neural networks. In: Advances in Neural Information Processing Systems, pp. 1097–1105 (2012)
25. Kuśmierz, Ł., Isomura, T., Toyoizumi, T.: Learning with three factors: modulating Hebbian plasticity with errors. Curr. Opin. Neurobiol. **46**, 170–177 (2017)

26. Kussul, E., Baidyk, T., Kasatkina, L., Lukovich, V.: Rosenblatt perceptrons for handwritten digit recognition. In: International Joint Conference on Neural Networks. Proceedings (Cat. No. 01CH37222), IJCNN 2001, vol. 2, pp. 1516–1520. IEEE (2001)

27. Law, C.C., Cooper, L.N.: Formation of receptive fields in realistic visual environments according to the Bienenstock, Cooper, and Munro (BCM) theory. Proc. Natl. Acad. Sci. **91**(16), 7797–7801 (1994)

28. LeCun, Y., Bottou, L., Bengio, Y., Haffner, P.: Gradient-based learning applied to document recognition. Proc. IEEE **86**(11), 2278–2324 (1998)

29. LeCun, Y., Cortes, C., Burges, C.: Mnist handwritten digit database (2010) http://yann.lecun.com/exdb/mnist 7, 23 (2010)

30. Li, G., Liu, M., Dong, M.: A new online learning algorithm for structure-adjustable extreme learning machine. Comput. Math. Appl. **60**(3), 377–389 (2010)

31. Liu, D., Yue, S.: Visual pattern recognition using unsupervised spike timing dependent plasticity learning. In: 2016 International Joint Conference on Neural Networks (IJCNN), pp. 285–292. IEEE (2016)

32. Lomo, T.: Frequency potentiation of excitatory synaptic activity in dentate area of hippocampal formation. In: Acta Physiologica Scandinavica. p. 128. BLACKWELL SCIENCE LTD PO BOX 88, OSNEY MEAD, OXFORD OX2 0NE, OXON, ENGLAND (1966)

33. Lüscher, C., Malenka, R.C.: NMDA receptor-dependent long-term potentiation and long-term depression (LTP/LTD). Cold Spring Harb. Perspect. Biol. **4**(6), a005710 (2012)

34. Magotra, A., kim, J.: Transfer learning for image classification using Hebbian plasticity principles. In: Proceedings of the 2019 3rd International Conference on Computer Science and Artificial Intelligence, pp. 233–238 (2019)

35. Mannor, S., Peleg, D., Rubinstein, R.: The cross entropy method for classification. In: Proceedings of the 22nd international conference on Machine Learning, pp. 561–568 (2005)

36. Nicoll, R.A.: A brief history of long-term potentiation. Neuron **93**(2), 281–290 (2017)

37. Nocedal, J., Wright, S.: Numerical Optimization. Springer, Heidelberg (2006)

38. Oja, E.: Simplified neuron model as a principal component analyzer. J. Math. Biol. **15**(3), 267–273 (1982)

39. Palacios-Filardo, J., Mellor, J.R.: Neuromodulation of hippocampal long-term synaptic plasticity. Curr. Opin. Neurobiol. **54**, 37–43 (2019)

40. Rosenblatt, F.: The perceptron: a probabilistic model for information storage and organization in the brain. Psychol. Rev. **65**(6), 386 (1958)

41. Russakovsky, O., et al.: ImageNet large scale visual recognition challenge. Int. J. Comput. Vision **115**(3), 211–252 (2015)

42. Sahoo, D., Pham, Q., Lu, J., Hoi, S.C.: Online deep learning: learning deep neural networks on the fly. arXiv preprint arXiv:1711.03705 (2017)

43. Seeliger, K., et al.: Convolutional neural network-based encoding and decoding of visual object recognition in space and time. NeuroImage **180**, 253–266 (2018)

44. Sejnowski, T.J., Tesauro, G.: Building network learning algorithms from Hebbian synapses. In: Brain Organization and Memory: Cells, Systems, and Circuits, pp. 338–355. Oxford University Press, New York (1989)

45. Serre, T.: Hierarchical Models of the Visual System. Springer Publishing Company, Incorporated (2015)

46. Shim, H.G., et al.: Long-term depression of intrinsic excitability accompanied by synaptic depression in cerebellar Purkinje cells. J. Neurosci. **37**(23), 5659–5669 (2017)

47. Simonyan, K., Zisserman, A.: Very deep convolutional networks for large-scale image recognition. arXiv preprint arXiv:1409.1556 (2014)

48. Szegedy, C., Ioffe, S., Vanhoucke, V., Alemi, A.A.: Inception-v4, inception-resnet and the impact of residual connections on learning. In: Thirty-First AAAI Conference on Artificial Intelligence (2017)

49. Szegedy, C., Vanhoucke, V., Ioffe, S., Shlens, J., Wojna, Z.: Rethinking the inception architecture for computer vision. In: Proceedings of the IEEE Conference on Computer Vision and Pattern Recognition, pp. 2818–2826 (2016)

50. Wadhwa, A., Madhow, U.: Bottom-up deep learning using the Hebbian principle (2016)

A Multiresolution Machine Learning Technique to Identify Exoplanets

Miguel Jara-Maldonado(iD), Vicente Alarcon-Aquino$^{(\boxtimes)}$(iD),
and Roberto Rosas-Romero(iD)

Department of Computing, Electronics and Mechatronics,
Universidad de las Americas Puebla,
Sta. Catarina Martir, 72810 San Andres Cholula, Puebla, Mexico
{miguel.jaramo,vicente.alarcon,roberto.rosas}@udlap.mx

Abstract. The discovery of planets outside our Solar System, called exoplanets, allows us to study the feasibility of life outside Earth. Different techniques such as the transit method have been employed to detect and identify exoplanets. The amount of time and effort required to perform such a task, hinder the manual examination of the existing data. Several machine learning approaches have been proposed to deal with this matter, though they are not yet unerring. Therefore, new models continue to be proposed. In this work, we present experimental results using the K-Nearest Neighbors, Random Forests, Convolutional Neural Network and the Ridge classifier models to identify simulated transit signals. Furthermore, we propose a methodology based on the Empirical Mode Decomposition and Ensemble Empirical Mode Decomposition techniques for light curve preprocessing. Following this methodology we prove that multiresolution analysis can be used to improve the robustness of the presented models.

Keywords: Empirical Mode Decomposition · Exoplanets · Light curves · Machine learning · Multiresolution Analysis · Synthetic transits

1 Introduction

Exoplanets (short for extra-solar planets) are planets found outside our Solar System. Discovering and studying them is important for obtaining statistical information about the properties of exoplanets and stellar systems, searching for planets found within the habitable zone (where liquid water could exist), and looking for life outside Earth. As a result, several missions have been launched to look for transiting exoplanets. Some examples of these missions are the Kepler [1,2], Convection, Rotation and Planetary Transits space observatory (CoRoT) [3], and Transiting Exoplanet Survey Satellite (TESS) [4] missions, among others. Transiting exoplanets are discovered by inspecting Light Curves (LCs) in order to look for periodic decrements in the light flux, caused by transits. However, there are different sources such as stellar variability (luminosity fluctuations

© Springer Nature Switzerland AG 2020
L. Martínez-Villaseñor et al. (Eds.): MICAI 2020, LNAI 12468, pp. 50–64, 2020.
https://doi.org/10.1007/978-3-030-60884-2_4

related to the regular activity of the star) and instrumental noise that introduce difficulties in this process. This is due to the fact that exoplanet transits can be confused with these signals, thus causing spurious detections.

During the exoplanet detection step, light flux fluctuations related to an exoplanet transit are searched for. This step generates a list of exoplanet candidates; which are carefully analyzed in order to determine whether the detected events are caused by exoplanets or not. The exoplanet identification step corresponds to the process of candidate vetting. This step can be a laborious and time consuming task that has to be performed by specialists. Nevertheless, several Machine Learning (*ML*) models have been proposed to automatize it. These models have proved highly accurate under certain Signal-to-Noise Ratio (*SNR*) conditions. For example, a dimensionality reduction metric, known as the Locality Preserving Projections (*LPP*) metric, which reduces the volume of data to analyse, is introduced in [5]. The limitation of this model is that it requires manual identification of the detrending method to use, and it cannot correctly preserve the shape of the transits found within highly-variable-star LCs. Another common method, for exoplanet identification, are decision trees (see [6–8], and [9]). Decision trees allow one to perform feature ranking, which can be used to recognise the most relevant features for exoplanet identification. However, they do not ensure an optimal configuration, and in some cases they depend on human intervention for the feature extraction process. Finally, [10–12], and [13] make use of deep learning techniques, which are capable of extracting their own characteristics for exoplanet identification. Nonetheless, these models depend on a proper hyper-parameter configuration; which is often obtained empirically, resulting on a non-optimal model. In this work, we test and compare the performance of the *k*-Nearest Neighbors (*KNN*), Ridge classifier, Random Forests (*RF*), and Convolutional Neural Network (*CNN*) models to identify signals of synthetic transiting exoplanets. Additionally, we compare these results with those obtained by using the LCs preprocessed with two Multiresolution Analysis (*MRA*) techniques as inputs for the models. Such MRA techniques are Empirical Mode Decomposition (*EMD*) and Ensemble Empirical Mode Decomposition (*EEMD*).

The rest of this paper is organized as follows. First, we provide a description of MRA in Sect. 2. Then, we give details of the KNN, Ridge, RF, and CNN models in Sect. 3. The approach proposed for implementing EMD and EEMD to the exoplanet identification ML models is presented in Sect. 4. Then, in Sect. 5 we report our experimental results obtained by using these ML models (as well as MRA) to identify transiting exoplanets signals. Finally, we summarize our conclusions in Sect. 6.

2   Multiresolution Analysis

MRA is used to divide a signal into different frequency components. These components correspond to features for analysis at different scales of resolution [14]. One technique for multiresolution analysis is the wavelet-based analysis, where a signal is reconstructed by using short-time duration components at different time positions and at different levels of time-scaling. According to [15], wavelets can be used to analyze a signal at different frequencies by using several decomposition levels. By decomposing the signal, it is possible to extract details of the signal that characterize its different frequency components. At lower resolutions, details correspond to larger building blocks, while at higher resolutions more detailed information of the signal can be obtained. One of the main issues with the Discrete Wavelet Transform (DWT) is that the signal has to undergo a downsampling process, which reduces the length of the signal. An example of how the downsampling process can hinder the exoplanet identification process is presented in [16]. If the LCs preprocessed with DWT are used as inputs for a CNN model, then the number of decomposition levels is limited to the length of the binned LCs. The reason behind this obstacle is that the architecture of CNNs consists of multiple layers, where downsampling (as an implementation of max pooling) of signals may take place. This limits the use of DWT with certain CNN configurations such as the one presented in [11], as shown in [16].

According to [17], EMD is an empirical non-linear analysis tool for complex non-stationary time series. As stated in [18], in contrast to other methods such as wavelet transforms [14,16], EMD does not make use of a predefined basis function. Instead, it iteratively decomposes the signal as a sum of Intrinsic Mode Functions ($IMFs$). IMFs are adaptively obtained by iterating a process called *sifting*; where the non-stationary time series data is separated into the locally non-overlapping higher frequency components of the signal. Once that the IMFs are obtained, further analysis may be performed by using the Hilbert spectral analysis, which, according to [19], would result in the Hilbert-Huang Transform (HHT). This method can be used to obtain a more physically meaningful time-frequency-energy description of a time series (e.g. LCs). Moreover, the original signal can be reconstructed without information loss or distortion, by superimposing all IMFs together with the residual. Also, EMD avoids the trend removal step, which often causes low-frequency terms injection in the resulting spectra. A flow chart illustrating the process of the EMD algorithm is presented in Fig. 1. Summarizing the process explained in [17,20], the local maxima and minimum of the original signal are found using cubic splines interpolation. These are averaged to obtain the envelope mean, which is subtracted from the signal. If the result is not an IMF, the process is repeated using the result of the subtraction as the new signal. In case the result is an IMF, it is subtracted from the signal to calculate the residual, which is used as the new signal until the residual is a monotonic function or constant. Other MRA techniques related to EMD are the Online EMD method ([21]) used for online applications and to deal with huge quantities of data; and the Ensemble EMD ($EEMD$, [19]) used to avoid obtaining IMFs with overlapped components. This is achieved by adding white noise of finite amplitude to the signal, and using the mean of several trials as the IMFs. These IMFs have a greater physical meaning because there are no more overlapped signals. The algorithm of EEMD is shown in Fig. 1. According to [20,22], this process consists in generating m realizations of Gaussian white noise, which are added to the original signal. Then, each of the new signals is decomposed by using EMD to get their IMFs. Finally, all the IMFs from the same mode are averaged to generate the EEMD IMF of that mode. The main limitation of the EMD based techniques is their lack of theoretical properties. For this reason, [23] proposed an alternative method, termed synchrosqueezed wavelet transform, derived from reassignment methods of wavelet coefficients. In this work, we test the performance of the exoplanet identification models by using LCs preprocessed with EMD and EEMD, to evaluate if they can be improved by using these MRA techniques.

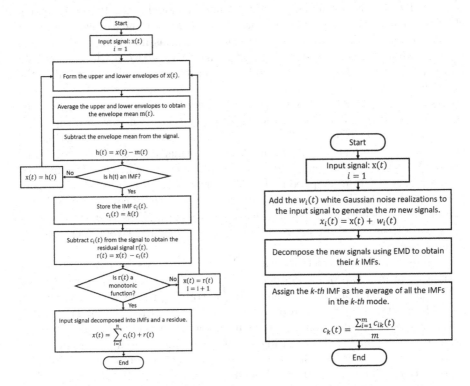

Fig. 1. Flow charts of the EMD (left) and the EEMD (right) algorithms.

3 Machine Learning Algorithms

ML models can be used to automatize several exoplanet discovery steps. The work in [24] is based on ML models to detect transiting signals within synthetic LCs. It is important to automate the exoplanet discovery pipeline because the amount of data available to look for planetary transits is huge (e.g. it is asserted in [25] that the CoRoT mission [3] produced $10,000$ to $12,000$ LCs sampled at 512s time interval with up to $25,000$ data points). In this work we focus in the exoplanet transit identification step, also termed vetting. It involves analyzing the detected signals, and retrieving a *yes* or *no* answer to the question *Is the detected signal caused by an exoplanet transit?*

According to [26], the KNN method has been widely used for data mining. It is based on the principle of associating similar features together. By doing so, it is capable of determining the class to which a new set of features belongs to. This is achieved by calculating the distance between an unclassified feature vector and an already labeled one, and looking for the k nearest neighbors to the unknown observation. Then, the feature vector is assigned to the class that most of the nearest neighbors belong to. Another model is the Ridge regression classifier. The targets are converted into binary data (i.e. the exoplanet and not exoplanet labels). Then, Ridge regression is used to classify the inputs according to the binary classes. As stated in [27], the difference between Ridge regression and Least Squares (LS) lies in a regularization term that helps to stabilize the algorithm.

As stated in [11,28], a CNN is a neural network model capable of learning from local features found within the entire input vector (in this case the LCs). The structure of a CNN generally consists of two stages for feature extraction and classification. The feature extraction stage is normally based on convolutional layers. At each convolutional layer, local data from a previous layer is convolved with a kernel function, mapped and pooled (usually implemented with subsampling). In other words, CNNs are usually formed by a set of convolutional layers and pooling layers. Finally, the classification stage of a CNN is similar to a multi-layer perceptron. The number and order of convolutional layers is empirically determined.

As mentioned in [6], decision trees classify the inputs by iteratively partitioning them into two branches, depending on whether the value of the inputs is greater or lower than a value that is set by training the model. Furthermore, for each partition step the entropy is reduced. The partition process is repeated until the entropy can no longer be reduced (or when the data split limit has been reached). Finally, the resulting set of splits can be used by the model to label new inputs. The RF classifier is composed by a combination of different decision trees. The training data is bootstrapped, meaning that it is replaced by using different training data subsets for each tree, which helps to decorrelate the trees. This process allows the model to avoid overfitting (i.e. to obtain a better performance when the testing inputs are very similar to the ones used for the training process).

4   Proposed Approach

We tested the transit identification performance of the KNN model with four different values of k, namely 3, 5, 7, and 9. We also tested the Ridge classifier model. Additionally, we tested the performance of such models by feeding them with LCs after EMD and EEMD analysis. For comparison we used the RF and CNN models from [16] (the CNN was originally presented in [11]). Detection performance was measured by computing the average accuracy, precision, recall, specificity, and execution time of each model after 100 iterations of each model. In order to obtain these metrics, it is necessary to analyze the True Positives (*TPs*), True Negatives (*TNs*), False Positives (*FPs*), and False Negatives (*FNs*). The accuracy $((TP + TN)/(TP + TN + FP + FN))$ determines the percentage of correct decisions made by the model. The precision $(TP/(TP + FP))$ is the ratio of correctly classified exoplanets over the number of signals identified as exoplanets. The recall $(TP/(TP + FN))$ obtains the percentage of correctly classified exoplanet signals. The specificity $(TN/(TN + FP))$ obtains the percentage of correctly classified non-exoplanet signals. Finally, the proposed exoplanet identification pipeline with MRA is shown in Fig. 2. In this figure, the first step involves acquiring the LCs from either the Real-LC or the 3-median datasets. We tested three different types of inputs for the ML models, namely, using the LCs without MRA, the IMFs obtained with EMD, or the IMFs obtained with EEMD. The ML models use these inputs to determine whether the signal belongs to an exoplanet transit or not.

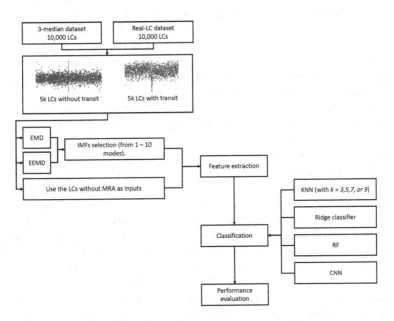

Fig. 2. Proposed exoplanet identification pipeline with multiresolution analysis. The LCs are used as inputs for the Machine Learning (*ML*) models. Then, the models output the label of the LCs, viz. exoplanet or not exoplanet.

We used the two datasets of simulated LCs from [16]. Both datasets are composed of 10,000 LCs that have 15,000 data points each. Half of the LCs in these datasets contain simulated transits created using the BATMAN model from [29].

The BATMAN Python package[1] allows one to simulate exoplanet transits with different limb darkening models; namely the uniform, linear, quadratic, logarithmic, exponential and nonlinear models. The calculations for such models are described in [29,30]. On the one hand, the *Real-LC* dataset was created using real LCs extracted from the Mikulsky Archive for Space Telescopes (*MAST*)[2]. The LCs chosen were those that contained signals marked as Non Transiting Planet (*NTP*) in the Q1-Q17 *Kepler* Data Release 24 (*DR24*, [7]). Then, the spline fitting method from [11] was applied to detrend these LCs. Lastly, the transit simulations obtained by the BATMAN model were added. On the other hand, the *3-median* dataset was created by using the simulated noisy photometric data model from [24] as base LCs. Then, the simulated transits were added to half of these LCs using the BATMAN model. Finally, a 3-median filter was used to detrend the LCs. Although the LCs are traditionally divided by the 3-median filter; the 3-median signal was used as input for the ML models instead of the result of the aforementioned division.

Once the LCs were generated, the folding and binning processes were used. During folding, the original LC is folded to center the transit event. This enhances the transit signal, and also provides a geometry that is easier to identify by the machine learning models. After folding the LCs, the binning process was used to set the length of all the LCs to 2048 data points. This length is similar to the 2001 data points used for the global view in [11]. This process consists in reducing the size of the data by averaging all the data points contained in each bin. The resulting LC is characterized by a length that matches the number of bins chosen. In the case of the datasets used, the 2048 bins represent the original 15,000 data points. For the original explanation of the datasets creation, the reader is referred to [16].

Each model was also tested by using the IMFs, obtained by applying EMD and EEMD to the binned LCs, as inputs. For the EMD technique, we used the PyEMD Python package. By doing so, we obtained a list that contained all the IMFs of each LC. We tested up to 10 modes. To do this, we used the nth IMFs for each LC, being n the mode that we wanted to analyze. Each IMF consisted of a 2048-sample time series, which is used as input to the ML models instead of the LCs. In some cases, EMD did not provide the same number of IMFs as the mode that we were testing. For those cases, the last IMF available was used (e.g.. if we wanted to test the fifth mode but there were only three IMFs available for that LC, we used the third IMF). EMD-based processing of the LCs took approximately 105 min for the 3-median dataset and approximately 65 min for the Real-LC dataset. Additionally, we used the *eemd* Matlab implementation presented in [22][3] to obtain the EEMD IMFs. We decomposed each LC with 1,000 iterations to obtain the EEMD IMFs, which is the same number of iterations used with EMD. Also, we set the number of realization to 500 (which is the

---

number of realizations of Gaussian white noise added to the data. This number of realizations is based on the configuration used in [22]). We saved these IMFs on a file that was then loaded in Python to test the performance of the models using these data. In the same way as EMD, the number of IMFs varies for each LC, and in those cases where the number of IMFs was lower than the mode desired, we used the last IMF available. Preprocessing the LCs using EEMD took approximately 238 h for the 3-median dataset and approximately 139 h for the Real-LC dataset.

5   Experimental Results

5.1   Model Setting

Four different classifiers (KNN, Ridge RF and CNN) were used to identify transit signals from the Real-LC and 3-median datasets. We used the scikit-learn Python API to configure our models. Parameters values for the KNN implementation are listed next.

- Number of neighbors (k): 3, 5, 7, and 9. We chose these values to evaluate the performance of the model given different k values.
- Nearest neighbors algorithm: brute-force search. This search was used since the length of the inputs was not too large.

The description of the configuration for the Ridge classifier is:

- Regularization strength (α): 1.0. We chose this value to avoid a strong regularization, while still reducing the variance of the estimates.
- The intercept was computed to add flexibility to the model.
- No normalization was applied because the LCs were already normalized during the folding and binning steps.
- Both classes had the same weights to avoid prioritizing one class.
- The LS solver was used to compare our results with the LS results presented in [16].

The configuration of the RF model is the same as the one described in [16], and it is listed next.

- Number of trees in the forest: 10 without limit of expansion (the branches could expand until becoming leaves).
- Split quality criteria: the Gini impurity criteria.
- Minimum number of samples to split a node: 2.
- Minimum samples on a leaf: 1.
- We built the trees by bootstrapping.

Finally, we used the same configuration for the CNN as in [16], which uses the architecture presented in [11]. This configuration is presented next.

- Batch size: 64.
- Number of epochs: 50.
- We used the Adam optimization algorithm.
- Stepsize (α): 10^{-5}.
- Exponential decay rates: $\beta_1 = 0.9$, $\beta_2 = 0.999$.
- $\epsilon = 10^{-8}$ (this is used to avoid dividing by zero during the parameters update).
- Loss function: categorical cross-entropy.

5.2   Simulation Results and Discussion

Each model was trained 100 times, and the performance of the model was tested at each training. In this way, each model was tested 100 times. The final metric (accuracy, precision, sensitivity, specificity and time) values were computed by averaging the 100 values corresponding to all the tests. For the case of the CNN, the model was trained once, and tested 100 times by using k-fold cross-validation. We only trained the CNN model once because of its very high computational time for training. Also, in order to avoid overfitting, we cross-validated the data with all the models. In total, for each iteration, we used 60% of the data for training and 40% of the data for testing. All the model implementations were run in a computer with an Intel Core i7-7700 HQ CPU, 16.0 GB of RAM, Windows 10 operative system of 64 bits, and a NVIDIA GeForce GTX 1060 graphics card.

The results are presented in Tables 1 and 2. In these tables, the best performance values obtained are highlighted by using boldface characters. Also, only the best results obtained with EMD and EEMD are presented, along with the results obtained without using MRA. We tested each ML model with every mode, i.e. from 1 to 10 IMFs. The results of the RF and CNN classifiers, without using the MRA technique, have been previously reported in [16]. It is noticeable that the results for each model, without the application of MRA to LCs, depend on the dataset. For instance, KNN outperformed all the other models in the Real-LC dataset. Nevertheless, its performance was poor in the 3-median dataset, where the best model in terms of accuracy was the RF model. In fact, the accuracy of all the KNN classifiers, tested with the 3-median dataset, was lower than 70%. These can be explained by observing the differences between the metrics. The models obtained a recall close to 100%, with the other metrics having a low percentage. This suggests that the models tended to classify all signals as exoplanet transits, even when they were not. We attribute this to the noise model used for the 3-median dataset. In the 3-median dataset, the transit signal is sometimes hidden by noise, giving the LCs a different shape than the expected U-shape. That irregular shape may cause the KNN model to average the transit signal with the noise found outside of the transit, causing the different accuracy results.

Among all the KNN configurations, the best results in terms of accuracy, precision and specificity, were obtained with k set to three neighbors (i.e. $k = 3$). However, as the number of neighbors is increased, the accuracy of the model drops. This is probably due to the fact that using more neighbors causes the model to average more data, thus loosing important details from each data point.

Table 1. Experimental results from the Real-LC dataset. Each value corresponds to the average of the 100 test iterations for each model.

Model	Accuracy (%)	Precision (%)	Specificity (%)	Recall (%)	Time (secs.)
KNN ($k = 3$)					
Without MRA	97.92	**98.92**	**98.94**	96.90	8.29
Using EMD and 7 IMFs	97.74	98.07	98.09	**97.38**	11.79
Using EEMD and 6 IMFs	**98.04**	98.81	98.83	97.25	**5.88**
KNN ($k = 5$)					
Without MRA	97.59	**98.64**	**98.67**	96.51	6.72
Using EMD and 7 IMFs	97.26	97.45	97.45	97.08	11.96
Using EEMD and 6 IMFs	**97.87**	98.60	98.63	**97.10**	**5.93**
KNN ($k = 7$)					
Without MRA	97.29	98.38	98.41	96.18	7.53
Using EMD and 7 IMFs	97.10	97.33	97.33	96.86	11.87
Using EEMD and 6 IMFs	**97.82**	**98.48**	**98.50**	**97.14**	**5.91**
KNN ($k = 9$)					
Without MRA	97.01	98.25	98.29	95.72	10.80
Using EMD and 7 IMFs	97.00	97.34	97.39	96.60	11.95
Using EEMD and 6 IMFs	**97.71**	**98.31**	**98.34**	**97.08**	**5.94**
Ridge Classifier					
Without MRA	85.19	**99.79**	**99.85**	70.60	6.21
Using EMD and 6 IMFs	**88.32**	92.07	92.79	83.84	10.18
Using EEMD and 9 IMFs	88.05	85.86	84.95	**91.14**	**5.13**
CNN					
Without MRA ([16])	91.46	97.55	91.46	85.21	46.74
Using EMD and 5 IMFs	91.67	**99.16**	91.67	83.98	135.89
Using EEMD and 6 IMFs	**97.13**	98.9	**97.15**	**95.32**	**44.32**
RF					
Without MRA ([16])	97.91	98.35	98.37	97.45	10.26
Using EMD and 7 IMFs	**98.43**	**98.8**	**98.81**	**98.04**	13.41
Using EEMD and 6 IMFs	98.17	98.48	98.49	97.84	**6.19**

Note: The best values for each dataset have been highlighted using bold characters.

In addition, there is not an evident relation between the number of neighbors used and the execution time of the algorithm. The best performing algorithm in terms of execution time was the Ridge classifier. This can be explained because it is the simplest model used in this work. Contrarily, the slowest model was the CNN, which is expected because of its computational complexity. Moreover, it is noticeable that, even though the Ridge classifier did not obtain the best accuracy percentage in the Real-LC dataset tests, it did obtain positive accuracy results with both datasets. Furthermore, it outperformed the LS model presented in [16], which was tested using the same datasets. The LS model reached an accuracy

Table 2. Experimental results from the 3-median dataset. Each value corresponds to the average of the 100 test iterations for each model.

Model	Accuracy (%)	Precision (%)	Specificity (%)	Recall (%)	Time (secs.)
KNN ($k = 3$)					
Without MRA	64.91	58.99	29.15	**100**	11.02
Using EMD and 9 IMFs	93.74	**90.80**	**89.97**	97.45	11.71
Using EEMD and 7 IMFs	**93.82**	89.70	88.43	99.12	**10.48**
KNN ($k = 5$)					
Without MRA	63.74	58.09	27.09	**100**	11.30
Using EMD and 9 IMFs	**93.75**	**90.27**	**89.27**	98.17	11.96
Using EEMD and 7 IMFs	93.21	88.72	87.18	99.14	**10.50**
KNN ($k = 7$)					
Without MRA	63.13	57.72	25.74	**100**	11.43
Using EMD and 9 IMFs	**93.61**	**89.84**	**88.66**	98.47	11.94
Using EEMD and 7 IMFs	92.97	88.35	86.72	99.13	**8.87**
KNN ($k = 9$)					
Without MRA	62.51	57.29	24.62	**100**	9.44
Using EMD and 9 IMFs	**93.60**	**89.69**	**88.45**	98.65	11.90
Using EEMD and 7 IMFs	92.63	87.80	85.98	99.16	**8.62**
Ridge classifier					
Without MRA	76.02	67.79	51.81	**99.87**	8.3
Using EMD and 6 IMFs	76.33	68.34	53.46	98.86	10.47
Using EEMD and 9 IMFs	**79.26**	**91.81**	**94.12**	64.68	**5.27**
CNN					
Without MRA ([16])	97.68	**99.94**	97.68	95.48	**54.17**
Using EMD and 1 IMFs	**99.32**	99.67	**99.32**	**98.99**	100.34
Using EEMD and 5 IMFs	95.39	94.43	95.39	96.6	161.93
RF					
Without MRA ([16])	**97.82**	**97.25**	**97.17**	**98.45**	9.42
Using EMD and 1 IMFs	97.57	96.84	96.73	98.40	13.97
Using EEMD and 6 IMFs	97.35	96.42	96.28	98.40	**6.11**

Note: The best values for each dataset have been highlighted using bold characters.

of 65.16% with the Real-LC dataset, and 37.99% with the 3-median dataset. This means that the Ridge classifier reaches an accuracy improvement of more than 20% for both datasets, probably caused by the regularization term and the intercept calculation.

We tested and compared the performance of the models using LCs preprocessed by EMD and EEMD. In most cases, the performance obtained using MRA is ameliorated. The classifier that achieves the highest improvement, based on the use of EMD and EEMD, is the KNN. As mentioned before, this model had a considerable difference in performance between the Real-LC and the 3-median datasets. By applying EMD or EEMD, the results improve approximately 30% for each k. This proves that using EMD or EEMD allows the models to perform similarly with both of the datasets presented. In all cases, the time taken to classify the LCs is increased by using EMD, even though it is not very significant in most cases. Contrarily, by using EEMD, the time is decreased except for the EEMD+CNN. Also, adding the MRA preprocessing step to the LC identification pipeline involves additional time. For instance, using EMD took 105 min for the 3-median dataset. However, this step can be performed only once, by storing the IMFs for further use of the corresponding mode. According to our results, we conclude that the best EMD- and EEMD-based models are the RF and CNN. On the one hand, the RF model seems to be the most robust model, because it has a good performance in both datasets. Furthermore, the use of MRA in RF does not improve too much any other metric than the time consumed by the model. On the other hand, the EMD+CNN does present an improvement in almost every metric after using MRA. Nevertheless, it did not obtain the best performance with the Real-LC dataset. Differently, the EEMD+CNN obtained an accuracy improvement of almost 6%. Moreover, the accuracy of the EMD+CNN attained more than 99% with the 3-median dataset, a percentage that no other model had.

Finally, we performed hypothesis tests in order to statistically validate the results reported in Tables 1 and 2. We applied the Welch's t-test to compare the results without MRA, and results based on EMD and EEMD to determine if there was a significative difference between the means of the results. In such tests, a p-value lower than a threshold which is typically 0.05 (e.g. [31]) is enough to statistically guarantee that the results are meaningfully different. The results of the Welch's t-tests where the p-values were greater than 0.05 (i.e. the only cases where there was no statistical difference between the results) are presented in Table 3. The rest of the p-values obtained were lower than that threshold, meaning that those results were statistically different than the ones obtained without using MRA techniques to preprocess the LCs.

Table 3. p-values obtained from the Welch's t-tests where the p-value is greater than 0.05.

Model	Metric	Dataset	MRA technique	p-value
KNN ($k = 9$).	Accuracy	3-median	EMD	0.78
RF.	Recall	Real-LC	EMD	0.27
RF.	Recall	3-median	EEMD	0.28
KNN ($k = 5$).	Precision	Real-LC	EEMD	0.39
KNN ($k = 9$).	Precision	Real-LC	EEMD	0.21
KNN ($k = 5$).	Specificity	Real-LC	EEMD	0.36
KNN ($k = 7$).	Specificity	Real-LC	EEMD	0.7
KNN ($k = 9$).	Specificity	Real-LC	EEMD	0.34

Note: A p-value higher than 0.05 means that the results are not different.

6 Conclusions

ML models can be used to automatize the process of vetting the detected exoplanet transit signals, in order to discard spurious detections. By doing so, it is possible to reduce the effort and to speed up the identification step, so that astronomers are provided with lists of planet candidates to perform follow-up observations on. Nevertheless, in order to automatize the aforementioned process, it is necessary to provide a model that can be robust to different sources of noise; while preserving the transit signal. In this work, we compared the performance of different ML models used for vetting exoplanet transits. We also compared their performance using three different types of inputs, namely the LCs preprocessed by EMD, EEMD and without preprocessing. We used real LCs and simulated LCs, which were injected with synthetic transits simulated using the BATMAN model. Four ML models were used, KNN, Ridge classifier, RF and CNN. Our results show that the accuracy and time performance of the models can be improved by using MRA techniques to preprocess the LCs, namely the EMD and EEMD techniques. It is noticeable that the presented models are limited by the type of data that is used as input for each model. For instance, the KNN model has an accuracy penalty of almost 30% between the results obtained with the Real-LC dataset and the 3-median dataset. We proved that the dependence of the results to the noise source can be avoided by using MRA techniques, which ensure the robustness of the models to different types of noise. Even more, in the case of the models that obtained the best results, such as RF, our experimental results demonstrate that the use of MRA to preprocess the LCs improves the time performance of the model without penalizing its accuracy. Processing more information in less time is important since the amount of information to be examined is very extensive. Examining more information in less time will allow us to provide astronomers with a more complete list of planet candidates. Also, the exoplanet study is a growing science field with many new telescopes being programmed such as the PLAnetary Trasits and Oscillations of stars mission (*PLATO*, [32]). It is desirable to examine the information already available to be able to keep up with the existing and emerging missions. Furthermore, we concluded that the advantage of using EMD and EEMD versus other MRA techniques, such as the DWT, is that there is no downsampling of the LCs, which is important for some models such as the CNN that require an specific number of inputs (see [16], where the CNN has to be reconfigured so it can use different decomposition levels as inputs). Future work will be done by testing the performance of the models using the synchrosqueezed wavelet transform [23]. This method will allow us to overcome the main limitation of the EMD based techniques, which is their lack of theoretical properties.

Acknowledgments. The authors would like to thank the Mexican National Council on Science and Technology (CONACyT) and the Universidad de las Americas Puebla (UDLAP) for their support through the doctoral scholarship program. This paper includes data collected by the Kepler mission and obtained from the MAST data archive at the Space Telescope Science Institute (STScI). Funding for the Kepler mission is provided by the NASA Science Mission Directorate. STScI is operated by the Association of Universities for Research in Astronomy, Inc., under NASA contract NAS 5–26555.

References

1. Borucki, W.J., et al.: Kepler planet-detection mission: introduction and first results. Science **327**, 977–980 (2010)
2. Basri, G., Borucki, W.J., Koch, D.: The Kepler mission: a wide-field transit search for terrestrial planets. New Astron. Rev. **49**, 478–485 (2005)
3. Auvergne, M., et al.: The CoRoT satellite in flight: description and performance. Astron. Astrophys. **506**, 411–424 (2009)
4. Ricker, G.R., et al.: Transiting exoplanet survey satellite (TESS). J. Astron. Telescop. Instrum. Syst. **1**, 014003 (2015)
5. Thompson, S.E., et al.: A machine learning technique to identify transit shaped signals. Astrophys. J. **812**, 46 (2015)
6. Catanzarite, J.H.: Autovetter planet candidate catalog for Q1–Q17 data release 24. Astronomy & Astrophysics (2015)
7. Coughlin, J.L., et al.: Planetary candidates observed by Kepler. VII. the first fully uniform catalog based on the entire 48-month data set (Q1–Q17 DR24). Astrophys. J. Supplement Ser. **224**, 12 (2016)
8. Armstrong, D., et al.: Automatic vetting of planet candidates from ground-based surveys: machine learning with NGTS. Monthly Not. Roy. Astron. Soc. **478**, 4225–4237 (2018)
9. Schanche, N., et al.: Machine-learning approaches to exoplanet transit detection and candidate validation in wide-field ground-based surveys. Monthly Not. Roy. Astron. Soc. **483**, 5534–5547 (2019)
10. Dattilo, A., et al.: Identifying exoplanets with deep learning. II. Two new superearths uncovered by a neural network in K2 data. Astron. J. **157**, 169 (2019)
11. Shallue, C.J., Vanderburg, A.: Identifying exoplanets with deep learning: a five-planet resonant chain around Kepler-80 and an eighth planet around Kepler-90. Astron. J. **155**, 94 (2018)
12. Ansdell, M., et al.: Scientific domain knowledge improves exoplanet transit classification with deep learning. Astrophys. J. **869**, L7 (2018)
13. Yu, L., et al.: Identifying exoplanets with deep learning. III. Automated triage and vetting of TESS candidates. Astron. J. **158**, 25 (2019)
14. Graps, A.: An introduction to wavelets. IEEE Comput. Sci. Eng. **2**, 50–61 (1995)
15. Bravo, J.P., Roque, S., Estrela, R., Leão, I.C., De Medeiros, J.R.: Wavelets: a powerful tool for studying rotation, activity, and pulsation in Kepler and CoRoT stellar light curves. Astron. Astrophys. **568**, A34 (2014)
16. Jara-Maldonado, M., Alarcon-Aquino, V., Rosas-Romero, R., Starostenko, O., Ramirez-Cortes, J.M.: Transiting exoplanet discovery using machine learning techniques: a survey. Earth Sci. Inf. **13**(3), 573–600 (2020). https://doi.org/10.1007/s12145-020-00464-7
17. Zeiler, A., et al.: Empirical mode decomposition - an introduction. In: Proceedings of the International Joint Conference on Neural Networks, pp. 1–8 (2010)

18. Mandic, D.P., ur Rehman, N., Wu, Z., Huang, N.E.: Empirical Mode Decomposition-based time-frequency analysis of multivariate signals: the power of adaptive data analysis. IEEE Sig. Process. Mag. **30**, 74–86 (2013)
19. Huang, N.E., Wu, Z.: A review on Hilbert-Huang transform: method and its applications to geophysical studies. Rev. Geophys. **46**, 1–23 (2008)
20. Fang, K., et al.: Comparison of EMD and EEMD in rolling bearing fault signal analysis. In: 2018 IEEE International Instrumentation and Measurement Technology Conference (I2MTC), pp. 1–5 (2018)
21. Fontugne, R., Borgnat, P., Flandrin, P.: Online empirical mode decomposition. In: IEEE International Conference on Acoustics, Speech and Signal Processing (ICASSP), pp. 4306–4310 (2017)
22. Torres, M.E., Colominas, M.A., Schlotthauer, G., Flandrin, P.: A complete ensemble empirical mode decomposition with adaptive noise. In: 2011 IEEE International Conference on Acoustics, Speech and Signal Processing (ICASSP), pp. 4144–4147 (2011)
23. Daubechies, I., Lu, J., Wu, H.T.: Synchrosqueezed wavelet transforms: an empirical mode decomposition-like tool. Appl. Comput. Harmon. Anal. **30**, 243–261 (2011)
24. Pearson, K.A., Palafox, L., Griffith, C.A.: Searching for exoplanets using artificial intelligence. Monthly Not. Roy. Astron. Soc. **474**, 478–491 (2018)
25. Tingley, B.: Improvements to existing transit detection algorithms and their comparison. Astron. Astrophys. **408**, L5–L7 (2003)
26. Mucherino, A., Papajorgji, P.J., Pardalos, P.M.: In: k-Nearest Neighbor Classification, pp. 83–106. Springer, New York (2009)
27. Theodoridis, S., Koutroumbas, K.: Pattern Recognition, vol. 4, 4th edn. Academic Press Inc., USA (2008)
28. Haykin, S.S.: Neural Networks and Learning Machines, 3rd edn. Pearson Education, Upper Saddle River (2009)
29. Kreidberg, L.: batman: BAsic transit model cAlculatioN in python. Publ. Astron. Soc. Pacific **127**, 1161–1165 (2015)
30. Mandel, K., Agol, E.: Analytic light curves for planetary transit searches. Astrophys. J. **580**, L171–L175 (2002)
31. Committee, E.S.: Statistical significance and biological relevance. EFSA J. **9**, 2372 (2011)
32. Rauer, H., et al.: The PLATO 2.0 mission. Exp. Astron. **38**, 249–330 (2014)

Outliers Detection in Multi-label Datasets

Marilyn Bello[1,2](✉), Gonzalo Nápoles[2,3], Rafael Morera[1], Koen Vanhoof[2],
and Rafael Bello[1]

[1] Computer Science Department, Universidad Central de Las Villas,
Santa Clara, Cuba
mbgarcia@uclv.cu
[2] Faculty of Business Economics, Hasselt University, Hasselt, Belgium
[3] Department of Cognitive Science and Artificial Intelligence, Tilburg University,
Tilburg, The Netherlands

Abstract. In many knowledge discovery applications, finding *outliers*, i.e. objects that behave in an unexpected way or have abnormal properties, is more interesting than finding *inliers* in a dataset. Outlier detection is important for many applications, including those related to intrusion detection, credit card fraud, and criminal activity in e-commerce. Several methods of outlier detection have been proposed, and even many of them from the perspective of Rough Set Theory, but at the moment none of them is specifically intended for multi-label datasets. In this paper, we propose a method that measures the degree of anomaly of an object in a multi-label dataset. This score or measure quantifies the degree of irregularity of an object with respect to the dataset. In addition, a method for generating anomalies in this type of datasets is proposed. From these synthetic datasets, the efficacy of the proposed method is proved. The results show the superiority of our proposal over other methods in the literature adapted to multi-label problems.

Keywords: Outlier detection · Outlier generation · Multi-label datasets · Rough set theory · Knowledge discovery

1 Introduction

The detection of outliers (anomalies or irregularities) is a key task in knowledge discovery. Roughly speaking, the process consists in detecting small groups of data objects that are deemed "exceptional" when compared with the rest of data, in terms of certain sets of properties. While there is no a single, generally accepted, formal definition of an outlier, Hawkins [10] defined an outlier as an observation that deviates so much from other observations as to arouse suspicions that it was generated by a different mechanism.

Initially, the main reason for outlier detection was to remove outliers from the training data, since some pattern recognition algorithms are quite sensitive to outliers in the data [1]. However, for many applications [4,9], such as fraud detection in e-commerce [22,23], it is more interesting to detect rare events than to common ones, from a knowledge discovery standpoint.

© Springer Nature Switzerland AG 2020
L. Martínez-Villaseñor et al. (Eds.): MICAI 2020, LNAI 12468, pp. 65–75, 2020.
https://doi.org/10.1007/978-3-030-60884-2_5

Generally speaking, the existing approaches for outlier detection can be classified into the following five categories [18]: distribution-based approach [24], depth-based approach [16], distance-based approach [17], density-based approach [6], and clustering approach [12]. In addition, some authors [13–15] have employed the Rough Set Theory (RST) [20] for detecting outliers. For instance, Shaari et al. [25] proposed a new method to detect outliers using the concept of Non-Reduct as defined in RST. Chen et al. [8] proposed an outlier detection algorithm based on the neighborhood rough set model. In [14] the authors proposed a boundary-based outlier detection method, while in [15] they presented a rough membership function-based outlier detection method, by virtue of the notion of rough membership function in rough sets.

Although many of these techniques have proven useful and effective in detecting outlier pattern, none of them are specifically intended to deal with multi-label datasets at the moment. In a multi-label dataset [11], every object x is described by a number of input features $\{f_1, f_2, \ldots, f_m\}$, and is associated with a set of labels $\{l_1, l_2, \ldots, l_k\}$ instead of a single class label. Hence in this type of problem, an observation can belong to several classes at the same time.

In this paper, we propose a method to detect outliers in multi-label dataset. With this goal in mind, we rely on the definition of *outlier* given by Barnet and Lewis [3]. They defined an outlier as an observation (or subset of observations) which appear to be inconsistent with the remainder of the dataset. This idea could be modeled by using the extended RST approach, in which the consistency of an object is defined from the relation between its predictive and decision part. In other words, if the object's similarity class (i.e., the objects that are similar to it taking into account its predictive characteristics) and its equivalence class (i.e., the objects that are identical to it taking into account its labels) are similar, it could be said that it is consistent with respect to the rest of the objects in the dataset. Then, the degree to which an object is an outlier could depend on the extent to which the object satisfies this relation. Therefore, our method provides an anomaly degree for each object in the dataset instead of using the binary labeling (i.e., whether the object is an anomaly or not). The degree assigned to each object will be between $[0, 1]$, where 0 denotes a normal object (inlier), whereas 1 indicates a strong anomaly (outlier).

The evaluation of our detection method is difficult due to the lack of multi-label datasets with objects that have already been identified as outliers. Thus, as a second contribution of our paper, we also propose a method that generates outliers for datasets reported in the multi-label literature. The idea is to build an object from those objects that are similar to it, and whose irregularity is caused by the variation of its behavior, in terms of their labels. This method not just allows assessing our method but also provides the machine learning community with a procedure to generate more changeling datasets.

The rest of the paper is organized as follows. In Sect. 2, we briefly introduce the fundamentals of the Rough Sets Theory. Section 3 presents the outlier generation method in multi-label datasets, and Sect. 4 describes the outlier detection method. Experimental results on benchmark problems are discussed in Sect. 5 while Sect. 6 concludes the paper.

2   Preliminaries on Rough Sets

RST is a methodology proposed in the early 1980's for handling uncertainty that is manifested in the form of inconsistent data [20]. The underlying notion behind the rough set analysis is the indiscernibility of objects. By modeling the indiscernibility as an equivalence relation, one can partition a finite universe of objects into a family of pair-wise disjoint subsets.

Let $DS = (\mathcal{U}, \Psi \cup \{d\})$ denote a decision system where $\mathcal{U}$ is a non-empty finite set of objects called the universe of discourse, Ψ denotes a non-empty finite set of features describing any object in $\mathcal{U}$, and $d \notin \Psi$ represents the decision class. In this mathematical formalism, an equivalence class $[x]_\Phi$ of $x \in \mathcal{U}$ comprises the set of objects in $\mathcal{U}$ that are deemed inseparable from x according to the information contained in the feature subset $\Phi \subseteq \Psi$. Two objects are considered inseparable if they have identical values for all features.

This definition is adequate for nominal features but is too rigid when dealing with numerical ones, given that marginal differences between two numerical values could toss two nearly identical objects into different inseparability classes. This problems can be alleviated in some extent by extending the concept of inseparability relation, and replacing the equivalence relation with a weaker binary relation [26]. Equation (1) shows an indiscernibility relation, where $0 \leq S(x, y) \leq 1$ is a similarity function. The similarity function could be formulated in a variety of ways. In this study, we assume that $S(x, y) = 1 - \delta(x, y)$, where $\delta(x, y)$ stands for the Heterogeneous Euclidean-Overlap Metric [29] between x and y. Hence, the similarity function can be written as follows:

$$R : xRy \Longleftrightarrow S(x, y) \geq \xi_1. \tag{1}$$

This weaker binary relation states that x and y are deemed inseparable as long as their similarity degree $S(x, y)$ exceeds a similarity threshold $0 \leq \xi \leq 1$, and defines a similarity class where $\bar{R}(x) = \{y \in U | yRx\}$.

3   Outlier Generation in Multi-label Datasets

A pivotal issue in evaluating outlier detection algorithms is the accessibility of benchmark datasets. In many cases, synthetic datasets are more suitable than authentic data [19] since we often know in advance what to expect. However, synthetic data have the disadvantage of not having the realism of authentic data. The method proposed in this section generates synthetic multi-label datasets with anomalies. In this paper, we use existing datasets in the multi-label literature, and introduce some new objects labeled as outlier. Those objects already existing in the dataset were labeled as inliers.

The method starts by building two sets $C(x)$ and $D(x)$ for each object x in the dataset. The former consists of all objects that are similar to x taking into account the input features, while the latter is the set of identical objects to x by considering the labels. Our approach pursues the fact that insofar as these two sets are similar, an outlier could be built. The next step consists in building an object whose feature values are the result of a process of aggregating the information of the objects contained in $C(x)$, and its decision values are the set of labels to which most of the objects in $D(x)$ do not belong to. As a result, we would have an object in the dataset that would be very similar to a set of objects in terms of its predictive characteristics, and at the same time, very different in terms of its labels. Algorithm 1 formalizes this idea.

Algorithm 1. Outlier Generation in Multi-label Datasets

1: $UsedSet = \{\}, OutliersSet = \{\}$
2: For each object $\forall x_i \in U : x_i \notin Used$, compute its similarity class $C(x_i)$, and its equivalence class $D(x_i)$
3: Compute the similarity (δ) as done in [9] between the information granules $C(x_i)$ and $D(x_i)$ by using the Equation (2),

$$\delta_i = \frac{|C(x_i) \cap D(x_i)|}{0.5|C(x_i)| + 0.5|D(x_i)|} \tag{2}$$

4: **if** $\delta_i \geq \xi_2$ **then**
5:     Build a outlier object $Out_i = [Out_{cond}, Out_{dec}]$, where Out_{cond} is derived from an features aggregation of all objects in $C(x_i)$, and $Out_{dec} = \{l_1, l_2, \ldots, l_k\}$ with $l_k = 0$ if most of the objects in $D(x_i)$ are labeled with that label, otherwise, $l_k = 1$
6:     $UsedSet = UsedSet \cup x_i$
7:     $OutliersSet = OutliersSet \cup Out_i$
8: **end if**

A similarity threshold (ξ_2) is established in order not to use in the construction of an outlier those objects that have a certain degree of anomaly. This is based on the criterion that the vicinity of a non-outlier object taking into account its condition and decision features must be similar.

It should be mentioned that, if the number of outliers is greater than the number of inliers, then inliers become noise and is not the purpose of our algorithm. We have to take into consideration that the number of outliers must always be considerably less than the number of inliers.

4   Outlier Detection in Multi-label Datasets

According to [2], a way to define outliers is to consider as such those points at which a function learned from the dataset results in an unusually large error. Since the learning process attempts to generalize the relation between inputs and outputs, it is expected a large error when processing objects having similar inputs but very different outputs. In the same way, if an object is very similar to a subset of objects according to its predictive features, it is reasonable to assume that it is labeled in a similar way to the objects in the subset, otherwise, this inconsistency could be considered an anomaly.

The method proposed in this section is based on the above idea, which relies on the RST consistency. It first builds a prototype from a subset of objects that are similar to each other. The prototypes represent the typical characteristics of the objects of a category instead of necessary or sufficient conditions. Prototypes can be abstractions (e.g., the result of an aggregation process) of universe objects, or they can be some observed objects themselves.

For each $x \in \mathcal{U}$, a similarity class −all objects that are similar to x taking into account their predictive features− is built. Next, we derive a prototype for each similarity class such that each prototype includes both predictive and decision part. This process is performed by using an aggregation operator, which aggregates the predictive and decision information of the objects in the similarity class of x. The average operator can be used as the aggregation operator if the feature value is numeric, while the mode can be used if the value is nominal. As a result, the resulting prototype will have as decision values the most common labels of the objects in the similarity class.

Finally, we compute the degree of anomaly of the x object by using the proximity to its associated prototype regarding the decision part. In other words, this degree will be determined by computing the distance between the set of labels associated with the object and its prototype. In our case, we used Hamming set distance [5]. Algorithm 2 formalizes this idea.

Algorithm 2. Outlier Detection in Multi-label Datasets

1: For each object $x_i \in U$, compute its similarity class $C(x_i)$ using the similarity relation defined in Equation 1, $x_i \notin C(x_i)$
2: Build a prototype $P_i = [P_{cond}, P_{dec}]$, where P_{cond} is derived from an features aggregation of all objects in $C(x_i)$, and $P_{dec} = \{l_1, l_2, \ldots, l_k\}$ with $l_k = 1$ if most of the objects in $C(x_i)$ are labeled with that label, otherwise, $l_k = 0$
3: Compute the anomaly degree of x_i from $HammingDistance(x_{i_{dec}}, P_{dec})$

The degree of anomaly obtained for each object in the dataset could be used to discern between weak outliers (noise) and strong outliers. A high degree indicates a significant difference in the behavior of an object, so that it would be considered a strong outlier. The advantage of this method is that it does not depend on the classification method used, which allows us to detect the outliers before any learning process is performed.

5   Results and Discussion

In this section, we carry some numerical simulations to evaluate the performance of the method of outlier detection proposed in this work. The first step consists in creating a group of datasets with outliers using the method proposed in Sect. 3. With this goal in mind, we adopt 10 multi-label datasets taken from the well-known RUMDR repository [7]. In these problems (see Table 1), the number of objects ranges from 207 to 10,491, the number of features goes from 72 to 635, and the number of labels from 6 to 400. Also, the last column of the table shows the number of outliers inserted in each dataset.

Table 1. Characterization of datasets used for simulations.

Name	# Objects	# Nominal features	# Numerical features	# Labels	# Outliers
Birds	708	2	258	19	63
Emotions	597	0	72	6	4
Genbase	679	1186	0	27	17
GnegativePseAAC	1397	0	441	8	5
GpositivePseAAC	521	0	441	4	2
HumanPseAAC	3131	0	441	14	25
PlantPseAAC	985	0	441	12	7
Scene	2410	0	294	6	3
VirusPseAAC	213	0	441	6	6
Yeast	2495	0	103	14	78

5.1   Performance of the Outlier Detection Method

According to [2], if an anomaly detection method is able to achieve a significant difference between the degree of anomaly of the objects labeled as normal (inliers), and those labeled as anomaly (outliers), we can confirm the quality of the method. From this point on, we conducted the experimental analysis. The results shown in this section were obtained by establishing the values of 0.95 and 0.90 for the ξ_1 and ξ_2 similarity thresholds, respectively. These values have been arbitrarily selected, so other alternatives are also possible.

Figure 1 portrays the average anomaly degree achieved for each object labeled as inliers, and outliers in each dataset. The results show how the proposed method for all the study cases is able to distinguish to a great extent between an inlier and outlier object. Since, the method in most cases assigns a value close to 0 to inliers, and close to 1 to outliers.

Table 2 shows a comparison of the performance of the proposed method against two algorithms reported in the literature: *Exact k-Nearest Neighbor Score* and *Average k-Nearest Neighbor Score* [2]. Both were adapted to the multi-label problem, and were selected because they also provide a score of anomaly for each object in a dataset. The second and third columns show the average of the anomaly degrees observed in the inliers and outliers, respectively. In addition, the last column in Table 2 shows the difference between both average values. The greater this difference, the better the performance, since it achieves a greater distinction between inlier and outlier objects.

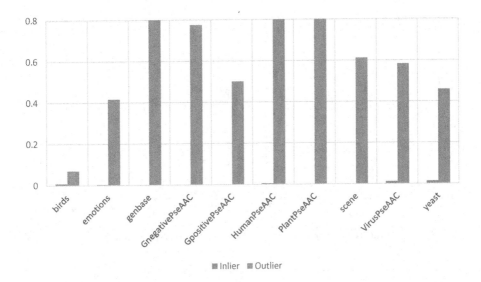

Fig. 1. Average anomaly degree observed for object labeled as inliers and outliers in each dataset adopted for simulation.

Table 2. Comparison against other methods in the literature. Boldface denotes the largest partition obtained between inliers and outliers.

	Inliers average	Outliers average	Difference
AverageKnnScore	0.2876294	0.2956309	0.0080015
ExactKnnScore	0.3055845	0.3285543	0.0229698
Proposal	0.0046806	0.5993862	**0.5947056**

The results suggest that our method is more effective in detecting outliers since it obtains a higher difference (i.e. over 0.59) than the other methods when discerning between an anomaly and a regular pattern. The reason for this is that these methods do not consider the relationship between the features and the labels in an object. This relation allows for more accurate results, even where there are objects that are isolated or in dense regions.

Figure 2 illustrates how the objects are distributed according to the anomaly degree computed by using the previous outlier detection methods. For each object in the dataset, we assign a random value between $[0, 1]$ to identify it on the x-axis, and then associate it with a degree of anomaly (i.e. the y-axis). In this way, the two colors in the plot represent whether the object is an outlier or not. Overall, this plot confirms the superiority of our proposal, since it achieves an outstanding partition between the objects that are outlier, and those that are not. In other words, most of the outliers (i.e, those objects labeled as "yes") have a high associated anomaly degree, and the opposite occurs in the case of the inliers (i.e, those objects labeled as "no").

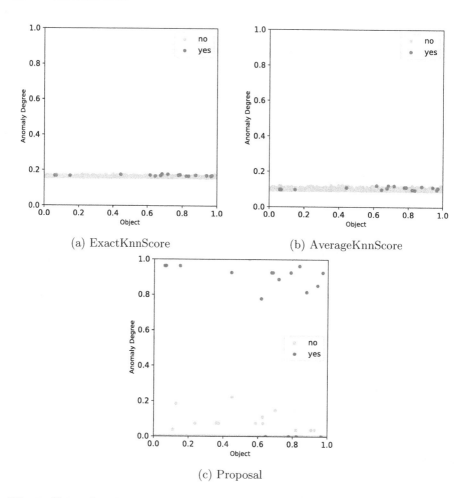

(a) ExactKnnScore   (b) AverageKnnScore

(c) Proposal

Fig. 2. Object distribution obtained for the *genbase* dataset from the anomaly degree estimated by each method. In this plot, universe objects labeled as "yes" are outliers while those labeled as "no" are inliers.

5.2   How Do Outliers Affect Multi-label Classifiers?

In the literature, it is frequently mentioned that the presence of outliers affects the performance of a classifier, but there are few studies verifying such claim [1]. As part of this study, we evaluated the effect of outliers on multi-label classifiers. To do this, we estimated the *Hamming Loss* (HL) value [11,21] by using a 10-fold cross validation scheme. The HL metric is probably the most used performance metric in multi-label scenarios. We considered three classifiers implemented in MULAN [27]: ML-kNN [31], RAkEL [28], and BP-MLL [30]. Those are considered state-of-the-art classifiers for multi-label classification.

Figure 3 shows the average HL values achieved by each method through the use of those datasets with outliers. It should be noted that for HL, small values show better results. The results show an increase of the HL values in those datasets that have anomalies. This confirms the sensibility of these classifiers to the presence of this type of objects. Similarly, the results indicate that BP-MLL seems to be slightly more vulnerable in these cases.

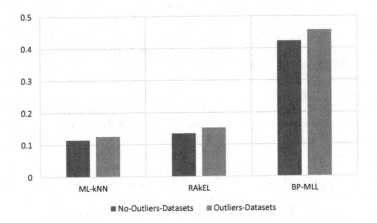

Fig. 3. Average HL values achieved by each classification model for multi-label datasets with and without outliers.

6 Conclusions

In this paper, we extended outlier detection to multi-label problems using the Pawlak's rough set theory. The method proposed is able to estimate the degree of anomaly of an object with respect to the others composing the dataset. As an additional contribution, we proposed a method for generating anomalies in a multi-label dataset, which allows for the validation of our method and other techniques to detect outliers in this type of problem.

The experimental study shows the superiority of our method over others existing in the literature, since it is more effective in distinguishing if an object is an outlier or not. Furthermore, we confirmed that the presence of these anomalies causes the performance of existing multi-label classifiers to decrease. The main advantage of the proposed methods is that they do not depend on any particular classification model. There are however two main issues to be mentioned. Firstly, the concept of outlier we used in this paper is based on the inconsistency, that is just a type of uncertainty. Secondly, one might wonder to what extent our outlier detection method is biased by the way we generate those outliers. Whichever the case might be, our research is a necessary step into overcoming of outliers in problems concerning multi-label pattern classification.

Moreover, as anomaly detection is of great interest in areas such as the financial and security sector, where it is essential not only to be able to detect anomalies, but also to understand what is considered an *outliers*, we find it interesting as future work to include the use of Explainable AI techniques.

References

1. Acuña, E., Rodriguez, C.: On Detection of Outliers and Their Effect in Supervised Classification, vol. 15. University of Puerto Rico at Mayaguez (2004)
2. Aggarwal, C.C.: Outlier analysis. Data Mining, pp. 237–263. Springer, Cham (2015). https://doi.org/10.1007/978-3-319-14142-8_8
3. Barnet, V., Lewis, T.: Outliers in Statistical Data (1994)
4. Basharat, A., Gritai, A., Shah, M.: Learning object motion patterns for anomaly detection and improved object detection. In: 2008 IEEE Conference on Computer Vision and Pattern Recognition, pp. 1–8. IEEE (2008)
5. Bookstein, A., Kulyukin, V.A., Raita, T.: Generalized hamming distance. Inf. Retrieval **5**(4), 353–375 (2002)
6. Breunig, M.M., Kriegel, H.P., Ng, R.T., Sander, J.: LOF: identifying density-based local outliers. In: Proceedings of the 2000 ACM SIGMOD International Conference on Management of Data, pp. 93–104 (2000)
7. Charte, F., Charte, D., Rivera, A., del Jesus, M.J., Herrera, F.: R ultimate multilabel dataset repository. In: Martínez-Álvarez, F., Troncoso, A., Quintián, H., Corchado, E. (eds.) HAIS 2016. LNCS (LNAI), vol. 9648, pp. 487–499. Springer, Cham (2016). https://doi.org/10.1007/978-3-319-32034-2_41
8. Chen, Y., Miao, D., Zhang, H.: Neighborhood outlier detection. Expert Syst. Appl. **37**(12), 8745–8749 (2010)
9. Gebhardt, J., Goldstein, M., Shafait, F., Dengel, A.: Document authentication using printing technique features and unsupervised anomaly detection. In: 2013 12th International Conference on Document Analysis and Recognition, pp. 479–483. IEEE (2013)
10. Hawkins, D.M.: Identification of Outliers, vol. 11. Springer, Netherlands (1980). https://doi.org/10.1007/978-94-015-3994-4
11. Herrera, F., Charte, F., Rivera, A.J., del Jesus, M.J.: Multilabel classification. Multilabel Classification, pp. 17–31. Springer, Cham (2016). https://doi.org/10.1007/978-3-319-41111-8_2
12. Jain, A.K., Murty, M.N., Flynn, P.J.: Data clustering: a review. ACM Comput. Surv. (CSUR) **31**(3), 264–323 (1999)
13. Jiang, F., Chen, Y.-M.: Outlier detection based on granular computing and rough set theory. Appl. Intell. **42**(2), 303–322 (2014). https://doi.org/10.1007/s10489-014-0591-4
14. Jiang, F., Sui, Y., Cao, C.: Outlier detection using rough set theory. In: Ślęzak, D., Yao, J.T., Peters, J.F., Ziarko, W., Hu, X. (eds.) RSFDGrC 2005. LNCS (LNAI), vol. 3642, pp. 79–87. Springer, Heidelberg (2005). https://doi.org/10.1007/11548706_9
15. Jiang, F., Sui, Y., Cao, C.: A rough set approach to outlier detection. Int. J. Gener. Syst. **37**(5), 519–536 (2008)
16. Johnson, T., Kwok, I., Ng, R.T.: Fast computation of 2-dimensional depth contours. In: KDD, pp. 224–228. Citeseer (1998)
17. Knorr, E.M., Ng, R.T., Tucakov, V.: Distance-based outliers: algorithms and applications. VLDB J. **8**(3–4), 237–253 (2000)
18. Kovács, L., Vass, D., Vidács, A.: Improving quality of service parameter prediction with preliminary outlier detection and elimination. In: Proceedings of the Second International Workshop on Inter-domain Performance and Simulation (IPS 2004), Budapest, vol. 2004, pp. 194–199 (2004)

19. Lundin, E., Kvarnström, H., Jonsson, E.: A synthetic fraud data generation methodology. In: Deng, R., Bao, F., Zhou, J., Qing, S. (eds.) ICICS 2002. LNCS, vol. 2513, pp. 265–277. Springer, Heidelberg (2002). https://doi.org/10.1007/3-540-36159-6_23

20. Pawlak, Z.: Rough sets. Int. J. Comput. Inf. Sci. **11**(5), 341–356 (1982)

21. Pereira, R.B., Plastino, A., Zadrozny, B., Merschmann, L.H.: Correlation analysis of performance measures for multi-label classification. Inf. Process. Manage. **54**(3), 359–369 (2018)

22. Porwal, U., Mukund, S.: Credit card fraud detection in e-commerce: an outlier detection approach. arXiv preprint arXiv:1811.02196 (2018)

23. Ramakrishnan, J., Shaabani, E., Li, C., Sustik, M.A.: Anomaly detection for an e-commerce pricing system. In: Proceedings of the 25th ACM SIGKDD International Conference on Knowledge Discovery & Data Mining, pp. 1917–1926 (2019)

24. Rousseeuw, P.J., Leroy, A.M.: Robust Regression and Outlier Detection, vol. 589. Wiley, New York (2005)

25. Shaari, F., Bakar, A.A., Hamdan, A.R.: Outlier detection based on rough sets theory. Intell. Data Anal. **13**(2), 191–206 (2009)

26. Slowinski, R., Vanderpooten, D.: A generalized definition of rough approximations based on similarity. IEEE Trans. Knowl. Data Eng. **12**(2), 331–336 (2000)

27. Tsoumakas, G., Spyromitros-Xioufis, E., Vilcek, J., Vlahavas, I.: Mulan: a java library for multi-label learning. J. Mach. Learn. Res. **12**(Jul), 2411–2414 (2011)

28. Tsoumakas, G., Vlahavas, I.: Random k-labelsets: an ensemble method for multilabel classification. In: Kok, J.N., Koronacki, J., Mantaras, R.L., Matwin, S., Mladenič, D., Skowron, A. (eds.) ECML 2007. LNCS (LNAI), vol. 4701, pp. 406–417. Springer, Heidelberg (2007). https://doi.org/10.1007/978-3-540-74958-5_38

29. Wilson, D.R., Martinez, T.R.: Improved heterogeneous distance functions. J. Artif. Intell. Res. **6**, 1–34 (1997)

30. Zhang, M.L., Zhou, Z.H.: Multilabel neural networks with applications to functional genomics and text categorization. IEEE Trans. Knowl. Data Eng. **18**(10), 1338–1351 (2006)

31. Zhang, M.L., Zhou, Z.H.: ML-KNN: a lazy learning approach to multi-label learning. Pattern Recogn. **40**(7), 2038–2048 (2007)

Implementation of a SVM on an Embedded System: A Case Study on Fall Detection

Luis Márquez-Ordaz[(✉)] and Hiram Ponce[(✉)]

Facultad de Ingeniería, Universidad Panamericana,
Augusto Rodin 498, 03920 Ciudad de México, Mexico
{0112601,hponce}@up.edu.mx

Abstract. Edge Computing seeks to bring Machine Learning as close as possible to the source events of interest, providing an almost instant interpretation to data acquired by sensors giving sense to raw data while addressing concerns of particular applications such as latency, privacy and server stress relieve. Due to a lack of research on this particular type of application, we are faced with difficulties both in software and hardware as embedded systems are known to possess serious limitations on its available processing resources. To address this, we make use of the concepts of edge computing and offline programming to accomplish a reliable machine learning model deployment on the microprocessor. By studying real case problem, we can get measurements on the resources required by such an application as well as its performance. In this study, we address the implementation of such an application in an embedded system focusing on the detection of human falls.

Keywords: Embedded system · Machine Learning · Edge computing · Deployed model · Fall detection

1 Introduction

Even though there have been embedded systems approaches on the fall detection field, specifically on the Internet-of-Things (IoT) area [10], this sort of application tends to rely on external servers to make the classification. In recent years, a new concept of edge computing [2] denotes the advantages of avoiding relying on servers to do the work. This saves problems of connectivity, high amount of data to process from different sources, privacy, among others.

In general, the efforts to pair machine learning and embedded systems does not seem to be widely implemented, and most of the times, they are particularly focused on a single platform. For example, there is an initiative into porting neural networks into microprocessors, comes in the form of a library called uTensor[1], but it is required the system to be able to be programmed under mBed[2].

---

[1] uTensor, "utensor," https://github.com/uTensor/uTensor, 2020.
[2] Mbed os. https://www.mbed.com/en.

L. Martínez-Villaseñor et al. (Eds.): MICAI 2020, LNAI 12468, pp. 76–87, 2020.
https://doi.org/10.1007/978-3-030-60884-2_6

Another example of these efforts is in hardware, OpenMV Cam H7[3] is a camera designed for embedded systems intended for vision that comes with an attached Cortex M7, the one caveat is that it needs a particular operating system called Mycropython[4] that is not the norm when handling embedded systems and will likely have a learning curve before implementing it. In this paper we describe a series of steps that will serve as example to implement machine learning on an embedded system using tools more widely spread.

For our real case subject of study we have selected Fall Detection, as stated by the World Health Organization (WHO), falls are the second leading cause of unintentional injury deaths worldwide [1]. Falls can be severe enough to require medical attention. They occur each year with injuries of degree as high as hip fracture, traumatic brain injuries, and upper limb injuries [6]. Such injuries repercussions can be mitigated if proper medical attention is given in the least amount of time. Thus, this is the importance of detecting this kind of events.

Different studies present many methods to monitor human activities, but there are three main approaches [9]: vision, environmental monitoring, and wearables. The first two depend on cameras and sensors strategically deployed in a particular area and they can collect data from anybody that enters into the designated zone; such that the method does not require any particular participation from the user. The second option, wearables, present a cheap option of monitoring. They rely mainly on a tri-axial accelerometer, some others rely on the combination of accelerometers and gyroscope, and sometimes they implement a single type of sensor or combination of all others [10].

From the compiled data in [8] we can note there are some methods commonly used for detecting falls. For instance, one of those is the use of a wearable in the wrist, this method focuses on triggering when certain data value surpasses a threshold. A practical and fairly simple implementation but it gets penalized with the lowest accuracy of all with less than 70%, while another method that makes use of an accelerometer data yields the highest accuracy overall 90%; and when pairing it with a machine learning algorithm and the position on the waist it gets up to over 97% of accuracy [8].

This paper presents an embedded system implementation for fall detection using support vector machines (SVM). In this work, we propose a methodology that comprises hardware selection, data acquisition, data preparation for training, offline training, data preparation for online testing, production model and evaluation. Throughout these steps, we implement a fully fall detection system on an ESP32 microprocessor. Our experiments show that the production model on this device is able to detect a fall and to classify simple activities prior defined to be recognized. Thus, the contribution of this work resides in the ability to deploy a machine learning model in a limited embedded system for fall detection, and the analysis of the impact on the computational resources (i.e., memory and execution time) with respect to the size of the input data required in the deployed machine learning model.

---

[3] Openmvcamh7. https://openmv.io/products/openmv-cam-h7.

[4] Micropython http://docs.micropython.org/en.

The rest of the paper is as follows. Section 2 presents the methodology for our proposed embedded system for fall detection using machine learning on-site. Section 3 describes the experimentation carried out in this work, and Sect. 4 shows the experimental results. Lastly, Sect. 5 concludes the paper and presents the future work.

2   Methodology

In this section, we explain the methodology conducted in our proposed fall detection system, running a machine learning algorithm in a microprocessor. In Fig. 1, we present a diagram depicting the general steps by which a model is trained, validated, exported and tested in production. Starting with hardware and software selection, a basic step that needs to be tailored for the needs of the application. Then, we go into data acquisition and data set creation, the better data structure we can get the easier it will be to handle in later stages and more plausible that is it to find a high rate model. Subsequently, we go into the model creation and selection, there are many structures a model can take and many variables it can use at the end. Finally, we describe the model implementation for production and its evaluation.

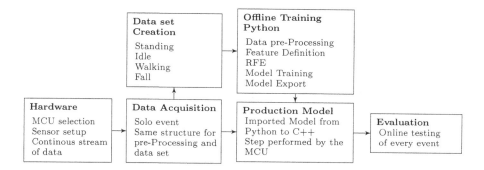

Fig. 1. Diagram detailing the proposed steps to implement a SVM in an embedded system

For the methodology, various aspects need to be addressed: hardware selection, data collection, and software selection.

2.1   Hardware Selection

Defining an embedded system depends on the author. Some define it as a module dedicated to a certain task, with limited resources, and dependant on another device to be programmed [7]. But this is a definition that describes the more traditional sense of the concept. In recent years, a new generation of microprocessors have been developed to address the requirements of the present era, especially

Internet of Things (IoT) requirements [5]. Specifically for machine learning, the starting requirement is the float precision. For this, it is expected the microprocessor to be capable of at least 32-bits operations. In addition, other attributes required are processor speed, flash capability and RAM memory.

The evolution through time in terms of processing power and resources of microprocessors several grade of magnitude recent microcontroller units (MCU's) posses almost four times the clock speed they possessed a decade before, today we can readily embedded systems with clock speeds of 200 MHz in contrast to the 16 MHz from years past. Another thing to pay attention is the increase in memory as well with values increasing from 2 KB to 300–500 KB. These features contribute to the recent interest in the implementation of machine learning models in the microprocessors, a feat previously unfeasible.

In this work, we use an ESP32 microprocessor although its architecture is not the mainstream, in contrast with the cortex line-up, it features an above average clock speed and RAM.

2.2 Data Acquisition

For the sensor we will be using a tri-axis accelerometer which, as observed in the published data sets in Martinez et al. [9], is the type of sensor that has the highest accuracy up to 97% in contrast to other options. The accelerometer of choice is the MPU-6050[5], this sensor in particular gives us not only raw gyroscope data and raw accelerometer data, but also gives us Yaw, Pitch and Roll with this data we can also calculate accelerations without the gravity, this means that the data we collect won't be polluted by the acceleration from gravity only reading accelerations directly related to the movement as well as world accelerations, this means that if the sensor is tilted we will still see data corresponding to the world axis not the ones related to the sensor position. With all this previous data we obtain a set of variables at a rate 20 Hz or 0.05 s in the following form: Yaw-Pitch-Roll-Acceleration X-Acceleration Y-Acceleration Z-Acc. X - Gravity-Acc. Y - Gravity & Acc. Z - World Acc X-World Acc. Y-World Acc. Z.

In Fig. 2, we can see a data comparison of two events, walk and fall. These measurement encompasses 4 s. On it, we can see the registered behavior of accelerations on the 3 axis and the 3 Euler angles of position. For the acceleration we can see that a normal walk (in blue) presents spikes that are within normal range, while a fall (in red) presents a sudden set of spikes that goes beyond range. In the 3 Euler angles we can see that for a walk the angles stay mostly constant while for a fall we can see an abrupt change of almost 90° from a rest position of zero.

2.3 Data Set Creation

Multiple datasets have been published for the study of fall detection: DLR Dataset, MobiFall Dataset, tFall, UMAFal, SisFall, UP-Fall Detection Dataset,

---

[5] Tdkinvensense. Availableonline: www.invensense.com/products/motion-tracking/6-axis/mpu6050 (2019).

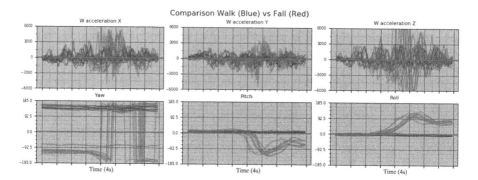

Fig. 2. Graphical representation of two movements, Walk (Blue) and Fall (Red). (Color figure online)

etc. (compilation found in Martinez et al. [8]). Two main types of approaches can be observed from these studies, the use of sensors that monitor an area (vision, vibration IR, etc.) and sensors attached to the monitored user better known as wearables.

This study is focused on the portable option of wearables that depend on microprocessors. Based on these observations of the data sets, we will use an accelerometer attached to the waist, according to Martinez et al. [8], this position seems to be the best from all other options with the highest accuracy of all of them.

We must remember that we are not only detecting falls but discerning them from other activities [8] referred as activities of daily living (ADL) and although they are not universally defined our focus will be detecting any kind of fall from standing, idle, sitting and walking.

2.4   Offline Training

The methodology for this study is divided in two main parts. First, it is the offline component which is where we will load our data set and train the model. Second, it is the production segment were we take the already trained model and load it into the microprocessor where data samples are classified periodically.

For the offline step, we will make use of Python [11] with the sklearn library. As resources at production level (MCU's) are scarce we are looking to leverage on the readily available tools this way we can obtain a final model capable of making predictions with the least amount of data and processing, this includes the pre-processing stage and the weights in the model, for that we will have to iterate the training reducing features and proposing new ones until we manage to achieve a model with the highest performance and the least amount of features.

In the following sub-sections, we will explain the steps since the acquisition of the raw data until the model is trained in Python and exported to C++.

A. Data Pre-processing

1) *Raw Data:* As explained on Sect. 2.2, a sample is a stream of data that spans across a window of 4 s at a rate 20 Hz, that means we get 60 points of each variable, counting 15 individual variables we end up with 900 total points per window. Three of those subsets describe the same redundant accelerations. So one approach would be just feed the model with a set of accelerations, a set of gyroscope data or a set of Euler angles (yaw, pitch, roll), or a combination of any of those sets.

2) *Feature Extraction:*   Another approach is to use basic statistical analysis for feature extraction. This will allow us to reduce drastically the amount of features present in the model, classic examples of this are mean, median, standard deviation. Other more complex approaches exist to find relationships between features, this can be process consuming so for this study we will focus on the basic ones.

B. Model Training

For the model we have chosen to implement an SVM model, as it yield pretty good results while maintaining a relatively reduced memory footprint. "What makes SVM attractive is the property of condensing information in the training data and providing a sparse representation by using a very small number of data points" [4].

SVM is a type of linear classifier that works by maximizing the margin between the separating hyper plane and the data [3]. SVM's are also known for their ability to use kernels that help separating non-linear separable data, we implement the lineal kernel trying to keep the processing necessary at minimal.

C. Feature Selection

We make use of recursive feature elimination (RFE) [12], which is an iterative method that first ranks the different features fed into the model, then by selecting and eliminating some of the less contributing ones it creates a new set of features with which it trains the model again, then it evaluates model using accuracy finding the best set of features. It is observed that we can achieve roughly the same accuracy with less features, sometimes higher accuracy can also be achieved. This helps in obtaining a model that requires less memory to work, that is faster and with the selection of the proper features an even more precise model can be achieved.

D. Model Evaluation

To evaluate the model performance we will use the accuracy indicator. When training a model there are a multiple of techniques and indicators used to evaluate its performance. The basic idea is to withheld certain amount of data from the training process and then use that unseen data to create prediction, as we know which class the retained data belongs to we can know if the model is doing a proper prediction or not.

For indicators, accuracy is the most straightforward of them. Given a certain amount of test samples what percentage of them were classified correctly, as see in (1), where tp, tn, fp and fn are the true positives, true negatives, false positives and false negatives, respectively. Accuracy is a good indicator of the model, specially if the percentage is high but other indicators must be taken into account to evaluate a model properly.

$$accuracy = \frac{tp + tn}{tp + fp + fn + tn} \tag{1}$$

Precision, as expressed in (2), represents the percentage of the samples labeled as a particular one was correct, low precision indicates a large amount of samples mislabeled as the wrong class.

$$precision = \frac{tp}{tp + fp} \tag{2}$$

Recall measures the percentage was labeled correctly, low recall indicates a class that has a high rate to be missclassified, as written in (3).

$$recall = \frac{tp}{tp + fn} \tag{3}$$

Lastly, F1-score in (4) is the relationship between the precision and the recall. The higher the F1-score the better the model is.

$$F1\text{-}score = 2 * \frac{recall * precision}{recall + precision} \tag{4}$$

E. Model Export

Once we have a model that is ready for production, the model we obtain is exported using sklearn porter[6] into C/C++. In this way, it should be able to run in most environments destined for programming embedded systems.

2.5   Production Model

The file that contains the exported model has an extension .cpp for C++. This means we need to structure the program so that the compiler can handle files in C and C++, this is easily achievable with the proper header files.

This file contains all the arrays necessary to describe the weights, vectors, coefficients and intercepts necessary for the SVM to work. This arrays are the principal contributors to the memory consumption, knowing this is valuable to obtain the real amount of memory the model requires. Once compiled the amount of memory can be visualized and if the required memory is more than the available it is possible the compilation to fail. In our case our selected MCU posses 512 KB of available RAM. We found that as the arrays are static values they can be declared as constant and be allocated not in the RAM memory but in the flash memory where we have at least 1 MB of available memory.

---

[6] Darius Morawiec, "Sklearn Porter", https://github.com/nok/sklearn-porter.

2.6   Classification

Once the data acquisition, the pre-processing functions and the production model are properly setup, the model will be able to classify any given data. The approach we are taking here is to give a data sample of 4 s every half a second this will give us a constant stream of classifications allowing us to act almost immediately when a case of interest occurs.

3   Experiments

For the experiments, we follow the methodology as explained in the corresponding Sect. 2. For the hardware, we use the ESP32 as the microprocessor and the MPU-6050 as the sensor. We collect the raw data via serial port and archive it in .csv file form. As for the dataset itself, we asked 5 subjects between the ages of 20 and 30 to perform the previously selected activities (fall, idle, sitting and walking), collecting 10 samples of each activity per person, each sample encompasses 4 s of movement data.

To evaluate the performance of the model on the microprocessor we measure two variables of interest: processing time and memory. For memory we compile the model in C then we register the memory needed according to the generated binary. The memory registered is the memory contributed by the SVM file alone. For processing time we measure the time it takes the model since it receives an array until it makes a prediction. This time refers only to the SVM prediction time and does not time the pre-process functions as they tend to contribute little to the process time. Finally we obtain the accuracy of the model in Python, using the Eq. 1 described in Sect. 2.4.

For this study we designed two experiments, each intended to address two different concerns of this research. The first focuses on the resources required by the SVM algorithm in the MCU, and second one focuses on creating a model that is the fittest for production implementation.

For the first experiment, we focused on measuring the performance on the microprocessor. For that, we used data of a single person to generate a set of models. The data used for this models is the raw data, as all of our data encompasses a time of 4 s, every channel should have a total amount of 80 points, these points will be the features in the model, in this way the more channels we use on the model the more complex it will be.

For the second experiment, we focused on creating a final model that can be used reliable on production and capable of classifying the movements from different people. This means our model has to be capable to perform reliable when it is presented with unseen data. Our approach was to train a model using data from just one person and then using that same model to classify data of the four remaining subjects.

4   Results

In this section we discuss the data obtained by the 2 experiments, the goal of the first experiment being the benchmarking of the algorithm in the microprocessor measurements of memory and processing time are provided. For the second experiment now that we have a good idea of the resources needed for a classification of events we focus on evaluating the model when exposed to previously unseen data. Process of feature selection is discussed and final accuracy values are provided.

4.1 First Experiment

As explained in Sect. 3, the intent of this first experiment is to gauge the resources required by the model and its performance overall. For this, we selected 2 variables, memory and time, as indicators of each, then by increasing the amount of data used to train we created a batch of models with different levels of complexity following which we compiled and ran them on the microprocessor from where we registered both variables of interest.

In Table 1, we show the collected data. We can observe that the more features the more memory and time are required by the model. We are using 4 classes across all the machine learning models. As shown in the table, the accuracy for raw data, as expected, is not satisfactory. After a simple pre-process of normalization the accuracy score increases, a process simple enough to be able to be implemented in the microprocessor. Another observation is that the same amount of features does not yield the same requirement of memory.

Table 1. Performance from collected datasets of different complexities.

No. of channels	Channels names	No. of features	Accuracy raw data	Accuracy normalized data	Memory (Bytes)	Process time (Seconds)
6	Yaw, Pitch, Roll, WA.X, WA.Y, WA.Z	480	0.79	1.00	93,012	0.025577
3	WA.X, WA.Y, WA.Z	240	0.71	1.00	44,992	0.013065
3	Yaw, Pitch, Roll	240	1.00	1.00	33,328	0.009825
2	W A.Y,W A.Z	160	0.71	1.00	24,840	0.004539
2	Yaw, Pitch	160	1.00	1.00	20,928	0.003904
1	Yaw	80	1.00	1.00	12,016	0.002819

In Fig. 3, we can see the relationship between the used features, memory and process time, with a behavior that is almost linear. As a reference, the most complex model requires 93 KB of the 500 KB available of RAM and takes 0.025 s to process, reminding the sensor refreshes at about 0.05 s we could make one prediction every time a new data arrives.

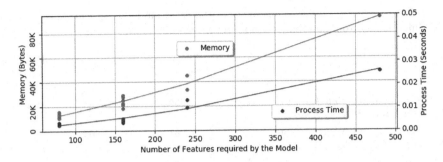

Fig. 3. Relationship between model complexity and resources required.

4.2 Second Experiment

In the second experiment, we follow the same procedure as for the first experiment, this time testing the same model with data from the four remaining people. We observed that raw data have an accuracy rate of 1 when the data is from the same person but when applied to unseen data the accuracy rate drops on average to less than 0.5.

To improve the accuracy rating for unseen data, we made use of more simpler features to describe the data channels. This allows the model to work the data with more general features reducing the model complexity. The new features include the mean, the variance and the standard deviation. This statistic analysis is applied to the 80 points that encompasses the 4 s samples, effectively reducing each channel to 3 features each. We focused on the accelerations and the Euler angles as we did on the first experiment, making this 6 channels from which we obtained 18 features.

To discern which of the proposed features were the most valuable we made use of RFE, this algorithm checks how much a particular feature is contributing to the model and iteratively eliminates one feature until certain accuracy is achieved, in the end we get a series of feature sets from where we can see the selected features correspondent accuracy. The results can be found in Table 2. One of the first things that got our attention is that neither mean nor the variance features contribute much to the model so we don't see them on the selected features. The next thing is that the model with the new features obtained an accuracy within acceptable ranges (more than 0.95). It is worth-noting that we are still using a model that has only seen data of one person to classify data from the four remaining subjects. The accuracy reported in Table 2 is from this unseen data. We can also observe that the models with the highest accuracy are not the ones with the highest number of features.

For the evaluation, we see that the accuracy achieved is almost perfect, correspondingly the precision and recall are pretty high above 0.95. We observe the model has no problems detecting and differentiating the classes of interest.

Table 2. Evaluation of different instances of the SVM model using feature selection, using information from four subjects not seen on training.

Features names	Accuracy unseen data	Precision	Recall	F1 score
Yaw Std, Pitch Std, Roll Std, W Accel X Std, W Accel Y Std, W Accel Z Std	0.969	0.97	0.97	0.97
Pitch Std, Roll Std, W Accel X Std, W Accel Y Std, W Accel Z Std	0.981	0.98	0.98	0.98
Roll Std, W A. X Std, W A. Y Std, W A. Z Std	0.981	0.98	0.98	0.98
Roll Std, W A. X Std, W A. Y Std	0.975	0.97	0.97	0.97
W A.X Std, W A.Y Std, W A.Z Std	0.981	0.98	0.98	0.98
Yaw Std, Pitch Std, Roll Std	0.4125	0.41	0.41	0.41

4.3   Discussion

In the first experiment, we proved that implementing a SVM in a microcontroller is viable and more so we mapped its performance although our experiment used only 4 classes, reducing the model complexity several degrees we still have a pretty good idea how a different model should behave in terms of expected classification time and memory requirements. Even though the most complex model we proposed in this study only used about a fifth of the available RAM, we must remember that we still have to share it across other functionalities that depending on the application can be as crucial as the prediction model; for example, it would be a communication module (WiFi or Bluetooth). It is not entirely the case where we were creating static arrays for the model to work those can be declared as constant and so be allocated in the flash memory that normally has more available space. This could potentially impact on the classification time, but is still an option to make use of all the resources available. We still have to be in mind full of memory space when talking about sensor data as these cannot be a constant. It must be allocated in the RAM, e.g. a camera sensor data.

On the second experiment, we focused on creating a final model that has a high rate of success. Through the different evaluation variables, we found out that raw data do not have good accuracy when presented with data that comes from different sources. Due to this, we had to make use of a different set of features to use in the model. These new set of features were appropriate and yielded excellent results. While our focus is entirely on detecting falls from any other activities, we can observe our proposed final model is capable of discerning from any of the 4 classes that we previously selected.

5   Conclusion

In this study, we focused on detecting falls from among other human activities with a focus on implementing it on an embedded system. We started this study with uncertainty on the viability of applying complex algorithms on a resource-constrained environment. We used tools that are readily available for the study and creation of models specifically the Python platform. This allowed us to re-design the model to be as optimal as possible to save resources in the final implementation. Then, the trained model was exported to C++ creating a sort of pipeline that allows us to create and train models quickly and implementing them on production almost seamlessly. For our case study, we managed to obtain a high rate accuracy of fall detection, and with the observed results the model can be a little more complex to be able to categorize more diverse human activities. With these results, we have a clear idea of the scalability and the resources of such implementations in the future. We are considering that other applications such as in handwritten recognition or robotics can be deployed easily into real-world production environments with computational resources constraints as embedded systems.

References

1. World Health Organization, falls (2020). http://www.who.int/mediacentre/factsheets/fs344/en/
2. Ai, Y., Peng, M., Zhang, K.: Edge computing technologies for internet of things: a primer. Digit. Commun. Netw. **4**(2), 77–86 (2018). https://doi.org/10.1016/j.dcan.2017.07.001
3. Amari, S., Wu, S.: Improving support vector machine classifiers by modifying kernel functions. Neural Netw. **12**(6), 783–789 (1999). https://doi.org/10.1016/S0893-6080(99)00032-5
4. Girosi, F.: An equivalence between sparse approximation and support vector machines. Neural Comput. **10**(6), 1455–1480 (1998)
5. Jovan Ivković, J.L.I.: Analysis of the performance of the new generation of 32-bit microcontrollers for IoT and big data application. In: 7th International Conference on Information Society and Technology ICIST 2017 (2017)
6. Kalache, A., et al.: World Health Organisation Global Report on Falls Prevention in Older Age
7. Haigh, K.Z., Mackay, A.M., Cook, M.R., Lin, L.G.: Machine Learning for Embedded Systems: A Case Study (2015)
8. Martinez-Villaseñor, L., Ponce, H., Brieva, J., Moya-Albor, E., Nuñez Martinez, J., Peñafort-Asturiano, C.: Up-fall detection dataset: a multimodal approach. Sensors **19**, 1988 (2019). https://doi.org/10.1016/j.neucom.2011.09.037
9. Mubashir, M., Shao, L.S.L.: A survey on fall detection: principles and approaches. Sciencedirect (2013). https://doi.org/10.1016/j.neucom.2011.09.037
10. Nooruddin, S., Islam, M.M., Sharna, F.A.: An IoT based device-type invariant fall detection system. Internet Things **9**, 100130 (2020). https://doi.org/10.1016/j.iot.2019.100130
11. Van Rossum, G., Drake, F.L.: Python 3 Reference Manual. CreateSpace, Scotts Valley (2009)
12. Zhou, Q., Zhou, H., Zhou, Q., Yang, F., Luo, L.: Structure damage detection based on random forest recursive feature elimination. Mech. Syst. Sign. Process. **46**(1), 82–90 (2014). https://doi.org/10.1016/j.ymssp.2013.12.013

Click Event Sound Detection Using Machine Learning in Automotive Industry

Ricardo Espinosa[1]($\boxtimes$) , Hiram Ponce[2] , Sebastián Gutiérrez[1] ,
and Eluney Hernández[1]

[1] Facultad de Ingeniería, Universidad Panamericana,
Josemaría Escrivá de Balaguer 101, Aguascalientes, 20290 Aguascalientes, Mexico
{respinosa,jsgutierrez,0232610}@up.edu.mx
[2] Facultad de Ingeniería, Universidad Panamericana,
Augusto Rodin 498, 03920 Ciudad de México, Mexico
hponce@up.edu.mx

Abstract. Artificial intelligence has been playing an important role when it comes to the automotive industry and its quality of assemblies in the production line, this is because since the arrival of the industry 4.0 it has been subject to change and continuous improvement. In the past, we've observed how many machine learning architectures have been used to create environmental sound classification systems in order to improve traditional systems, thus overcoming efficiency issues with great results. In this work, we present a machine learning solution/approach for click event sound detection using audio sensors that are used in the assembly of electric harnesses for engines, this being done on an automotive production line, where we divided our workflow into: data collection, pre-processing, feature extraction, training and inference and finally the detection of the click event sounds. We created a dataset that is composed by 25,000 audio files that have an average duration of 0.025 seconds per click sound with the purpose of training a Multi-layer Perceptron and bring it into the inference phase. In order to test this approach, we've performed various implementations in a laboratory and in the real automotive industry. We obtained 95.23% in F1-Score Metric in a laboratory, while in real conditions, we obtained less reliable results, as 84.00% as the best results.

Keywords: Audio signal processing · Events sound recognition · Feature extraction · Machine learning · MLP · Neural network · Signal spectral characteristics · Supervised learning

1 Introduction

In Mexico, 97.9% of the Gross Domestic Product (GDP) of the automotive industry in 2017 includes car manufacturing as the most important activity in

© Springer Nature Switzerland AG 2020
L. Martínez-Villaseñor et al. (Eds.): MICAI 2020, LNAI 12468, pp. 88–103, 2020.
https://doi.org/10.1007/978-3-030-60884-2_7

this industry [1, 2]. When speaking of auto parts production, Mexico remained as the fifth largest producer worldwide and was the largest in Latin America in 2017. Due to the fast integration of electronic and software components, the basis of the automotive industry is changing remarkably. We can also note that is not feasible to have automation systems because of the reduced space in some production lines and that the involvement of humans in production stages is still necessary to assure certain quality standards, since the products must be assembled without any kind of defects.

In the automotive industry, the automobiles factories are still employing workers in specific tasks, in this way allowing operations such as the assembly of the seating, steering wheels, belts and other parts that form the interior and exterior of the vehicle. Because of this and the transport of different components of the vehicles and the performance of unvaried movement, employees have been exposed to many risk factors, as well as problems such as overloads, like stress, an excess of tiresome movements that involve poor non-physical postures, as well as deterioration in assembly quality [3].

The literature addresses a brilliant method to picture data identified with assembly and quality in the creation of cars, permitting the control of imperfection data in a manner arranged to the worker of the assembly line [4]. Different examinations have executed acoustic quality control systems in their creation lines with good outcomes, likewise applying machine learning because of the distinctive commotion situations inside the enterprises [5].

As an aspect of giving an answer for the issues that emerge in car creation lines, the current work proposes the usage of a machine learning model for sound events detection utilizing sound sensors in the get together of electric bridles for motors on a car creation line, where the computerization of the process gets practically impossible to execute.

We define the electrical connections of an engine as a set of cables, terminals, connectors, clips, tapes, among other components that carry an electrical signal from one point to another. They have been involved in several quality problems in productions lines for the assembly of motor parts in cars, specifically when installing them using harnesses. When connecting one or more harnesses into the motor, there's the doubt if this connection has been made accurately, since the dependability of the connections is based on a sound (a click). Accordingly to that, this research work offers a method of verification using an ultrasonic microphone and considering the click sounds generated during the connection procedure through a multi-layered perceptron, in this way we can assure an appropriate assembly of 6 harnesses in the engine, helping the operator in this way.

Various classification and detection studies have been proposed through machine learning techniques for sound detection. As we know, in this way it is possible to classify whale species based on their whistles [6]; emotions and physiological needs of newborn babies can be detected using artificial intelligence [7]. In addition, we can include the detection of uncommon sounds in the streets (crying for help), shootings inside urban environments, and illegal forest activities, as well as other others [8, 9].

Even though there are multiple studies that have been able to classify audio signals under experimental noise conditions with the use of deep learning, there is very few information available in the literature on diagnosing car engine failures using a detection system and machine learning. This few mentioned works include: [10] presented ML techniques of audio samples to detect an engine failure; [11] reported a model-based fault diagnostics systems using ML for detecting and locating multiple classes of faults in a automotive electric drive; and one of the most remarkable ones is [12], that presented a new diagnostic framework namely Probabilistic Committee Machine (PCM) that combines feature extraction, a parameter optimization algorithm, and multiple Sparse Bayesian Extreme Learning Machines (SBELM) to form an intelligent diagnostic framework, allowing to determine both single and simultaneous-faults for car engines. It should be noted that in these studies the diagnosis is carried out experimentally outside the production lines, where it could help laborers carry to accomplish special tasks within a production line.

Therefore, we present an application developed and tested into a manufacturing enterprise, being able to detect appropriate assembly from harnesses connections using MLP as a traditional machine learning algorithm, which was implemented and tested to detect click events sound within a real assembly production line. During 3 months of production, there were 25,000 click events of 0.025 s of duration, which in addition to being recorded by an ultrasonic microphone that was allowed to record up to 22,000 Hz from real work scenarios, were collected into a dataset, which was later used in this work.

This proposal of this research is about to present an application of ML proposition for determining failures of the assembly parts of a vehicle by using sound detection events of harnesses.

The rest of this work is organized as follows: Sect. 2 presents the previous and related work. Section 3 provides the proposal description. Section 4 describes the use case. Section 5 presents the experimental results of the study and a discussion, and Sect. 6 concludes the research paper.

2   Background and Related Work

Research in areas such as music and speech have been heavily studied for over a decade, having examples such as [13–17]. Nevertheless, fields like environmental sound recognition, event detection and audio pattern recognition have not received as much attention as the previous mentioned topics. A group of research works and methods that could relate to our research has been included in [18]. Some of those talk about surveillance [19], acoustic event detection (AED) [20] and time-frequency audio features [21]. Sound classification and recognition commonly relies on traditional, handmade features like Mel Frequency Crespal Coefficients (MFCCs) [22], which have been shown to be sensitive to background noise found in urban environments [23]. Unsupervised feature learning has also been studied when talking about the previous topics [24].

Sound recognition systems have mostly focused on speech and music signals, however, events sound recognition systems have received more debate/attention in recent years. A survey of different features extraction methods used in sound recognition systems is described in [24]. The effect of ambient background noise on event classification performance in real life recordings is studied in [25], with an achieved accuracy of 24%, which was obtained by classifying sound events into 61 classes reporting how background noise makes sound events classification and detection a hard task.

Traditional ML techniques have been characterized for their reliability in AED to improve the detection of acoustic events, this task is performed by a regression via classification based approach along with the random forest technique. As far as we are aware, this is the first time in which machine learning is applied to sound detection events of harnesses, with the objective of improving the quality of manufacturing in the automotive industry.

3   Description of the Proposal

In this section, we describe the methodology for developing our proposal. In this research we followed the approach presented by Babaee et al. in [26], that is being applied in a real case on a production line of electric harnesses for motors in an automotive industry, which includes: data gathering, pre-processing, feature extraction and training, and inference stages. Figure 1 shows the methodology we used for our application. A detailed description of these steps are presented following.

Fig. 1. Our proposal of click sound events recognition methodology

3.1   Sound Data Collection

In the traditional workflow for sound event detection systems and in general machine learning related problems, one of the most challenging phases is data collection. Some very important aspects that must integrate audio signals for reliable sound events recognition systems are the audio clips, sampling rate, frequency of signals and the number of audio channels.

Starting from the above, in order to build our own dataset we focus only on the click event sounds inside the collected audio clips and other alike sounds with frequencies greater than 10 kHz. These sounds were segmented in time windows of 0.025 s duration. This period of time was selected as a period of time to detect click events extracting the average time that the click events take in all the data

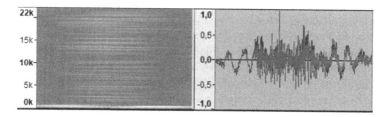

Fig. 2. A spectrogram and waveform of a click event with 0.025 s of duration

collected as shown in Fig. 2. The dataset is integrated by 25,000 samples of 0.025 s windows of duration balanced and labeled with 1 indicating a correct click sound assembly and 0 to opposite.

3.2　Pre-processing

Pre-processing of information is critical for building a reliable machine learning application. Recording the assembly production line's sounds involves background noise, and because of that, we implemented pre-processing in three steps: noise reduction, pre-emphasis filter and an onset detection algorithm for segmentation as show in Fig. 3. In this particular work we added a segmentation phase from the original methodology of the collected audio to then continue with feature extraction, which can be later used with the finality of improving data analysis [26] and finding ideal features. In this case, this were robustness against noise, easy adaptability, easy implementation, and containing necessary smoothing characteristics [27].

In the noise reduction step, we used an algorithm based on spectral gating algorithm to suppress the noise in the audio and to preserve more information from the original data than retained by standard techniques. Noise gates are used by Spectral Gating Based Noise Reduction technique in the Fourier domain to separate reasonable image structure from background noise, using the statistics of local neighborhoods in the signal [28]. As an example of this, Kiapuchinski et al. [29] used spectral noise gating to filter out the background noise in birds' chirping (birds' songs).

The pre-emphasis step was applied with noise-reduced audio signal, which allows us to amplify higher frequencies as shown in (1) where the signal is represented as x, time t and α is the filter coefficient. This step is very useful in several ways: the frequency spectrum gets balanced, since high frequencies usually have smaller magnitudes compared to lower frequencies, thus avoiding numerical problems throughout the Fourier transformation operation and might also improve the Signal-to-Noise Ratio (SNR). As examples of this step's uses, there's objective cardiac event detection [30] and speech emotion recognition system [31].

$$y(t) = x(t) - \alpha x(t - 1) \tag{1}$$

In the third step we compute onset detection algorithm using spectral flux algorithm based on maximum filter vibrato suppression technique to locate onset events by picking peaks in an onset strength envelope in high frequencies to then proceed with feature extraction.

These timestamps allow detection of sound click events locations Using these timestamps we extract time windows of 0.025 s subtracting 1024 samples from the collected filtered audio by the spectral flux based onset algorithm to then be processed to feature extraction phase as shown in Fig. 3. As observable, they allow to detect the possible locations of the click sound events. It should be noted that the three mentioned were implemented using Python 3.7 and Librosa, which is a library for audio analysis implemented in Python [32].

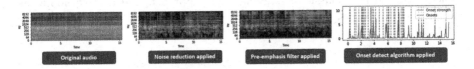

Fig. 3. Our proposal work flow to pre-processing and segmentation phase

3.3 Feature Extraction

Feature extraction is a general method where input space is transformed into a lower dimensional space that preserves the majority of its relevant information. As we mentioned before, robustness against noise, easy adaptability, easy implementation, and containing necessary smoothing characteristics are the ideal features.

For this work, we implemented a combined approach of the following five features: Mel Frequency Crespal Coefficients (MFCCs), Mel-Scaled Spectrogram, Chromogram, Spectral Centroid (SF) and Tonnetz Representation (TR).

The first mentioned has the following main uses in this research:

- As a feature extraction method in sound events detection systems and speech recognition systems. As an example, [33] and [34] used MFCCs features with a Deep Neural Network as an inference method to recognize different speakers.
- They are deeply used in audio analysis and detection systems due to the ability to model the vocal tract shape in a short time power spectrum. The previous mentioned are computed using a psycho-acoustically motivated filterbank, then a logarithmic compression and a discrete cosine transformation (DCT) are applied. Finally, the 12–15 lowest DCT coefficients are returned to represent the MFCCs feature vector [35].
- Used in identification and tracking of timbre fluctuations in a sound file, where this last one tends to be inadequate in a distinguishable representation of pitch classes and harmony [35]. Rich information is provided by using Spectral Centroid information with MFCC for speech and music discrimination tasks [36–38] Oppositely, in order to deal with pitch classes and harmony, we computed a Chromogram applying the Short-Time Fourier Transform (STFT) [32].

– The Tonnetz representation measures the tonal centroid of a sound based on harmonic changes [28].

These features are significant in the classification procedure by using our dataset with correct and incorrect click sounds. To perform this, we implemented a t-Distributed Stochastic Neighbor Embedding (t-SNE) algorithm as shown in Fig. 4. This method consists of mapping the high-dimensional state-vectors onto a low-dimensional space without losing important information on the relatedness of the component [39]. Thus, the graph in Fig. 4 can gives us insights on the efficiency of these features to explain correctness or not in the click sounds. Furthermore, it is noticeable that these classes cannot be separated by a linear classifier, thus more complex nonlinear models are required. In this respect, we implemented MLP as classic machine learning approach to deal with nonlinear classification problems.

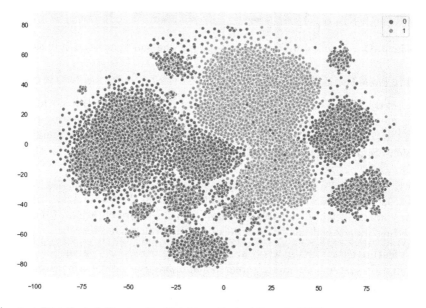

Fig. 4. t-Distributed Stochastic Neighbor Embedding (t-SNE) implemented in our dataset with 25,000 audio clips with Mel Frequency Crespal Coefficients, Mel-scaled spectogram, chromogram, spectral centroid and Tonnetz representation, features extracted

3.4   Learning and Detection

In a machine learning algorithm, this step looks forward to train and test the output from feature engineering to detect the event sound with inputs from the audio sensors.

This method approaches have been widely applied into automatic sound recognition areas. specifically, it has been deeply studied in multiple speech recognition tasks with robustness. In [40] improve phoneme recognition accuracy under different noise types achieving using MFCC and Fast Fourier Transform (FFT) as combined features.

Multi-layer Perceptron is a classic machine learning model and the approach used in this work, MLP is a neural network that uses a back-propagation algorithm in order to adjust the weights between the connections in the network. The MLP network can integrate 3 types of layers: input layer, hidden layers and the output layer [41], where each layer is built by units ("neurons") involved in a learning procedure with a simple activation function. The activation functions are divided into 2 types: linear activation functions and nonlinear activation functions [42]. In this research, we implemented Rectified Lineal Unit (ReLU) and Logistic Activation functions both from nonlinear functions. Stochastic Gradient Descent (SGD) is used in this work in order to update the weights, thus minimizing the loss.

4   Use Case

Our proposal is a click event sound detection system based on a ML approach in order to satisfy a multinational industry's problematic inside of its assembly line production. The process can be described as follows: the connection of six electric harnesses connected manually by an operator inside the engine. The main requirement of the company in question was a system that helps the process made by operators to guarantee an appropriate connection of 6 plastic harnesses with only the sound the harness produces when it is connected correctly. It has to be emphasized that this process is performed in an environment particularly noisy and is full of the noises of processes like supply processes, machinery working, alerts, etc. This process is made by different workers at different times of day, this entails different aspects in the right connection of the harnesses, such as the applied force in the connection and distinct sounds throughout the day. In order to explain the use case applied in this problematic, this section is divided in the same phases as the previous section: sound data collection, pre-processing, feature extraction and learning and detection.

4.1   Sound Data Collection

To complete this phase we developed a desktop software based on .Net framework 4.0 technology to automatically record and store the sounds of harness connection routines directly from assembly production lines. Each stored file contains the sounds of 6 harness connections sounds with an appropriate assembly made manually by workers in a real assembly line.

During this 3 months of data collection contained different types of noise can be heard including: the click sound events, principally the noise came from another process in the same assembly production line, metal shocks originated by the same connection process, machinery working and external sounds as workers talking.

All the files were collected with one audio signal sensed by an ultrasonic microphone "Ultramic UM200K" which was placed on top of operations at a range of 35 cm from the workstation where the harnesses are connected, thus offering freedom of movement for workers, in order to be able to record sounds up to 22,000 Hz of the frequency with a sample rate of 44,100 Hz and as WAV audio file format without any treatment applied. The dataset obtained was composed by 25,000 samples of 0.025 s windows of duration.

4.2   Pre-processing

Here we divided the pre-processing phase in three tasks: noise reduction, pre-emphasis filtering and onset detection algorithm to segmentation step. In the noise reduction task, we stored the first 0.5 s of each audio in order to record only the noise that will be denoised in all the audio clip. This allowed us to dynamically apply noise reduction depending on real noise of every audio clip. Pre-emphasis filtering was applied with Python 3.7 using (1) and $\alpha = 0.97$, thus balancing the frequency spectrum since high frequencies usually have smaller magnitudes compared to lower frequencies.

The last task to be applied was the onset detection algorithm, which was implemented by using Librosa library to perform a maximum filter vibrato suppression algorithm, which detects high frequency changes between 10 kHz and 22 kHz in the recorded audio clips. As a result of this step, we obtained the timestamps of the event sounds including the correct click sounds as shown in Fig. 3.

4.3   Feature Extraction

As we mentioned before, we implemented the extraction of five features (Mel Frequency Crespal Coefficients (MFCCS) [34], Mel-scaled spectogram [36], chromogram [37], spectral centroid (SC) [38] and Tonnetz representation (TR) [29] using the Librosa library package, and then combined into a 213 length vector. To obtain these features the process was carried out with sample rate 44.1 kHz, 22 kHz as maximum frequency and 60 number of MFCCs. We defined a vector with all of the features combined. This vector contains all the features, thus summing a length of 213 representing 0.025 s windows.

4.4   Learning and Detection

In this step we trained and tested a MLP algorithm, following the same methodology described in Fig. 1 in order to test its performance in laboratory and in assembly production line.

For the machine learning implementation we used the sklearn3 framework. As described, the clicks sound data set is integrated from two different classes with 25,000 samples collected. In order to train MLP algorithm, we split the data into a training set (70%) and a testing set (30%). The training data contains 17,500 audio clips and testing data 7,500 both with 213 features extracted from 0.025 s click event audio clips. The testing data contains the other 30% (7,500) of data vectors with the same information.

Each feature vector is pre-processed with an standard scalar function as in (2) where u is the mean of the training samples, s is the standard deviation of the training samples, and z is the standardized value.

$$z = \frac{(x - u)}{s} \tag{2}$$

The architecture of this method was selected by a cross validation process.

The architecture for the MLP had a 213 units length input layer and one hidden layer with 256 units to finally obtain the detection. The MLP was built with activation function = "ReLU", shuffle = 1, initial learning rate = 0.001, solver = "stochastic gradient" and maximum epochs = 50 as shown in Fig. 5.

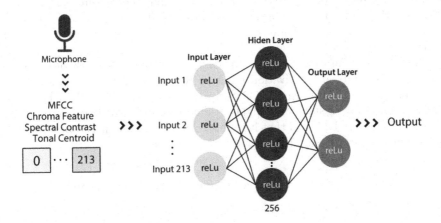

Fig. 5. Our proposal of MLP architecture to click event sound detection

5   Experimental Results

To evaluate our proposal in a real assembly production line, the experiments were executed in two branches: (i) experiments with MLP in laboratory and (ii) testing the MLP model in the assembly production line.

In order to measure the performance of our model, we tested the following in a laboratory: accuracy, sensitivity, specificity, precision and a F1-score as the metrics. We notice this from (3) to (7), where: TP (true positives), TN (true negatives), FP (false positives), FN (false negatives).

$$accuracy = \frac{TP + TN}{TP + TN + FP + FN} \tag{3}$$

$$precision = \frac{TP}{TN + FP} \tag{4}$$

$$sensitivity = \frac{TP}{TP + FP} \tag{5}$$

$$specificity = \frac{TN}{TN + FP} \tag{6}$$

$$F1 - score = 2 * \frac{precision * sensitivity}{precision + sensitivity} \tag{7}$$

5.1 Experiments with MLP in Laboratory

In Table 1, it is seen that MLP as traditional machine learning technique can handle with the click event detection task in laboratory testing according with the results obtained from a cross validation process, exploring two different activation function (ReLU) and (Logistic) and 3 different number of neurons 64,128,256 all tests with 1 hidden layer, obtaining the best result with 95.23% in F1-Score metric the combination of 256 neurons in hidden layer with activation function ReLU.

The best configuration for this experiment was obtained with one hidden layer with 256 units and activation function ReLU, according with the results this configuration accomplished 97.35% in specificity and 95.23% in F1-Score metric. From these results, we might assume that our MLP approach using sklearn3 library can be found that it is able to generalize and it is robust enough performing click event sound detection task in laboratory.

Table 1. Performance obtained by the MLP model in laboratory.

MLP architecture	Activation function	Accuracy (%)	Precision (%)	Sensitivity (%)	Specificity (%)	F1-Score (%)
64	RELU	94.05	95.40	95.40	92.88	94.13
128	RELU	93.68	96.02	96.02	91.48	93.69
256	**ReLU**	**94.99**	**93.19**	**93.19**	**97.35**	**95.23**
64	Logistic	94.19	94.19	94.87	93.73	94.30
128	Logistic	94.51	94.51	94.78	94.50	94.64
256	Logistic	94.64	93.86	93.86	95.82	94.83

5.2   Testing the MLP Model in a Real Assembly Production Line

Lastly, we conducted an experiment for clicks event sound detection implementing in real assembly production line testing our MLP model with 1 hidden layer with 256 neurons and activation function (ReLU). In this case, the tests were measured testing the model with 300 different tests of good harnesses assembly in real conditions assembled by the same person and then being processed in the same computer with processor Intel Core i-7 and 8 GB RAM.

To define a process as a good assembly the operator have to connect 6 harnesses in to the motor, this sequence is recorder in order to analyze it each one with both trained algorithms. This sequence was performed with the same computer for the model.

The results of this experiment are included in Table 2. We can see that the performance for the MLP approach achieved 84.00% of efficiency having problems with the right detection of the click event sounds in noisy environment.

5.3   Discussion

This work describes a methodology based on a machine learning approach for the click event sounds detection, the experiments were performed in laboratory and with real conditions in an assembly production line from a multinational automotive industry achieving good results.

The results support the evidence about the good results of our proposed methodology of click event sounds detection system using traditional ML using MLP (95.23% of the F1-score). Our model then achieved 84% of efficiency. The efficiency of our model achieved 84% of efficiency in assembly production line was calculated by 300 tests with 6 click connections each one. The efficiency achieved in the assembly production line could be limited by the amount of tests made in real conditions and the noise involved in that time.

A consideration to be made is that our MLP approach could be less generalized (e.g. overfitted) in the training step and producing mistakes on detection in real conditions. One possible limitation of our proposal is the occlusion of sound. Since we used a mono-sensor, occlusion might have happened between the connector and the microphone which can directly affect sound detection of clicks. In addition, real-world sounding conditions are not controlled nor studied in this work.

Table 2. Performance obtained by the MLP algorithm in an assembly production line.

Model	Number of tests	Test OK	Test NG	Efficiency (%)
MLP	300	252	48	84.00%

6   Conclusions

In this paper, we presented a click events sound detection system using audio sensors in the assembly of electric harnesses for engines on an automotive production line through ML techniques. In addition, we combined 5 features: Mel Frequency Crespal Coefficients (MFCCS), Mel-scaled spectogram, chromogram, Spectral Centroid (SF) and Tonnetz Representation (TR) from 0.025 s of duration audio clips. We conducted different experiments for: benchmarking our proposal with a conventional MLP machine learning model in laboratory and extending our model in real conditions in assembly production line.

From the experimental results, we concluded that MLP machine learning approach conducts reliable and robust behavior in laboratory and in real conditions of click sound being more accurate especially with unknown sounds and noisy environment as assembly production line.

Lastly, future work considers to implement this approach using spectogram and mel-spectogram images of the sounds in order to take more advantage of a deep learning 2D-CNN approach and to analyze and propose improvements to issues of occlusion of sound and another noise reduction methods.

References

1. National Institute of Statistics and Geography (INEGI), Collection of sectoral and regional studies. Knowing the Automotive Industry, November 2018
2. Mexican Automotive Industry Association (AMIA), Dialogue with the Automotive Industry (2018)
3. Błaszczyk, A., Zygmańska-Jabłońska, M., Wegner-Czerniak, K., Ogurkowska, M.B.: Evaluating progressive overload changes of the musculoskeletal system in automobile industry workers. Polish J. Environ. Stud. **29**(4), 2579–2586 (2020). https://doi.org/10.15244/pjoes/111883
4. Gewohn, M., Beyerer, J., Usländer, T., Sutschet, G.: Smart information visualization for first-time quality within the automobile production assembly line. In: IFAC-PapersOnLine (2018). https://doi.org/10.1016/j.ifacol.2018.08.333
5. Grollmisch, S., Abeßer, J., Liebetrau, J., Lukashevich, H.: Sounding industry: challenges and datasets for industrial sound analysis. In: European Signal Processing Conference (2019). https://doi.org/10.23919/EUSIPCO.2019.8902941
6. Jiang, J.J., et al.: Whistle detection and classification for whales based on convolutional neural networks. Appl. Acoust. **150**, 169–178 (2019)
7. Chang, C.-Y., Tsai, L.-Y.: A CNN-based method for infant cry detection and recognition. In: Barolli, L., Takizawa, M., Xhafa, F., Enokido, T. (eds.) WAINA 2019. AISC, vol. 927, pp. 786–792. Springer, Cham (2019). https://doi.org/10.1007/978-3-030-15035-8_76
8. Khamparia, A., Gupta, D., Nguyen, N.G., Khanna, A., Pandey, B., Tiwari, P.: Sound classification using convolutional neural network and tensor deep stacking network. IEEE Access **7**, 7717–7727 (2019)

9. Zinemanas, P., Cancela, P., Rocamora, M.: End-to-end convolutional neural networks for sound event detection in urban environments. In: Conference of Open Innovation Association, FRUCT (2019)

10. Siegel, J., Kumar, S., Ehrenberg, I., Sarma, S.: Engine misfire detection with pervasive mobile audio. In: Berendt, B., Bringmann, B., Fromont, É., Garriga, G., Miettinen, P., Tatti, N., Tresp, V. (eds.) ECML PKDD 2016. LNCS (LNAI), vol. 9853, pp. 226–241. Springer, Cham (2016). https://doi.org/10.1007/978-3-319-46131-1_26

11. Murphey, Y.L., Masrur, M.A., Chen, Z.H., Zhang, B.: Model-based fault diagnosis in electric drives using machine learning. IEEE/ASME Trans. Mech. (2006). https://doi.org/10.1109/TMECH.2006.875568

12. Wong, P.K., Zhong, J., Yang, Z., Vong, C.M.: Sparse Bayesian extreme learning committee machine for engine simultaneous fault diagnosis. Neurocomputing (2016). https://doi.org/10.1016/j.neucom.2015.02.097

13. McCowan, I.A., Pelecanos, J., Sridharan, S.: Robust speaker recognition using microphone arrays. In: 2001: A Speaker Odyssey - The Speaker Recognition Workshop (2001)

14. Shuyang, Z., Heittola, T., Virtanen, T.: Active learning for sound event classification by clustering unlabeled data. In: ICASSP, IEEE International Conference on Acoustics, Speech and Signal Processing - Proceedings (2017). https://doi.org/10.1109/ICASSP.2017.7952256

15. Karbasi, M., Ahadi, S.M., Bahmanian, M.: Environmental sound classification using spectral dynamic features. In: ICICS 2011–8th International Conference on Information, Communications and Signal Processing (2011). https://doi.org/10.1109/ICICS.2011.6173513

16. Khunarsal, P., Lursinsap, C., Raicharoen, T.: Very short time environmental sound classification based on spectrogram pattern matching. Inf. Sci. (2013). https://doi.org/10.1016/j.ins.2013.04.014

17. Huang, Z., Jia, X., Guo, Y.: State-of-the-art model for music object recognition with deep learning. Appl. Sci. (2019). https://doi.org/10.3390/app9132645

18. Salamon, J., Bello, J.P.: Unsupervised feature learning for urban sound classification. In: ICASSP, IEEE International Conference on Acoustics, Speech and Signal Processing - Proceedings (2015). https://doi.org/10.1109/ICASSP.2015.7177954

19. Harma, A., McKinney, M.F., Skowronek, J.: Automatic surveillance of the acoustic activity in our living environment. In: 2005 IEEE International Conference on Multimedia and Expo, p. 4, July 2005

20. Khan, M.K.S., Al-Khatib, W.G.: Machine-learning based classification of speech and music. Multimedia Syst. 12(1), 55–67 (2006)

21. Yamakawa, N., Kitahara, T., Takahashi, T., Komatani, K., Ogata, T., Okuno, H.G.: Effects of modelling within-and between-frame temporal variations in power spectra on non-verbal sound recognition. In: Proceedings of 2010 International Conference on Spoken Language Processing, Makuhari, Citeseer, pp. 2342–2345 (2010)

22. Böck, S., Widmer, G.: Maximum filter vibrato suppression for onset detection. In: 16th International Conference on Digital Audio Effects, Maynooth, Ireland (2013)

23. Mitrovic̀, D., Zeppelzauer, M., Eidenberger, H.: On feature selection in environmental sound recognition. In: Proceedings of the International Symposium (ELMAR 2009), Zadar, Croatia, 28–30 September 2009, pp. 201–204 (2009)

24. Chachada, S., Kuo, C.C.J.: Environmental sound recognition: a survey. APSIPA Trans. Signal Inf. Process. (2014). https://doi.org/10.1017/ATSIP.2014.12

25. Mesaros, A., Heittola, T., Eronen, A., Virtanen, T.: Acoustic event detection in real life recordings. In: Proceedings of 18th European Signal Processing Conference (EUSIPCO), pp. 1267–1271 (2010)

26. Hakkani-Tur, D., Riccardi, G., Gorin, A.: Active learning for automatic speech recognition. In: Proceedings of the IEEE International Conference on Acoustics, Speech, and Signal Processing (ICASSP), pp. 3904–3907 (2002)

27. Babaee, E., Anuar, N.B., Wahab, A.W.A., Shamshirband, S., Chronopoulos, A.T.: An overview of audio event detection methods from feature extraction to classification. Appl. Artif. Intell. **31**(9–10), 661–714 (2017). https://doi.org/10.1080/08839514.2018.1430469

28. Harte, C., Sandler, M., Gasser, M.: Detecting harmonic change in musical audio. In: Proceedings of the 1st ACM Workshop on Audio and Music Computing Multimedia, pp. 21–26 (2006)

29. Kiapuchinski, D.M., Erig Lima, C.R., Alves Kaestner, C.A.: Spectral noise gate technique applied to birdsong preprocessing on embedded unit. In: IEEE International Symposium on Multimedia, pp. 24–27 (2012)

30. Twomey, N., Flach, P.A.: A machine learning approach to objective cardiac event detection. In: Proceedings - 2014 8th International Conference on Complex, Intelligent and Software Intensive Systems, CISIS 2014 (2014). https://doi.org/10.1109/CISIS.2014.75

31. Cai, L., Hu, Y., Dong, J., Zhou, S.: Audio-textual emotion recognition based on improved neural networks. Math. Probl. Eng. (2019). https://doi.org/10.1155/2019/2593036

32. McFee, B., et al.: Librosa: audio and music signal analysis in python. In: Proceedings of the 14thPython in Science Conference, pp. 18–25 (2015)

33. Dhonde, S.B., Jagade, S.M.: Mel-frequency cepstral coefficients for speaker recognition: a review. Int. J. Adv. Eng. Res. Dev. **2**(05) (2015). https://doi.org/10.21090/ijaerd.0205157

34. Hourri, S., Kharroubi, J.: A deep learning approach for speaker recognition. Int. J. Speech Technol. **23**(1), 123–131 (2019). https://doi.org/10.1007/s10772-019-09665-y

35. Beigi, H.: Fundamentals of Speaker Recognition. Springer, Boston (2011). https://doi.org/10.1007/978-0-387-77592-0

36. Jiang, D.-N., Lu, L., Zhang, H.-J., Tao, J.-H., Cai, L.-H.: Music type classification by spectral contrast feature. In: Proceedings of 2002 IEEE International Conference on Multimedia and Expo, ICME 2002, vol. 1, pp. 113–116. IEEE (2002)

37. Kamarudin, N., Al-Haddad, S.A.R., Hashim, S.J., Nematollahi, M.A., Bin Hassan, A.R.: Feature extraction using spectral centroid and mel frequency cepstral coefficient for Quranic accent automatic identification. In: 2014 IEEE Student Conference on Research and Development, SCOReD 2014 (2014). https://doi.org/10.1109/SCORED.2014.7072945

38. Wu, X., Gong, H., Chen, P., Zhong, Z., Xu, Y.: Surveillance robot utilizing video and audio information. J. Intell. Robot. Syst. **55**, 403–421 (2009). https://doi.org/10.1007/s10846-008-9297-3

39. Cieslak, M.C., Castelfranco, A.M., Roncalli, V., Lenz, P.H., Hartline, D.K.: T-distributed stochastic neighbor embedding (t-SNE): a tool for eco-physiological transcriptomic analysis. Marine Genomics **51**, 100723 (2020). https://doi.org/10.1016/j.margen.2019.100723

40. Dabbaghchian, S., Sameti, H., Ghaemmaghami, M.P., BabaAli, B.: Robust phoneme recognition using MLP neural networks in various domains of MFCC features. In: 2010 5th International Symposium on Telecommunications, IST 2010 (2010). https://doi.org/10.1109/ISTEL.2010.5734123

41. Rumelhart, D.E., Hinton, G.E., Williams, R.J.: Learning representations by back-propagating errors. Nature (1986). https://doi.org/10.1038/323533a0

42. Grossberg, S.: Nonlinear neural networks: principles, mechanisms, and architectures. In: Pattern Recognition by Self-Organizing Neural Networks. The MIT Press (1991)

Convolutional Neural Network for Classification of Diabetic Retinopathy Grade

Vanessa Alcalá-Rmz[1(✉)], Valeria Maeda-Gutiérrez[1],
Laura A. Zanella-Calzada[2], Adan Valladares-Salgado[3],
José M. Celaya-Padilla[1], and Carlos E. Galván-Tejada[1]

[1] Unidad Académica de Ingeniería Eléctrica, Universidad Autónoma de Zacatecas,
Jardín Juarez 147, Centro, 98000 Zacatecas, Zac, Mexico
{vdrar.06,valeria.maeda,jose.celaya,ericgalvan}@uaz.edu.mx
[2] LORIA (Université de Lorraine, CNRS, Inria),
Campus Scientifique BP 239, 54506 Nancy, France
laura.zanella-calzada@univ-lorraine.fr
[3] Unidad de Investigación Médica en Bioquímica, Hospital de Especialidades, Centro
Médico Nacional Siglo XXI. Instituto Mexicano del Seguro Social. Mexico City,
Av. Cuauhtémoc 330, Col. Doctores, Del. Cuauhtémoc,
06720 Ciudad de México, Mexico
adan.valladares@imss.gob.mx

Abstract. Diabetic Retinopathy (DR) represents an important group of lesions found in the retina of patients who suffer from diabetes mellitus, affecting around one out of three patients and presenting a global prevalence of approximately 34.6%. Besides, DR is characterized as being the leading cause of vision loss in adults. Its diagnosis consists on a series of screening tests to obtain digital photographs of the retina, to find the grade of the evolution of the disease, which can be classified into four grades. The early detection and diagnosis of DR are fundamental to prevent its evolution. In this paper it is proposed the implementation of the Convolutional Neural Network (CNN), VGGNet-like, which is a model focused in the classification of images based on object recognition and detection. The main objective is the classification of a set of images containing the four different grades in the evolution of DR. The datasets used are the Indian Diabetic Retinopathy Image Dataset and the Diabetic Retinopathy Detection. The performance of the CNN proposed is evaluated through a statistical analysis based on accuracy, the loss function and area under the curve (AUC). The results present statistically significant values, obtaining 0.81 of accuracy, 0.49 of loss function and, 0.71 of micro-average and 0.72 of macro-average in the AUC. According to the results, it is possible to conclude that the CNN implemented can classify DR into its different grades in patients with presence of diabetes mellitus, obtaining a preliminary Computer-Aided Diagnosis tool that could be supportive for the diagnosis of the evolution of DR.

Keywords: Diabetic Retinopathy · Computer-aided diagnosis · VGGNet-like

© Springer Nature Switzerland AG 2020
L. Martínez-Villaseñor et al. (Eds.): MICAI 2020, LNAI 12468, pp. 104–118, 2020.
https://doi.org/10.1007/978-3-030-60884-2_8

1   Introduction

Diabetes is a noncommunicable disease and one of the most common metabolic disorders in the world, increasing in numbers and significance [36,37]. In 2013, 382 million people had diabetes and, it is estimated that 592 million people will have diabetes by 2035 and, according to the International Federation of Diabetes, 642 million by 2040, mainly affecting young and elderly sectors of population [13,34]. One of the consequences of being diagnosed with diabetes is the increasing risk of develop a number of serious health issues, such as cardiovascular disease, kidney disease (diabetic nephropathy), nerve disease (diabetic neuropathy), eye disease (diabetic retinopathy), pregnancy complications or oral complications [18]. The most common microvascular complication of diabetes is diabetic eye disease, which is the result of chronic high blood glucose levels causing damage to the retinal capillaries, including diabetic retinopathy (DR) and Diabetic Macular Oedema (DMO) [2].

DR is an eye condition that is composed of a characteristic group of injuries found in the retina of individuals having diabetes mellitus, taking place when high blood sugar levels cause damage to blood vessels in the retina. These blood vessels can swell, leak or they can close, stopping blood from passing through that can cause loss of vision and blindness. Based on some studies, the global prevalence for any DR is approximately 34.6% [39], representing the main reason of loss of vision in working-age adults (20–65 years), being estimated that one of three people with diabetes have DR and one of ten people will develop a threatened vision by this disease [17]. There are not DR symptoms in the early stages, for that reason, a person can suffer DR without knowing of it. As DR gets worse, the patient will notice symptoms such as: increasing number of floaters, having blurry vision, having vision that changes sometimes from blurry to clear, seeing blank or dark areas in the field of vision, having poor night vision and noticing colors appear faded or washed out losing vision [30]. To obtain a diagnostic and monitor the patient, it is necessary to perform a series of a screening tests, where a diagnostic tool is used to obtain digital photographs of the retina after the images are classified in grades [9].

Taking advantage of digital computing technology advances, some studies have implemented image processing, pattern recognition, and artificial neural networks (ANN) to develop computer-aided diagnosis (CADx) systems. The purpose of these systems is to assist the clinicians in the diagnosis process [31]. The general process of a framework for a CADx system is described: the first step consists of the imaging acquisition that is recorded using the appropriate imaging system. Then, the captured images are pre-processed by the implementation of algorithms to isolate a specific region from the rest of the image [35]. To characterize the extracted segments, features such as textures and shapes can be extracted with a biomedical knowledge base. After this step, a supervised classifier can be implemented and trained using the available features extracted. Therefore, the diagnosis can be performed by comparing the feature patterns between the test sample and the trained patterns in the classifier features [25, 26]. An example of algorithms that can be implemented is ANN, which has been studied for many years to solve classification problems including image classification. An advantage of ANNs is that the algorithm could be generalized to solve different kinds of problems using similar designs [16].

Among the different types of ANN are found convolutional neural networks (CNNs). The aim of CNNs is the processing of data with known grid-like shape, such as 2D image data or 1D time-series data [24]. CNN consists of a multi-stage neural network which is composed of some filter stages and one classification stage. The purpose of filter stages is to extract features from the inputs and it can contain four different types of layers, convolutional layer, batch normalization layer, activation layer and pooling layer. Finally the classification stage corresponds to a multi-layer perceptron, which is comprised of several fully-connected layers [20,28].

In this study, CNN is used to classify the different grades of diabetic retinopathy based on a database composed of a series of images related to DR grades. The main contribution of this work is that, given a DR image, using a CNN can be determined the specific grade of DR that a subject presents, giving a preliminary tool that could be supportive for the improvement of the diagnosis of this disease [5,21].

1.1   Related Work

Recently, the classification of medical images using CNN has been a relevant topic. There are works that have been focused in this area, e.g. the proposal of Xu et al. [38], who present the deep CNN-based early automated detection of DR using fundus image. They implement a CNN focusing on the automatic classification of DR images, based on the color fundus image. They used 800 labeled images to train the neural network and 200 images to evaluate the performance of the trained neural network, reporting a value of 94.5% of accuracy.

Gulshan et al. [14] propose a deep learning algorithm with the objective of detecting DR and diabetic macular edema in retinal fundus photographs. They used a dataset with 9,963 images from 4,997 patients, using 80% of the total images to train the CNN and the remaining 20% for the tuning step, achieving an AUC of 0.991, the sensitivity of 90.3% and specificity of 98.1%.

Kalia et al. [22] compare three different algorithms with the purpose of detecting DR. SVM algorithms present a recognition rate of 87%, texture classifier using neural network, 91%, and pre-trained architecture of CNN, 92%. On the other hand, Arora et al. [3] propose a CNN architecture to classify DR into five different classes. They performed experiments using a set of 1000 sample images, reporting an accuracy value of 74%.

On the other hand, Ghosh et al. [11], proposed to automate the method of diabetic retinopathy screening using color fundus retinal photography. The authors implemented a CNN composed by six layers: convolutional, maxpooling, activation, dropout, fully connected and classification layer. The model was able to classify five stages of DR (No DR, Mild, Moderate, Severe and Proliferative). The experimental results showed a precision for each class: 0.882 (class 0), 0.403 (class 1), 0.704 (class 2), 0.365 (class 3) and 0.628 (class 4).

Another approach of diabetic retinopathy, is that proposed by Lam et al. [23] which presents an evaluation of well-known architectures of CNNs, GoogleNet, and AlexNet. In this work, their models were able to attain an accuracy of 74.5%, 68.8%, and 57.2% on 2-ary, 3-ary, and 4-ary classification models, respectively, using transfer learning.

Finally, Singla et al. [33] implement different versions of the support vector machine (SVM) algorithm is presented. This proposal focus on the detection of DR, obtaining as results 98.75% accuracy for the linear SVM, 96.25% for the to Twin SVM with hinge loss and, 96.25% for the Twin SVM with pinball loss.

As it is shown, there are many papers that describe the implementation of different machine learning and deep learning techniques using the DR diagnosis as objective, reporting significant results in accuracy terms in most of them, however, some of the presented works are not able to classify the DR grade. So, in this paper we propose a CNN that is able to classify DR grade into five different classes, presenting results that overcome the state of the art.

2   Materials and Methods

The methodology followed for the classification of the DR grade, description of the data and the validation of the results are presented in this section. This process is shown in Fig. 1. Section A) refers to data acquisition, making a recompilation of the Indian Diabetic Retinopathy Image Dataset (IDRiD) and the Diabetic Retinopathy Detection Kaggle dataset. In section B) is presented the pre-processing step where images are prepared. Section C) corresponds to the implementation of the CNN for the classification of the images according to DR grade. Finally, in the CNN validation, the Area Under the Receiver Operating Characteristic Curve (AUC-ROC), accuracy and loss function are calculated in Section D).

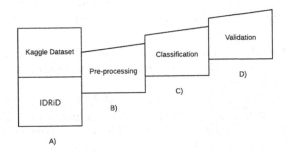

Fig. 1. Flowchart of the methodology followed. A) IDRiD and Kaggle datasets recompilation, B) Image pre-processing, C) Image classification based on the CNN and D) Validation of the CNN performance.

2.1 Dataset Description

The dataset used for the development of this work is a combination of the IDRiD and the Diabetic Retinopathy Detection Kaggle dataset. The dataset is comprised by five classes, where *No DR* class means that a patient has a normal retina, being labeled as 0; *mild* class refers to hemorrhages and microaneurysms, being labeled as 1; *moderate* class corresponds to extensive microaneurysm, intraretinal hemorrhage and hard exudates, being labeled as 2; *severe* class means venous abnormalities, large blot hemorrhages, venous beading, being labeled as 3 and *proliferative DR* class corresponds to new vessels formation either at the disc, being labeled as 4.

In Fig. 2 is shown an example of each class.

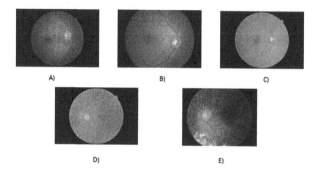

Fig. 2. Samples of DR grades. **A)** No DR, **B)** Mild, **C)** Moderate, **D)** Severe and **E)** Proliferative DR.

The dataset is comprised by 2,644 DR images that are divided as follows: *No DR* class includes 500 images, the *mild* class includes 510 images, the *severe* class includes 515 images (each one corresponding to 19% from the total images), the *moderate* class includes 518 images (corresponding to the 20%) and *proliferative DR* class including 601 images (corresponding to 23%).

Indian Diabetic Retinopathy Image Dataset (IDRiD). The IDRiD dataset, which is divided into three parts: segmentation, disease grading and localization. For this work, there was used the disease grading part. It consists of original color fundus images and ground-truth labels for diabetic retinopathy and diabetic macular edema severity grade (divided into train and test set). The dataset is available in http://biomedicalimaging.org/2018/challenges/.

Diabetic Retinopathy Detection Dataset. The Kaggle dataset collect large numbers of fundus images and high-resolution retina images took in a variety of imaging conditions, from diabetic patients for a competition to detect DR by different deep learning models [27]. This dataset was provided by the Kaggle coding website (https://www.kaggle.com/c/diabetic-retinopathy-detection/data).

2.2 Data Preprocessing

In the data preprocessing, the raw pixel intensities of the images are scaled, normalizing the pixel values in a range between zero and one. This normalization is used to remove distortions caused by lights and shadows in an image. Besides, a neural network usually processes inputs using small weight values, and inputs with large integer values can slow down the learning process. For that reason, it is good practice to normalize the pixel values.

After the normalization step, the dataset is randomly divided and balanced in two sets. The first one represents a training set, is comprised of 1,851 DR images and corresponding to 70% of the total images. The second set represents the test set, is composed by 793 DR images and corresponding to the remaining 30% of the total images.

2.3 Data Classification

The objective of this stage is to classify the DR images according to its DR grade. For this purpose, it is implemented VGGNet-like, which is a CNN that is a small version of VGGNet, in Python 3.7.4 (a programming language that allows to work quickly and integrate systems more effectively [8]), using the packages Keras 2.3.1, Tensorflow 2.1.0, Numba 0.48.0 and Sklearn 0.22.1. Tensorflow is an open-source software library for dataflow programming across a range of tasks. It is a symbolic math library and is also used for machine learning applications such as neural networks [12]. Keras, a high-level ANN API written in Python, is designed to enable fast experimentation with deep ANN. It focuses on being user-friendly, modular, and extensible. It was developed as part of the research effort of project ONEIROS (Open-ended Neuro-Electronic Intelligent Robot Operating System) [6]. Numba, is a compiler for Python. This package offers to speed up the code with high performance functions. In other words, pass from CPU (Central Processing Unit) to a GPU implementation (Graphics Processing Unit) of the software kernel [19].

VGGNet is a model presented by Simonyan et al. [32], which obtained second place in the classification task of ImageNet Large Scale Visual Recognition (ILSVRC) in 2014. This model was developed for object recognition and detection, being its main contribution to the demonstration that the deep of the network improves the classification performance significantly. VGGNet-like, is the small and compact version of VGGNet. This model is optimized by decreasing the depth quantity and filter size while retaining its original architecture.

In general, the structure of VGGNet-like consists of five convolutional layers and three maxpooling layers.

The activation function used for all the layers is a Rectified Linear Unit (ReLU). This activation function is required once the input has been calculated. It becomes the activation value. Then, an output function can be applied in charge of transforming the input value in the output value of node [10]. In a simple way, the activation function is a function that limits the signal output to a finite value. A common activation function used in the implementation of

CNN for deep learning is ReLU, especially for the hidden layers. As shown in Eq. 1, ReLU function indicates the input will be equal to the same if the value is greater or equal to zero, otherwise, the output will correspond to zero. This function presents a non-differentiable activation at z = 0.

$$ReLU(z) = \begin{cases} \text{si } z < 0 & 0 \\ \text{si } z \geq 0 & z \end{cases} \tag{1}$$

ReLU activation function is the simplest, being faster when training a large ANN. On the other hand, it has less problem with the fading of the gradients in deep models, but a disadvantage that it entails is that CNN can stop the process it is carrying out if it is one of the very high learning rate. For the output layer, the activation function used is Softmax, which is based on a general logistic function. It compressed a vector of arbitrary values into a vector of values ranging (0,1). The Softmax function can be calculated with Eq. 2, where $\sigma(z)$ refers to the K-dimensional vector, z [4].

$$\sigma(z)_j = \frac{e^{z_j}}{\sum_{K=1}^{K} e^{z_k}}, j = 1, ..., K \tag{2}$$

For this work, the optimization algorithm used is Adam, which is based on the stochastic gradient descent algorithm. Since the epoch number is configurable, 50–300 epochs are used, where each epoch corresponds to the training iteration, and the mini-batch is set to 32. The VGGNet-like structure implemented is shown in Table 1.

2.4   Evaluation

To evaluate and test the performance of the model, there were calculated the loss function and accuracy on each epoch, as well as the ROC curve based on the average of the general behavior of VGGNet-like. When the value of the loss function goes down, it indicates that the model is fitting better to the data that is trying to model, looking for the global minimum which represents the minimum error. Additionally, the loss function optimizes the network feeding back with information on the system capacity [1]. The algorithm chosen to calculate the loss function in this work was "categorical cross-entropy", which is included in the Keras package, and it is able to calculate the cross-entropy parameter specifically in categorical classification problems. This method compares the distribution of the prediction with the ground truth distribution, where the probability is set to 1 for the target class and 0 for the other classes (see Eq. 3).

$$L(y, \widehat{y}) = -\sum_{j=0}^{M} \sum_{i=0}^{N} (y_{ij} * log(\widehat{y}_{ij})) \tag{3}$$

The accuracy calculates the average performance of the CNN based on the difference between the classification calculated and the real classification, as

Table 1. Structure of VGGNet-like.

Layer (type)	Output shape	Param #
Input	(96, 96, 32)	–
Conv 1	(96, 96, 32)	896
Activation	(96, 96, 32)	0
Batch normalization	(96, 96, 32)	128
Max pooling	(32, 32, 32)	0
Dropout	(32, 32, 32)	0
Conv 2	(32, 32, 64)	18,496
Activation	(32, 32, 64)	0
Batch normalization	(32, 32, 64)	256
Conv 3	(32, 32, 64)	36, 928
Activation	(32, 32, 64)	0
Batch normalization	(32, 32, 64)	256
Max pooling	(16, 16, 64)	0
Dropout	(16, 16, 64)	0
Conv 4	(16, 16, 128)	73,856
Activation	(16, 16, 128)	0
Batch normalization	(16, 16, 128)	512
Conv 5	(16, 16, 128)	147, 584
Activation	(16, 16, 128)	0
Batch normalization	(16, 16, 128)	512
Max Pooling	(8, 8, 128)	0
Dropout	(8, 8, 128)	0
Flatten	(8192)	0
Dense	(1024)	8389632
Activation	(1024)	0
Batch normalization	(1024)	4,096
Dropout	(1024)	0
Dense	(5)	5,125
Activation	(5)	0

Total parameters: 8, 678, 277

Trainable parameters: 8, 675, 397

Non-trainable parameters: 2, 880

shown in Eq. 4. Calculating the accuracy as 1-error, V_pred is the classification value calculated and V_true is the true classification value. It doesn't optimize the network but it obtains this value for each of the models, giving the option to select the model that presents the better performance [29].

$$error = V_{pred} - V_{true} \qquad (4)$$

The accuracy function selected is "categorical-accuracy" from the Keras package. This function evaluates if the index of the maximal true value is equal to the index of the maximal predicted value.

Generally, the quality of learning algorithms is evaluated by analyzing how well they perform on test data. The first one is the ROC curve, which is commonly used performance measure in supervised classification, and it is calculated based on the sensitivity and specificity. These parameters are based on true positives (TP), true negatives (TN), false positives (FP), and false negatives (FN).

- TP: indicates the number of instances that are positive and correctly identified.
- TN: indicates the number of negative cases that are negative and correctly identified.
- FP: indicates the negative instances that are misclassified as positive cases.
- FN: indicates the positive cases that are misclassified as negative.

Sensitivity or recall refers to the proportion of subjects with a positive condition that is correctly classified and it is calculated with Eq. 5 [15].

$$Sensitivity = \frac{TP}{TP + FP} \tag{5}$$

Specificity refers to the proportion of subjects with a negative condition that is correctly classified and it is calculated with Eq. 6 [15].

$$Specificity = \frac{TN}{TN + FN} \tag{6}$$

Sensitivity and specificity help to evaluate the effectiveness of the algorithm on binary problems.

The ROC curve of each class is calculated, as well as the ROC curve of the macro-average and micro-average. The micro-average refers to the amount of the total true positives, false positives and false negatives for different sets, and there are calculated with Eq. 7, where TP_1 is the true positives of one set, TP_2 is the true positives of a second set, FP_1 is the false positives of the first set and FP_2 is the false positives of the second [7].

$$Micro - average = \frac{TP_1 + TP_2}{TP_1 + TP_2 + FP_1 + FP_2} \tag{7}$$

Finally, the macro-average is factor to calculate the average accuracy in different arbitrary sets, obtained with Eq. 8, where A_1 is the average of one set and A_2 is the average of a second set.

$$Macro - average = \frac{A_1 + A_2}{2} \tag{8}$$

3   Results

In this section are the results obtained for the proposal of this paper.

The dataset used for the development of the methodology, which contains a total of 2644 DR images, is balanced and divided in two sub-datasets, where 70% of the images correspond to each class assigned to the training dataset (344 - No DR, 362 - Mild, 376 - Moderate, 356 - Severe and 412 - Proliferative DR). The remaining 30% of the images assigned to the testing dataset (156 - No DR, 148 - Mild, 142 - Moderate, 159 - Severe, 189 - Proliferative DR).

To determine the optimal number of epochs, CNN is tested manually changing the values of the hyperparameters based on the time of performance, accuracy, loss function, and AUC for each class, as is shown in Table 2. The numbers of epoch evaluated are 50, 100, 150, 200, 250 and, 300. Based on the metrics mentioned, it is determined 150 as the optimal number.

Table 2. Accuracy, loss function, AUC per class and time of performance based on the different number of epochs.

Epochs number	Accuracy	Loss function	AUC					Performance time (s)
			No DR	Mild	Moderate	Severe	Proliferative	
50	0.8058	0.4886	0.67	0.64	0.61	0.61	0.66	198.9436
100	0.7972	0.4927	0.69	0.68	0.59	0.66	0.66	390.4843
150	**0.8065**	**0.4870**	**0.79**	**0.67**	**0.65**	**0.69**	**0.79**	**579.6239**
200	0.7899	0.5824	0.76	0.66	0.61	0.71	0.77	777.3275
250	0.7960	0.5060	0.79	0.71	0.64	0.74	0.79	970.8505
300	0.7660	0.7064	0.73	0.63	0.61	0.67	0.75	1169.1128

Figure 3 shows the behavior of the accuracy through the epochs, where the orange line represents the training data, obtaining an accuracy value of 0.83, and the blue line corresponds to test data, obtaining an accuracy value of 0.80.

On the other hand, Fig. 4 shows the behavior of the loss function, where the orange line represents the training data, obtaining a loss function value of 0.43, and the blue line corresponds to the testing data, obtaining a loss function value of 0.48.

It is important to mention that the accuracy and loss function is able to measure the behavior of the classification of DR grades, but the accuracy is a parameter that may provide a superior value than the real when there are biases in the data. Due to, it is also calculated the AUC parameter for each class, as well as the micro and macro-average.

Figure 5 Shows the ROC curves obtained by the CNN performance. The ROC curve calculated for the micro-average is presented with the dotted pink line, getting an AUC value of 0.71. The ROC curve calculated for the macro-average is shown with the dotted dark blue line, presenting an AUC value of 0.72. The ROC curve corresponding to class 0 (normal retina) is presented with

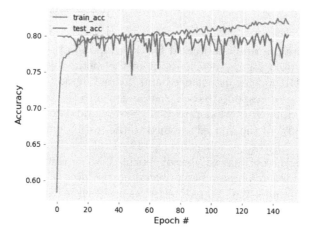

Fig. 3. Accuracy behavior.

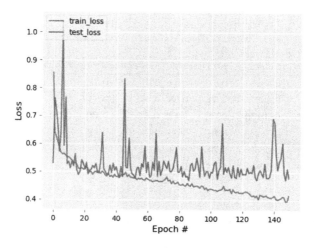

Fig. 4. Loss function behavior.

the aqua line, presenting an AUC value of 0.79. The ROC curve for class 1 (mild DR) is presented with the dark orange line, obtaining an AUC value of 0.67. The ROC curve for class 2 (moderate DR) is shown with the light blue line, with an AUC value of 0.65. The ROC curve for class 3 (severe DR) is presented with the green line, presenting an AUC value of 0.69. The ROC curve for class 4 (proliferative DR) is presented with the purple line, presenting an AUC value of 0.79.

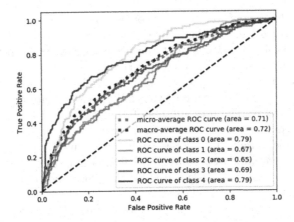

Fig. 5. ROC curves obtained with the average performance of the CNN. (Color figure online)

4   Discussion and Conclusions

The purpose of this work is the classification of images, based on the VGGNet-like model, represents a grade of DR into five classes: No DR, mild, moderate, severe and proliferative DR. The data set used is contained by 2,644 DR images, which were normalized and divided into two subsets in a balanced and random way. The first subset used for CNN training. In this step were tested a different number of epochs (50, 100, 150, 200, 250, and 300) and different metrics were calculated and analyzed (accuracy, loss function, AUC for each class, and performance time) for the selection of the optimal number of epochs. The second subset used for testing VGGNet-like behavior, the last stage corresponds to the validation, applied to both subsets. This step allows us to measure the performance parameters like accuracy and loss function values, as is shown in Figs. 3 and 4. The behavior is similar in both training and testing steps, which means the model obtained from VGGNet-like may classify DR grades from known images with similar performance as the unknown images. Due to, the model developed is considered a generalized model.

In the training stage, the accuracy obtained is around 80%. This value indicates that 80% of the time, the images will be correctly classified into one of the five possible classes. Furthermore, in Fig. 4 the loss function is decreasing in both cases, training, and testing steps, this implies an approximation to the global minimum.

On the other hand, the last evaluation corresponds to know the ROC curves for each class shown in Fig. 5 the class 0 achieved an AUC of 0.79, which means that 79% of the images are correct for this class, the AUC of class 1 was 0.67, this corresponds to 67% of correct classification, class 2 obtained 0.65, this refers to 65% of images correctly classified, class 3 achieved 0.69, this means that 69% of the severity images were correctly classified in a correct form in this class, and finally, class 4 gets an AUC of 0.79, this corresponds to 79% of proliferative DR images that are correct in this class. Also, it is shown the ROC curves for micro-average, which obtains an AUC of 0.71 and macro-average with an AUC of 0.72, this means that the DR images were correctly classified in around 72%. Micro-average and macro-average may have similar behavior because the calculate of macro-average are based on true positives/false positives rate using a complete data set, and micro-average uses subsets of images. It is important to mention that the obtained results are more than a random classification, because the percentage obtained in all ROC values are higher than 64%.

The results were validated through an evaluation step, being possible to conclude that the dataset was adequate for this work, demonstrating that it is possible to classify the five DR classes.

In addition, compared to the work of Ghosh et al. [11], this research presents higher values in the results obtained in some classes as is shown in Table 3.

Table 3. Comparison of precision obtained for class.

	Class 0	Class 1	Class 2	Class 3	Class 4
Results obtained	0.882	0.403	0.704	0.365	0.628
Gosh et al. [11]	0.79	0.67	0.65	0.69	0.79

Furthermore, in the work proposed by Lam et al. [23], their models were-able to get 74.5%, 68.8% and 57.2% of accuracy, compared with this work, which achieve an accuracy of 80.65%.

For the implementation of this method, there was necessary the use of a GPU GeForce GTX 1060 to optimize the performance time.

Moreover, it could be interesting to propose a data set with DR images of Mexican subjects, looking to improve the health of the Mexican diabetic population with this complication, through the implementation of this model into a health support software tool.

References

1. Antona Cortés, C.: Herramientas modernas en redes neuronales: la librería keras (2017)
2. Antonetti, D.A., Klein, R., Gardner, T.W.: Diabetic retinopathy. MEDLINE **366**(13), 1227–1239 (2012)
3. Arora, M., Pandey, M.: Deep neural network for diabetic retinopathy detection. In: 2019 International Conference on Machine Learning, Big Data, Cloud and Parallel Computing (COMITCon), pp. 189–193. IEEE (2019)
4. Carlini, N., Wanger, D.: Towards evaluating the robustness of neural network (2017)
5. Chae, S., Kwon, S., Lee, D.: Predicting infectious disease using deep learning and big data. Int. J. Environ. Res. Public Health **15**(8) (2018). https://doi.org/10.3390/ijerph15081596

6. Chollet, F.: Keras: deep learning library for theano and tensorflow. https://keras.io/k. Accessed June 2018
7. Chollet, F.: Keras: deep learning libary for theano and tensofrflow (2011). https://keras.io/k
8. What is python? https://www.python.org/doc/essays/blurb/. Accessed Sept 2018
9. Corcóstegui, B., et al.: Update on diagnosis and treatment of diabetic retinopathy: a consensus guideline of the working group of ocular health (Spanish society of diabetes and Spanish vitreous and retina society). J. Ophthalmol. **2017** (2017)
10. Freeman, J.A., Skapura, D.M.: Algorithms, applications, and programming techniques. In: Neural Networks. Addison Wesley (1991)
11. Ghosh, R., Ghosh, K., Maitra, S.: Automatic detection and classification of diabetic retinopathy stages using CNN. In: 2017 4th International Conference on Signal Processing and Integrated Networks (SPIN), pp. 550–554. IEEE (2017)
12. Google: Tensorflow. https://www.tensorflow.org/. Accessed June 2018
13. Guariguata, L., Whiting, D.R., Hambleton, I., Beagley, J., Linnenkamp, U., Shaw, J.E.: Global estimates of diabetes prevalence for 2013 and projections for 2035. Diabetes Res. Clin. Pract. **103**(2), 137–149 (2014)
14. Gulshan, V., et al.: Development and validation of a deep learning algorithm for detection of diabetic retinopathy in retinal fundus photographs. JAMA **316**(22), 2402–2410 (2016)
15. Hanley, J.A., McNeil, B.J.: The meaning and use of the area under a receiver operating characteristic (ROC) curve. Radiology **143**(1), 29–36 (1982)
16. Hubel, D.H., Wiesel, T.N.: Receptive fields of single neurones in the cat's striate cortex. J. Physiol. **148**(3), 574–591 (1959)
17. IDF: Diabetes and the eye (2020)
18. IDF: Diabetes complications (2020)
19. Index, P.P.: Numba documentation (2020). http://numba.pydata.org/numba-doc/latest/index.html. Accessed 25 Apr 2020
20. Ioffe, S., Szegedy, C.: Batch normalization: Accelerating deep network training by reducing internal covariate shift. arXiv preprint arXiv:1502.03167 (2015)
21. Irles, C., et al.: Estimation of neonatal intestinal perforation associated with necrotizing enterocolitis by machine learning reveals new key factors. Int. J. Environ. Res. Public Health **15**(11) (2018). https://doi.org/10.3390/ijerph15112509
22. Kalia, A.A., Uttarwar, V.U.: Identification of diabetic retinopathy from fundus images using machine learning. Natl. J. Comput. Appl. Sci. **2**(2), 1–4 (2019)
23. Lam, C., Yi, D., Guo, M., Lindsey, T.: Automated detection of diabetic retinopathy using deep learning. In: AMIA Summits on Translational Science Proceedings 2018, p. 147 (2018)
24. LeCun, Y., Bottou, L., Bengio, Y., Haffner, P.: Gradient-based learning applied to document recognition. Proc. IEEE **86**(11), 2278–2324 (1998)
25. Lee, H., Chen, Y.P.P.: Cell cycle phase detection with cell deformation analysis. Expert Syst. Appl. **41**(6), 2644–2651 (2014)
26. Lee, H., Chen, Y.P.P.: Image based computer aided diagnosis system for cancer detection. Expert Syst. Appl. **42**(12), 5356–5365 (2015)
27. Lin, G.M., et al.: Transforming retinal photographs to entropy images in deep learning to improve automated detection for diabetic retinopathy. J. Ophthalmol. **2018** (2018)
28. Lu, W., Liang, B., Cheng, Y., Meng, D., Yang, J., Zhang, T.: Deep model based domain adaptation for fault diagnosis. IEEE Trans. Ind. Electron. **64**(3), 2296–2305 (2016)

29. Nye, M., Saxe, A.: Are efficient deep representations learnable? pp. 1–4 (2017)
30. AAO: What is Diabetic Retinopathy? (2020)
31. Rolim, C.O., Koch, F.L., Westphall, C.B., Werner, J., Fracalossi, A., Salvador, G.S.: A cloud computing solution for patient's data collection in health care institutions. In: 2010 Second International Conference on eHealth, Telemedicine, and Social Medicine, pp. 95–99. IEEE (2010)
32. Simonyan, K., Zisserman, A.: Very deep convolutional networks for large-scale image recognition. arXiv preprint arXiv:1409.1556 (2014)
33. Singla, M., Soni, S., Saini, P., Chaudhary, A., Shukla, K.K.: Diabetic retinopathy detection using twin support vector machines. In: Jain, L.C., Virvou, M., Piuri, V., Balas, V.E. (eds.) Advances in Bioinformatics, Multimedia, and Electronics Circuits and Signals. AISC, vol. 1064, pp. 91–104. Springer, Singapore (2020). https://doi.org/10.1007/978-981-15-0339-9_9
34. Summaty, E.: IFD diabetes atlas (2016)
35. Tourassi, G.D., Delong, D.M., Floyd Jr., C.E.: A study on the computerized fractal analysis of architectural distortion in screening mammograms. Phys. Med. Biol. 51(5), 1299 (2006)
36. Whiting, D.R., Guariguata, L., Weil, C., Shaw, J.: IDF diabetes atlas: global estimates of the prevalence of diabetes for 2011 and 2030. Diabetes Res. Clin. Pract. 94(3), 311–321 (2011)
37. WHO: Global status report on noncommunicable diseases 2010 (2010)
38. Xu, K., Feng, D., Mi, H.: Deep convolutional neural network-based early automated detection of diabetic retinopathy using fundus image. Molecules 22(12), 2054 (2017)
39. Yau, J.W., et al.: Global prevalence and major risk factors of diabetic retinopathy. Diabetes Care 35(3), 556–564 (2012)

Classifiers Ensemble of HMM and d-Vectors in Biometric Speaker Verification

Juan Carlos Atenco-Vazquez[1(✉)], Juan C. Moreno-Rodriguez[1],
Israel Cruz-Vega[1], Pilar Gomez-Gil[1], Rene Arechiga[2],
and Juan Manuel Ramirez-Cortes[1]

[1] National Institute of Astrophysics, Optics and Electronics, Puebla, Mexico
atencovaz@gmail.com
[2] Electrical Engineering Department, New Mexico Tech, Socorro, USA

Abstract. This paper presents a novel approach on text-dependent biometric speaker verification (SV) based on the ensemble of two feature extraction and classification processes using Hidden Markov Models in a Universal Background Model framework (HMM-UBM) and d-Vectors derived from a Deep Learning Network (DNN) structure. Once the individual SV systems are trained, a third classifier is trained/tuned over individual test scores in the same dataset using three different approaches for comparison purposes: Multilayer Perceptron (MLP), Support Vector Machine (SVM) with three different kernels, and a Fuzzy Inference System (FIS). Obtained results over a proprietary speech database in Spanish, indicate an improved performance, providing an Equal Error Rate (EER) within the range of 0.7%–2.54% when classifier ensembles are used, versus an EER of 3.6% and above obtained in average with individual classifiers. Results in detail corresponding to comparison of the several approaches used in this experimental work are further described.

Keywords: Speaker verification · Voice biometrics · HMM-UBM · Machine learning · d-vectors · FIS · SVM · MLP

1 Introduction

Nowadays, speaker verification is a very active research topic in both, text dependent and text independent modalities, with a broad range of biometric applications. In the first case the uttered words are limited to a small set, while in the second case there is no restriction on the vocabulary, with the corresponding limitations of each case [2,5]. Among the most relevant techniques existing in the state of the art of automatic speaker recognition, Hidden Markov Models, Gaussian Mixture Models (GMM) and i-vectors stand out due to their excellent characteristics and performance [9,22,23], however new approaches are constantly explored in this research area, specially on applications based on small utterances. Reference [8] presents a series of experiments using the mentioned

© Springer Nature Switzerland AG 2020
L. Martínez-Villaseñor et al. (Eds.): MICAI 2020, LNAI 12468, pp. 119–131, 2020.
https://doi.org/10.1007/978-3-030-60884-2_9

techniques and different features with a good performance comparison based on analysis of lexical content, fixed-phrase, and prompted-phrase conditions. Among the proposed techniques to improve verification performance in text-dependent modality there are recent approaches on the use of deep neural networks (DNN) to extract speech features, or as a complete end-to-end systems [7]. Reference [18] presents an approach on the use a DNN for extraction of speaker embeddings and it provides a comparison to i-vectors, concluding that these two representation are complementary and their fusion may improve performance at different scales on several operating points. Other works have addressed the topic through the use of convolutional neural networks (CNN) to extract the speaker embeddings, exploring new loss functions [24], and recent approaches propose robust embeddings called x-vectors [19] and their extraction using a special type of DNN and a long short term memory (LSTM) recurrent neural network (RNN) [20]. These type of representations has shown to be a compact and very robust solution under experimentation in several conditions using proprietary and public datasets.

A relevant strategy in the area of machine learning aimed to improve performance of multiple classifiers is their fusion or integration into ensemble schemes. This approach has been conceived to overcome possible weaknesses of single classifiers and take advantage of individual properties. In [16] several numerical methods are presented based on two frameworks of ensembles: independent and dependent. In an independent framework the original dataset can be divided into mutually exclusive or overlapping subsets. These subsets are used to train several classifiers in parallel, and further a combination method is applied to output the final classification. On the other hand in a dependent framework a first classifier is trained, its output is used to train a second classifier and so on, using as many classifiers as required in a serial way. This approach allows the system to take advantage of the partial knowledge acquired in each classifier, finally the outputs of each trained system are combined. A study on the optimal number of classifiers is elaborated in [3]. In that reference the authors address the ensemble problem in a geometrical framework, with classifiers fusion at score level. The score vectors generates a surface in the Euclidean space called score-polytope, which is further processed through aggregation rules and mapping functions. Concerning to biometric frameworks, there are four levels in which two or more systems can be combined: sensors, features, decision and score. In [11] and [6] extensive reviews of fusion levels and methods for multimodal biometric systems can be found. Some of these methods include feature concatenation, weighted sum, SVM, ANN, GMM, FIS, and others, and they could be applied at several fusion levels and several combination of biometric traits aiming to perform multimodal classification. Examples of recent works reported in the literature are: Reference [10], in which weighted sums and products are used to fuse three classifiers on face, fingervein and fingerprint recognition at score level. Similarly, Ref. [1] presents a bimodal biometric system on finger vein and palm vein traits, in which the extracted features are matched using a distance metric, and then, classification fusion at score level is carried out through a fuzzy inference system.

The approach of using score level fusion based on modular neural networks and fuzzy inference systems on the biometric modality of iris recognition is presented in Ref. [12] with good results.

In this work, text dependent HMM-UBM and DNN-based d-vectors system are fused using several binary classifiers at score level, and a performance comparison of the different cases is presented. Both SVS were trained independently and the resulting test scores are used as the training data entered to the fusion system. The rest of the paper is organized as follows: Section 2 presents theoretical background and concepts associated to HMM and d-vectors in Speaker Verification. Section 3 presents a brief description of the fusion system and classifiers used in this work. In Sect. 4, description of the experimental development and details of the database created for these experiments are presented. Finally, results and concluding remarks are presented in Sects. 5 and 6, respectively.

2   Biometric Speaker Verification Based on Classifiers Ensemble; Theoretical Background

Figure 1 shows the block diagram of the proposed scheme on biometric speaker verification (SV) based on classifiers ensemble using HMM-UBM and DNN-based d-Vectors. A brief description of the theoretical concepts corresponding to each part is presented in the following sections.

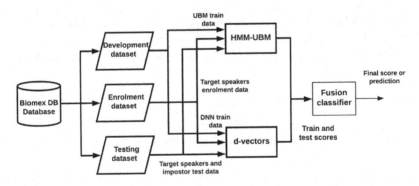

Fig. 1. Block diagram of the ensemble of classifiers.

2.1   HMM-UBM Speaker Verification System

HMM is a statistical approach used for dealing with temporal stochastic data, and it has been widely used in speech analysis. Figure 2 shows a typical representation of an HMM. The model can be regarded as a finite state machine defined by a set of states $\Omega = (S_1, S_2, S_3, ..., S_M)$, a set of possible observations $\mathbf{O} = (O_1, O_2, O_3, ..., O_M)$, a transition probability matrix $A = [a_{ij}]$, and an output probability distribution $B = [b_i(k)]$. The stochastic nature of HMM

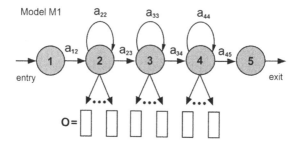

Fig. 2. Hidden Markov Model representation with three hidden states.

is manifested in the transition of states governed by the transition matrix A as it is in the observation's generation given by B, being both probabilistic events. Detailed concepts on Hidden Markov Models can be found elsewhere [13].

The HMM-UBM system is comprised of two parts: Universal Background Model (UBM), and Target Speaker Model (TSM). UBM is a model that pools speech features of a set of speakers which are not part of the target speakers neither the impostor set. The target speaker model (TSM) contains the speech characteristics of a particular speaker, built from the UBM using Maximum A Posteriori (MAP) adaptation [15]. The UBM is formed by a set of HMMs trained at word level with each model representing a digit from 0 to 9. The TSM is composed of 10 HMMs with a similar design of the UBM, as shown in the Fig. 3. Each HMM has been designed to contain 8 states and 1 gaussian mixture per state. The UBM is considered gender independent, so the models were trained with balanced data of male and female speakers. TSMs were generated by adapting the UBM parameters with the MAP technique using the enrollment speech data provided by the target speakers.

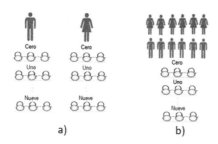

Fig. 3. a) Examples of target speaker models. b) Universal background model.

The matching of a test speech sample with a particular speaker model during the identity verification process is carried out through the Logarithmic Likelihood Ratio (LLR) [15] given by Eq. 1.

$$\Lambda(\mathbf{X}) = \log p(\mathbf{X}|\lambda_S) - \log p(\mathbf{X}|\lambda_{UBM}), \tag{1}$$

where $p(\mathbf{X}|\lambda_S)$ represents the likelihood that a speech sample $\mathbf{X}$ has been generated by the TSM λ_S, and $p(\mathbf{X}|\lambda_{UBM})$ is the likelihood that some specific sample has been generated by the UBM. The decision on acceptance or rejection of the claimed identity is made by comparing the quotient of these two quantities with a previously specified threshold.

2.2 DNN-Based d-Vectors Speaker Verification System

The use of Deep Neural Networks (DNN) in speaker verification is rapidly increasing as a very promising research field [7]. A very interesting approach is the use of DNN to extract speaker related features taken from some layer, which is the case with the so called d-vectors [21]. In a first stage, the network is trained with speaker features at frame level using data from the development set, thus making it gender independent. Silence segments are removed from speech data. In a second stage, once the DNN is trained, speech enrollment samples of a particular target speaker are fed into the network and the outputs of the last hidden layer are extracted, creating thus a unique speaker embedding called d-vector. Since every enrollment sample produces a hidden layer output, the embedding is obtained by applying some operator, such as *average* or *max* to the corresponding outputs [4]. In this work, d-vectors were obtained by averaging the outputs. In the case of test speech samples for target and impostor speakers, a d-vector is extracted per sample, and no further operation is required. The dimensionality of the embeddings depends on the number of neurons of the last hidden layer of the network.

Table 1. Deep network topology for d-vectors extraction.

Layer	Type	Neurons	Act. function
1	Dense	250	Relu
2	Dense	250	Relu
3	Dropout	250	Relu
4	Dense	250	Relu
5	Dense	30	Softmax

In this work, speech features were obtained through the logarithm of the energies derived from a 40 bands filter bank, with filters uniformly distributed in the range located 300 Hz to 8 kHz forming a single frame. Furthermore, a context window is formed by concatenation of 41 frames: a central frame, 30 frames on the left (past information) and 10 segments on the right (future information), providing a resultant input with a dimension of 1640. This approach provided a solid representation of speech characteristics in support of the DNN learning process. Table 1 shows the deep network topology for d-vectors extraction. The training of the network was carried out through 20 epochs, with a batch size of

1000, a learning rate of 0.001, categorical cross entropy as the loss function, and a dropout layer with a 0.5 activation probability. Since the development subset is comprised of 30 speakers the output layer has 30 neurons, delivering d-vectors with a dimension of 250 elements.

In order to obtain a match score, the cosine distance between the d-vectors of a target speaker and a speech sample was calculated according to the Eq. 2. Verification is further obtained by comparing the cosine distance with a specified threshold.

$$\cos\theta_{similarity} = \frac{A \cdot B}{\|A\| \|B\|} \tag{2}$$

3   Classifiers Ensemble of HMM and d-Vectors

Classifiers fusion in biometric systems can be carried out at four different levels: sensors, feature vectors, scores and decision making. For the purpose of this work on speaker verification, the use of score level fusion becomes pertinent since those scores contain discriminant information between target speakers and impostors and it is directly available from classifiers output [1]. In classifiers ensemble two cases are distinguished according to the used dataflow: dependent and independent frameworks [16]. In the first case the data produced by the output of the first classifier is used as training data for a second classifier and so on. In the second case all classifiers are trained with subsets of a main database, which can be exclusive or overlapped while the classifiers are trained in parallel. In this work, we used the approach of fusion at score level with an independent assembly scheme, using the same database to train both classifiers independently. Consequently, three different classifiers were implemented for fusion purposes: Multilayer Perceptron (MLP), Support Vector Machine (SVM) with three different kernels and a Mamdani Fuzzy Inference System (FIS). A brief description of each classifier is presented as follows.

3.1   Multilayer Perceptron

MLP is widely used in classification tasks for both cases, binary and multiclass. In our work the scores generated by the two base systems are the inputs of the MLP and the output is the decision to accept or reject the identity of a test speaker. In this regard, with this classifier it is not necessary to establish a comparison threshold for decision making. The MLP topology is shown in the Table 2. The training process was carried out using a batch size of 8 during 20 epochs, a learning rate of 0.001 and a categorical cross entropy cost function. The output layer is conformed by two neurons containing the decision of acceptance or rejection of a test speaker.

Table 2. MLP topology for verification systems fusion.

Layer	Type	Neurons	Act. function
1	Dense	10	Relu
2	Dense	10	Relu
3	Dense	2	Softmax

3.2 Support Vector Machine

Support Vector Machine (SVM) is a statistical learning method based on a structural risk minimization procedure adequate to be used in non-linear classification problems. Geometrically speaking, the algorithm constructs separating hyperplanes that are optimal in the sense that the classes are separated with the largest margin and minimum classification error. The algorithm maps through the use of a kernel function, the input data to higher dimensional feature space where such hyperplane is constructed. The kernel choice depends on the problem to solve. SVM is a very well known technique and details can be consulted elsewhere [14]. In this work a SVM was used in the classifiers fusion process of the base systems through several experiments using three different kernels: gaussian, linear and cubic polynomial. The kernel equations are shown below.

$$Gaussian : G(x_j, x_k) = exp(-||x_j - x_k||^2) \tag{3}$$

$$Linear : G(x_j, x_k) = x_j^T x_k \tag{4}$$

$$Polynomial : G(x_j, x_k) = (1 + x_j^T x_k)^q \tag{5}$$

where x_j and x_k are p-dimensional vectors representing observations or data points j and k. In Eq. 5, q takes the value 3 since a polynomial cubic kernel was used.

3.3 Fuzzy Inference System

In this section, FIS-based fusion at score level of the classifiers based on HMM-UBM and DNN d-Vectors, is described. The scheme corresponds to a Mamdani type FIS with membership functions of each input created using scores histograms obtained from both, HMM-UBM and d-vectors. The histograms showed the overlapping point of the scores generated by target speaker and impostor test samples in each SVS. In the case of HMM-UBM scores, target and impostor scores are centered at the origin, with negative values indicating that the test sample corresponds to an impostor subject, and positive values indicating a target speaker. In the d-vectors system the threshold was found to be located in 0.9. The histogram corresponding to HMM-UBM scores showed a bigger overlapping around the value of 0, meanwhile, d-vectors histogram showed a noticeable smaller overlapping. Several experiments were conducted in order to define the number, type, and parameters of the membership functions. The system fuzzy rules shown in Fig. 4d are written to cover all possible cases of the fuzzy inputs, aiming to accept the claimed identity if the scores of both systems are labeled as highly similar, which provided a high performance results. In HMM-UBM input case, since the overlap of target speaker and impostors scores was significantly larger than d-vectors scores, five gaussian functions were defined. The FIS output was defined using two symmetric gaussian functions within a range of $[0, 1]$, so there is equal chance to accept or reject a speech sample, and the decision relies only on the statistical distribution of the fuzzy input data. Figure 4 shows the fuzzy sets and membership rules used in the experiment which provided the best results.

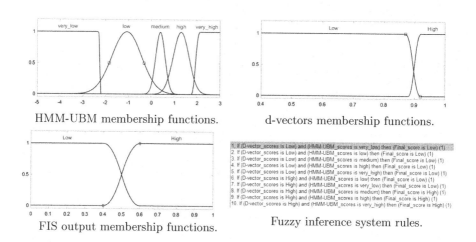

HMM-UBM membership functions.   d-vectors membership functions.

FIS output membership functions.   Fuzzy inference system rules.

Fig. 4. Inputs, output and rules of the fuzzy inference system.

4   Experimental Development

4.1   Database

As part of this project we generated a speech database in Spanish named BIOMEX-DB, with a protocol corresponding to a text-dependent, short utterances, and password-associated case, oriented to speaker verification biometric experiments. Speech samples were recorded at a sampling rate of 16 kHz in a noiseless anechoic chamber. The database has 51 speakers: 26 males and 25 females, and each volunteer recorded 10 speech samples for enrollment and 10 for tests with duration of 20 s each. The enrollment data is comprised of the utterances of 10 randomly arranged digits, the test data has utterances of 4 random digits. The database was split into three sets: development, target speakers and impostors sets. The development set is comprised of 15 male and 15 female speakers in equal proportion to prevent a bias towards a certain gender; the enrollment set is comprised of 10 target speakers with utterances of 10 randomly arranged digits, and the evaluation set is composed with test samples of 10 target speakers and 11 impostors with utterances of 4 random digits. Since the experiment was conceived as text dependent, each target speaker was assigned a unique four digits password.

4.2   Training and Evaluation

The feature vectors extracted from speech data are based on short term Mel Frequency Cepstral Coefficients (MFCC), which has become the standard in speaker verification [17]. The vectors were formed by MFCC energy coefficients, Delta, and Delta-Delta coefficients, corresponding to first and second derivative, respectively. In Fig. 5 the scores generated by the base systems can be separated into the classes of target speakers and impostors, each point represent the score generated by the HMM-UBM and d-vectors for the same test sample. UBM and DNN were trained with the development subset of 10 target speakers and 11 impostors. In the first evaluation, a target speaker utters correctly a previously assigned password. In the second evaluation, an impostor knows the password of a target speaker, therefore, this evaluation aims to test the systems capacity to distinguish between target speakers and impostors, when impostors know the password of the target speakers. The evaluation consisted of 10 iterations corresponding to 10 available passwords. In a particular iteration every target speaker has a unique password to test against 11 impostors that know all target speakers passwords, in the next iteration the passwords are randomly assigned to other target speakers and son on. The evaluation stops when the 10 passwords have been assigned to each target speaker.

Fusion systems were trained with the scores generated by the base systems. There were 100 samples of the accepted class and 1100 sample of the rejected class. The MLP was trained with 140 samples (70 accepted and 70 rejected), 20 samples for validation (10/10) and 1030 test samples (20/1010). SVM had 160 training samples (80/80) and the rest was used for testing. The output of this fusion system is a score of 1 if the test sample is classified as an accepted target speaker or 0 in the opposite case. Since the FIS membership functions were designed using histograms to define the parameters, all scores generated by the SVS were utilized as test samples. Figure 6 shows a three dimensional mapping of the scores of Fig. 5 once they are fed into the FIS.

5   Results

Figure 5 shows a scatter plot of scores corresponding to the target speakers as the accepted class and the impostors as the rejected class, obtained from both, HMM-UBM and d-Vectors. Figure 6 shows the output scores of the ensemble with FIS fusion represented in a three dimensional space. Figure 7 shows the Receiver Operating Characteristics (ROC) curve corresponding to the seven experiments reported in this work: the first two obtained from individual SV

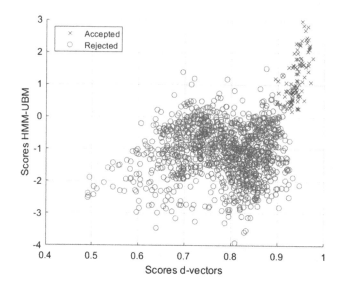

Fig. 5. Scatter plot for the scores generated by the base systems.

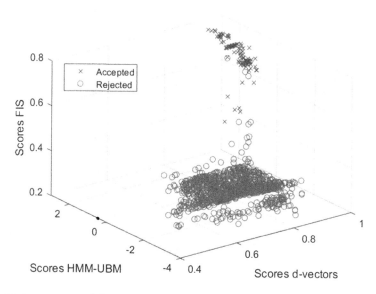

Fig. 6. Output scores of the ensemble with FIS fusion represented in a three dimensional space.

systems (HMM-UBM and d-Vectors), and the rest obtained from the described ensembles with the specified classifier fusion scheme.

Table 3 presents the results of evaluation of the base systems and compares them with the performance of the ensemble with the three fusion classifiers,

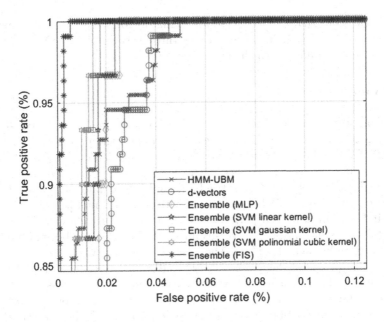

Fig. 7. Receiver operating characteristics curve

Table 3. Performance measures comparison.

System	EER (%)	Accuracy (%)
HMM-UBM	3.63	92.56
d-vectors	3.64	96.19
Ensemble (MLP)	3.12	94.27
Ensemble (SVM gaussian kernel)	2.84	93.42
Ensemble (SVM lineal kernel)	2.94	93.8
Ensemble (SVM polinomial cubic kernel)	2.54	95.71
Ensemble (FIS)	0.727	99.66

in the case of the SVM three kernels were tested. The results are expressed in terms of Equal Error Rate (EER), which is defined as the point in which false acceptance rate and false rejection rate intersects, and Verification Accuracy, which is defined as the number of correctly accepted or rejected samples divided by the total amount of test samples. It can be seen that the ensemble systems have an improved performance in comparison to the base systems. It is observed that HMM-UBM has the worst accuracy because of the scores of both classes are more overlapped than the scores of the other systems as discussed in Sect. 3. Regarding the d-vectors, accuracy is better overall than the ensembles with MLP and the three kernels of the SVM. In contrast the ensemble systems have a smaller EER value than the base systems, being the MLP ensemble the approach with the larger EER. In the case of the three kernels of the SVM the best performance is obtained with the cubic kernel.

6   Conclusions

A novel approach on text-dependent SV based on the fusion of two classifiers using HMM-UBM and DNN-based d-Vectors on the proprietary database BIOMEX DB has been presented. The fusion was carried out at score level by a third classifier, which was trained with the test scores generated through the base systems. The ensemble was carried out using three different approaches for comparison purposes: MLP, FIS, and SVM with three different kernels. Obtained results indicate an improved performance of classifier ensembles, with an EER within the range of 0.7%–2.54% versus an EER of 3.6% and above obtained in average with individual classifiers. The best performance was obtained with the FIS ensemble providing an EER of 0.727 and accuracy of 99.66% in average. Optimization schemes such as those based on genetic algorithms or adaptive neuro-fuzzy inference systems can be explored aiming to improve performance on the obtained results. Summarizing, ensembles provided the best overall results and they proved to be a good alternative to improve recognition. This approach may be used to train several systems independently with different types of speech data and make them robust against a wide variety of conditions, then fused them to obtain a integral and more secure ensemble. This fusion scheme can be used to explore alternatives of multimodal biometrics based on speech in combination with other modalities.

References

1. Bharathi, S., Sudhakar, R.: Biometric recognition using finger and palm vein images. Soft. Comput. **23**(6), 1843–1855 (2018). https://doi.org/10.1007/s00500-018-3295-6
2. Bhukya, R.K., Prasanna, S.M., Sarma, B.D.: Robust methods for text-dependent speaker verification. Circuits Syst. Signal Process. **38**(11), 5253–5288 (2019)
3. Bonab, H., Can, F.: Less is more: a comprehensive framework for the number of components of ensemble classifiers. IEEE Trans. Neural Netw. Learn. Syst. **30**(9), 2735–2745 (2019)
4. Chen, Y.h., Lopez-Moreno, I., Sainath, T.N., Visontai, M., Alvarez, R., Parada, C.: Locally-connected and convolutional neural networks for small footprint speaker recognition. In: Sixteenth Annual Conference of the International Speech Communication Association (2015)
5. Das, R.K., Prasanna, S.M.: Investigating text-independent speaker verification systems under varied data conditions. Circuits Syst. Signal Process. **38**(8), 3778–3801 (2019)
6. Fierrez, J., Morales, A., Vera-Rodriguez, R., Camacho, D.: Multiple classifiers in biometrics. Part 1: fundamentals and review. Inf. Fus. **44**, 57–64 (2018)
7. Irum, A., Salman, A.: Speaker verification using deep neural networks: A. Int. J. Mach. Learn. Comput. **9**(1) (2019)

8. Liu, Y., He, L., Tian, Y., Chen, Z., Liu, J., Johnson, M.T.: Comparison of multiple features and modeling methods for text-dependent speaker verification. In: 2017 IEEE Automatic Speech Recognition and Understanding Workshop (ASRU), pp. 629–636. IEEE (2017)
9. Maghsoodi, N., Sameti, H., Zeinali, H., Stafylakis, T.: Speaker recognition with random digit strings using uncertainty normalized HMM-based i-vectors. IEEE/ACM Trans. Audio Speech Lang. Process. **27**(11), 1815–1825 (2019)
10. Mehdi Cherrat, E., Alaoui, R., Bouzahir, H.: Convolutional neural networks approach for multimodal biometric identification system using the fusion of fingerprint, finger-vein and face images. PeerJ Comput. Sci. **6**, e248 (2020)
11. Modak, S.K.S., Jha, V.K.: Multibiometric fusion strategy and its applications: a review. Inf. Fus. **49**, 174–204 (2019)
12. Mozumder, A.I., Begum, S.A.: Iris recognition using modular neural network and fuzzy inference system based score level fusion. Int. J. Adv. Res. Comput. Sci. **8**(7), 604–610 (2017)
13. Nguyen, L.: Tutorial on hidden Markov model. Appl. Comput. Math. **6**(4–1), 16–38 (2017)
14. Nguyen, L.: Tutorial on support vector machine. Applied and Computational Mathematics **6**(4–1), 1–15 (2017)
15. Reynolds, D.A., Quatieri, T.F., Dunn, R.B.: Speaker verification using adapted gaussian mixture models. Digit. Signal Proc. **10**(1–3), 19–41 (2000)
16. Rokach, L.: Ensemble-based classifiers. Artif. Intell. Rev. **33**(1–2), 1–39 (2010)
17. Sahidullah, M., Kinnunen, T.: Local spectral variability features for speaker verification. Digit. Signal Proc. **50**, 1–11 (2016)
18. Snyder, D., Garcia-Romero, D., Povey, D., Khudanpur, S.: Deep neural network embeddings for text-independent speaker verification. In: Interspeech, pp. 999–1003 (2017)
19. Snyder, D., Garcia-Romero, D., Sell, G., Povey, D., Khudanpur, S.: X-vectors: Robust DNN embeddings for speaker recognition. In: 2018 IEEE International Conference on Acoustics, Speech and Signal Processing (ICASSP), pp. 5329–5333. IEEE (2018)
20. Tang, Y., Ding, G., Huang, J., He, X., Zhou, B.: Deep speaker embedding learning with multi-level pooling for text-independent speaker verification. In: ICASSP 2019–2019 IEEE International Conference on Acoustics, Speech and Signal Processing (ICASSP), pp. 6116–6120. IEEE (2019)
21. Variani, E., Lei, X., McDermott, E., Moreno, I.L., Gonzalez-Dominguez, J.: Deep neural networks for small footprint text-dependent speaker verification. In: 2014 IEEE International Conference on Acoustics, Speech and Signal Processing (ICASSP), pp. 4052–4056. IEEE (2014)
22. Xing, Y., Tan, P., Wang, X.: Speaker verification normalization sequence kernel based on gaussian mixture model super-vector and Bhattacharyya distance. J. Low Freq. Noise Vibr. Active Control 1461348419880744 (2019)
23. Yao, S., Zhou, R., Zhang, P.: Speaker-phonetic i-vector modeling for text-dependent speaker verification with random digit strings. IEICE Trans. Inf. Syst. **102**(2), 346–354 (2019)
24. Zhou, J., Jiang, T., Li, Z., Li, L., Hong, Q.: Deep speaker embedding extraction with channel-wise feature responses and additive supervision softmax loss function. In: INTERSPEECH, pp. 2883–2887 (2019)

Reducing the Risk of Premature Birth Through an Expert System Based on a Neural Network

Nayeli Montalvo-Romero[1]([✉]), Aarón Montiel-Rosales[1],
Albero Alfonso Aguilar-Lasserre[2] [iD], and Gregorio Fernández-Lambert[3] [iD]

[1] Industrial Engineering Division, National Technology of Mexico/HTI of Purísima del Rincón, Purísima del Rincón, Guanajuato, Mexico
{nayeli.mr,aaron.mr}@purisima.tecnm.mx
[2] Division of Postgraduate Studies and Research, National Technology of Mexico/TI of Orizaba, Orizaba, Veracruz,, Mexico
albertoaal@hotmail.com
[3] Division of Postgraduate Studies and Research, National Technology of Mexico/HTI of Misantla, Misantla, Veracruz, Mexico
gfernandezl@misantla.tecnm.mx

Abstract. Health is a matter of government and society´s attention. The World Health Organization defines health as a state of complete physical, mental, and social well-being, and is not just the absence of conditions or illnesses. Good maternal womb health is a predominant factor in the physical and mental development of the individual, in the stage of maturity. However, multiple factors influence during the gestation process, *e.g.*, amniotic fluid, fetal abnormality, intergenic interval, cervical incompetence, feeding, age, urinary tract infections; and that, they affect an adequate gestation of the baby generating irrigation of premature birth. This paper addresses the development of an Expert System based on an Artificial Multi-Layer Neural Network modeled with medical expertise; able to predict the estimated weeks of gestation while providing the treatment that helps reduce the risk of preterm birth. The results found show that the neural network predicts the weeks of gestation with an estimated deviation of one week-one day, while the Expert System has an efficiency of 93.33%.

Keywords: Expert System · Multi-Layer Artificial Neural Network · Expertise · Preterm birth

1 Introduction

The quality of life begins from the moment of conception; an adequate gestation process in the mother´s womb may well ensure a healthy life. It is ideal that the gestation time of a baby, be between 39 weeks 0/7 days and 40 weeks 6/7 days; by this time the baby has been properly trained and is ready to continue its development outside the mother´s womb [1].

On the other hand, if the baby is born before 37 weeks it suffers from premature birth, an unwanted situation. Preterm birth according to the World Health Organization

© Springer Nature Switzerland AG 2020
L. Martínez-Villaseñor et al. (Eds.): MICAI 2020, LNAI 12468, pp. 132–144, 2020.
https://doi.org/10.1007/978-3-030-60884-2_10

(WHO) occurs almost spontaneously, however, it can also be triggered by early induction of uterine contractions or cesarean delivery, either for medical or non-medical reasons; the most common causes of preterm birth are causes of multiple pregnancies, infection, chronic illness (diabetes and/or hypertension), or some other cause that is often unidentified [2].

In *ibidem*, about 15 million babies are considered to be born worldwide each year before reaching completion, *i.e.*, more than one in 10 births; however, it is estimated that more than 60% of preterm births occur in Africa and South Asia; in low-income countries, an average of 12% of children are born early, compared to 9% in higher-income countries; poorer families are at increased risk of preterm birth.

According to *ibídem*, more than 80% of newborn deaths occur as a result of premature birth, complications during labor or delivery, and infections such as sepsis, meningitis, and pneumonia. In [3], an estimated 5% are extreme preterm births, 15% are very premature births, and the rest represent moderate to late preterm births. In addition to this, the rate of re-entry and mortality is also higher than those born at term [4–6]. In [7], every year 1.09 million children under the age of 5 die from direct complications from being born before the full 37 weeks of pregnancy. Finally, in [8], it is estimated that approximately one million premature children die each year from complications in childbirth.

Premature babies who manage to survive to suffer from some form of lifelong disability, *e.g.*, there is intellectual limitation originating in early stages [9, 10]; likewise, the musculoskeletal system has loss of dexterity, loss or absence of voluntary contraction force and hypotonia [11, 12]; finally, for moms, better performance of babies is associated in cognitive tasks and worse in fine motor skills activities and permanence of the object [11, 13]. Preterm birth is associated with a lack of quality health care during pregnancy and childbirth; this includes, *e.g.*, the promotion of a healthy lifestyle, good nutrition, disease detection and prevention, counseling for family planning, and support for women suffering from family violence.

With adequate medical care, the risk of preterm birth decreases considerably. So, it is possible to define what, the quality of health care is defined as the degree to which health services improve desired health outcomes. Care before, during, and after pregnancy is critical to ensuring a positive experience for both the baby and the mother.

The field of Artificial Intelligence emanates from trying to make machines think, *i.e.*, to create machines capable of reacting, in certain circumstances; the European Commission's High-Level Expert Group on Artificial Intelligence proposes the following definition for AI systems [14]: "Artificial intelligence (AI) systems are software (and possibly also hardware) systems designed by humans that, given a complex goal, act in the physical or digital dimension by perceiving their environment through data acquisition, interpreting the collected structured or unstructured data, reasoning on the knowledge, or processing the information, derived from this data and deciding the best action(s) to take to achieve the given goal. AI systems can either use symbolic rules or learn a numeric model, and they can also adapt their behaviour by analysing how the environment is affected by their previous actions...". The AI field includes logic, probability, and continuous mathematics; perception, reasoning, learning, and action; and everything from micro-electronic controllers to planetary robotic explorers [15].

In [16–19], some of the main techniques used in the field of AI are presented, such as Petri Nets, Expert System, Fuzzy Logic, Artificial Neural Networks, Evolutionary Computing, Genetic Algorithms, Genetic Programming, and Theory Chaos.

Another need in the field of AI is the emulation of human reasoning in a computer system, as an expert would do in an area of knowledge, through the Expert System (ES) [20–22].

The present research work addresses the development of an ES to support the medical decision-making process in the area of gynecology and pediatrics, in the monitoring and control of neonatal treatment, from the determination of the weeks of gestation, so that the newborn is born to the end; through, *e.g.*, proper determination of medical treatments, food recommendations, and psychological care.

With the proper implementation of the tool, the follow-up of the patient to the recommendations and the accompaniment of the doctor; the newborn is born at the end, which represents a lower risk of presenting physical and mental problems, at the same time that a benefit is obtained to the family, society and the government.

The rest of the paper is organized as follow: in Sect. 2 reviews the work related to the premature birth; in Sect. 3 is divided into five parts: the first part included getting cases for the database; the second part contains the debugging variables, through expert knowledge; the third explains the parameterizing the neural network; the fourth presents the integration of the Expert System, and the fifth parts describe the Expert System performance. Finally, Sect. 4 discusses conclusions and future work.

2 Related Work

The prediction of preterm birth can well be made by ultrasonographic measurement of the cervix, and that is that the risk of preterm birth increases inversely with cervical length; being the simplest and most reproducible examination of all [23], at the same time, then maternal abdominal palpation.

Also, some studies are carried out during the gestational quarters; that is: during the first trimester a preterm birth screening may be used to predict preterm birth [24]; during the second trimester, at [25, 26] it was determined that cervical length by transperineal ultrasonography may be a useful tool in preterm birth prediction; while Tekniker (Research and Technology Centre), who is a member of the Basque Research and Technology Alliance (BRTA), is developing a technology device called "Fine Birth", which uses torsion wave-based technology to observe changes in uterine tissue stiffness along with an AI algorithm, to determine the risk of premature birth over the next seven days [27], this technology may well be applicable during the second and third trimesters of gestation. In addition to these studies in [28], the QUiPP App prototype is presented; a tool that predicts the risk of spontaneous preterm birth—one that occurs between 22 and 36 weeks 6 days after the last period— by evaluating cervical length using transvaginal ultrasound and quantitative fetal fibronectin test results of the cervical-vaginal fluid.

Some other efforts have chosen to use regression analysis as a forecasting tool; *e.g.* [29–35] uses predictive models based on multiple logistic regression, while regression analysis is performed using an Artificial Neural Network (ANN) system in [36]; these are developed in the field of classification, prediction, and the determination of behavior patterns. They are a highly recommended tool in real cases, where information processing is massive, inaccurate, and distorted. ANN's, they're "… computational networks which attempt to simulate, in a gross manner, the decision process in networks of nerve cell (neurons) of the biological (human or animal) central nervous system. This simulation is a gross cell-by-cell (neuron-by-neuron, element-by-element) simulation. It borrows from the neurophysiological knowledge of biological neurons and of networks of such biological neurons" [37].

In addition to quantitative studies, in [38–40] the usefulness of the qualitative fetal fibronectin test in cervical secretion is evaluated as a predictor of preterm birth in pregnant women with risk factors in first-level care units. Similarly, a categorical exit variable of a decision tree using algorithm C5.0 allows evaluating cases of risk of preterm birth, traveling the root while checking different rules until reaching the node, preterm birth, or nonterm birth [41].

It is apparent from the previous information that the rate of detection of preterm birth in the first trimester is less than 30%; achieves a higher performance of sonographic biometrics detection during the third trimester; while screening at 30–34 weeks gestation identifies approximately 80% of preterm births, but only 50% of those who give birth to the term, with a positive screening rate of 10% [42].

While it is true that various studies allow estimating the weeks of gestation, these require physical interaction. The proposed Expert System can provide a non-invasive diagnosis by not resorting to an additional study on the baby and the pregnant mother; this because some approaches consider analysis from attributes, others simply consider the value of a parameter in the estimate, some others more robust in modeling do consider the behavior of multiple dependent and independent variables where the correlation between those variables is analyzed. In addition to the above, the revised studies do not include the medical experience; at the same time that they do not integrate diagnosis and suggestion of a treatment that allows prolonging the weeks of gestation, in such a way that the newborn is born at the end; that is why, this research proposes the development of an ES, based on techniques in the field of AI capable of predicting the week of the birth of a newborn, and from this support the process of making medical decisions when integrating a treatment, to reduce the risk of preterm birth.

3   Development of the Expert System

The ES, feeds on variables defined and validated by experts in the area of gynecology-obstetrician and pediatrics, which in turn are collected from clinical records, thus forming a database. However, with the database a Multi-Layer Artificial Neural Network (MANN) is configured that can predict the estimated weeks of gestation appropriately; based on this information, the ES provides a diagnosis validated by the knowledge of the experts; which, allows to improve the conditions of the mother and the newborn, so that it is born in the end, if the recommendations are followed properly. The use of this tool is considered, because it can analyze complex information, with quantitative and qualitative variables, both in inputs and outputs (MANN); and, this, in turn, is strengthened with knowledge, of specialists in the clinical area. The ES developed is implemented on the intranet of a particular hospital of León, Guanajuato-Mexico.

To support the medical decision-making process in the face of gestation monitoring; it is proposed, the development of an ES based on a MANN considering the expertise of specialists in the area of gynecology-obstetrician and pediatrics (see Fig. 1). In the proposed ES knowledge base, it consists of the input and output event data; the inference engine is performed by learning—updating synoptic weights—; while the explanation subsystem is integrated by the MANN model and characteristics; finally learning is obtained through MANN training.

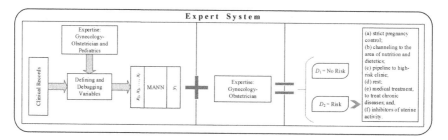

Fig. 1. Expert system design.

3.1   Getting Cases for the Database

The study is carried out in a private hospital in León, Guanajuato-Mexico; where, with the support of the areas of gynecology-obstetrician and pediatrics, access is obtained to the clinical records of patients who suffered and not a preterm birth. The processing of information is based on the Regulations of the General Health Law on Health Research. Based on the information contained in the dossiers, the experts define the variables of interest by categorizing them into the background, which in turn are divided into non-pathological, pathological, and gynecological; also include medical complications during pregnancy; and, a socioeconomic study.

Clinical records under study include patients who had a normal birth and preterm birth, during the period March 2018 to December 2018; however, information is obtained from those files during January 2019; the study comprises 77 cases out of a total of 380, obtained from a simple random sampling with a confidence level of 95% and a margin of error of 10%, sampling was carried out due to the complexity in access to the information and available resources.

3.2   Debugging Variables, Through Expert Knowledge

With the support of the areas of gynecology-obstetrician and pediatrics, 29 variables were first defined; of which, after an analytical process by the experts, these variables were purged, consisting of study 17 independent variables and 1 dependent variable. In Table 1, the qualitative variables describing the different level of presence of a state require coding because the software used in this study—Matlab R2019a— does not allow the entry of categorical values, *e.g.*, the variable "Food" is defined in 1 for "Normal", 2 for "Hyperfat" and 3 for "Hypocaloric"; whereas in those variables where it is required to represent the absence or presence of a condition a binary quantitative variable, *e.g.*, is established in the variable "Chronic diseases" the value 0 represents that the condition has not been presented, while 1 represents that it does.

Table 1. Variables of interest.

Variable	Name	Type	Levels	Risk
x_1	Maternal Age	Quantitative	Age	< 20 or 35>
x_2	BMI	Quantitative	Value	< 18.5 or> 30
x_3	Power	Qualitative	1: Normal; 2: Hyperfat; 3: Hypocaloric	Hyperfast or Hypocaloric
x_4	Hygiene	Qualitative	1: Good; 2: Regulad; 3: Bad	Bad
x_5	Chronic diseases	Qualitative	0: No; 1: Yes	Yes
x_6	Intergenic interval	Quantitative	Year. month	< 2
x_7	Current scenario number	Quantitative	Value	> 5
x_8	Cesaria would	Quantitative	Value	> 1
x_9	Abortion	Qualitative	0: No; 1: Yes	Yes
x_{10}	Gestational hypertension	Qualitative	0: No; 1: Yes	Yes
x_{11}	Uterine bleeding	Qualitative	0: No; 1: Yes	Yes
x_{12}	Amniotic fluid	Quantitative	1: Oligohydramnios; 2: Normal; 3: Polyhydramnios	Oligohydramnios or Polyhydramnios
x_{13}	Cervicovaginal infections	Qualitative	0: No; 1: Yes	Yes
x_{14}	Preeclampsia	Qualitative	0: No; 1: Yes	Yes
x_{15}	Anemia	Qualitative	0: No; 1: Yes	Yes
x_{16}	Low-lying placenta	Qualitative	0: No; 1: Yes	Yes
x_{17}	Urinary tract infections	Qualitative	0: No; 1: Yes	Yes
y_1	Weeks of gestation	Quantitative	Value	< 37

3.3   Parameterizing the Neural Network

A neural network is trained to predict the estimated weeks of gestation. For this, various neural network configurations were iteratively trained and tested in Matlab R2019a, evaluating their performance; resulting in a better-performing MANN, resulting in the reasonable increase of layers and neurons in these the estimation error decreases, due to the pattern of behavior of the dataset. The best-performing MANN has the following configuration: (a) an input layer, which contains the input variables of interest; (b) four hidden layers—5 neurons in the first layer, 15 neurons in the second, 10 neurons in the third, and 3 neurons in the fourth—; and finally, (c) an output layer, which contains the output variable of interest.

The MANN is a Feed Forward Back Propagation Net (FFBPN), with a Levenberg-Marquardt (LM) Backpropagation Algorithm as a training function, a Gradient Descent with Momentum (GDM) as an adaptive learning function, and finally, as a performance function of the MANN, the Mean Squared Error (MSE) is established; because an FFBPN is used, inputs and outputs are normalized before training the network so that all data takes values between $[-1.1]$. The database was divided into three subsets: training, validation, and testing, consisting of 70%, 15%, and 15%, respectively, while the training parameters used were those predefined in the software [43]. The difference between the expected value of the estimator and the actual value of the training parameter is 2.4888; in Fig. 2 the behavior of the MSE during such training is shown.

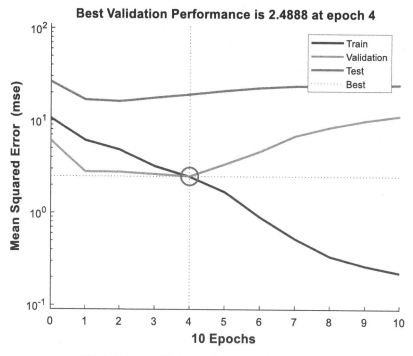

Fig. 2. Better validation performance, during training.

Obtained the best configuration, we proceed to validate its performance in the face of new cases; validation is carried out with cases collected from January to June 2019. Figure 3, shows that there is a one-week-one-day estimate deviation, which in turn MANN is validated by experts considering it to be acceptable medical information.

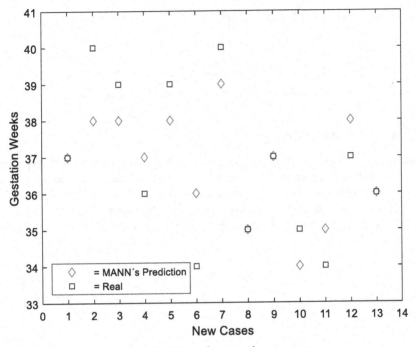

Fig. 3. MANN's performance in new cases.

3.4 Integration of the Expert System

With the validation of the MANN, the type of diagnosis is integrated into the ES; for this, the expertise of the area of gynecology-obstetrician is included to the prognosis of the weeks of gestation, in such a way that the ES provides the treatment recommended by knowledge of the medical area (Fig. 1). According to the specialists, it is possible to have two types of diagnosis: D_1, the diagnosis in which a safe pregnancy is expected, while the presence of a D_2, represents a diagnosis in which there is a risk of preterm birth. When D_1 is presented, the control of pregnancy continues normally, however when a D_2 is presented, care measures are required, being the treatments suggested by the gynecology-obstetrician specialist: (a) strict pregnancy control; (b) channeling to the area of nutrition and dietetics; (c) pipeline to a high-risk clinic; (d) rest; (e) medical treatment, to treat chronic diseases; and, (f) inhibitors of uterine activity. The system developed is implemented on the hospital intranet and supports medical personnel to establish the appropriate treatment to allow for a run-in gestation time, from the diagnosis from the pattern of behavior of the variables (see Fig. 4).

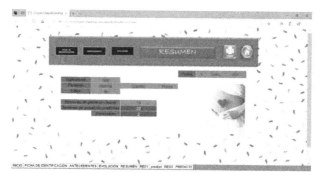

Fig. 4. ES's performance in the face of new cases.

3.5 Expert System Performance

During the period from March to November 2019, ES was used as a tool for 103 patients who agreed to be diagnosed by the system and who came to the doctor during the first trimester of gestation; of these, 15 was estimated that their due date would be before 37 weeks, preterm birth; with this information, the ES supported medical experts in diagnosing diagnosis (D_2) and in turn assigning the treatment that increased the weeks of gestation (see Fig. 5).

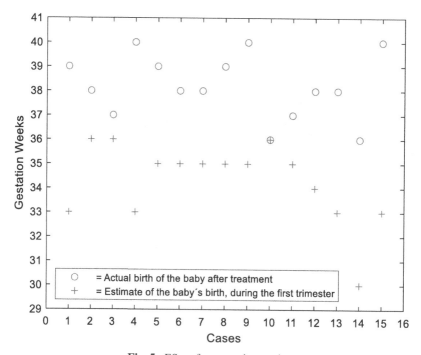

Fig. 5. ES performance in practice.

The suggested treatment for these cases consisted of 40.00% in strict pregnancy control and high-risk clinic pipeline, 13.33% pipeline to the area of nutrition and dietetics, while it was suggested at 33.33% rest, eventually, 13.33% of patients required specialized medical treatment to treat chronic diseases. The efficiency shown by ES in the face of prognosis, diagnosis, and treatment is 93.33%; having an average increase of 4 weeks gestation, on cases under study.

4   Conclusions and Future Work

Triggering a preterm birth is based on the behavior of a set of risk factors; what it generates, a complex activity for doctors in determining the treatment that allows achieving delivery to the end, and thus avoid all the complications that are generated to the baby and the mother. The proposed Expert System supports the decision-making process in the area of gynecology-obstetrician in determining the type of treatment to be followed by the patient in the gestation period according to her clinical history.

The Expert System, based on predictions of the weeks of gestation and the analysis of the experts determines the treatment; with this information, the doctor relies on the assignment of the type of treatment necessary to allow the newborn to be born to the end; having this way, less risk of physical and mental problems, which inherently brings benefit to family, society, and government. On the one hand, (a) the family enjoys a baby in conditions suitable for growth and development; (b) society develops a positive mood for the good birth of the baby; and finally, (c) the government will have financial savings by improving health care, avoiding the allocation of recourse to rehabilitation treatments, wages, and supplies to care for patients who may have had premature birth and who require specialized care for the development of their psychomotor abilities.

The ES shows to be a tool capable of providing reliable estimates; this is always associated with the MANN adequately representing behavioral parameters while being considered the expertise of specialists in the area of gynecology-obstetrician and pediatrics. During MANN training it was observed that a minimum number of neurons in the hidden layers hinder adequate learning, while an excessive number of neurons cause an over-workout. Experts are being worked to strengthen the system by considering other variables, e.g., ultrasound results and maternal blood testing. Considering these feasible—according to medical specialists— will improve the performance of the system.

The proposed Expert System is a tool to support the decision-making process, at no time does it attempt to replace the experience or knowledge of specialist physicians in the area; this can be a tool to support pregnancy control in patients living in precarious areas, it can also serve as a training tool in the formation of human capital in the medical area.

References

1. ACOG. Definition of Term Pregnancy. American College of Obstetricians and Gynecologists (2019). https://www.acog.org/Clinical-Guidance-and-Publications/Committee_Opinions/Committee_on_Obstetric_Practice/Definition-of-Term-Pregnancy. Accessed 07 Jan 2020

2. WHO. Preterm Birth. In: World Health Organization, February 2018. https://www.who.int/news-room/fact-sheets/detail/preterm-birth. Accessed 06 Jan 2020

3. Donoso, B., Oyarzún, E. Parto Prematuro. In: Medwave. 12(8), pp. e5477 September 2012. https://doi.org/10.5867/medwave.2012.08.5477

4. Fernández, T., Ares, G., Carabaño, I., Sopeña, J.El: Prematuro Tardío: El Gran Olvidado. Pediatría Atención Primaria **14**(55), e23–e29 (2012)

5. Gouyon, J.B., Iacobelli, S., Ferdynus, C., Bonsante, F.: Neonatal problems of late and moderate preterm infants. In: Seminars in Fetal and Neonatal Medicine, 3(17), pp. 146–152 June 2012

6. Escobar, G.J., et al.: Unstudied infants: outcomes of moderately premature infants in the neonatal intensive care unit. Arch. Dis. Child. –Fetal Neonatal Ed. **91**(4), F238–F244 (2006)

7. Lawn, J.E., Kinney, M.: Preterm birth: now the leading cause of child death worldwide. In: American Association for the Advancement of Science (2014). https://stm.sciencemag.org/content/6/263/263ed21.short. Accessed 07 Jan 2020

8. Liu, L., et al.: Global, regional, and national causes of under-5 mortality in 2000–2015: an updated systematic analysis with implications for the sustainable development goals. Lancet **388**(10063), 3027–3035 (2016)

9. Rodríguez, G., Vivas, S., Cangelosi, M., Schapira, I.: Avatares en prematuros de 3 a 5 años y sus Madres. Revista del Hosp. Materno Infantil Ramón Sardá **27**(4), 152–154 (2008)

10. Abbott, A.: The brain, interrupted: babies are increasingly surviving premature birth–but researchers are only beginning to understand the lasting consequences for their mental development. Nature **518**(7537), 24–27 (2015)

11. De Fraga, D.A., Linhares, M.B.M., Carvalho, A.E.V., Martinez, F.E.: Desenvolvimento de Bebês Prematuros Relacionado a Variáveis Neonatais e Maternas. Psicologia em Estudo **13**(2), 335–344 (2008)

12. Silva, C.C.V.: Atuação da Fisioterapia através da Estimulação Precoce em Bebes Prematuros. Rev Eletrôn Atualiza Saúde **5**(5), 29–36 (2017)

13. Rossel, C., Carreño, T., Maldonado, M. E. Afectividad en Madres de Niños Prematuros Hospitalizados. Un mundo Desconocido. In: Revista Chilena de Pediatría, 73(1), 15–21 (2002)

14. The European Commission´s High-Level Expert Group on Artificial Intelligence: A Definition of AI: Main Capabilities and Scientific Disciplines, Brussels (2018)

15. Russell, S.J., Norvig, P.: Artificial Intelligence: a Modern Approach, 3rd edn. Pearson Education Limited, Malasya (2016)

16. Nilsson, N.J.: Artificial Intelligence: a New Synthesis, p. 513. Morgan Kaufmann Publishers Inc., San Francisco–California (1998)

17. Vas, P.: Artificial-Intelligence-based Electrical Machines and Drives: Application of Fuzzy. In: Neural, Fuzzy-neural, and Genetic-algorithm-based Techniques, p. 625. Oxford University Press, New York (1999)

18. Bäck, T.; Schwefel, H.P.: An overview of evolutionary algorithms for parameter optimization. In: Massachusetts Institute of Technology (1993). https://doi.org/10.1162/evco.1993.1.1.1 (1993)

19. Tettamanzi, A., Tomassini, M.: Soft Computing: Integrating Evolutionary. In: Neural, and Fuzzy Systems, p. 328. Springer Science & Business Media, New York (2013)

20. López, O.: Computer-assisted creativity: emulation of cognitive processes on a multi-agent system. Expert Syst. Appl. **9**(40), 459–3470 (2013). https://doi.org/10.1016/j.eswa.2012.12.054

21. Zuzčák, M.; Zenka, M.: Expert system assessing threat level of attacks on a hybrid SSH honeynet. In: Comput. Secur. (92) (2020). https://doi.org/10.1016/j.cose.2020.101784

22. Szu, H.: Third gen AI as human experience based expert systems. In: Kozma, R., Alippi, C., Choe, Y., Morabito, F.C. (eds.) Artificial Intelligence in the Age of Neural Networks and Brain Computing, pp. 53–78. Academic Press, Cambridge (2019). https://doi.org/10.1016/b978-0-12-815480-9.00003-7
23. Ordóñez, E. B. Evaluación Sonográfica del Cuello Uterino en la Predicción del Parto Prematuro. Primera Parte. In: Rev. Obstet. Ginecol.-Hosp. Santiago Oriente Dr. Luis Tisné Brousse, 1(1), pp. 64–68 (2006)
24. Molina, F.S., Touzet, G.B., Martínez, T., Nicolaides, K.H.: Cribado de Parto Pretérmino en el Primer Trimestre de la Gestación. In: Progresos de Obstetricia y Ginecología, 57(6), 274–279 (2014). https://doi.org/10.1016/j.pog.2014.04.005
25. Navarro, Y., et al.: A. Longitud Cervical en el Segundo Trimestre por Ecografía Transperineal para la Predicción de Parto Pretérmino. In: Perinatología y Reproducción Humana, 30(2), 63–68 (2016) https://doi.org/10.1016/j.rprh.2016.06.003
26. Huertas, E., Valladares, E.A., Gómez, C.M.: Longitud Cervical en la Predicción del Parto Pretérmino Espontáneo. Revista peruana de Ginecología y Obstetricia 56(1), 50–56 (2010)
27. Urtasun, J. Un Dispositivo Portátil para Diagnóstico de Parto Prematuro Inminente. Tekniker (2020). https://www.tekniker.es/media/uploads/noticias/NP_ProyectoFineBirth_ES.pdf. Accessed 16 July 2020
28. Watson, H.A., et al.: Development and validation of predictive models for QUiPP App v.2: tool for predicting preterm birth in asymptomatic high risk women. Ultrasound Obstet. Gynecol. 55(3), 348–356 (2020). https://doi.org/10.1002/uog.20401
29. Shah, P.S., Ye, X.Y., Synnes, A., Rouvinez-Bouali, N., Yee, W., Lee, S.K.: Canadian neonatal network. prediction of survival without morbidity for infants born at under 33 weeks gestational age: a user-friendly graphical tool. Arch. Dis Child. Fetal Neonatal Ed 97(2), 110–115 (2012). https://doi.org/10.1136/archdischild-2011-300143
30. Ambalavanan, N., et al.: Outcome trajectories in extremely preterm infants. Pediatrics 130(1), 115–125 (2012). https://doi.org/10.1542/peds.2011-3693
31. Ge, W.J., Mirea, L., Yang, J., Bassil, K.L., Lee, S.K., Shah, P.S.: Prediction of neonatal outcomes in extremely preterm neonates. Pediatrics 132(4), 876–885 (2013). https://doi.org/10.1542/peds.2013-0702
32. Ravelli, A.C.J., et al.: Antenatal prediction of neonatal mortality in very premature infants. Euro. J. Obstet. Gynecol. Reprod. Biol. 176, 126–131 (2014). https://doi.org/10.1016/j.ejogrb.2014.02.030
33. Márquez-González, H., et al.: Development and validation of the neonatal mortality score-9 mexico to predict mortality in critically ill neonates. Archivos Argentinos de Pediatría 113(3), 213–220 (2015). https://doi.org/10.5546/aap.2015.213
34. Schmidt, B., et al.: Investigators-caffeine. prediction of late death or disability at age 5 years using a count of 3 neonatal morbidities in very low birth weight infants. J. Pediatr 167, 982–986 (2015). https://doi.org/10.1016/j.jpeds.2015.07.067
35. King, C.P., Da Silva, O., Filler, G., Lopes, L.M.: Online calculator to improve counseling of short-term neonatal morbidity and mortality outcomes at extremely low gestational age (23–28 weeks). Am. J. Perinatol. 33(9), 910–917 (2016). https://doi.org/10.1055/s-0036-1581131
36. Podda, M., Bacciu, D., Micheli, A., Bellù, R., Placidi, G., Gagliardi, L.: A machine learning approach to estimating preterm infants survival: development of the preterm infants survival assessment (PISA) predictor. Sci. Rep. 8(1), 1–9 (2018)
37. Graupe, D.: Principles of Artificial Neural Networks: Advanced Series on Circuits and Systems. World Scientific Publishing Co. Pte. Ltd, Singapore (2013)
38. López, L.R., et al.: Utilidad de una Prueba Cualitativa para la Detección de Fibronectina Fetal en Secreción Cervicovaginal como Predictor de Parto Prematuro. In: Perinatología y Reproducción Humana, 29(4), (2015). https://doi.org/10.1016/j.rprh.2016.02.002

39. Zamora, F., Fernández, G., Pérez, M., Pérez, M.C., Maris, C.A.: Valor de la Fibronectina Fetal en Secreciones Cervicales en la Predicción del Parto Pretérmino en Pacientes con Membranas Íntegras. Rev Obstet Ginecol Venez **60**(1), 15–22 (2000)

40. Althabe, F., Carroli, G., Lede, R., Belizán, J.M., El Althabe, O.H.: Parto Pretérmino: Detección de Riesgos y Tratamientos Preventivos. Revista Panamericana de Salud Pública **5**, 373–385 (1999)

41. Abad, I. Modelo Predictivo de Parto Prematuro basado en Factores de Riesgo. (Tesis de Maestría). Universidad de Oviedo. Oviedo, España (2016)

42. Ciobanu, A., Rouvali, A., Syngelaki, A., Akolekar, R., Nicolaides, K.H.: Prediction of small for gestational age neonates: screening by maternal factors, fetal biometry, and biomarkers at 35–37 weeks' gestation. Am. J. Obstet. Gynecol. **220**(5), 486 (2019). https://doi.org/10.1016/j.ajog.2019.01.227

43. MathWorks. neural network toolbox—user´s guide. Massachusetts: The MathWorks, Inc. Natick. (2017)

Impact of Memory Control on Batch Learning in Human Activity Recognition Scenario in Comparison to Data Stream Learning

Leandro Miranda$^{(\boxtimes)}$, José Viterbo , and Flávia Bernardini

Fluminense Federal University, Niterói, RJ 24210-346, Brazil
leandromiranda@id.uff.br, {viterbo,fcbernardini}@ic.uff.br

Abstract. Human Activity Recognition (HAR) has gained attention in many studies in the ubiquitous computing area. Due to its high demand in recent years, various researchers use the sensors data stream to infer activities. In general, state-of-the-art literature uses batch machine learning approaches for constructing inference models. One disadvantage of batch learning is that many algorithms may present high memory consumption in the training phase. On the other hand, adaptive algorithms based on data stream learning can also be used. However, its disadvantage is that the model may need a high volume of data to converge. Thus, in this work, we compare the behavior of batch learning and online learning algorithm for constructing inference models in HAR scenarios. For this, we used in our methodology a *memory control module* for restricting memory consumption in batch learning. Our results show that models constructed using batch learning are much sensitive to memory consumption.

Keywords: Human Activity Recognition · Batch models · Stream learning models

1 Introduction

Human Activity Recognition (HAR), based on sensors data, has emerged as a key research area in mobile and ubiquitous computing. Activity recognition systems focus on inferring the current activities of users by leveraging the rich sensory environment [9, 21]. Systems that can recognize human activities from sensor data may support important applications in healthcare, social networks, environmental monitoring and etc. [17, 26, 28]. For instance, consider a person executing a daily activity, and suddenly, the person falls. In this case, the system should detect the falling and actuate with some advice. In another example scenario, the system needs to detect whether an older adult had his lunch or not, or whether he had taken his medicines, or even if he is bleeding due to the impact caused by the fall.

© Springer Nature Switzerland AG 2020
L. Martínez-Villaseñor et al. (Eds.): MICAI 2020, LNAI 12468, pp. 145–157, 2020.
https://doi.org/10.1007/978-3-030-60884-2_11

HAR systems need reasoning methods to infer high-level knowledge about the user and/or the environment. In general, HAR systems use several machine learning approaches to construct models for inference, such as distance-based [20,34], probability-based [2,4], optimization-based [19,23,25], and rules-based [14,30]. Most of the state-of-the-art works propose the use of models based on batch machine learning. These models can lead to segmented data and extract the pattern of a (relatively) low volume of data. However, the disadvantages of batch learning algorithms are: (i) they can need high processing capacity and high memory consumption; and (ii) they consider the data distribution is stationary [8,35], *i.e.*, the data distribution does not evolve over time. Regarding the disadvantage (i), distance-based models are the ones that most consume memory among all the approaches, due to memorizing data. Probabilistic-based (more specifically the Naive Bayes family of algorithms) and rules-based (or tree-based) are most simple, due to the facility of calculating probabilities and defining rules, respectively. However, when retraining batch models (given some frequency-time) happens (due to the new data stream), the systems that use batch learning tend to consume much memory. The consumption happens due to having to store the entire stream. This consumption is necessary to reconstruct a new model when using batch learning algorithms [1].

On the other hand, Online Models (*OM*) [11] (constructed using Online or Data Stream Learning algorithms) were presented in the literature with more flexibility to lead non-stationary distribution data. Moreover, Online Models act on scenarios where data distribution changes are present. In this way, *OM* appears as a solution for systems with low memory resources. The model incorporates new information for data segmentation of activities, which evolves high speed, detecting changes, and adapting the activities models to the most recent information. However, these models feed on recently labeled data. Furthermore, they require a minor computational cost. On the other hand, these models may require too much data to converge [5], as each instance is seen by the algorithm only once, which may lead to a minor potential for generalization when compared to batch algorithms.

In scenarios with limited hardware resources (such as HAR in smartwatches, mobiles, and other wearable technologies), there is a high demand for cheaper algorithms for constructing inference models. They should be able to deal with concept drift. They should need a low volume of labeled data. Another example of a scenario is the real-time classification of complex activities. In this case, devices with limited resources need to be maintained by a solid infrastructure to lead data coming from heterogeneous sensors and support the machine learning model's storage. In these special scenarios, when dealing with large amounts of data that need to be processed locally and timely, there may also be a need for infrastructure that supports fog [7]. The fog computing paradigm is an extension of cloud computing between the edge and cloud of the network. The fog has been widely accepted as a reasonable alternative to the cloud when large data may be processed locally [7,9].

Considering this panorama, analyzing the performance of batch models and online models focused on memory consumption is crucial. The objective is to verify the impact in batch models with similar resources to online models, considering the quality of inference. To this end, memory consumption must be fixed for batch models, similar to the online learning models. In this way, our aim in this work is to analyze the robustness of batch models constructed considering limited memory resources, compared to online models. To this end, we created a *memory control module* that manages memory consumption when new data arrives to construct new batch models. Our focus is on verifying if the batch learning models on this setup can obtain the same results versus online learning algorithms.

This work is organized as follows: Sect. 2 describes the HAR systems concepts; and approaches related to machine learning. Section 3 describes an overview of the state-of-the-art, according to HAR and machine learning. Section 4 describes the experiment setup and detail the *memory control module* for constrained of memory consumption in batch models. Section 5 presents how we conducted the experiments, including the datasets and parameters of the models. Section 6 presents our experimental analysis, aiming to evaluate the performance of all algorithms. Section 7 presents our final remarks about this work.

2   Background

This section describes the design from collected data from low-cost devices as electronic sensors or mobiles—afterward, the difference between batch models and online models.

2.1   HAR Design

HAR intends to observe human-related actions to understand what activities (or routines) individuals perform within a period. For example, a system could detect when a human is standing, lying down, cooking, driving, among many other activities. HAR is composed of two areas [33]: *Atomic Activity Recognition* and *Complex Activity Recognition*. Atomic activity recognition represents the repetition of a simple daily activity such as walking, jogging, sitting, cycling, and so forth. Complex activity recognition involves recognizing activities with a tricky and repetitive pattern. For Vyas et al. [33], atomic activities achieve complex activity recognition. Examples of complex activities are cooking, washing the plants, washing the room, driving a car, etc.

Figure 1 describes all steps in HAR. Firstly, the sensor (raw) data is collected. A sliding window is used with a specific time interval (size window w) and an overlapping size value. Many approaches use a fixed-width sliding window where we are only interested in the w most recent transactions with fixed-width size. The others are eliminated [16,24]. For the preprocessing and feature extraction, the data via multiple sources undergoes through a cleaning and enrichment process: The system selects relevant features; eliminates inconsistent and redundant data; correct missing values; removes outliers; validates activity. After this step, we have diverse feature vectors that enable us to have training data for classification. Afterward, the inference process occurs in these systems, in general, using algorithms based on machine learning. For acquiring the necessary knowledge, these systems have a reasoning engine that accomplishes a mathematical model with trained knowledge. In the next subsection, we focus on two machine learning approaches for creating these models: Batch and Online (Stream) Learning. After the inference step, the system is a reasonably straightforward task. It provides methods to deliver actual activity to the service customer.

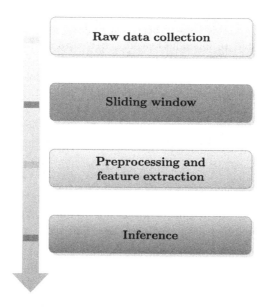

Fig. 1. Steps of HAR inference process.

2.2 Machine Learning Algorithms and Techniques

This section resumes concepts about two paradigms: batch learning (BM) and online (or data stream) learning (OM). In batch learning, all training datasets are available in memory. An algorithm learns a mathematical model after processes all data iteratively. Mainly, the examples are generated according to a stationary random distribution [10]. We potentially have a huge amount of automatic data collection when facing a scenario where sensors are connected to the system. Considering a set of sensors where they send real-time data to several devices using data based on the transient data stream, batch learning may face a big challenge. Over the years, batch research has engaged in machine learning algorithms. However, the high demand requires mathematical models that can process a large volume of information, which evolves over time, according to some non-stationary distribution.

Online (or data stream) learning techniques can modify the current model by adding new information [5]. In the presence of a non-stationary distribution, the system must incorporate knowledge adaptation strategies. Some fragmented information is no longer necessary in the current state of the problem. In HAR systems, continuous data stream evolves over time. In general, variations in dataset distribution and concept evolution are expected to be learned. Older observations become obsolete for the current state observation. The changes can occur either due to changes in variables that are no longer observed or in changes in the characteristic properties of the observed properties.

3 Literature Review

HAR systems have become a relevant research area over the years due to their relevance for different application scenarios. The principal researches use two approaches: the use of image data [12,18], or sensory data. First, the video-frames are collected in sequence to develop gestures or movements of users [12,22]. However, the computational cost is extremely expensive and becomes impractical in technologies where memory consumption is restricted.

Based on these limitations, the start-of-the-art literature presents many HAR techniques that are using sensors directly sustained by the users. For the development of atomic activities, some studies use collected data from smartphones using a simple sensor (accelerometer); and heterogeneous sensors such as accelerometer, gyroscope, step detector, and geomagnetic with multiples devices. For the development of complex activities, Reyes et al. use an accelerometer with a simple device (smartphone). Liu et al. use multiples sensors such as gyroscope, accelerometer, and magnetic field sensors. However, none of them care about the use or control of memory consumption when fitting their reasoning techniques (machine learning models).

There are just a few works that tackle HAR with machine learning models considering the limitation of memory consumption. Therefore, cheaper learning algorithms and models, in the way that they consume a lower quantity of memory, may be present in these systems to assist the inference in these activities. Some studies have adopted strategies that deal with reduced memory [15,29,31,32]. All of them use batch learning algorithms. However, none of them explicitly considers restriction in memory consumption and do not compare the two approaches (batch and online). This comparison is important, especially when consumption resources are limited.

4 Our Experimental Methodology

As described in Sect. 2.1, the HAR process can be divided into various steps, as illustrated in Fig. 1: *Raw data collection, Sliding window, Preprocessing and feature extraction,* and *Inference. Raw data collection* collects data from differents datasets described on Sect. 5.1. For *Preprocessing*; our study fuses data from different sensors. Each dataset describes its sensors (e.g. accelerometer, gyroscope). The feature extraction is different for each dataset. Section 5.2 describes the features of construction for each dataset.

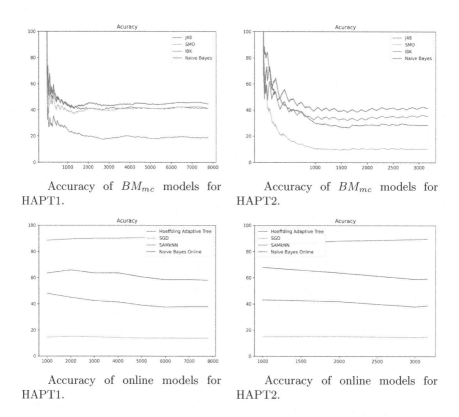

Accuracy of BM_{mc} models for HAPT1.

Accuracy of BM_{mc} models for HAPT2.

Accuracy of online models for HAPT1.

Accuracy of online models for HAPT2.

Fig. 2. Comparison between BM_{mc} models and online models using HAPT1 and HAPT2 by accuracy.

The key point in this work is the inference step. Our assumption is that batch learning, and online algorithms models are limited by memory size. Thus, we created a *memory control module* that helps to fit the batch models (BM_{mc}), under a respective memory size of the model. Algorithm 1 describes the *memory control module* for fitting models (BM_{mc}). Let x_i be a new segment of the stream, and M be the memory size for constructing the model. For this value, we selected the memory size used by an online model within the same learning approach (probabilistic-based, rules-based, and so on). Let S (security samples) be a set of samples that offers initial information for (BM_{mc}). We used 7% of samples for the initial fit distributed uniformly per each class. Registry R is a subset of the dataset with recent x_i labeled instances. This registry is similar to a buffer for control the sample sequence. Its objective is maintaining the model

Algorithm 1. Memory control module for (BM_{mc})

Input: $\mathbf{x}_i$, incoming segment stream; $\mathbf{y}_i$ predicted label for x_i, incoming stream;
   M: size of memory cap; S = security samples; Registry R
Output: A model BM_{mc} with size at most size M.
1: BM_{mc} is created under S samples
2: **repeat**
3:     $\mathbf{y}_i \leftarrow Classify(\mathbf{x}_i, BM_{mc})$;
4:     $R \leftarrow R \bigcup x_i$.
5:     $Retrain(BM_{mc}, x_i)$
6:     **if** $size(BM_{mc}) > M$ **then**
7:         $BM_{mc} \leftarrow \emptyset$
8:         **repeat**
9:             Take $x_i \in R$
10:            $Retrain(BM_{mc}, x_i)$
11:            $i \leftarrow i + 1$
12:        **until** There no are object in R **or** $size(BM_{mc}) > M$
13:    **end if**
14: **until** There are no stream x_i.

updated with the new data arriving in the stream, considering a time-frequency. The algorithm retrain BM_{mc} model for each new segment x_i. This element is stored in R. If the memory of BM_{mc} is much larger than M, the algorithm uses the most recent labeled instances $x_i \in R$. The order in the sequence x_i and x_{i+1} is preserved.

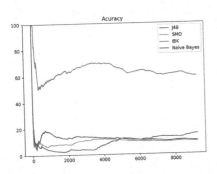

Fig. 3. Accuracy of BM_{mc} models for REALDISP.

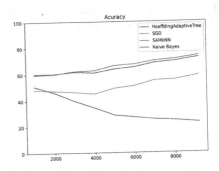

Fig. 4. Accuracy of online models for REALDISP.

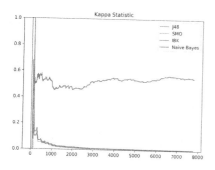

Kappa statistic of BM_{mc} models for HAPT1.

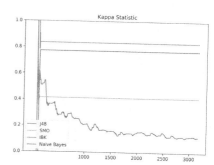

Kappa statistic of BM_{mc} models for HAPT2.

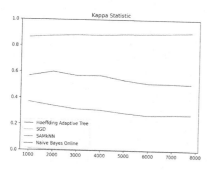

Kappa statistic of online models for HAPT1.

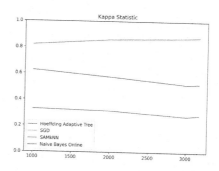

Kappa statistic of online models for HAPT2.

Fig. 5. Comparison between BM_{mc} models and Online Models using HAPT1 and HAPT2 by Kappa Statistic.

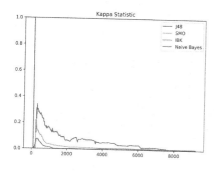

Fig. 6. Kappa statistic of BM_{mc} models for REALDISP.

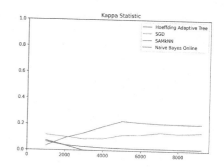

Fig. 7. Kappa statistic of online models for REALDISP.

Algorithm 2. Retrain function

Input: $\mathbf{x}_i$, incoming segment stream; A model BM_{mc} with size at most size M
1: the system gathered all object $(OBJs)$ used on model BM_{mc}
2: BM_{mc} is trained as from $OBJs \bigcup x_i$

5   Materials and Methods

5.1   Datasets

We selected the datasets HAPT[1] (two parts), REALDISP [2]. The HAPT dataset
has two sub-datasets: HAPT1 and a HAPT2. We used the two datasets individually due to the different number of samples. Thus, it allows us to create one thin
dataset and one big dataset. The choice of all datasets is due to the lack of studies involving datasets with labeled data concerning transition labels. This format
of the dataset may allow support to develop complex human activities [27].

The description of all datasets is present in Table 1. This table describes the
total of activities (number of classes); window size is the quantity of data under
the window and information about overlapping. The total of segments is the
number of samples for test and training models. Each segment is created by a
sliding window, and lastly, the number of features extracted. More details about
the execution process are described in the next subsection.

Table 1. Description of datasets.

Datasets	*HAPT*	*REALDISP*
Total of activities	12	33
Total of users	30	17
Window size (segments)	128 ($\approx$2.56 s)	200 ($\approx$4 s)
Total of segments (number of samples)	7767 (HAPT1) 3162 (HAPT2)	9213
Type of sliding window	Fixed-width sliding windows (50% overlap)	Fixed-width sliding windows (50% overlap)
Total of features	53	200

---

[1] https://bit.ly/3frazYN.
[2] https://bit.ly/35N4ZM8.

5.2   Experimental Setup

Firstly, the data flow as a stream in raw data format. For data segmentation, we used a fixed size of the sliding window. In this technique, a window is moved over the data stream to extract a data segment with a fixed size that is then used in subsequent processing steps. In this work, there is a 50% overlapping for all datasets.

After, the process of feature extraction is applied. For HAPT, we used the extracted feature processing based by Anguita et al. [3]). We generated 53 features enrolling in this dataset. For REALDISP, we used 200 features for construction. Its calculation is based on mean, standard deviation, variance in x, y, and z. All of this, we have a set of features (named by F), and we created $\|F\|$ as a feature. We represented all features as a vector V. The authors create a histogram in V_x, V_y, V_z. We gathered all features, so we created A_i with 40 features. This dataset has five devices ($i = 5$) distributed on the body. Thus we created A_i for each device and gathered all features. So, we have 200 features.

We selected four batch learning algorithms and four online learning algorithms at the level of comparison between the two types of learning. To deal with different types of distribution and model construction methods, we chose for each approach of learning: an optimization-based algorithm, a distance-based algorithm, a probabilistic-based algorithm, and a rules-based (using trees). The batch algorithms are SMO, KNN ($k = 5$), Naive Bayes, and J48 (C4.5), considering all are implemented in WEKA [13]. The algorithms with an online approach are SGD, SAMkNN ($k = 5$), Naive Bayes (online version), and Hoeffding Adaptive Tree. All classifications algorithms are implemented on framework MOA [6]. The choice of these algorithms is due to their robustness and performance. The choice of the k value for the distance-based algorithms (SAMkNN and KNN) is due to the presence of satisfactory results.

During the stream processing, the batch models have a restricted memory consumption size M, according to the function *memory control module*. The M generated by the SGD is the value of M capsize for the SMO. The M of KNN value is the maximum consumption calculated by SAMkNN; the M value of Naive Bayes in the batch is equivalent to the memory consumption of the Naive Bayes online version.

Finally, we performed a quantitative analysis between each algorithm, using accuracy and Kappa Statistic as an evaluation metric. As an evaluation strategy, the most commonly used in environments with data stream was used prequential [11]. Prequential allows the calculation of the error rate of algorithms (accumulated sum of a loss functions between the prediction and observed values). This evaluation is best, especially in scenarios in non-stationary data distributions [11].

6   Analysis of Results

This section describes an analysis of the results of all experiments. Figures 2, 3 and 4 show results about accuracy in datasets HAPT (train and test),

REALDISP respectively. We compared BM_{mc} models to online models with the same method. We observed that distance-based algorithms (composed by KNN and SAMkNN) in these scenarios show oppositive results for HAPT datasets (dataset with the fewer segment data). Probabilistic-based methods (composed by Naive Bayes and Naive Bayes online) show middling and similar results. Both of them do not offer good accuracy for big datasets as REALDISP. Overall, optimization-based methods (composed by SMO and SGD) show a limited accuracy, except for SGD using REALDISP. While rule-based method as J48 as Hoeffing Adaptative Tree is a non-accentuated decrease in the learning curve, its convergence is faster than other models. In general, for all algorithms, the result shows that online models have the best results; however, BM_{mc} models have a relation between the level of memory consumption and quality of accuracy. Increased consumption can improve the result of the accuracy metric. However, under big datasets, exhibited in Figs. 3 and 4, batch models do not show good results to online methods, except for IBK.

Concerning to Kappa metric, Figs. 5, 6, 7 show all results. For HAPT1, J48 executed a straightforward result; however, the other datasets, the performance was low. For online learning, SAMkNN has the best results. For HAPT2, two approaches obtained similar order for the evolution models. Distance-based and rules-based had substantial results. About the REALDISP dataset, neither batch models neither online models acquired good results. Overall, online learning obtains the best results, in particular, using distance-based models. The lack of new data (in quantity) shows the principal limitation for the batch model. Overall, strategies using online learning have better results than batch models with restricted memory using evaluation metrics.

7   Conclusion

Considering the scenario where computational resources are limited, effective strategies are welcome for HAR. Systems that require agile decision making must fit into resource restrictions, such as memory size. In this way, this paper presents a comparative analysis between batch machine learning models considering restriction in memory consumption and online learning algorithms. We used collected data from sensors available in benchmark datasets presented in the literature. The goal is to identify whether batch learning algorithms with limited memory resources can be robust compared to online learning algorithms.

In our study, we compared four batch learning with limited memory size to four online learning algorithms. These algorithms follow different learning approaches: distance-based learning, rules-based learning, probability-based learning, and optimization-based learning. Our results show that batch models are more sensitive to low data volume and low memory size than online models. According to the reduced memory consumption, batch learning presented difficulty in generalizing the models. Online models converge fast and show good results, in particular to SAMkNN. As future work, we intend to implement this scenario in ambient intelligence, dealing with complex activity recognition.

References

1. Abdallah, Z.S., Gaber, M.M., Srinivasan, B., Krishnaswamy, S.: Activity recognition with evolving data streams: a review. ACM Comput. Surv. **51**(4), 71:1–71:36 (2018)
2. Alam, M.G.R., Haw, R., Kim, S.S., Azad, M.A.K., Abedin, S.F., Hong, C.S.: EM-psychiatry: an ambient intelligent system for psychiatric emergency. IEEE Trans. Industr. Inf. **12**(6), 2321–2330 (2016)
3. Anguita, D., Ghio, A., Oneto, L., Parra, X., Reyes-Ortiz, J.L.: A public domain dataset for human activity recognition using smartphones. In: ESANN (2013)
4. Asghari, P., Soleimani, E., Nazerfard, E.: Online human activity recognition employing hierarchical hidden markov models. J. Ambient Intell. Humaniz. Comput. **11**(3), 1141–1152 (2020)
5. Bifet, A., Gavalda, R., Holmes, G., Pfahringer, B.: Machine Learning for Data Streams with Practical Examples in MOA. MIT Press, Cambridge (2018)
6. Bifet, A., Holmes, G., Kirkby, R., Pfahringer, B.: MOA: massive online analysis. J. Mach. Learn. Res. **11**, 1601–1604 (2010). http://portal.acm.org/citation.cfm?id=1859903
7. Bonomi, F., Milito, R., Zhu, J., Addepalli, S.: Fog computing and its role in the internet of things. In: Proceedings of the First Edition of the MCC Workshop on Mobile Cloud Computing, pp. 13–16 (2012)
8. Cardoso, H., Moreira, J.: Improving human activity classification through online semi-supervised learning. In: STREAMEVOLV@ECML-PKDD, September 2016
9. Concone, F., Re, G.L., Morana, M.: A fog-based application for human activity recognition using personal smart devices. ACM Trans. Internet Technol. (TOIT) **19**(2), 1–20 (2019)
10. Frank, E., Hall, M.A., Witten, I.H.: Data Mining: Practical Machine Learning Tools and Techniques, 4th edn. Morgan Kaufmann, Burlington (2016)
11. Gama, J., Sebastião, R., Rodrigues, P.P.: Issues in evaluation of stream learning algorithms. In: Proceedings of the 15th ACM SIGKDD International Conference on Knowledge Discovery and Data Mining, pp. 329–338 (2009)
12. Garcia-Garcia, A., Orts-Escolano, S., Oprea, S., Villena-Martinez, V., Martinez-Gonzalez, P., Garcia-Rodriguez, J.: A survey on deep learning techniques for image and video semantic segmentation. Appl. Soft Comput. **70**, 41–65 (2018)
13. Hall, M., Frank, E., Holmes, G., Pfahringer, B., Reutemann, P., Witten, I.H.: The WEKA data mining software: an update. SIGKDD Explor. **11**(1), 10–18 (2009)
14. Huang, Z., Lin, K.J., Tsai, B.L., Yan, S., Shih, C.S.: Building edge intelligence for online activity recognition in service-oriented IoT systems. Future Gener. Comput. Syst. **87**, 557–567 (2018)
15. Kotthaus, H., Korb, I., Lang, M., Bischl, B., Rahnenführer, J., Marwedel, P.: Runtime and memory consumption analyses for machine learning R programs. J. Stat. Comput. Simul. **85**(1), 14–29 (2015)
16. Krishnan, N.C., Cook, D.J.: Activity recognition on streaming sensor data. Pervasive Mob. Comput. **10**, 138–154 (2014)
17. Lara, O.D., Labrador, M.A., et al.: A survey on human activity recognition using wearable sensors. IEEE Commun. Surv. Tutor. **15**(3), 1192–1209 (2013)
18. Lima, E., Vieira, T., de Barros Costa, E.: Evaluating deep models for absenteeism prediction of public security agents. Appl. Soft Comput. 106236 (2020)
19. Madeira, R., Nunes, L.: A machine learning approach for indirect human presence detection using IoT devices. In: 2016 Eleventh International Conference on Digital Information Management (ICDIM), pp. 145–150. IEEE (2016)

20. Mane, Y.V., Surve, A.R.: CAPM: context aware provisioning middleware for human activity recognition. In: 2016 International Conference on Advanced Communication Control and Computing Technologies (ICACCCT), pp. 661–665, May 2016

21. Mehrang, S., Pietilä, J., Korhonen, I.: An activity recognition framework deploying the random forest classifier and a single optical heart rate monitoring and triaxial accelerometer wrist-band. Sensors **18**(2), 613 (2018)

22. Miranda, L., Vieira, T., Martínez, D., Lewiner, T., Vieira, A.W., Campos, M.F.: Online gesture recognition from pose kernel learning and decision forests. Pattern Recogn. Lett. **39**, 65–73 (2014)

23. Mshali, H., Lemlouma, T., Moloney, M., Magoni, D.: A survey on health monitoring systems for health smart homes. Int. J. Ind. Ergon. **66**, 26–56 (2018)

24. Nguyen, H.-L., Woon, Y.-K., Ng, W.-K.: A survey on data stream clustering and classification. Knowl. Inf. Syst. **45**(3), 535–569 (2014). https://doi.org/10.1007/s10115-014-0808-1

25. Punj, R., Kumar, R.: Technological aspects of WBANs for health monitoring: a comprehensive review. Wirel. Netw. 1–33 (2018)

26. Raychoudhury, V., Cao, J., Kumar, M., Zhang, D.: Middleware for pervasive computing: a survey. Pervasive Mob. Comput. **9**(2), 177–200 (2013)

27. Reyes-Ortiz, J.L., Oneto, L., Samà, A., Parra, X., Anguita, D.: Transition-aware human activity recognition using smartphones. Neurocomputing **171**, 754–767 (2016)

28. Rodrigues, J.J., Compte, S.S., De la Torre Diez, I.: e-Health Systems: Theory and Technical Applications. Elsevier, Amsterdam (2016)

29. Saha, S., Duwe, H., Zambreno, J.: An adaptive memory management strategy towards energy efficient machine inference in event-driven neuromorphic accelerators. In: 2019 IEEE 30th International Conference on Application-specific Systems, Architectures and Processors (ASAP), vol. 2160, pp. 197–205. IEEE (2019)

30. Sansrimahachai, W., Toahchoodee, M.: Mobile-phone based immobility tracking system for elderly care. In: 2016 IEEE Region 10 Conference (TENCON), pp. 3550–3553. IEEE (2016)

31. Si, S., Hsieh, C.J., Dhillon, I.S.: Memory efficient kernel approximation. J. Mach. Learn. Res. **18**(1), 682–713 (2017)

32. Starzyk, J.A., He, H.: Spatio-temporal memories for machine learning: a long-term memory organization. IEEE Trans. Neural Netw. **20**(5), 768–780 (2009)

33. V Vyas, V., Walse, K., Dharaskar, R.: A survey on human activity recognition using smartphone. Proc. Comput. Scie. **5** (2017)

34. Vales-Alonso, J., Chaves-Diéguez, D., López-Matencio, P., Alcaraz, J.J., Parrado-García, F.J., González-Castaño, F.J.: SAETA: a smart coaching assistant for professional volleyball training. IEEE Trans. Syst. Man Cybern.: Syst. **45**(8), 1138–1150 (2015)

35. Yao, L., Sheng, Q.Z., Ruan, W., Li, X., Wang, S., Yang, Z.: Unobtrusive posture recognition via online learning of multi-dimensional RFID received signal strength. In: 2015 IEEE 21st International Conference on Parallel and Distributed Systems (ICPADS), pp. 116–123. IEEE (2015)

Automated Characterization and Prediction of Wind Conditions Using Gaussian Mixtures

Magali Arellano-Vázquez[1,2(✉)], Carlos Minutti-Martinez[3],
and Marlene Zamora-Machado[4]

[1] INFOTEC Center for Research and Innovation in Information and Communication Technologies, Mexico City, Mexico
[2] National Council for Science and Technology, Mexico (CONACYT), Mexico City, Mexico
marellano@conacyt.mx
[3] Institute of Research in Applied Mathematics and Systems, National University of Mexico, Mexico City, Mexico
carlos.minutti@iimas.unam.mx
[4] Autonomous University of Baja California, Tijuana, Mexico
zamora.marlene@uabc.edu.mx

Abstract. The behavior of the wind in each region is given according to its orography and geographical position where phenomena such as sea breezes or valley or mountain winds, which are characteristic of specific areas, may occur. Thus, the wind's behavior in a region is a complex system that depends on multiple factors, which interact. The design of models for the characterization of wind systems in specific regions is a problem at various scales. Information such as wind speed and direction, obtained from anemometers at weather stations, represent the data that provides the most information to current models, however, other highly correlated variables such as relative humidity and atmospheric pressure are generally not used. The method proposed in this work uses the four previously mentioned meteorological variables to detect discrete wind states, managing to reproduce the classifications made by experts independently, *i.e.*, without training the algorithm to reproduce it. Hence, it is consistent with the expert knowledge while validating it. The methods is tested using meteorological data from weather stations located in Mexico City. The information obtained due to the generated classification serves to facilitate the prediction and projection of wind energy production and for the characterization of environmental, local phenomena.

Keywords: Automated wind characterization · Wind prediction · Gaussian kernels and clustering

© Springer Nature Switzerland AG 2020
L. Martínez-Villaseñor et al. (Eds.): MICAI 2020, LNAI 12468, pp. 158–168, 2020.
https://doi.org/10.1007/978-3-030-60884-2_12

1   Introduction

The wind's behavior in a region is a complex system that depends on multiple variables, most of which are unknown or difficult to quantify. The design of wind system characterization models in specific regions is a problem at numerous scales. Wind speed and direction information obtained from anemometers at weather stations represent the data that provide the most information in current models; however, more variables can correlate with weather phenomena, such as relative humidity and atmospheric pressure. Wind behavior is influenced by local terrain conditions, variables such as wind direction and speed, relative humidity, and atmospheric pressure, among others. This study presents a proposal with a multidisciplinary approach, using the wind state concept, which is based on the hypothesis that wind systems overlap states. It is proposed to use a mixture model based on the Gaussian multivariable mixture method, with the motivation of the possibility that the correlation of these variables that influence the behavior of the wind may contain subsets of wind "state" hidden in the data.

Studies on local winds have been carried out in Mexico City, in which the presence of three winds throughout the day has been identified (Fig. 1), which are affected when there are meteorological fronts in the Pacific Ocean and the Gulf of Mexico [3–5,7], other authors have identified up to 9 wind patterns throughout the year [1]. The wind's behavior is influenced by local terrain conditions, variables such as wind direction and speed, relative humidity, and atmospheric pressure, among others. Mexico City is located within the Valley of Mexico basin, a flat area surrounded by mountains with an average height between 600 and 800 meters above the valley floor. The Sierra de Guadalupe surrounds the city to the north, the Sierra de las Cruces to the west, the Sierra del Ajusco to the south, and the Sierra Nevada to the east, the latter including the Iztlacihuatl (5200 m.a.s.l.) and Popocatepetl (5400 m.a.s.l.) volcanoes. The quantity and distribution of the mountains, make Mexico City and its metropolitan area terrain of high complexity, influencing the meteorology and how the pollutants behave in the atmosphere [6]. Urbanization causes cities to experience higher temperatures than the surrounding countryside; this phenomenon is known as "urban heat island" [8]. Local winds influence air quality and the distribution of pollutants.

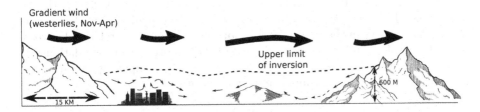

Fig. 1. Schematic illustration of drainage airflow over the Mexico basin [7]

In recent years, especially in 2016, environmental contingencies [9] have become more frequent and are a hazardous phenomenon, especially for children, particularly in the northern part of Mexico City. It has been shown that several lung morphology changes related to exposure to O_3 with a predominantly restrictive pattern. During the winter, the phenomenon of thermal inversion occurs. The environmental contingency plan is not activated because it depends on the concentration of O_3 in the environment; however, with the appearance of the thermal inversion, other pollutants are found in large concentrations in the environment. A three-year study supports the hypothesis that long-term exposure to ambient air pollutants is associated with children's lung growth deficits [11].

2   Methodology

2.1   Gaussian Mixture Model

In statistics, a mixture model is a probabilistic model used to represent different sub-populations within a larger population, through the combination of many probability density functions where each component of the function could be interpreted as a "probability" or the likelihood of the existence of each sub-population in each spatial coordinate.

In this case, the main population would be the characteristic wind of an area due to the location, and the sub-populations would be any other kind of winds product of the change of the different conditions in the area. If Gaussian distributions are used for the mixture model, this is known as the Gaussian Mixture Model (GMM). The GMM is a parametric probability density function represented as the sum of Gaussian component densities [10], represented by:

$$G(\boldsymbol{\theta}) = G(X, \mu_i, \Sigma_i) = \sum_{i=1}^{N_k} \omega_i N(X, \mu_i, \Sigma_i) \tag{1}$$

where ω_i is a weight for the i-th Gaussian distribution with mean μ_i and covariance matrix Σ_i. N_k is the number of components in the mixture, and X is the vector of spatial coordinates.

Unlike other clustering methods such as K-Means, the GMM can take into account the correlation between variables related to the phenomena being studied and use this information to identify groups within the population. In addition, the value of the estimated parameters has a direct interpretation with the phenomena. For example, the variance of each group provides a direct measure of the homogeneity of the group. In addition, the estimated correlation between pairs of variables can be used as a measure of the importance of the relationship between those variables in identifying the group, and comparing whether this relationship had a different importance in other groups.

2.2   Implementation

The hypothesis is that through the analysis of climatic data sets, it is possible to characterize the behavior of wind and therefore take actions that reduce health damage during environmental contingencies or thermal inversions. A wind state is defined as a region in velocity phase space containing available wind speeds that have a standard probability distribution function that characterizes them as a group [12]. We postulate that wind states exist physically but are stochastically determined by the site's geographic and climatic conditions; it is challenging to model them from fundamental hydrodynamic equations. Clustering methods are an alternative for discovering wind states in long-period data series. If clustering preserves the relationship with the wind's physical state, it could be the basis for the automatic recognition of wind patterns.

The proposed method is tested using meteorological data from stations located in the Mexico City area. These stations are presented in Fig. 2. There are several public data sources available, the REDMET database, which belongs to the Mexico City air quality monitoring system and the Automatic Weather Stations operated by the National Water Commission (Comisión Nacional del Agua or CONAGUA), being the last one which provided the data used for this work, including the following variables: wind speed, wind direction, atmospheric pressure, and relative humidity.

Fig. 2. Geographical location of Ecoguardas, ENCB1, ENCB2 and Tezontle stations in Mexico City, managed by CONAGUA [2]

Information is available on the occurrence of environmental contingencies [9], and the three characteristic Mexico City's wind flows provide a framework for evaluating the results obtained by the GMM method.

Using data from REDMET and CONAGUA, the weather stations with information in most years were used to study wind conditions in the relevant areas.

To visualize this information it is necessary to consider that there are two primary cycles, first the daily cycle, that is to say, the winds that occur throughout the day (in principle the day and the night), it is sought that in the visualization the duration of these can be distinguished and in average the hour in which they appear. It also seeks to appreciate the annual cycle, that is, the changes that are a consequence of the year's seasons that can be identified when they begin, which are more noticeable.

3   Results

Figure 3 shows the grouping of winds using GMM for the GAM weather station. Through a Principal Component Analysis (PCA), the three main components of the data are presented to determine the variables that most influence the groups. These variables were mainly wind direction and wind speed, so from now on, the speeds concerning wind direction are used to show the groups.

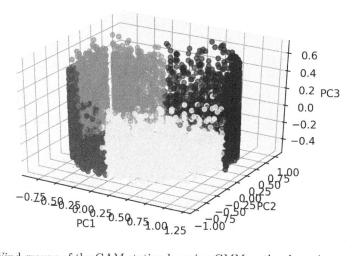

Fig. 3. Wind groups of the GAM station by using GMM as the clustering method and PCA to present the groups.

So far, by analyzing the Ecoguardas station, four daily wind states have been automatically identified Fig. 4; three of them have been reported in the literature, proving the effectiveness of the techniques used. Three air masses have been identified that push air into the basin: the channeled flow from Chalco, the west winds over the Toluca, and the flow over the Ajusco to the south. The wind circulation in the Mexico City basin is characterized by a gap that crosses the mountain pass in the southeast and extends towards the basin [4]. This takes place almost every day, with different strength and depth. The grouping obtained by GMM identifies the three winds mentioned in the literature and wind in the central zone, an area where it has a higher incidence of thermal inversion.

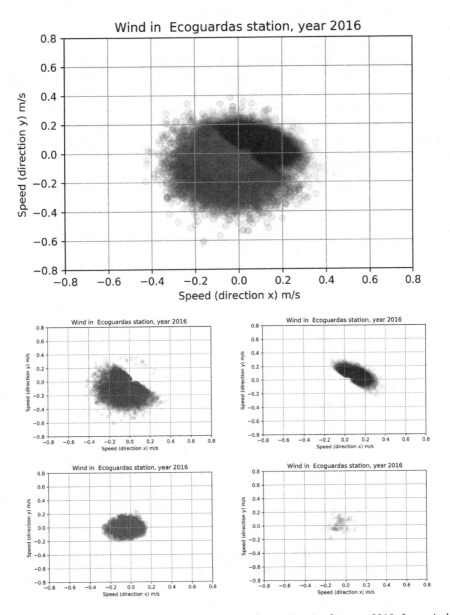

Fig. 4. Grouping of wind data from the Ecoguardas station in the year 2016, four wind states are identified, with three main wind states, (a) Wind state 1 (day) (b) Wind state 3, low pressure weather front and (c) Wind state 4 (night).

In Fig. 4, the wind states for the Ecoguardas station in the year 2016 can be seen. According to the results of the GMM, when separating the wind states from the Ecoguardas station, the visualization of them is observed in Fig. 4, separated in the three predominant states: a low meteorological pressure state, and day and night states.

Employing time series analysis, and the classification of the wind states obtained from the GMM, the information on the behavior of the variables is aligned. Figure 5 shows the typical behavior in March of the meteorological variables of temperature, relative humidity, wind direction, and wind speed. During the day corresponding to wind state 1 and wind state 2. The wind state 2, is another kind of wind in the morning day around 0:00 hours to 7:00 am of the wind, marked with the red box, in midday it reached a temperature of 27.6 °C with a decrease in relative humidity to 21%, and during the afternoon-night which is state 4, it reached 9.5 °C with an increase in relative humidity of 67% marked with the blue box.

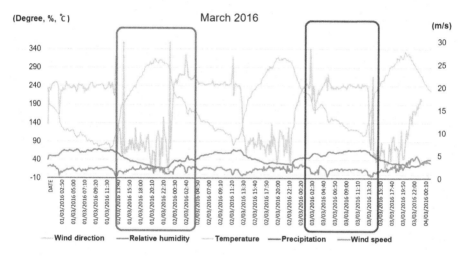

Fig. 5. Typical behavior of wind state 1 and 2 in the morning in the red box and wind state 4 in the afternoon-nigh in the blue box (Color figure online)

For the year 2016 in the Ecoguardas station, in the wind that corresponds to the day (wind state 1 is 28.72%, and wind state 2 is 23.18%), it represents 51.9% of the presence in the annual data, which makes it the state with a more significant presence. Wind state 4, which corresponds to the night, has 29.5% of the presence of the data, there is 18.3% of erroneous data in the taking of readings from the Ecoguardas weather station, especially in data with night schedule, which explains the low percentage of wind data in this state. Furthermore, the wind states 3, represent 0.25%, a low presence, could be a wind state in transition. The developed method was applied to the measurements of the Tezontle, and Escuela Nacional de Ciencias Biológicas (ENCB 2) sites for the year 2016. The clusters obtained for these sites are shown in Fig. 7.

Figure 7 shows the wind states for Tezontle, where the results obtained are 62.7% for wind state 3, which corresponds to night; wind state 2, is day with 19%, and states 1 and 4, are states in transition between day and night with 10% and 8%, respectively. At the Tezontle station there was only 0.02% of non-existent data.

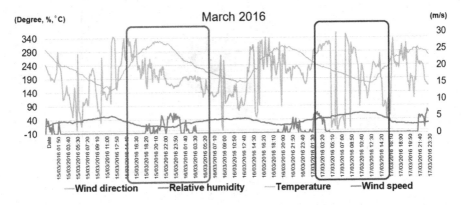

Fig. 6. Daytime behavior of weather variables at Tezontle station. In the red box, the day is marked, corresponding to wind state 2, and with variations between wind state 1 or 4. And in the blue box, the temperature increase is marked, corresponding to the night period. (Color figure online)

There is more variation in wind direction in the Tezontle data, in Fig. 6 we can see the daytime behavior of the meteorological variables. In the red box the behaviour corresponding to the day is marked, which belongs to wind state 2, with variations between wind state 1 or 4. In the blue box, the increase in temperature is marked, which corresponds to the night period. The time of the graph is in Universal Time Coordinated (UTC).

For the ENCB 2 site, the day and night wind states are divided from the first six months of January through the beginning of June, the wind state 1 is day with 22.84% and the wind state 3 is night with 22.31%, and the following six months the wind state 4 is day with 24.74% and the wind state 2 is night with 30%. There was 0.05% of non-existent data. For this weather station, unlike the other two, the GMM method separates the day and night states, indicating that, within the 6-month periods mentioned, the variation between these two moments is greater than that which occurs throughout the year.

4   Summary and Conclusions

By applying the GMM model with four variables, a more accurate description of the wind states is obtained by differentiating between winds generated by high

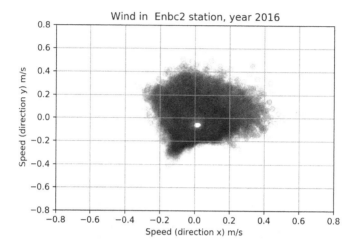

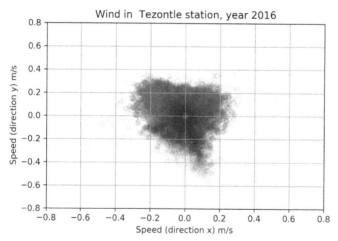

Fig. 7. Results for the site of ENCB2 and Tezontle site. Each site is different, because of the orography, and topographic conditions of the terrain, the dominant direction of wind speed will change.

and low-pressure centers. With the application of this method to other sites where there is an energy potential or where it is necessary to study the behavior of the wind, it would be saving time in the detection of wind states, since when carrying out surface wind analysis the time is higher than with the method proposed in this work. The advantage of the method is that using four variables, it is possible to identify winds generated in the same quadrant with high speeds, but different atmospheric pressure. Knowing this type of wind study will help change the wind states present through different years to make predictions of the wind's states.

The results indicate that local daytime and nighttime wind conditions account for 80% of the winds' presence, and a missing data set of 18% is analyzed. With the method, they are automatically identified using 4 meteorological variables: wind speed, wind direction, relative humidity, and atmospheric pressure, decreasing the time of analysis in the handling of information. Likewise, the method makes a difference with the wind state 3, since they are low-pressure winds. The advantage of this method is that analyses can be performed for several stations simultaneously, and significant wind patterns can be found in a specific area. As future work, it is proposed to identify specific meteorological phenomena and study the data around those dates to look for some wind precursor to them.

The code developed for this wind characterization work can be found under the name **WindClAI**, at: https://github.com/estudiovientos/saw.

Acknowledgments. This work was partially supported by project UABC-PTC-705, and project 735 from Cátedras CONACYT, project "Fortalecimiento del laboratorio Nacional de Internet del Futuro". A respectable acknowledgement to the Comisión Nacional del Agua (CONAGUA) for supplying the data.

References

1. Carreón-Sierra, S., Salcido, A., Castro, T., Celada-Murillo, A.T.: Cluster analysis of the wind events and seasonal wind circulation patterns in the Mexico City region. Atmosphere 6(8), 1006–1031 (2015)
2. CONAGUA: Map of automated weather stations, August 2020. https://smn.conagua.gob.mx/tools/GUI/EMAS.php
3. De Foy, B., et al.: Mexico City basin wind circulation during the MCMA-2003 field campaign. Atmos. Chem. Phys. Discuss. 5(3), 2503–2558 (2005). https://hal.archives-ouvertes.fr/hal-00303903
4. De Foy, B., Clappier, A., Molina, L.T., Molina, M.J.: Distinct wind convergence patterns in the Mexico City basin due to the interaction of the gap winds with the synoptic flow. Atmos. Chem. Phys. 6(5), 1249–1265 (2006). https://doi.org/10.5194/acp-6-1249-2006. https://www.atmos-chem-phys.net/6/1249/2006/
5. de Foy, B., et al.: Basin-scale wind transport during the milagro field campaign and comparison to climatology using cluster analysis. Atmos. Chem. Phys. 8(5), 1209–1224 (2008). https://doi.org/10.5194/acp-8-1209-2008. https://www.atmos-chem-phys.net/8/1209/2008/

6. Jauregui, E.: Heat island development in Mexico City. Atmos. Environ. **31**(22), 3821–3831 (1997). https://doi.org/10.1016/S1352-2310(97)00136-2. http://www.sciencedirect.com/science/article/pii/S1352231097001362
7. Jauregui, E.: Local wind and air pollution interaction in the Mexico basin. Atmósfera **1**(3) (2011). https://www.revistascca.unam.mx/atm/index.php/atm/article/view/25944
8. Mexico City Government: Calidad del aire en la ciudad de méxico. informe anual 2016, August 2020. http://www.aire.cdmx.gob.mx/descargas/publicaciones/flipping-book/informe_anual_calidad_aire_2016v1/informe_anual_calidad_aire_2016.pdf
9. Mexico City Government: Sistema de monitoreo de la calidad del aire de la CDMX, August 2020. http://www.aire.cdmx.gob.mx/descargas/ultima-hora/calidad-aire/pcaa/pcaa-historico-contingencias.pdf
10. Reynolds, D.: Gaussian Mixture Models, Encyclopedia of Biometrics. Springer, Heidelberg (2009). https://doi.org/10.1007/978-0-387-73003-5_196
11. Rojas-Martinez, R., et al.: Lung function growth in children with long-term exposure to air pollutants in Mexico City. Am. J. Respir. Crit. Care Med. **176**(4), 377–384 (2007). https://doi.org/10.1164/rccm.200510-1678OC. pMID: 17446338
12. Sánchez-Pérez, P.A., Robles, M., Jaramillo, O.A.: Real time markov chains: Wind states in anemometric data. J. Renew. Sustain. Energy **8**(2), 023304 (2016). https://doi.org/10.1063/1.4943120. http://scitation.aip.org/content/aip/journal/jrse/8/2/10.1063/1.4943120

A Survey on Freezing of Gait Detection and Prediction in Parkinson's Disease

Lourdes Martínez-Villaseñor[1](✉), Hiram Ponce[1], and Luis Miralles-Pechuán[2]

[1] Facultad de Ingeniería, Universidad Panamericana,
Augusto Rodin 498, 03920 Ciudad de México, Mexico
lmartine@up.edu.mx, hponce@up.edu.mx
[2] Ireland's Centre for Applied Artificial Intelligence (CeADAR),
University College Dublin, Dublin, Ireland
luis.miralles@ucd.ie

Abstract. Most of Parkinson's disease (PD) patients present a set of motor and non-motor symptoms and behaviors that vary during the day and from day-to-day. In particular, freezing of gait (FOG) impairs their quality of life and increases the risk of falling. Smart technology like mobile communication and wearable sensors can be used for detection and prediction of FOG, increasing the understanding of the complex PD. There are surveys reviewing works on Parkinson and/or technologies used to manage this disease. In this review, we summarize and analyze works addressing FOG detection and prediction based on wearable sensors, vision and other devices. We aim to identify trends, challenges and opportunities in the development of FOG detection and prediction systems.

Keywords: Freezing of gait · FOG detection · FOG prediction · Parkinson · Machine learning

1 Introduction

In the last decade, technology-based applications have been developed for the diagnosis, monitoring, and therapy of Parkinson's disease (PD). Sensors, mobile communications, cloud computing, advanced data analysis, and the Internet of Things have transformed healthcare for chronic and complex diseases [10]. With regard to PD, these technologies can improve the sensitivity, precision, reproducibility and feasibility with which the complex and diverse changes in motor and non-motor behavior of patients are captured [10]. It is difficult to reliably assess fluctuating events, capture rare incidents such as falls and freeze-up, or evaluate behaviors that occur outside the clinical examination room. Freezing of gait (FOG) is associated with PD and is considered among the most incapacitating complex symptoms [6]. FOG is related to an increased risk of fall occurrence, loss of independence, and impaired quality of life in PD patients [11].

This research has been funded by Universidad Panamericana through the grant "Fomento a la Investigación UP 2020", under project code UP-CI-2020-MEX-11-ING.

© Springer Nature Switzerland AG 2020
L. Martínez-Villaseñor et al. (Eds.): MICAI 2020, LNAI 12468, pp. 169–181, 2020.
https://doi.org/10.1007/978-3-030-60884-2_13

The important relationship between FOG and falls [5,18,27] and deterioration of Parkinson's patient autonomy supports the need to detect episodes of FOG. In order to avoid FOG in patients, it is necessary to develop a FOG prediction model and then, design personalized strategies and treatments to improve their quality of life. We can find in the literature, approaches based on wearable devices [26], vision systems [16] and WiFi devices [36] to detect and predict FOG events.

In this paper, we present a literature review of the state of the art in FOG detection and prediction. Previous reviews focus on technologies for diagnosis, monitoring and therapy of PD [10,29]. For instance, Pardoel et al. [26] recently presented a review on FOG detection and prediction, but they focused only on wearable-sensor-based approaches. In our current survey, we included papers based on wearable sensors, vision and other devices. We aim to identify trends, challenges and opportunities in the development of FOG detection and prediction systems.

The rest of the paper is organized as follows. In Sect. 2, we provide a brief introduction to FOG phenomenon, and present a detailed review of the most cited works addressing FOG detection and FOG prediction. In Sect. 3 we present trends, challenges and opportunities for FOG detection and prediction. Lastly, in Sect. 4, we concluded the paper and propose future work.

2 Freezing of Gait Detection and Prediction

In this section, we provide a brief introduction to the phenomenon namely FOG, and we review relevant works on FOG detection and prediction. This review includes approaches based on vision, wearable sensors and other devices.

2.1 Freezing of Gait

Gait disorder or FOG is a phenomenon identified by brief, transient episodes or marked reduction in forwarding foot progression despite the intent to walk [24,38]. Patients describe it as being unable to take their feet off the ground and it occurs when starting, turning, or continuing to walk. It can last a few seconds or occasionally exceed 30 seconds [32]. It is more commonly observed in patients with advanced Parkinson's stages, but can also occur spontaneously in the early stages of the disease [5]. According to Macht et al. [19], FOG is more common in men than in women and less frequent in patients who have the symptom of tremors. FOG is one of the most common symptoms in PD and it is one of the main factors that limit autonomy, impairs the patient's quality of life and sometimes, it is the reason for transferring patients to a care home [5]. Thus, FOG is frequently associated with falls [5].

The pharmacological treatment for FOG is commonly done with Levodopa (dopaminergic medication). FOG episodes generally appear in off state (periods with a no-effect level of medication). Nevertheless, PD patients are often resistant to medical treatment [4,5], and increasing medication often presents side-effects [35]. Hence, pharmacological treatment is difficult and do not always help.

Non-medicinal therapeutic strategies have been proposed to manage FOG. Gait performance can be improved with auditory and/or visual cues [12,35]. FOG detection and prediction systems can identify when PD patients need help, and cueing in the right moment can get the patient going. If the prediction is before FOG, then, cueing can prevent it from happening, reducing the risk of fall.

2.2 FOG Detection and Prediction

Following, we present a review of the most cited works related to FOG detection and prediction. A summary of FOG detection systems are shown in Tables 1 and 2, while Table 3 summarizes FOG prediction systems.

Statistical and Threshold-Based Approaches for FOG Detection. Starting in the early 2000s, initiatives that automatically detect FOG events have begun to emerge. This detection refers to pointing out when a FOG episode is happening. In the last two decades, wearable inertial sensors with tri-axial accelerometer, gyroscope and magnetometer, have commonly been used to detect FOG. Early works apply threshold-based methods and handcrafted features for FOG detection as described next.

One of the first FOG detection works is presented by Han et al. [13]. The authors propose a portable monitoring system based on accelerometers positioned on the ankles of patients suffering from freezing gait and people with a normal gait. They used the Fast Fourier Transform (FFT) and amplitude analysis to identify the characteristics of each gait. Four-level Daubechies wavelet was used to discriminate between normal and FOG.

Moore et al. [23] designed an ambulatory monitoring device and algorithm using the frequency characteristics of vertical leg movement captured with an accelerometer placed on the left shank of eleven PD patients. Subjects were between 45 and 72 years old. They were asked to walk around some internal corridors requiring to negotiate a narrow doorway and three obstacles. Special conditions of levodopa/carbidopa medication combination on and off were considered in this study. They detected FOG with a threshold-based approach obtaining a 78% FOG detection and 89% accuracy.

Delval et al. [8] carried out a study where they cause FOG in patients and with a set of quantitative markers detected the occurrence of FOG. They recorded 10 patients and 10 healthy subjects on a treadmill with a video camera using a 3D motion analysis system. Ten markers were attached to heels, toes, ankles, shoulders, and over vertebra T10. Special conditions were considered as obstacles and the patients were in off-state. In that work, FOG detection was based on threshold and frequency analysis.

Bächlin et al. [4] developed a FOG detection system based on three accelerometers using Moore's threshold-based algorithm [23]. When the system detected an episode of FOG, a metronome provided stimuli to the patient to help him/her to get back on track. Six out of eight patients that experienced FOG reported an improvement of gait with the system assistance.

Azevedo et al. [3] proposed a FOG detector that included gait pattern analysis based on one inertial sensor positioned on the lower extremity. From its results, it concludes that the frequency-based analysis is not enough to reliably detect the FOG and that it is necessary to predict, not only detect, when a FOG event will occur. They added cadence and stride analysis to their method for a better classification.

With the aim of evaluating gait patterns in Parkinson's patients, Djurić-Jovičić et al. [9] proposed a method based on inertial sensors positioned on both shanks to classify gait patterns. It also identified normal and abnormal gait using an expert rule-based system from twelve PD patients that walked along a complex pathway. They used a rule-based classification method for FOG identification and classification.

In the work of Pham et al. [30], the authors presented a subject-independent FOG detection system based on feature selection techniques using correlation and clustering metrics. The novelty of this proposal is that it is independent of the subject.

Another example of a FOG detection system using wearable accelerometers with video recording to label the event is the work presented by Zach et al. [40]. Their conclusion is that it is possible to detect FOG with a single accelerometer in the lumbar region.

Table 1 summarizes these works, presenting the equipment used and their placement, the number and type of subjects in the study, the activities and conditions, the methods employed for FOG detection, and the results obtained.

Artificial Intelligence Approaches for FOG Detection. In contrast to previous works, here, we highlight relevant works on FOG detection, but only those that apply artificial intelligence methods.

Pepa et al. [28] investigation was one of the firsts using soft computing techniques for FOG detection. They developed a fuzzy algorithm to fuse information related to freeze index, energy, cadency variation and the ratio of the derivative of the energy. They built an architecture based on a smartphone. Their results showed that the system was able to identify FOG episodes with 83.33% sensitivity and 92.33% specificity on average.

Cole et al. [7] presented a solution based on dynamic neural networks (DNN) to detect FOG from signals, collected by three accelerometers and an electromyographic surface dressed by patients, obtaining good detection results. An important contribution of this work is that they recorded a database of unscripted and unconstrained activities of daily living of PD patients in which FOG also occurred.

Mazilu et al. [22] proposed a wearable assistant consisting of a smartphone and wearable accelerometers to detect FOG using machine learning techniques. They used Random Forest (RF), Decision Trees (C4.5), Näive Bayes (NB),

Table 1. Relevant works in FOG detection not based on artificial intelligence.

Author/Year	Equipment/ Placement	Subjects	Activity/ conditions	Methods	Results
(Han et al. 2003) [13]	Two biaxial accelerometers/Each ankle Camera as reference	5 normal 2 patient movement disorder	Walked on level ground and turn repeatedly	FFT, 4-level Daubechies wavelet	Not comparable
(Moore et al. 2008) [23]	IMU/left shank and Digital videocamera	11 males (9 PD) Age 45 to 72	Walked around a corridor with at least 2 turns, obstacles and doorway/ on and off state	Threshold-based	78% FOG events detected 89% accuracy
(Deval et al. 2010) [8]	3D Motion analysis system/10 markers:heels,toes,ankles, shoulders, over T10 vertebra Videocamera	10 patients PD with FOG (off-state) 10 controls	Treadmill walking with obstacles	Threshold frequency analysis	83% FOG detection
(Bächlin et al. 2009) [4]	3D accelerometers and 3D gyroscope (left thigh and shank, and belt) earphones	11 PD patients (8 off-state 2 on-state)	Walking -Straight line -Random walk -Entering and exiting rooms	Threshold-based	73.1% sensitivity 81.6% specificity
(Zach et al. 2015) [40]	3D accelerometer/waist Camera	23 PD patients	Walking rapidly, full turns	Frequency and threshold analysis	75% sensitivity 76% specificity
(Azevedo et al. 2014) [3]	One 3D accelerometer/lower limb	4 PD patients	Walk along a corridor	Threshold +cadence and stride criterion	
(Djurić-Jovičić et al. 2014) [9]	two IMUs/both shanks	12 PD patients (off-state)	Walk along a complex pathway	Detection and classification Rule-based classification	78% to 100% sensitivity 94.6% to 100% specificity
(Pham et al. 2017) [30]	3D accelerometers/shank,thigh,lower back	DAPHNet dataset 10 PD patients	Walking -Straight line -Random walk -Entering and exiting rooms	Anomaly score detector	94% sensitivity 84% specificity

Multi-Layered Perceptron (MLP), AdaBoost with C4.5, and Bagging with C4.5. Their results present an average sensitivity of 98.35% and an average specificity of 99.72%.

Ahlrichs et al. [1] presented a FOG detector based on one waist-worn accelerometer and Support Vector Machines (SVM) classifier. They recorded twenty PD patients performing scripted general activities. A special condition was that patients were recorded in on and off state of medication. Their results showed an accuracy of 98.7%.

Rodriguez et al. [31] presented a machine learning algorithm to detect FOG episodes. Support Vector Machines (SVM) were their choice for FOG detection. Their system is based on a single 3D accelerometer worn in the waist with the aim of detecting FOG "in real life". Twenty-one PD patients in off and on periods performed two sets of scripted activities. These activities were related to daily living. They reported that medication influenced the motor response of the patients.

In recent years, deep learning approaches are commonly used for FOG detection [6,17,20,28,33,36,39]. The most relevant ones are reviewed below.

For example, Kim et al. [17] and Pepa et al. [28] proposed a new sensing device, a smartphone placed in the trouser pocket, to find a more practical way to monitor PD patients and detect FOG. They applied a method based on convolutional neural networks (CNN) to extract discriminative features automatically from sensors embedded in an Android smartphone. They compared the performance of CNN classifier with RF, and CNN showed a 20% higher sensitivity than the RF classifier.

In order to achieve automatic feature learning and discrimination for FOG, Xia et al. [39] also proposed a FOG detection system based on CNN. They used the dataset created by Bachlin et al. [4]. They performed patient-dependent and patient-independent experiments. The best results were reported in the patient-dependent experiments. We present the patient-independent results in Table 2 in order to compare them with Bächilin's results.

Camps et al. [6] proposed an eight-layered CNN architecture for FOG detection. They based the data collection in one accelerometer placed on the left side of the waist. Twenty-one PD patients performed at least three tests standing up from a chair or a sofa, walking 6 m, making turns, walking the 6 m back to the chair or sofa, and sitting down on it. They included some complexity by adding FOG detection when cleaning a cup, carrying a glass of water, typing in a computer, brushing one's teeth, and drawing and erasing on a sheet of paper. The authors' comparative results support the fact that deep learning approaches present high sensitivity and specificity.

On the other hand, in order to avoid obtrusiveness of wearable sensors, vision-based approaches were presented in the last few years. Relevant works are summarized following.

Sun et al. [34] presented an action recognition algorithm based in a Spatial Attention Network and 3D CNN to learn a FOG candidate region. Using the same dataset, Hu et al. [16] proposed one of the first vision-based approaches for automatic FOG detection. They introduced an architecture of graph convolutional neural network using video data with the aim of developing a straightforward method. In their proposal, they constructed a directed graph to represent the anatomic joints extracted from FOG assessment videos. This graph representation allows the characterization of FOG gait patterns. They recorded videos collected from 45 PD patients.

Tahir et al. [36] proposed a WiFi sensing system for unobtrusive detection of FOG symptoms in PD patients. They demonstrated that their WiFi system can detect channel state information (CSI) amplitude variations generated in FOG episodes. Their system was able to discriminate FOG symptoms from walking, sitting-standing, and voluntary stops. Multi-resolution time-frequency scalograms were used for feature extraction and a very deep multi-class CNN was presented for deep transfer learning of scalograms for FOG detection. They reported a sensitivity of 97% and a specificity of 100% in their results.

Table 2. Relevant works in FOG detection based on artificial intelligence.

Author/Year	Equipment/ Placement	Subjects	Activity/ conditions	Methods	Results
(Pepa et al. 2014) [28]	Smartphone/hip	18 PD patients	TUG activities	Threshold+Fuzzy Logic	83.33% sensitivity 92.33% specificity
(Cole et al. 2011) [7]	3D accelerometers/ forearm,thigh and shin Electromyographic (EMG)/shin Camera	10 PD patients	Unscripted and unconstrained activities of daily living	Linear classifier + dynamic neural network	73.1% sensitivity 81.6% specificity
(Mazilu et al. 2012) [22]	Smartphone and 3D accelerometer- s/shank,thigh,lower back	DAPHNet dataset 10 PD patients	Walking -Straight line -Random walk -Entering and exiting rooms	Random Forest C4.5 Näive Bayes MLP AdaBoost with C4.5 Bagging with C4.5	98.35% sensitivity 99.72% specificity
(Ahlrichs et al. 2016) [1]	3D accelerometer/waist	20 PD patients (on and off-state)	Normal activities	Support Vector Machine	98.7% accuracy
Rodriguez 2017 [31]	3D accelerometer/waist	21 PD patients (on and off-state)	Activities od daily living	Support Vector Machine (SVM)	93.8% sensitivity 90.1% specificity
(Kim et al. 2018) [17]	Smartphone/trouser pocket	32 PD patients	walking, turning around, opening and entering doors	Convolutional Neural Network (CNN)	93.8% sensitivity 90.1% specificity
(Xia et al. 2018) [39]	3D accelerometers and 3D gyroscope (left thigh and shank, and belt) earphones	11 PD patients (8 off-state 2 on-state)	Walking -Straight line -Random walk -Entering and exiting rooms	CNN	69.3% sensitivity 90.60% specificity
(Camps et al. 2018) [6]	One accelerometer/waist left side	21 PD patients	walking and complex activities	CNN	91.9% sensitivity 89.5% specificity
(Hu et al. 2019) [16]	Clinical videos	45 PD patients	TUG activities	Graph CNN	81.9% sensitivity 82.1% specificity
(Sun et al. 2018) [34]	Clinical videos	45 PD patients	TUG activities	3-dimensional CNN	81.9% sensitivity 82.1% specificity
(Tahir et al. 2019) [36]	CSI measurements of WiFi devices	15 PD patients	TUG activities	Graph CNN	81.9% sensitivity 82.1% specificity

Table 2 shows a summary of the previous works based on FOG detection using artificial intelligence techniques. The table consists of the equipment and placement, the number and type of subjects, the activities and conditions, the methods employed for FOG detection, and the results obtained in the studies.

FOG Prediction. There are fewer works addressing FOG prediction than those related to FOG detection. Acevedo et al. [3] highlight the importance of predicting FOG instead of detecting it to provide cues on real-time preventing FOG events from happening and therefore, diminishing fall risk.

Table 3 summarizes some important works described below related to FOG prediction in PD patients. The table contains information about equipment and placement, type of subjects, activities and conditions, methods implemented for FOG prediction, and obtained results.

In the work of Assam and Seidl [2], the authors proposed a robust FOG predictive model in PD patients. They used wavelets to predict and extract unique signature features for FOG. In the same way, Handojoseno et al. [15] used electroencephalography (EEG) to predict FOG using wavelets and other spectral features obtained from the Fourier transform of the EEG signals.

Mazilu et al. [21] presented an interesting method that included an electrocardiography (ECG) and a skin conductance analysis to find statistical differences before an episode of FOG. The prediction, however, had exploratory results using the one-way analysis of variance (ANOVA) and mutual information.

Zia et al. [41] proposed layered recurrent networks (LRN), a special type of neural networks, for predicting FOG in PD patients. The underlying of using this machine learning model is that LRN can capture time dependencies on signals from 3D accelerometers placed in the body.

In [25], Palmerini et al. used inertial sensors to identify and quantify gait characteristics before FOG occur based in a threshold method, i.e. linear discriminant analysis. The results were preliminary and no prediction system has been built with this method.

Using deep learning, Torvi et al. [37] studied the performance of Long Short-Term Memory (LSTM) architectures and domain adaptation algorithms to predict FOG episodes in PD patients. They used transfer learning schemes to develop a prediction model for a particular subject.

3   Trends, Challenges and Opportunities Regarding FOG Detection and Prediction

In this section, we compile the trends, challenges and opportunities regarding FOG detection and prediction, from the relevant works described above.

3.1   Trends

Sensors. From the review of the previous describe works, we can observe that accelerometers, gyroscopes and magnetometers are the most commonly used sensors for FOG detection and prediction. Nevertheless, other sensors are implemented, namely electroencephalography (EEG) [14] and electromyography (EMG) [7]. In order to build a less obtrusive system, some authors are using sensors embedded in smartphones to collect PD patients data [17,22,28]. Furthermore, wearable sensors and smartphones need to be worn or carried by the patient continuously. This makes them uncomfortable. To address these issues vision-based approaches, like the systems proposed by Hu et al. [16] and Sun et al. [34], have been studied. However, these systems are sensitive to lighting conditions, obstructions and have privacy issues [36]. New modalities of data collection have been explored to address all these inconveniences like CSI measurements of WiFi devices presented by Tahir et al. [36].

Table 3. Works in FOG prediction.

Author/Year	Equipment/ Placement	Subjects	Activity/ conditions	Methods	Results
(Assam and Seidl 2014) [2]	3D accelerometers in shank, thigh, lower back	DAPHNet dataset 10 PD patients	Walking: -Straight line, -Random walk, -Entering and exiting rooms	Wavelets	Overall performance of over 90%
(Handojoseno et al. 2015) [15]	4-channel electroen-cephalography (EEG) on head	16 PD patients	Walking	Fourier transform, wavelets	Sensitivity of 86%, specificity of 74.4%, accuracy of 80.2%
(Mazilu et al. 2015) [21]	Electrocardiography (ECG) and skin-conductance in chest and fingers	CuPiD dataset with 11 PD patients	Walking: -Ziegler protocol, -Figure eight, -Straight line, -Circles, -Random walk	One-way analysis of variance and mutual information	Overall performance of 71.3%
(Zia et al. 2016) [41]	3D accelerometers in shank, thigh, lower back	DAPHNet dataset with only 3 PD patients	Walking: -Straight line, -Random walk, -Entering and exiting rooms	Layered recurrent networks	overall precision of 62.7%, Overall sensitivity of 34.7%
(Palmerini et al. 2017) [25]	3 inertial wearables in lower back and two shins	CuPiD dataset with 11 PD patients	Walking: -Ziegler protocol, -Figure eight, -Straight line, -Circles, -Random walk	Linear discriminant analysis classifier	AUC of 76%, sensitivity of 83%, specificity of 67%
(Torvi et al. 2018) [37]	3D accelerometers in shank, thigh, lower back	DAPHNet dataset 10 PD patients	Walking: -Straight line, -Random walk, -Entering and exiting rooms	LSTM and transfer learning	Overall performance of over 90%

Algorithms. During the first decade of the 2000s, most algorithms were based on hand-crafted statistical features and simple threshold on the freezing index or rule-based algorithms, see Table 1. In the second decade of the 2000s, artificial intelligence methods became relevant for FOG detection and prediction. Fuzzy logic in conjunction with threshold methods was used by Pepa et al. [28]. Well-known machine learning classifiers such as decision trees, RF, SVM, MLP, and Näive Bayes were also used to address the FOG detection problem, as shown in Table 2. Hence, more recently, deep learning approaches have gained interest to manage this problem. CNNs are the preferred method for FOG detection.

3.2 Challenges

The characteristics of human gait pattern are highly particular for each person [37]. FOG events are also influenced by the state of patient medication (On an Off), the severity of Parkinson's disease, and other personal factors. Experimental protocols must take these variables into account to improve the quality of machine learning models.

The creation of data sets using subjects with different characteristics, diverse modalities, and more participants, is recommended for the development of FOG detection and prediction systems, and for a better comparison between their models. It is unpractical and difficult to study FOG events in real life because FOG episodes are difficult to provoke [8]. Since databases are usually unbalanced, data augmentation strategies can be useful to address this issue. Additionally, as participants are PD patients, ethical and medical aspects must be carefully considered.

Each data collection modality has drawbacks as stated above. For example, acceleration sensors must be calibrated for each subject when using threshold methods. Some methods of acquirement can be used indoors and other outdoors. Nevertheless, it is important to develop practical systems to monitor PD patients to detect and predict FOG in order to allow an independent and secure life. These systems must be usable and accurate [31].

3.3   Opportunities

Detection vs Prediction. As described in this review, there are two main focuses of research around FOG in PD patients: detection and prediction. In the first case, FOG episodes are discriminated from other activities, while in the second, FOG episodes are predicted for preventing possible issues on health. It is clear that FOG detection has been studied more than FOG prediction. But, it is important and relevant for this active area of research, to anticipate FOG events in order to prevent falls or injuries in subjects. Thus, new perspectives and studies are required for a better understanding of how to predict FOG episodes in a less obtrusive and more accurate fashion.

Robust Methods. In the same way, since FOG prediction is crucial in the development of systems for prevention, new and better methods are required. As shown in this review, artificial intelligence methods and, specifically, those related to machine and deep learning approaches are being implemented. These methods are important because they can tackle complex problems related to the variations of gait from person to person. Also, they have been more accurate models than before, and they can work with images and not only with sensor signals. In addition, a key feature in deep learning approaches is transfer learning, specially, when dealing with FOG prediction in different people's gaits. Thus, there are opportunities in the development and implementation of new and robust artificial intelligence methods focusing on FOG prediction.

4   Conclusions

In this paper, we reviewed the state-of-the-art in FOG detection and prediction. We mainly focused our attention on the types of sensors used (i.e. wearables, vision-based and ambient sensors) and the methods employed (from threshold and statistical methods to artificial intelligence and deep learning approaches). This review includes the analysis of vision-based approaches that were not found in other surveys on the topic.

Furthermore, we identified trends in this research field such as the need for less obtrusive sensors and more accurate algorithms for FOG detection and prediction. In terms of challenges, we identified that thresholding impacts on the performance of FOG detection and prediction systems, that FOG depends on subject to subject, and that there are still many difficulties to use these systems in real life. Lastly, a few opportunities were pointed out to develop new FOG prediction systems as well as the implementation of robust methods.

For future work, we are considering to extend this review with other gait symptoms associated with PD, and to extend the details of the different artificial intelligence methods implemented in this research field.

References

1. Ahlrichs, C., et al.: Detecting freezing of gait with a tri-axial accelerometer in Parkinson's disease patients. Med. Biol. Eng. Comput. **54**(1), 223–233 (2016)
2. Assam, R., Seidl, T.: Prediction of freezing of gait from parkinson's disease movement time series using conditional random fields. In: Proceedings of the Third ACM SIGSPATIAL International Workshop on the Use of GIS in Public Health, pp. 11–20 (2014)
3. Azevedo Coste, C., Sijobert, B., Pissard-Gibollet, R., Pasquier, M., Espiau, B., Geny, C.: Detection of freezing of gait in parkinson disease: preliminary results. Sensors **14**(4), 6819–6827 (2014)
4. Bachlin, M., et al.: Potentials of enhanced context awareness in wearable assistants for parkinson's disease patients with the freezing of gait syndrome. In: 2009 International Symposium on Wearable Computers, pp. 123–130. IEEE (2009)
5. Bloem, B.R., Hausdorff, J.M., Visser, J.E., Giladi, N.: Falls and freezing of gait in Parkinson's disease: a review of two interconnected, episodic phenomena. Move. Disord.: Off. J. Move. Disord. Soc. **19**(8), 871–884 (2004)
6. Camps, J., et al.: Deep learning for freezing of gait detection in Parkinson's disease patients in their homes using a waist-worn inertial measurement unit. Knowl.-Based Syst. **139**, 119–131 (2018)
7. Cole, B.T., Roy, S.H., Nawab, S.H.: Detecting freezing-of-gait during unscripted and unconstrained activity. In: 2011 Annual International Conference of the IEEE Engineering in Medicine and Biology Society, pp. 5649–5652. IEEE (2011)
8. Delval, A., et al.: Objective detection of subtle freezing of gait episodes in Parkinson's disease. Mov. Disord. **25**(11), 1684–1693 (2010)
9. Djurić-Jovičić, M.D., Jovičić, N.S., Radovanović, S.M., Stanković, I.D., Popović, M.B., Kostić, V.S.: Automatic identification and classification of freezing of gait episodes in Parkinson's disease patients. IEEE Trans. Neural Syst. Rehabil. Eng. **22**(3), 685–694 (2013)
10. Espay, A.J., et al.: Technology in Parkinson's disease: challenges and opportunities. Mov. Disord. **31**(9), 1272–1282 (2016)
11. Forsaa, E., Larsen, J., Wentzel-Larsen, T., Alves, G.: A 12-year population-based study of freezing of gait in Parkinson's disease. Parkinsonism Relat. Disord. **21**(3), 254–258 (2015)
12. Ghai, S., Ghai, I., Schmitz, G., Effenberg, A.O.: Effect of rhythmic auditory cueing on parkinsonian gait: a systematic review and meta-analysis. Sci. Rep. **8**(1), 1–19 (2018)

13. Han, J.H., Lee, W.J., Ahn, T.B., Jeon, B.S., Park, K.S.: Gait analysis for freezing detection in patients with movement disorder using three dimensional acceleration system. In: Proceedings of the 25th Annual International Conference of the IEEE Engineering in Medicine and Biology Society (IEEE Cat. No. 03CH37439), vol. 2, pp. 1863–1865. IEEE (2003)

14. Handojoseno, A.A., Shine, J.M., Nguyen, T.N., Tran, Y., Lewis, S.J., Nguyen, H.T.: The detection of freezing of gait in Parkinson's disease patients using EEG signals based on wavelet decomposition. In: 2012 Annual International Conference of the IEEE Engineering in Medicine and Biology Society, pp. 69–72. IEEE (2012)

15. Handojoseno, A.A., Shine, J.M., Nguyen, T.N., Tran, Y., Lewis, S.J., Nguyen, H.T.: Analysis and prediction of the freezing of gait using eeg brain dynamics. IEEE Trans. Neural Syst. Rehabil. Eng. **23**(5), 887–896 (2014)

16. Hu, K., et al.: Vision-based freezing of gait detection with anatomic directed graph representation. IEEE J. Biomed. Health Inf. **24**(4), 1215–1225 (2019)

17. Kim, H.B., et al.: Validation of freezing-of-gait monitoring using smartphone. Telemed. e-Health **24**(11), 899–907 (2018)

18. Latt, M.D., Lord, S.R., Morris, J.G., Fung, V.S.: Clinical and physiological assessments for elucidating falls risk in Parkinson's disease. Movem. Disord.: Off. J. Move. Disord. Soc. **24**(9), 1280–1289 (2009)

19. Macht, M., et al.: Predictors of freezing in Parkinson's disease: a survey of 6,620 patients. Mov. Disord. **22**(7), 953–956 (2007)

20. Masiala, S., Huijbers, W., Atzmueller, M.: Feature-set-engineering for detecting freezing of gait in parkinson's disease using deep recurrent neural networks. arXiv preprint arXiv:1909.03428 (2019)

21. Mazilu, S., Calatroni, A., Gazit, E., Mirelman, A., Hausdorff, J.M., Tröster, G.: Prediction of freezing of gait in Parkinson's from physiological wearables: an exploratory study. IEEE J. Biomed. Health Inf. **19**(6), 1843–1854 (2015)

22. Mazilu, S., et al.: Online detection of freezing of gait with smartphones and machine learning techniques. In: 2012 6th International Conference on Pervasive Computing Technologies for Healthcare (PervasiveHealth) and Workshops, pp. 123–130. IEEE (2012)

23. Moore, S.T., MacDougall, H.G., Ondo, W.G.: Ambulatory monitoring of freezing of gait in Parkinson's disease. J. Neurosci. Methods **167**(2), 340–348 (2008)

24. Nutt, J.G., Bloem, B.R., Giladi, N., Hallett, M., Horak, F.B., Nieuwboer, A.: Freezing of gait: moving forward on a mysterious clinical phenomenon. Lancet Neurol. **10**(8), 734–744 (2011)

25. Palmerini, L., Rocchi, L., Mazilu, S., Gazit, E., Hausdorff, J.M., Chiari, L.: Identification of characteristic motor patterns preceding freezing of gait in Parkinson's disease using wearable sensors. Front. Neurol. **8**, 394 (2017)

26. Pardoel, S., Kofman, J., Nantel, J., Lemaire, E.D.: Wearable-sensor-based detection and prediction of freezing of gait in Parkinson's disease: a review. Sensors **19**(23), 5141 (2019)

27. Paul, S.S., Canning, C.G., Sherrington, C., Lord, S.R., Close, J.C., Fung, V.S.: Three simple clinical tests to accurately predict falls in people with Parkinson's disease. Mov. Disord. **28**(5), 655–662 (2013)

28. Pepa, L., Ciabattoni, L., Verdini, F., Capecci, M., Ceravolo, M.: Smartphone based fuzzy logic freezing of gait detection in Parkinson's disease. In: 2014 IEEE/ASME 10th International Conference on Mechatronic and Embedded Systems and Applications (MESA), pp. 1–6. IEEE (2014)

29. Pereira, C.R., Pereira, D.R., Weber, S.A., Hook, C., de Albuquerque, V.H.C., Papa, J.P.: A survey on computer-assisted parkinson's disease diagnosis. Artif. Intell. Med. **95**, 48–63 (2019)

30. Pham, T.T., et al.: Freezing of gait detection in Parkinson's disease: a subject-independent detector using anomaly scores. IEEE Trans. Biomed. Eng. **64**(11), 2719–2728 (2017)

31. Rodríguez-Martín, D., et al.: Home detection of freezing of gait using support vector machines through a single waist-worn triaxial accelerometer. PloS One **12**(2), e0171764 (2017)

32. Schaafsma, J., Balash, Y., Gurevich, T., Bartels, A., Hausdorff, J.M., Giladi, N.: Characterization of freezing of gait subtypes and the response of each to levodopa in parkinson's disease. Eur. J. Neurol. **10**(4), 391–398 (2003)

33. Sigcha, L., Costa, N., Pavón, I., Costa, S., Arezes, P., López, J.M., De Arcas, G.: Deep learning approaches for detecting freezing of gait in Parkinson's disease patients through on-body acceleration sensors. Sensors **20**(7), 1895 (2020)

34. Sun, R., Wang, Z., Martens, K.E., Lewis, S.: Convolutional 3D attention network for video based freezing of gait recognition. In: 2018 Digital Image Computing: Techniques and Applications (DICTA), pp. 1–7. IEEE (2018)

35. Sweeney, D., Quinlan, L.R., Browne, P., Richardson, M., Meskell, P., ÓLaighin, G., et al.: A technological review of wearable cueing devices addressing freezing of gait in Parkinson's disease. Sensors **19**(6), 1277 (2019)

36. Tahir, A., et al.: WiFreeze: multiresolution scalograms for freezing of gait detection in Parkinson's leveraging 5G spectrum with deep learning. Electronics **8**(12), 1433 (2019)

37. Torvi, V.G., Bhattacharya, A., Chakraborty, S.: Deep domain adaptation to predict freezing of gait in patients with Parkinson's disease. In: 2018 17th IEEE International Conference on Machine Learning and Applications (ICMLA), pp. 1001–1006. IEEE (2018)

38. Weiss, D., et al.: Freezing of gait: understanding the complexity of an enigmatic phenomenon. Brain **143**(1), 14–30 (2020)

39. Xia, Y., Zhang, J., Ye, Q., Cheng, N., Lu, Y., Zhang, D.: Evaluation of deep convolutional neural networks for detection of freezing of gait in Parkinson's disease patients. Biomed. Signal Process. Control **46**, 221–230 (2018)

40. Zach, H., et al.: Identifying freezing of gait in parkinson's disease during freezing provoking tasks using waist-mounted accelerometry. Parkinsonism Relat. Disord. **21**(11), 1362–1366 (2015)

41. Zia, J., Tadayon, A., McDaniel, T., Panchanathan, S.: Utilizing neural networks to predict freezing of gait in Parkinson's patients. In: Proceedings of the 18th International ACM SIGACCESS Conference on Computers and Accessibility, pp. 333–334 (2016)

ZeChipC: Time Series Interpolation Method Based on Lebesgue Sampling

Luis Miralles-Pechuán[1]($\boxtimes$) , Matthieu Bellucci[1], M. Atif Qureshi[2] ,
and Brian Mac Namee[1]

[1] Ireland's Centre for Applied AI (CeADAR), University College Dublin,
Dublin, Ireland
{luis.miralles,brian.macnamee}@ucd.ie
matthieu.bellucci@gmail.com

[2] Ireland's Centre for Applied AI (CeADAR), Technological University Dublin,
Dublin, Ireland
MuhammadAtif.Qureshi@tudublin.ie

Abstract. In this paper, we present an interpolation method based on Lebesgue sampling that could help to develop systems based time series more efficiently. Our methods can transmit times series, frequently used in health monitoring, with the same level of accuracy but using much fewer data. Our method is based in Lebesgue sampling, which collects information depending on the values of the signal (e.g. the signal output is sampled when it crosses specific limits). Lebesgue sampling contains additional information about the shape of the signal in-between two sampled points. Using this information would allow generating an interpolated signal closer to the original one. In our contribution, we propose a novel time-series interpolation method designed explicitly for Lebesgue sampling called ZeChipC. ZeChipC is a combination of Zero-order hold and Piecewise Cubic Hermite Interpolating Polynomial (PCHIP) interpolation. ZeChipC includes new functionality to adapt the reconstructed signal to concave/convex regions. The proposed methods have been compared with state-of-the-art interpolation methods using Lebesgue sampling and have offered higher average performance.

Keywords: Lebesgue sampling interpolation method · Event-based interpolation · Signal reconstruction using Lebesgue sampling · Time series interpolation method

1 Introduction

Nowadays, a lot of time series data is produced, which represents the state of the environment over a period of time [1,2]. These data points are generally captured by a piece of equipment called a sensor. The sensor can detect different events or changes in the environment and quantify the changes in the form of various

M. Atif Qureshi—Senior Author and provided level of mentorship.

L. Martínez-Villaseñor et al. (Eds.): MICAI 2020, LNAI 12468, pp. 182–196, 2020.
https://doi.org/10.1007/978-3-030-60884-2_14

measures such as temperature, pressure, noise, or light intensity. A limitation of collecting data points is the frequency at which the sensor records the changes or events. The more frequently a sensor records a reading, the more expensive the running cost is. Likewise, the less frequent the sensor records the reading, the more difficult it is to capture and reconstruct the original behaviour of the event.

In practice, all signals have to be sampled because the number of points in a continuous environment is infinite. Capturing readings more often is economically more expensive due to the amount of data being stored, transmitted, and processed. The challenge while performing sampling is to preserve the vital information in the less amount of data points so that the objective of recording changes is met.

The periodic or Riemann sampling [5] is a conventional approach of sampling in the time series data. In this approach, the data is captured periodically, i.e. at an equidistant time intervals such as each second or each microsecond. Even though the approach is simple to implement, the shortcoming is that, when the sampled data fail to indicate changes that happen between the interval (also known as frequency aliasing), sampling needs to be readjusted at a higher frequency, resulting into more data collection. Due to this pitfall, many research findings advocated for the use of Lebesgue sampling, instead of Riemann sampling [7].

In the Lebesgue sampling, time-series data is sampled whenever a significant change takes place or when the measurement passes a certain limit [6]. The overall intuition of the Lebesgue sampling is to save unnecessary data from being stored, processed, or transmitted, which represents either no change or a trivial change compared to the previous data point.

In this contribution, it is proposed an interpolation method called ZeChipC to reconstruct the time series data sampled using Lebesgue sampling. ZeChipC uses **Ze**ro-order hold and **PChip** interpolation with a **C**oncavity/Convexity functionality improvement[1]. To the best of our knowledge, this is the first interpolation method designed exclusively for Lebesgue sampling. The proposed methods have a higher performance because they exploit the particular properties of this kind of sampling.

The rest of the paper is organised as follows. In Sect. 2, it has been elaborated a review of the state-of-the-art about the Lebesgue sampling technique. In Sect. 3, it is presented the proposed interpolation method called ZeChipC, along with its simpler versions (ZeLi, ZeLiC and ZeChip). In Sect. 4, two experiments using 67 different data sets are carried out. The objective of the first experiment is to compare the performance of the proposed methods against that of the state-of-the-art interpolation methods for Lebesgue sampling. The objective of the second experiment is used to compare the performance of Lebesgue and Riemann sampling with approximately the same number of samples and with the same methods. This is very useful in order to decide which is the best

---

[1] The implementation code for the proposed algorithms can be found in: https://github.com/shamrodia74/ZeLiC.

combination of sampling and interpolation methods when time series need to be sampled. Finally, in Sect. 5, the conclusions of the research are shown along with some possible future directions.

2   State of the Art

Lebesgue sampling is an alternative to the traditional approach called Riemann, which samples time series at a constant frequency. Instead of periodically taking samples from a system like most health monitoring systems, the event-based method takes samples only when a predefined event happens, as shown in Fig. 1. Some examples of typical events could be a sudden change in the signal, the signal reaching a preset limit, the arrival of a data package, or a change in the state of a system [1]. Even though Lebesgue sampling is more accurate than Riemann sampling, it is less extended because it is more difficult to implement [1]. Sampling using methods based on Lebesgue will allow developing systems with many advantages such as lower energy consumption and less bandwidth required. In systems based on Lebesgue less information needs to be processed, transmitted and stored.

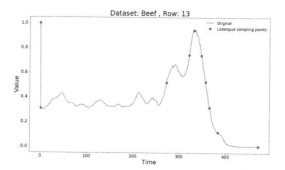

Fig. 1. Lebesgue sampling takes points based on the output value of the signal. In this particular case, when the absolute difference is higher than 0.2.

In recent years, a great interest has aroused in applications implementing event-based sampling. For example, the "Send on Delta" algorithm takes advantage of Lebesgue sampling to reduce the information transmitted by wireless networks, frequently used in health monitoring systems, in order to increase the lifetime of the sensors' batteries. Under this scheme, the sampling is performed only when there is a deviation in the signal higher than the delta value. Results show that by using this approach, it is possible to increase the lifetime of the sensors without any loss of quality in the resolution of the signals [8].

It is also interesting pointing out the convenience of using event-based sampling in the Fault Diagnosis and Prognosis (FDP) which are widely applied in the daily care of elderly (e.g. fall detection or human activity detection). In the last years, it has been increasingly difficult to manage microcontrollers and embedded systems due to the volume of the information collected by sensors and to the complexity of the programs that they implement [13].

Lebesgue sampling can minimise energy consumption, storage space, computation time and the amount of data to be transmitted which turns out into enormous advantages for the development of systems that require to collect time-series related to heath attributes [12]. It is therefore very interesting for companies who are in charge of developing health systems, as it significantly reduces the expense, without a negative impact on the precision of the measures.

In summary, the traditional approach for sampling and digital control has been working well in many applications in the health domain for many years. However, there are new domains where Riemann sampling has significant problems that can be easily solved by implementing Lebesgue sampling.

3   ZeChipC Lebesgue Sampling Interpolation Method

In this section, first, we give some information that can be extracted from sampling based on events to develop methods that either need less sampled points to achieve a similar accuracy level than the state-of-the-art methods or that given the same amount of points, achieve higher accuracy. For the sake of the reading understanding, in the following lines, we will explain all the previously developed methods until we finally developed the ZeChipC algorithm. Therefore, we first describe in detail the development of ZeLi, our first and simplest interpolation method proposed for Lebesgue sampling. Following, we describe ZeLiC, which is an improved version of ZeLi with new functionality to adapt it to convex and concave regions. And lastly, we propose a method called ZeChipC, which is basically an adaptation of ZeLiC that uses PCHIP instead of Linear interpolation so that it can represent signals with curve regions.

3.1   Tolerated Region

In order to understand how ZeLi (our first method) works, we have to introduce a new concept called tolerated region and why is it important for ZeLi. There are many possible implementations of Lebesgue sampling for time series such as sampling a point when it crosses a preset limit or when the percentage variation is higher than a given threshold. Our particular implementation of Lebesgue sampling is based on the variation of the signal. In other words, when the sensor detects that a point has a difference from the previous sampled point greater than a given threshold, then the point is captured. We can express this same idea in mathematical terms in the following way. Let y_i be the first sample of a signal and t the threshold, where $t > 0$. Then, the sensor captures the next point called y_{i+1} if and only if $|y_{i+1} - y_i| \geq t$.

Lebesgue sampling indirectly gives information on the behaviour of the signal between the two consecutive samples. It can be deduced that all the points between two pair of consecutive sampled points (not necessarily consecutive in time intervals) are inside an interval delimited by the threshold, as shown in Fig. 2.

We know this because if the value of a point of the interval was out of the interval, this point would have been captured. Just remember that points are not sampled while the signal stays inside this allowed region. The *tolerated region* can be defined as $[y_i - t, y_i + t]$, where t (threshold) is the maximum allowed value of change.

As shown in Fig. 2, if the difference between two consecutive sampled points a and b of a time series is very large in a given interval, we know that an abrupt change has happened (otherwise the point would have been collected earlier). On the other hand, if the difference between the sampled points is very small, it is quite probable that a smooth change has taken place. This simple principle is the basis on which our interpolation algorithms for Lebesgue sampling (ZeLi, ZeLiC, ZeChip, and ZeChipC) have been developed.

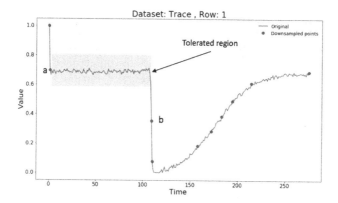

Fig. 2. The point b is very far away from the tolerated region of the point a, so we can deduce that an abrupt change has taken place.

In other words, any y in the interval I between the two points is inside the tolerated region. We can therefore significantly reduced the region of the possible values of y when performing the interpolation and therefore reducing the error when comparing the original signal with the reconstructed one.

3.2   ZeLi Interpolation Algorithm

From the information that can be extracted from the tolerance region, we will develop a set of methods to interpolate time series sampled with the Lebesgue approach. The simplest method and the first that is going to be explained is called ZeLi. The rest of the methods are improvements with respect to this first method.

Combination of Zero-Order Hold and Linear Interpolation. ZeLi interpolation combines **Ze**ro-order hold interpolation and **Li**near interpolation, which explains the origin of its name to reconstruct the original signal from the sampled signal as shown in Fig. 3. To decide whether to apply Zero-order hold (ZOH) or Linear interpolation, the *tolerance ratio* parameter is used. The *tolerance ratio* is a constant value that multiplies the interval of the tolerated region, that is: $[(y_i - t) * tolerance\,ratio, (y_i + t) * tolerance\,ratio]$, creating a new interval called increased tolerated region.

Therefore, the ZeLi algorithm contemplates two possible cases:

1. If the examined point is outside of the increased tolerance region, then ZOH interpolation is used.
2. Otherwise, Linear interpolation is used.

The justification of the algorithm is as follows. We know that all the points between two captured points should be in the tolerated region. If the difference between the values of the points is small, it is quite possible that between the two sampled points the signal follows a linear trend with small variations around it, therefore Linear interpolation is used. On the other hand, to minimise the error when the difference between the two sample points is very large (an abrupt change is presented), we interpolate all the points using ZOH. Although ZOH interpolation does not represent continuous signals in a smooth way, it is a very effective mechanism since it satisfies that all the values of the interval between a given point and the next point [a,b) are in the tolerated region. ZOH interpolation minimises the error because it keeps all the values in the middle of the tolerated region R_i, dividing by two the maximal possible error.

A visual intuition of this method can be seen in Fig. 3. When the signal crosses the threshold in a continuous way, Linear interpolation would be used. This is because it can be assumed that the values of the previous points close to b will have similar values (obviously, the further those points are from b, the less probable this assumption would be). By contrast, if an abrupt change is presented, then the last but one point and all the previous points were somewhere in the limited region R_i. However, we cannot deduce a trend because the change is so abrupt. Due to this lack of information, we choose to minimise the maximal error by using ZOH interpolation. Since ZOH interpolation uses a horizontal line (same values for y-axis for all the points of the region) followed by a straight line to interpolate.

3.3 ZeLiC Interpolation Method

One of the disadvantages of using simple methods such as linear interpolation and ZOH is that they are not able to adapt smoothly to the signal when there is a change in the sign of the slope. To sort this out, we have developed new functionality to improve the performance of ZeLi when convex/concave regions are presented.

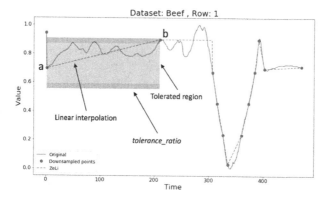

Fig. 3. ZeLi combines ZOH with Lineal interpolation. Between a and b ZeLi applies Line interpolation.

Convex/Concave Regions on Time Series. The shape of the signal when a slope change is presented is generally a convex or concave region. When Lebesgue sampling is used, a lack of information about the shape of the signal is presented when the signal changes the sign of the slope between two sampled points x_i and x_{i+1}, and that change takes place inside the tolerance region (i.e. before the signal hits the threshold). Additionally, neither Linear nor ZOH are able to adapt to convex or concave regions of a signal since those two methods connect the pairs of points individually.

In order to improve the adaptation of the proposed methods, we have studied the case of convexity and concavity, which are the inflexion points of a function. A function is convex if the line segment between any two points on the graph of the function lies above or on the graph. If we assume that the function f follows the trend of the sampled points, that is to say, if the values of f for a particular region are decreasing and, at some point, they start increasing, then, we can assume that f is convex on the interval I_i. At this point, it is important to remind that this is based on assumptions, we do not have enough information to support the assumptions, except the values and position of the sampled points.

3.4 ZeChip Interpolation Algorithm

ZeLi is based on a combination of ZOH and Linear interpolation, and in consequence, it shares some limitations of those type of interpolation. ZeLi is able to approximate time series with a high precision when they are composed of straight lines, that is to say, signals for which their first and second derivative present very constant values. However, when the signal function has curved lines, it is not possible to represent it using ZeLi.

We can apply the same idea of combining two interpolation methods as in ZeLi but replacing Linear interpolation with PCHIP interpolation. This new method is called ZeChip and is able to adapt much better to those signals that present curves regions. In addition, the new method will include the advantages of PCHIP; a fast and powerful interpolation method that allows to represent regions using curved lines and obtaining a great precision. One of the shortcomings of ZeChip with respect to ZeLi is that, because it uses PCHIP interpolation instead of Linear interpolation, it has a higher complexity cost. Therefore, for the same given points, ZeChip will take more time to generate the interpolated signal than ZeLi.

4   Experiments

So far, we have discussed our proposed methods from a theoretical perspective. Still, to have certain evidence that our contribution can have a meaningful impact, we need to demonstrate that the proposed methods have a better general performance than that of the state-of-the-art. To this end, we have decided to perform the experiments using a large number of databases. We want to test the performance of our models against other interpolation methods under Lebesgue sampling. Besides that, we want to compare the performance of our method with Lebesgue sampling with the performance of other interpolating methods with Riemann sampling with a similar number of samples, so we can recommend that approach when time series need to be sampled.

4.1   Preparation of the Experiments

To perform the experiments, we followed the methodology explained in Fig. 4. First, we downsampled the original time series (using Lebesgue or Riemann sampling), then we reconstructed the original signals from the downsampled data (using Linear, PCHIP, ZOH... interpolation methods) and finally, we compared the original signal with the reconstructed one, using RMSE, to evaluate the performance of the different interpolation methods.

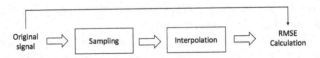

Fig. 4. The methodology to calculate the best interpolation method is based on the RMSE between the original signal and the reconstructed one.

There are many metrics in the state-of-the-art to calculate the difference between the original signal and the reconstructed signal. In this research, we applied a prevalent metric called root-mean-square-error (RMSE). The RMSE has been used in many research works to calculate the efficiency of the interpolation techniques [9,14]. To this end, all the signals of all the datasets have been individually normalised between "0" and "1".

In order to conduct the experiments, we applied some of the most popular time series interpolation methods in state of the art such as ZOH, Linear interpolation, PCHIP, Shannon, Lasso, Natural Neighbour, Cubic, Multiquadric, Inverse Multiquadric, Gaussian, Quintic and Thin-Plate. This functions have been implemented using the Radial Basis Function (RBF) approximation/interpolation in python based on the books [4] and [11].

We have applied two different approaches strategies to downsample the signals:

– Lebesgue sampling: Our implementation of Lebesgue sampling is based on the absolute difference between the sampled values.
– Riemann sampling: The Riemann sampling is performed by using the same (or slightly higher) average number of points than in Lebesgue sampling but using a fix time interval over time.

To perform the experiments, all the signals of all the datasets have been interpolated between "0" and "1". The values of the parameters for the developed methods (ZeLi, ZeLiC, ZeChip, and ZeChipC) were: *tolerance ratio = 1.15, min distance = 3, and previous distance = 3.*

The objective of the first experiment is to evaluate the performance of our proposed method for interpolating time series from Lebesgue sampling. To this end, we compared our methods with those of the state-of-the-art. In this experiment, we applied Lebesgue sampling based on the difference between the values with a threshold of 0.05^2.

The goal of the second experiment is a bit more ambitious than the one of the first experiment. We want to demonstrate that the best technique to interpolate and reconstruct any signal is to use Lebesgue sampling and our best-proposed method; ZeChipC. To this end, we will conduct a similar experiment to the first one, but this time with the same number of samples for both Lebesgue sampling and Riemann sampling. We will select 15% of the total samples of the signal for both Riemann and Lebesgue sampling. In the case of Lebesgue, we will tune the value of the threshold until selecting the same or slightly less (never more) number of samples than in Riemann sampling.

To carry out the experiments, we used Python 3.6.1 with Anaconda custom (x86_64). We used a MacBook with macOS High Sierra with the following features. 2.3 GHz Intel Core i5, 8 GB 2133 MHz, L2 Cache:256 KB, L3: 4 MB.

4.2 Data Sets

The experiments have been conducted over the 67 databases of a repository called "The UEA and UCR time series classification repository" [2]. Some of the datasets have the training set and the testing set to perform classification techniques. Since we are not doing classification, we have simply joined the training set and testing set in a single dataset for each dataset of the repository.

---

[2] Note that all the signals had been scaled between "0" and "1". From this perspective, 0.05 means a 5% difference in the maximum change between the possible values.

4.3   Experiment I

Figure 5 shows an illustrative summary of the performance of the best eight combinations of interpolation methods and sampling strategies. It could be possible that a method is strongly penalised in some dataset, and this will undermine its performance severely. To avoid this, we also calculated the average position, as displayed in Fig. 6. We can see that the position order of the median RMSE is the same as the order in terms of the average position of the Ranking.

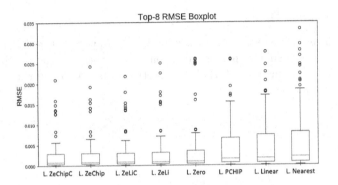

Fig. 5. Boxplot of the RMSE of the top-8 methods for all the 67 datasets, ordered by the median value.

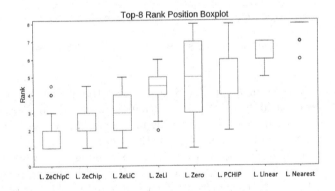

Fig. 6. Boxplot of the rank position of the top-8 methods for all the 67 datasets.

Figure 5 shows the box-plot of the RMSE score of the top-8 interpolation methods. In this plot, the interpolation methods are sorted by the 50th percentile, and from the Figure, it can be seen that ZeChipC performs best for the Lebesgue sampling and it produces least errors while reconstructing the signal. Furthermore, it can be observed that interquartile range is smaller in magnitude compared to the rest of methods and as well whisker is at lower RMSE value, which establishes that ZeChipC performs very well in the overall spread of the reconstruction from the sampled single.

Likewise, Fig. 6 shows a similar conclusion where ZeChipC is the winner in terms of the rank position of the reconstructed signal. The 50th percentile indicates that ZeChipC half of the time is a clear winner compared to the rest of the interpolation methods. Similarly, the interquartile range and the whisker establishes that overall ZeChipC outperforms the rest of the interpolation methods.

4.4   Experiment II

In this experiment, results are shown in the same way as in the first one. First, in Fig. 7, it is shown the performance based on the average RMSE of each combination (sampling and interpolation methods) using 15% of the samples for each of the 67 datasets.

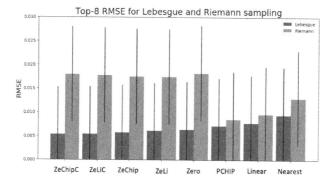

Fig. 7. RMSE of the top-8 methods for all the 67 datasets.

As in the first experiment, in Fig. 8, it is shown the average position of the best 12 methods of the dataset. We can see that the order of the positions of the Average Ranking is similar to that with the median RMSE value. For example, the order for the first eight combinations is the same.

We can also see that ZeChipC with Lebesgue sampling is the winner in terms of the rank position of the reconstructed signal. The 50th percentile shows that ZeChipC half of the time is the clear winner compared to the rest of the interpolation methods. Similarly, the interquartile range and the whisker establishes that overall ZeChipC outperforms the rest of the interpolation methods.

4.5   Discussion of the Experiments

The interpolation method that offers the best performance in both experiments is ZeChipC. This method implements three ideas that have been presented throughout the paper.

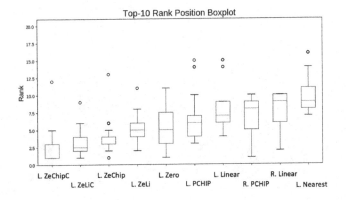

Fig. 8. Boxplot of the rank position of the top-10 methods for all the 67 datasets.

First, it uses ZOH interpolation, which allows ZeChipC to adapt to abrupt changes. This improvement is shared by the other three developed methods (ZeLi, ZeLiC and ZeChip), and it can be clearly appreciated when we compare in experiment I the performance of ZeLi against Linear interpolation or ZeChip against PCHIP interpolation. ZOH is the only interpolation technique that guarantees that all the points are in the tolerated region which allows representing the shape of the signal more accurately. We can see a clear example of this in Fig. 9 where PCHIP interpolation is out of the tolerated region while ZeChip is respecting it.

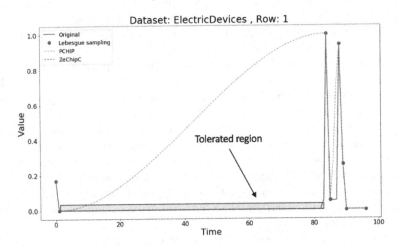

Fig. 9. PCHIP is interpolating outside the tolerated region and so, its performance is low.

Second, ZeChipC includes new functionality to adapt to concave and convex regions. It is interesting to see that this improvement means an increment of

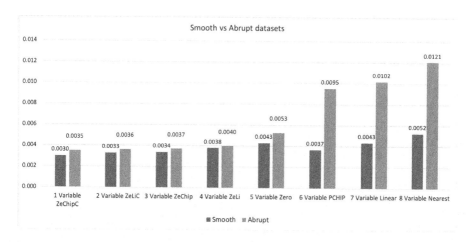

Fig. 10. Average RMSE of the 15 smoother datasets against the 15 abrupter ones.

8.06% of ZeChipC with respect ZeChip (which does not implement the convexity/concavity functionality) in the first experiment and of 7.36% in the second. In the same way, there is an improvement of ZeLiC against ZeLi of 10.88% and 10.89% in the first and second experiments respectively.

The third and last idea consists of implementing PCHIP interpolation instead of Linear interpolation. The increase in the performance of this approach can be appreciated when ZeChip is compared against ZeLi, and when ZeChipC is compared against ZeLiC. In the first experiment, ZeChip has an improvement of 8.82% against ZeLi while in the second experiment, it has an improvement of 5.94%. In the same way, ZeChipC has an improvement against ZeLiC of 5.94% in the first and of 2.22% in the second.

In addition, it is worth stressing that the ZOH interpolation is better than Linear interpolation and even better than PCHIP interpolation. In fact, it is better than any other interpolation technique when Lebesgue sampling is used. PCHIP is the second best and Linear the third best. This is a confirmation that using ZOH for the algorithms ZeChipC and ZeLiC (as well as ZeChip and ZeLi) as a combination of these methods is a good idea. Regarding the rest of the methods, it seems that Lebesgue PCHIP, variable near, variable linear and variable ZOH always remain ahead of the rest of the methods. Our results strengthen the claims regarding that sampling based on Lebesgue sampling is more accurate than Riemann sampling (either in fixed or uniform with the same number of samples).

On the other hand, we could think that ZeChipC is not better because for some data sets simply because it has been in a better average position. To argue for the ZeChipC we have two arguments. In the position ranking, it has won 53 times out of 67 in the first experiment and 37 in the second. Furthermore, if we see the average position, it has been the first method in both experiments, 2.18 in the first experiment and 2.63 in the second.

Lastly, time-series smoothness is a concept that has been studied in detail in several investigations [3]. One of the most frequent ways of measuring it, and the one applied in our research is by calculating the standard deviation of the differences between the points (1st derivative). The lower the SD, the smoother the time series is.

The differences between the proposed methods and the rest of the methods are enlarged when the databases have a large number of changes. As it is shown in Fig. 10, when the signals of a dataset have abrupt changes, the state-of-the-art methods do not "understand" that the change has occurred between the last tracked point and the previous instant and as a result, the signal is drawn out of the tolerance region as shown in Fig. 9.

5   Conclusion

Throughout this investigation, we have developed an interpolation methodology that requires a smaller number of samples to achieve the same precision. This methodology is a solid basis on which systems related to ambient assisted living could be developed. Those systems could monitor time series related to health user attributes such as blood pressure, respiration, temperature, etc. but requiring fewer samples which makes them more efficient.

The main reason why the developed methods (ZeLi, ZeLiC, ZeChip and ZeChipC) have better results compared to the other interpolation methods is that the interpolation is performed by taking into account the Lebesgue sampling characteristics. That is to say, when there is an abrupt change ZOH interpolation is applied, otherwise (when there is a smooth change) Linear and PCHIP interpolation are applied. The proposed methods detect that there has been an abrupt change because the newly captured sample is far away from the tolerated region. Additionally, this decision can be optimised depending on the dataset using the tolerance ratio parameter.

On the other hand, the convexity/concavity functionality has performed very well. We can guess that when there is a change of sign in the slope of a signal, a concavity/convexity region has happened. Additionally, accurately calculating the exact point where the signal changes the slope and approximating its shape is a very complex and wide issue, although the applied implementation performed very well and boosted the performance of both methods: ZeLiC and ZeChipC.

The developed methods have been implemented based on the absolute difference with respect to the last sampled point. However, it is easily adaptable to another kind of events in the health care domain that trigger sensors. For example, the sensor could be triggered when the output signal crosses a certain limit or when the percentage variation is higher than a preset limit. Using the same approach; Linear or PCHIP interpolation for smooth transitions and ZOH for abrupt changes will still be effective.

From the assumptions and contributions of this research, new and more effective interpolation methods could be designed. Lebesgue sampling is known in academia, but it is important to develop reliable and adapted tools to encourage the industry to make a transition to Lebesgue sampling.

Acknowledgements. This publication has emanated from research conducted with the support of Enterprise Ireland (EI), under Grant Number IP20160496 and TC20130013.

References

1. Åström, K.J., Bernhardsson, B.: Comparison of periodic and event based sampling for first-order stochastic systems. IFAC Proc. Volumes **32**(2), 5006–5011 (1999)
2. Bagnall, A., Lines, J., Vickers, W., Keogh, E.: The UEA and UCR time series classification repository (2018). http://timeseriesclassification.com. http://timeseriesclassification.com
3. Barnes, R.: Variogram tutorial. Golden, CO: Golden. Software. http://www.goldensoftware.com/variogramTutorial.pdf (2003)
4. Fasshauer, G.E.: Meshfree Approximation Methods with MATLAB, vol. 6. World Scientific, Singapore (2007)
5. Hamilton, J.D.: Time Series Analysis, vol. 2. Princeton University Press, Princeton (1994)
6. Heemels, W., Johansson, K.H., Tabuada, P.: An introduction to event-triggered and self-triggered control. In: 2012 IEEE 51st Annual Conference on Decision and Control (CDC), pp. 3270–3285. IEEE (2012)
7. Meng, X., Chen, T.: Optimal sampling and performance comparison of periodic and event based impulse control. IEEE Trans. Autom. Control **57**(12), 3252–3259 (2012)
8. Miskowicz, M.: Send-on-delta concept: an event-based data reporting strategy. Sensors **6**(1), 49–63 (2006)
9. Mühlenstädt, T., Kuhnt, S.: Kernel interpolation. Comput. Stat. Data Anal. **55**(11), 2962–2974 (2011)
10. Sayakkara, A., Miralles-Pechuán, L., Le-Khac, N.A., Scanlon, M.: Cutting through the emissions: feature selection from electromagnetic side-channel data for activity detection. Forensic Sci. Int. Digital Invest. **32**, 300927 (2020)
11. Schimek, M.G.: Smoothing and Regression: Approaches, Computation, and Application. Wiley, Hoboken (2013)
12. Yan, W., Zhang, B., Wang, X., Dou, W., Wang, J.: Lebesgue-sampling-based diagnosis and prognosis for lithium-ion batteries. IEEE Trans. Ind. Electron. **63**(3), 1804–1812 (2016)
13. Zhang, B., Wang, X.: Fault diagnosis and prognosis based on lebesgue sampling. University of South Carolina Columbia United States, Technical report (2014)
14. Žukovič, M., Hristopulos, D.: Environmental time series interpolation based on spartan random processes. Atmos. Environ. **42**(33), 7669–7678 (2008)

Machine Leaning Based Urdu Language Tutor for Primary School Students

Fatima Khalil[1], Farva Sardar[1], Mehreen Gull[1], Muhammad Aslam[1(✉)],
Nafees Ahmad[1], and A. M. Martinez-Enriquez[2]

[1] Department of CS, University of Engineering and Technology Lahore, Lahore, Pakistan
fatimakhalilahmedbutt@gmail.com, farvasardar495@gmail.com,
gmehreen06@gmail.com, maslam@uet.edu.pk, nafeesahmad361@yahoo.com
[2] Department of CS, CINVESTAV, Mexico City, Mexico
ammartin@cinvestav.mx

Abstract. Our proposed system is an offline android application named as "Urdu mu-all-um". The final design is demonstrated through various android mobiles. The application consists of writing and reading of Urdu alphabets and words as well as reading of counting, grammar, idioms, proverbs, phrases, vocabulary, dialogues and chat-bot in Urdu language. We designed reading module to teach pronunciation of Urdu alphabets, words, and counting by creating data sets which include images and media player chunks. Media player is recording of pronunciation for each alphabet, word, and counting. Writing module teaches the writing by tracing on the canvas that was developed through Android Studio. In addition to tracing, a sub-part for practice is added for evaluation of the user by creating a model on Jupyter using python in deep learning and tensor flow and then the model was deployed into Android Studio. The sections on grammar, idioms, proverbs, phrases, vocabulary and dialogues are designed by using data through web services. Urdu chat-bot is designed by using wit.ai framework and preact. The project provides different basics of the language that are imperative for learning Urdu at a single platform.

Keywords: Chat-bot · Evaluation · Media player · Tensor flow · Urdu language · Primary education · Online teaching and learning

1 Introduction

It is hard to think our existence without mobile phone. With the passage of time mobile phones are becoming more advance and brilliant. Smart phones is the type of mobile phones and are distinguished from feature phones because of its hardware and operating system (OS) [1]. Android mobile is a class of smart phones as it has Android OS installed in it. The phone today in our hand took a journey of 26 years to reach 2019. Kids as well as adults these days like to have an Android mobile. This gadget has proved helpful in learning but in addition to this, mobile phone has negative impact as well [2]. Android mobiles have play store to install Android apps. These apps are of different types.

© Springer Nature Switzerland AG 2020
L. Martínez-Villaseñor et al. (Eds.): MICAI 2020, LNAI 12468, pp. 197–207, 2020.
https://doi.org/10.1007/978-3-030-60884-2_15

One of them is education in this category of play store one can see learning apps. According to the most popular Google play store app categories research, educational apps take 8.95 of the percentage in the total share of apps used. This ratio shows the importance of educational apps in current time period [3].

In play store we can see number of apps related to language learning but when it comes for Urdu language, ratio is very small and the apps which are present there do not cover much of Urdu modules and data in a single application. People spend most of their time using smart phone either in learning, playing games or in free time [6]. This reason made us to develop an Android app that has maximum of the modules so we designed and developed "Urdu Mu-all-um". The developed app takes place in the times of Covid-19 staying at home, thinking that this can be very beneficial for teachers as well as students to learn reading and writing of Urdu language. "Urdu mu-all-um" is an Android app that has the following modules: writing, reading, Urdu grammar, idioms, proverbs, phrases, dialogues, chat-bot, and vocabulary.

The *Reading* module treats Urdu alphabets, words, and counting. Reading of alphabets is being taught by using a feature in Android studio media player. Similarly, Reading of words is being taught by using images. These images have the particular alphabet, word from that alphabet, and picture of object that is being taught. On the side of image there is a Speaker button, by clicking on the button audio of word can be hear multiple times. *Counting* is taught by the same technique by using image and voice. From 1 to 10, image and voice both are used but from 11 to 100 only voice is used. Next, *Writing* of alphabets and words. *Tracing* teaches users how to write Urdu alphabets and words, and the animation presents a demo of the writing [8]. This module includes a *Practice* feature too. In Practice, only empty screen is provided where a student can write Urdu and Evaluation feature will tell him/her the accuracy of work done. This feature is implemented by using Tensor Flow [4]. Next modules are Urdu grammar, idioms, proverbs, phrases, dialogues, and vocabulary. In all these modules, data is shown on the screen by using Web services. Web services means that data is uploaded on a Website instead of copying it in project folder so that it can be updated when needed so that after each app update, data automatically starts showing in app. Only selective data is added in each of these modules. For grammar there are noun (isam), verb (fail), hurf, sentence (jumla), meaning full words (kalma) and word (lafaz). For idioms and proverbs, five sentences from each alphabet is added. In case of phrases, some scenarios are added that are asking for help, greetings, saying thank you, solving a misunderstanding, and wishing someone something. For dialogues, the scenarios consider hospital, hotel, restaurant, shop, and for your introduction. The vocabulary includes 22 scenarios: name of days, name of months, periods of time, color name, fruits, vegetable, body parts, clothing, flowers, emotions, professions, food, family relations, animals, birds, common materials, furniture, health, personality types, spices, vehicles, and weather.

Last but not the least module in our project is the Urdu chat-bot. This chat-bot provides a platform where students can test/practice their Urdu learning Skills. This module helps students to know how to interact with people in different scenarios. This is designed by using wit.ai framework [11] and preact.

2 Related Work

Nowadays, there are many Android applications that helps us to learn Urdu by providing different functionality. These Android applications contain various features and functionalities. Some of the most prominent applications that are available on google play store are:

- Kids Urdu qaida and Urdu for kids
- Learn Urdu language-speak Urdu in 10 days
- Speak Urdu: learn Urdu language offline
- Learn Urdu
- Kids Urdu learner: Urdu qaida, games and poems.
- Learn Urdu alphabets with phonics
- Kids education learn Urdu alphabets

The most important feature provided by these applications is to help users to read, learn, and speak Urdu language, like Urdu alphabets, words, and counting with the help of pictures and phonics sound. Users also learn to pronounce fruits, animals, and color name. Moreover, these Urdu app also helps to understand and learn Urdu grammar. These apps also contain feature to learn to write Urdu alphabets with the help of Tracing. But there is no Urdu applications that cover all the aspects of Urdu language, for instance, there is no app that helps users to write, read, and speak Urdu in an easy way. Mostly, currently present apps mainly cover the reading part of Urdu learning and writing part of Urdu learning is mostly ignored in these apps. These Urdu applications did not focus on the basic structure of Urdu grammar. There is no module in these applications where the users can evaluate their learned skills in Urdu language. So, our goal is to build an Android application in a single platform to support users in learning how to read, write, and to speak Urdu language in the most easily and interesting way.

The most important constructed module is about writing that helps users to not only write Urdu alphabets and words with help of Tracing but users will also be able to check their writing skills in Urdu by practicing on Canvas [7]. Thus, writing module has two sub features that are Tracing and Evaluation. Tracing feature is basically for new users which are not familiar with Urdu language. There exist many methods to design Tracing modules. Android Studio provides different classes and libraries which can help us to draw. Android Studio allow to draw anything even it is some shape, path or bitmap with help of few classes and libraries. One of the most important class which we have used in the implementation of Tracing module is Canvas class. Canvas is a class in Android studio that helps to do 2D drawing of different objects on the screen.

We have designed the Tracing module in such way that user can draw on object of class and then we pass this object to the onDraw (Canvas) method of MyCanvas class [10]. But this feature is also present in many Urdu applications and we have taken the idea of Tracing module for our application from these Urdu applications and we have added an extra animation feature of Urdu alphabets/word in the Tracing module. These animations guide users about how to write/trace the given alphabet/words.

The goal of the second sub-feature of Writing module is the Evaluation, a very important functionality for our application. Current applications for Urdu learning provides Canvas/clear screen, on which users practice their learned skills, but there is no a functionality in these applications to evaluate the user skills in the Urdu language. So, we have designed a module to support users to check their skills in the language knowledge. The implemented Evaluation module is based on Deep Learning [5]. The main target of this machine learning technique is to understand and gather information about the structure of given data set and fit that dataset into a Model that helps in the design of a module which involves automate decision-making.

We have applied the supervised learning method for our application that trains the Models on the bases of given input data and output data that are labels defined by the developer. The main task of this method is to train the Model so that it will able to "learn" to find the errors by comparing its actual outputs with the "learned" outputs and with the help of this comparison we can improve our Model. In the Evaluation module, we have provided a clear screen/Canvas to users on which they can write alphabets and our trained Model will check the accuracy of the written alphabets.

The Reading is the next designed module and we have taken the help on this idea from the currently present Urdu applications. Mostly applications provide features which help users to read and speak the Urdu alphabets with the help of the phonics of alphabets and message type text. Some Urdu learning applications also provide features that support users to speak Urdu proverbs, idioms, and phrases with help of phonics and message type text. But there is no application which covers all the parts that can support users to read and speak Urdu properly. So, we have designed a Reading module for reading and speaking Urdu alphabet and words based on phonics and message type text. Moreover, we have designed a Grammar module for learning the Urdu grammar structure. For this purpose, we have used the object of class of MediaPlayer to control the playing of audios/videos.

Our Chatterbox module provides a platform where students can test/practice their Urdu learning skills. This Chatterbox teach students how to interact with people in different scenarios. The Chatterbox uses the withal framework and react as this framework was one of those frameworks which were supporting Urdu. This Chat bot module provides different scenarios for selection to start chatting with the bot.

3   Urdu Mu-all-um: Proposed Work

In this project, we are going to design and develop an Android application that will help the students or any person who wants to learn Urdu language. This application has different modules as menu that are writing, reading of Urdu grammar, idioms, proverbs, phrases, conversation, vocabulary and Chatbot. To accomplish this project and to develop an Android Application we divided the modules in following main parts:

– Tracing Module
– Evaluation Module
– Reading Urdu grammar, proverbs, idioms, phrases and dialogues
– Chatbot

Through Tracing, writing of words and alphabets is taught. By Evaluation, app is evaluating the accuracy of writing. In reading of Urdu grammar, proverbs, idioms, phrases and dialogues, web services are used. To develop the Chatbot, wit.ai framework is used [9].

Tracing Module: the writing sub-module helps users to learn how to write Urdu alphabets, words, and counting. There are many ways to implement the Tracing module, we mainly focus on Draw the paths/shapes/bitmap, on two ways:

1. View object in the layout file (XML).
2. On Canvas object and pass it to the onDraw (Canvas) method of related class.

The former uses a static/predefined graphics, i.e., for applications that do not change and remain static. Thus, it is good when we simply draw graphics without changing dynamically.

As our application's main focus is to allow the users to draw on their own and drawing on Canvas, we have used the second method to draw the paths/shapes/bitmap on Canvas object. It is best way, because users need to redraw the paths/shapes/bitmap. Basically, Canvas is a class in Android studio which helps to produce 2D drawing of different objects on the screen. We have designed and implemented the Tracing feature in Android studio based on four basic components:

- A bitmap or view that helps to hold the pixels of the part of screen where the Canvas has been drawn.
- A Canvas on which we can run the drawing commands.
- Drawing commands which gives the instruction to Canvas what to draw.
- Paint object that contains the information of style and color. It basically helps to draw shapes/paths on Canvas.

We have also used another method of Canvas class which is clipping (that defines geometrically which portion of the Canvas the user will be able to see in the view.) We have also used the class of Animation Drawable to display animation which help the user in Tracings (This animation will teach the user that how can we trace/write the given alphabet). The class of AnimationDrawable object, made possible to treat frame by frame animations with the help of graphics present in the Drawable folder of res directory of Android. We have defined the AnimationDrawable in XML file in the Drawable folder of res directory of Android that contain a single list of graphics, i.e., animation-list and series of nested items tags.

Evaluation Module: is the second sub-module of the Writing module, which allows users to check or evaluate their skills in Urdu writing. This module provides a clear screen/Canvas to users on which they can write alphabet and the Trained Model checks the accuracy of the written alphabet. There exist many ways to implement the Evaluation module. We have designed it with Deep learning [5] to understand and gather information about the structure of given dataset and fit that dataset into Model that can help us when we need to design a module which involves automate decision-making.

Deep learning is based on ANN applying supervised, unsupervised or semi-supervised learning process [5]. Neural Networks are arranged into hidden layers that contain the set of interconnected nodes to carry out the learning process. Our research focus in two mostly used learning process:

- Supervised learning Model trains labeled data.
- Unsupervised learning is trained on unlabeled data.

In Unsupervised Learning, given data is not labeled and the goal of the Unsupervised Learning is to understand and learn the hidden patterns in data-sets and to learn the features. But in our application, we have used the method of Supervised Learning in which we have provided the system with dataset with labels and system will be trained on this dataset and will "learn" to find the errors by comparing its actual outputs with the "learned" outputs and with the help of this comparison we can improve our Model. Deep learning contain networks that can do supervised learning from dataset. Deep learning is AI (Artificial Intelligence) function that can works in the same way as human brain and made decision on the basis of learned patterns. In deep learning, Models are trained with help of large set of data that is labeled and with help of neural network architectures that has many hidden layers. Deep Learning use neural network architectures, that's why deep learning Models are also known as deep neural networks. They are known as "deep" because there are many layers in the neural network which are hidden. The artificial neural networks in deep learning built and function like human brain with many hidden layers. We have used Tensor-flow [4] which is an open source platform to build and train Models and with it we can easily deploy our Models to Android studio. We have designed and implemented the module of Evaluation by implementing the following methods:

- Dataset to train the Model: We have downloaded data for training of our Model in Urdu from kaggle which contain more 50,000 images of Urdu alphabets and counting [5]. This dataset contain images of handwritten Urdu alphabets and counting that are 28×28 pixels in size.
- Creating the neural network architecture: Neural network architecture includes elements like number of layers in the network, number of nodes in each layer and pattern in which the nodes are connected between layers. As the concept of artificial neural network is originated from the working structure of human brain. In artificial neural network, nodes works in the same way as neurons. As brain works in a way that neurons pass the signals around the brain, nodes accepts some values from previous nodes as input and perform some operation on these values and then pass the new value to other nodes as output. We have designed neural network architecture for our Model in which each layer is fully connected to all other layers.

  - We used the Deep neural networks as it contain multiple layers and multiple layers among the input dataset and output label allow the network to do feature learning at different stages of abstraction, which makes the network to generalize itself in a better way.

- There are some components of NN that we have to predefine as they will not be updated in the process of training which are learning rate, number of training steps/number of iterations, size of batch and dropout/threshold.
- The main important task in building architecture of NN is to define learning rate. Learning rate helps to reach the accuracy point. Larger learning rate has tendency to converge faster but they can go past the optimal values as they are updated [11].
- The next important parameter in building architecture of NN is to define the number of iterations that describes the number of steps Model will perform the training procedure.
- The parameter size of batch represents the number of training data we are going to use at each training step. The dropout parameter defines the threshold at which we excludes some nodes randomly. We have defined some computational nodes that have some weights related to them. The value of these weights affects the accuracy of prediction. These weights are required to make predictions from given input. If the prediction comes out to be correct then it is good. If the prediction comes out to be wrong, then we simply need to adjust the value of weights associated with nodes to improve the accuracy of prediction. The parameters which can help to adjust the value of weights associated with nodes are ACCURACY and LOSS.
- Training and testing procedure includes functionalities like feeding the data as input and check if Model provides correct result. If result are not correct then values of parameters will be adjusted on the basis of the fact that how much our prediction comes out wrong [11]. Every time, when network/Model iterates through the training images batch, the network updates the value of parameters so that the value of the loss can be reduced. Before the process of training, we have described our method for the Evaluation of accuracy so that we can display it on small batches of dataset while we train. These values of accuracy helped us to check that from the first to last iteration in training process how much loss has been reduced and how much accuracy has been increased. That thing helped us to keep track of many things like whether or not we have pass through the enough number of iterations to reach point of optimal accuracy. In the training process, the values of the parameters like weight and bias are adjusted to reduce the loss for coming training steps. As the learning process works, we see that loss reduces and then we have halted training and use the network as a Model. During the training process, the parameters like weight and bias has learned some values which we save in the checkpoint file *.ckpt on hard disk. Then we have saved the definition of our Model in *.pb file and learned values of variable in *.ckpt file. Lastly, we have merged the *.pb file and *.ckpt file into a single *.pb file and freeze all the variable nodes into constant nodes.

Reading Urdu Grammar, Proverbs, Idioms, Phrases and Dialogues: We have designed the reading module in our application in such way that it will help the user to read and learn to speak Urdu in easy way. We have designed our module in such a way that it contain recording/audio of alphabets which will help the user that how can they speak the alphabets in Urdu. Reading module has another part which contain the recording of words against each alphabets. Moreover, reading module has another part which can help the user to learn Urdu counting. Our other modules like proverbs, idioms, phrases and dialogues helps the user how to read and speak different proverbs, idioms, phrases and dialogues in Urdu with help of audio and message text. We have used the object of class MediaPlayer implementation of reading, proverbs, idioms, phrases and dialogues modules. Media player class help us that how can we control the audio files. Media player is an Android class which helps us to use by default media player services like playing audio. We can use a media player class by using the static method create() of the media player class. This method gives the object of media player class. After creating the object, we have called a method to start audio.

Web Services: Our main focus is to provide an offline application to the user so that user will be able to learn Urdu language even if there is data connection available. For this purpose, we have used the file storage system in our application. We have stored our files in the applications and if there is a need to update that data then application will update the data in the background along with the running application. But application need data connection for the updating of files. System will update the file with the help of AsyncTask class which will help to start a process in another thread from the UI thread and then will the run some code in the running UI thread after the process is completed. The code which is running in the background will be done in the method of doInBackground, means the downloading of files is done with the help of this method. Then the result of the process in the UI thread is done with help of another method. With this method, the file which has been downloaded in the background will be posted on the screen of device with help of the method.

Chatbot: We have trained our Chatbot in wit.ai framework using entities. Our code files are explained below.

1) **Variables.env:** Variables.env file in the root of our Chatbot directory has the following things:

   - PORT7777
   - WIT_ACCESS_TOKEN
   - PUSHER_ APP_ID
   - PUSHER_ APP_KEY
   - PUSHER_APP_SECRET

   We can grab our wit.ai server access token by heading to the settings under API details. Pusher related keys and IDs etc. are got from pusher Website.

2) Setting up pusher channels for real-time responses: We head over to the Pusher Website and sign up for a free account. Select Channels apps on the sidebar, and hit Create Channels app to create a new app. Once our app is created, we retrieve credentials from the Keys tab, then add the following to our variables.env file:

   a. PUSHER_APP_ ID = < your app id>
   b. PUSHER_APP_KEY = < your app key>
   c. PUSHER_APP_SECRET < your app secret>
   d. PUSHER_APP_CLUSTER = <your app cluster>

3) **Style.css:** This file add style to app front end.

4) **Index.js:** The state of the application is initialized with two values: userMessage which contains the value of whatever the user types into the input field, and conversation which is an array that will hold each message in the conversation. The 'handleChange' function runs on every keystroke to update userMessage which allows the displayed value to update as the user types. When the user hits the Enter button the form will be submitted and handleSubmit will be invoked. 'handleSubmit' updates the conversation state with the contents of the user's message and sends the message in a POST request to the/chat endpoint which we will soon setup in our app's server component, before clearing the input field by setting userMessage to an empty string.

5) **Server.js:** There is a/chat endpoint that receives messages from the frontend of our app and sends it off to the Wit message API. Whatever response is received is then logged to the console.

4 Results

The result of this project is an Android application which is Urdu Mu-all-um. Main menu has options for all the modules so user can select according to his/her choice. Selecting reading module, user can see three options on screen, Haroof (Alphabets), Alfaz (Words), Ginti (Counting). After clicking on words, a list of alphabets appear. Click on desired alphabet read word as shown (Fig. 1).

Fig. 1. Layout for reading Urdu words

Selecting writing module, user has two options on screen, Haroof (Alphabets), Alfaz (Words). Select according to your interest and following type of screen will appear for Tracing (Fig. 2).

Fig. 2. Layout for tracing Urdu alphabets

If user select practice option in writing module an empty screen appears where user can write and Evaluation takes place as in below image an alphabet is practiced on screen as shown below (Fig. 3).

Fig. 3. Layout for practicing Urdu alphabets

Other modules work on same method as by selecting any of these modules like grammar, proverbs, idioms, phrases, dialogues and vocabulary, a screen appears and user can select one option and can read according to the selected module. Similarly, by clicking on the Chatbot option, user can write messages and get responses from it [9].

5   Conclusion

In the proposed work, data set is developed that are images, audio files, text files and excel sheets based on questions and answers for particular scenarios. Reading and writing of

Urdu language is added to this project. To teach writing of Urdu alphabets and words, canvas is used. It is difficult to detect the accuracy of user's Urdu writing skills so, evaluation approach is used to check the accuracy of Urdu alphabets by using tensor flow. Reading of Urdu words, alphabets, counting, grammar, proverbs, idioms, vocabulary is added to app using images, media player and web services. Chatbot is also developed by using wit.ai framework. In short, we tried our best to develop a responsive and efficient system to teach basics of Urdu language. We plan to improve the work in reading and writing, from each alphabet only one word is being taught so data can be increased in these modules so that user can learn more than one thing.

References

1. Parasuraman, S.: Smartphone usage and increased risk of mobile phone addiction: a concurrent study. Int. J. Pharma. Investig. **7**(3), 125–131 (2017)
2. Mushroor, S., Haque, S., Amir, R.A.: The impact of smart phones and mobile devices on human health and life. Int. J. Commun. Med. Pub. Health **7**(1), 9–15 (2019)
3. Martin, W., Sarro, F., Jia, Y., Zhang, Y., Haman, M.: A survey of app store analysis for software engineering. IEEE Trans. Softw. Eng. **43**(1), 817–847 (2017)
4. Ahmed, F.G.: TensorFlow A Guide to Build Artificial Neural Networks using Python, pp 7–11. LAP LAMBERT Academic Publishing (2017)
5. Weihs, C., Ickstadt, K.: Data science: the impact of statistics. Int. J. Data Sci. Anal. **6**(3), 189–194 (2018). https://doi.org/10.1007/s41060-018-0102-5
6. Adeleke, A.G.: Influence of time-on-phone on undergraduates academic achievement in nigerian universities. Am. J. Educ. Res. **5**(5), 564–567 (2017)
7. Syed, A.Z., Aslam, M., Martinez-Enriquez, A.M.: Associating targets with SentiUnits: a step forward in sentiment analysis of Urdu text. Artifi. Intell. Rev. **41**(4), 535–561 (2012). https://doi.org/10.1007/s10462-012-9322-6
8. Basit, R.H., Aslam, M., Martinez-Enriquez, A.M., Syed, A.: Semantic similarity analysis of urdu documents. In: Carrasco-Ochoa, J.A., Martínez-Trinidad, J.F., Olvera-López, J.A. (eds.) MCPR 2017. LNCS, vol. 10267, pp. 234–243. Springer, Cham (2017). https://doi.org/10.1007/978-3-319-59226-8_23
9. Alaa, A.Q.: Improvement of chatbot semantics using wit. ai and word sequence kernel: education chatbot as a case study. Int. J. Modern Edu. Comp. Sci. (IJMECS) **11**(3), 16–22 (2019)
10. Margaret, Q., Marie, B.: Moving beyond tracing: the nature, availability and quality of digital apps to support children's writing. J. Early Child Literacy (2019)
11. Martín, A.: TensorFlow: learning functions at scale. In: Proceedings of the 21st ACM SIGPLAN International Conference on Functional Programming, p. 1 (2016)

Evolutionary and Metaheuristic Algorithms

Selection Schemes Analysis in Genetic Algorithms for the Maximum Influence Problem

Abel García-Nájera[⊠], Saúl Zapotecas-Martínez, and Roberto Bernal-Jaquez

Departamento de Matemáticas Aplicadas y Sistemas, Universidad Autónoma
Metropolitana Unidad Cuajimalpa, Av. Vasco de Quiroga 4871,
Col. Santa Fe Cuajimalpa, 05300 México, D.F., Mexico
{agarcian,szapotecas,rbernal}@cua.uam.mx

Abstract. Information spread in social network is a current prime target for a number of sectors, namely politics, marketing, research, education, finance, etc. Information diffusion through the network has been modeled in different manners, all of them using their own dynamics. The main goal is to maximize the influence with the minimum number of starting users. This problem is known as the influence maximization problem, which is known to be NP-hard. This is why several proposals based on heuristics and meta-heuristics have appeared in order to tackle the problem. Interesting results have been published, however, many studies have concentrated exclusively on the results and the analysis of the algorithms components has been left aside. We believe it is also important to know what features of the algorithms are meaningful in order for the algorithms to perform well. This is why we analyze a couple of selection schemes in a genetic algorithm. Our results revealed that one of the selection schemes perform better for a certain class of networks.

Keywords: Maximum influence problem · Genetic algorithms · Selection schemes

1 Introduction

Social networks play an important role nowadays. Many businesses, academic institutions, government agencies, and people in general rely on information diffusion on social networks. From marketing to political campaigns have been successful by broadcasting information through this kind of networks [5,6].

Actually, what these applications look for, is to reach the maximum audience in the social network by starting with the smallest number of users of that network. This problem is known as the influence maximization problem. In this problem, information diffusion has been modeled in several manners and depending on the model, information could have different reach.

© Springer Nature Switzerland AG 2020
L. Martínez-Villaseñor et al. (Eds.): MICAI 2020, LNAI 12468, pp. 211–222, 2020.
https://doi.org/10.1007/978-3-030-60884-2_16

It has been proved that the influence maximization problem is NP-hard [13], this is why heuristics and metaheuristics have been employed for solving a variety of real problem instances.

Despite a number of studies have proposed population-based metaheuristics to solve the problem, they have not analyzed what the impact of the operators involved in the techniques is for maximizing information diffusion, particularly the selection schemes in evolutionary algorithms.

In order to bridge this gap, in the present study we focus on analyzing two selections schemes, namely (μ, λ) and $(\mu + \lambda)$. We have embedded each of these schemes in a genetic algorithm for solving four real instances of the influence maximization problem.

Our results suggest that the $(\mu + \lambda)$ selection scheme does not perform better than the (μ, λ) scheme, at least in the four instance networks used in this study.

The rest of this paper is structured as follows. In Sect. 2, we introduce the influence maximization problem, explain three information diffusion models and provide related literature review. Section 3 briefly introduces the components of a genetic algorithm and accounts for the two selection schemes that are analyzed. In Sect. 4, the genetic algorithm employed in this study is described. The experimental set-up and results analysis are discussed in Sect. 5. Finally, In Sect. 6 we provide our conclusions and present some ideas for future work.

2   Influence Maximization Problem

A social network can be modeled as a graph $G = (V, E)$, with the set of vertices V representing individuals and the set E of edges representing connections or relationships between two individuals. Influence is propagated in the network according to a stochastic diffusion model.

The influence maximization problem can be defined as follows. Given a social network graph G, a specific influence diffusion model, and a number k, the influence maximization problem is to find a *seed set* $K \subset V, |K| = k$, such that, under the influence diffusion model, the expected number of vertices influenced by the seed set K, regarded as the influence spread, is the maximum possible.

Certainly, every influence diffusion model has its own dynamics. We can find in the literature several models that have been used for the problem at hand. In the next section, three of these models are described.

2.1   Influence Diffusion Models

In this section, three diffusion models, namely *independent cascade*, *weighted cascade*, and *linear threshold*, are outlined.

Independent Cascade
In the independent cascade (IC) model, the *influence probability* p_{ij}, with which node i activates its neighbor j, can be computed as follows:

$$p_{ij} = 1 - (1 - p)^{w_{ij}} \tag{1}$$

where $p \in [0,1]$ is the *activation probability* and w_{ij} denotes the weight of the edge (i,j). Specifically, if the targeted social network is unweighted, the values of active probability for all edges equal to p.

Weighted Cascade

In the case of the weighted cascade (WC) model, the probability that node i activates node j is slightly different. The activation probability p_{ij} can be determined by the reciprocal of the in-degree number of node j, and it can be calculated as

$$p_{ij} = \frac{a_{ij}}{|N_j^{(in)}|} \qquad (2)$$

where $a_{ij} = 1$ if node j is one of the neighbors of node i and 0 otherwise. $N_j^{(in)}$ is the set of incoming neighbors of node j in a directed graph. Especially, if the graph is undirected, $|N_j^{(in)}|$ is the degree of node j.

Linear Threshold

In the linear threshold (LT) model, for any node i, all its neighbors that were just activated at previous time stamp, together make a try to activate that node. This activation process will be successful if the sum of the incoming active neighbor's probability becomes either greater than or equal to the node's threshold θ_i, i.e. if

$$\sum_{\substack{\forall j \in N_i^{(in)} \\ j \in \mathcal{A}_t}} p_{ji} \geq \theta_i \, , \qquad (3)$$

then, i will become active at time stamp $t+1$. $\mathcal{A}_t$ is the set of active nodes at time t. This method will be continued until no more activation is possible.

2.2   Previous Studies on Influence Maximization

According to Banerjee et al. [1], social influence on networks has been analyzed since early 2000 and they have recently surveyed relevant studies which tackle the problem by means of heuristic and metaheuristic techniques.

Given that the present study analyzes two selection schemes as part of a metaheuristic approach, we review some recent works that tackle the problem by means of this kind of techniques.

Bucur and Iacca [2] analyzed influence on social networks by means of a genetic algorithm, which aim was to maximize influence while setting the size of the seed. They showed that, by using simple genetic operators, it is possible to find in feasible runtime solutions of high-influence that are comparable, and occasionally better, than the solutions found by a number of known heuristics.

Gong et al. [8] proposed a discrete particle swarm optimization algorithm to optimize the local influence criterion, which can provide a reliable estimation for the influence propagations in independent and weighted cascade models. The representations and update rules for the particles were redefined and they introduced a degree-based heuristic initialization strategy and a network-specific local search strategy to speed up the convergence.

Zhang et al. [19] proposed a genetic algorithm to solve the influence maximization problem. Through multi-population competition, using this algorithm they achieved an optimal result while maintaining diversity of the solutions. They tested their method with real networks and their genetic algorithm performed slightly worse than the greedy algorithm but better than other algorithms.

As we can see, previous work did not analyze throughly the components of their proposals. On the contrary, the study we present here, aims at remedy this situation.

3   Natural Selection Schemes in Genetic Algorithms

3.1   Components of Genetic Algorithms

Since its introduction in the 1970s [10], genetic algorithms (GAs) have been a flexible and a practical tool to solve several problems in the areas of science and engineering. Nowadays, GAs constitute a well-stablished area of research which is inspired by the process of natural selection observed in species. GAs work at the genotypic level and normally do not adopt a self-adaptation mechanism as the evolutionary strategies. Normally, GAs adopt a mating selection, recombination, and a natural selection mechanism to approximate an optimal solution. Additionally, there is another operator called elitism which plays a crucial role in GAs. This operator retains the best individual produced at each generation, and passes it intact (i.e. without being recombined or mutated) to the next generation. In [16], Rudolph showed that a GA requires elitism to converge to the optimum. For this reason, elitism is a mechanism that has become a standard operator in evolutionary algorithms. Thus, the main components into GAs are described below.

Solution Encoding. Solution encoding is related to how a solutions is represented. As the structure of a solution varies from problem to problem, a solution of a particular problem can be represented in a number of ways.

Initial Population. A population consist in a number of individuals encoded under a determined criterion. As is standard practice for GAs, the initial population is chosen randomly with the aim of covering the entire search space.

Fitness Assignment. At each generation of evolution, the objective function is evaluated for every solution in the population, and each individual is assigned a fitness value which drives the natural selection process. When solving a single-objective problem, the fitness assigned to an individual is set according to its single objective function value.

Mating Selection. The evolutionary process requires some stochastic function for selecting *parent* individuals from the population, according to their fitness, to undergo mating (or recombination) to create an *offspring*. The fittest individuals should be more likely to be selected, but low-fitness individuals should also be given a small chance, with the aim of not allowing the algorithm to be too greedy.

Recombination. Recombination is the process of generating one or more children solutions from two parent solutions, preferably in a manner that maintains and combines the desirable features from both parents. It is a simple imitation of the complex process that occurs between pairs of chromosomes in biological systems.

Perturbation. Mutation is a variation operator that uses only one parent solution and create one child solution by applying some kind of randomized change to the representation. That is, once an offspring solution has been generated, a further stochastic change is applied with probability P_m.

Natural Selection. The final stage of each evolutionary cycle is the selection of individuals to form the next generation. There are several possibilities for coupling this operator into evolutionary algorithm. However, the comma and plus selections are the most used schemes into GAs. In this investigation, these two strategies are of importance which are studied within complex network problems.

3.2 (μ, λ)- and $(\mu + \lambda)$-Selection Schemes

Since the early 1980s, the performance of natural selection strategies into evolutionary algorithms have been studied [4,7,9,11,12,15,17,18]. A generational genetic algorithm generates a set of solutions at each generation. Thus, the offspring solutions replace the parents $((\mu, \lambda)$-selection) or compete with them and survive the best individuals $((\mu+\lambda)$-selection). Traditionally, the number of children is equal to the number of parents, i.e., $\mu = \lambda$. As it was discussed in some studies [7,15,18], the natural selection schemes in evolutionary algorithms provide different balance between exploration and exploitation. Their performance goes hand in hand with the nature of the problems they are intended to solve. For this reason, the study of different schemes is of particular importance when used to find solutions to real-world applications, where the characteristics of the problem are unknown. To contrast the differences of these schemes, we show the general framework of GAs based on the principles (μ, λ) and $(\mu + \lambda)$ in Algorithms 1 and 2, respectively. It is worth noticing that in the case of $(\mu + \lambda)$ selection scheme, the elitism is implicitly given by the selection of the best solutions (see line 8 in Algorithm 2). On the other hand, an elitism strategy has to be explicitly given in the (μ, λ) selection (see lines 8–10 in Algorithm 1).

4 Maximum Influence Problem Adaptation

Since the maximum influence problem requires solutions to define the seed set of nodes, the most natural way to encode such solutions is the integer representation. This encoding considers a vector of size k, the size of seed set K, in which

---

Algorithm 1: Genetic algorithm with the (μ, λ) selection scheme.

Input: Number of generations G_{max}
Output: An evolved population P

1   $t = 0$
2   Generate an initial population P_t
3   **while** $t < G_{max}$ **do**
4      $Q = crossover(P_t)$
5      $Q' = mutation(Q)$
6      $evalute(Q')$
7   // Elitism
8      $p_b = best\_solution(P_t)$
9      $q_w = worst\_solution(Q')$
10     $P_{t+1} = Q' \setminus \{q_w\} \cup \{p_b\}$
11     $t = t + 1$
12 **end**
13 **return** P_t

Algorithm 2: Genetic algorithm with the $(\mu + \lambda)$ selection scheme.

Input: Number of generations G_{max}
Output: An evolved population P

1   $t = 0$
2   Generate an initial population P_t
3   **while** $t < G_{max}$ **do**
4      $Q = croosover(P_t)$
5      $Q' = mutation(Q)$
6      $evalute(Q')$
7      $T = P_t \cup Q'$
8      $P_{t+1} = select\_best(T)$
9      $t = t + 1$
10 **return** P_t

---

each dimension of the vector is assigned an integer in the set $V = \{1, 2, \ldots, |V|\}$. An example of this representation is shown in Fig. 1. In this example, a seed set of size 10 is considered, which are selected from the set $V = \{1, 2, \ldots, 1000\}$.

Initial population is filled with randomly generated individuals, where each individual is a random selection of k nodes that represent the seed set K. With respect to the fitness function, the independent cascade diffusion model introduced above was adopted to assign fitness to individuals. Individuals that propose a seed set that activates a larger number of nodes, are assigned a higher fitness.

Mating selection is carried out by means of the binary tournament selection method, where two individuals are randomly chosen and the fittest win the tournament, which is selected to be recombined.

Fig. 1. Solution encoding: integer representation.

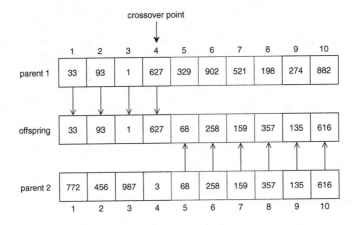

Fig. 2. Recombination procedure: one-point crossover

Regarding the variation operators, for the recombination process, the one-point crossover has been adopted: A crossover point on the parent solutions is randomly selected. All information before that point is copied from one of the parents to the child. To complete the solution, all data beyond that point is copied from the second parent. An example of this operator is shown in Fig. 2.

In the case of the mutation operator, the uniform mutation has been selected, which, for each node in the seed set, selects a random node with probability P_m.

After crossover and mutation, it could be the case that one offspring considers a duplicate node. In this scenario, the individual is not repaired. That is, the seed set that proposes this individual will contain less than k nodes.

5   Experimental Set-Up and Results

Our experiments have two aims. On the one hand, we are interested in the convergence of the genetic algorithm when it considers the two selection schemes under analysis. On the other hand, we would like to know if the genetic algorithm achieves a larger influence with any of the selection schemes. We describe next the experimental set-up that will help us to accomplish these two goals.

Table 1. Main features of the four real social network data sets considered for the analysis of the selection schemes.

Name	Type	$|V|$	$|E|$	r	Description
ca-HepTh	Undirected	9,877	25,998	2.63	Collaboration network of arXiv High Energy Physics Theory
ca-GrQc	Undirected	5,242	14,496	2.77	Collaboration network of arXiv General Relativity
wiki-Vote	Directed	7,115	103,689	14.57	Wikipedia who-votes-on-whom network
ego-Facebook	Undirected	4,039	88,234	21.85	Social circles from Facebook (anonymized)

5.1 Experimental Set-Up

In order to assess the two selection schemes, four data sets from real social networks have been selected from the Stanford Large Network Dataset Collection [14]. These social networks were also considered in [2,3,8]. The chosen benchmarks, along with their respective main features, are described in Table 1. This Table shows the name of the benchmark network, its type, the number of nodes $|V|$ and edges $|E|$, the ratio $r = |E|/|V|$ between the number of edges and nodes, and some basic description of the network.

The genetic algorithm was executed 30 times with each selection scheme for solving every benchmark network and varying the seed size to 10, 20, 30, 40, and 50. The parameters of the genetic algorithm were set to traditional values [10]: population size = 100, crossover probability = 0.9, mutation probability = 0.1. The genetic algorithm ran for 1000 generations in each repetition.

The experiments were performed in a computer with Intel Xeon Gold 6130 CPU at 2.10 GHz, 64 cores.

5.2 Convergence Analysis

For the first aim, Fig. 3 shows the average convergence plots for the four benchmark networks and for each seed size. We can observe that, when it is set with the $(\mu + \lambda)$ and with the (μ, λ) schemes, the genetic algorithm has a similar convergence pattern for the ego-Facebook network with seed sizes 10, 20, and 50. For seed sizes 30 and 40, the convergence present a slight difference.

Something analogous occurs for the wiki-Vote network, however, in this case, the average convergence is slightly different only for the case seed size 40.

Contrary to the previous two benchmark networks, for the ca-GrQc and ca-HepTh networks, the algorithm with the (μ, λ) scheme converged significantly better than the algorithm with the $(\mu+\lambda)$ scheme for all seed sizes. It is worthy to

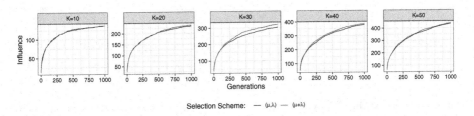

(a) ego-Facebook network.

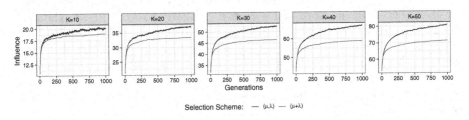

(b) wiki-Vote network.

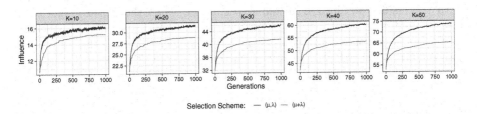

(c) ca-GrQc network.

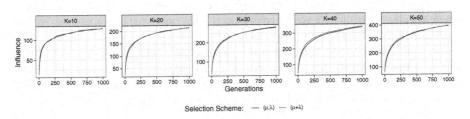

(d) ca-HepTh network.

Fig. 3. Average convergence of the genetic algorithm using the two selection schemes (μ, λ) and $(\mu + \lambda)$.

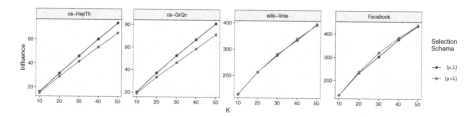

Fig. 4. Influence achieved by the genetic algorithm when set with the two selection schemes using different seed set sizes in the adopted social networks.

note that, in these cases, the difference in the convergence between both selection schemes is larger while the seed size is larger. This behavior is not present in the ego-Facebook and wiki-Vote networks.

Overall, since there is no important difference in convergence in two out of the four benchmark networks and for the other two the algorithm with the (μ, λ) scheme achieve a superior convergence, we can conjecture that the algorithm converges more adequately with the (μ, λ) selection scheme.

5.3 Maximum Influence

Regarding our second aim, Fig. 4 shows the average maximum influence achieved for each benchmark network and seed size. Similarly to what Fig. 3 exhibited, the genetic algorithm reached nearly the same maximum influence with both selection schemes for the ego-Facebook and the wiki-Vote networks. However, for the ca-GrQc and ca-HepTh networks, the maximum influence is significantly broader when the algorithm is set with the (μ, λ) selection scheme than when it is set with the $(\mu + \lambda)$ scheme for all seed sizes. With this result, our previous conjecture remains.

5.4 Final Remarks

With the results obtained from our experiments, when the genetic algorithm is configured with the (μ, λ) selection scheme, it performs significantly better than when it is configured with the $(\mu + \lambda)$ scheme. However, this improved performance is evident on networks with ratios $r = |E|/|V|$ below 3, which is the case of the two benchmark networks ca-HepTh and ca-GrQc.

6 Conclusions

In this study, we have analyzed two selection schemes in a genetic algorithm for solving the influence maximization problem in social networks, specifically, the (μ, λ) and $(\mu + \lambda)$ selection schemes. In order to validate the performance of each selection scheme, we have tested the algorithm in four real social networks publicly available.

The experimental set-up was conducted in order to analyze the performance of the two selection schemes regarding convergence and maximum influence.

Results indicate that both selection schemes perform practically similarly, for both convergence and maximum influence, for all set seed sizes in two benchmark networks which have low ratios (<3) between $|E|$ and $|V|$.

On the other two benchmark networks, which have higher ratios (>14) between $|E|$ and $|V|$, selection scheme (μ, λ) had a significantly better performance, both in convergence and maximum influence, than selection scheme $(\mu + \lambda)$ for all set seed sizes. Particularly interesting in these cases is the fact that the (μ, λ) genetic algorithm improved its performance as the set seed increased in size.

Given these interesting results, more experimentation is necessary in order to prove our conjectures. For instance, more benchmark networks have to be considered with different ratios $|E|/|V|$. Other characteristics of the networks can also be taken into account, for example diameter, number of triangles, and average clustering coefficient, among others.

References

1. Banerjee, S., Jenamani, M., Pratihar, D.K.: A survey on influence maximization in a social network. Knowl. Inf. Syst. **62**, 3417–3455 (2020). https://doi.org/10.1007/s10115-020-01461-4

2. Bucur, D., Iacca, G.: Influence maximization in social networks with genetic algorithms. In: Squillero, G., Burelli, P. (eds.) EvoApplications 2016. LNCS, vol. 9597, pp. 379–392. Springer, Cham (2016). https://doi.org/10.1007/978-3-319-31204-0_25

3. Bucur, D., Iacca, G., Marcelli, A., Squillero, G., Tonda, A.: Improving multi-objective evolutionary influence maximization in social networks. In: Sim, K., Kaufmann, P. (eds.) EvoApplications 2018. LNCS, vol. 10784, pp. 117–124. Springer, Cham (2018). https://doi.org/10.1007/978-3-319-77538-8_9

4. Dahal, K.P., McDonald, J.R.: Generational and steady-state genetic algorithms for generator maintenance scheduling problems. In: Artificial Neural Nets and Genetic Algorithms, pp. 259–263. Springer, Vienna (1998). https://doi.org/10.1007/978-3-7091-6492-1_57

5. Enli, G.: Twitter as arena for the authentic outsider: exploring the social media campaigns of trump and Clinton in the 2016 US presidential election. Eur. J. Commun. **32**(1), 50–61 (2017)

6. Francia, P.L.: Free media and twitter in the 2016 presidential election: the unconventional campaign of Donald Trump. Soc. Sci. Comput. Rev. **36**(4), 440–455 (2018)

7. Goldberg, D.E., Deb, K.: A comparative analysis of selection schemes used in genetic algorithms. In: Rawlins, G.J. (ed.) Foundations of Genetic Algorithms, vol. 1, pp. 69–93. Elsevier, Amsterdam (1991)

8. Gong, M., Yan, J., Shen, B., Ma, L., Cai, Q.: Influence maximization in social networks based on discrete particle swarm optimization. Inf. Sci. **367**, 600–614 (2016)

9. Grefenstette, J.J.: Optimization of control parameters for genetic algorithms. IEEE Trans. Syst. Man Cybern. **16**(1), 122–128 (1986)

10. Holland, J.H.: Adaptation in Natural and Artificial Systems. University of Michigan Press, Ann Arbor (1975)
11. Jiang, S., Yang, S.: A steady-state and generational evolutionary algorithm for dynamic multiobjective optimization. IEEE Trans. Evol. Comput. **21**(1), 65–82 (2017)
12. Jones, J., Soule, T.: Comparing genetic robustness in generational vs. steady state evolutionary algorithms. In: Proceedings of the 8th Annual Conference on Genetic and Evolutionary Computation, New York, NY, USA, pp. 143–150. ACM (2006)
13. Kempe, D., Kleinberg, J., Tardos, É.: Maximizing the spread of influence through a social network. In: Proceedings of the Ninth ACM SIGKDD International Conference on Knowledge Discovery and Data Mining, pp. 137–146. ACM (2003)
14. Leskovec, J., Krevl, A.: SNAP Datasets: Stanford large network dataset collection, June 2014. http://snap.stanford.edu/data
15. Noever, D., Baskaran, S.: Steady-state vs. generational genetic algorithms: a comparison of time complexity and convergence properties. Technical report, Santa Fe Institute (1992)
16. Rudolph, G.: Convergence of evolutionary algorithms in general search spaces. In: Proceedings of IEEE International Conference on Evolutionary Computation, pp. 50–54. IEEE (1996)
17. Schaffer, J.D., Caruana, R.A., Eshelman, L.J., Das, R.: A study of control parameters affecting online performance of genetic algorithms for function optimization. In: Proceedings of the Third International Conference on Genetic Algorithms, pp. 51–60. Morgan Kaufmann Publishers Inc., San Francisco (1989)
18. Vavak, F., Fogarty, T.C.: Comparison of steady state and generational genetic algorithms for use in nonstationary environments. In: Proceedings of IEEE International Conference on Evolutionary Computation, pp. 192–195. IEEE (1996)
19. Zhang, K., Du, H., Feldman, M.W.: Maximizing influence in a social network: improved results using a genetic algorithm. Phys. A **478**, 20–30 (2017)

A Comparative Analysis of Evolutionary Learning in Artificial Hydrocarbon Networks

Hiram Ponce[1]([⊠])[iD] and Paulo Souza[2][iD]

[1] Universidad Panamericana, Facultad de Ingeniería,
Augusto Rodin 498, 03920 Ciudad de México, Mexico
hponce@up.edu.mx
[2] Department of Knowledge Based Mathematical Systems, Johannes Kepler
University Linz, 4040 Linz, Austria
paulo.de_campos_souza@jku.at

Abstract. Artificial hydrocarbon networks (AHN) is a supervised learning model that is loosely inspired on the interactions of molecules in organic compounds. This method is able to model data in a hierarchical and robust way. However, the original training algorithm is very time-consuming. Recently, novel training algorithms have been applied, including evolutionary learning. Particularly, this training algorithm employed particle swarm optimization (PSO), as part of the procedure. In this paper, we present a benchmark of other meta-heuristic optimization algorithms implemented on the training method for AHN. In this study, PSO, harmony search algorithm, cuckoo search, grey wolf optimization and whale optimization algorithm, were tested. The experimental results were done using public data sets on regression and binary classification problems. From the results, we concluded that the best algorithm was cuckoo search optimization for regression problems, while there is no evidence that one of the algorithms performed better for binary classification problems.

Keywords: Machine learning · Artificial organic networks · Supervised learning · Meta-heuristic optimization · Regression · Classification.

1 Introduction

Machine learning provides intelligent solutions to complex problems, assisting with the automation of procedures to obtain assertive and quick answers. Each approach has different techniques and styles to solve problems. However, machine learning models require to find the most suitable parameters to perform the best [3].

To solve the problems that arise in the definition of parameters in intelligent models, several approaches have emerged to assist in the search for optimal parameters, where techniques such as k-fold and cross-validation stand out

© Springer Nature Switzerland AG 2020
L. Martínez-Villaseñor et al. (Eds.): MICAI 2020, LNAI 12468, pp. 223–234, 2020.
https://doi.org/10.1007/978-3-030-60884-2_17

[18]. These techniques are useful but have high computational consumption for solving problems. To address more effective techniques, evolutionary learning incorporates characteristics from the behavior of living beings in nature to solve problems. Thus, supported by the behavior of specific groups of animals, the problems and parameters are solved with a focus on optimal solutions [19].

Based on the concepts of problem-solving, meta-heuristics incorporate the behavior of groups of animals to solve them. It should be noted that there are several meta-heuristics inspired by animals, such as lions, elephants, and bats, among many others [20]. Researchers observed hunting or defense behaviors and incorporated the computational context into these types of actions. In this case, it is expected that using heuristics inspired by nature, optimality problems will be solved as if they were approaches to search for food or to defend against enemy attacks.

Meta-heuristic optimization approaches have been used to solve these issues [5]. They consist of a high-level procedure designed to search for, generate, or select a heuristic, which provides a sufficiently right solution to the optimization problem. In other words, a meta-heuristic is a generative process that combines concepts of diversification (exploration), used to perform searches in large portions of the search space, and intensification (exploitation), used to refine a candidate solution from local search. These strategies guide the search process for near global solutions. Techniques based on meta-heuristics consist of simple local searches and complex learning procedures, usually inspired by some biological strategy or behavior in nature [5]. These approaches are known to have a wide range of complex problem solving, such as cluster [6] problem solving, wireless sensor networks [7,10], course schedule problem-solving in a university [1], complex networks [8], and many others.

Artificial hydrocarbon networks (AHN) are machine learning models capable of solving complex pattern classification and regression problems. Recently, this model was proposed by Ponce et al. [16] based on the behavior of organic molecules. The model has been widely explored in different applications [13,14,17]. However, this model requires high-intensive computational resources to be trained [14].

In order to identify efficient and evolutionary approaches for training parameters of AHN models, this paper aims to evaluate the application of five evolutionary meta-heuristics to define the parameters known as molecular centers. These optimization methods are particle swarm optimization, harmony search algorithm, cuckoo search, grey wolf optimization and whale optimization algorithm. The training algorithm for AHN based on meta-heuristics will be subjected to classification tests of binary patterns and regression tests with real data sets, in different contexts and complexities.

The contribution of this paper is the comparative analysis of evolutionary techniques to optimize the AHN model and the insights provided for future training algorithms design. Two metrics have been evaluated to say the predictability performance of the model and the execution time in training.

The rest of the paper is organized as follows. In Sect. 2, the methodology proposed in this paper is presented. Section 3 presents the experimental results, and discussion is provided in Sect. 4. Finally, the conclusions and possible extensions of the work are presented in Sect. 5.

2   Evolutionary Learning for Artificial Hydrocarbon Networks

This section presents an overview of AHN and the meta-heuristic optimization algorithms implemented in the comparative analysis.

2.1   Artificial Hydrocarbon Networks

AHN is a supervised learning method, proposed by Ponce and Ponce [15], that models data using carbon networks as inspiration. It loosely simulates the chemical rules involved in hydrocarbon molecules to find a way for representing the structure and behavior of data [17]. The main feature of this model is to package data in units so-called molecules. Then, packages are organized and optimized through heuristic mechanisms based on chemical assumptions that are encoded in the training algorithm. The key features of AHN are threefold: modular organization of data, structural stability of data-packages and inheritance of packaging information [13].

As described above, the main unit of information is the molecule. It consists of a kernel function parameterized with a set of weights, as written in (1) where $x \in \mathbb{R}^n$ is the feature vector of the input data, H_i is a set of weights namely the hydrogen values, σ is a vector namely the carbon value and $k \leq 4$ is the maximum number of hydrogen values associated to one molecule. Jointly, those weights are known as molecular parameters, and they resemble to the hydrogen and carbon atoms of a hydrocarbon molecule in nature.

$$\varphi(x,k) = \sum_{r=1}^{n} \sigma_r \sum_{i=1}^{k \leq 4} H_{ir} x_r^i \tag{1}$$

Molecules are arranged in groups namely compounds. The latter are structures that represent nonlinearities in molecules. Those compounds are associated with a functional behavior as expressed in (2), where m is the number of molecules in the compound and Σ_j is a partition of the input x such that $\Sigma_j = \{x | \arg\min_j(x - \mu_j) = j\}$, and $\mu_j \in \mathbb{R}^n$ is the center of the jth molecule [13]. In fact, $\Sigma_{j_1} \cap \Sigma_{j_2} = \emptyset$ if $j_1 \neq j_2$. The compound behavior written in (2) is known as linear chain of m molecules since it is similar to organic chains in chemical nature [17].

$$\psi(x) = \begin{cases} \varphi_1(x,3) & x \in \Sigma_1 \\ \varphi_2(x,2) & x \in \Sigma_2 \\ \cdots & \cdots \\ \varphi_{m-1}(x,2) & x \in \Sigma_{m-1} \\ \varphi_m(x,3) & x \in \Sigma_m \end{cases} \tag{2}$$

Compounds can interact among them in definite ratios α_t, namely stoichiometric coefficients or simply weights, forming a mixture $S(x)$. It is represented as shown in (3); where, c is the number of compounds in the mixture and α_t is the weighted factor of the t-th compound [17].

$$S(x) = \sum_{t=1}^{c} \alpha_t \psi_t(x) \tag{3}$$

Literature has reported different training algorithms for AHN. They differ in terms of how to approach the learning process of the molecular parameters and the centers of molecules. For example, the simplest and original method [17] implements the least square estimates (LSE) to learn the molecular parameters and the gradient descent to learn the centers of molecules. In [14] authors implements the Moore-Penrose pseudo-inverse to find the molecular parameters and particle swarm optimization (PSO) to learn the centers of molecules. Recently, authors in [13] implemented the stochastic parallel extreme (SPE-AHN) training algorithm that is a fast and reliable method based on the latter training method, but running parallel processing and stochastic learning.

In this work, we use the SPE-AHN training algorithm as part of the inspiration into this benchmark. For our proposal, we show Algorithm 1. It describes the training process using a generalized meta-heuristics. This algorithm sets the lower and upper bounds, lb and ub, of the individuals in the meta-heuristics, and the number of the individuals N in the population. An individual p_i, for all $i = 1, \ldots, N$, is encoding the centers of molecules such that $p_i = (\mu_1, \ldots, \mu_m)$ fulfills. Then, additional settings for the proper meta-heuristics is also set up. After that, the meta-heuristics evaluates an individual into the objective function obj proposed in Algorithm 2. This objective function learns the molecular parameters using the Moore-Penrose pseudo-inverse in one-shot. It is important to highlight that the tuning of molecular parameters is running in parallel, as suggested in [13]. Also, the objective function of the individuals in the meta-heuristic optimization method is evaluated in parallel to accelerate the training procedure, according to [13].

2.2 Overview of Meta-heuristic Optimization Methods

In this work, we implement five meta-heuristic optimization methods to compare the training procedure in AHN. Following, we describe the meta-heuristics implemented for this benchmark, to say: particle swarm optimization (PSO), harmony search algorithm (HSA), cuckoo search (CS), grey wolf optimization (GWO), and whale optimization algorithm (WOA).

Algorithm 1. SPE-AHN training algorithm modification using a generalized meta-heuristics.

Input: the training data set $\Sigma = (x, y)$, the number of molecules in the compound $m \geq 2$ and the batch size $0 < \beta \leq 1$.
Output: the trained compound ψ.

1: Set the lower and upper bounds of individuals, lb and ub, respectively.
2: Set the number of individuals N in the population, and parameter settings of the meta-heuristics.
3: Apply the meta-heuristics algorithm evaluating, in parallel, the individuals into the objective function `obj`.
4: Build the best AHN-model using the best individual.
5: **return** ψ.

Algorithm 2. Objective function `obj` for individual evaluation.

Input: the individual $p_i = (\mu_1, \ldots, \mu_m)$, the training data set $\Sigma = (x, y)$ and the number of molecules in the compound $m \geq 2$.
Output: the overall error E in the model and the trained compound ψ.

1: Create the structure of a new compound with m molecules.
2: Set the centers of molecules using p_i.
3: **parfor** $j = 1$ to m **do**   // run in parallel
4:     $\Sigma_j \leftarrow$ do a subset of Σ using μ_j.
5:     $\mathbf{w} \leftarrow$ calculate the weights of φ_j using Moore-Penrose pseudo-inverse.
6:     $\{H_j, \sigma_j\} \leftarrow$ compute the molecular parameters using $w_{ir} = \sigma_r H_{ir}$ and $H_{1r} = 1$.
7:     $E_j \leftarrow$ compute the error in molecule.
8: **end parfor**
9: Compute the overall error $E = \sum_j E_j$.
10: Build the behavior of compound ψ using all φ_j already calculated.
11: **return** E, ψ.

Particle Swarm Optimization (PSO). A technique created in the mid-90s and to this day acts as one of the most relevant techniques in bio-inspired optimization. PSO initializes the population at random and it updates positions scanning the search space of optimal values [9]. The operation of PSO simulates the feeding behavior of birds. In PSO, birds have been replaced by particles, and they act by inspecting the problem space. Each of these structures can be pointed in a different direction of the region, with different speeds. Particles close to the target are called optimal particles, and they guide the other particles involved in the problem. The optimum values define the updating criteria for each generation of the algorithm. In each iteration, particles update following the best solution so far obtained by itself and the best particle. [9]. The algorithm iterates until a stopping criteria.

Harmony Search Algorithm (HSA). It is based on building a song's harmonic tones, and it is inspired on the behavior of musicians who are looking for tones that have the same harmony as a song, a factor that is similar to the search for optimal solutions to a complex problem. This meta-heuristic method comprises different steps. The first one is the initialization of memory which consists of random assignments of possible solutions to the problem. The second step is the improvement of the initial solutions through a harmonic consideration rate that, in general, can allow for mutations in the proposed solutions, but new solutions in HSA make full use of all individuals of the initial solutions. The third and fourth steps are responsible for updating the initial solutions and for repeating steps two and three, respectively [4].

Cuckoo Search (CS). The parasitic behavior of cuckoo birds so that their eggs are hatched together with eggs from other animals inspired CS [21]. In order to use the nests of other birds, cuckoo females can camouflage their eggs so that they resemble those in the host nest, thus allowing the perpetuation of the species. This adaptation allows cuckoo eggs to suffer less with abandonment or destruction, as when several birds identify eggs of other species, they may discard or abandon them. As the cuckoo eggs hatch earlier, the cuckoo females can also adapt to the song of the animals with which they share the nest. When this action is successful, the children are usually fed by the host mother. In this method, each cuckoo egg is a candidate solution to the optimization problem and nests represent local search in the space.

Grey Wolf Optimization (GWO). Grey wolves and their hunting method have inspired an optimization approach. Mirjalili et al. [12] created an approach that mimics the hunting behavior of wolves in the wild, in addition to defining the hierarchy during the procedures for obtaining food, which similarly is the search for the optimum point of a solution. Four types of grey wolves such as alpha, beta, delta, and omega, are used to simulate the leadership hierarchy. Besides, three main stages of hunting, the search for prey, the fencing of prey, and the attack of prey, are implemented to perform the optimization [12].

Whale Optimization Algorithm (WOA). The humpback whale is an animal that has unusual behaviors when they are hunting for food. They use spirals of bubbles that emerge from the surface, surrounding the prey and enabling the attack [11]. Humpback whales can recognize the location of possible prey and use resources to surround them. As the position of the ideal design in the search space is not known a priori, WOA assumes that the best current solution is the target prey or is close to the ideal. After defining this search individual, other whales will try to update their positions regarding the prey. To carry out the attack (find the optimum point), WOA uses the bubble net attack choosing the circling mechanism, defining the update position of the spiral, performing the exploration phase to search for its prey (using bubbles in circular or spiral) until it finds its prey [11].

3   Experimentation

To assess the performance of AHN in using optimization techniques to find the best training parameters for the model, we will compare the results of the model with different evolutionary approaches. To perform this comparison, datasets commonly used for pattern classification and regression are used to verify the performance of the models. Thus, it is able to evaluate with robust criteria the values referring to the accuracy of the model in performing machine learning tasks using evolutionary approaches. The criteria used for the evaluation of binary pattern classification datasets are accuracy (4) and the area under the ROC curve (5), where, TP = true positive, TN = true negative, FN = false negative and FP = false positive.

$$ACC = \frac{TP + TN}{TP + FN + TN + FP} \tag{4}$$

$$AUC = \frac{sensitivity + specificity}{2} \tag{5}$$

In this context, specificity (7) and sensitivity (6) are also defined.

$$sensitivity = \frac{TP}{TP + FN} \tag{6}$$

$$specificity = \frac{TN}{TN + FP} \tag{7}$$

Likewise, in the regression tests, the evaluation criteria is the root mean squared-error (RMSE) as shown in (8), where y is the target, $\hat{y}$ is the estimation from the model, and q is the number of samples. That is a frequently used measure of the differences between values (sample or population values) predicted by the AHN model, and the values observed.

$$RMSE = \sqrt{\frac{\sum_{i=1}^{q}(y_i - \hat{y}_i)^2}{q}} \tag{8}$$

In all tests the time (in seconds) will also be collected.

The data samples in the test were randomly selected. We computed the metrics in 30 repetitions for each of the datasets evaluated and for each model analyzed. The features involved in the process were normalized with mean zero and unit variance. All outputs of the model were normalized to the range $[-1, 1]$ in the case of classification problems. The initial number of molecules in all models were fixed to = 5. The same was done for the batch size equals to 0.02. For better representations, the models analyzed were represented by these acronyms: PSO-AHN, HSA-AHN, CS-AHN, GWO-AHN, and WOA-AHN representing respectively the optimization techniques of particle swarm optimization, harmony search algorithm, cuckoo search, grey wolf optimization, and whale optimization algorithm. All the experiments were run in a computer Core 2 Duo, 2.27 GHz wiith 3-GB RAM using MATLAB.

Datasets were retrieved from a repository specialized in machine learning problems (UCI Machine Learning Repository [2]). To evaluate the training proposal for AHN in this paper, we use databases with different features, as shown in Table 1.

Table 1. Datasets used in the classification and regression experiments.

Dataset	Acronym	Features	Training samples	Testing samples
Classification				
Haberman	HAB	3	214	92
Transfusion	TRA	4	523	225
Liver Disorder	LIV	6	242	103
Pulsar	PUL	8	12,529	5,369
Regression				
Air Quality	AIQ	2	192	80
Carbon Nanotubes	CAR	5	6,698	2,870
Abalone	ABA	8	2,874	1,393

4   Results and Discussion

Table 2 presents the results of the classification of binary patterns in each of the experiments carried out, highlighting the best in bold values.

For the Haberman (HAB) database, the models maintained similar behaviors in the classification of patterns. It is noteworthy that, in average values, the model that uses PSO in training has better results in accuracy, sensitivity, and AUC. For the transfusion-related (TRA) database, the best results were obtained by the model that uses GWO. Except for the execution time and specificity, all other indexes were leading for this model. When analyzing the results of liver diseases (LIV), the model that had the best accuracy was the one where its parameters were defined with HSA, but specificity, sensitivity and time of execution were better in other models used in the benchmark. Finally, the technique that uses CS works efficiently in the evaluation of pulsars (PUL). Figure 1 presents the results graphically.

Table 3 presents the results for the regression problems. Highlighted values in bold were the best found in each dataset. As shown, CS performs the best, outstanding in two out three datasets evaluated. It should be noted that the models maintained results close to RMSE and training time, demonstrating the ability to define parameters with meta-heuristic optimization techniques. Figure 2 shows the results obtained graphically.

As shown in the results, meta-heuristic optimization methods are able to serve as training algorithms for AHN. It is evident that all meta-heuristic optimization methods in binary classification datasets perform similarly, while CS

Table 2. Performance results for binary classification.

Algorithm	Dataset	Accuracy (%)	AUC	Sensitivity	Specificity	Training time (s)
PSO-AHN	HAB	**75.14 ± 4.22**	**0.5712 ± 0.0228**	**0.1612 ± 0.0011**	0.9812 ± 0.0002	0.2314 ± 0.0014
HSA-AHN		74.42 ± 5.85	0.5681 ± 0.0314	0.1487 ± 0.0003	0.9875 ± 0.0001	**0.2101 ± 0.0098**
CS-AHN		75.03 ± 4.94	0.5702 ± 0.0142	0.1506 ± 0.0003	**0.9898 ± 0.0002**	0.2258 ± 0.0014
GWO-AHN		74.89 ± 3.97	0.5698 ± 0.0104	0.1498 ± 0.0005	**0.9898 ± 0.0001**	0.2358 ± 0.0116
WOA-AHN		74.25 ± 6.02	0.5641 ± 0.0140	0.1581 ± 0.0003	0.9701 ± 0.0001	0.2087 ± 0.0104
PSO-AHN	TRA	76.29 ± 3.25	0.6125 ± 0.0013	0.4287 ± 0.0015	**0.7963 ± 0.0078**	**0.3628 ± 0.0042**
HSA-AHN		78.69 ± 1.97	0.6014 ± 0.0009	0.4628 ± 0.0001	0.7400 ± 0.0024	0.3928 ± 0.0022
CS-AHN		79.14 ± 2.24	0.6095 ± 0.0004	0.4926 ± 0.0007	0.7264 ± 0.0014	0.3997 ± 0.0042
GWO-AHN		**79.15 ± 2.29**	**0.6305 ± 0.0012**	**0.5029 ± 0.0003**	0.7581 ± 0.0017	0.4118 ± 0.0002
WOA-AHN		79.11 ± 1.83	0.6234 ± 0.0021	0.4995 ± 0.0003	0.7473 ± 0.0057	0.4287 ± 0.0052
PSO-AHN	LIV	66.87 ± 0.0788	0.5987 ± 0.0836	**0.6250 ± 0.0117**	0.5724 ± 0.0126	0.5120 ± 0.0140
HSA-AHN		**69.54 ± 0.0674**	**0.6205 ± 0.0423**	0.6114 ± 0.0009	0.6296 ± 0.0071	0.5102 ± 0.0012
CS-AHN		67.74 ± 0.1021	0.5688 ± 0.0381	0.6724 ± 0.0012	0.5686 ± 0.0101	**0.4998 ± 0.0174**
GWO-AHN		68.47 ± 0.0643	0.5967 ± 0.0511	0.5981 ± 0.0207	0.5953 ± 0.0407	0.5401 ± 0.0080
WOA-AHN		67.15 ± 0.0243	0.5981 ± 0.0701	0.4987 ± 0.0041	**0.6975 ± 0.0107**	0.5608 ± 0.0011
PSO-AHN	PUL	96.89 ± 0.0041	0.9651 ± 0.0015	**0.9948 ± 0.0001**	0.9354 ± 0.0001	**25.1840 ± 0.0147**
HSA-AHN		97.14 ± 0.0058	0.9587 ± 0.0043	0.9785 ± 0.0004	0.9389 ± 0.0012	32.2658 ± 0.2602
CS-AHN		**97.99 ± 0.0044**	**0.9745 ± 0.0021**	0.9851 ± 0.0011	0.9639 ± 0.0071	37.6587 ± 0.3607
GWO-AHN		96.18 ± 0.0043	0.9651 ± 0.0104	0.9759 ± 0.0013	0.9543 ± 0.0007	36.1218 ± 0.1642
WOA-AHN		97.12 ± 0.0043	0.9702 ± 0.0025	0.9659 ± 0.0017	**0.9745 ± 0.0007**	41.1911 ± 0.4621

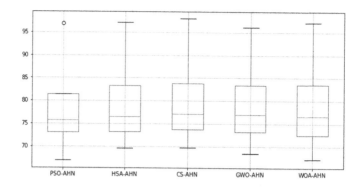

Fig. 1. Graphical representation of accuracy for classification problems.

outperformed in regression datasets. These results should be treated as preliminary since the conditions of the datasets were not varied and the number of features in all datasets are not very different among them. In addition, the training time is not excessive for none of the datasets, except for PUL which we assume it is for the number of samples. In this regard, the present work is limited by the fixed conditions in the experimentation that should be addressed in a future work.

Table 3. Performance results for regression.

Algorithm	Dataset	RMSE	Training time (s)
PSO-AHN	AIQ	1.5247 ± 0.0054	0.2147 ± 0.0005
HSA-AHN		1.8417 ± 0.0172	0.0620 ± 0.0184
CS-AHN		**1.1512 ± 0.0021**	**0.0590 ± 0.0015**
GWO-AHN		1.1914 ± 0.0147	0.2184 ± 0.0187
WOA-AHN		2.0502 ± 0.3243	0.2951 ± 0.0147
PSO-AHN	CAR	**4.2364 ± 0.0766**	2.5829 ± 0.2611
HSA-AHN		4.3291 ± 0.4160	**0.3634 ± 0.0664**
CS-AHN		5.581 ± 4.3297	3.1736 ± 0.1314
GWO-AHN		5.6983 ± 5.9530	2.4477 ± 0.2460
WOA-AHN		4.512 ± 0.7843	1.6987 ± 0.0118
PSO-AHN	ABA	0.6985 ± 0.0058	0.0436 ± 0.0009
HSA-AHN		0.7154 ± 0.0021	**0.0403 ± 0.0056**
CS-AHN		**0.6815 ± 0.0047**	0.0876 ± 0.0051
GWO-AHN		0.8154 ± 0.0030	0.0377 ± 0.0140
WOA-AHN		0.7112 ± 0.0010	0.0087 ± 0.0019

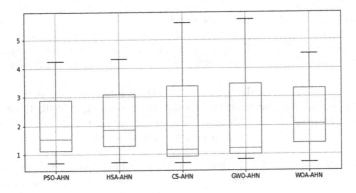

Fig. 2. Graphical representation of RMSE for regression problems.

5 Conclusions

In this work, we presents a comparative analysis of five meta-heuristic optimization methods implemented as training algorithms for AHN models. It evaluates the predictability power (accuracy and AUC) of the trained AHN models and the training time consumption.

Results showed that there is no evidence that any of the five meta-heuristic optimization algorithms applied were better for binary classification. But, CS was clearly better in training AHN models for regression datasets. In terms of the training time, it was not excessive in any case, except in one dataset that is slightly larger in samples than the others. But, in all the cases, the training algorithms performed in less than 45 s.

For future work, we will address training performance of AHN wth more complicated and varied datasets to measure other performance in the meta-heuristic optimization methods. Also, other meta-heuristic optimization methods will be tested.

References

1. Abdullah, S., Burke, E.K., McCollum, B.: A hybrid evolutionary approach to the university course timetabling problem. In: 2007 IEEE Congress on Evolutionary Computation. pp. 1764–1768. IEEE (2007)
2. Asuncion, A., Newman, D.: Uci machine learning repository (2007)
3. Bengio, Y.: Gradient-based optimization of hyperparameters. Neural Comput. **12**(8), 1889–1900 (2000)
4. Geem, Z.W., Kim, J.H., Loganathan, G.V.: A new heuristic optimization algorithm: harmony search. Simulation **76**(2), 60–68 (2001)
5. Glover, F.W., Kochenberger, G.A.: Handbook of metaheuristics. Springer Science & Business Media, Berlin (2006)
6. Handl, J., Knowles, J.: An evolutionary approach to multiobjective clustering. IEEE Trans. Evol. Comput. **11**(1), 56–76 (2007)

7. Harizan, S., Kuila, P.: Evolutionary algorithms for coverage and connectivity problems in wireless sensor networks: a study. In: Das, S.K., Samanta, S., Dey, N., Kumar, R. (eds.) Design Frameworks for Wireless Networks. LNNS, vol. 82, pp. 257–280. Springer, Singapore (2020). https://doi.org/10.1007/978-981-13-9574-1_11

8. Karimi, F., Lotfi, S., Izadkhah, H.: Multiplex community detection in complex networks using an evolutionary approach. Expert Syst. Appl. 146, 113184 (2020)

9. Kennedy, J., Eberhart, R.: Particle swarm optimization. In: Proceedings of ICNN 1995-International Conference on Neural Networks. vol. 4, pp. 1942–1948. IEEE (1995)

10. Kuila, P., Gupta, S.K., Jana, P.K.: A novel evolutionary approach for load balanced clustering problem for wireless sensor networks. Swarm Evol. Comput. 12, 48–56 (2013)

11. Mirjalili, S., Lewis, A.: The whale optimization algorithm. Adv. Eng. Software 95, 51–67 (2016). https://doi.org/10.1016/j.advengsoft.2016.01.008

12. Mirjalili, S., Mirjalili, S.M., Lewis, A.: Grey wolf optimizer. Adv. Eng. Software 69, 46–61 (2014). https://doi.org/10.1016/j.advengsoft.2013.12.007

13. Ponce, H., de Campos Souza, P.V., Guimarães, A.J., González-Mora, G.: Stochastic parallel extreme artificial hydrocarbon networks: an implementation for fast and robust supervised machine learning in high-dimensional data. Eng. Appl. Artif. Intell. 89, 103427 (2020)

14. Ponce, H., González-Mora, G., Morales-Olvera, E., Souza, P.: Development of fast and reliable nature-inspired computing for supervised learning in high-dimensional data. In: Rout, M., Rout, J.K., Das, H. (eds.) Nature Inspired Computing for Data Science. SCI, vol. 871, pp. 109–138. Springer, Cham (2020). https://doi.org/10.1007/978-3-030-33820-6_5

15. Ponce, H., Ponce, P.: Artificial organic networks. In: Electronics, Robotics and Automotive Mechanics Conference (CERMA). pp. 29–34. IEEE (2011)

16. Ponce, H., Ponce, P.: Artificial hydrocarbon networks: a new algorithm bio-inspired on organic chemistry. Int. J. Artif. Intell. Comput. Res. 4(1), 39–51 (2012)

17. Ponce-Espinosa, H., Ponce-Cruz, P., Molina, A.: Artificial organic networks. Artificial Organic Networks. SCI, vol. 521, pp. 53–72. Springer, Cham (2014). https://doi.org/10.1007/978-3-319-02472-1_3

18. Rodriguez, J.D., Perez, A., Lozano, J.A.: Sensitivity analysis of k-fold cross validation in prediction error estimation. IEEE Trans. Pattern Anal. Mach. Intell. 32(3), 569–575 (2009)

19. Sinha, A., Malo, P., Deb, K.: A review on bilevel optimization: from classical to evolutionary approaches and applications. IEEE Trans. Evol. Comput. 22(2), 276–295 (2017)

20. Sun, J., Garibaldi, J.M., Hodgman, C.: Parameter estimation using metaheuristics in systems biology: a comprehensive review. IEEE/ACM Trans. Comput. Biol. Bioinform. 9(1), 185–202 (2011)

21. Yang, X.S., Deb, S.: Cuckoo search via lévy flights. In: 2009 World Congress on Nature & Biologically Inspired Computing (NaBIC). pp. 210–214. IEEE (2009)

Fatty Chain Acids Risk Factors in Sudden Infant Death Syndrome: A Genetic Algorithm Approach

Karen E. Villagrana-Bañuelos[1]([✉]) [iD], Laura A. Zanella-Calzada[2] [iD],
Irma E. Gonzalez-Curiel[1] [iD], Jorge I. Galván-Tejada[1] [iD],
and Carlos E. Galván-Tejada[1] [iD]

[1] Universidad Autónoma de Zacatecas,
Jardín Juarez 147, Centro, Zacatecas 98000, Zac, Mexico
{kvillagrana,irmacuriel,gatejo,ericgalvan}@uaz.edu.mx
[2] LORIA (INRIA, CNRS, Université de Lorraine), Campus Scientifique BP 239,
54506 Nancy, France
laura.zanella-calzada@univ-lorraine.fr

Abstract. Medicine and artificial intelligence (AI) have made great progress, since they have achieved unprecedented knowledge and explanations about how the human body works and about some diseases that seemed to have no way of preventing, diagnosing or treating or simply help make those processes more efficient. Sudden infant death syndrome (SIDS) could benefit from AI, since to date it has not been possible to clarify what actually causes it, devices to monitor vital signs have been used so far, an recently was made a predictive model to predict results from an autopsy in infants, however, further investigation is necessary to more effectively prevent. The main objective of this work is to be able to find a set of factors related to short chain fatty acids (SCFA) that could help to understand the risk of SIDS. Was used a public dataset named "Analysis of SCFA profile in infants dying of SIDS compared to infants dying of controls", that contained SCFA values, of deceased children, labels them as SIDS death and from another cause (control). For pre-processing some variables were removed from the dataset. An analysis was performed with a feature ranking with genetic algorithm (GA) and risk analysis using the information of SCFAs and their relationship with SIDS, is presented. The median was calculated for each of the SFCA, which served to form two groups necessary to evaluate the risk difference and the risk relationship depending on the amount of acids present for each subject. As results, Octanoic acid represents a risk difference of 18% for the population with an amount less than 3.5 uM and an individual risk of 1.28 times. On the other hand, hexanoic and propinoic acids present a risk difference of less than 11% with a lesser amount of 23 and 128 uM respectively, as well as an individual risk of approximately 0.85 times. As conclusion there is 18% higher risk of developing SIDS if octanoic acid is less than 3.5 uM or 1.28 times greater risk. On the other hand, with hexanoic and propionic acid, they agree that there is an 11% lower risk of developing SIDS (of manner independent), if the values are less than 23 uM and 128 uM, respectively.

© Springer Nature Switzerland AG 2020
L. Martínez-Villaseñor et al. (Eds.): MICAI 2020, LNAI 12468, pp. 235–245, 2020.
https://doi.org/10.1007/978-3-030-60884-2_18

Keywords: SIDS · SCFA · Genetic algorithm · Risk ratio · Risk difference · Machine learning · Artificial intelligence

1   Introduction

Interdisciplinary research is a necessity that allows scientific and technological advance; one of the disciplines that has been favored is medicine, which together with artificial intelligence (AI), have made great progress, since they have achieved unprecedented knowledge and explanations about how the human body works and about some diseases that seemed have no way to prevent, diagnose or treat [30] or simply help to make those processes more efficient, for example with predictive models [2,3,8,19,20,33].

Sudden infant death syndrome (SIDS) represents a challenge, due to its great complexity, so it can benefit from the relationship described above. SIDS can be described as the death of babies less than one year of age, known previously healthy, i.e. without apparent cause, after an autopsy, and exhaustive research. In the United States, SIDS represents the leading cause of death among infants one month to one year of age, and there has been little or no improvement in the mortality rate from this cause since the 1990s [11].

This disease causes great impact in society, especially parents, as it attacks without warning and leaves few or no clues about the cause that produces it. It is considered multi-factorial [14,22], since there multiple factors that can be causing it [7,18,28,31]; however, a definitive explanation has not been reached.

One of the explanations of this syndrome is related to the inborn errors of metabolism (IEM) [31], which are disorders caused by mutations in genes that encode enzymes with a specific role in metabolism [6].

Within the IEM are the disorders of beta oxidation of fatty acids [6], which can affect different enzymes, since they intervene in the metabolism of fatty acids, e.g. acyl-CoA dehydrogenase where there are three isoenzymes specializing in long-chain (less than 18 carbon atoms) fatty acids, medium-chain (less than 14) and short-chain (less than 8) [13]. According to literature, middle chain fatty acids and SIDS have been linked [1,12,15,23]; however, research has shown the need to explore other types of acids [21].

An approach that has been widely used by research in different fields, such as medicine, to try to find information that cannot be easily identified by a human being, are machine learning algorithms. Among these algorithms are genetic algorithms (GA), which their main purpose is to analyze and find knowledge from the information contain in complex and large datasets [26], resembling the process that is developed biologically in natural selection. GA takes into consideration a set of features that are influencing an outcome feature, in the same way as variables influences biological processes and synergy between genes, proteins and metabolites. Then, starting from random populations of data, the objective is to find the top most significant features to be used to develop a statistical model that describes the relationship between these features, using mechanisms such as higher rate of replication of the more effective features, mutation for the generation of variants and crossover for the improvement of combinations [29], such as the work by Yang et al. [32], in which the combinations of the metabolism of steroid hormones and the genes involved in breast cancer were analyzed through GA and statistical techniques, successfully detecting the differences between cancer cases breast and non-cancerous cases [32].

SIDS has been studied extensively from the medical field [11], without being the exception of the engineering area, the latter has focused on monitoring vital signs, issuing alarms to tutors, in an attempt to prevent it [9,27], recently Booth et al. [5], carried out a predictive model to predict the results of a childhood autopsy in the syndrome of unexpected infant death, which demonstrates the need to continue investigating these disorders using machine learning techniques, and try to find characteristics that help their prevention and develop computer assisted diagnosis (CAD) systems.

Based on this, the main objective of this work is to be able to find a set of factors related to short chain fatty acids (SCFAs) (which are naturally produced in the colon by the fermentation of carbohydrates and proteins that are accessible to the microbiota [10]) that could help to understand the causes of SIDS. For this purpose, it is proposed the development of a statistical analysis, based on a GA, that allows to describe the relationship between the information of SCFAs and SIDS. After evaluating the relation of the different fatty acids with respect to the diagnosis of SIDS, and obtaining a rank of them, evaluate in terms of risk, the relation of the three main acids, allowing to have evidence for a possible screening of particular acids, as well as a metric that helps to the attention and surveillance depending on the risk.

2 Materials and Methods

This section describes in detail the public data set with the profile of SCFAs, as well as the tools used to develop this work. A flowchart of the methodology followed is presented in Fig. 1.

2.1 Data Set Description

The dataset used for this work is publicly available in the NIH Common Fund's National Metabolomics Data Repository, "Analysis of SCFA profile in infants dying of SIDS compared to infants dying of controls". These data were provided by the University of Michigan, Biomedical Research Core Facilities and describes a case-control study, short chain fatty acid profile for all subjects, and sudden infant death labelling available.

The data set is entitled "SCFA profile in babies dying from SIDS" and it is comprised by the data of 18 patients, five controls (death by other factors) and 13 cases (diagnosis of sudden infant death). The features contained in the data

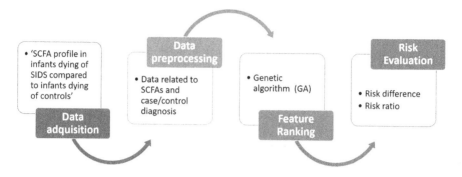

Fig. 1. Flowchart of the methodology proposed to rank and study SCFAs affecting SIDS.

were calculated postmortem by cold extraction measured by electron ionization gas chromatography mass spectrometry (EI GC-MS) without derivatization, and they are described in Table 1. The unit of these values is uM.

Table 1. Features contained in the "SCFA profile in babies dying from SIDS" dataset.

	Feature	Chemical Formula
1	Postmortem interval PMI hours	-
2	Gestational age weeks	-
3	Postnatal age weeks	-
4	Isopentanoic acid (Isovaleric acid)	$(CH_3)_2CH(CH_2)COOH$
5	Octanoic acid (Caprylic acid)	$CH_3(CH_2)_6COOH$
6	Propanoic acid (Propionic acid)	CH_3CH_2COOH
7	Isobutanoic acid (Isobutyric acid)	$(CH_3)_2CHCO_2H$
8	Butanoic acid (Butyric acid)	$CH_3(CH_2)_2COOH$
9	Hexanoic acid (Caproic acid)	$CH_3(CH_2)_4COOH$
10	Pentanoic acid (Valeric acid)	$CH_3(CH_2)_3COOH$
11	Ethanoic acid (Acetic acid)	CH_3COOH

Despite the fact that octanoic acid is included in this data set as a short chain, and although there is controversy since the literature usually includes it as a medium chain fatty acid [16], some sources of information [13] mention that until to eight carbons, it can be considered as short chain, therefore, we will consider it in this work as such.

2.2 Data Availability

This data is available at the NIH Common Fund's National Metabolomics Data Repository (NMDR) website, https://www.metabolomicsworkbench.org, the Metabolomics Workbench, where it has been assigned Project ID PR000512. The data can be accessed directly via it's Project doi: 10.21228/M8GQ27. This work is supported by NIH grant U2C-DK119886.

2.3 Data Preprocessing

The preprocessing performed for this study consists of manually removing data related to gestational, postnatal and postmortem periods, leaving only data related to SCFAs and case/control diagnosis.

2.4 Feature Ranking

For the significance ranking of SCFAa with respect to SIDS, an approach for feature selection based on a GA, is used for this study.

The GALGO package (implemented in R [24]), which uses GA for selecting feature subsets, starts its procedure from a random population of feature subsets of a given size. In GALGO, genes represent features whereas chromosomes represent a set of n features that are included in the multivariate model. Each of these chromosomes are tested for its ability to predict an outcome feature, measuring the level of accuracy, based on a fitness function. The general principle is to substitute the initial population with a new population contained by variants of chromosomes with higher classification accuracy. This process is repeated a given number of times to achieve a desired level of accuracy. The operators used for the improvement in the chromosome population are mainly based on the process of natural selection, (1) selection, (2) mutation and (3) crossover [29].

Therefore, the data set comprised by cases and controls feeds GALGO, evolving in a set of multivariate models to finally obtain models with higher fit. The rank is obtained depending on the frequency with which the features appear in these models generated throughout the evolutionary process.

2.5 Risk Evaluation

To evaluate the fatty acid ordered by the GA, an assessment in terms of population risk is used, i.e. absolute risk (risk difference) and relative risk (risk ratio).

Risk Difference. The risk difference is defined as the difference in risk of those with the condition, such as a disease, between the exposed and unexposed group, Eq. 1.

$$RD = risk\,of\,exposure\,group - risk\,of\,unexposed\,group, \tag{1}$$

Risk Ratio. The relative risk or risk ratio is the ratio between the exposed and unexposed group, calculated by Eq. 2.

$$RR = \frac{risk\,of\,exposure\,group}{risk\,of\,unexposed\,group}, \tag{2}$$

3   Experiments and Results

After data preprocessing, there information of 18 subjects was contained in the dataset, five controls and 13 cases. Each one described by the measured values in uM of the eight SCFAs. Among the features, it was found that four of them presented outliers, as shown in Fig. 2; however, since they do not correspond to the same observation, they were decided to be kept.

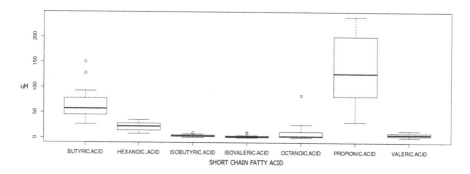

Fig. 2. Boxplot of each of the short chain fatty acids, to know the distribution and possible outliers in them

For the selection of the most significant features, the GA, GALGO [29], was used through its R package optimized for bioinformatics applications.

Table 2. Setup parameters for the configuration of the analysis with GALGO.

Parameter	Description
Input data	SFCAs profile from the 18 subjects
Outcome	Diagnostic of case/control (1/0)
Classification method	Nearest Centroid[a]
Accuracy target	100%[b]
Chromosome size	Chromosomes comprised by 5 genes (features)[c]
Generations	200 generations[d]
Evolutionary cycle	100 evolutionary cycles[e]

[a] Chosen given the low computational cost allowing a fast gene ranking.
[b] Chosen to force the mutation and get the best possible fit.
[c] Chosen based on suggested in bioinformatics literature [17,29].
[d] Chosen to evolve and acquire a good representation of the possible solutions.
[e] Chosen to generate random initial populations.

After 200 evolution cycles, all processes reach a stability of 92% of fitness, as shown in Fig. 3. This process generates the ranking of genes with those that reappear more frequently throughout these cycles. Figure 4 shows ordered the features representing SFCAs related to SIDS, according to their frequency of appearance in the different chromosomes, in descendent order.

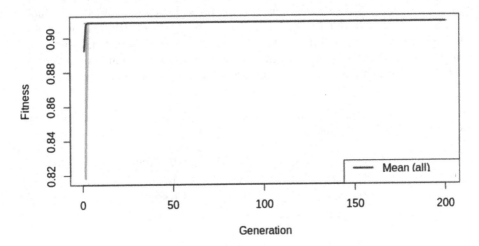

Fig. 3. Evolution, in terms of accuracy, of the 100 models (chromosomes) over 200 generations.

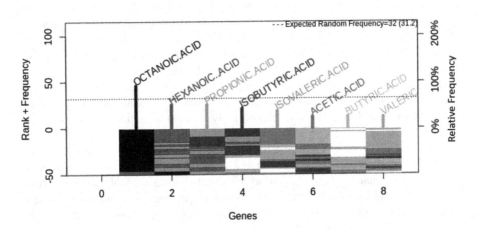

Fig. 4. Gene rank after 100 evolutionary process of 200 generations each. SFCAs ordered by frequency.

Once the feature ranking is obtained through the AG, the three main SCFAs are evaluated in terms of risk to the population. To assess the population, the median of each of the selected SCFAs is calculated to constitute two groups required to calculate the risk. The median is selected to split and comprise both groups, since allows to give a more representative value of the samples even when the presence of outliers.

The Table 3 shows the median calculated for each of the SFCAs, which serves to conform the two groups necessary to evaluate the difference in risk and the risk ratio depending on the amount of acids present for each subject. Octanoic acid presents an risk difference of 18% for the population with an amount less than 3.5 uM and an individual risk of 1.28 times. On the other hand, Hexanoic and Propinoic acids present 11% minor risk difference with an amount less of 23 and 128 uM respectively, as well as an individual risk approximately 0.85 times.

Table 3. Risk difference and Risk ratio in the sample from three main short chain fatty acids related to SIDS after GA ranking.

SCFA	Median	Risk difference	Risk ratio
Octanoic	3.50	0.18	1.28
Hexanoic	23.00	−0.11	0.86
Propionic	128.00	−0.11	0.86

4   Discussion and Conclusions

In this work, an analysis based on a GA and risk analysis using the information of SCFAs and their relationship with SIDS, is presented. A data set composed by the profile of SCFAs, previously evaluated as death by other situation or by SIDS, is used. The main purpose is to identify the risk of SIDS in infants.

As observed in Table 3, there is 18% higher risk of developing SIDS if octanoic acid is less than 3.5 uM, or there is a 1.28-fold higher risk.

On the other hand, with hexanoic and propionic acid, they agree that there is an 11% lower risk of developing SIDS (of manner independent), if the values are less than 23 uM and 128 uM, respectively; the same as 0.86 times more less risk of suffering it.

Finding that there is a relationship between SCFA values in babies who died from SIDS, it allows to generalize, in the sense that it is unknown whether or not the patients had a diagnosed metabolic disease, both control cases and those labeled SIDS; which supposes that regardless of presenting or not presenting a diagnosed metabolic disease, it is possible to predict an increased risk of suffering from SIDS with the value of the mentioned acids.

The SCFA, which was identified with the GA that best identifies patients with SIDS, was octanoic acid, even assuming that the possible link to various metabolic disorders (which is assumed to be labeled in the database) is completely ruled out with the diagnosis of SIDS) even with the multiple techniques to diagnose them [4], and taking into account the multifactorial nature of this pathology, it is premature to say that octanoic acid can be used as a biochemical marker to identify the increased potential risk of SIDS.

Also the results regarding hexanoic and propionic acids are promising, in the sense that when they are present below the levels described, they could be considered as protective factors, clarifying that when they are present at the levels previously described, it does not ensure that they will not suffer a fatal event.

However, the fact of being identified these acids, among a population unknown for diagnosis of IEM, and having the low probability described in the literature [25], of suffering it, provides encouraging results, to build indicators that help prevention of the SIDS.

The foregoing will generate a potential line of research that allows babies to be sampled, at least with respect to these acids for reasons of cost, and to create a database that allows identifying the average values that are considered to be within the normal range. This could be complemented with a record of octanoic, propionic and hexanoic acids values in patients of the same age range who die from any other reason, contrasted with cases of death from SIDS.

References

1. Arens, R., et al.: Prevalence of medium-chain acyl-coenzyme a dehydrogenase deficiency in the sudden infant death syndrome. J. Pediatr. **122**(5), 715–718 (1993)
2. Atabaki-Pasdar, N., et al.: Predicting and elucidating the etiology of fatty liver disease: a machine learning modeling and validation study in the imi direct cohorts. PLoS Med. **17**(6), e1003149 (2020)
3. Böcker, S., Broeckling, C., Schymanski, E., Zamboni, N.: Computational metabolomics: from cheminformatics to machine learning (dagstuhl seminar 20051). In: Dagstuhl Reports, vol. 10. Schloss Dagstuhl-Leibniz-Zentrum für Informatik (2020)
4. Boles, R.G., Martin, S.K., Blitzer, M.G., Rinaldo, P.: Biochemical diagnosis of fatty acid oxidation disorders by metabolite analysis of postmortem liver. Hum. Pathol. **25**(8), 735–741 (1994)
5. Booth, J., et al.: Machine learning approaches to determine feature importance for predicting infant autopsy outcome. medRxiv (2020)
6. Chávez-Ocaña, S., Bravata-Alcántara, J.C., Sierra-Martínez, M.: Errores innatos del metabolismo, una mirada a un tópico poco valorado. Revista del Hospital Juárez de México **85**(3), 159–167 (2018)
7. Duncan, J.R., Byard, R.W.: SIDS Sudden Infant and Early Childhood Death: The Past, the Present and the Future. University of Adelaide Press, Adelaide (2018)
8. Fang, X., Liu, Y., Ren, Z., Du, Y., Huang, Q., Garmire, L.X.: Lilikoi v2. 0: a deep-learning enabled, personalized pathway-based r package for diagnosis and prognosis predictions using metabolomics data. bioRxiv (2020)
9. Gallo, X.L., Lechón, S., Mora, S., Vallejo-Huanga, D.: Marrsids: Monitoring assistant to reduce the risk of sudden infant death syndrome. In: 2019 XXII Symposium on Image, Signal Processing and Artificial Vision (STSIVA), pp. 1–4. IEEE (2019)
10. Gill, P., van Zelm, M.J., M, P.G.: Review article: short chain fatty acids as potential therapeutic agents in human gastrointestinal and inflammatory disorders. Aliment Pharmacol. Ther. **48**, 15–34 (2018)

11. Hageman, J.R.: The sids summit. Pediatr. Ann. **49**(1), e1–e2 (2020)
12. Kaku, N., et al.: Diagnostic potential of stored dried blood spots for inborn errors of metabolism: a metabolic autopsy of medium-chain acyl-coa dehydrogenase deficiency. J. Clin. Pathol. **71**(10), 885–889 (2018)
13. Koolman, J., Röhm, K.H.: Bioquímica. Médica Panamericana, Madrid, España (2005)
14. Kugener, B., et al.: Sudden infant death syndrome: a multifactorial disease. In: Mathematical Modelling in Biomedicine, pp. 57–57 (2019)
15. Li, Y., Zhu, R., Liu, Y., Song, J., Xu, J., Yang, Y.: Medium-chain acyl-coenzyme a dehydrogenase deficiency: six cases in the chinese population. Pediatr. Int. **61**(6), 551–557 (2019)
16. Martínez, C.V., Blanco, A., Nomdedeu, C.L.: Alimentación y nutrición: manual teórico-práctico. Ediciones Díaz de Santos (2005)
17. Martínez-Torteya, A., Rodríguez-Rojas, J., Celaya-Padilla, J.M., Galván-Tejada, J.I., Treviño, V., Tamez-Peña, J.G.: MRI signal and texture features for the prediction of MCI to alzheimer's disease progression. In: Medical Imaging 2014: Computer-Aided Diagnosis, vol. 9035, p. 903526. International Society for Optics and Photonics (2014)
18. Moon, R.Y., Hauck, F.R.: Risk factors and theories. SIDS Sudden Infant and Early Childhood Death: The Past, the Present and the Future. University of Adelaide Press, Adelaide (2018)
19. Oh, T.G., et al.: A universal gut-microbiome-derived signature predicts cirrhosis. Cell Metabolism (2020)
20. de Oliveira Lima, E., et al.: Metabolomics and machine learning approaches combined in pursuit for more accurate paracoccidioidomycosis diagnoses. mSystems **5**(3), e00258 (2020)
21. Opdal, S., Rognum, T.: The sudden infant death syndrome gene: does it exist? Pediatrics **114**(4), e506–12 (2004)
22. Otagiri, T., et al.: Cardiac ion channel gene mutations in sudden infant death syndrome. Pediatr. Res. **64**(5), 482–487 (2008)
23. Prakash, S.: Beta (β)-oxidation of fatty acid and its associated disorders. Int. J. **5**(1), 158–172 (2018)
24. R Core Team: R: A Language and Environment for Statistical Computing. R Foundation for Statistical Computing, Vienna, Austria (2020). https://www.R-project.org/
25. Rosenthal, N.A., Currier, R.J., Baer, R.J., Feuchtbaum, L., Jelliffe-Pawlowski, L.L.: Undiagnosed metabolic dysfunction and sudden infant death syndrome-a case-control study. Paediatr. Perinatal Epidemiol. **29**(2), 151–155 (2015)
26. Sanchita, G., Anindita, D.: Evolutionary algorithm based techniques to handle big data. In: Techniques and Environments for Big Data Analysis, pp. 113–158. Springer (2016). https://doi.org/10.1007/978-3-319-27520-8_7
27. Shamsir, S., Hassan, O., Islam, S.K.: Smart infant-monitoring system with machine learning model to detect physiological activities and ambient conditions. In: 2020 IEEE International Instrumentation and Measurement Technology Conference (I2MTC), pp. 1–6. IEEE (2020)
28. Tester, D.J., et al.: Cardiac genetic predisposition in sudden infant death syndrome. J. Am. Coll. Cardiol. **71**(11), 1217–1227 (2018)
29. Trevino, V., Falciani, F.: Galgo: an r package for multivariate variable selection using genetic algorithms. Bioinformatics **22**(9), 1154–1156 (2006)

30. Tugizimana, F., Engel, J., Salek, R., Dubery, I., Piater, L., Burgess, K.: The disruptive 4IR in the life sciences: Metabolomics. In: The Disruptive Fourth Industrial Revolution, pp. 227–256. Springer (2020). https://doi.org/10.1007/978-3-030-48230-5_10
31. Van Rijt, W.J., et al.: Inborn errors of metabolism that cause sudden infant death: a systematic review with implications for population neonatal screening programmes. Neonatology **109**(4), 297–302 (2016)
32. Yang, C.H., Lin, Y.D., Chuang, L.Y., Chang, H.W.: Evaluation of breast cancer susceptibility using improved genetic algorithms to generate genotype SNP barcodes. IEEE/ACM Trans. Comput. Biol. Bioinform. **10**(2), 361–371 (2013)
33. Yin, P.N., et al.: Histopathological distinction of non-invasive and invasive bladder cancers using machine learning approaches. BMC Med. Inf. Decis. Making **20**(1), 1–11 (2020)

Best Paper Award, First Place

An NSGA-III-Based Multi-objective Intelligent Autoscaler for Executing Engineering Applications in Cloud Infrastructures

Virginia Yannibelli[1]([⊠]), Elina Pacini[2,3,4], David Monge[2], Cristian Mateos[1], and Guillermo Rodriguez[1]

[1] ISISTAN (UNICEN-CONICET), Tandil, Buenos Aires, Argentina
{virginia.yannibelli,cristian.mateos,
guillermo.rodriguez}@isistan.unicen.edu.ar
[2] ITIC, UNCUYO, Mendoza, Argentina
{epacini,dmonge}@uncu.edu.ar
[3] CONICET, Mendoza, Argentina
[4] Facultad de Ingeniería, UNCuyo, Mendoza, Argentina

Abstract. Parameter Sweep Experiments (PSEs) are commonplace to perform computer modelling and simulation at large in the context of industrial, engineering and scientific applications. PSEs require numerous computational resources since they involve the execution of many CPU-intensive tasks. Distributed computing environments such as Clouds might help to fulfill these demands, and consequently the need of Cloud autoscaling strategies for the efficient management of PSEs arise. The Multi-objective Intelligent Autoscaler (MIA) is proposed to address this problem, which is based on the Non-dominated Sorting Genetic Algorithm III (NSGA-III), while aiming to minimize makespan and cost. MIA is assessed utilizing the CloudSim simulator with three study cases coming from real-world PSEs and current characteristics of Amazon EC2. Experiments show that MIA significantly outperforms the only PSE autoscaler (MOEA autoscaler) previously reported in the literature, to solve different instances of the problem.

Keywords: Parameter Sweep Experiments · Cloud autoscaling · Multi-objective evolutionary algorithm · CloudSim · Amazon EC2

1 Introduction

Scientific computing involves large-scale computer modelling and simulation, and requires large amounts of computer resources to satisfy the ever-increasing resource intensive nature of performed experiments, being PSEs [1] a representative example. For instance, the PSE in [1] discusses a large strain viscoplastic constitutive model. A plane strain plate with a central circular hole under imposed displacements stretching the plate has been studied. By varying certain parameters (e.g. viscosity), several study cases were obtained, which must be run in parallel.

© Springer Nature Switzerland AG 2020
L. Martínez-Villaseñor et al. (Eds.): MICAI 2020, LNAI 12468, pp. 249–263, 2020.
https://doi.org/10.1007/978-3-030-60884-2_19

A kind of parallel infrastructure that improves the execution of scientific applications is Clouds [2]. This paradigm permits the on-the-fly acquisition of fully-configured infrastructures through virtualization technologies. Different types of Virtual Machine (VM) provide a wide spectrum of hardware and software configurations under a pay-per-use scheme. Prices differ according to the type of instance acquired, which represent in turn a combination of available virtual CPUs and maximum RAM/disk space. Moreover, prices may also vary according to the pricing model of the Cloud provider. Firstly, on-demand VMs can be accessed for a fixed price typically charged by hour of use. Secondly, spot VMs have fluctuating prices over time, which tend to decrease during low demand periods. In this article, the Amazon Elastic Compute Cloud (EC2) nomenclature is adopted, and VMs are referred to as instances.

In Clouds, the workloads are very often from applications with different computing requirements. Autoscaling strategies [3, 4] deal with the dynamic resizing of the infrastructure according to the application demands and constraints (i.e. determining the number/type of instances to use) and the online scheduling of such tasks on the acquired instances. These are two interdependent problems to be solved simultaneously. Since scientific applications usually comprise many tasks, and that a wide spectrum of instance types and pricing models are available, determining beforehand the right amount and type of necessary instances is not a trivial problem. In this article, the autoscaling problem for scientific applications, more specifically PSEs, is addressed, where the price model of on-demand instances is considered. The problem is formulated as minimizing the makespan of all tasks and the monetary cost. Although spot instances are generally much cheaper than their on-demand counterpart, they are subject to sudden terminations by the provider, i.e., spot instances compromise cost and reliability. The termination criteria, at least for the case of Amazon EC2, is not public [5]. In addition, delaying task execution due to the use of spot instances might be harmful. For example, when PSEs are executed it is important to control that there are no failures in their tasks because, from the disciplinary user perspective, it is very important to quickly obtain and analyze the complete model results by varying the values of one or more variables of interest. If failures occur in some of the tasks this strongly impacts the results analysis.

Most Cloud autoscaling strategies have been proposed for the efficient management of workflow applications and mainly subject to deadline constraints [6–8]. Although workflows are useful to model many scientific applications, these approaches are not appropriate for managing PSEs. The main difference is that in PSEs there are no inter-task dependencies, and tasks are somewhat homogeneous but resource-intensive, which determines a completely different autoscaling scenario. Only in [9], the authors have addressed a PSE autoscaling problem, aiming at reducing the makespan, monetary cost, and the potential impact of out-of-bid errors. However, the authors considered the use of (unreliable) spot instances. Such autoscaler is called Multi-objective Evolutionary Autoscaler (MOEA) and is based on the multi-objective evolutionary algorithm NSGA-II.

Specifically, this article aims to provide a new Cloud autoscaler for PSEs, and thus brings in the following contributions:

- A reformulation of the PSE autoscaling problem addressed in [9], resulting in a new autoscaler called Multi-objective Intelligent Autoscaler (MIA), which is based on the algorithm NSGA-III. To the best of the authors' knowledge, autoscalers based on

NSGA-III have not been reported previously in the literature. Besides, this algorithm has demonstrated to be very efficient regarding other known algorithms, such as NSGA-II, for solving various NP-Hard problems [10, 11].

- An experimental validation of MIA, showing that it outperforms MOEA [9]. Experiments consider three study cases, involving a viscoplastic problem and an elastoplastic problem from the Computational Mechanics domain, and an ensemble of the two PSEs, over simulated Cloud environments. PSE execution data derived from these applications, actual Amazon EC2 instance data, and real Amazon EC2 on-demand prices were also considered to offer a realistic experimental testbed.

The remainder of the article is organized as follows. Section 2 describes the mathematical formulation of the addressed problem. Section 3 describes the proposed MIA autoscaler. Section 4 describes the study cases considered for evaluating MIA. Section 5 presents the performed experiments by using the well-known CloudSim simulator [12], and also the results of statistical significance tests that back up the conclusions. Section 6 reports on relevant related work. Finally, Sect. 7 concludes this article.

2 Multi-objective Autoscaling Problem

Autoscaling PSEs in public Clouds (e.g., Amazon EC2, Google Cloud, Microsoft Azure) implies determining the number and type of VM instances necessary to execute PSE tasks, and scheduling these tasks on the instances, so that the predefined optimization objectives are met. This problem is recognized in the literature as a multi-objective NP-Hard problem [9].

PSEs model numerical experiments which involve many computational tasks, and usually require several hours or days to be completed. In practice, when a PSE is executed, the execution, duration and cost of the tasks differ according to the instances employed.

In a public Cloud, instances of different types of VMs have different characteristics regarding number of processors, processing power, memory size, memory speed, disk size, etc. Besides, instances of different types of VMs have different monetary cost. In this respect, instances of VMs can be acquired under different pricing models which determine the cost of instances and their behavior.

In this work, it is considered that instances are charged for every hour, i.e. the on-demand pricing model. For the remainder of this article, instances acquired under this model will be referred as on-demand instances.

The utilization of on-demand instances is considered because they are not subject to failures that can abruptly terminate the execution of the tasks assigned to them. Thus, unlike in [9], the utilization of on-demand instances guarantees that the execution of the tasks is not abruptly terminated.

The PSE autoscaling problem addressed here involves two interrelated problems. The first problem implies to determine a scaling plan describing the number and type of instances to request to the Cloud provider for the next hour (i.e., the virtual infrastructure setting). The second problem implies scheduling the tasks of the PSE on such virtual infrastructure.

As both problems are interdependent, they need to be solved periodically during the execution of the PSE to fit the infrastructure to the PSE workload, and schedule the tasks while pursuing the selected optimization objectives.

2.1 Mathematical Formulation of the Problem

Given I, the set of instance types available, and $n = |I|$ the number of instance types, a scaling plan X is defined as a vector $x^{od} = (x_1^{od}, x_2^{od}, \ldots, x_n^{od})$. The ith component of the vector, where $i \in [1, n]$, is a number ranging from 0 and the maximum number of instances for that type. This limit is established by the Cloud provider for the current autoscaling stage (i.e., for the next hour).

Problem Formulation. Given T, the set of PSE tasks considered for the current autoscaling stage, the multi-objective problem corresponding to this autoscaling stage is defined as shown in Eq. (1), subject to a set of constraints which define both the current state of the PSE execution and the current Cloud infrastructure load state.

$$min(Makespan(X), Cost(X)). \tag{1}$$

Optimization Objectives. $Makespan(X)$ is the expected execution time. Given the set of tasks T, a greedy scheduling algorithm is used to approximate this time. Each task is scheduled to an instance using the earliest completion time (ECT) criterion, which schedules a task to the instance promising the earliest completion time.

$Makespan(X)$ is shown in Eq. (2). $ST(t)$ represents the start time of the task t, and d_t represents the duration of the task t. The values of these terms are estimated by the mentioned scheduling algorithm based on the ECT criterion.

$$Makespan(X) = \max_{t \in T}\{ST(t) + d_t\} - \min_{t \in T}\{ST(t)\}. \tag{2}$$

$Cost(X)$ is the monetary cost of running all the instances indicated in x^{od} for the current autoscaling stage. This function is formally defined in Eq. (3), where x_i^{od} represents the number of instances of type i, and $price_i$ is the monetary cost of one instance of the type i for one hour of computation.

$$Cost(X) = \sum_{i=1}^{n} x_i^{od} \times price_i. \tag{3}$$

Constraints. The constraints shown in Eq. (4) set the possible number of instances of each type. Formally:

$$X_i^{min} \leq x_i^{od} \leq X_i^{max}. \tag{4}$$

where X_i^{max} and X_i^{min} are the upper and lower bounds of the number of instances regarding the type i for the current autoscaling stage. Specifically, X_i^{min} refers to the number of running instances of type i which are processing at least one task assigned during a previous autoscaling stage. The Cloud provider cannot terminate instances that are executing tasks assigned during previous autoscaling stages.

The constraint in Eq. (5) establishes that at least one instance must be acquired in the current autoscaling stage. Formally:

$$\sum_{i=1}^{n} x_i^{od} \geq 1. \tag{5}$$

3   MIA Autoscaler

During the execution of a given PSE, it is necessary to solve the multi-objective autoscaling problems corresponding to the different autoscaling stages, as mentioned in Sect. 2 and formally detailed in Sect. 2.1.

To solve each multi-objective autoscaling problem, an autoscaler based on the well-known multi-objective evolutionary algorithm NSGA-III [13] is proposed. This autoscaler develops three phases. First, the autoscaler addresses the multi-objective autoscaling problem by using the algorithm NSGA-III to obtain an approximation to the optimal Pareto set. Then, the autoscaler chooses the solution that best satisfies a predefined selection criterion. Finally, the autoscaler reconfigures the infrastructure according to the scaling plan represented by such a solution, and then initiates tasks scheduling. These three phases of the MIA autoscaler are shown in Fig. 1, and are described below.

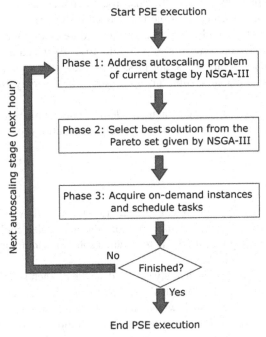

Fig. 1. Phases of the MIA autoscaler

3.1 First Phase

NSGA-III [13] is a multi-objective evolutionary algorithm widely studied in the literature. This algorithm begins creating a random initial population with s solutions, where s is a predefined number. In this case, each solution represents a feasible scaling plan, and is encoded like the vector x^{od}.

In each generation t, an offspring population Q_t with s solutions is firstly created by applying crossover and mutation operators to randomly selected solutions from the current population P_t having s solutions. In relation to the crossover and mutation operators, NSGA-III uses the well-known Simulated Binary Crossover (SBX) and Polynomial Mutation (PM) [13].

Once the offspring Q_t is created, the best s solutions from the combined current and offspring population $R_t = P_t \cup Q_t$ are selected to create a new population P_{t+1} with s solutions for the next generation. To achieve this, solutions are sorted according to non-domination levels as $\{F_1, F_2, \ldots\}$. Then, each non-domination level is selected one at a time to build the new population P_{t+1}, starting from F_1, until the size of P_{t+1} is greater or equal than s. When the size of P_{t+1} is equal to s, the next generation is started with P_{t+1}. Otherwise, when the size of P_{t+1} exceeds s, the last non-domination level selected F_l is not fully included into P_{t+1}. Specifically, the solutions from level F_1 to level F_{l-1} are included into P_{t+1}, and the k remaining solutions ($k = s - |F_1 \cup \ldots \cup F_{l-1}|$) are selected from level F_l so that P_{t+1} has s solutions.

To select the k remaining solutions from level F_l, a selection process based on reference points is applied by NSGA-III. This process creates a set of reference points widely and uniformly distributed on the normalized hyper-plane inherent to the optimization objectives of the multi-objective problem addressed by the algorithm. Then, the process emphasizes the selection of solutions from F_l which are associated with each of these reference points. Thus, this process promotes the selection of diverse and well-distributed non-dominated solutions, to preserve the diversity and distribution of the new population P_{t+1}.

The algorithm ends its execution when a predefined number of evaluations is reached. As result, the Pareto set (i.e., the set of non-dominated solutions) of the last generation is provided by the algorithm.

3.2 Second Phase

The autoscaler selects one solution from the Pareto set provided by NSGA-III, to solve the autoscaling problem. To select this solution, the autoscaler applies a predefined selection criterion. This is meant mainly to obtain a solution autonomously without the need of a human decision maker.

The applied selection criterion analyzes the distance of each solution of the Pareto set to an ideal solution, and then selects the solution which minimizes such distance. In this case, the ideal solution is such whose makespan and cost is equal to 0. Then, the distance of a solution of the Pareto set to this ideal solution is calculated by applying the well-known L_2 norm. In this respect, the L_2 norm is calculated considering both the distance between the makespan values of the two solutions and the distance between the costs of the two solutions. Thus, the selection criterion considers the trade-off of each solution of the Pareto set between both optimization objectives. The makespan and the cost of each solution of the Pareto set are calculated by Eqs. (2) and (3), respectively.

3.3 Third Phase

Considering the selected solution in the previous phase, the autoscaler acquires the number of instances for each type in I. Then, the autoscaler schedules the tasks in T on the acquired instances, by using the ECT criterion. As was detailed in Sect. 2.1, I refers to the set of instance types, and T refers to the set of PSE tasks considered for the current autoscaling stage.

4 Study Cases

The study cases considered for evaluating MIA are described in detail below.

4.1 PSE Applications

PSEs are experiments based on software simulation. Executing a PSE means obtaining as much output data as (model) input values are varied. When designing a PSE, each task is fed with an input file that has a determined configuration of its parameters values. Below, three real-world engineering problems are described, to evaluate the performance of the proposed autoscaler when the PSE-tasks are executed in a Cloud.

The first PSE studies a plane strain plate with a central circular hole [1]. The plate has a dimension of 18×10 m, with a radius equals to 5 m. Figure 2.a illustrates the plate geometry, the scheme of spatial discretization and the boundary conditions that are utilized in the numerical simulations. The number of elements of the 3D finite element mesh used is 1.152. In the study, imposed displacements at 18 m were applied until a final displacement of 2 m was achieved in 400 equal time steps each. A viscosity material parameter η was chosen as the variation parameter for generating the PSE-tasks. The parameter was varied as $\eta = \{1.10^8 \text{ Mpa}\} \cup \{x \times 10^y \text{ Mpa}, x = 1, 2, 3, 4, 5, 7 \text{ and } y = 4, 5, 6, 7\}$. Varying this parameter is useful in areas such as industrial design to determine resistance or flexibility of materials.

A second PSE studies the behavior of elastoplastic buckling of cruciform columns [14], which is used for comparing the total deformation and plasticity incremental theories [14]. Figure 2.b shows the column geometry used in the numerical simulations. The initial geometry has a length L equal to 50 mm and a cross section of 10 mm and 1 mm of width and thickness, respectively. The mesh elements number was equal to 2.176. The rotation of the cross section was imposed as initial imperfection along the column length. The angle parameter α was chosen as the variation parameter for generating the PSE-tasks, and varied as $\alpha_n = \alpha_{n-1} + 0.25$, where $\alpha_0 = 0.5$ and $n = 1, 2,..., 30$. The variation of an angle parameter may be useful to other applications such as seismic protection of structures, where it is important to know the sensitivity to the size of the imperfection.

Finally, a third PSE (ensemble) was included, which is derived from the two above described PSE applications. The execution of this application consists of dispatching to run the tasks of both PSEs at the same time, which is a realistic Cloud execution scenario.

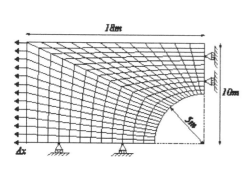
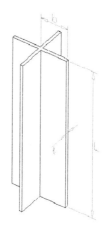

a. Geometry of the plane strain plate   **b.** Geometry of the cruciform column

Fig. 2. PSE applications

The applications were named as Plate3D, Cruciform and Ensemble. Then, for each PSE, different sizes (*small, medium and large*) were defined based on the number of tasks to run, namely 30, 100, and 300 tasks for Plate3D and Cruciform, and 60, 200 and 600 tasks for Ensemble. The greater the number of tasks to execute, the deeper the parameters exploration performed by the PSEs.

4.2 On-Demand Instances

Table 1 shows the characteristics of the on-demand instance types used in the experiments, extracted from Amazon EC2 (first column). Then, in the second column, the number of available virtual CPUs for each instance type is depicted. Next, columns three and four show the relative computing power of the VMs taking into account all the virtual CPUs (ECUtot) and the relative performance of one of the CPUs (ECU), respectively. Finally, column five presents the price per hour of computation expressed in USD.

Table 1. Instances characteristics (Amazon EC2 instances from the US-west region)

VM type	vCPU	ECUtot	ECU	Price [USD]
t2.micro	1	1	1	0.013
m3.medium	1	3	2	0.07
c3.2xlarge	8	28	3.5	0.42
r3.xlarge	4	13	3.25	0.35
m3.2xlarge	8	26	3.25	0.56

5 Computational Experiments

To evaluate the proposed MIA autoscaler, it is compared with the MOEA autoscaler [9]. To the best of the authors' knowledge, MOEA is the only autoscaler for PSEs in public Clouds previously proposed in the literature.

Below, the main characteristics of the MOEA autoscaler are presented. Then, the experimental settings used to evaluate the MIA and MOEA autoscalers are detailed. Finally, the experimental results are presented and analyzed.

5.1 MOEA Autoscaler

MOEA autoscaler [9] is based on NSGA-II [15]. This autoscaler develops three phases to solve a given multi-objective autoscaling problem. First, the autoscaler solves the multi-objective autoscaling problem using NSGA-II, to approximate the optimal Pareto set. Then, the autoscaler selects a solution from the obtained set according to a given selection criterion. Finally, the autoscaler applies such solution (i.e. scaling plan), and schedules the tasks.

Hence, the phases developed by MOEA are similar to those developed by MIA. However, these autoscalers differ regarding the multi-objective algorithm used in the first phase to address the multi-objective autoscaling problem. Specifically, MOEA utilizes the algorithm NSGA-II, and MIA utilizes the algorithm NSGA-III. The algorithm NSGA-III has been proposed in the literature to improve the performance of NSGA-II [13].

Both algorithms start creating a random initial population. In each generation, the algorithms apply the same crossover and mutation operators (i.e., SBX and PM) to create an offspring population from the current population. However, these algorithms differ significantly regarding the selection process employed to define which solutions from the combined current and offspring population will be present in the new population.

In NSGA-II, the selection process considers first the non-domination level of the solutions in the combined population, and then the crowding distance of these solutions. The crowding distance represents the distance of a solution to its neighboring solutions in the population. Then, the process emphasizes the selection of non-dominated solutions with larger crowding distances. Thus, the process promotes the selection of diverse, but potentially not-so-well-distributed, non-dominated solutions.

Unlike NSGA-II, in the algorithm NSGA-III, the selection process considers first the non-domination level of the solutions in the combined population, and then the association of these solutions to the reference points. In this respect, the process uses a set of diverse reference points (i.e., a set of reference points widely and uniformly distributed). Then, the process emphasizes the selection of non-dominated solutions which are associated with each of these reference points. Thus, this process promotes the selection of both diverse and well-distributed non-dominated solutions.

5.2 Experimental Settings

The MIA and MOEA autoscalers were evaluated on the studied applications and sizes, using the CloudSim toolkit [12]. Considering that these autoscalers are based on non-deterministic algorithms, each autoscaler was run 30 times on each studied application and size. For each run, the results obtained regarding different metrics, including makespan in seconds and cost in USD, were recorded.

To develop the runs of MIA, the parameter settings detailed in Table 2 for the algorithm NSGA-III regarding each studied application and size were considered. Such settings were selected based on an exhaustive preliminary sensitivity analysis. In this respect, to determine the best setting of NSGA-III for each application and size, 640 different settings were considered, then 30 runs of NSGA-III were developed for each setting, and finally the setting maximizing the average hypervolume (HV) value of the Pareto sets obtained by NSGA-III was selected.

Table 2. Selected parameter settings.

Application	Size	*max Eval.*	*pop. Size*	*reference PointSetSize*	*sbx rate*	*sbx dist.*	*pm rate*	*pm dist.*	HV (hyper-volume)
Plate3D	30	23301	156	102	0.85	35.90	0.25	51.20	0.843
	100	24832	156	141	0.92	54.70	0.30	32.40	0.840
	300	24832	156	154	0.92	54.70	0.30	32.40	0.836
Cruciform	30	5883	156	129	0.87	16.80	0.36	2.75	<0.001
	100	22535	156	129	0.87	16.80	0.36	2.75	0.330
	300	22535	156	129	0.87	16.80	0.36	2.75	0.330
Ensemble	60	22535	156	129	0.87	16.80	0.36	2.75	0.586
	200	12785	156	153	0.99	3.43	0.14	44.50	0.787
	600	24832	156	154	0.92	54.67	0.33	32.40	0.750

To develop the runs of MOEA, the parameter settings suggested in [9] for the algorithm NSGA-II regarding the studied applications and sizes were considered. However, a new value (i.e., a higher value) was defined for the parameter *maxEvaluations* of NSGA-II. Specifically, the parameter *maxEvaluations* of NSGA-II was set with the value used for the parameter *maxEvaluations* of NSGA-III. Thus, both algorithms utilize the same termination condition (i.e., same number of evaluations) regarding each studied application and size. This is very important to offer a fair assessment of the autoscalers.

5.3 Experimental Results

Table 3 presents the obtained experimental results. Columns 4–5 present the average values for makespan in seconds and cost in USD, respectively. Columns 6–7 present the average makespan relative percentage difference regarding MOEA (average makespan RPD) and the average cost relative percentage difference regarding MOEA (average cost RPD), respectively. These two metrics are described in detail below for clarity. Finally, column 8 presents the average value for the L_2-norm which considers the makespan and cost resulting from the experiments. This L_2-norm aggregates the metrics which are interesting for the multi-objective autoscaling problem addressed.

Table 3. Results obtained from the experiments. For the metrics average makespan, average cost and average L_2-norm, lower values represent better results. Note that bold values are better than those obtained by the MOEA autoscaler, and the symbol * indicates the best value. For the metrics average makespan RPD and average cost RPD, positive values represent favourable results.

Application	Size	Autoscaler	Makespan	Cost	Makespan RPD	Cost RPD	L_2-norm
Plate3D	30	MIA	**1235.522 ***	0.633	0.555	−0.522	**0.51 ***
		MOEA	2779.389	0.416 *	–	–	0.97
	100	MIA	**1436.633 ***	**1.703 ***	0.452	0.107	**0.48 ***
		MOEA	2619.889	1.906	–	–	0.97
	300	MIA	**1592.078 ***	**4.243 ***	0.207	0.578	**0.41 ***
		MOEA	2008.4598	10.056	–	–	0.99
Cruciform	30	MIA	2766.078	**1.670 ***	0	0.125	**0.64 ***
		MOEA	2766.078	1.915	–	–	0.76
	100	MIA	2777.167	**5.370 ***	0	0.206	**0.39 ***
		MOEA	2777.167	6.765	–	–	0.65
	300	MIA	2789.822	**15.870 ***	0	0.004	**0.68 ***
		MOEA	2789.822	15.937	–	–	0.98
Ensemble	60	MIA	3028.511	**2.430 ***	−0.070	0.565	**0.43 ***
		MOEA	2818.411 *	5.584	–	–	0.56
	200	MIA	**3248.811 ***	**7.900 ***	0.036	0.262	**0.51 ***
		MOEA	3369.122	10.706	–	–	0.95
	600	MIA	**3220.833 ***	**22.355 ***	0.125	0.297	**0.48 ***
		MOEA	3682.856	31.781	–	–	1.12

In relation to the metric average makespan RPD, this metric analyzes the percentage difference of the average makespan of MIA respecting the average makespan of MOEA by the next formula $((m^t - m)/m^t)$, where m^t represents the average makespan of MOEA and m represents the average makespan of MIA. When this difference is positive, this means that MIA has achieved a makespan saving (a decrease in average makespan) in relation to MOEA. Higher positive values represent better average makespan savings. When this difference is negative, this means that MIA has achieved an increase in average makespan respecting MOEA. Higher negative values represent higher average makespan increases. Similarly, the metric average cost RPD analyzes the percentage difference of the average cost of MIA respecting the average cost of MOEA by the next formula ($((c^t - c)/c^t)$), where c^t represents the average cost of MOEA and c represents the average cost of MIA.

According to Table 3, regarding the average makespan values, MIA has obtained a better performance than MOEA in five of the nine studied applications and sizes (i.e., Plate3D with 30, 100, and 300 tasks, and Ensemble with 200 and 600 tasks), reaching very good makespan savings (around 50% in some cases). Both autoscalers have obtained the same performance for Cruciform with the different sizes. Regarding Ensemble with 60 tasks, the performance of MIA has been slightly worse than that of MOEA. Specifically, MIA achieved an increase in average makespan of 7% regarding MOEA.

Regarding the average cost values, MIA has obtained a better performance than MOEA in eight of the nine studied applications and sizes, reaching very good cost savings (around 60% in some cases and 30% in some other cases).

In relation to the average values obtained regarding the metric L_2-norm, MIA has obtained a much better performance than MOEA, in all the studied applications and sizes. This is mainly because MIA outperforms MOEA in eight of the studied cases considering cost, and outperforms (equals) MOEA in five (three) of the studied cases considering makespan.

To ascertain the significance of the improvements reached by MIA regarding MOEA, a statistical significance test was applied on the results obtained from the experiments for the L_2-norm. Given that the L_2-norm provides a joint analysis of the makespan and cost resulting from the experiments, it is considered that the L_2-norm is appropriate and useful to develop the statistical significance test. Regarding the results obtained from the experiments for the L_2-norm, each autoscaler was run 30 times on each studied application and size, and thus obtained 30 results for the L_2-norm in relation to each studied application and size. The Mann-Whitney test [16] was applied on the results obtained by MIA and MOEA regarding each studied application and size, using $\alpha = 0.001$. According to this test, MIA reached significant improvements in terms of the L_2-norm. Note that such test was applied because the results obtained by each autoscaler for the L_2-norm regarding each studied application and size do not fit the normal distribution, as confirmed with the Shapiro-Wilk test applied with $\alpha = 0.001$.

6 Related Work

Many works have addressed the efficient execution of Cloud-based scientific applications. However, most of them focus on task scheduling [17–24]. Furthermore, no works have addressed autoscaling for PSEs by multi-objective metaheuristics using only on-demand instances, and simultaneously, minimizing makespan and monetary cost. In [9], an autoscaler for PSEs, named MOEA, was presented. This autoscaler, however, considers spot instances that are subject to abrupt Cloud provider terminations. Consequently, the assigned tasks must be re-scheduled to other instances, affecting the makespan.

In [3], an autoscaler for workflow applications, named SIAA, which considers only spot instances, was proposed. SIAA minimizes makespan based on a maximum cost (i.e. budget constraints). To address the lack of reliability of spot instances, a heuristic for tasks scheduling minimizes the negative effects of out-of-bid errors. In [7], a cost-efficient based scheduling strategy was proposed for leasing VMs from Clouds and executing workflows while meeting given deadline constraints. Workflow tasks are scheduled considering spot instances. In [25], the execution of large-scale applications on Clouds considering spot instances was proposed. A dynamic algorithm for scheduling applications is employed to reduce the monetary cost, disregarding makespan minimization.

In [4], an autoscaler for scientific workflows subject to budget constraints was presented, which considers spot instances. The goal was to help the service providers to dynamically provision and allocate their cloud resources in a cost-efficient way. In [8], an autoscaler for workflows was proposed, which considers spot instances and minimizes makespan. The main workflow task characteristics are learned over time.

In [26], an approach that uses hybrid clusters of private and public Clouds, and spot instances for reducing costs, was presented. Hence, a checkpointing strategy was implemented to save the tasks progress before a Cloud provider terminates a spot instance. In [6], a dynamic strategy for provisioning of Cloud resources for workflows named delay-based dynamic scheduling was proposed, which considers spot instances. This strategy minimizes the monetary cost subject to deadline constraints. The scheduler dynamically rents new instances considering the execution state and the estimated execution times of the tasks to meet the deadline. Note that the methods in [26] and [6] do not exploit metaheuristics.

In [27] and [28], approaches for the execution of workflow applications in Cloud were proposed, which are based in multi-objective evolutionary algorithms. In [27], the approach is based on the algorithm NSGA-III, and aims to minimize the cost and makespan and maximize VMs utilization. In [28], the approach is based on NSGA-II, and minimizes makespan and cost. These approaches focus only on task scheduling without considering the automatic, dynamic scaling of the Cloud infrastructure.

7 Conclusions

In this article, we proposed an autoscaler for PSEs in public Clouds (e.g., Amazon EC2), which periodically determines the right number and type of instances of VMs to be acquired to execute the tasks inherent to a given PSE. Two relevant optimization objectives were considered: the minimization of the makespan and the monetary cost. Besides, the utilization of on-demand instances was considered because these are not subject to failures that can abruptly terminate the execution of the tasks assigned. The autoscaler, named MIA, is based on the well-known multi-objective evolutionary algorithm NSGA-III.

MIA was evaluated on three real-world PSEs, considering different sizes per PSE. Moreover, on-demand instances of different types of VMs available in Amazon EC2 were considered. These applications and instance types were considered to provide diverse realistic experimental settings. Then, the performance of MIA was compared with that of the MOEA autoscaler (the only PSE autoscaler previously reported in the literature). Based on the performance comparison developed, MIA has significantly outperformed MOEA in both optimization objectives, in the applications and sizes considered. Thus, it can be concluded that the proposed MIA autoscaler represents a better alternative to solve the addressed autoscaling problem.

In future works, other relevant optimization objectives will be incorporated into the problem addressed. Besides, other multi-objective evolutionary algorithms (e.g., E-NSGA-III) will be evaluated in the context of the proposed autoscaler.

References

1. García Garino, C., Ribero Vairo, M.S., Andía Fagés, S., Mirasso, A.E., Ponthot, J.-P.: Numerical simulation of finite strain viscoplastic problems. J. Comput. Appl. Math. **246**, 174–184 (2013)
2. Mauch, V., Kunze, M., Hillenbrand, M.: High performance cloud computing. Future Gen. Comput. Syst. **29**(6), 1408–1416 (2013)
3. Monge, D., Garí, Y., Mateos, C., García Garino, C.: Autoscaling scientific workflows on the cloud by combining on-demand and spot instances. Comput. Syst. Sci. Eng. **32**(4), 291–306 (2017)
4. Mao, M., Humphrey, M.: Scaling and scheduling to maximize application performance within budget constraints in cloud workflows. In: 27th International Symposium on Parallel & Distributed Processing, pp. 67–78 (2013)
5. George, G., Wolski, R., Krintz, C., Brevik, J.: Analyzing AWS Spot Instance Pricing. In: Proceedings of the 2019 IEEE International Conference on Cloud Engineering (IC2E), pp. 222–228 (2019)
6. Cai, Z., Li, X., Ruiz, R., Li, Q.: A delay-based dynamic scheduling algorithm for bag-of-task workflows with stochastic task execution times in clouds. Future Gen. Comput. Syst. **71**, 57–72 (2017)
7. Li, J., Su, S., Cheng, X., Song, M., Ma, L., Wang, J.: Cost-efficient coordinated scheduling for leasing cloud resources on hybrid workloads. Parallel Comput. **44**, 1–17 (2015)
8. De Coninck, E., Verbelen, T., Vankeirsbilck, B., Bohez, S., Simoens, P., Dhoedt, B.: Dynamic autoscaling and scheduling of deadline constrained service workloads on IaaS clouds. J. Syst. Softw. **118**, 101–114 (2016)
9. Monge, D., Pacini, E., Mateos, C., García Garino, C.: Meta-heuristic based autoscaling of cloud-based parameter sweep experiments with unreliable virtual machines instances. Comput. Eng. **69**, 364–377 (2018)
10. Campos Ciro, G., Dugardin, F., Yalaoui, F., Kelly, R.: A NSGA-II and NSGA-III comparison for solving an open shop scheduling problem with resource constraints. In: 8th IFAC Conference on Manufacturing Modelling, Management and Control MIM 2016. IFAC-PapersOnLine vol. 49(12), pp. 1272–1277 (2016)
11. Yi, J.-H., Deb, S., Dong, J., Alavi, A.H., Wang, G.-G.: An improved NSGA-III algorithm with adaptive mutation operator for big data optimization problems. Future Gen. Comput. Syst. **88**, 571–585 (2018)
12. Calheiros, R., Ranjan, R., Beloglazov, A., De Rose, C., Buyya, R.: Cloudsim: a toolkit for modeling and simulation of cloud computing environments and evaluation of resource provisioning algorithms. Softw. Pract. Experience **41**(1), 23–50 (2011)
13. Deb, K., Jain, H.: An evolutionary many-objective optimization algorithm using reference-point based non-dominated sorting approach, part i: solving problems with box constraints. IEEE Trans. Evol. Comput. **18**(4), 577–601 (2014)
14. Makris, N.: Plastic torsional buckling of cruciform compression members. J. Eng. Mech. **129**(6), 689–696 (2003)
15. Deb, K., Pratap, A., Agarwal, S., Meyarivan, T.: A fast and elitist multiobjective genetic algorithm: NSGA-II. IEEE Trans. Evol. Comput. **6**(2), 182–197 (2002)

16. Mann, H.B., Whitney, D.R.: On a test of whether one of two random variables is stochastically larger than the other. Ann. Math. Stat. **18**(1), 50–60 (1947)
17. Arunarani, A.R., Manjula, D., Sugumaran, V.: Task scheduling techniques in cloud computing: A literature survey. Future Gen. Comput. Syst. **91**, 407–415 (2019)
18. Masdari, M., ValiKardan, S., Shahi, Z., Azar, S.I.: Towards workflow scheduling in cloud computing: a comprehensive analysis. J. Netw. Comput. Appl. **66**, 64–82 (2016)
19. Pacini, E., Mateos, C., García Garino, C.: Distributed job scheduling based on swarm Intelligence: a survey. Comput. Electr. Eng. **40**(1), 252–269 (2014)
20. Adhikari, M., Nandy, S., Amgoth, T.: Meta heuristic-based task deployment mechanism for load balancing in IaaS cloud. J. Netw. Comput. Appl. **128**, 64–77 (2019)
21. Kalra, M., Singh, S.: A review of metaheuristic scheduling techniques in cloud computing. Egypt. Inf. J. **16**(3), 275–295 (2015)
22. Casas, I., Taheri, J., Ranjan, R., Wang, L., Zomaya, A.Y.: Ga-eti: An enhanced genetic algorithm for the scheduling of scientific workflows in cloud environments. J. Comput. Sci. **26**, 318–331 (2018)
23. Hu, H., et al.: Multi-objective scheduling for scientific workflow in multicloud environment. J. Netw. Comput. Appl. **114**, 108–122 (2018)
24. Srichandan, S., Kumar, T.A., Bibhudatta, S.: Task scheduling for cloud computing using multi-objective hybrid bacteria foraging algorithm. Future Comput. Inf. J. **3**(2), 210–230 (2018)
25. Lu, S., et al.: A dynamic hybrid resource provisioning approach for running large-scale computational applications on cloud spot and on-demand instances. In: International Conference on Parallel and Distributed Systems, pp. 657–662 (2013)
26. Calatrava, A., Romero, E., Moltó, G., Caballer, M., Alonso, J.M.: Self-managed cost-efficient virtual elastic clusters on hybrid cloud infrastructures. Future Gen. Comput. Syst. **61**, 13–25 (2016)
27. Wangsom, P., Lavangnananda, K., and Bouvry, P.: The application of nondominated sorting genetic algorithm (NSGA-III) for scientific-workflow scheduling on cloud. In: Proceedings of the 8th Multidisciplinary International Conference on Scheduling: Theory and Applications, pp. 269–287 (2017)
28. Thant, P.T., Powell, C., Schlueter, M., Munetomo, M.: Multiobjective level-wise scientific workflow optimization in IaaS public cloud environment. Sci. Program. (2017)

The Improvement Direction Mapping Method

Salvador Botello-Aceves[1]($\boxtimes$) (ID), S. Ivvan Valdez[2] (ID),
and Arturo Hernández-Aguirre[1] (ID)

[1] Centro de Investigación en Matemáticas, A.C., Jalisco S/N,
Col. Valenciana CP: 36023, Guanajuato, Gto, Mexico
{salvador.botello,artha}@cimat.mx
[2] Centro de Investigación en Ciencias de Información Geoespacial,
Contoy 137 Esq. Chemax, Col. Lomas de Padierna, Querétaro, Qro, Mexico
svaldez@centrogeo.edu.mx

Abstract. The Improvement Direction Mapping (IDM) is a novel multi-objective local-search method, that independently steers a solution set towards promising regions by computing improvement directions in the objective space and transform them, into the variable space, as search directions. The IDM algorithm consists of two main sub-tasks 1) the computation of the improvement directions in the objective space 2) the transformation of directions from the objective space to the variable space. The transformation from the objective to the variable space is carried out via a pseudo-inverse of the Jacobian matrix. The goal of this paper is two fold: it introduces the main IDM algorithm and three approaches to determine improvement directions, and then it explores the trade-off of either approach by performing statistical analysis on the experimental results. The approaches are based on: 1) Pareto dominance, 2) aggregation functions, and 3) indicator functions. A set of well-known benchmark problems are used to compare the three proposed improvement directions and the Directed Search method. This paper is devoted to introduce the IDM algorithm for multi-objective optimization, nonetheless, the application of IDM for hybridizing stochastic-global-search algorithms is straight forward.

Keywords: Multi-objective optimization · Multi-objective local search

1 Introduction

Multi-objective Optimization Problems (MOPs) seek to simultaneously optimize a set of two or more conflicting objectives. Multi-objective optimization methods (MOOM) are classified based on the preference scheme. A priori methods assign a

S. I. Valdez is supported by the Consejo Nacional de Ciencia y Tecnología, CONACYT México, Cátedra 7795.

A. Hernández-Aguirre—We acknowledge support from Proyecto FORDECyT No. 296737 "Consorcio en Inteligencia Artificial".

© Springer Nature Switzerland AG 2020
L. Martínez-Villaseñor et al. (Eds.): MICAI 2020, LNAI 12468, pp. 264–283, 2020.
https://doi.org/10.1007/978-3-030-60884-2_20

default preference value to each objective before the optimization process [13]. A posteriori methods look for a finite set of solutions, without the assumption of their relative position, that adequately represent the set of all non-dominated solutions, called the Pareto set (PS), and their corresponding image called the Pareto front (PF). In general, the image of the solution set, now called the solution front (SF), is expected to fulfill three characteristics: 1) *Convergence* to the true PF, minimizing the distance between the solution front and the true PF. 2) *Distribution* of the solutions in the solution front so that each solution adequately represents a similar fragment of the true PF. 3) *Spread* measures the distances between the extreme solutions, which is the extension of the solution front.

Multi-objective evolutionary algorithms (MOEAs) have proven to be a versatile a posteriori MOOMs for solving MOPs. These algorithms perform stochastic perturbations to the current solution set to generate an offspring population, they are compared to select a new solution set using a dominance measure. We can classify the algorithms according to their dominance measure. The first generation of MOEAs applies the Pareto dominance raking. The second generation of MOEAs uses two different dominance measure: 1) Indicators-based algorithms measure the contribution of each solution to the SF. 2) Decomposition-based algorithms decompose the objective space, solving a set of mono-objective problems.

The Improvement Direction Mapping (IDM) method is a multi-objective local search optimization method that differs from MOEAs as follows: The IDM method proposes improvement directions in the objective space and transforms them into the variable space as search directions, and then, displaces each solution and applies a dominance measure. The IDM method is consists of two fundamental problems: 1) the improvement directions computation, and 2) the transformation function computation.

There are multi-objective local search optimization methods in the literature that use first or second-order information to direct the search for unconstrained problems. The Steepest Descent Direction [8] applies quadratic programming to determine a descent direction, in the variable space, so that the range of the Jacobian matrix decreases, being null for an optimal solution. The Normal-Boundary Intersection [3] uses a fixed set of attainment vectors in the objective space, which are used to find a set of descent directions whose image is normal to a set of achievement vectors. The Pareto Descent Method [11] computes a set of descent directions by solving a linear programming problem based on descent cones. The Gradient Subspace Approximation [22] presents a way to compute descent directions by exploiting the information from the nearest solution, given as the most common direction (greedy) within the neighborhood. Note that our approach seems similar to them since in the first sub-task we compute descend directions in the function space, however, we then perform the descent direction in variable space by computing the mapping from the objective space to variable space (second sub-task). The so-called Directed Search method is related to our approach [23], however, it is limited to direct the search by a set of fixed directions in the objective space under a transformation based on the Jacobian matrix.

This paper introduces three improvement directions computation proposals. The first approach is based on a geometric formulation to compute search directions as the: normal vectors to the current SF, using Pareto dominance as the dominance measure, this approach maintains the trade-off between objectives for each solution, which favors the distribution on the front. The second is a Quasi-Newton approach using aggregation functions to compute the improvement directions, so that each solution is displaced towards a reference vector, to adequately distribute all solutions on the PF. The third approach proposes improvement directions that increase the contribution of each solution in the SF by means of a binary indicator.

Section 2 presents the required concepts for the discussion of the proposed methods. Section 3 introduces the improvement direction mapping method. The three methods for the computation of the improvement directions based on different dominance measures are presented in Sect. 4. Section 5 presents the experiments comparing the improvement direction mapping method with the proposed improvement direction computation methods. The results are discussed. Finally, Sect. 6 presents conclusions and future work.

2   Background

This section presents concepts of Multi-objective Optimization Problems (MOPs), for instance, dominance measures, and performance metrics. They are used for developing the proposals and to compare them.

2.1   Multi-objective Optimization Problem

A MOP seeks to find a set of non-dominated solutions that improve a set of two or more conflicting objectives. In general, a MOP consists of three basic mathematical entities: 1) the *decision variables*, 2) the *objective functions*, and 3) the *constraints* impose limits on the search domain. In this work, only the box constraints over the decision variables are considered, in consequence, the MOP is described as in Eq. (1).

$$\min_{\mathbf{x}} \quad \mathcal{F}(\mathbf{x}), \tag{1}$$

where $\mathbf{x} \in \mathbf{X} \in \mathbb{R}^n$ are the decision variables bounded as $x_i^L \leq x_i \leq x_i^U \ \forall i = 1, \ldots, n$, $\mathcal{F} : \mathbb{R}^n \to \mathbb{R}^m$ is the objectives vector, and $f_i \in \mathcal{F} : \mathbb{R}^n \to \mathbb{R}$ are the objective functions.

Pareto Concepts. According to [24], a candidate solution x_1 dominates another candidate solution x_2, $x_1 \prec x_2$, if

$$f_i(x_1) \leq f_i(x_2) \quad \forall i = 1, \ldots, n \tag{2}$$

and

$$\exists j : f_j(x_1) < f_j(x_2) \quad j \in 1, \dots, n \tag{3}$$

When one or more of these relations is not satisfied, x_1 does not dominate x_2, $x_1 \not\prec x_2$.

Pareto Set (PS). The set of non-dominated vectors are known as a Pareto set. A candidate solution x^* is said to be Pareto optimal if:

$$\nexists x \in X : x \prec x^* \tag{4}$$

Pareto Front (PF). The image in the function space of the corresponding PS is called the Pareto front.

2.2 Dominance Measures

Very often multi-objective optimization methods apply a dominance measure (DM) to quantify the contribution of each solution to the solution set and to apply operators for improving it. This section is dedicated to present and discuss three dominance measures. The first ranks a solution according to a front it belongs to. The second transforms the solutions employing an aggregation function, then measures the distance vector among them. The third measures the contributions of each solution to the solution set.

DM Based on Pareto Dominance ranks each solution by the front to which it belongs to. The objective values of the current set of candidate solutions are compared to determine the non-dominated solutions, the image of this first non-dominated set is the rank-1 front, this set is removed from the candidate solutions and the remaining solutions are compared a second time, the image of this second non-dominated set is the rank-2 set, and so on until all solutions have an assigned rank. This ranking is useful to compare solutions from different fronts, but it does not distinguish between individuals belonging to the same front, thus, a distribution operator is commonly added to measure the solution clustering, such as the crowding distance [5].

DM Based on Aggregation Functions explicitly decomposes the MOP into scalar optimization sub-problems by a discretization of the objective space. At each generation, the selected set is composed of the best solutions found for each subproblem employing an aggregation function as a DM. Aggregation coefficient vectors adjust the value of the aggregation function in such a way that they prioritize combinations of groups of objectives, provoking the decomposition of the objective space, such that:

$$g(\mathcal{F}(\mathbf{x})|\lambda) : \mathbb{R}^n \to \mathbb{R} \tag{5}$$

where g is the aggregation function, depending on the objective functions $\mathcal{F}(\mathbf{x}) \in \mathbb{R}^m$ and the aggregation coefficient vector $\lambda \in \mathbb{R}^m$. It should be emphasized that $\sum_i^m \lambda_i = 1$ and $\lambda_i \geq 0$.

DM Based on Binary Indicators measures the contributions of each solution within the solution set, using a scalar indicator such as hypervolume, the search is guided by the set of solutions with the greatest contributions.

2.3   Performance Metrics

This section briefly presents the performance metrics used to compare the different algorithms analyzed in this work.

Usually, four properties are measured to characterize the performance of a front **A**: 1) *Cardinality*, given as the number of non-dominated solutions in **A** [19]. 2) *Convergence*, measures the distance from **A** to a reference front, commonly, the optimal theoretical PF [19]. 3) *Diversity* refers to the relative distance among the solutions in **A** [4]. 4) *Extension* qualifies the range of values covered by the solutions in **A** [26]. This work uses two unary indicators [21], for describing one or more characteristics of the approximation set:

Hypervolume ratio (HV$_r$) is the relation of the dominated region of the solution set **A** and that of the reference set $\mathcal{R}^*$, that is:

$$HV_r = \frac{HV_\mathbf{A}}{HV_{\mathcal{R}^*}} \tag{6}$$

The hypervolume [25] is the **only unary Pareto compliant indicator**. It is defined as the dominated enclosed volume, bounded by a reference point and **A**

$$HV = \left\{ \bigcup_i vol(\mathbf{a}) \Big| \mathbf{a} \in \mathbf{A} \right\} \tag{7}$$

Modified inverted generational distance (IGD+). It was shown in [15], that Inverted generational distance (IGD) [1,17] is a non-Pareto compliant metric, thus, to circumvent this issue, the IGD+, **a weakly-Pareto complaint version of the IGD** indicator, was introduced. It reports how far, on average, a solution of the reference set $\mathcal{R}^*$ is from the interference hypervolume generated by the closest solution within the solution set **A**, given as:

$$IGD = \frac{1}{|\mathcal{R}^*|} \sum_{i=1}^{|\mathcal{R}^*|} \min_{\mathbf{a} \in \mathbf{A}} ||\hat{\mathbf{d}}_i(\mathbf{a}, \mathbf{r}_i)||_p \tag{8}$$

where $|\mathcal{R}^*|$ is the cardinality of the reference set, p is a normalization coefficient for the norm operator $||\cdot||$, usually $p = 2$, and $\hat{\mathbf{d}}_i(\mathbf{a}, \mathbf{r}_i)$ is the modified difference vector between the i-th solution in the reference front, $\mathbf{r}_i \in \mathcal{R}^*$, and the closest solution $\mathbf{a} \in \mathbf{A}$, given as:

$$\hat{d}_i^{(j)}(\mathbf{a}, \mathbf{r}_i) = \max\{0, d_i^{(j)}(\mathbf{a}, \mathbf{r}_i)\} \quad \forall j = 1, \dots, m \tag{9}$$

where $\hat{d}_i^{(j)}(\mathbf{a}, \mathbf{r}_i)$ is the j-th component of the modified distance and $d_i^{(j)}(\mathbf{a}, \mathbf{r}_i) = a^{(j)} - r_i^{(j)}$ is the j-th component of the distance from $\mathbf{r}_i$ to $\mathbf{a}$.

3   The Improvement-Direction Mapping Method

The Improvement Direction Mapping method is a multi-objective optimization method that displaces a solution set using local directions, proposing *improvement directions in the objective space*, and transforming them to *search directions in the variable space*, so that the evaluation of the displaced solution corresponds to the proposed improvement direction, so that:

$$\mathbf{p} = \{\mathbf{p} \in \mathbb{R}^m | \mathbf{x} + \mathbf{H}(\mathbf{x}, \mathbf{p}) \triangleleft \mathbf{x}\} \tag{10}$$

where $\mathbf{p}$ is the search direction and $\mathbf{H}$ is the transformation function from the objective space to the variable space at $\mathbf{x}$. The $\triangleleft$ operator is used to indicate that a solution is better than another, in this case, the solution $\mathbf{x} + \mathbf{H}(\mathbf{x}, \mathbf{p})$ is better than $\mathbf{x}$, by means of a dominance measure (Pareto Dominance, Indicator, aggregation function, etc.). Displacing a solution in the $\mathbf{p}$ direction implies Eq. (11), that is to say, the vector from $\mathcal{F}(\mathbf{x} + \mathbf{H}(\mathbf{x}, \mathbf{p}))$ to $\mathcal{F}(\mathbf{x})$ must be parallel to the improvement direction.

$$\frac{\mathbf{p}^\mathsf{T} \mathbf{y}}{||\mathbf{p}|| \, ||\mathbf{y}||} = 1 \tag{11}$$

where $\mathbf{y} = \mathcal{F}(\mathbf{x} + \mathbf{H}(\mathbf{x}, \mathbf{p})) - \mathcal{F}(\mathbf{x})$ is the difference vector of the objective values. Each solution should be displaced so it achieved at least one of three objectives: 1) it outperforms the current solution, 2) it improves the distribution of the solutions on the Pareto front, 3) it increases the extent of the Pareto front.

Algorithm 1 presents the pseudocode of the Improvement Direction Mapping (IDM) method. Initially, $g = 0$, the step sizes $\mathbf{a} \in \mathbb{R}^\mu$ are initialized for a population $\mathcal{X}_g \in \mathbb{R}^{\mu \times n}$ of size μ, generated randomly from a uniform distribution. The offspring population is $\mathcal{O}_g \in \mathbb{R}^{\mu \times n}$. In line 3, the improvement directions $\mathcal{P}_g \in \mathbb{R}^{\mu \times m}$ are computed according to the dominance measure. Until a stop condition is met, for each individual in the population, the search direction $d\mathbf{x} \in \mathbb{R}^n$ is computed using the transformation of the improvement direction $\mathbf{p}_k \in \mathcal{P}_g$ from the objective space to the variable space, and values are assigned for a step size bisection process. As long as the step size is greater than $1e-6$ and the counter l is less than 3, the k-th offspring $\mathbf{o}_k \in \mathcal{O}_g$ is created as the offset of the k-th individual $\mathbf{x}_k \in \mathcal{X}_g$ in the search direction. If $\mathbf{x}_k$ is "better" than $\mathbf{o}_k$, the step size is reduced by a factor of 0.5, otherwise, the step size is updated. After computing a new offspring population, it is added to the current population and a selection operator applies the DM and generates a new population $\mathcal{X}_{g+1}$. With the new population, the improvement directions $\mathcal{P}_{g+1}$ are computed and the next generation is carried out, $g = g + 1$.

We decouple the method into two parts: 1) the improvement directions computation in line 3 and 19, and 2) the transformation function between the objective space and the variable space.

Algorithm 1. Improvement Directions Mapping Pseudocode

1: Set generation counter $g = 0$
2: Initialize population, offspring population and step size $[\mathcal{X}_g, \mathcal{O}_g, \mathbf{a}] = \text{Initialize}(\mu)$
3: Compute improvement directions $\mathcal{P}_g = \text{Directions}(f, \mathcal{X}_g)$
4: **while** Stop criteria $\neq$ True **do**
5:    **for** $k = 1$ to μ **do**
6:       Compute search directions $d\mathbf{x} = \mathbf{H}(\mathbf{x}_k, \mathbf{p}_k)$
7:       Set step size bisection parameters $\hat{\alpha} = a_k$, $\overline{\alpha} = 0$, $l = 0$
8:       **while** $\hat{\alpha} > 1e-6$ & $l < 3$ **do**
9:          Compute k-th offspring $\mathbf{o}_k = \mathbf{x}_k + (\overline{\alpha} + \hat{\alpha})d\mathbf{x}$
10:          **if** $\mathbf{x}_k \vartriangleleft \mathbf{o}_k$ **then**
11:             Resize bisection step size $\hat{\alpha} = 0.5\hat{\alpha}$
12:          **else**
13:             Update bisection step size $\overline{\alpha} = \overline{\alpha} + \hat{\alpha}$
14:          **end if**
15:          Add counter $l = l + 1$;
16:       **end while**
17:       Update step size $a_k = \overline{\alpha} + \hat{\alpha}$
18:    **end for**
19:    Update   Population   and   improvement   directions $[\mathcal{X}_{g+1}, \mathcal{P}_{g+1}]$ $=$ UpdatePop_&_Directions$(f, \mathcal{X}_g, \mathcal{O}_g)$
20:    Add counter $g = g + 1$
21: **end while**
22: **return** $\mathcal{X}_g$

Regarding the transformation between spaces, to transform differential vectors in the variable space, $d\mathbf{x}$, to differential vectors in the objective space, $d\mathbf{f}$, a Jacobian matrix $\mathbf{J}$ is used as shown in Eq. (12).

$$d\mathbf{f} = \mathbf{J}(\mathbf{x})d\mathbf{x} \tag{12}$$

where $d\mathbf{x} \in \mathbb{R}^n$ is the search direction on the variable space, $d\mathbf{f} \in \mathbb{R}^m$ is the improvement direction in the objective space and $\mathbf{J}(\mathbf{x}) \in \mathbb{R}^{m \times n}$ is a numerical approximation to a Jacobian matrix evaluated on $\mathbf{x}$. Applying the inverse formulation, the transformation function between spaces is given as a linear transformation, as it is shown in Eq. (13).

$$\mathbf{H}(\mathbf{x}, \mathbf{p}) = \mathbf{J}^\dagger \mathbf{p} \tag{13}$$

where $\mathbf{J}^\dagger$ is the pseudo inverse of the Jacobian matrix evaluated at $\mathbf{x}$, computed as $\mathbf{J}^\dagger = \mathbf{V}\mathbf{D}^{-1}\mathbf{U}^\intercal$, where $\mathbf{U} \in \mathbb{R}^{m \times m}$, $\mathbf{D} \in \mathbb{R}^{m \times n}$ and $\mathbf{V} \in \mathbb{R}^{n \times n}$ are: the orthogonal matrix in the objective space, the diagonal and orthogonal matrix in the variable space from a SVD decomposition of the Jacobian matrix. In the IDM method, once the improvement and search directions are computed, an adaptive calculation of the step size controls the displacement. Hence, the calculation of the pseudo inverse is modified as:

$$\hat{\mathbf{J}}^\dagger = \mathbf{V}\mathbf{I}\mathbf{U}^\intercal \tag{14}$$

where $\mathbf{I} \in \mathbb{R}^{m \times n}$ is the identity matrix, and $\hat{\mathbf{J}}^\dagger$ is the normalized pseudo inverse. This modified pseudo inverse only takes into account the rotation on the variables space by setting all singular values to one, anticipating that the Jacobian is poorly conditioned, thus, misadjusting the scale of the search direction and with the possible pay off of steering the solution towards unpromising areas.

4   Computation of the Improvement Directions

This section is dedicated to studying the computation of the improvement directions, thus, for a given solution $\mathbf{x}$ in the current solution set, at least one of the three objectives must be met, such as the following:

- Minimization in the objective space: the improvement direction must produce that the objective values of the current solution $\mathbf{x}$ are greater or equal than those of the displaced solution, $f_i(\mathbf{x}) \geq f_i(\mathbf{x}) + p_i \ \forall i = 1, \ldots, m$. This requires that all components in the improvement direction are less than or equal to 0.
- Distribution maintenance: to maintain the quality of the solutions within the current solutions, the improvement direction must meet a distribution criteria.
- Front full-extension: since one aspect of the quality of the approximation to the PF is given by the extension of the solutions, it is desirable that the improvement directions extend the range of the current Pareto front.

The three objectives of the improvement directions can be controlled such that the dominance measures provide the necessary information to steer the search, maintaining an adequate distribution, increasing the spread of solutions and improving the current front.

From Eq. 10, three different methods to compute improvement directions are proposed in the following sections.

4.1   Computing the Improvement Directions Using the Pareto Front

A geometric approach is proposed that allows directing the search while trying to keep the trade-off given by the computation of a tangent vector to a local quadratic approximation of the solution set, and a perpendicular vector to such tangent vector.

Computation of the Tangent Vector. The trade-off indicator quantifies the conflict between two objectives of a particular solution, given as $T_{i,j} = df_i/df_j$ for the i-th and j-th objective. For m objectives, a Trade-off matrix is constructed, where each component i, j indexes is the i-th and j-th objectives. Thus, each component of the upper triangular matrix is the inverse of its counterpart. Such matrix is computed as $\mathbf{T} = df dg^\mathsf{T}$, where $dg_i = 1/df_i \ \forall i = 1, \ldots, m$, and the objective difference vector df is computed by differentiating a regression model. Our goal is to extract the tangent vector from the trade-off matrix. A deeper analysis of the computation of the tangent vector is presented in [2].

Computing the Improvement Directions. Once the local tangent vector to the current front is computed, the next step is to compute a perpendicular vector. There is an infinite set of vectors perpendicular to a local tangent vector $d\mathbf{f}$, all contained in the same hyperplane, thus, the perpendicular vector is computed as the projection of a reference vector $\mathbf{z}_r$, given as the vector from a point in the SF to the zenith point, on the hyperplane, as it is shown in Eq. (15), where $\mathbf{p} \in \mathbb{R}^m$ is the improvement direction proposal.

$$\mathbf{p} = \mathbf{z}_r - \frac{\mathbf{z}_r \cdot d\mathbf{f}}{||d\mathbf{f}||^2} d\mathbf{f} \tag{15}$$

4.2 Computing the Improvement Directions Using Aggregation Functions

Since the aggregation function is a transformation of a MOP into a scalar problem, it is natural to propose search directions, in the variable space, that minimize the aggregation function. Two proposals for the minimization of the aggregation function are presented in this section, the first uses the gradient vector of the aggregation function. The second is a quasi-Newton approach.

The computation of the improvement vector is given by the gradient vector of the aggregation function, in Eq. (5), with respect to the decision variables. By the chain rule, the partial differentiation of the aggregation function with respect the i-th decision variable is given as:

$$\frac{\partial g}{\partial x_i} = \sum_{j=1}^{m} \frac{\partial g}{\partial f_j} \frac{\partial f_j}{\partial x_i} \tag{16}$$

Rearranging, the gradient of the aggregation function with respect to the decision variables is given as:

$$\nabla_{\mathbf{x}} g = \mathbf{J}^{\mathsf{T}} \nabla g \tag{17}$$

where ∇g is the gradient vector of the aggregation function with respect to the objectives. From the second-order Taylor approximation, the improvement direction is given as:

$$\left(\nabla_{\mathbf{x}}^2 g\right)^{-1} \nabla_{\mathbf{x}} g \tag{18}$$

where $\mathbf{p}$ is the search direction, $\nabla_{\mathbf{x}} g$ is the gradient vector of the aggregation function with respect to the decision variables, computed as presented in Eq. (17) , and $\nabla_{\mathbf{x}}^2 g$ is the Hessian matrix with respect to the decision variables of the aggregation function, where the i, j component is computed, using the chain rule, as:

$$\frac{\partial^2 g}{\partial x_i \partial x_j} = \sum_{k=1}^{m} \left(\frac{\partial^2 f_k}{\partial x_i \partial x_j} \frac{\partial g}{\partial f_k} + \frac{\partial f_k}{\partial x_i} \sum_{l=1}^{m} \frac{\partial^2 g}{\partial f_l \partial f_k} \frac{\partial f_l}{\partial x_j} \right) \tag{19}$$

The first term in Eq. (19) is the contributions of the each objective function given by the importance of the gradient of the aggregation function. The second term transforms the Hessian matrix to the variable space. Rearranging Eq. (19) we obtain Eq. (20)

$$\nabla_x^2 g = \sum_{k=1}^{m} \left(\frac{\partial g}{\partial f_k} \nabla^2 f_k \right) + \mathbf{J}^\intercal \nabla^2 g \mathbf{J} \qquad (20)$$

where $\nabla^2 f_k$ is the Hessian matrix of the k-th objective function with respect to the decision variables, $\frac{\partial g}{\partial f_k}$ is the fist order derivative of the aggregation function with respect to function f_k, and $\nabla^2 g$ is the hessian matrix of the aggregation function with respect to the objective functions.

Similar to the Levenberg-Marquardt method, once the Hessian is inverted, as it converges towards the minima, the first term can lead to numerical inconsistencies, so it is omitted, and the Hessian matrix of the aggregation function with respect to the decision variables are given as $\nabla_x^2 g = \mathbf{J}^\intercal \nabla^2 g \mathbf{J}$. Substituting in Eq. (18) and rearranging:

$$\mathbf{p} = -\mathbf{J}^{-1} \nabla^2 g^{-1} \nabla g \qquad (21)$$

In this work, the Penalized Boundary Intersection (PBI) is used as the aggregation function. It uses a penalty to the boundary intersection (BI) [3,18]. From the geometric point of view, a solution on the Pareto Front can be approximated as the intersection of a set of uniformly distributed straight lines and the Pareto front, thus, BI decomposition can handle the problem of non-convex Pareto fronts. In practice, the PBI decomposition is often used to solve multiple constrained MOPs. The i-th subproblem is formulated as follows:

$$\min g^{PBI}(\mathbf{x}|\lambda, \mathbf{z}) = d_1 + \theta d_2 \qquad (22)$$

where

$$d_1 = \frac{\hat{\mathbf{f}}^T \lambda}{||\lambda||}; \quad d_2 = \left|\left| \hat{\mathbf{f}} - d_1 \frac{\lambda}{||\lambda||} \right|\right|$$

$\hat{\mathbf{f}} = \mathbf{F}(\mathbf{x}) - \mathbf{z}$, $\mathbf{z}$ is the reference point given as the minimum known value for each objective, θ is a default penalty parameter and the operator $||\cdot||$ is the L_2 norm. Notice that d_1 measures the distance of the objective values to the reference point by the projection of the aggregation coefficient vector. d_2 measures the distance from the objective vector to the aggregation coefficient vector as the distance between the projection d_1 on the direction of λ and $\mathbf{f}$. The first differentiation of Eq. 22 is given as:

$$\nabla g^{PBI}(\mathbf{x}|\lambda, \mathbf{z}) = \mathbf{h} - \frac{\theta}{d_2} \left(\hat{\mathbf{f}} - d_1 \mathbf{h} \right) \qquad (23)$$

where $h_i = \frac{\lambda_i}{||\lambda||}$ for $i = 1, \ldots, m$. Notice that Eq. (21) requires the Hessian of the aggregation function with respect to the objectives, thus, the second differentiation of Eq. 22 is given as:

$$\nabla^2 g^{PBI}(\mathbf{x}|\lambda, \mathbf{z}) = \frac{\theta}{d_2}\left(\mathbf{I} - \left(1 - \frac{d_1^2}{d_2^2}\right)\mathbf{h}\mathbf{h}^\mathsf{T} + \frac{d_1}{d_2^2}\left(\hat{\mathbf{f}}\mathbf{h}^\mathsf{T} + \mathbf{h}\hat{\mathbf{f}}^\mathsf{T}\right)\right) \quad (24)$$

where $\mathbf{I} \in \mathbb{R}^{m \times m}$ is the identity matrix. In order to compute the improvement vector in Eq. 21, the gradient of the aggregation function with respect to the function is given by Eq. 23 and the Hessian of the aggregation function with respect to functions is given by Eq. 24.

4.3   Computation Based on the R2 Indicator

This indicator [10] is based on utility functions which map a vector $\mathbf{y} \in \mathbb{R}^m$ to a scalar value $u \in \mathbb{R}$ to measure the quality of two Pareto front approximation sets. For a given finite set of weights $\mathcal{V} \in \mathbb{R}^{M \times m}$, the R_2 indicator is written as [28]:

$$R_2(\mathbf{A}, \mathcal{V}, \mathbf{z}) = \frac{1}{|\mathcal{V}|}\sum_{\nu \in \mathcal{V}} \min_{\mathbf{a} \in \mathbf{A}} u(\mathbf{a}, \nu, \mathbf{z}) \quad (25)$$

$\mathbf{A} \in \mathbb{R}^{N \times m}$ is the current Pareto front, $\mathbf{z} \in \mathbb{R}^m$ is the utopian point, computed as in [20], and $u(\mathbf{a}, \nu, \mathbf{z})$ is an utility function. The contribution of a solution $\mathbf{a} \in \mathbf{A}$ to the R_2 indicator is defined as:

$$C_{R_2}(\mathbf{a}) = R_2(\mathbf{A}, \mathcal{V}, \mathbf{z}) - R_2(\mathbf{A} \setminus \{\mathbf{a}\}, \mathcal{V}, \mathbf{z}) \quad (26)$$

The improvement direction based on indicators is computed by the first derivative of Eq. 26, given as:

$$\nabla_{\mathbf{f}} C_{R_2}(\mathbf{x}) = \frac{1}{|\mathcal{V}|}\sum_{\nu \in \mathcal{V}} \begin{cases} \mathbf{0} & \text{if } u(\mathbf{x}, \nu, \mathbf{z}) \neq \min_{\mathbf{a} \in \mathbf{A}} u(\mathbf{a}, \nu, \mathbf{z}) \\ \nabla_{\mathbf{f}} u(\mathbf{a}, \nu, \mathbf{z}) & \text{else} \end{cases} \quad (27)$$

where $\nabla_{\mathbf{f}} u(\mathbf{a}, \nu, \mathbf{z})$ is the utility gradient. Notice that if solution $\mathbf{a}$ does not contributes to the approximation set $\mathbf{A}$, no direction is computed, thus, an alternative direction is given as $\mathbf{p} = \mathbf{z} - \mathbf{a}$. In this case we use the standard weighted Tchebycheff function as the utility function, given by $u(\mathbf{a}, \nu, \mathbf{z}) = \max_{j=1,\ldots,m} \nu_j |z_j - a_j|$, hence, the utility gradient is computed as:

$$\frac{\partial}{\partial f_j} u(\mathbf{a}, \nu, \mathbf{z}) = \begin{cases} \nu_j & \text{if } j | \max_{j=1,\ldots,m} \nu_j |z_j - a_j| \\ 0 & \text{else} \end{cases} \quad (28)$$

5   Experiments

In this section, we compare the three methods for the computation of the improvement directions. The IDM based on Pareto dominance (IDM) applies the Pareto dominance ranking and the crowding distance within the selection operator in order to compute the new population. The IDM based on the aggregation function (IDM/PBI) uses the Penalized Boundary Intersection (PBI) aggregation function to replace the current solution with the solution that minimizes the aggregation function. Finally, the IDM based on binary indicators (IDM/R2) applies the R2 indicator to discard the solutions with the lesser contributions. The aim of this experiment is to show the competence of the IDM method for solving a set of well-known benchmark problems. The three improvement directions computations are compared with a similar approach: the Directed Search (DS) method [23]. The DS method steers the search under a set of fixed and equispaced directions in the objective space, through a transformation based on the Jacobian pseudoinverse. Note that the pioneer DS is actually a version of the IDM, using the weighted sum aggregation function with the identity matrix as the Hessian.

Table 1. Problems set description

Problem	m	n	Domain	FE	ref	Description					
						F1	F2	F3	F4	F5	F6
FON	2	10	$[-4, 4]$	5e3	$[1, 1]$	2	S	F	2,3	U	T
POL	2	2	$[-\pi, \pi]$	5e3	$[16, 30]$	4	N	T	2,4	U	F
ZDT1	2	30	$[0, 1]$	5e3	$[2, 2]$	3	S	F	1	U	T
ZDT2	2	30	$[0, 1]$	5e3	$[2, 2]$	2	S	F	1	U	T
ZDT3	2	30	$[0, 1]$	5e3	$[2, 2]$	4	S	F	1	U	F
ZDT4	2	10	$[0, 1]$	1e4	$[2, 2]$	3	S	F	1	M	T
ZDT6	2	10	$[0, 1]$	5e3	$[2, 2]$	2	S	T	2	M	T
DTLZ1	2	7	$[0, 1]$	5e3	$[2, 2]$	1	S	F	2	M	T
DTLZ2	2	12	$[0, 1]$	5e3	$[2, 2]$	2	S	F	2	U	T
DTLZ3	2	12	$[0, 1]$	1e4	$[2, 2]$	2	S	F	2	M	T
DTLZ4	2	12	$[0, 1]$	5e3	$[2, 2]$	2	S	T	2	U	T

The Fonseca (FON)[9], Poloni (POL), ZDT[1-4, 6][27], and the DTLZ[1,-4] [6] problems are featured in this experiment. DTLZ[5-7] are discarded since they present a degenerate front in lower objective dimensions [12,14]. A description of the problems set is presented in Table 1, where F1 presents the PF geometry features (1: Linear, 2: Concave, 3: Convex and 4: Disconnected). F2 presents the parameter dependencies feature, that is, objectives of a test problem can be separable or non-separable (S: Separable, N: Non-separable). F3 describes the

Bias feature, that is, if more solutions are placed on some regions than in others (T: True, F: false). F4 describes the objective landscape features (1: One-to-one, 2: Many-to-one, 3: Flat regions, 4: Isolated optima). F5 presents the local multi-frontal feature(U: Uni-frontal, M: Multi-frontal). F6 shows the continuity of the Pareto set feature (T: True, F: False). The parameter setting used for this benchmark are: number of objectives $m = 2$, number of decision variables for FON $n = 10$, POL $n = 2$, ZDT[1–3] $n = 30$, ZDT[4,6] $n = 10$, DTLZ1 $n = 7$ and DTLZ[2,4] $n = 12$. For the four compared methods, the parameters are set as: population size $\mu = 50$, initial step size $\alpha = 1$, 5000 function evaluations for all problems except for ZDT4 and DTLZ3, which use 10000 function evaluations.

Table 2. Mean and standard deviation of the Hypervolume ratio (HV-r) and the Modified Inverse Generational Distance (IGD+) performance indicators. The higher the value of the HV-r indicator the better, whilst for the IGD+, the lower the better. The information is gathered by 30 independent runs.

		DS		IDM		IDM/PBI		IDM/R2	
		mean	*(±std dev)*	*mean*	*(±std dev)*	*mean*	*(±std dev)*	*mean*	*(±std dev)*
FON	HV-r	0.0011	(±0.0000)	**0.9299**	**(±0.0137)**	*0.8504*	*(±0.2364)*	0.0523	(±0.1302)
	IGD+	0.7732	(±0.0000)	**0.0252**	**(±0.0168)**	*0.0934*	*(±0.1552)*	0.5668	(±0.2027)
POL	HV-r	0.9110	(±0.0495)	*0.9766*	*(±0.0480)*	0.9736	(±0.0046)	**0.9849**	**(±0.0036)**
	IGD+	0.7547	(±0.2904)	**0.1965**	**(±0.1403)**	*0.6802*	*(±0.7671)*	0.9543	(±0.4832)
ZDT1	HV-r	0.7678	(±0.1040)	**0.9801**	**(±0.0236)**	0.9055	(±0.0333)	*0.9769*	*(±0.0055)*
	IGD+	0.2870	(±0.1699)	**0.0294**	**(±0.0247)**	0.0727	(±0.0349)	*0.0469*	*(±0.0110)*
ZDT2	HV-r	0.6803	(±0.0706)	**0.7645**	**(±0.1372)**	*0.6949*	*(±0.1646)*	0.6001	(±0.0000)
	IGD+	0.2417	(±0.0752)	**0.1987**	**(±0.1102)**	*0.2506*	*(±0.1415)*	0.3337	(±0.0000)
ZDT3	HV-r	0.4788	(±0.0703)	**0.8486**	**(±0.0823)**	0.7577	(±0.1362)	*0.8291*	*(±0.0527)*
	IGD+	0.6289	(±0.1285)	**0.1358**	**(±0.0691)**	*0.1922*	*(±0.1368)*	0.2170	(±0.0728)
ZDT4	HV-r	0.0000	(±0.0000)	0.0000	(±0.0000)	0.0000	(±0.0000)	0.0000	(±0.0000)
	IGD+	43.2239	(±9.8774)	**27.9589**	**(±7.9136)**	38.4730	(±10.6775)	*28.2765*	*(±6.7774)*
ZDT6	HV-r	0.8581	(±0.1021)	*0.9754*	*(±0.0270)*	**0.9919**	**(±0.0022)**	0.9746	(±0.0057)
	IGD+	0.1497	(±0.0972)	0.0219	(±0.0065)	**0.0048**	**(±0.0003)**	*0.0449*	*(±0.0095)*
DTLZ1	HV-r	0.0000	(±0.0000)	**0.0140**	**(±0.0767)**	0.0000	(±0.0000)	0.0000	(±0.0000)
	IGD+	**7.2145**	**(±2.9234)**	21.0724	(±10.4668)	*14.3250*	*(±5.6631)*	21.5870	(±6.3842)
DTLZ2	HV-r	0.9810	(±0.0056)	*0.9949*	*(±0.0015)*	**0.9959**	**(±0.0004)**	0.9790	(±0.0017)
	IGD+	0.0443	(±0.0162)	*0.0110*	*(±0.0029)*	**0.0093**	**(±0.0008)**	0.0523	(±0.0050)
DTLZ3	HV-r	0.0000	(±0.0000)	0.0000	(±0.0000)	0.0000	(±0.0000)	0.0000	(±0.0000)
	IGD+	**42.6333**	**(±11.9019)**	83.5140	(±40.1095)	*64.9695*	*(±16.1718)*	146.6646	(±38.4433)
DTLZ4	HV-r	0.7841	(±0.1430)	**0.8734**	**(±0.1183)**	0.6820	(±0.1360)	*0.8616*	*(±0.0926)*
	IGD+	0.2861	(±0.1766)	**0.1894**	**(±0.1548)**	0.4295	(±0.1780)	*0.2391*	*(±0.1323)*

Table 2 presents the mean and standard deviation of the hypervolume ratio and modified inverse generational distance of 30 independent executions. The reference points, used by the hypervolume ratio performance indicator, for each problem are shown in the sixth column of Table 1. The best and the second-best mean of each indicator for each problem is highlighted in bold and italics, respectively.

Note that for most of the problems the Pareto dominance-based IDM out-performs the other three compared methods, it is the best in 13 out of 22 performance values and 4 out of 22 is the second best. Although it is not the most competitive in the most complex problems, such as the DTLZ. For this case, the aggregation function-based IDM outperforms the other two methods, with 4 of 22 indicators as the best and 8 of 22 indicators as the second best, with the best performance in DTLZ problems. It is imprecise to define which of the following two methods is better since the DS is the best in 2 of 22 performance values and the indicator-based IDM is the best in 1 of 22 and 8 of 22 is second best. It is worth to mention that none of the four compared methods reach the reference front for the HV-r of the ZDT4 and DTLZ3 problems. Regarding the ZDT4, the problem is highly multimodal since it contains 21^9 local PFs, stagnating the search, similar to the DTLZ1 problem. For the DTLZ3, the objective space is too large compared to the step size, so it requires more function evaluations to reach the PF.

Table 3. First, second and third best algorithm based on the sorting of the median value of the Hypervolume ratio (HV-r) and the Modified Inverse Generational Distance (IGD+) performance indicators for 30 independent runs. The p-value of the non-parametric Wilcoxon rank sum test between the ith and $i + 1$th best median algorithm is presented.

		1° place	(p-value)	2° place	(p-value)	3° place	(p-value)
FON	HV-r	IDM/PBI	(0.0061)	IDM	(0.0000)	DS	(0.7446)
	IGD+	IDM	(0.0007)	IDM/PBI	(0.0000)	IDM/R2	(0.0000)
POL	HV-r	IDM	(0.0000)	IDM/R2	(0.0000)	IDM/PBI	(0.0000)
	IGD+	IDM	(0.0007)	IDM/PBI	(0.0000)	DS	(0.0000)
ZDT1	HV-r	IDM	(0.0000)	IDM/R2	(0.0000)	IDM/PBI	(0.0000)
	IGD+	IDM	(0.0000)	IDM/R2	(0.0000)	IDM/PBI	(0.0000)
ZDT2	HV-r	IDM	(0.0000)	DS	(0.0000)	IDM/PBI	(0.0000)
	IGD+	IDM	(0.0000)	DS	(0.0000)	IDM/PBI	(0.0000)
ZDT3	HV-r	IDM	(0.0000)	IDM/R2	(0.0000)	IDM/PBI	(0.0000)
	IGD+	IDM	(0.0007)	IDM/PBI	(0.0000)	IDM/R2	(0.0000)
ZDT4	HV-r	DS	(0.0000)	IDM	(0.0061)	IDM/PBI	(0.0000)
	IGD+	IDM/R2	(0.0000)	IDM	(0.0007)	IDM/PBI	(0.0000)
ZDT6	HV-r	IDM/PBI	(0.0061)	IDM	(0.0000)	IDM/R2	(0.7446)
	IGD+	IDM/PBI	(0.0007)	IDM	(0.0000)	IDM/R2	(0.0000)
DTLZ1	HV-r	DS	(0.0000)	IDM	(0.0061)	IDM/PBI	(0.0000)
	IGD+	DS	(0.0000)	IDM/PBI	(0.0007)	IDM	(0.0000)
DTLZ2	HV-r	IDM/PBI	(0.0061)	IDM	(0.0000)	DS	(0.7446)
	IGD+	IDM/PBI	(0.0007)	IDM	(0.0000)	DS	(0.0000)
DTLZ3	HV-r	DS	(0.0000)	IDM	(0.0061)	IDM/PBI	(0.0000)
	IGD+	DS	(0.0000)	IDM/PBI	(0.0007)	IDM	(0.0000)
DTLZ4	HV-r	IDM	(0.0000)	IDM/R2	(0.7446)	DS	(0.0000)
	IGD+	IDM	(0.0000)	IDM/R2	(0.0000)	DS	(0.0000)

Table 3 show the sorting of the compared methods based on the median of the hypervolume ratio (HV-r) and the Modified Inverse Generational Distance (IGD+)performance indicators for the 30 independent runs, and the p-value of the non-parametric Wilcoxon rank sum test [16] between the ith and the $i + 1$th best-sorted methods is presented.

The Wilcoxon rank sum test "measures" the order in which the observations from the two samples fall. That is, the Wilcoxon rank sum test the hypothesis that the distribution of a performance indicator of a solution set $\mathbf{A}$, $p(\mathbf{A})$, is the same as the distribution of the performance indicator of solution set $\mathbf{B}$, $p(\mathbf{B})$, given as $H_0 : \mathbf{A} = \mathbf{B}$. Such hypothesis tries to detect location shifts between both distribution, $p(\mathbf{A}) \neq p(\mathbf{B})$, thus, our alternative hypothesis $H_1 : \mathbf{A} \neq \mathbf{B}$ is the the two sided-alternative hypothesis, where the alternative hypotheses, where $p(\mathbf{A})$ shifts to the right of $p(\mathbf{B})$, $H_1 : \mathbf{A} > \mathbf{B}$, and where $p(\mathbf{A})$ shifts to the left of $p(\mathbf{B})$, $H_1 : \mathbf{A} < \mathbf{B}$, are united. The presented p-value displays a logical value indicating the test decision. The result indicates a rejection of the null hypothesis, and indicates an error in rejecting the null hypothesis at 5% significance level for this work. That is, given a p-value lower than 0.05, the null hypothesis is rejected and the shift between the distribution is given by the median of $p(\mathbf{A})$ and $p(\mathbf{B})$. For the HV-r performance indicator, a positive(right) shift indicates that the method $\mathbf{A}$ performs better than method $\mathbf{B}$, $m(\mathbf{A}) - m(\mathbf{B}) > 0$, where $m(\mathbf{A})$ and $m(\mathbf{B})$ is the median of the performance indicator of method $\mathbf{A}$ and $\mathbf{B}$, respectively. In the case of the IGD+, a negative(left) shift indicates that the method $\mathbf{A}$ performs better than method $\mathbf{B}$, $m(\mathbf{A}) - m(\mathbf{B}) < 0$. The presented results supports the discussed conclusions presented in Table 2, where the IDM method based on Pareto dominance better approximate solutions to the PF and such solutions are better distributed, for 11 of 22 performance indicators.

Additionally, Fig. 1 shows boxplots of the mean of a bootstrapping resampling [7] of the performance indicators for each problem within the problem benchmark set for the 30 independent runs of the Directed Search (DS) method, the IDM based on Pareto Dominance (IDM), the IDM based on aggregation functions (IDM/PBI) and the IDM based on binary indicators (IDM/R2). The method with the best result is highlighted in green. Similar to Table 2, Fig. 1 shows that the method that consistently delivers a "better" Pareto front is the IDM based on Pareto dominance, outperforming all other methods in 6 out of 11 problems with hypervolume indicator, and better-distributed fronts, with 6 out of 11 problems with the modified inverse generational distance indicator. Note IDM based on aggregation functions computes well distributed fronts, and outperforms the remaining 2 methods in 6 out of 11 problems with the modified inverse generational distance indicator. It is not possible to argue that the DS method is better than the IDM based on binary indicator, because the DS method shows better dispersion of solutions in 2 of the 11 problems, but it is the worst in 6 of the 9 remaining.

Figure 2 presents the front with the best hypervolume of the 30 runs for the DS method (blue square), IDM based on Pareto dominance (orange diamond), IDM based on aggregation functions (yellow star), and IDM based on binary

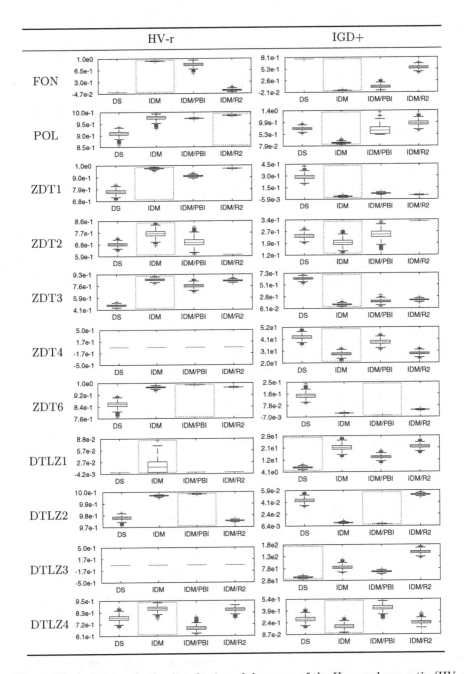

Fig. 1. On the left hand side: distribution of the mean of the Hypervolume ratio (HV-r), higher is better, and on the right hand side: the Modified Inverse Generational Distance (IGD+), lower is better, by means of a bootstrap re-sampling method over the 30 independent runs.

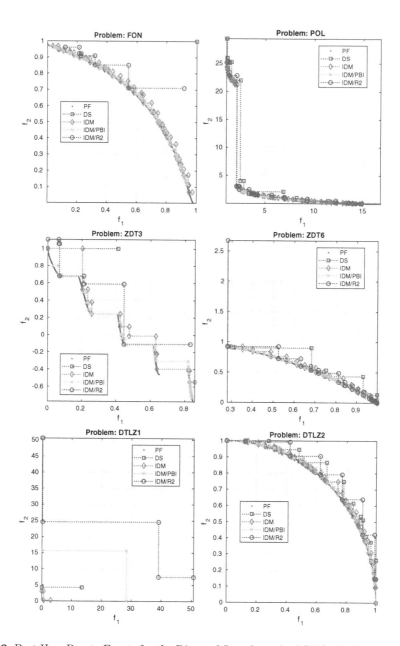

Fig. 2. Best Hv-r Pareto Fronts for the Directed Search method (DS), the Improvement Direction Mapping based on Pareto dominance (IDM), the Improvement Direction Mapping based on aggregation function (IDM/PBI) and the Improvement Direction Mapping based on binary indicator (IDM/R2).

indicators (purple circle). The reference front PF for each problem is shown in red. In the case of the IDM based on aggregation functions, in general, it distributes all the solutions on the reference front, having complications at the extreme solutions, contrary to the IDM based on binary indicators, which usually reaches the extreme solutions of the reference front. This can be noticed in the extreme solutions of the POL, ZDT3, and ZDT6 problems. The DS performs favorably on the POL and DTLZ2 problems, although it is not competitive in all the others, being unable to displace the solutions on the FON problem. In summary, the Pareto dominance based IDM deliver the best convergence to the reference front while the IDM based on aggregation function delivers a better distribution.

6   Conclusions

In this article, we introduce three procedures for computing improvement directions based on three dominance measures, for the solution of multi-objective problems. The contributions are various: the computation of improving directions in the objective space without the need of any apriori information, the use of different dominance measures to compute the improving directions, not only are proposals for approaching the solution of multi-objective problems, but the mathematical development and results presented in this work shed light on the different features of dominance measures such as Pareto dominance, aggregation functions and indicators used in MOEAS.

Additionally, one of the most challenging problems for the local search method applied to highly multi-modal and complex problems is the instability of maps or transformations from the objective space to the variable space. Nevertheless, in future work we will discuss deeply this issue, the proposed transformations and numerical techniques, such as replacing the singular values matrix by the identity and adapting the descent step, avoids numerical instabilities, and is essential for avoiding numerical singularities and erroneous searches.

The three improvement direction computation methods are compared using a set of well-known bi-objective benchmark problems in order to characterize the competitiveness in: approximating the PF, distributing, and spreading of the solutions. Furthermore, we introduce the general form of the IDM, then we specify the application with different dominance measures, each dominance measure produces an instance of an IDM method, from this point of view the pioneer DS method, in the state of the art, according to the mathematical formulae introduced here, is an instance of the IDM that uses the weighted sum aggregation function with the identity matrix as the Hessian.

On one hand, the results show that the Pareto dominance-based IDM, consistently, has a closer approximation to the PF, while the IDM based on aggregation functions produces the best distribution of the solutions, due to the dominance measurement scheme, where each solution referees to a coefficient aggregation vector to minimize the distance to the coefficient aggregation vector and the ideal point. On the other hand, the IDM is not competitive in multi-front problems, due to the characteristics of local search methods. Regarding this issue, a promising line of research is the IDM hybridization as a local search operator, with global search engines, such as MOEAs.

References

1. Bosman, P.A.N., Thierens, D.: The balance between proximity and diversity in multiobjective evolutionary algorithms. IEEE Trans. Evol. Comput. **7**(2), 174–188 (2003)
2. Botello-Aceves, S., Hernandez-Aguirre, A., Valdez, S.I.: Computation of the improvement directions of the pareto front and its application to MOEAs. In: Proceedings of the 2020 Genetic and Evolutionary Computation Conference. GECCO' 2020, Association for Computing Machinery, New York, NY, USA, pp. 480–488 (2020). https://doi.org/10.1145/3377930.3390165
3. Das, I., Dennis, J.E.: Normal-boundary intersection: a new method for generating the pareto surface in nonlinear multicriteria optimization problems. SIAM J. Optim. **8**(3), 631–657 (1998). https://doi.org/10.1137/S1052623496307510
4. Deb, K.: Multi-Objective Optimization Using Evolutionary Algorithms. John Wiley & Sons, New York (2001)
5. Deb, K., Pratap, A., Agarwal, S., Meyarivan, T.: A fast and elitist multiobjective genetic algorithm: Nsga-ii. IEEE Trans. Evol. Comput. **6**(2), 182–197 (2002)
6. Deb, K., Thiele, L., Laumanns, M., Zitzler, E.: Scalable Test Problems for Evolutionary Multiobjective Optimization, pp. 105–145. Springer, London (2005). https://doi.org/10.1007/1-84628-137-7_6
7. Dixon, P.M.: Bootstrap resampling. Encyclopedia of environmetrics, vol. 1 (2006)
8. Fliege, J., Svaiter, B.F.: Steepest descent methods for multicriteria optimization. Math. Methods Oper. Res. **51**(3), 479–494 (2000)
9. Fonseca, C.M., Fleming, P.J.: An overview of evolutionary algorithms in multiobjective optimization. Evol. Comput. **3**(1), 1–16 (1995)
10. Hansen, M.P., Jaszkiewicz, A.: Evaluating the Quality of Approximations to the Non-Dominated Set. Department of Mathematical Modelling, Technical Universityof Denmark, IMM, Kongens Lyngby (1994)
11. Harada, K., Sakuma, J., Kobayashi, S.: Local search for multiobjective function optimization: Pareto descent method. In: Proceedings of the 8th Annual Conference on Genetic and Evolutionary Computation. GECCO' 2006, Association for Computing Machinery, New York, NY, USA, pp. 659–666 (2006). https://doi.org/10.1145/1143997.1144115
12. Huband, S., Hingston, P., Barone, L., While, L.: A review of multiobjective test problems and a scalable test problem toolkit. IEEE Trans. Evol. Comput. **10**(5), 477–506 (2006)
13. Hwang, C., Masud, A.S.M.: Multiple Objective Decision Making–Methods and Applications: A State-of-the-Art Survey. Springer Science & Business Media, New York (2012)
14. Ishibuchi, H., Masuda, H., Nojima, Y.: Pareto fronts of many-objective degenerate test problems. IEEE Trans. Evol. Comput. **20**(5), 807–813 (2016)
15. Ishibuchi, H., Masuda, H., Tanigaki, Y., Nojima, Y.: Modified distance calculation in generational distance and inverted generational distance. In: Gaspar-Cunha, A., Henggeler Antunes, C., Coello, C.C. (eds.) Evolutionary Multi-Criterion Optimization, pp. 110–125. Springer International Publishing, Cham (2015)

16. Lam, F.C., Longnecker, M.T.: A modified Wilcoxon rank sum test for paired data. Biometrika **70**(2), 510–513 (1983). https://doi.org/10.1093/biomet/70.2.510
17. Li, M., Zheng, J.: Spread assessment for evolutionary multi-objective optimization. In: Ehrgott, M., Fonseca, C.M., Gandibleux, X., Hao, J.K., Sevaux, M. (eds.) Evolutionary Multi-Criterion Optimization, pp. 216–230. Springer, Berlin Heidelberg (2009)
18. Messac, A., Ismail-Yahaya, A., Mattson, C.: The normalized normal constraint method for generating the pareto frontier. Struct. Multi. Optim. **25**(2), 86–98 (2003). https://doi.org/10.1007/s00158-002-0276-1
19. Okabe, T., Jin, Y., Sendhoff, B.: A critical survey of performance indices for multi-objective optimisation. In: The 2003 Congress on Evolutionary Computation. CEC' 2003, vol. 2, pp. 878–885, December 2003. https://doi.org/10.1109/CEC.2003.1299759
20. Phan, D.H., Suzuki, J.: R2-IBEA: R2 indicator based evolutionary algorithm for multiobjective optimization. In: 2013 IEEE Congress on Evolutionary Computation, pp. 1836–1845 (2013)
21. Riquelme, N., Von Lücken, C., Baran, B.: Performance metrics in multi-objective optimization. In: 2015 Latin American Computing Conference (CLEI), pp. 1–11, October 2015. https://doi.org/10.1109/CLEI.2015.7360024
22. Schütze, O., Alvarado, S., Segura, C., Landa, R.: Gradient subspace approximation: a direct search method for memetic computing. Soft Comput. **21**(21), 6331–6350 (2017). https://doi.org/10.1007/s00500-016-2187-x
23. Schütze, O., Martín, A., Lara, A., Alvarado, S., Salinas, E., Coello, C.A.C.: The directed search method for multi-objective memetic algorithms. Comput. Optim. Appl. **63**(2), 305–332 (2015). https://doi.org/10.1007/s10589-015-9774-0
24. Van Veldhuizen, D.A., Lamont, G.B.: Multiobjective evolutionary algorithms: analyzing the state-of-the-art. Evol. Comput. **8**(2), 125–147 (2000). https://doi.org/10.1162/106365600568158
25. Zitzler, E.: Evolutionary Algorithms for Multiobjective Optimization: Methods and Applications. Ph.D. thesis, Swiss Federal Institute of Technology Zurich, Computer Engineering and Networks Laboratory (1999)
26. Zitzler, E., Deb, K., Thiele, L.: Comparison of multiobjective evolutionary algorithms: empirical results. Evol. Comput. **8**(2), 173–195 (2000). https://doi.org/10.1162/106365600568202
27. Zitzler, E., Deb, K., Thiele, L.: Comparison of multiobjective evolutionary algorithms: empirical results. Evol. Comput. **8**(2), 173–195 (2000). https://doi.org/10.1162/106365600568202
28. Zitzler, E., Knowles, J., Thiele, L.: Quality assessment of pareto set approximations. In: Branke, J., Deb, K., Miettinen, K., Słowiński, R. (eds.) Multiobjective Optimization. LNCS, vol. 5252, pp. 373–404. Springer, Heidelberg (2008). https://doi.org/10.1007/978-3-540-88908-3_14

A Genetic Programming Framework for Heuristic Generation for the Job-Shop Scheduling Problem

E. Lara-Cárdenas⬛, X. Sánchez-Díaz⬛, I. Amaya⬛, J. M. Cruz-Duarte⬛,
and J. C. Ortiz-Bayliss(✉)⬛

Tecnologico de Monterrey, School of Engineering and Sciences, Av. Eugenio Garza
Sada 2501, 64849 Monterrey, NL, Mexico
a00398510@itesm.mx, {sax,iamaya2,jorge.cruz,jcobayliss}@tec.mx

Abstract. The Job-Shop Scheduling problem is a combinatorial optimization problem present in many real-world applications. It has been tackled with a colorful palette of techniques from different paradigms. Particularly, hyper-heuristics have attracted the attention of researchers due to their promising results in various optimization scenarios, including job-shop scheduling. In this study, we describe a Genetic-Programming-based Hyper-heuristic approach for automatically producing heuristics (dispatching rules) when solving such a problem. To do so, we consider a set of features that characterize the jobs within a scheduling instance. By using these features and a set of mathematical functions that create interactions between such features, we facilitate the construction of new heuristics. We present empirical evidence that heuristics produced by our approach are competitive. This conclusion arises from comparing the makespan of schedules obtained from our proposed method against those of some standard heuristics, over a set of synthetic Job-Shop Scheduling problem instances.

Keywords: Hyper-heuristics · Job-Shop scheduling · Genetic Programming

1 Introduction

Combinatorial optimization problems are widespread in everyday processes, liaised with both academic and industrial applications. A particular example of such combinatorial optimization problems resides in Job-Shop Scheduling (JSS), where the solving process requires to assign a set of tasks within jobs to a set of machines in such a way that they minimize the makespan (completion time). A JSS problem is inherent to any manufacturing process where it is imperative to schedule an optimal production plan.

Several variations of JSS have risen throughout the years [12,30]. Likewise, different methods for solving them have appeared in the literature since 1956 [35].

© Springer Nature Switzerland AG 2020
L. Martínez-Villaseñor et al. (Eds.): MICAI 2020, LNAI 12468, pp. 284–295, 2020.
https://doi.org/10.1007/978-3-030-60884-2_21

For example, some authors have tackled the Dynamic Flexible JSS problem where there is uncertainty in processing times [22,34,36]. Others have considered the Deterministic No-Wait JSS version, whose primary goal is to find a schedule that minimizes the makespan [3,23,24]. Since the search space of such problems is usually huge, exhaustive exploration is impractical. Hence, solving JSS problems usually relies on approximation techniques. Some illustrative examples include the dispatching rules proposed by Blackstone *et al.* [17], and the *shifting bottleneck* procedure employed by Adams *et al.* [1]. Such dispatching rules refer to low-level heuristics that can either construct or modify a schedule. The main advantage of these approaches is their low computational cost, which means they deliver quick solutions. Nonetheless, their inability to guarantee optimality emerges as a side-effect. Thus, heuristics are usually applied in practice to solve hard combinatorial optimization problems, including the JSS problem [27].

One way of surmounting the optimality drawback is to incorporate more robust search techniques. There are several works following this path, including strategies such as Tabu Search [13,26], and Guided Local Search with Branch-and-Bound [2]. However, there are also approaches based on Genetic Algorithms [19,32], Genetic Search [31], and Genetic Programming [25]. Of course, these strategies also include hybrids [33] and other approaches [8,18,28]. Moreover, there is another strategy that emerged recently: Hyper-Heuristics (HHs) [9]. A HH extends the ideas proposed by Fisher and Thompson [14] and Crowston [10] in the early 1960s: a combination of priority dispatching rules should perform better than any of the rules in isolation. HHs represent a particular application where the idea is to automate the design or selection of the available heuristics. According to Burke *et al.* [5], HHs can be classified into two main categories: methodologies that select from a fixed set of heuristics and those that generate new heuristics. The former produces a mapping between the states of the problem and a feasible heuristic. Otherwise, generation HHs identify critical parts of existing heuristics to create new ones [6,16].

Particularly, the literature contains some interesting works within the intersection of hyper-heuristics and the JSS problem. For example, Chaurasia *et al.* proposed a HH based on evolutionary algorithms and a guided heuristic for JSS problem instances [7]. Similarly, Garza-Santisteban *et al.* studied the feasibility of using the well-known Simulated Annealing to train HHs [15]. More recently, Lara-Cárdenas *et al.* implemented Neural Networks for improving the performance of existing HHs for the JSS problem [21].

In this work, we explore a novel idea for contributing to the state-of-the-art about generation HHs. Our model combines features that characterize the individual jobs within the instances, while other similar approaches from the literature reuse components from existing heuristics. The main benefit of this particularity is that we require no information from other heuristics or criteria to produce new competent ones. We tackle the JSS problem through an approach based on Genetic Programming (GP) for producing new heuristics. GP is an evolutionary algorithm that borrows ideas from the theory of natural evolution to build a program represented as a tree-like data structure [20]. The method evolves programs through three genetic operators: selection, crossover, and mutation. In GP, crossover and mutation are specifically designed to work with the tree-like data structure. This algorithm relies on an objective function to evaluate the programs, and then, the programs with the best objective values are more likely to survive to future generations. Thus, our hyper-heuristic model produces heuristics (or dispatching rules) by combining the features that characterize the jobs in a JSS problem. Merging this material allows to encapsulate significant human-derived expertise to reuse for improving performance. Our experiments offer empirical evidence that the newly-produced heuristics can be specialized for specific groups of instances, and that they outperform the best standard heuristics. Although our model is tested on JSS problems, it may be applied to other problem domains with ease, as long as they rely on heuristics that guide the search.

The remainder of this document is organized as follows. Section 2 presents the basic concepts related to this work. Subsequently, Sect. 3 describes the proposed approach and how it produces heuristics for the JSS problem. Section 4 discusses the experiments and main results achieved with such an approach. Finally, Sect. 5 remarks the most relevant conclusions and some future research directions.

2   Background

A Job-Shop Scheduling (JSS) problem is described by a set of jobs and a set of machines. Each job contains a list of tasks that must be processed in a specific order. Solving the JSS problem requires that the machines handle all the tasks in each job, in their corresponding order. Each task has a processing time on a particular machine since not all the machines can process all tasks. A feasible schedule must then satisfy that tasks of all jobs have been assigned to one suitable machine in a valid order of execution. The time needed to complete such a schedule is known as the *makespan*. All the solving methods considered in this work focus on yielding schedules that minimize such a value.

In the following lines, we briefly describe some relevant concepts related to this study: the available heuristics, the instances we used, the features to characterize the jobs within such instances, and the performance metrics for evaluating the methods under analysis.

2.1   Heuristics

For this work, we select heuristics based on reports in the same area [15,21]. Thus, we only consider those that build a solution from scratch by making one decision per step (*i.e.*, constructive heuristics). For the JSS problem, these heuristics decide which job to process next among all the available options. Such a decision is made at each stage of the search. Withal, we describe the selected heuristics as follows:

Shortest Processing Time (SPT) picks the activity with the shortest processing time, from the available activities to schedule.

Longest Processing Time (LPT) chooses the activity with the longest processing time, from the available activities yet to schedule.

Maximum Job Remaining Time (MRT) first takes the job that requires the most time to finish (*i.e.*, the one with the largest sum of the processing times of its activities yet to be scheduled). Then, it returns the first possible activity (in precedence order) that corresponds to such a job.

Most Loaded Machine (MLM) takes the machine with the maximum total processing time (the one with the largest sum of the processing times of the activities that it has allocated) from the available machines. Then, it selects the activity with the shortest processing time, from the activities that can be allocated on the selected machine.

Least Loaded Machine (LLM) works similar to MLM, but it chooses the machine with the minimum total processing time from the set of machines. Then, it selects the activity with the shortest processing time from the activities that can be allocated on the selected machine.

Earliest Start Time (EST) finds the job that has the earliest possible starting time at the current problem state, by considering the available activities yet to be scheduled. Then, it picks the activity corresponding to that job.

In all cases, these heuristics break ties by using the index of the job that coincides to its belonging activity; they prioritize small values.

2.2   Instances

All the instances considered for this research were synthetically produced by using the algorithm proposed by Taillard [29]. This algorithm produces JSS problem instances with a specific number of jobs and machines, specified by the user. The jobs' processing times are generated uniformly on an interval from 1 to 99, using the random generator proposed by Bratley *et al.* [4]. For this investigation, we set the parameters of the instance generator as recommended by Taillard [29]. We produced 25 JSS problem instances, with ten machines and ten jobs. We then split those instances into training and testing sets by using 15 and 10 instances. These sets are mutually exclusive, which means that each instance appears only in one of the two sets.

2.3   Job Characterization

In this work, the job characterization relies on six features that capture the state of the jobs and allow the creation of new heuristics. Such features are described below:

APT calculates the ratio between the sum of the processing times of the processed activities of the job and that of the whole list of the activities of the job. This feature pictures the completion percentage of the scheduling process for the job.

DPT determines the ratio between the standard deviation of the processing times of the processed activities and their mean value.

SLACK obtains the ratio between the slack (available machine time), and the makespan of the current schedule.

DNPT describes the ratio between the standard deviation and the mean processing times of all the unscheduled activities for each job.

NAPT is the complement of APT. It calculates the ratio between the sum of the processing times of unscheduled activities of the job and the sum of the processing times of the complete list of activities of the job (including scheduled ones).

NJT determines the sum of the processing times normalized for each job. Then, it divides such an amount by the number of pending jobs. It only applies to the pending jobs.

2.4 Performance Metrics

To evaluate the performance of the methods studied in this work, we employ two metrics. The first one is the makespan, which represents the value of the completion time of the schedule produced by a particular method on a specific instance. Then, the smaller the makespan, the better the performance. We have mainly used the total makespan determined as the sum of all the makespans per instance on the test set. The second metric is the success rate, which estimates the relative performance of the methods under study. The success rate represents the fraction of cases where one particular process 'succeeds' against another one by reducing the makespan in a specific instance. With the success rate, the closer the value to 1, the better the performance. In other words, the success rate indicates the proportion, from the total instances, where a technique (a hyper-heuristic, in our experiments) outperforms another model on the test set.

Using these metrics, we evaluated the performance of the heuristics produced and compared them against the human-made heuristics and a synthetic Oracle H*. Hence, H* represents the best possible schedule obtained utilizing the six heuristics to solve each particular instance. Since this value cannot be known in advance, H* is infeasible in practice. However, it is useful for comparison purposes, as we show in this investigation.

3 The Hyper-heuristic Approach

This model focuses on the generation of heuristics for the JSS problem utilizing Genetic Programming (GP). The heuristics produced by our approach contain an internal function that combines the features, which characterize a job in the JSS problem, by using a set of available operations. We consider this feature combination as a high-level feature that increases the discriminative power of the individual features. When the solving process summons a heuristic, such a heuristic evaluates all the available jobs employing its internal function. Then, the heuristic schedules the next available task in the job with the smallest evaluation. After scheduling a task, the solving process requires a new call to the heuristic (with its corresponding function evaluations) before scheduling another task. This process is repeated until the instance is solved.

As mentioned before, the evolution of such heuristics (actually, their internal functions) is achieved through a GP-based approach. A tree-like structure represents a function, as the example depicted in Fig. 1. We can interpret such a structure as the function $f(x_1, x_2, x_3) = x_1 + (x_2 - x_3)$. In this function, x_1, x_2, and x_3 can be features that characterize the jobs in the instance. All the features considered for this work are dynamic, then the heuristics produced are dynamic as well. In our context, being dynamic means that the values change as the solving process takes place. Thus, one internal function may return different values for the same job at different moments of the solution process.

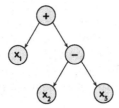

Fig. 1. A tree-like structure that encodes the function $f(x_1, x_2, x_3) = x_1 + (x_2 - x_3)$

The evolutionary process that powers the hyper-heuristic (HH) model is the component responsible for creating new heuristics by evolving their internal functions. The HH model requires three inputs: the training instances and the terminal and function sets. This model uses the training instances to evaluate the performance of the heuristics throughout the evolutionary process. The two last inputs (the terminal and function sets) are a requirement imposed by GP, which uses those sets to generate and modify the functions. In the GP's tree-like structures, leaf nodes always contain an element from the terminal set, while the rest of the nodes always contain an element from the function set. In this work, the terminal set is composed of features that characterize jobs, as described in Sect. 2.3 and the ephemeral constant $R \in [-1, 1]$. The function set contains six simple operations: addition $(+)$, subtraction $(-)$, multiplication $(\times)$, protected division $(/)$, minimization (min), and maximization (max). All these operations take two operands each.

The evolutionary process starts with 30 randomly initialized individuals, using the ramped half-and-half method for this purpose. This process runs for 100 generations. For crossover and mutation, we considered rates of 0.9 and 0.05, respectively. Finally, for selecting the individuals for mating, we used a tournament selection of size two. At the end of the 100 generations, the model returns the individual with the smallest objective value as the resulting heuristic. At this point, the heuristic becomes ready to solve unseen instances.

The objective function within the evolutionary process estimates how well the heuristics will cope with unseen instances by considering two crucial components when dealing with a set of instances.

The function $f(x)$ regards both the time for completing all the schedules (f_a) and the variation in the results from one instance to another (f_b), as given

$$f(x) = f_a(x) + f_b(x) = \frac{1}{n}\sum_{i=1}^{n} C_i + \sqrt{\frac{1}{n}\sum_{i=1}^{n} |C_i - \bar{C}|^2}, \qquad (1)$$

where C_i stands for the makespan of the schedule for instance i in the test set, and $\bar{C}$ is the average makespan of all the instances in the test set.

The rationale behind reducing the total makespan is evident: the sooner the schedules are completed, the better the solutions. Plus, the reason for minimizing the standard deviation of the results is more difficult to appreciate. We expect that, by also minimizing the deviation of the makespans of the schedules produced by the heuristics, we are likely to avoid extreme cases where one heuristic is desirable for some instances but entirely useless for others. The proposed fitness function then aims to render heuristics that show a good and steady performance in different instances.

4   Experiments and Results

In this work, we generated 30 heuristics for the JSS problem by using the GP-based hyper-heuristic approach. These heuristics are labeled with the prefix 'HGP'. Additionally, and for comparison purposes, we also built 30 hyper-heuristics by employing the model proposed by Garza-Santisteban *et al.*, which relies on Simulated Annealing (SA) to produce a method capable of switching heuristics as the solving process takes place [15]. These hyper-heuristics are labeled with the prefix 'HHSA'. The 30 HGPs and the 30 HHSAs were compared against the human-made heuristics defined in Sect. 2.1. To evaluate the performance of each method, we used two metrics: the success rate and the reduction in total makespan when solving the test set. Table 1 summarizes the performance of the methods produced. Due to space restrictions, we only show the results of the best three performers per method.

Based on the results from Table 1, we can observe that the best method for the test set was one of the heuristics produced with our approach: HGP22. This heuristic generated schedules that represent essential savings in time concerning the schedules provided by human-made heuristics. For example, when compared against SPT, it saves 132 h to complete all the schedules for the instances in the test set. That is more than five days earlier than with the best heuristic for the test set. The reductions are even more significant for the rest of heuristics.

Although HGP22 proved to be a competent heuristic, not all the heuristics we produced seem to have the same quality. Regarding the results obtained by HGP16 and HGP21, they are, in all cases, outperformed by any of the HHSA methods. Then, it may be the case that the competent behavior of HGP22 may

Table 1. Success rate and time savings (in hours) of the three best heuristics produced with the proposed approach (HGPs) and the three best hyper-heuristics built with SA [15] (HHSAs) when compared against the human-made heuristics on the test set. An arrow (↑) before the time savings indicates that, for that particular case, the method required additional hours to complete the schedules of the test set (no savings were obtained). The best method is highlighted in bold.

Method	SPT	LPT	MRT	MLM	LLM	EST
HGP16	(0.4, ↑100)	(0.5, 613)	(0.7, 42)	(0.4, 156)	(0.8, 611)	(0.8, 1154)
HGP21	(0.4, ↑103)	(0.6, 610)	(0.6, 39)	(0.7, 153)	(0.9, 608)	(1.0, 1151)
HGP22	**(0.5, 132)**	**(0.7, 845)**	**(0.7, 274)**	**(0.6, 388)**	**(0.8, 843)**	**(1.0, 1383)**
HHSA03	(0.5, 51)	(0.6, 764)	(0.6, 193)	(0.5, 307)	(0.7, 762)	(1.0, 1305)
HHSA06	(0.4, 34)	(0.8, 747)	(0.6, 176)	(0.6, 290)	(0.9, 745)	(0.9, 1288)
HHSA11	(0.6, 72)	(0.7, 785)	(0.6, 214)	(0.6, 328)	(0.9, 783)	(0.9, 1326)

be an exceptional situation challenging to replicate if we rerun the model. Future work should include a more in-depth analysis of the model behavior.

So far, we have shown that it is possible to improve upon the results from human-made heuristics by employing the heuristics generated by the GP-based approach. However, we have not yet analyzed how these results look when comparing the heuristics and hyper-heuristics against the best possible outcome by using the human-made heuristics, *i.e.*, the Oracle (H*). The total makespan of H* on the test set was 7846 h while the total makespans of HGP22, HGP16, and HGP21 were 8205, 8437, and 8440 h, respectively. These makespans are similar for the hyper-heuristics produced by using Simulated Annealing, HHSA11, HHSA03, and HHSA06, which required 8265, 8286, and 8303 h to finish their schedules. When we compare the best performer of each method, HGP22 and HHSA11, we observe a difference of 60 h that favors HGP22. It is essential to mention that neither HGP22 nor HHSA11 can improve the total makespan of the Oracle, but they achieve it on a per-instance basis. The success rates of HGP22 and HHSA11 are 0.4 and 0.3, respectively, which indicates that they indeed improved the best possible result from the human-made heuristics for some specific instances in the test set.

Deepening on the reductions in the makespan for some specific instances, Fig. 2 depicts the distribution of makespan differences (in hours) of the HGPs and HHSAs when they are compared against H* (drawn as a red line). The human-made heuristics are omitted in this chart since they are already represented in the Oracle's behavior. In this plot, values below zero mean that the method improved the best schedule produced with the human-made heuristics. It is interesting to notice that HGP16 has a considerable variation in the makespans of the schedules it produces. For some instances, the schedule obtained has a very small makespan. However, for some others, it pays the price, and their schedules are among the worst in the makespan. In other words, their results are not consistent, which results in an overall performance that sits below the other

HGPs and HHSAs. But, it achieves significant savings in some isolated instances, savings that no other method can achieve.

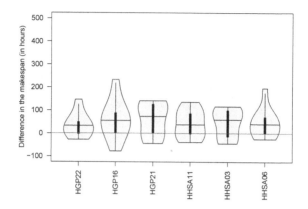

Fig. 2. Distribution of the makespan of the three best heuristics produced with the proposed approach (HGPs) and the three best hyper-heuristics produced with SA [15] (HHSAs) when compared against H* (red line) on the test set. (Color figure online)

Finally, we conducted two pairwise two-tailed t-tests with a significance level of 5% to validate our results statistically. Although HGP22 and HHSA11 obtained good results on an individual level (some specific instances), we observed that they failed to reduce the total makespan of H* in the test set. Nonetheless, we scrutinized if the statistical evidence suggests differences in the performance of such methods. The tests were conducted on the pairs (HGP22, H*) and (HHSA11, H*). The p-values for these tests were 0.1323 and 0.1033, respectively. Then, the statistical evidence suggests that both HGP22 and HHSA11 are similar to the Oracle in terms of makespan for the test set.

5 Conclusions

In this study, we proposed an approach based on Genetic Programming (GP) for tackling the Job-Shop Scheduling (JSS) problem. The model produces new heuristics by combining features that characterize jobs within the instance being solved; this makes our model unique. To the best of our knowledge, other generation hyper-heuristic approaches rely on components of existing heuristics, which are reused. In our case, we do not have this limitation. Thus, the proposed model is free to explore and produce heuristics that explode a criterion that probably has never been seen before, since the evolutionary process creates a function that reflects such a criterion. However, the solution model now depends on the expressiveness of the features that describe the jobs.

In general, the GP-based approach favors the creation of heuristics that outperform the Oracle, at least for some instances in the test set. This was inferred from the results presented in Table 1 and Fig. 2. However, we are aware that our training and test sets are quite short, and to validate our proposal thoroughly, we require to test it on a more extensive and diverse collection of instances. We plan to expand the set of training and test instances in the future. As future work, we would like to explore other features to characterize the jobs within the instance and compare the performance of the refined model against other existing generation hyper-heuristic models from the literature. Also, we consider that a combination of selection and generation hyper-heuristics might be possible by extending the model described in this document. We think that the model could use a hyper-heuristic that chooses among heuristics most of the time but generate completely new heuristics when the situation requires it. These new heuristics would be available for selection in future cases, extending the heuristic pool as the model deals with more instances. Furthermore, we plan to implement this GP-based approach in continuous optimization problems, for example, to create brand-new search operators [11].

Acknowledgments. This research was partially supported by CONACyT Basic Science Project under grant 287479 and ITESM Research Group with Strategic Focus on Intelligent Systems.

References

1. Adams, J., Balas, E., Zawack, D.: The shifting bottleneck procedure for job shop scheduling. Manage. Sci. **34**(3), 391–401 (1988)
2. Balas, E., Vazacopoulos, A.: Guided local search with shifting bottleneck for job shop scheduling. Manage. Sci. **44**(2), 262–275 (1998)
3. Bozejko, W., Gnatowski, A., Pempera, J., Wodecki, M.: Parallel tabu search for the cyclic job shop scheduling problem. Comput. Ind. Eng. **113**, 512–524 (2017). https://doi.org/10.1016/j.cie.2017.09.042
4. Bratley, P., Fox, B.L., Schrage, L.E.: A Guide to Simulation. Springer Science & Business Media, Berlin (2011)
5. Burke, E.K., Hyde, M.R., Kendall, G.: Providing a memory mechanism to enhance the evolutionary design of heuristics. In: IEEE Congress on Evolutionary Computation, pp. 1–8. IEEE (2010)
6. Burke, E.K., Hyde, M.R., Kendall, G., Woodward, J.: Automatic heuristic generation with genetic programming: evolving a jack-of-all-trades or a master of one. In: Proceedings of the 9th Annual Conference on Genetic and Evolutionary Computation, pp. 1559–1565 (2007)
7. Chaurasia, S.N., Sundar, S., Jung, D., Lee, H.M., Kim, J.H.: An evolutionary algorithm based hyper-heuristic for the job-shop scheduling problem with no-wait constraint. In: Yadav, N., Yadav, A., Bansal, J.C., Deep, K., Kim, J.H. (eds.) Harmony Search and Nature Inspired Optimization Algorithms. AISC, vol. 741, pp. 249–257. Springer, Singapore (2019). https://doi.org/10.1007/978-981-13-0761-4_25
8. Chong, C.S., Low, M.Y.H., Sivakumar, A.I., Gay, K.L.: A bee colony optimization algorithm to job shop scheduling. In: Proceedings of the 2006 Winter Simulation Conference, pp. 1954–1961. Winter Simulatrion Conference, Monterey, California December 2006. https://doi.org/10.1109/WSC.2006.322980

9. Cowling, P., Kendall, G., Soubeiga, E.: A hyperheuristic approach to scheduling a sales summit. In: Burke, E., Erben, W. (eds.) PATAT 2000. LNCS, vol. 2079, pp. 176–190. Springer, Heidelberg (2001). https://doi.org/10.1007/3-540-44629-X_11

10. Crowston, W.B., Glover, F., Trawick, J.D., et al.: Probabilistic and Parametric Learning Combinations of Local Job Shop Scheduling Rules. Technical report, Carnegie inst of tech pittsburgh pa graduate school of industrial administration (1963)

11. Cruz-Duarte, J.M., Ivan, A., Ortiz-Bayliss, J.C., Conant-Pablos, S.E., Terashima-Marín, H.: A primary study on hyper-heuristics to customise metaheuristics for continuous optimisation. In: 2020 IEEE Congress on Evolutionary Computation (CEC), pp. 1–8 (2020)

12. Cunha, B., Madureira, A.M., Fonseca, B., Coelho, D.: Deep reinforcement learning as a job shop scheduling solver: a literature review. In: Madureira, A.M., Abraham, A., Gandhi, N., Varela, M.L. (eds.) Hybrid Intelligent Systems, pp. 350–359. Springer International Publishing, Cham (2020)

13. Fattahi, P., Messi Bidgoli, M., Samouei, P.: An improved tabu search algorithm for job shop scheduling problem trough hybrid solution representations. J. Qual Eng. Product. Optim. 3(1), 13–26 (2018). https://doi.org/10.22070/jqepo.2018.1360.1035

14. Fisher, H.: Probabilistic learning combinations of local job-shop scheduling rules. Ind. Sched. 225–251 (1963)

15. Garza-Santisteban, F., et al.: A Simulated Annealing Hyper-heuristic for job shop scheduling problems. In: 2019 IEEE Congress on Evolutionary Computation (CEC), pp. 57–64. IEEE (June 2019). https://doi.org/10.1109/CEC.2019.8790296, https://ieeexplore.ieee.org/document/8790296/

16. Grendreau, M., Potvin, J.: Handbook of Metaheuristics. International Series in Operations Research & Management Science, vol. 146 (2010)

17. Blackstone, J.H., Phillips, D.T., Hogg, G.: A state-of-the-art survey of dispatching rules for manufacturing job shop operations. Int. J. Product. Res. 20, 27–45 (1982)

18. Huang, K.L., Liao, C.J.: Ant colony optimization combined with taboo search for the job shop scheduling problem. Comput. Oper. Res. 35(4), 1030–1046 (2008)

19. dao-er ji, R.Q., Wang, Y.: A new hybrid genetic algorithm for job shop scheduling problem. Comput. Oper. Res. 39(10), 2291–2299 (2019). https://doi.org/10.1016/j.cor.2011.12.005

20. Koza, J.R., Koza, J.R.: Genetic Programming: on the Programming of Computers by Means of Natural Selection, vol. 1. MIT press, Cambridge (1992)

21. Lara-Cárdenas, E., Sánchez-Díaz, X., Amaya, I., Ortiz-Bayliss, J.C.: Improving hyper-heuristic performance for job shop scheduling problems using neural networks. In: Martínez-Villaseñor, L., Batyrshin, I., Marín-Hernández, A. (eds.) Advances in Soft Computing, pp. 150–161. Springer International Publishing, Cham (2019)

22. Lin, J.: Backtracking search based hyper-heuristic for the flexible job-shop scheduling problem with fuzzy processing time. Eng. Appl. Artif. Intell. 77186–196, (2019). https://doi.org/10.1016/j.engappai.2018.10.008

23. Masood, A., Mei, Y., Chen, G., Zhang, M.: Many-objective genetic programming for job-shop scheduling. In: 2016 IEEE Congress on Evolutionary Computation (CEC), pp. 209–216. IEEE, Vancouver, Canada (July 2016). https://doi.org/10.1109/CEC.2016.7743797

24. Miyashita, K.: Job-shop scheduling with genetic programming. In: Proceedings of the 2nd Annual Conference on Genetic and Evolutionary Computation, pp. 505–512. GECCO 2000, Morgan Kaufmann Publishers Inc., San Francisco, CA, USA (2000)

25. Nguyen, S., Zhang, M., Johnston, M., Tan, K.C.: Genetic programming for job shop scheduling. In: Bansal, J.C., Singh, P.K., Pal, N.R. (eds.) Evolutionary and Swarm Intelligence Algorithms. SCI, vol. 779, pp. 143–167. Springer, Cham (2019). https://doi.org/10.1007/978-3-319-91341-4_8

26. Nowicki, E., Smutnicki, C.: A fast taboo search algorithm for the job shop problem. Manag. Sci. **42**(6), 797–813 (1996)

27. Sánchez, M., Cruz-Duarte, J.M., Ortiz-Bayliss, J.C., Ceballos, H., Terashima-Marín, H., Amaya, I.: A systematic review of hyper-heuristics on combinatorial optimization problems. IEEE Access **8**(1), 1–28 (2020). https://doi.org/10.1109/access.2020.3009318

28. Sha, D., Hsu, C.Y.: A hybrid particle swarm optimization for job shop scheduling problem. Comput. Ind. Eng. **51**(4), 791–808 (2006)

29. Taillard, E.: Benchmarks for basic scheduling problems. Euro. J. Oper. Res. **64**(2), 278–285 (1993). https://doi.org/10.1016/0377-2217(93)90182-M, project Management and Scheduling

30. Türkyılmaz, A., Şenvar, Ö., Ünal, I., Bulkan, S.: A research survey: heuristic approaches for solving multi objective flexible job shop problems. J. Intell. Manufact. February 2020. https://doi.org/10.1007/s10845-020-01547-4, http://link.springer.com/10.1007/s10845-020-01547-4

31. Uckun, S., Bagchi, S., Kawamura, K., Miyabe, Y.: Managing genetic search in job shop scheduling. IEEE Intell. Syst. **8**(5), 15–24 (1993)

32. Wang, L., Cai, J.C, Ming, L.: An adaptive multi-population genetic algorithm for job-shop scheduling problem. Adv. Manufact. 1–8 (2016). https://doi.org/10.1007/s40436-016-0140-y

33. Wang, L., Zheng, D.Z.: An effective hybrid optimization strategy for job-shop scheduling problems. Comput. Oper. Res. **28**(6), 585–596 (2001)

34. Yska, D., Mei, Y., Zhang, M.: Feature construction in genetic programming hyper-heuristic for dynamic flexible job shop scheduling. In: Proceedings of the Genetic and Evolutionary Computation Conference Companion on - GECCO 2018, pp. 149–150. ACM Press, New York, USA (2018). https://doi.org/10.1145/3205651.3205741

35. Zhang, J., Ding, G., Zou, Y., Qin, S., Fu, J.: Review of job shop scheduling research and its new perspectives under Industry 4.0. J. Intell. Manufact. **30**(4), 1809–1830 (2017). https://doi.org/10.1007/s10845-017-1350-2

36. Zhou, Y., Yang, J.J., Zheng, L.Y.: Hyper-Heuristic Coevolution of Machine Assignment and Job Sequencing Rules for Multi-Objective Dynamic Flexible Job Shop Scheduling. IEEE Access **7**, 68–88 (2019). https://doi.org/10.1109/ACCESS.2018.2883802

A Genetic Algorithm Approach for a Truck and Trailer Routing Problem in a Loading/Unloading Bays Application

Ana Bricia Galindo-Muro[1]([⊠]), Jaime Mora-Vargas[1],
Miguel Gastón Cedillo-Campos[2], and Fabiola Regis-Hernández[1]

[1] Tecnologico de Monterrey, Estado de Mexico, Mexico
a01657186@itesm.mx, {jmora,fregisher}@tec.mx
[2] Instituto Mexicano del Transporte, Queretaro, Mexico
gaston.cedillo@imt.mx

Abstract. Nowadays urban mobilities represent a necessity more than a challenge. Urban centers have a large vehicle congregation in the streets, causing difficulties in the last mile operations for urban freight. Further to the traffic problems, authorities imposed strict regulations in the cities for freight vehicles. As a consequence of both of these limitations, the freight vehicles can't optimally execute their activities. In this research, a Genetic Algorithm is developed for the resolution of the Truck and Trailer Routing Problem (TTRP). Urban freight dynamics for loading/unloading bays are represented through Mixed-Integer Linear Programming (MILP) model. The obtained results for instances up to 100 customers shows that the approach presented provides competitive solutions with the best known in the area.

Keywords: Loading bays · Truck and Trailer · Mixed-Integer Linear Programming · Genetic algorithm

1 Introduction

Urban mobility is a determinant factor for economic development and the quality of life of citizens. It is also a link between people and service centers, required for coexistence. Nowadays, decision-makers are looking for initiatives that promote wellness and prosperity in urban areas where freight transport is an intrinsic activity [1], which also contributes to an entity's economic progress [2]. However, transport activities can produce detrimental effects on the environment and the health of citizens [3].

In the last years, a new customer service model has been developing. Companies offer a variety of products and deliveries in less time possible, which present new logistics challenges. One of the first decisions that the companies take to accomplish demand is to increase the vehicle fleet, which promotes more vehicles to be on the streets. To have a large concentration of freight vehicles, all of

© Springer Nature Switzerland AG 2020
L. Martínez-Villaseñor et al. (Eds.): MICAI 2020, LNAI 12468, pp. 296–310, 2020.
https://doi.org/10.1007/978-3-030-60884-2_22

them looking for a space to execute their loading and unloading operations in an urban center is now a challenge. In the case of historical downtown, the streets are very narrow and unable to deal with high vehicle demand, so this is even a more significant problem [5]. The parking problem is one of the reasons why the last-mile is considering the most inefficient part of the supply chain [6]. The last mile is the distance from a central depot or a offloading point to the final delivery destination. Even the last-mile is performing in a short section; this represents 28% of the total transport cost [7] New urban planning strategies are focused on reducing the negative impact of freight transport. Some actions that might help in high vehicle demand areas are: *a)* better use of parking areas, *b)* optimal vehicle utilization, and *c)* optimal distribution routes [8]. However, in order to implement all those actions simultaneously it might be complicated. Therefore, this article focus on those parking areas, denoted as loading/unloading bays. Bays represent a window of opportunity to improve the collection and delivery operations, assuring street access for all vehicles, and reducing traffic congestion [9]. This paper is organized as follows: Sect. 2 of the article describes the main contributions in the loading/unloading bays studies and the in Truck and Trailer models. Section 3 presents the Truck and Trailer Routing Problem extension for the loading/unloading bays application. The genetic algorithm description is presented in Sect. 4. The results for the model application in the benchmark instances are reported in Sect. 5. Finally, conclusions for this investigation are provided in Sect. 6.

2 Literature Review

2.1 The Truck and Trailer Routing Problem

The Truck and Trailer Routing Problem (TTRP), introduced by [11], has been studied since 1993. The TTRP has two sets of customers: *truck-customer* and *trailer-customer*. Both the truck and the trailer have a determined capacity. Trailer-customers can be served by a vehicle with a trailer, but the truck-customer can not [10]. The reason for having two kinds of clients is because some small stores do not have the infrastructure where a large vehicle can park. Some additional concepts for the TTRP are the next: *Road train:* a truck pulling a trailer. *Classical circuit:* a route covered by a truck alone, and *Sub-tour:* a route covered by a truck alone, that starts from a trailer-store and that comes back to the same trailer-store [11]. In [4], restrictions on the TTRP model proposed in [11] are considered. One restriction points that a truck-store can be in a sub-tour or a classical circuit. The author proposed a Tabu Search method to solve the TTRP and performed 21 different experiments in his investigation. Nowadays, the database proposed by [4] has been used by several authors like [12,14–16,34,36,37] in the last few years.

The TTRP has been studied from the ideas presented by different authors with different resolution methods that go from Tabu Search [14], Simulated Annealing [12,13,35], Branch and Price [17], Branch and Cut [34], Local Search

[18], Greedy algorithms [10,15,19], Genetic algorithms [20,21], Swarm Intelligence algorithms [16], Iterative local search (randomized variable neighborhood descent with granular speedup) [37], and Backtracking Search Algorithm [36].

Table 1. A summary of the papers on TTRPs.

	Fleet type	Time Windows	Formulation	Solution method
[11]	Heterogeneous	Yes	–	Heuristic
[4]	Homogeneous	–	–	Heuristic
[14]	Homogeneous	–	–	Heuristic
[12]	Homogeneous	–	–	Heuristic
[13]	Heterogeneous	Yes	–	Heuristic
[15]	Homogeneous	–	ILP	Heuristic
[17]	Heterogeneous	Yes	MILP	Exact/Heuristic
[18]	Homogeneous	Yes	–	Heuristic
[29]	Heterogeneous	Yes	MILP	Optimization Software
[36]	Homogeneous	–	–	Metaheuristic
[37]	Homogeneous	–	–	Hybrid Metaheuristic
Our work	Homogeneous	Yes	MILP	Metaheuristic

Table 1 shows a summary of the mentioned works features and which of these features we incorporate into our problem. Some investigations shared features like heterogeneous fleet and time windows constraints. Restriction capacities differ from author to author. Even though most of them worked with a fleet of trucks and trailers with homogeneous capacity. Some real world TTRP applications include grocery store distribution plan [11], fuel oil delivery [17], container terminals [21], last- mile operations for natural disasters [34], and juice delivery [29].

Even though some researchers have applied a heterogeneous fleet in the TTRP, we select and homogeneous fleet in this first approach to study the performance of a fleet with the same capacity in the urban freight operations; also, a heterogeneous fleet is a complicated element, it shall be deemed for a future investigation.

2.2   Loading and Unloading Bays

The loading and unloading bays are halt areas not suitable for parking. A driver can stop their vehicle in a bay to perform freight loading and unloading operations without disrupting traffic flow to the commercial and industrial activities in a limited radius. As a result, delivery areas have an impact on local traffic and the flow of goods [22]. Currently, loading/unloading bays are some of the most popular tools implemented in cities to improve urban freight operations [23], some characteristics of the bay are that they operate under time restrictions and can be one or more spaces available [24]. There are different perspectives on the loading/unloading bays research in literature. Some objectives consider modifying policies in order to improve the use of bays. Another approach is focused on location improvement or even the search for the optimal vehicle for freight operations. Authors like [25–27], presented a baseline on the loading/unloading bays investigation.

The research topics are summarized as follows: quantification of delivery areas requirements, design proposal, and simulations, bays operation simulation, quantification of demand of loading/unloading bays, public policies recommendations, new location proposals of bays and actual infrastructure modifications, optimization models with cost constraints, and booking systems. According to the research topics mentioned above, we can split the loading/unloading bays investigation in two areas. On one hand, there is the theoretical and empirical work that has proposed methods for the design and operation of delivery areas in several stages. On the other hand, some works have not focused entirely on organizational practices; but rather, on the study of the impact of implementation or change of the configuration of delivery spaces on mobility, congestion, and anarchic parking practices [28].

3   The TTRP for Loading/Unloading Bays

Lopez-Ramos et al. [29] proposes a different approach on the loading/unloading bays research. The authors proposed a Truck and Trailer Routing model extension to assign loading/unloading bays to delivery trucks. The model consists of several depots and time windows in the Historical downtown of the city of Queretaro in Mexico.

The model evaluation was implemented using *"Route Optimizer"*, a PTV Group^{TM} optimization software with real data from food companies.

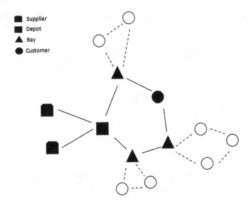

Fig. 1. Example of a TTRP solution

The experiment studied the daily delivery of fruit juice with one vehicle. The data consist of 147 customers demanding 117 boxes of juice. The results showed that the travel distances by trucks reduced from 106.6 km to 46.1 km. The 106.6 km distance was regularly traveled by the juice company.

In contrast with the contributions mentioned above, in this paper, we proposed a TTRP model as a complement of the first approach for the research [29] in Queretaro city, Mexico. We consider a cumulative demand, time window restrictions for bays and clients; as well as a cost function. For a better understanding of a feasible TTRP solution we provide Fig. 1. In the figure, we have two suppliers visiting a depot. The loading/unloading bays are represented by triangles. Each customer attended by a truck is represented as a black circle and the white circle is a customer attended from a bay. In this example, we assume that we have a distribution center. The suppliers leave the product at the depot, then a truck (or multiple trucks) leaves the depot to delivers the products. According to the customer location and demand, the truck can visit a bay or a customer (black circle). In the figure, the truck starts with a bay that supplies two customers (white circles), then visits a customer (black circle) and continues with another two bays.

3.1   Mathematical Model

In this section, we provide the mathematical formulation of the TTRP. Before presenting the mathematical structure, the sets, parameters, and decision variables are listed in Table 2.

The model aims at minimizes the costs of delivering a product to customers in the study area. In (1), the term minimizes the operation cost of the trucks used; the second term reduces the cost of visiting a client, and finally, the cost for using a bay is also lowered.

$$min \sum_{k \in K} \sum_{i,j \in B} X_{ijk} C_{ijk} + \sum_{b \in B} \sum_{i,j \in (S-CL)} V_{ij} C_{jb} + \sum_{k \in K} \sum_{b \in B} Y_{bk} C_{bk} \qquad (1)$$

Constraints (2–3) require that each customer and bay node be visited by a truck or delivery man only once.

$$\sum_{b \in B} \sum_{k \in K} Y_{bk} \leq 1 \qquad (2)$$

$$\sum_{i,j \in (S-CL)} V_{ij} \leq 1 \qquad (3)$$

Constraint (4) require that the sum of the cumulative demand do not exceed the total trucks capacity, i.e., the sum of all the trucks capacity.

$$d_j^+ \leq \sum_{k \in K} \sum_{i,j \in B} X_{ijk} W_k \qquad (4)$$

Time windows constraints are represented in (5)–(7). Constraints (5) are for bays and constraints (6) are for customers. Moreover, we need to ensure that

Table 2. Sets, parameters, and decision variables of the proposed model.

Sets	
A	set of arcs where $(i,j)\|i,j \in K; i,j \in B; i,j \in S - CL; i \neq j$
S	set of nodes where S contain $AL \cup CL$: and $AL =$ warehouse and $CL =$ clients
K	trucks
B	bays

Parameters	
w_k	capacity of truck k
d_j	product demand of client j
e_{bk}	earliest arrival time of truck k to bay b
a_{bk}	latest arrival time of truck k to bay b
e_j	earliest arrival time to client j
a_j	latest arrival time to client j
c_{ijk}	operation cost of truck k for moving from node i to j
c_{jb}	operation cost of bay b for moving from node i to j
c_{bk}	operation cost if bay b is used by truck k
at_j	arrival time to client j
at_b	arrival time to bay b
st_j	service time j

Decision variables	
x_{ijk}	binary variable equal to 1 if truck k visits node j after node i, 0 otherwise
v_{ij}	binary variable equal to 1 if client j is visited after client i to accomplish their demand, 0 otherwise
y_{bk}	binary variable equal to 1 if a truck k visits a bay b, 0 otherwise

the arrival time of vehicles do not exceed the time interval $[e_{bk}, a_{bk}]$ and $[e_j, a_j]$. Constraint (7) defines the arrival time to one node, where M represents a large constant.

$$e_{bk} \leq X_{ijk}at_b \leq a_{bk} \qquad \forall k \in K, j \in B \tag{5}$$

$$e_j \leq Y_{bk}at_j \leq a_j \qquad \forall j \in (S - CL) \tag{6}$$

$$t_{ij} + at_{b_j} + st_i - (1 - x_{ijk})M \leq at_{b_j+1} \tag{7}$$

Constraint (8) ensures that only one vehicle is on the bay. Constraint (9) ensures that the cost of the bays visited in the routes is evaluated.

$$Y_{bk_j} + Y_{bk_{j+1}} = 1 \tag{8}$$

$$X_{ijk} \leq Y_{bk} \tag{9}$$

Finally constraints (10)–(12) impose the integrity of the binary variables.

$$X_{ijk} \in 1, 0 \qquad \forall k \in K, i, j \in B \tag{10}$$

$$V_{jn} \in 1, 0 \qquad \forall i, j \in (S - CL) \tag{11}$$

$$Y_{bk} \in 1, 0 \qquad \forall k \in K, b \in B \tag{12}$$

4 The Genetic Algorithm

In the last five years, different methods have been suggested in order to solve a TTRP problem, Genetic Algorithm (GA) is one of them. In [21], we could see a GA application with a TTRP model in a container terminal. The GA is a flexible tool that supports multi-objective problems like TTRP, returning a suite of potential solutions and provides optimization over a large space state. The adaptability of the GA makes this method relatively easy to implement in complex formulations. However, in the loading/unloading bays problems, we have not seen a GA contribution, so this is an opportunity area to extend the loading/unloading bays approaches. Genetic Algorithms are search mechanisms based on principles of natural selection and genetics [30], they operate under a set code, possibly big but finite. From the set, some samples are taken and evaluated according to what we want to get. Later, the elements *(individuals)* that best accomplish those objectives are selected.

In a GA, the strings which are candidate solutions to the search problem, are referred to as *chromosomes*, the alphabets are referred to as *genes* and the values of genes are called *alleles*.[31]. There are different ways to represent chromosomes; binary, and not binary coding. We applied not binary coding for this problem. In problems like TTRP, the individuals are represented by an integer or a character in the chromosome. Each individual *(customer)* has an identification number, so one allele is one customer [32].

The pseudo-code is shown in Algorithm 1.

The GA works with a Vehicle Routing Problem with Time Window (VRPTW) characteristics. We differentiate the VRPTW coding from the TTRP establishing: several bay nodes, one depot, and several customers. The depot node has different operation times in comparison to bays and customers, so there are multiple time windows. The first and last allele in the chromosome is the depot. The second node in the route can be a customer or a bay. The selection is according to the node coordinates. Finally, the bay node has no demand and can be visited in the route by grouping the closest customer nodes. We accomplish the TTRP characteristics indicating that we have a bay customer and a no-bay customer. A client can be attended directly from a vehicle or a bay.

4.1 Chromosome Encoding

The structure of the chromosome consists of a series of nodes. Natural numbers are used to encode all the nodes in the network. In the example of Fig. 2, we have

---

Algorithm 1. Genetic Algorithm

1: **procedure** MAIN PROCEDURE
2:    Initialize parameters *population, generations*
3:    Generate Population size $P = pop\_size$
4:    Generate distance matrix
5:    *Fitness* = Rate the initial population children
6:    **repeat**
7:        **for** *pop_size* **do**
8:            *ParentSelection* = Select parents (*parent1, parent2*)
9:            *GenerateChildren* = $Crossover(parent1, parent2) = child1, child2$
10:           Mutation(*children*)
11:           Keep the new children generated
12:           Repeat from 7 to 9 to generate the new population
13:       **end for**
14:       Elite population *elitism* = Keep best individuals from children population
15:       *population* = best children
16:   **until** complete all the n generations = $generation_n$
17: **end procedure**

---

three trucks. The first gene is composed of the permutation of natural numbers (0, 1, 8, 6, 9, 13, 0) where 0 is the depot, 1 and 6 are bays and 8, 9, and 13 are customers. Therefore, the route can start with a customer node or with a bay node. In example of Fig. 2, the first vehicle procedure will be as follows: a vehicle leaves the depot, goes to bay 1, and serves customer 8, later visits bay 6, and visits customers 9 and 13 and returns to the depot.

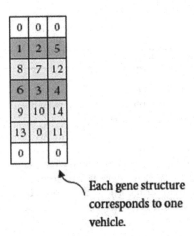

Each gene structure corresponds to one vehicle.

Fig. 2. Chromosome composition.

4.2   Operators Parameter Description

Selection, mutation, and crossover operators are described in this section. The method selected for each operator was chosen according to the algorithm performance.

Selection. The selection operator allows getting the best individuals because we raise our adaption level in the population. The tournament method selects two individuals that compete. This method allows us to get the best of those two. The pseudo-code for the tournament selection is shown in algorithm 2.

Crossover. In GA, reproduction means that given two previously selected individuals according to their fitness score, these individuals will be part of the next generation, or maybe their genetic codes will be exchanged to create a child (hybrid code). With that action, the genetic codes were crossed. In Partially Mapped Crossover (PMX), two parents are randomly selected and two random crossover sites are generated. Alleles within the two crossover sites of a parent are exchanged with the alleles corresponding to those mapped by the other parent. The cycle crossover method was also used, but we do not get good results for this problem.

The pseudo-code for PMX is shown in Algorithm 3.

Mutation. In evolutionary strategies, mutation is the primary variation/search operator [31]. The objective of mutation is to create a new individual who explores regions that have not been visited yet. These individuals will search for new solutions that might be better for the ones already gotten.

For this research, we select an inversion mutation method. In this procedure, a range of genes are selected and the values within that set are inverted. Algorithm 4 explains this procedure.

Algorithm 2. Tournament selection

1: **function** POPULATION
2:     $PopCopy = poblacion$ Create a copy of population
3:     $IndividualsSelected = []$ Create an empty variable
4:     **for** i in range of selection size k **do**
5:         shuffle $PopCopy$
6:         $tournament = PopCopy[: k]$
7:         **if** If a individual has the best score **then**
8:             save as "minimum" $IndividualsSelected$
9:         **else if** If the individual has the worst score **then**
10:             save as "maximum" in $IndividualsSelected$
11:         **end if**
12:     **end for**
13:     **return** $IndividualsSelected$
14: **end function**

Algorithm 3. Partially Mapped Crossover (PMX)

1: **function** PARENT1, PARENT2
2:     Check if both chromosomes have the same lenght
3:     $LenghtCromo = lenght(parent1)$
4:     $child1 = parent1$
5:     $child2 = parent2$
6:     Establish the slice points a and $b = MappZone$ in a chromosome
7:     **for** i into the slice points **do**
8:         swapped the genes between the slice point of $child1$ and $child2$
9:         put the rest genes outside a and b again in the chromosome
10:    **end for**
11:    **return** $child1, child2$
12: **end function**

Algorithm 4. Inversion Mutation

1: **function** SLICE POINT
2:     $SlicePoint1 = suffle(0, LenghtChromo - 3)$
3:     $SlicePoint2 = suffle(SlicePoint1 + 2, LenghtChromo - 1)$
4:     **return** $SlicePoint1, SlicePoint2$
5: **end function**
6: **function** INVERSION
7:     $SlicePoint1, SlicePoint2$ =SLICEPOINTS
8:     Swapped genes between $SlicePoint1, SlicePoint2$
9:     **return** mutated chromosome
10: **end function**

---

5 Experiments and Results

In order to test the efficiency of the proposed algorithm, we designed a series of numerical experiments based on the Solomon Benchmark dataset [33] The GA was coded in Python and the experiments were run on a computer with Intel Core i7 running at 2.21 GHz under Windows 10 (64 bits) with 12 GB of RAM. A design of experiments was made to establish the parameter's value for initial population, mutation, and crossover values. The best parameter combination for this research was: *Mutation rate: 0.1, Crossover rate: 0.9* and, *Initial population: 150*. The "stop" criteria for this GA was according to a maximum number of generations. In this case, there were 1,500 and, the cost used in these experiments was $0.4 pesos. There are six types of data sets in the Solomon Benchmark. In this research, we used four of them. The best results reported in the literature are provided in Table 3.

Solutions obtained with our GA are on table 4. Computational experiments show competitive results in the four selected instances. The genetic algorithm was executed 30 times per database. The graphs presented expressed the *best* result for each database experiment. Figure 3a–7d show the changes in the optimum results with the run of the GA in all the instances analyzed. Offline performance graphs show the best individual in each generation according to their

Table 3. Solomon benchmark instances.

Instance	Distance	Number vehicles	Type
C101	828.94	10	Euclidean distance
C201	591.56	3	Euclidean distance
R101	1650.80	19	Euclidean distance
R201	1252.37	4	Euclidean distance

Table 4. Results for Solomon instances.

Instance	Best reported	Best	Average	Worst
C101	828.94	814.84	922.53	1013.66
C201	591.56	560.39	663.17	860.52
R101	1650.80	1105.10	1116.66	1414.40
R201	1252.37	989.89	1224.75	1428.92

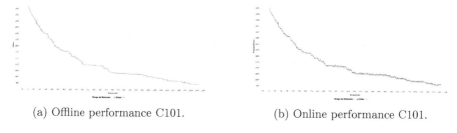

(a) Offline performance C101.　　　　(b) Online performance C101.

Fig. 3. Results of C101.

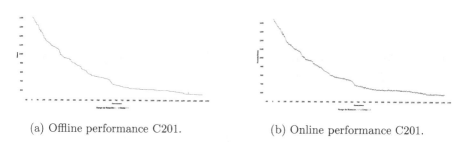

(a) Offline performance C201.　　　　(b) Online performance C201.

Fig. 4. Results of C201.

fitness score. Online performance express the mean fitness value of all the individuals in each generation.

An optimal solution had reached convergence when the generation was up to around 1300 in the case of R101 in Fig. 5a. In the case of C101 (Fig. 3a and 4a) was until generation 1350 just as C201. R201 database reached convergence until generation 1400 (Fig. 6a).

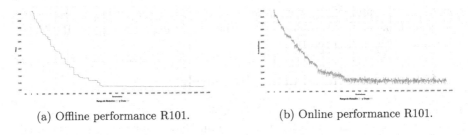

(a) Offline performance R101.

(b) Online performance R101.

Fig. 5. Results of R101.

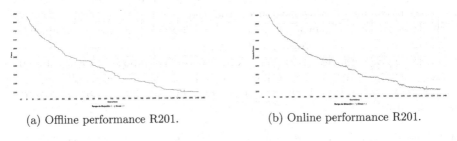

(a) Offline performance R201.

(b) Online performance R201.

Fig. 6. Results of R201.

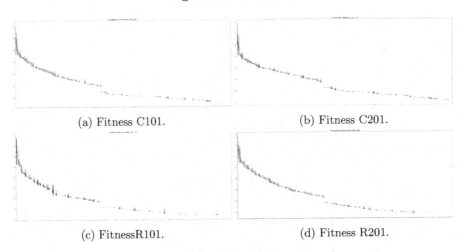

(a) Fitness C101.

(b) Fitness C201.

(c) FitnessR101.

(d) Fitness R201.

Fig. 7. Fitness result per generation.

In the online performance of Fig. 4b and Fig. 6b, it can be concluded that the fitness value in the C201 and R201 databases has less noise. The experiments gave more stable fitness values in their individuals, mean values per generation remain constant. This behavior does not happen in the C101 and R101 results, we could see it more clearly in R101. We expressed the fitness function per individual in each generation from Fig. 7a–7d. With the evolution of the GA, we can see that the interquartile range goes down in the four experiments. In the results of C101 and C201, there is more dispersion in the fitness values in the first generations and, we could see the variation in the fitness value of R101 that has peaks in the last generations.

6   Conclusions and Future Research

In this paper, a Genetic algorithm formulation for the solution of a Truck and Trailer Routing Problem in a loading/unloading bays application was proposed. The GA formulation was coded according to a MILP model presented in Sect. 3 for a future urban freight analysis application. We used Solomon benchmark instances to evaluate GA performance. From the results of the experiments made with the benchmark instances, we can conclude that our GA gave us comparable results against the presented in the literature.

Currently, the application of the GA in real loading/unloading bays problems is analyzed. Data from a Historical downtown in Mexico has been collected and, for further research, we will use the information and present the obtained results with the GA.

Acknowledgment. The first author would like to thank CONACyT (Consejo Nacional de Ciencia y Tecnología) for the financial support of her Master studies under Scholarship 921004.

References

1. Cedillo Campos, G., Fransoo, J.C.: Distribución Urbana Inteligente de Mercancías. In: InterTraffic Conference, Mexico (2019a)
2. Velázquez-Martínez, J.C., Fransoo, J.C., Blanco, E.E., Valenzuela-Ocaña, K.B.: A new statistical method of assigning vehicles to delivery areas for CO2emissions reduction. Transp. Res. Part D: Transp. Environ. **43**, 133–144 (2016). https://doi.org/10.1016/j.trd.2015.12.009
3. Demir, E., Bektaş, T., Laporte, G.: A review of recent research on green road freight transportation. Eur. J. Oper. Res. **273**, 775–793 (2014). https://doi.org/10.1016/j.ejor.2013.12.033
4. Chao, I.M.: A tabu search method for the truck and trailer routing problem. Comput. Oper. Res. **29**(1), 33–51 (2002). https://doi.org/10.1016/S0305-0548(00)00056-3
5. Jaller, M., Holguín-Veras, J., Hodge, S.: Parking in the city. Transp. Res. Rec. **2379**, 46–56 (2013). https://doi.org/10.3141/2379-06
6. Letnik, T., Farina, A., Mencinger, M., Lupi, M., Božičnik, S.: Dynamic management of loading bays for energy efficient urban freight deliveries. Energy **159**, 916–928 (2018). https://doi.org/10.1016/j.energy.2018.06.125
7. Roca-Riu, M., Estrada, M.: An evaluation of urban consolidation centers through logistics systems analysis in circumstances where companies have equal market shares. Procedia Soc. Behav. Sci. **39**, 796–806 (2012). https://doi.org/10.1016/j.sbspro.2012.03.148
8. Dezi, G., Dondi, G., Sangiorgi, C.: Urban freight transport in Bologna: planning commercial vehicle loading/unloading zones. Procedia-Soc. Behav. Sci. **2**, 5990–6001 (2010). https://doi.org/10.1016/j.sbspro.2010.04.013

9. Moufad, I., Jawab, F. (2018). The Determinants of the performance of the Urban Freight Transport-An Empirical Analysis: International Colloquium on Logistics and Supply Chain Management. LOGISTIQUA (2018). https://doi.org/10.1109/LOGISTIQUA.2018.8428296

10. Grechikhin, I.S.: Iterative local search heuristic for truck and trailer routing problem. Springer Proc. Math. Statist. **197**, 67–76 (2017). https://doi.org/10.1007/978-3-319-56829-4-6

11. Semet, F., Taillard, E.: Solving real-life vehicle routing problems efficiently using tabu search. Ann. Oper. Res. **41**(4), 469–488 (1993). https://doi.org/10.1007/BF02023006

12. Lin, S.W., Yu, V.F., Chou, S.Y.: Solving the truck and trailer routing problem based on a simulated annealing heuristic. Comput. Oper. Res. **36**(5), 1683–1692 (2009). https://doi.org/10.1016/j.cor.2008.04.005

13. Lin, S.W., Yu, V.F., Lu, C.C.: A simulated annealing heuristic for the truck and trailer routing problem with time windows. Expert Syst. Appl. **38**(12), 15244–15252 (2011). https://doi.org/10.1016/j.eswa.2011.05.075

14. Scheuerer, S.: A tabu search heuristic for the truck and trailer routing problem. Comput. Oper. Res. **33**, 894–909 (2006). https://doi.org/10.1016/j.cor.2004.08.002

15. Villegas, J.G., Prins, C., Prodhon, C., Medaglia, A.L., Velasco, N.: A GRASP with evolutionary path relinking for the truck and trailer routing problem. Comput. Oper. Res. **38**, 1319–1334 (2011). https://doi.org/10.1016/j.cor.2010.11.011

16. Wang, C., Zhou, S., Gao, Y., Liu, C.: A self-adaptive bat algorithm for the truck and trailer routing problem. Engineering Computations (Swansea, Wales) (2018). https://doi.org/10.1108/EC-11-2016-0408

17. Drexl, M.: Branch-and-price and heuristic column generation for the generalized truck-and-trailer routing problem. Revista de Metodos Cuantitativos Para La Economia y La Empresa **12**(1), 5–38 (2011)

18. Derigs, U., Pullmann, M., Vogel, U.: Truck and trailer routing - Problems, heuristics and computational experience. Comput. Oper. Res. **40**(2), 536–546 (2013). https://doi.org/10.1016/j.cor.2012.08.007

19. Batsyn, M., Ponomarenko, A.: Heuristic for a real-life truck and trailer routing problem. Procedia Comput. Sci. **6**, 778–792 (2014). https://doi.org/10.1016/j.procs.2014.05.328

20. Li, T., Yang, W.-Y., Wang, L., Cai, C., Liang, K.-K.: Research on site selection of logistics nodes in expressway service area considering truck and trailer vehicle routing problem. CICTP **2019**, 4938–4949 (2019). https://doi.org/10.1061/9780784482292.425

21. Ma, H., Tao, L., Hu, X.: Container swap trailer transportation routing problem based on genetic algorithm. Math. Probl. Eng. **2018**, 1–15 (2018). https://doi.org/10.1155/2018/6523764

22. Delaître, L., Routhier, J.L.: Mixing two French tools for delivery areas scheme decision making. Procedia-Soc. Behav. Sci. **2**, 6274–6285 (2010). https://doi.org/10.1016/j.sbspro.2010.04.037

23. Iwan, S., Małecki, K.: Utilization of cellular automata for analysis of the efficiency of urban freight transport measures based on loading/unloading bays example. Transp. Res. Procedia **25**, 1021–1035 (2017). https://doi.org/10.1016/j.trpro.2017.05.476

24. Alho, A.R., de Abreu e Silva, J.: Analyzing the relation between land-use/urban freight operations and the need for dedicated infrastructure/enforcement-Application to the city of Lisbon. Res. Transp. Bus. Manage. **11**, 85–97 (2014). https://doi.org/10.1016/j.rtbm.2014.05.002

25. Dablanc, L.: Freight transport for development toolkit: Urban Freight. In: The International Bank for Reconstruction and Development / The World Bank (2009)

26. Gonzalez-Feliu, J., Muñuzuri, J., Cedillo-Campos, G., Ambrosini, C., Taniguchi, E., Chiabaut, N.: Restrictions d'accès au centre-ville: à la recherche du véhicule optimal urbain. Logistique Manage. **23**(2), 31–44 (2015). https://doi.org/10.1080/12507970.2015.11673822

27. Holguín-Veras, J., Amaya Leal, J., Sánchez-Diaz, I., Browne, M., Wojtowicz, J.: State of the art and practice of urban freight management. Transportation Research Part A: Policy and Practice (2018). https://doi.org/10.1016/j.tra.2018.10.037

28. Imane, M., Fouad, J.: Proposal methodology of planning and location of loading/unloading spaces for urban freight vehicle: a case study. Adv. Sci. Technol. Eng. Syst. J. **4**(5), 273–280 (2019). https://doi.org/10.25046/aj040534

29. López Ramos, F., Cedillo Campos, G., Fransoo, J. C., Santana Reynoso, A.: Multi-depot truck and trailer routing problem with multiple time windows. In: International Congress on Logistics and Supply Chain (CiLOG) (2018)

30. Holland, J.H.: Adaptation in Natural and Artificial Systems. MIT Press/Bradford Books editions, New York (1975)

31. Sastry, K., Goldberg, D., Kendall, G.: Genetic algorithms. In: Burke, E.K., Kendall, G. (eds.) Search Methodologies. Springer, Boston, MA (2005). https://doi.org/10.1007/0-387-28356-0-4

32. Kuri, A., Galaviz, J.: Algorítmos Genéticos. Sociedad Mexicana de Inteligencia Artificial (2007)

33. Solomon, M.M.: Best known solutions identified by heuristics (2005). http://web.cba.neu.edu/msolomon/heuristi.htm

34. Bartolini, E., Schneider, M.: A two-commodity flow formulation for the capacitated truck-and-trailer routing problem. Discrete Appl. Math. **275**, 3–18 (2020). https://doi.org/10.1016/j.dam.2018.07.033

35. Maghfiroh, M.F., Hanaoka, S.: Dynamic truck and trailer routing problem for last mile distribution in disaster response. J. Human. Logist. Supp. Chain Manage. (2018). https://doi.org/10.1108/JHLSCM-10-2017-0050

36. Yuan, S., Fu, J., Cui, F., Zhang, X.: Truck and trailer routing problem solving by a backtracking search algorithm. J. Syst. Sci. Inf. **8**(3), 253–272 (2020). https://doi.org/10.21078/JSSI-2020-253-20

37. Accorsi, L., Vigo, D.: A hybrid metaheuristic for single truck and trailer routing problems. Transportation Science (2020). https://doi.org/10.1287/trsc.2019.0943

Soft Computing

A Tensor-Based Markov Decision Process Representation

Daniela Kuinchtner$^{(\boxtimes)}$ ⓘ, Felipe Meneguzzi$^{(\boxtimes)}$ ⓘ, and Afonso Sales$^{(\boxtimes)}$ ⓘ

Pontifical Catholic University of Rio Grande do Sul (PUCRS),
Porto Alegre, RS 90619-900, Brazil
`daniela.kuinchtner@edu.pucrs.br`,
{`felipe.meneguzzi,afonso.sales`}`@pucrs.br`

Abstract. A Markov Decision Process (MDP) is a sequential decision problem for a fully observable and stochastic environment. MDPs are widely used to model reinforcement learning problems. Researchers developed multiple solvers with increasing efficiency, each of which requiring fewer computational resources to find solutions for large MDPs. However, few of these solvers leverage advances in tensor processing to further increase solver efficiency, such as Google's TPUs (https://cloud. google.com/tpu) and TensorFlow (https://www.tensorflow.org/). In this paper, we formalize an MDP problem in terms of Tensor Algebra, by representing transition models of MDPs compactly using tensors as vectors with fewer elements than its total size. Our method aims to facilitate implementation of various efficient MDP solvers reducing computational cost to generate monolithic MDPs.

Keywords: Artificial intelligence · CANDECOMP/PARAFAC decomposition · Compact transition model · Markov Decision Process · Tensor algebra · Tensor decomposition

1 Introduction

Markov Decision Processes (MDPs) are the underlying model for optimal planning for decision theoretic agents in stochastic environments [11]. Several works proved MDPs are useful in a variety of sequential planning applications where uncertainty is crucial to account in the process [15], such as Autonomous Robots [4,6] and Machine Maintenance [1]. These concepts are essential for theory and algorithms of modern reinforcement learning [17, Ch. 1].

Examples of extensively developed methods for solving MDPs are Linear and Dynamic Programming algorithms [17, Chs 3 and 4]. The main problem with these solvers is in virtually any real-life domain the state space is large enough that solvers cannot compute policies for tabular representations of MDPs in reasonable time. This limitation is often referred to as *the curse of dimensionality*, since the number of states grows exponentially with the number of state variables [3]. By contrast, many large MDPs can be modeled compactly

© Springer Nature Switzerland AG 2020
L. Martínez-Villaseñor et al. (Eds.): MICAI 2020, LNAI 12468, pp. 313–324, 2020.
https://doi.org/10.1007/978-3-030-60884-2_23

if their structure is exploited in the representation [11]. A method to represent large MDPs in a compact representation is called *Factored Markov Decision Process* (Factored MDP). Factored MDPs allow compact representations of complex uncertain dynamic systems [12] and often allow for an exponential reduction in representation complexity.

In this paper we propose a compact representation of the transition model of an MDP using tensor decomposition. Tensor decomposition aims to extract data from arrays, allowing to represent an array with fewer elements than its total size. Tensor decomposition is applied in several applications, such as: signal processing, computer vision, data mining, neuroscience, etc. [13]. In our particular method, we use a tensor decomposition called CANDECOMP/PARAFAC (CP), which decomposes a tensor as sums of rank-one tensors. Our method is to decompose the MDP problem into smaller tensor components, aiming to improve efficiency of MDP solvers.

2 Background

2.1 Markov Decision Process

Richard Bellman introduced Markov Decision Process (MDP) in 1957 [2]. An MDP is a sequential decision problem for a fully observable and stochastic environment. The way an agent transitions through an MDP is by sequential decision making, i.e., choosing actions which lead from one state to another. State transitions and decision making in MDPs are characterized by: i) a stochastic transition system, which determines probabilities to which state the decision making agent reaches after taking an action; and ii) the *Markov property*, which dictates every transition between states depends exclusively on the last visited state, rather than the history of states before that [17, Ch. 3, p. 49].

An MDP is formally defined as a tuple $\mathcal{M} = \langle \mathcal{S}, \mathcal{A}, \mathcal{P}, \mathcal{R}, \gamma \rangle$ [17, Ch. 3, p. 48–49], where i) $\mathcal{S}$ is the state space; ii) $\mathcal{A}$ is the action space; iii) $\mathcal{P}$ is a transition probability function $\mathcal{P}(s' \mid s, a)$; iv) $\mathcal{R}$ is a reward function; and v) $\gamma \in [0..1]$ is a discount factor. More specifically, at each time step t the agent interacts with the environment by taking an action $a_t \in \mathcal{A}$ in state $s_t \in \mathcal{S}$. As a consequence, the agent receives a reward r_{t+1} (also known as r') $\in \mathcal{R}$ and reaches a new state s_{t+1} (also known as s') $\in \mathcal{S}$ with probability $\mathcal{P}(s_{t+1} \mid s_t, a_t)$ given the transition probability function [17, Ch. 3, p. 48]. A transition model describes the stochastic outcome of each action in each state, denoted by $\mathcal{P}(s_{t+1}|s_t, a_t)$, to determine the probability of reaching state s_{t+1} if action a is taken in state s [16, Ch. 17, p. 645-646].

The way an agent behaves in an environment is by following a policy, which maps states to actions. A policy is a solution for the MDP; an *optimal policy* (π^*) maximizes the reward an agent receives over the long run. After taking an action at a state, the environment provides feedback to the agent in terms of an immediate reward [17, Ch. 1, p. 6]. The interaction with the environment terminates when the agent reaches one of the terminal states.

2.2   Tensor Algebra

Leopold Kronecker [14] proposed a tensor-based operation, called *Kronecker product*, represented by $\otimes$. The Kronecker product is used in Tensor Algebra, extension of Linear Algebra, allowing generalization of matrices where more than two dimensions can be represented.

Aiming to improve efficiency of MDP solvers, we propose a representation of transition models using *tensor decomposition*, extension of Tensor Algebra. Our method is to decompose the problem into smaller component elements to improve runtime of the solution.

Tensor Decomposition. The process that factorizes a tensor into sums of individual components is called CANDECOMP (canonical decomposition) and PARAFAC (parallel factors). This method provides a parallel proportional analysis and an idea of multiple axes for analysis [13]. We illustrate in Fig. 1 a CANDECOMP/PARAFAC decomposition of a third-order tensor and define three dimensions (i, j, k) of tensor $\mathcal{X}$ by $x_{ijk} = a_i b_j c_k$. The *order* of a tensor is the number of dimensions.

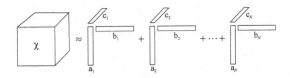

Fig. 1. CANDECOMP/PARAFAC decomposition example.

In the third-order tensor example $\mathcal{X} \in \mathbb{N}^{I*J*K}$, where N is a positive integer and $a_n \in \mathbb{N}^I$, $b_n \in \mathbb{N}^J$, and $c_n \in \mathbb{N}^K$ for n = 1, ..., N; we can express the sum of individual components as

$$\mathcal{X} \approx \sum_{n=1}^{N} (a_n \otimes b_n \otimes c_n). \tag{1}$$

3   Computational Cost of a Regular Method

Markov Decision Process with large state spaces arise frequently when applied to real world problems. Optimal solutions to such problems exist, but may not be computationally tractable, as the required processing scales exponentially with number of states. Related work contemplates comparisons of factored MDPs experimental results with traditional approaches. However, in order to compare a small example with our method, in this section we show the ineffectiveness of a regular method, called *Bellman's Operator Method*, to generate the stochastic outcome of state transition for a 4×3 grid (Fig. 2).

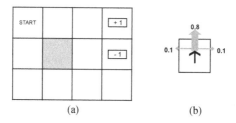

Fig. 2. (a) A simple 4×3 environment grid and (b) an illustration of the transition model of the environment. Adapted from [16, Ch. 17, p. 646].

In Fig. 2 the interaction with the environment terminates when the agent reaches one of the terminal states, marked by +1 or –1 rewards. The agent's actions in a given state, in this example, are *North, East, West* and *South*, where the expected outcome occurs with probability 0.8, but with probability 0.1 the agent moves at right angles to the intended direction and with probability 0.0 the agent moves at opposite direction. A collision with a wall (the shaded square and/or the limits of the environment) results in no movement [16, Ch. 17, p. 645-646].

In order to illustrate the disadvantage of Bellman's operator method, we calculate its computational cost by Eq. 2 based on Fig. 2 example.

$$
\prod_{i=1}^{A} a_i \times \prod_{j=1}^{A} a_j \times \prod_{k=1}^{S} s_k \times \prod_{l=1}^{S} s_l \quad \Longrightarrow \quad O(|A|^2 \times |S|^2) \tag{2}
$$

In the example proposed, $A = 4$ and $S = 12$ resulting in a computational cost of 2,304 multiplications, because all actions multiplied by all states provides the stochastic outcome.

4   Proposed Method Formalization

We now introduce a Markov Decision Process (MDP) compact representation using Tensor Algebra, since none of the related work leverage advances in tensor-based computation to further increase solver efficiency. Our method is to represent an MDP using tensors to decompose the transition probability model into smaller components, with the goal to solve MDPs leveraging advances in Tensor Processing. Our formalization represents an approximate result of Bellman's operator method by sums of tensors component. This proposal allows the implementation to improve runtime of the solution, solving smaller problems faster than the original.

4.1   Definition of MDPs

We propose a Markov Decision Process formalization only for two-dimensional grids using concepts of Tensor Algebra, as follows:

$\mathcal{X}$ set of states x, where $\mathcal{X} = \{x_1, x_2, x_3, ..., x_X\}$ and $X = |\mathcal{X}|$ is the number[1] of rows x;

$\mathcal{Y}$ set of states y, where $\mathcal{Y} = \{y_1, y_2, y_3, ..., y_Y\}$ and $Y = |\mathcal{Y}|$ is the number of columns y;

$\mathcal{S}$ set of all states xy, where $x \in \mathcal{X}$, $y \in \mathcal{Y}$, $\mathcal{S} = \{s_1, s_2, s_3, ..., s_S\}$ and $S = |\mathcal{S}|$ is the number of states xy;

$\mathcal{E}$ environment matrix of order X rows by Y columns.

$\mathcal{M}$ transition model matrix of order X×Y rows by X×Y columns.

Definition 1. Set of states $\mathcal{X}$ and $\mathcal{Y}$ contain $|\mathcal{X}|$ states x and $|\mathcal{Y}|$ states y, respectively, where[2] $x \in [1..X]$ and $y \in [1..Y]$.

Definition 2. The position (xy) is obtained through the function $\mathcal{E}(xy)$, where $x \in \mathcal{X}$ and $y \in \mathcal{Y}$.

Four subsets are also applied to formalize an MDP:

$\mathcal{A}$ set of actions, where $\mathcal{A} = \{a_1, a_2, a_3, ..., a_A\}$ and $A = |\mathcal{A}|$ is the number of actions;

$\mathcal{O}$ set of obstacles, where $\mathcal{O} = \{(o_{xy1}), (o_{xy2}), ..., (o_{xyO})\}$ and $O = |\mathcal{O}|$ is the number of obstacles;

$\mathcal{T}$ set of terminals, where $\mathcal{T} = \{(t_{xy1}), (t_{xy2}), ..., (t_{xyT})\}$ and $T = |\mathcal{T}|$ is the number of terminals;

$\mathcal{R}$ set of rewards, where $\mathcal{R} = \{[(xy_1), r_1], [(xy_2), r_2], ..., [(xy_{XY}), r_R]\}$ and $R = |\mathcal{R}|$ is the number of rewards.

Definition 3. A tuple of rewards $\mathcal{R}$ $[(xy), r]$ is composed by: i) (xy), position xy in the environment where $x \in \mathcal{X}$ and $y \in \mathcal{Y}$; and ii) r, respective reward of the state.

By using a formalization with tensors, we exploit the representation in a way MDP becomes more compact. Therefore, we solve an MDP by creating functions that precompute wherever possible the actions, the obstacles and the terminals of a problem, minimizing computational cost.

4.2   State Transition Probability Matrix

In order to represent the stochastic outcome of actions, we formalize the *state transition probability matrix*, as:

$\mathcal{P}$ set of state transition probabilities, where $\mathcal{P} = \{$ $[p_{11'}(a_1, a_1')]$, $[p_{12'}(a_1, a_2')]$, ..., $[p_{1A'}(a_1, a_A')]$, $[p_{21'}(a_2, a_1')]$, $[p_{22'}(a_2, a_2')]$, ..., $[p_{2A'}(a_2, a_A')]$, ..., $[p_{A1'}(a_A, a_1')]$, $[p_{A2'}(a_A, a_2')]$, ..., $[p_{AA'}(a_A, a_A')]\}$ and $P = |\mathcal{P}|$ is the number of state transition probabilities.

---

[1] The notation adopted is $|\mathcal{X}|$ to define the cardinality of a set $\mathcal{X}$.

[2] The notation adopted is $[i..j]$ referring to a number in range from i to j, inclusive, belonging to set of natural numbers; and notation $[i, j]$ refers to a number within range i to j, including number of real numbers.

Definition 4. Matrix $\mathcal{P}$ is defined by $A \times A$, covering transition probabilities (p) between a current state (xy) and a target state ($x'y'$) of the environment with a desired action (a) and the probability of that action happening (a').

4.3   Limits

In order to define environment limits, we introduce two fundamental sets:

$\mathcal{D}$ set of dimensions of the environment matrix, where $\mathcal{D} = \{d_1, d_2, d_3, ..., d_D\}$ and $D = |\mathcal{D}|$ is the number of dimensions;
$\mathcal{L}$ set of limits of the environment matrix, where $\mathcal{L} = \{[\alpha(d1), \Omega(d1)], [\alpha(d2), \Omega(d2)], ..., [\alpha(d_D), \Omega(d_D)]\}$ and $L = |2 \times \mathcal{D}|$ is the number of limits.

Definition 5. Set of limits $\mathcal{L}$ is defined by the number of dimensions $|\mathcal{D}|$ multiplied by 2. Thus, we consider an initial limit, defined by α, and a final limit, defined by Ω, for each dimension. We define *limit states* as collision with walls, specifically environment's limits.

4.4   Successor States

In order to precompute a new-reachable state ($x'y'$) of a current state (xy), we define a concept of *successor states* by:

$succ_a(xy)$ is a valid-reachable successor state $x'y'$, from xy and an action a.

Definition 6. Successor states for a specific set of actions $\mathcal{A} = \{North, East, West, South\}$ and for a two-dimensional environment matrix $x \in \mathcal{X}$ and $y \in \mathcal{Y}$, are defined by:

7.1. *if $a = North$, then*
   if *$x \neq \alpha(\mathcal{X})$, then $x'=x-1$ and $y'=y$;*
   else *$x = \alpha(\mathcal{X})$, then $x'=x$ and $y'=y$*

7.2. *if $a = East$, then*
   if *$y \neq \Omega(\mathcal{Y})$, then $x'=x$ and $y'=y+1$;*
   else *$y = \Omega(\mathcal{Y})$, then $x'=x$ and $y'=y$*

7.3. *if $a = West$, then*
   if *$y \neq \alpha(\mathcal{Y})$, then $x'=x$ and $y'=y-1$;*
   else *$y = \alpha(\mathcal{Y})$, then $x'=x$ and $y'=y$*

7.4. *if $a = South$, then*
   if *$x \neq \Omega(\mathcal{X})$, then $x'=x+1$ and $y'=y$;*
   else *$x = \Omega(\mathcal{X})$, then $x'=x$ and $y'=y$*

In Definition 6, we only deal with collision with environment's limits, thus a valid successor state can belong to set of obstacles ($\mathcal{O}$).

5   Bellman's Operator Method Optimizations

In this section we propose four optimizations of Bellman's operator method in order to reduce computational cost. The first optimization eliminates zero-probabilities of state transition $\mathcal{P}$:

$\mathcal{Z}^{(a)}$ set of actions with non-zero state transition probabilities of action a, where $\mathcal{Z}^{(a)} = \{[p_{11'}(a_1, a_1')], [p_{12'}(a_1, a_2')], [p_{13'}(a_1, a_3')], ..., [p_{1Z'}(a_1, a_Z')]\}$ and $Z^{(a)} = |\mathcal{Z}^{(a)}|$ is the number of non-zero state transition probabilities of action a. Therefore, $\mathcal{Z}^{(a)} \subset \mathcal{P}$.

The second optimization is focused on eliminating terminal states. The third optimization eliminates obstacle states as we address in set $\mathcal{V}$.

$\mathcal{V}$ set of valid states, where $\mathcal{V} = \{v_1, v_2, v_3, ..., v_V\}$ and $V = |\mathcal{V}|$ is the number valid states. Valid states are determined by excluding obstacles and terminal states of $\mathcal{S}$. Therefore, $\mathcal{V} \subset \mathcal{S}$.

Finally, the fourth optimization is focused on representing transition models of MDPs with tensor decomposition as third-order tensors.

$\mathcal{C}^{(a)}$ set of tensor components of action a. The set $\mathcal{C}^{(a)}$ is a third-order tensor, where $\mathcal{C}^{(a)} = \{[xy_1, x'y_1', \mathcal{P}(a, a')_1], [xy_2, x'y_2', \mathcal{P}(a, a')_2], ..., [xy_C, x'y_C', \mathcal{P}(a, a')_C]\}$ and $C^{(a)} = |\mathcal{V} \times \mathcal{Z}^{(a)}|$ is the number of tensor components of action a.

Definition 7. Each action constitutes a third-order tensor (i.e., $|\mathcal{D}| = 3$). Each tensor component is composed by: i) xy, which is the current state; ii) $x'y'$, is the intended state; and iii) $\mathcal{P}(a, a')$, is the probability of state transition.

In Fig. 3 we illustrate the Definition 7 of tensor components.

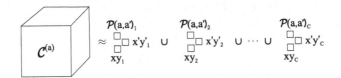

Fig. 3. Definition of a 3th-order tensor of action a.

6   Algorithm

In this section we propose a tensor-based algorithm to generate compact transition models, as we modeled in our formalization. Algorithm 1 consists in composing the set of components $\mathcal{C}^{(a)}$ at each iteration with a set of values $[xy, x'y', \mathcal{P}(a, a')]$, where xy is the current state, $x'y'$ is the target state and $\mathcal{P}(a, a')$ is the probability of state transition.

As previously mentioned, $succ_a(xy)$ can return successor states $(x'y')$ belonging to set of obstacles $(\mathcal{O})$. In order to address this issue, in lines 8–9 we define target states as current ones, i.e., no movement is performed.

Algorithm 1: Tensor-based algorithm to generate transition models of MDPs.

1: **for** $\forall a \in \mathcal{A}$ **do**
2:    **for** $\forall x \in \mathcal{X}$ **do**
3:      **for** $\forall y \in \mathcal{Y}$, where $xy \notin \mathcal{T}$ and $xy \notin \mathcal{O}$ **do**
4:        **for** $\forall a' \in \mathcal{A} \mid \mathcal{P}(a, a') \neq 0$ **do**
5:          $x'y' = \text{succ}_{a'}(xy), \, x' \in \mathcal{X}, \, y' \in \mathcal{Y}$
6:          **if** $x'y' \notin \mathcal{O}$ **then**
7:            $\mathcal{C}^{(a)} \leftarrow \mathcal{C}^{(a)} \cup [xy, x'y', \mathcal{P}(a, a')]$
8:          **else**
9:            $\mathcal{C}^{(a)} \leftarrow \mathcal{C}^{(a)} \cup [xy, xy, \mathcal{P}(a, a')]$
10:          **end if**
11:        **end for**
12:      **end for**
13:    **end for**
14: **end for**

---

7 Proposed Method Computational Cost Analysis

In this section we use Fig. 2 (see Sect. 3) as example to explain the formalization and optimizations of our proposed method. As we defined in Sect. 4.1, the first properties are:

$\mathcal{X} = \{1, 2, 3\}$ and $|\mathcal{X}| = 3$ states x;
$\mathcal{Y} = \{1, 2, 3, 4\}$ and $|\mathcal{Y}| = 4$ states y;
$\mathcal{S} = \{11, 12, 13, 14, 21, 22, 23, 24, 31, 32, 33, 34\}$ and $|\mathcal{S}| = 12$ states xy;
$\mathcal{A} = \{N, E, W, S\}$ and $|\mathcal{A}| = 4$ actions;
$\mathcal{O} = \{(22)\}$ and $|\mathcal{O}| = 1$ obstacle state;
$\mathcal{T} = \{(14), (24)\}$ and $|\mathcal{T}| = 2$ terminal states;
$\mathcal{R} = \{[(11), -3], [(12), -3], [(13), -3], [(14), 100], [(21), -3], [(22), -3], [(23), -3],$
$[(24), -100], [(31), -3], [(32), -3], [(33), -3], [(34), -3]\}$ and $|\mathcal{R}| = 12$ rewards.

In Sect. 4.2 we define the state transition probability matrix, and in Sect. 4.3 we define the dimensions and the limits of an environment. Based on Fig. 2, we formalize these properties as:

$\mathcal{P} = \{[[0.8(N,N')], [0.1(N,E')], [0.1(N,W')], [0.0(N,S')]], [[0.1(E,N')],$
$[0.8(E,E')], [0.0(E,W')], [0.1(E,S')]], [[0.1(W,N')], [0.0(W,E')], [0.8(W,W')],$
$[0.1(W,S')]], [[0.0(S,N')], [0.1(S,E')], [0.1(S,W')], [0.8(S,S')]]\}$ and $|\mathcal{P}| = 4{\times}4 = 16$ state transition probabilities;
$\mathcal{D} = \{\mathcal{X}, \mathcal{Y}\}$ and $|\mathcal{D}| = 2$ dimensions;
$\mathcal{L} = \{[\alpha(\mathcal{X}), \Omega(\mathcal{X})], [\alpha(\mathcal{Y}), \Omega(\mathcal{Y})]\}$, where $\alpha(\mathcal{X}) = 1$, $\Omega(\mathcal{X}) = 3$, $\alpha(\mathcal{Y}) = 1$, $\Omega(\mathcal{Y}) = 4$ and $|\mathcal{L}| = 4$ limits.

Finally, we define the optimizations of Bellman's operator method (see Sect. 5), as follows:

$\mathcal{Z}^{(N)} = \{[0.8(N, N')], [0.1(N, E')], [0.1(N, W')]\}$ and $|\mathcal{Z}^{(N)}| = 3$ non-zero state transition probabilities for action North (N);

$\mathcal{Z}^{(E)} = \{[0.1(E, N')], [0.8(E, E')], [0.1(E, S')]\}$ and $|\mathcal{Z}^{(E)}| = 3$ non-zero state transition probabilities for action East (E);

$\mathcal{Z}^{(W)} = \{[0.1(W, N')], [0.8(W, W')], [0.1(W, S')]\}$ and $|\mathcal{Z}^{(W)}| = 3$ non-zero state transition probabilities for action West (W);

$\mathcal{Z}^{(S)} = \{[0.1(S, E')], [0.1(S, W')], [0.8(S, S')]\}$ and $|\mathcal{Z}^{(S)}| = 3$ non-zero state transition probabilities for action South (S);

$\mathcal{V} = \{11, 12, 13, 21, 23, 31, 32, 33, 34\}$ and $|\mathcal{V}| = 9$ valid states.

$\mathcal{C}^{(N)} = \{[xy_1,\ x'y_1',\ \mathcal{P}(N, N')_1],\ [xy_2,\ x'y_2',\ \mathcal{P}(N, E')_2],\ ...,\ [xy_{27},\ x'y_{27}',\ \mathcal{P}(N, W')_{27}]\}$ and $|\mathcal{V} \times \mathcal{Z}^{(N)}| = 27$ tensor components;

$\mathcal{C}^{(E)} = \{[xy_1,\ x'y_1',\ \mathcal{P}(E, N')_1],\ [xy_2,\ x'y_2',\ \mathcal{P}(E, E')_2],\ ...,\ [xy_{27},\ x'y_{27}',\ \mathcal{P}(E, S')_{27}]\}$ and $|\mathcal{V} \times \mathcal{Z}^{(E)}| = 27$ tensor components;

$\mathcal{C}^{(W)} = \{[xy_1,\ x'y_1',\ \mathcal{P}(W, N')_1],\ [xy_2,\ x'y_2',\ \mathcal{P}(W, W')_2],\ ...,\ [xy_{27},\ x'y_{27}',\ \mathcal{P}(W, S')_{27}]\}$ and $|\mathcal{V} \times \mathcal{Z}^{(W)}| = 27$ tensor components;

$\mathcal{C}^{(S)} = \{[xy_1,\ x'y_1',\ \mathcal{P}(S, E')_1],\ [xy_2,\ x'y_2',\ \mathcal{P}(S, W')_2],\ ...,\ [xy_{27},\ x'y_{27}',\ \mathcal{P}(S, S')_{27}]\}$ and $|\mathcal{V} \times \mathcal{Z}^{(S)}| = 27$ tensor components.

In order to demonstrate the idea of tensor components generated by Algorithm 1, we show the components of tensor $\mathcal{C}^{(N)}$, where we express the dimensions (i, j, k) of $\mathcal{C}^{(N)}$ by $c_{ijk}^N = xy_c, x'y_c', \mathcal{P}(N, a')_c$, as follows:

$[11_1, 1'1_1', \mathcal{P}(N, N')_1]$ $[21_{10}, 1'1_{10}', \mathcal{P}(N, N')_{10}]$ $[32_{19}, 3'2_{19}', \mathcal{P}(N, N')_{19}]$

$[11_2, 1'2_2', \mathcal{P}(N, E')_2]$ $[21_{11}, 2'1_{11}', \mathcal{P}(N, E')_{11}]$ $[32_{20}, 3'3_{20}', \mathcal{P}(N, E')_{20}]$

$[11_3, 1'1_3', \mathcal{P}(N, W')_3]$ $[21_{12}, 2'1_{12}', \mathcal{P}(N, W')_{12}]$ $[32_{21}, 3'1_{21}', \mathcal{P}(N, W')_{21}]$

$[12_4, 1'2_4', \mathcal{P}(N, N')_4]$ $[23_{13}, 1'3_{13}', \mathcal{P}(N, N')_{13}]$ $[33_{22}, 2'3_{22}', \mathcal{P}(N, N')_{22}]$

$[12_5, 1'3_5', \mathcal{P}(N, E')_5]$ $[23_{14}, 2'4_{14}', \mathcal{P}(N, E')_{14}]$ $[33_{23}, 3'4_{23}', \mathcal{P}(N, E')_{23}]$

$[12_6, 1'1_6', \mathcal{P}(N, W')_6]$ $[23_{15}, 2'3_{15}', \mathcal{P}(N, W')_{15}]$ $[33_{24}, 3'2_{24}', \mathcal{P}(N, W')_{24}]$

$[13_7, 1'3_7', \mathcal{P}(N, N')_7]$ $[31_{16}, 2'1_{16}', \mathcal{P}(N, N')_{16}]$ $[34_{25}, 2'4_{25}', \mathcal{P}(N, N')_{25}]$

$[13_8, 1'4_8', \mathcal{P}(N, E')_8]$ $[31_{17}, 3'2_{17}', \mathcal{P}(N, E')_{17}]$ $[34_{26}, 3'4_{26}', \mathcal{P}(N, E')_{26}]$

$[13_9, 1'2_9', \mathcal{P}(N, W')_9]$ $[31_{18}, 3'1_{18}', \mathcal{P}(N, W')_{18}]$ $[34_{27}, 3'3_{27}', \mathcal{P}(N, W')_{27}]$

As the third-order tensor representation $\mathcal{C}^{(a)} \in \mathbb{C}^{I*J*K}$, we express the sum of individual components by Eq. 3.

$$\mathcal{C}^{(a)} \approx \sum_{c=1}^{C} (xy_c \otimes x'y_c' \otimes \mathcal{P}(a, a')_c) \tag{3}$$

Where C is a positive integer and $xy_c \in \mathbb{C}^I$, $x'y_c' \in \mathbb{C}^J$, and $\mathcal{P}(a, a')_c \in \mathbb{C}^K$ for $c = 1, ..., C$. Thus, we write Eq. 3 as

$$C_{ijk} \approx \sum_{c=1}^{C} (xy_{ic}, x'y_{jc}', \mathcal{P}(a, a')_{kc}) \text{ for } i = 1, ..., I; j = 1, ..., J; k = 1, ..., K.$$

Therefore, we define the computational cost of our optimizations previously mentioned by Eq. 4 and its respective complexity (O).

$$\prod_{i=1}^{A} a_i \times \prod_{j=1}^{C^{(a_i)}} c_j \times \prod_{k=1}^{D} d_k \quad \Longrightarrow \quad O(|C^{(a)}| \times |A| \times |D|) \qquad (4)$$

In example proposed, $C^{(a_i)} = 27$, $A = 4$ and $D = 3$, resulting in a computational cost of 324 multiplications.

8 Related Work

A method to represent large MDPs in a compact representation is called factored MDPs. The idea of representing a large MDP using a factored model was first proposed by Boutilier et al. [5]. The benefit of using such a representation is the state transition model can be compactly represented using one of several methods, the most common being a Dynamic Bayesian Network (DBN). This technique allows a compact representation of the transition model, by exploiting the fact the transition of a variable often depends only on a small number of other variables [11].

Guestrin et al. [9–11] developed three approaches to solve factored MDPs using DBNs, respectively. The first approach introduces an efficient planning algorithm for cooperative multiagent dynamic systems. The second approach proposes an approximation scheme to the solution using an approximate value function with a compact representation. The third approach presents two approximate solution algorithms using factored MDPs, where the first algorithm uses approximate linear programming, and the second one uses approximate dynamic programming. All three approaches prove to be able to deal with problem of exponentially large representations of vectors.

Delgado et al. [7] use Markov Decision Process with Imprecise Transition Probabilities (MDP-IP), due to the necessity when transition probabilities are imprecisely specified [8]. Thus, the authors introduce the factored MDP-IP, by proposing to replace the usual Dynamic Bayes Networks (DBNs) used in factored MDPs by Dynamic Credal Networks (DCNs). Results show up to two orders of magnitude speedup in comparison to traditional dynamic programming approaches.

In general, all proposed methods and algorithms in related work prove decomposing the representation into smaller subsets (a factored representation) allows an exponential reduction in representation size of structured MDPs. Moreover, no single method proving superior in all applications is provided, so it still remains an active area of research. In our approach, instead of using DBNs and DCNs to represent transition models of factored MDPs, we provide a representation of MDPs using tensor decomposition, concept of Tensor Algebra, which represents a multidimensional tensor by sums of separable arrays.

9 Conclusion and Future Work

Since investigating methods for efficiently determining optimal or near-optimal policies remains an active area of research, in this paper we formalize an MDP using Tensor Algebra to represent transition models compactly, aiming to allow developers to implement efficient MDPs solvers. In Table 1 we show a comparison of computational cost required to create the transition model of the 4×3 grid example (Fig. 2) of our approach and Bellman's operator method.

Table 1. Computational cost comparison

Method	Number of multiplications
Bellman's operator method	2,304
Proposed method	324
Complexity reduction	85.94 %

We compose out method by sums of tensors components, which represents an approximate result of Bellman's operator method. This optimized proposal enables a complexity reduction of 85.94% compared to the regular method.

Therefore, as future work, we plan to: i) generalize our formalization for N-dimensional environments; ii) compile Relational Dynamic Influence Diagram Language (RDDL)[3] representations into tensor algebra; iii) implement the solution using tensors as we modeled; and iv) solve MDPs leveraging advances in Tensor Processing Frameworks that run on Graphics Processing Units (GPUs) to further increase solver efficiency, by processing each action apart and at the same time.

In closing, we envision this kind of formalization will allow developers to implement efficient MDP solvers. Moreover, in the lack of solvers leveraging advances in tensor processing, the tensor-based representation is a potential stand-in solution, as computational cost calculations show it provides complexity reduction compared to the regular method.

References

1. Amari, S.V., McLaughlin, L., Hoang, P.: Cost-effective condition-based maintenance using markov decision processes. In: RAMS 2006. Annual Reliability and Maintainability Symposium, pp. 464–469 (2006)
2. Bellman, R.: A markovian decision process. J. Math. Mech. **6**(5), 679–684 (1957)
3. Bellman, R.E.: Dynamic Programming. Dover Publications Inc, New York USA (1957)
4. Boger, J., Hoey, J., Poupart, P., Boutilier, C., Fernie, G., Mihailidis, A.: A planning system based on markov decision processes to guide people with dementia through activities of daily living. IEEE Trans. Inf Technol. Biomed. **10**(2), 323–333 (2006)
5. Boutilier, C., Dearden, R., Goldszmidt, M.: Exploiting structure in policy construction. In: Proceedings of the 14th International Joint Conference on Artificial Intelligence - IJCAI 1995, Vol. 2. pp. 1104–1111. Morgan Kaufmann Publishers Inc., San Francisco, California, USA (1995). http://dl.acm.org/citation.cfm?id=1643031.1643043

---

[3] https://github.com/ssanner/rddlsim

6. Cassandra, A.R., Kaelbling, L.P., Kurien, J.A.: Acting under uncertainty: discrete bayesian models for mobile-robot navigation. In: Proceedings of IEEE/RSJ International Conference on Intelligent Robots and Systems. IROS 1996. vol. 2, pp. 963–972 (1996)

7. Delgado, K.V., Sanner, S., de Barros, L.N.: Efficient solutions to factored mdps with imprecise transition probabilities. Artif. Intell. **175**(9), 1498–1527 (2011). https://doi.org/10.1016/j.artint.2011.01.001

8. Delgado, K.V., Sanner, S., de Barros, L.N., Cozman, F.G.: Efficient solutions to factored mdps with imprecise transition probabilities. In: Proceedings of the Nineteenth International Conference on International Conference on Automated Planning and Scheduling. ICAPS 2009, pp. 98–105. AAAI Press (2009). http://dl.acm.org/citation.cfm?id=3037223.3037237

9. Guestrin, C., Koller, D., Parr, R.: Multiagent planning with factored mdps. In: Proceedings of the 14th International Conference on Neural Information Processing Systems: Natural and Synthetic. NIPS 2001, pp. 1523–1530. MIT Press, Cambridge, Massachusetts, USA (2001). http://dl.acm.org/citation.cfm?id=2980539.2980737

10. Guestrin, C., Koller, D., Parr, R.: Solving factored pomdps with linear value functions. In: Planning under Uncertainty and Incomplete Information. IJCAI 2001, pp. 67–75. Seattle, Washington, USA (2001)

11. Guestrin, C., Koller, D., Parr, R., Venkataraman, S.: Efficient solution algorithms for factored mdps. J. Artif. Int. Res. **19**(1), 399–468 (2003)

12. Guestrin, C.E.: Planning Under Uncertainty in Complex Structured Environments. Ph.D. thesis, Stanford University, Stanford, California, USA (2003)

13. Kolda, T.G., Bader, B.W.: Tensor decompositions and applications. SIAM Rev. **51**(3), 455–500 (2009). https://doi.org/10.1137/07070111X

14. Kronecker, L.: Über einige interpolationsformeln für ganze funktionen mehrerer variabeln. Lect. Acad. Sci. **21**(1865), 133–141 (1865)

15. Puterman, M.L.: Markov Decision Processes: Discrete Stochastic Dynamic Programming, 1st edn. John Wiley & Sons Inc, New York, New York, USA (1994)

16. Russell, S., Norvig, P.: Artificial Intelligence: A Modern Approach, 3rd edn. Prentice Hall Press, Upper Saddle River, New Jersey, USA (2009)

17. Sutton, R.S., Barto, A.G.: Reinforcement learning: An introduction. MIT press, Cambridge, Massachusetts, USA (2018)

Object-Based Goal Recognition Using Real-World Data

Roger Granada$^{(\boxtimes)}$, Juarez Monteiro$^{(\boxtimes)}$, Nathan Gavenski$^{(\boxtimes)}$,
and Felipe Meneguzzi$^{(\boxtimes)}$

School of Technology, Pontifícia Universidade Católica do Rio Grande do Sul,
Porto Alegre, RS, Brazil
{roger.granada,juarez.santos}@acad.pucrs.br,
nathan.gavenski@edu.pucrs.br, felipe.meneguzzi@pucrs.br

Abstract. Goal and plan recognition of daily living activities has attracted much interest due to its applicability to ambient assisted living. Such applications require the automatic recognition of high-level activities based on multiple steps performed by human beings in an environment. In this work, we address the problem of plan and goal recognition of human activities in an indoor environment. Unlike existing approaches that use only actions to identify the goal, we use objects and their relations to identify the plan and goal towards which the subject in the video is pursuing. Our approach combines state-of-the-art object and relationship detection to analyze raw video data with a goal recognition algorithm to identify the subject's ultimate goal in the video. Experiments show that our approach identifies cooking activities in a kitchen scenario.

Keywords: Goal recognition · Relationship detection · Object detection

1 Introduction

Goal recognition is the task of recognizing agents' goals, given a model of the environment dynamics in which the agent operates and a sample of observations about its behavior [25]. These observations can be events provided by sensors or actions performed by an agent. Goal recognition has several real-world applications, such as human-robot interaction [28], recognizing navigation goals [14], and recipe identification [10,12]. Most approaches of goal recognition rely on plan libraries [3] to represent the agent behavior. However, recent advances use classical planning instead of plan libraries, showing that automated planning techniques can efficiently recognize goals and plans [18]. Although much effort has been focused on improving the recognition algorithms themselves [18], recent research has focused on the quality of the domain models used to drive such algorithms [1,2,17]. Unlike most approaches that assume that a human domain engineer can provide an accurate and complete domain model for the plan recognition algorithm, recent work on goal recognition use the latent space [1,2] to

© Springer Nature Switzerland AG 2020
L. Martínez-Villaseñor et al. (Eds.): MICAI 2020, LNAI 12468, pp. 325–337, 2020.
https://doi.org/10.1007/978-3-030-60884-2_24

overcome this limitation. These approaches build planning domain knowledge from raw data using a latent representation of the input data. However, building such domain knowledge requires training an autoencoder with states where a transition of two subsequent images can represent the action.

In this paper, we explore the quality of automatically generated domain models that require minimal or no-interference of the human domain engineer. We evaluate our approach empirically using an existing kitchen-centered dataset. Since there is limited data for goal recognition based on videos, we manually annotated the dataset with bounding boxes and relationships between objects. Using this dataset, we perform experiments to compare both domain models, showing that a domain model built with minimal human interference achieves higher accuracy for most of the goals.

2   Background

2.1   Object and Relationship Detection

Object detection aims to determine whether there are any instances of objects from given categories in an image and return their spatial location and extent dimensions [15]. It is widely used in computer vision from simple tasks, such as surface inspection [27], to complex tasks, as autonomous robots operating in unstructured real-world environments [29]. Recently, approaches that learn raw data features, such as the ones based on deep learning [21,32] have advanced state-of-the-art results. Deep learning is present in many architectures developed over the past few years, such as Faster R-CNN [21] and FSAF [32].

Visual relationship detection (VRD) aims to accurately localize a pair of objects and determine the predicate between them [13]. Recently, VRD has attracted more and more research attention in artificial intelligence since it is a step further on the understanding of images [33]. Nevertheless, recognizing individual objects is generally not sufficient to understand the relation of multiple items in a real-world scenario. VRD plays a crucial role in image understanding since it reflects the relationship between two objects, including relative positions (*e.g.*, *on*, *above*, *etc.*), actions (*e.g.*, *holding*, *moving*, *etc.*), as well as the human-object interactions such as *person holding ball*.

The task of recognizing relations between objects is represented by the widely adopted convention [16] that characterizes each relationship as a triplet in the form (s, r, o), where s and o are the subject and object categories of the relationship predicate r, respectively, *e.g.*, (*person, move, pan*), (*bowl, on, table*). Recent methods focus on identifying triplets containing relationships by using deep neural networks [13,33]. Other approaches describe the creation of a scene graph that contains the relationship between pairs of objects [31].

2.2   Goal Recognition

Plan recognition is the task of recognizing how agents achieve their goals based on a set of observed interactions in an environment. Goal recognition is a particular case of plan recognition in which only the goal is recognized [25]. Interactions in goal recognition can be some possible observed events performed by an agent in an environment, as well as actions/activities (*e.g.*, *cook*, *drive*), and changing properties in an environment (*e.g.*, *at home*, *at work*, *resting*). Recognizing agent goals and plans is vital to monitor and anticipate the agent behavior, such as in stories and life understanding [4], and educational environments [26].

Unlike relationship detection that identifies the predicate of a pair of objects to understand the scene better, goal recognition concentrates on identifying high-level, complex goals by exploiting relationships between predicates that are observations of the plan. Relationships between predicates are often encoded as a STRIPS-style [8] domain, which is used for *plan recognition as planning* (PRAP), since PRAP uses planning domains to generate hypotheses of possible plans consistent with observations [19].

Formally, we model planning domains of the agents being observed following a STRIPS [8] domain model $\mathcal{D} = \langle \mathcal{R}, \mathcal{O} \rangle$, where: $\mathcal{R}$ is a set of predicates with typed variables. Such predicates are associated with relations between objects in a grounded problem representing binary facts. Grounded predicates represent logical values according to some interpretation as facts, which are divided into two types: positive and negated facts, as well as constants for truth ($\top$) and falsehood ($\bot$). The set $\mathcal{F}$ of positive facts induces the state-space of a planning problem, which consists of the power set $\mathbb{P}(\mathcal{F})$ of such facts, and the representation of individual states $S \in \mathbb{P}(\mathcal{F})$. $\mathcal{O}$ is a set of operators $op = \langle pre(op), \mathit{eff}(op) \rangle$, where $\mathit{eff}(op)$ can be divided into positive effects $\mathit{eff}^+(op)$ (the add list) and negative effects $\mathit{eff}^-(op)$ (the delete list). An operator op with all variables bound is called action and the collection of all actions instantiated for a specific problem induces a state transition function $\gamma(S, a) \mapsto \mathbb{P}(\mathcal{F})$ that generates a new state from the application of an action to the current state. An action a instantiated from an operator op is applicable to a state S iff $S \models pre(a)$ and results in a new state S' such that $S' \leftarrow (S \cup \mathit{eff}^+(a))/\mathit{eff}^-(a)$.

A planning problem within $\mathcal{D}$ and a set of typed objects Z is defined as $\mathcal{P} = \langle \mathcal{F}, \mathcal{A}, \mathcal{I}, G \rangle$, where: $\mathcal{F}$ is a set of facts (instantiated predicates from $\mathcal{R}$ and Z); $\mathcal{A}$ is a set of instantiated actions from $\mathcal{O}$ and Z; $\mathcal{I}$ is the initial state ($\mathcal{I} \subseteq \mathcal{F}$); and G is a partially specified goal state, which represents a desired state to be achieved. A plan π for a planning problem $\mathcal{P}$ is a sequence of actions $\langle a_1, a_2, ..., a_n \rangle$ that modifies the initial state $\mathcal{I}$ into a state $S \models G$ in which the goal state G holds by the successive execution of actions in a plan π. Modern planners use the *Planning Domain Definition Language* (PDDL) as a standardized domain and problem representation medium [9], which encodes the formalism described here.

Bringing this all together, a goal recognition problem is a tuple $\mathcal{P}_{GR} = \langle \mathcal{D}, \mathcal{F}, \mathcal{I}, \mathcal{G}, O \rangle$, where $\mathcal{D}$ is a planning domain; $\mathcal{F}$ is the set of facts; $\mathcal{I} \subseteq \mathcal{F}$ is an initial state; $\mathcal{G}$ is the set of possible goals, which include a correct hidden goal G^* (*i.e.*, $G^* \in \mathcal{G}$); and $O = \langle o_1, o_2, ..., o_n \rangle$ is an observation sequence of executed actions, with each observation $o_i \in \mathcal{A}$, and the corresponding action being part of a valid plan π that sequentially transforms $\mathcal{I}$ into G^*. The solution for a goal recognition problem is the correct hidden goal $G \in \mathcal{G}$ that the

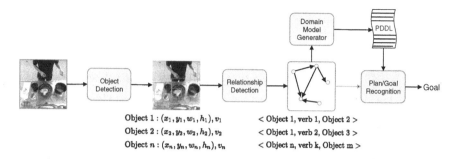

Fig. 1. Pipeline for goal recognition containing object detection, relationship recognition, planning domain generation and goal recognition modules.

observation sequence O of a plan execution achieves. An observation sequence O contains actions representing an optimal or sub-optimal plan that achieves a correct hidden goal, and this observation sequence can be full or partial. A full observation sequence represents the whole plan that achieves the hidden goal, *i.e.*, 100% of the observed actions. A partial observation sequence represents a sub-sequence of the plan for the hidden goal, such that a certain percentage of the actions actually executed to achieve G^* could not be executed.

3   Goal Recognition Using Relationship Information

In order to generate a domain representation of the environment from raw data, we perform the following processes (as illustrated in Fig. 1): (a) Object detection that identifies and extracts a set of bounding boxes from the raw data that contain objects. (b) Relationship detection that extracts important relations between objects. (c) Domain model generation that converts relationships extracted from a module (b) into a STRIPS [8] domain model. Although (a) and (b) processes are nontrivial, there are significant research on both subjects recently [21,31,32]. In this paper, we address these problems by training off-the-shelf architectures with our dataset and consider that the resulting relationships contain a particular noise given each model's accuracy. The output of the relationship recognition module contains triplets with the relationship of the two objects, which can be represented as a scene graph [31].

Our contribution in this paper relies on generating domain models for goal recognition using minimal or no-interference from domain engineers. Upon using minimal interference, the human domain engineer has to define verbs and predicates in the extraction of complex relationships. Considering a no-interference domain generation, the STRIPS domain model is entirely generated from data.

3.1   Planning Domain Generation with Minimal Interference

To generate the planning domain model, we extract all relationships annotated in the ground truth of the training set and build a scene graph [31], as illustrated

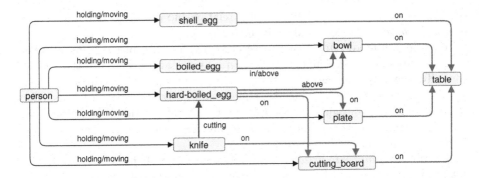

Fig. 2. Direct multigraph generated using an excerpt of the relationships from *boiled-egg* recipe. For simplicity, multiple edges are grouped into a single edge with relationships represented with a dash division. (Color figure online)

in the excerpt in Fig. 2. A scene graph is a directed multigraph $G = (V, E)$ containing relationships between objects, where V is a set of vertices containing the subjects and objects of a list of relationships, and E is a set of directed edges containing the relationship between objects. The direction of the arrow in the graph comes from the relationship of the *subject* to the *object*. For example, the relationship (*knife, cutting, hard-boiled_egg*) generates the red arrow in Fig. 2.

From the scene graph, we can extract complex relationships between vertices. Here, we denominate a complex relationship as a relationship with more than two vertices. For example, from the excerpt scene graph presented in Fig. 2, we can extract the relationship (*person, holding, boiled-egg, above, bowl*). We use the complex relationships to create the domain model.

This process considers a minimal interference of the human domain engineer since he only has to decide what verbs generate complex relationships. In our experiments, we identify four sets of actions. The four types of actions are: *handling actions*, *moving actions*, *cutting actions*, and *metamorphic actions*.

Handling actions are the actions associated with persons manipulating objects. The multigraph denotes this action by vertices connected to the *holding* edge. From these vertices and edge, we generate three actions: *hold, take*, and *put*. The *hold* action considers the vertices connected to the edge *holding*. For example, in Fig. 2, we extract the action (*person, hold, shell_egg*). In order to generate *take* and *put* actions, the *relationship* in the triplet (*subject, relationship, object*) must be *holding* and the *object* must have at least one edge with another vertex in the multigraph where this edge is a preposition. Using the Fig. 2, we extract the complex relationships (*person, take, shell-egg, on table*) and (*person, put, shell-egg, on, table*).

Moving actions occur when objects change their position in the scene. The multigraph denotes this action by vertices connected to the *moving* edge. To generate the action *moving*, the *relationship* in the triplet must be *moving* and the *object* must have at least two edges in the multigraph identified by prepositions. For example, we extract the complex relationship (*person, moving, hard-boiled-*

egg, on, plate) from Fig. 2. This complex relationship describes that the *person* moves the *hard-boiled-egg* to place it *on* the *plate*.

Cutting actions occur when an object is divided into pieces using another object. The multigraph denotes this action by vertices connected to the *cutting* edge. To generate the *cutting* action, the *relationship* in the triplet (*subject, relationship, object*) must be *cutting*, and the *object* must have at least one edge containing a preposition. For example, in Fig. 2, we extract this action from the edges connecting *knife, hard-boiled-egg* and *cutting-board* as (*knife, cutting, hard-boiled-egg, on, cutting-board*).

Finally, *metamorphic actions* occur when an object changes its form. Different forms can be seen in Fig. 2 as the many names to describe an egg (*shell-egg, boiled-egg,* and *hard-boiled-egg*). In order to create this action, we consider as pre-conditions all the relationships that appear in the frame before the first appearance of the new form of the object. For example, in order to generate the *boiled-egg*, the frame before its first appearance contains the relationships where the *shell-egg* must be in the *pan* (*shell-egg, in, pan*), the *person* must be *holding* the *pan* (*person, holding, pan*) and the *pan* must not be *on* the *stove* (*pan, on, stove*).

3.2   Planning Domain Generation with No-Interference

To generate the planning domain model without human interference, we consider all relationships annotated in the ground truth of the training set. Using the annotated relationships, we create a binary vector containing all possible relations of the domain. An action is generated any time a transition occurs, *i.e.*, when some relationship changes between two frames. We encode these transitions in a binary vector containing all the possible relationships that appear in training data. This approach is similar to the one performed by Amado *et al.* [1]. However, instead of deriving binary vectors from an autoencoder, we consider a binary vector composed by all the relationships containing in the training set. Having generated binary vectors considering all transitions between frames, we derive a set of actions by performing a bit-wise comparison using each state before a transition s and the state after a transition s'. This process is summarized in Algorithm 1, where a modified XOR operation (XOR_E) on both states generates the effect of the transition, and a modified version of the XNOR operation ($XNOR_P$) generates the preconditions of candidate actions.

As described by Amado *et al.* [1], the *Effect XOR* (XOR_E) operation (Line 5) computes the *effect* of the action when applying a state s. This operation outputs 1 for *positive effects, i.e.*, when a bit changes from 0 in s to 1 in s', and -1 for *negative effects, i.e.*, when a bit changes from 1 in s to 0 in s'. When multiples transitions result in the same effect, we apply the *Precondition XNOR* ($XNOR_P$) operation (Line 10) to identify which bits do not change in all the set of states s of the transitions. The idea is that a bit that appears in all transitions with the same effect must be a necessary predicate to execute this action. The $XNOR_P$ operation outputs 1 for *positive preconditions, i.e.*, when the bit is 1 in all states that generate the effect, and -1 for *negative preconditions, i.e.*, when

---

Algorithm 1. Learn actions of a planing domain [1]

Require: Set of transitions T
1: **function** ACTION-LEARNER(T)
2:     $E \leftarrow \langle\rangle$ ▷ Map of actions
3:     $A \leftarrow \langle\rangle$ ▷ Set of generated actions
4:     **for all** $(s, s') \in T$ **do**
5:         $\text{eff} \leftarrow XOR_E(s, s')$
6:         $E(\text{eff}) \leftarrow E(\text{eff}) \cup s$
7:     **for all** $\text{eff} \in E$ **do**
8:         $\text{pre} \leftarrow \emptyset$ ▷ Derived pre-condition
9:         **for all** $s \in E(\text{eff})$ **do**
10:             $\text{pre} \leftarrow XNOR_P(\text{pre}, s)$
11:         $A \leftarrow A \cup \langle\text{pre}, \text{eff}\rangle$
12:     **return** A

---

the bit is 0 in all states that generate the effect. Using the Algorithm 1, we can generate the PDDL domain model with a compressed number of actions.

3.3   Goal Recognition Problem

Before setting up the goal recognition problem, we must have a planning problem. We generate the planning problem by extracting the relationships existent in the first frame of the videos and the goal as the relationships existent in the last frame. As described in Sect. 2.2, we represent a goal recognition problem as a tuple $\mathcal{P}_{GR} = \langle \mathcal{D}, \mathcal{F}, \mathcal{I}, \mathcal{G}, O \rangle$, where the domain $\mathcal{D}$ we compute using Algorithm 1, facts $\mathcal{F}$ are represented by a binary vector encoding all possible relationships. We compute the initial state $\mathcal{I}$ as the intersection of the relationships existent in the initial frame of all videos of the training set. This set of relationships are converted to a binary vector representing the initial state. We generate the set of candidate goals $\mathcal{G}$ as the intersection of the relationships presented in the last frame of each recipe, and then encode the resulting relationships into a binary vector. Finally, for each frame of the test set, we derive the observations O by encoding the relationships presented in the frame into a binary vector representing the state.

After building a goal recognition problem, we can apply off-the-shelf goal recognition techniques, such as [18,19]. The output of such techniques is the goal with the highest probability of being the correct one.

4   Experiments

In this section we describe the dataset we use in the experiments, the annotation process, the training of the detectors and the goal recognition execution. In order to evaluate our models, we generated a dataset by altering the level of observability available to the algorithm. We set five different percentages of observability: 100%, 70%, 50%, 30% and 10%. We also compare both approaches using real-world data extracted using a visual relationship detector [13].

4.1   Dataset

Previous work on goal recognition using a kitchen scene dataset [12] has the drawback of using limited dataset. Koller *et al.* [12] affirm that a thorough evaluation was not possible due to the small number of annotated videos. Their work uses a subset of MPII Cooking 2 dataset [22] annotated with objects that contains only two different performed recipes. Since a large number of images with ground truth object bounding boxes are critical for learning object detectors using a neural network, we decide to manually annotate a dataset with objects and relationships between objects.

The Kitchen Scene Context based Gesture Recognition dataset[1] (KSCGR) [23] is a fine-grained kitchen dataset that contains videos of 7 different subjects creating five menus for cooking eggs in Japan: *ham and eggs, omelet, scrambled egg, boiled egg*, and *kinshi-tamago*. The original ground truth annotation of the dataset aims to recognize cooking actions and comprises of 8 cooking gestures performed by the subject. The dataset is divided into *training, validation*, and *test* sets [10], where the *training* set contains 4 subjects, each of them performing 5 recipes, the *validation* set contains 1 subject performing 5 recipes, and the *test* contains 2 subjects, each performing 5 recipes. We select this dataset since it has been used for goal recognition [10].

4.2   Dataset Annotation

The dataset annotation consists of two tasks: the bounding boxes annotation and the relations annotation. For each task, we use two subjects that follow a similar protocol that dictates first to watch the video containing the recipe being performed and then annotate all bounding boxes and relations existent in each video frame. Finally, the subjects must generate a file for each video containing all annotated data. For bounding box annotation, we generate a list containing 30 category labels used at least in one recipe. The category labels contains: *person, baked egg, boiled egg, broken egg, hard-boiled egg, mixed egg, shell egg, ham egg, kinshi egg, scrambled egg, omelette, ham, pan, frying pan, pan handle, pan lid, bowl, chopstick, cutting board, dishcloth, glass, knife, milk carton, oil bottle, plate, saltshaker, spoon, turner, table*, and *stove*. The released dataset annotation[2] contains 2,356,829 instance-level annotations for objects. Both subjects annotate a single video, and we measure the quality of inter-annotator agreement using the Cohen's Kappa [5]. We consider a correct agreement if the bounding boxes have an intersection over union (IoU) greater than 0.7. Using this criteria, we achieve a $\kappa = 0.99$, indicating almost perfect agreement between annotators.

The process of relationship annotation aims to identify relations between objects that are interesting for the performed task. We consider 6 types of relations predicates: 3 spatial relations (*in, on*, and *above*) and 3 action relations (*cutting, holding*, and *moving*). Applying these predicates, we manually created

---

[1] http://www.murase.m.is.nagoya-u.ac.jp/KSCGR/.

[2] https://github.com/rogergranada/kscgr_annotation.

a list containing 164 relations between the 30 category labels that reflects the interesting relations between two objects in the dataset. This list characterizes each relationship as a triplet (s, r, o), where s and o are the subject and object categories respectively, and r is the relationship predicate. For example, a relation for a *ham on* the *cutting board* is identified as $(ham, on, cutting\ board)$. The complete dataset annotation contains 2,269,151 triples for all 35 videos of the dataset. We compute the inter-annotator agreement using a single video annotated by both subjects, resulting in a $\kappa = 0.87$, indicating an almost perfect agreement.

4.3   Object and Relationship Detection

In order to generate triplets for our experiments, we train an off-the-shelf object and relationship detectors. It is important to note that our approach is independent of both detectors, although their accuracy may influence the final results. We use the Faster R-CNN [21] as object detector and VDR-DSR [13] as a relationship detector. We trained the Faster R-CNN using a VGG-16 [24] as the base network. We loaded weights pre-trained in PASCAL VOC 2007 dataset [7] and freeze the first five convolutional layers. In the other layers, we use a learning rate of 1e−3, which decreased by a factor of 10 after every epoch. VRD-DSR [13] uses the RoI features from Faster R-CNN to use as the visual appearance features and spatial location cues. As we previously extracted features from Faster R-CNN, we can perform only predicate detection using VRD-DSR. In such task, VRD-DSR predicts the correlated predicates given a pair of localized objects. We train the VRD-DSR using the VGG-16 as the backbone network for 20 epochs. We use Adam optimizer [11] for all networks and set the learning rate to 1e-5.

4.4   Goal Recognition

To test our approaches' ability to recognize goals using only the relationships between objects, we perform goal recognition using a landmark-based heuristics [18], which is the current state-of-the-art in goal and plan recognition. Following the current goal recognition research, we evaluate our approaches in terms of accuracy and spread using different observability levels. We set five different percentages of observability: 100%, 70%, 50%, 30% and 10%. Finally, we test our approaches using the real-world data from the VRD-DSR relationship detector.

Table 1 summarizes the goal recognition performance using our approaches for all recipes of the test set, where *Obs* is the percentage of the plan that is actually observed; $|O|$ is the average number of observations; *Acc* (Accuracy) represents the average number of problems in which the correct goal was among the recognized goals; $S_{\mathcal{G}}$ (Spread of goal $\mathcal{G}$) is the average number of returned goals when multiple-goal hypotheses were tied in the recognition algorithm.

As we can see, the accuracy for *Boiled egg* was the highest when compared with the other recipes. It justifies since the *Boiled egg* recipe is the most dissimilar recipe. While the other recipes uses the *frying pan* to prepare the egg, the *Boiled egg* uses the *pan*. The egg is also different in this recipe, since it is not broken

Table 1. Experimental results on Goal Recognition problems using domain model with minimal human interference.

Obs	Boiled egg			Ham egg			Kinshi egg			Omelette			Scrambled egg		
	$|O|$	Acc	S_G	$|O|$	Acc	S_G	$|O|$	Acc	S_G	$|O|$	Acc	S_G	$|O|$	Acc	S_G
10	591	1.00	3.36	575	0.76	1.64	513	0.13	2.17	585	0.67	1.74	521	0.58	2.41
30	1774	1.00	3.31	1727	0.77	1.65	1540	0.12	2.10	1758	0.48	2.16	1564	0.60	2.45
50	2957	1.00	3.41	2879	0.76	1.65	2568	0.11	2.15	2931	0.42	1.99	2608	0.58	2.45
70	4139	1.00	3.38	4031	0.77	1.64	3596	0.13	2.14	4103	0.52	1.94	3651	0.60	2.39
100	5914	1.00	3.39	5759	0.76	1.65	5137	0.12	2.15	5863	0.48	2.19	5217	0.59	2.41
VRD	5914	1.00	3.43	5759	0.65	1.54	5137	0.11	2.07	5863	0.56	2.31	5217	0.44	2.50

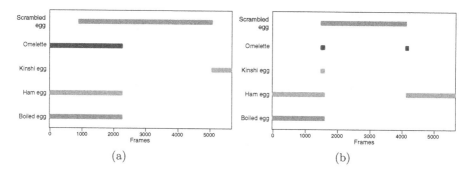

Fig. 3. Examples of possible goals in goal recognition for (a) *Kinshi* and (b) *Ham* eggs.

into the container. A counter point is illustrated by the *Kinshi egg* recipe, that achieved the lowest accuracy of all recipes. Figure 3 (a) illustrates the output of the goal recognizer to the *Kinshi egg* recipe, where we can see that in most frames the recipe *Scrambled egg* is predicted as the correct recipe. In fact, both recipes are very similar, when the *egg* is being cooked in the *frying pan*. However, in *Kinshi egg*, the *person* cuts the *egg* after taking it out of the *frying pan*, which represents the change in the correct goal by the goal recognizer in the last frames. Figure 3 (b) illustrates the candidate goals for *Ham egg*, where *Scrambled egg* is predicted mainly in parts of the video where the *egg* is in *frying pan*.

Table 2 shows the results achieved when using the domain model without human interference. When dealing with our automatically generated domain model, it seems that the plan focus on *Scrambled egg* actions, since in most plans this action is the candidate goal with the highest number of achieved landmarks. The unique case where it does not infer the *Scrambled egg* goal occurs when we feed the observations from *Boiled egg* recipe.

When using real-world data from the visual relationship detector (VRD), there is not a large difference between the scores achieved by using missing observations. As the goal recognizer is based on landmarks, the most of the noisy data do not interfere the goal prediction. When comparing our results with the results achieved by Granada *et al.* [10], our approach using a minimal inference can achieve a highest number of correct goals. In that work, some goals were never achieved since missing information would lead to wrong plans in the plan library. As our work considers more than the sequence of actions to determine the correct goal, we improve the goal recognition process.

Table 2. Experimental results on Goal Recognition problems using domain model with no human interference (data-driven).

	Boiled egg			Ham egg			Kinshi egg			Omelette			Scrambled egg		
Obs	$|O|$	Acc	S_g	$|O|$	Acc	S_g	$|O|$	Acc	S_g	$|O|$	Acc	S_g	$|O|$	Acc	S_g
10	591	1.00	1.97	575	0.12	1.89	513	0.26	2.46	585	0.04	2.47	521	0.97	2.70
30	1774	1.00	1.95	1727	0.22	1.79	1540	0.24	2.42	1758	0.04	2.47	1564	0.98	2.71
50	2957	1.00	1.96	2879	0.23	1.79	2568	0.25	2.43	2931	0.04	2.49	2608	0.98	2.69
70	4139	1.00	1.96	4031	0.21	1.82	3596	0.25	2.42	4103	0.04	2.47	3651	0.97	2.67
100	5914	1.00	1.97	5759	0.25	1.77	5137	0.25	2.43	5863	0.04	2.49	5217	0.97	2.69
VRD	5914	1.00	1.96	5759	0.23	1.68	5137	0.26	2.33	5863	0.04	2.43	5217	0.97	2.73

5 Related Work

Amado *et al.* [1] combines goal recognition techniques with deep autoencoders to generate domain theories from data streams. A pair of images is encoded into an autoencoder generating a 72 bits vector representation of the transition. These pairs of states are fed into an Action Learner to generate the domain model. Their experiments are evaluated in simple problems, such as Hanoi Tower and MNIST 8-Puzzle datasets. Using a kitchen scenario, Koller *et al.* [12] proposes a goal recognition approach that infers goals from video using spatial object annotation traces. In order to find the goal, their technique matches the properties of detected objects to the preconditions of planning operators, using a knowledge base. Unlike our method, they build a domain model using domain engineering.

Granada *et al.* [10] perform goal recognition using the KSCGR [23] dataset. Their approach modifies a symbolic plan recognition approach called Symbolic Behavior Recognition (SBR) to work with a Convolutional Neural Network (CNN). The CNN identifies individual actions from raw images that are then processed by a goal recognition algorithm that uses a plan library describing possible overarching activities to identify the subject's ultimate goal in the video. Although their approach uses the same KSCGR dataset, plan libraries limit the goal recognition process, since some recipes contain actions that appear only in the test set and not in the training set.

6 Conclusion

This paper describes two approaches for goal recognition using the relationship between objects in a kitchen scenario. The first approach uses minimum interference of a human domain engineer, while the second approach is totally data-driven. In order to perform experiments, we annotate a dataset of actions occurring in a kitchen scenario and make it freely available. Experiments using both models shows that the model using a minimal human interference achieves better results when comparing with the automatically generated domain model.

As future work, we plan to test different objects and relationship detectors [6,30] to verify their influence in the outcome results. We intend to test other goal recognizers such as probabilistic plan recognizers [20] and plan recognition algorithms to deal with incomplete domain models to handle inconsistencies and noise generated by the domain model generator.

References

1. Amado, L., Pereira, R., Aires, J.P., Magnaguagno, M., Granada, R., Meneguzzi, F.: Goal recognition in latent space. In: Proceedings of the 2018 International Joint Conference on Neural Networks, pp. 4841–4848 (2018)
2. Asai, M., Fukunaga, A.: Classical planning in deep latent space: bridging the subsymbolic-symbolic boundary. In: Proceedings of the Thirty-Second AAAI Conference on Artificial Intelligence, pp. 6094–6101 (2018)
3. Avrahami-Zilberbrand, D., Kaminka, G.A.: Fast and complete symbolic plan recognition. In: Proceedings of the 19th International Joint Conference on Artificial Intelligence, pp. 653–658 (2005)
4. Charniak, E., Goldman, R.: Plan recognition in stories and in life. Mach. Intell. Pattern Recogn. **10**(1), 343–351 (1990)
5. Cohen, J.: A coefficient of agreement for nominal scales. Educ. Psychol. Measur. **20**(1), 37–46 (1960)
6. Dai, B., Zhang, Y., Lin, D.: Detecting visual relationships with deep relational networks. In: Proceedings of the 2017 IEEE Conference on Computer Vision and Pattern Recognition, pp. 3298–3308 (2017)
7. Everingham, M., Van Gool, L., Williams, C.K., Winn, J., Zisserman, A.: The pascal visual object classes (VOC) challenge. Int. J. Comput. Vis. **88**(2), 303–338 (2010)
8. Fikes, R., Nilsson, N.: Strips: a new approach to the application of theorem proving to problem solving. Artif. Intell. **2**(3–4), 189–208 (1971)
9. Fox, M., Long, D.: Pddl2.1: an extension to pddl for expressing temporal planning domains. J. Artif. Intell. Res. **20**, 61–124 (2003)
10. Granada, R., Pereira, R., Monteiro, J., Barros, R., Ruiz, D., Meneguzzi, F.: Hybrid activity and plan recognition for video streams. In: The AAAI 2017 Workshop on Plan, Activity, and Intent Recognition (2017)
11. Kingma, D.P., Ba, J.: Adam: a method for stochastic optimization. arXiv preprint arXiv:1412.6980 (2014)
12. Koller, M., Patten, T., Vincze, M.: Plan recognition from object detection traces (preliminary report). In: The AAAI 2020 Workshop on Plan, Activity, and Intent Recognition (2020)
13. Liang, K., Guo, Y., Chang, H., Chen, X.: Visual relationship detection with deep structural ranking. In: Proceedings of the Thirty-Second AAAI Conference on Artificial Intelligence, pp. 7098–7105 (2018)
14. Liao, L., Fox, D., Kautz, H.: Hierarchical conditional random fields for GPS-based activity recognition. In: Thrun, S., Brooks, R., Durrant-Whyte, H. (eds.) Robotics Research, vol. 28, pp. 487–506 (2007). https://doi.org/10.1007/978-3-540-48113-3_41

15. Liu, L., et al.: Deep learning for generic object detection: a survey. Int. J. Comput. Vis. **128**, 261–318 (2020)
16. Liu, W., et al.: SSD: single shot multibox detector. In: Leibe, B., Matas, J., Sebe, N., Welling, M. (eds.) ECCV 2016. LNCS, vol. 9905, pp. 21–37. Springer, Cham (2016). https://doi.org/10.1007/978-3-319-46448-0_2
17. Pereira, R.F., Meneguzzi, F.: Landmark-based heuristics for goal recognition. In: Proceedings of the Thirty-Second AAAI Conference on Artificial Intelligence, pp. 8127–8128 (2018)
18. Pereira, R.F., Oren, N., Meneguzzi, F.: Landmark-based heuristics for goal recognition. In: Proceedings of the Thirty-First AAAI Conference on Artificial Intelligence, pp. 3622–3628 (2017)
19. Ramírez, M., Geffner, H.: Plan recognition as planning. In: Proceedings of the 21st International Joint Conference on Artifical Intelligence, pp. 1778–1783 (2009)
20. Ramírez, M., Geffner, H.: Probabilistic plan recognition using off-the-shelf classical planners. In: Proceedings of AAAI-10, pp. 1121–1126 (2010)
21. Ren, S., He, K., Girshick, R., Sun, J.: Faster R-CNN: towards real-time object detection with region proposal networks. In: Proceedings of the 28th International Conference on Neural Information Processing Systems, pp. 91–99 (2015)
22. Rohrbach, M., et al.: Recognizing fine-grained and composite activities using hand-centric features and script data. Int. J. Comput. Vis. **119**(3), 346–373 (2016)
23. Shimada, A., Kondo, K., Deguchi, D., Morin, G., Stern, H.: Kitchen scene context based gesture recognition: a contest in ICPR2012. In: Jiang, X., Bellon, O.R.P., Goldgof, D., Oishi, T. (eds.) WDIA 2012. LNCS, vol. 7854, pp. 168–185. Springer, Heidelberg (2013). https://doi.org/10.1007/978-3-642-40303-3_18
24. Simonyan, K., Zisserman, A.: Very deep convolutional networks for large-scale image recognition. In: arXiv preprint arXiv:1409.1556 (2014)
25. Sukthankar, G., Goldman, R.P., Geib, C., Pynadath, D.V., Bui, H.H.: Plan, Activity, and Intent Recognition: Theory and Practice, 1st edn. MKP Inc. (2014)
26. Uzan, O., Dekel, R., Seri, O., Gal, Y.K.: Plan recognition for exploratory learning environments using interleaved temporal search. AI Mag. **36**(2), 10–21 (2015)
27. Wang, Y., Liu, M., Zheng, P., Yang, H., Zou, J.: A smart surface inspection system using faster R-CNN in cloud-edge computing environment. Adv. Eng. Inf. **43** (2020)
28. Wang, Z., et al.: Probabilistic movement modeling for intention inference in human-robot interaction. Int. J. Robot. Res. **32**(7), 841–858 (2013)
29. Yang, S., Wang, J., Wang, G., Hu, X., Zhou, M., Liao, Q.: Robust RGB-D slam in dynamic environment using faster R-CNN. In: Proceedings of the 3rd IEEE International Conference on Computer and Communications, pp. 2398–2402 (2017)
30. Zellers, R., Yatskar, M., Thomson, S., Choi, Y.: Neural motifs: scene graph parsing with global context. In: Proceedings of the 2018 IEEE Conference on Computer Vision and Pattern Recognition, pp. 5831–5840 (2018)
31. Zhang, J., Shih, K.J., Elgammal, A., Tao, A., Catanzaro, B.: Graphical contrastive losses for scene graph parsing. In: Proceedings of the 2019 IEEE Conference on Computer Vision and Pattern Recognition, pp. 11535–11541 (2019)
32. Zhu, C., He, Y., Savvides, M.: Feature selective anchor-free module for single-shot object detection. In: Proceedings of the 2019 IEEE Conference on Computer Vision and Pattern Recognition, pp. 840–849 (2019)
33. Zhu, Y., Jiang, S.: Deep structured learning for visual relationship detection. In: Proceedings of the Thirty-Second AAAI Conference on Artificial Intelligence, pp. 7623–7630 (2018)

Comparing Multi-issue Multi-lateral Negotiation Approaches for Group Recommendation

Silvia Schiaffino$^{(\boxtimes)}$, Ariel Monteserin, and Emanuel Quintero

ISISTAN (CONICET-UNCPBA), Campus Universitario, Tandil, Argentina
`silvia.schiaffino@isistan.unicen.edu.ar`

Abstract. Recommender systems help users to deal with information overload when trying to find interesting items to consume in a certain domain (e-commerce, education, entertainment, tourism). Recommendations have been traditionally made to individuals, but in the last years recommender systems have been applied to group of users. Several aggregation techniques have been proposed to generate group recommendations, but most of them present some shortcomings when trying to satisfy the whole group evenly. In addition to recommendations to multiple users, it also arises the need of recommending multiple items to each group. In this context, this work proposes a multi-agent approach that uses a multi-agent system to make recommendations to a group of users using negotiation techniques. This approach also considers the recommendation of multiple items. Two alternatives within the approach were evaluated in the movies domain with promising results.

Keywords: Group recommendation · Negotiation · Multi-issue recommendations · Multi-agent systems

1 Introduction

When a user wants to consume a certain item through the Internet, i.e. watch a movie, read a book, buy clothes, he/she has an overwhelming amount of potential interesting items to process. Recommender Systems [15] have emerged as a solution to this information overload problem. Recommender systems allow us to find an item that matches with our preferences in domains in which the number of available items is high (i.e. e-commerce, movies, tourism and music, among others). Over the years, several techniques have been proposed to generate recommendations. Most of these techniques were developed to assist single users instead of group of users. However, many activities are nowadays carried out by group of users such as watching a movie, listening to music, or taking a tour. Several group recommender systems (GRS) have proposed the use of aggregation techniques to generate recommendations to groups: profile aggregation, ranking aggregation, and recommendation aggregation. However, these

© Springer Nature Switzerland AG 2020
L. Martínez-Villaseñor et al. (Eds.): MICAI 2020, LNAI 12468, pp. 338–350, 2020.
https://doi.org/10.1007/978-3-030-60884-2_25

aggregation techniques have some shortcomings: for example, when using average as aggregation technique the recommendation might not satisfy the whole group in an even way [1,3]. Recently, other approaches have been proposed to build group recommender systems, such as multi-agent systems (MAS) [16,19]. MAS are systems composed of multiple intelligent agents that interact among them to achieve a certain goal [20,21]. Particularly, when they have to reach a decision, these agents might participate in a negotiation process that is inspired in the way humans behave to reach a consensus. It is presumed that negotiating a set of items will lead to recommendations that satisfy the parties involved more uniformly, since the decision is agreed by all users. An instance of a MAS-based GRS using negotiation is MAGReS [19], although other implementations are also possible. In MAGReS, this negotiation process is multi-lateral and single-issue, and based on MCP (Monotonic Concession Protocol) [5]. However, when this negotiation takes place in a multidimensional solution space (i.e. considering multiple items or considering multiple issues in an item), it turns into a complex process. In this context, making recommendations to multiple users that are negotiating multiple items has several challenges. The difficulties of negotiating multiple items must be considered: deciding how the items will be negotiated, finding a utility function to evaluate the set of items, and trying to find multidimensional solutions that are Pareto optimal. In this work we extend MAGReS negotiation for enabling multiple issues with these challenges in mind. We compare a multi-lateral multi-issue protocol that enables multiple agents negotiate multiple items at the same time, based on the notion of package deal, against a repetitive single-issue multi-lateral negotiation (sequential approach). We evaluated the two alternatives in the movies domain with promising results.

The rest of the article is organized as follows. In Sect. 2, we describe some related works. In Sect. 3 we present our proposed approach. Then, in Sect. 4 we describe the experiments we carried out to compare the different alternatives for recommending multiple items. Finally, in Sect. 5 we present our conclusions and outline some future works.

2   Related Work

Making recommendations to groups of users began to be investigated in the RS field during the last decade [3]. Traditional GRS can be classified into three main categories according to the way in which they generate the recommendations: (i) recommendation aggregation [1], by producing individual recommendations for every member of the group and then merging those recommendations; (ii) preference aggregation [12], by combining the individuals' preferences/ratings in order to obtain a group evaluation for each candidate item; and (iii) model/profile aggregation [4], by merging individuals' models into a single group model first and then generating suggestions based on that model. Some disadvantages of aggregation approaches have been discussed in [11].

MAS have been applied in several areas and domains [20]. Regarding MAS being applied to GRS, only a few works have been reported, mostly in the tourism domain and using negotiation approaches [2,8,9,16,17]. As far as we know, there are no GRS based on MAS that apply multi-issue negotiation. The multi-issue or multi-dimensional multilateral negotiation has been studied in [14,22]. It is usually characterized by being used where the parties involved in the negotiation recognize that there are differences of interest in the items but there is also the concept of cooperation between them (since if it were not, it would be intractable for simultaneous negotiations), with which they try to seek an agreement that can be beneficial to all parties [7]. There are three ways to negotiate multiple items [10,13]: i) Package deal: items are negotiated as a package; ii) Simultaneous negotiation: items are negotiated simultaneously but independently; iii) Sequential negotiation: items are negotiated sequentially, one after the other. According to the analysis carried out in [6], for each of the configurations presented in the literature, the best way to negotiate multiple items is "Package deal". It was found to be the only option that generates an optimal Pareto solution. However, Package deal is computationally more complex than the other two.

3   Proposed Approach

In this work we propose an approach that allows multiple agents to negotiate multiple items at the same time. This approach is an extension of the MAGReS group recommendation system [19]. MAGReS (Multi Agent Group Recommender System), consists of 2 main modules: negotiation module and group recommendation generation module (see Fig. 1). In MAGReS, this negotiation process is multi-lateral and single-issue. This work focuses on the extension and modification of the negotiation and recommendation generation modules so that the system allows recognizing proposals made up of multiple items, and being able to carry out negotiations on them.

A negotiation in which multiple items are involved varies radically from those where only one item is negotiated for three main reasons: the choice of a utility function for the agents, the space of solutions goes from being one-dimensional to n-dimensional, and trying to achieve an optimal Pareto solution. In addition, as said before, there are different ways of negotiating items [10,13]. In [19], individual items were negotiated between multiple agents, now these agents must agree to negotiate multiple items. In [6] it was found that the optimal way to negotiate multiple items is in the form of "Package Deal", where the individual items are grouped into a "package" allowing them to be negotiated all together as a single entity. We adopted this technique for our approach.

The negotiation module is in charge of selecting the items that are recommended for the group and to do so, it uses a MAS. In this MAS each agent (known as UserAgent) acts as a representative of a group member and participates in a negotiation process in which it is decided which items could be recommended to the group. Each agent knows the preferences of the member of the group it represents and it has a profile of his/her behavior, which determines how it should behave during the negotiation. User preferences are modeled as the ratings assigned to items the user has voted for in the past. The agent's

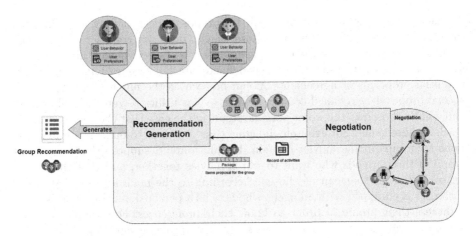

Fig. 1. Proposed approach

behavior profile corresponds to the set of strategies that the agent can use to resolve certain aspects of the negotiation. Additionally, each agent is able to predict the rating that the user would assign to an item that she has not seen yet, and to generate recommendations for its user, that is, lists of items that the agent considers would be pleasant to the user. In the negotiation process, agents interact exchanging proposals according to the guidelines established by a negotiation protocol. The candidate proposals of each agent are built from the recommendations made by a SUR (single user recommender) for the user represented by the agent. Regarding the SUR, it should be noted that MAGReS is not tied to a specific SUR. This means that if it is necessary, the SUR currently used by MAGReS can be changed by another. There are many negotiation protocols, however, only a few of them take into account the properties considered necessary for the protocols to be used in MAGReS: i) it imitates the negotiation process carried out by humans; ii) it has support to carry out multilateral and multi-attribute negotiations. Taking these considerations into account, the MAGReS negotiation module uses MCP, which was proposed in [5].

3.1 Items and Proposals Utility

Let $A = \{ag_1, ag_2, ..., ag_n\}$ be a finite set of N cooperative agents, and let $X = \{x_1, x_2, ..., x_m\}$ be a finite set of potential agreements or proposals, each containing a set of items that can be recommended to one of the agents. Each agent $ag_1 \in A$ has a utility function $U_i : X \rightarrow [0, 1]$ that assigns to each proposal $x_j \in X$ a value that indicates how satisfied the user represented by ag_i will be with the set of items contained in proposal x_j, where 0 means not satisfied and 1 means very satisfied. In MAGReS, each agent ag_i internally has access to a SUR, to which it requests to generate a list of recommended items. These items are part of the set of candidate proposals $X_i \subseteq X$ (the proposals that the agent will use in the negotiation) for the agent.

Each agent orders its list of candidate proposals decreasingly according to their utility value, and it discards those that it does not consider to be good enough to be proposed to the other agents; that is, those whose utility value is less than a certain threshold or, agent-defined threshold value. Thus, the set of potential proposals or agreements X can be seen as the union of all X_i and a special proposal x_{CD} called conflict deal. x_{CD} has utility 0 (zero) for all agents and will be chosen as the worst possible result in the case that the agents cannot reach an agreement. For example, imagine that you want to make recommendations to groups in the movies domain. In this context, suppose that there is a group of three friends who want to watch movies together, and that there is a set of M movies that can be chosen. According to the main idea of MAGReS, each user is equipped with an agent who acts as a personal assistant and is able to access their profile in order to know their preferences. For simplicity, it is assumed that the user profile contains only the ratings given by the user to a subset of the movies available in M. A rating rt_i is the value (in the range $[0, 1]$) assigned by the user u_i to the given item. Additionally, the utility function of each $ag_i \in A$ agent for an item that makes up one of the proposals is defined according to Eq. 1:

$$
U_i(x_j) = \begin{cases} rt_i(x_j) & if\ x_j \in R_i \\ SUR_i(x_j) & if\ x_j \notin R_i \end{cases} \tag{1}
$$

where R_i is the list of items voted by user i and $SUR_i(x_j)$ is the rating predicted by the SUR_i if the item has not been voted. As mentioned above, each proposal that an agent will propose and negotiate with the others is composed of multiple items. Therefore, each of these proposals, called Composite Proposal (CP), must have a function with which its utility can be calculated, taking into account the items it contains. There are different ways to calculate this value, however there are no formalized methods that lead to an optimal function, since it is not a trivial job. In this work we use the average utility of the items in a proposal, where k is the number of items in a proposal CP (Eq. 2).

$$
U_i(CP) = \frac{\sum_{j=0}^{k} U_i(x_j)}{k} \tag{2}
$$

3.2   MCP Negotiation Protocol

MCP is a multilateral negotiation protocol that was proposed in [5] for negotiations in multi-agent systems. It is characterized by imitating, in a simplified way, the negotiation process carried out by human beings when they try to reach a consensus when making a decision on a certain issue. In MCP, agents participate in rounds of negotiation, each agent making proposals that must be evaluated by the other agents, until an agreement is reached or the negotiation ends with a conflict. Notice that in the multi-issue version, each proposal is composed of multiple items.

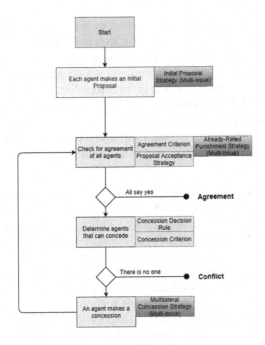

Fig. 2. Multilateral Monotonic Concession protocol.

Figure 2 shows the operation of the MCP protocol. Initially, each agent makes an initial proposal in accordance with its Initial Proposal Strategy; for example, the agent proposes its first N favorite items within the items not voted by his/her user if the strategy that follows is the so-called Egocentric (it always chooses the proposal with the highest utility value for the agent). Then, the initial proposals of all agents are exchanged in order to determine if an agreement could be reached. The notion of agreement is defined in terms of the usefulness of a given proposal for agents, and an agreement regarding a proposal is considered to exist if the proposal meets the requirements established by the Agreement Criterion (AC). For example, an AC might consider that an agreement occurred if and only if there was a proposal that was accepted by all the agents involved in the negotiation. Whether or not an agent accepts a proposal depends on: i) Proposal Acceptance strategy (PrA); and ii) Already-Rated Punishment strategy (ARP) used by the agent. The first one models the different acceptance criteria of a user and the second one helps to model the opinion of users regarding proposals that contain items that they have already consumed/voted on. If during a negotiation round an agreement is reached, the proposal on which the agreement was reached is chosen and the negotiation ends. If more than one proposal meets the criteria, one is chosen randomly from among them. Conversely, if an agreement is not reached, one or more of the agents must concede.

The fact that an agent makes a concession implies that the agent changes its current proposal for an "inferior" one (for example, in terms of utility), in the hope that an agreement will be reached in the next round of negotiations. Before choosing the agent to concede, it is necessary to determine which of the agents have the possibility to do so. For example, there may be agents who have exhausted their candidate proposals and, therefore, have no other alternatives to propose. The Concession Criterion is used to select the agent that must concede. Once the set of agents that can make a concession has been defined, the Concession Decision Rule (CDR) is used to choose the agent that must grant the concession. Finally, those agents that must concede will select their next proposal using the defined Multilateral Multi-issue Concession strategy (MMC).

Initial Proposal Strategy (IPr): An Initial Proposal (IPr) strategy is the strategy that models the way agents select their initial proposal, that is, the one they will make in the first round of negotiation. This strategy was not formalized in the MCP proposed by Endriss, and was formalized in [19]. Although this strategy could have many variants, it was decided that in MAGReS the anonymous variant proposed in [5] should be kept, which was called Egocentric. The Multi-Issue Egocentric strategy is based in the assumption that the agent that uses it only thinks about the best option for itself without caring about the rest of the agents. Thus, according to this variant, the first proposal of an $ag_i \in A$ agent will always consist of a proposal made up of the k items with the greatest utility values for itself, which have not yet been consumed by user u_i.

Agreement Criteria: The Agreement Criterion (AC) models the requirements that must be met in order to consider that an agreement has occurred between the agents that are part of the negotiation. For example: a potential AC might consider that an agreement occurred if the majority or all of the agents have accepted the proposal. MAGReS uses a particular agreement criterion, which was proposed in [5] and was called the Multilateral Agreement Criterion (MAC). This AC determines that an agreement has occurred between the agents if the proposal of any of them was accepted by all the other agents. Formally, there is an agreement if and only if there is an agent $ag_i \in A$ such that its proposal x_i is accepted by all other agents $ag_k \in A$.

Proposal Acceptance Strategy (PrA Relaxed): An agent ag_i accepts a proposal x_k if it is as good as its own proposal x_i or it is at least close to be. Equation 3 formalizes this strategy where $relaxPercentage(rp)$ is a value in the $[0, 0.2]$ range. This parameter might vary from one agent to another depending on the user. The higher the rp value, the more relaxed the user represented by ag_i is to evaluate proposals. Other variants of this strategy are available in MAGReS, but we selected this one because it reported better results than the others.

$$accepts(ag_i, x_k) = TRUE \ if \ U_i(x_i) * (1 - relaxPercentage) \tag{3}$$

Already-Rated Punishment strategy: The Already-Rated Punishment (ARP) strategy, proposed in [19], allows modeling different ways of penalizing the usefulness of proposals that contain items that the user has voted in the past, which can be positive or negative depending on the user. Formally, ARP materializes as an additional factor in the utility function, thereby indirectly affecting agent decision processes. As a result, the agent utility function initially defined in Eq. 1 is redefined as Eq. 4 indicates.

$$U_i(x_j) = \begin{cases} rt_i(x_j) * (1 - penalty_i(x_j)) & x_j \in R_i \\ SUR_i(x_j) & x_j \notin R_i \end{cases} \tag{4}$$

where $penalty_i(x_j)$ is the penalization (a value in the $[0,1]$ range) applied by the ARP that agent ag_i uses when it evaluated proposal x_j, which contains an item that user u_i has already voted ($x_j \in R_i$), R_i is the list of items voted by user u_i and $SUR_i(x_j)$ is the rating predicted by SUR_i (if the item in x_j has not been voted by the user, i.e. $x_j \notin R_i$). There are different strategies to materialize the penalty in the value of the utility, currently at MAGReS there are 5 alternatives namely, Easy Going, Flexible, Minimum Satisfaction, Flexible Plus and Taboo. Considering the results previously obtained in [19], only the one that provided the best results will be used: Taboo. This variant allows modeling those users who under no circumstances would accept to receive a proposal containing an item they have already voted. The penalty applied to proposals with these characteristics causes their utility to become null, that is $penalty_i(x_j) = 1$

Finally, in the multi-issue case, in order to calculate the set penalty, it was decided not to compute one for the group, but to each item in the set. Then the utility function for the group will be calculated in the same way as previously done, where the penalty is $penalty_i(CP) = (\sum_{j=0}^{k} penalty_i(x_j))/k$ where k is the number of item in the composite proposal CP.

Multilateral Multi-issue Concession Strategy: In contrast to the single-issue strategies, multi-issue strategies are divided into two sub-strategies. The first of them is based on choosing which item will be removed from the current proposal of each agent (x_{del}), while the second is the choice of the item that will be added in the new proposal generated (x_{new}). Both strategies can be of two types, reactive (depending on other users) or non-reactive (it does not depend on other users). Notice that both strategies can be reactive, non-reactive, or one of each type. Taking into account this idea, we define thee multi-issue concession strategies:

- Egocentric: the agent acts in a self-centered way without taking other users into account. This strategy replaces the item with less utility in the current proposal with a candidate item with highest utility, where the utility of the new item is not greater than the utility of the removed item. That is $U_i(x_{del}) > U_i(x_{new})$.
- Reactive: this strategy removes an item from the current proposal following the same idea that the egocentric one. However, the choice of the new item

is carried out following a reactive strategy. In this case, when the agent must decide which element will be added, it observes the items of each current proposal with highest utility that the other agents offered. Once each of these items has been obtained, the agent calculates the average utility of that items and searches for a candidate item that has a value similar to that average.

– Double Reactive: This strategy is reactive both to remove an item and to add a new one. That is, each agent, who is not the one that must concede, evaluates which of the items of the current proposal is the least useful to them (i.e. it has less utility), the item that is chosen by the majority of the agents is removed. Finally, x_{new} is selected following the same criterion of Reactive strategy.

4   Experimental Evaluation

In this section we describe, first the goals of the experiments and the experimental settings. Then, we detail the metrics used to compare the approaches. Finally, we describe the results obtained.

4.1   Goals and Experimental Settings

The goal of the experiments was comparing two alternatives for multi-lateral multi-issue recommendation to groups. We compared the approach described in Sect. 3 based on the notion of package deal, named as multi-issue model, against a sequential approach using MAGReS single-issue recommendations. The different approaches were implemented using the Mahout framework[1]. We evaluated three versions of the multi-issue model according to the three multi-issue concession strategies defined above. Regarding to the concession strategy of the single-issue model, we use Desire Distance, which is the strategy that reported the best results in [19].

To evaluate MAGReS in this domain, the MovieLensLatestSmall[2] dataset was used, which is one of the MovieLens datasets provided by GroupLens. This dataset was chosen due to the small size of its rating matrix and because it is one of the most commonly used in the literature. This dataset contains information about 668 users, 10,329 movies and 105,339 ratings.

For the experiments, random groups were generated based on the users present in the dataset. Thus, 45 groups were created: 15 of size 3 (that is, they have 3 members), 15 of size 4 and 15 of size 5. The number of items to be recommended is given by parameter k, which can adopt values 2, 5 and 10. For each group, each approach generated a recommendation taking into account the movies available in the dataset.

---

[1] http://mahout.apache.org/.

[2] https://grouplens.org/datasets/movielens/.

4.2   Metrics

We computed different metrics in order to compare the proposed approaches from two points of view: users satisfaction and information privacy. We evaluated user satisfaction by computing three metrics: Group Satisfaction (GS), Member Satisfaction Dispersion (MSD) and Fairness (F). GS measures the level of satisfaction of a group with respect to an item (or a set of items). The level of satisfaction of a group g with respect to an item x_j is calculated using Eq. 5:

$$GS(Xj) = \frac{\sum_{i=0}^{n} S_i(x_j)}{n} \tag{5}$$

where n is the number of members in g and $S_i(x_j)$ is the level of satisfaction of member i regarding item x_j. Taking into account this formula, GS of a recommendation r (set of items) is computed as the average of the GS metric for each item of r. MSD measures how uniformly group members were satisfied: the lower MSD is, the more uniformly satisfied these members will be. MSD of an item x_j is computed as the standard deviation of the group satisfaction of the group members (with respect to that item). Moreover, MSD of a recommendation r is computed as the average of the MSD metric for each item of r. GS and MSD were proposed in [19]. Fairness was proposed in [18] to evaluate a group recommendation. This metric is defined as the percentage of the group members who were satisfied by the recommendation. To determine which users were satisfied, the authors of [18] define a threshold $th = 3.5$ stars out of 5 stars (the equivalent of 0.7 of 1), and any member whose level of satisfaction is higher than th is considered satisfied. For the experiments, it was decided to keep $th = 0.7$ and this metric was extended to apply it to multi-item recommendations.

Regarding the information privacy metrics, given two approaches to generate recommendations a_1 and a_2, it is considered that a_1 generates better recommendations than a_2, with respect to the amount of "revealed" information, if it reveals less information when it generates the recommendations. For this reason, we defined in [19] the utility function information leak (UFIL) metric. $UFIL(ag_i, x_j)$ measures the amount of information leaked by agent ag_i during the negotiation in which the agents reached an agreement on item x_j. This metric is computed as $itemsWUR(ag_i, x_j)/itemsTotal(ag_i)$, where $itemsWUR(ag_i, x_j)$ is the number of items for which ag_i revealed the utility value during the negotiation and $itemsTotal(ag_i)$ is the number of items on which ag_i can reveal information (that is, all the items that can be recommended to the user u_i).

4.3   Results

Table 1 presents a comparison of the different metrics computed. Notice that the best results for each configuration are in bold, while the best results for each approach are underlined. As we can see, regarding to GS metric, the sequential model performed slightly better than the multi-issue model. Among the multi-issue concession alternatives, the double reactive concession was the best.

Table 1 also compares the Member Satisfaction Dispersion (MSD) obtained by each model. Here, the results are also very similar, but in contrast to GS, some configurations of the multi-issue model outperformed the sequential model. The same occurred with the Fairness. In both MSD and Fairness, the best results within the multi-issue alternatives were obtained by the double reactive concession strategy.

Table 1. Comparison of metrics GS, MSD, Fairness (F) and UFIL.

Model	Multi-issue model												Sequential model			
Concession strategy	Egocentric				Double reactive				Reactive				Desire distance			
k	n	GS	MSD	F	UFIL	GS	MSD	F	UFIL	GS	MSD	F	UFIL	GS	MSD	F	UFIL
2	3	0.876	0.072	0.977	**0.144**	0.881	0.072	0.977	0.145	0.876	0.072	0.98	**0.144**	**0.888**	0.07	1	0.229
2	4	0.839	0.103	0.9	**0.166**	0.851	0.09	0.933	0.199	0.839	0.103	0.93	**0.166**	0.863	0.082	**0.967**	0.3
2	5	0.839	0.089	0.906	**0.202**	0.85	**0.082**	0.932	0.255	0.839	0.088	0.91	**0.202**	**0.855**	0.086	**0.944**	0.422
5	3	0.845	0.084	0.953	**0.148**	0.874	0.062	0.98	0.164	0.841	0.086	0.93	0.153	**0.879**	0.069	0.977	0.338
5	4	0.82	0.105	0.833	**0.174**	0.843	0.081	0.95	0.205	0.823	0.102	0.85	0.176	**0.855**	**0.081**	0.932	0.434
5	5	0.806	0.091	0.882	**0.21**	0.835	0.075	0.92	0.267	0.805	0.092	0.88	0.219	**0.847**	0.076	**0.946**	0.586
10	3	0.83	0.09	0.887	0.199	0.867	**0.057**	0.98	0.165	0.831	0.101	0.93	**0.159**	0.869	0.063	0.977	0.486
10	4	0.813	0.101	0.8825	0.198	0.786	0.071	0.88	0.179	0.817	0.1	0.89	0.176	0.848	0.082	0.932	0.63
10	5	0.804	0.086	0.892	**0.215**	0.834	0.083	0.92	0.268	0.803	0.089	0.86	**0.215**	0.836	0.074	0.932	0.759

Finally, Table 1 shows the comparison of utility function information leak (UFIL). Taking into account this metric, we can observe that all the configurations of the multi-issue model clearly outperformed the sequential model with all the concession alternatives.

In summary, the experimental results showed the advantages of modeling the negotiation by using a multi-issue protocol instead of a sequential one. Although the GS and MSD were really similar, we have checked that more than 50% of the items recommended by multi-issue and sequential models were different. We think that this can be explained due to the fact that the SUR tends to predict high ratings in a high number of movies. Future works will aim to test this hypothesis in other domains. In addition, multi-issue models better kept privacy of user information than the sequential model. It is worth noticing that this fact is key in both recommender systems and negotiation protocols.

5   Conclusions and Future Work

We have presented an extension of MAGReS, a multi-agent based group recommender system. The extension considers multiple issues/items. Two variants of the approach have been developed and compared when recommending multiple items, a repetitive version of a multi-lateral MCP protocol (sequential model) and a multi-issue multi-lateral variant of MCP. The results obtained were very similar for the two variants regarding to group satisfaction, with better results for the multi-issue version regarding to privacy information. As a future work we plan to evaluate the approach in other domains, in which the items are not of the same type, but they form a package recommendation (for example, a package composed of movie, restaurant and pub). Moreover, we will evaluate other multi-issue multi-lateral protocols.

Acknowledgements. This work has been partially supported by CONICET PIP Project 112-201501-00030 and ANPCyT PICT Project 2016-2973.

References

1. Baltrunas, L., Makcinskas, T., Ricci, F.: Group recommendations with rank aggregation and collaborative filtering. In: Proceedings of RecSys 2010, pp. 119–126. ACM (2010)
2. Bekkerman, P., Sarit, K., Ricci, F.: Applying cooperative negotiation methodology to group recommendation problem. In: ECAI Workshop on Recommender Systems (2006)
3. Cantador, I., Castells, P.: Group recommender systems: new perspectives in the social web. Recommender Systems for the Social Web. Intelligent Systems Reference Library, vol. 32, pp. 139–157. Springer, Heidelberg (2012). https://doi.org/10.1007/978-3-642-25694-3_7
4. Christensen, I., Schiaffino, S.: A hybrid approach for group profiling in recommender systems. J. Univ. Comput. Sci. **20**(4), 507–533 (2014)
5. Endriss, U.: Monotonic concession protocols for multilateral negotiation. In: Proceedings of AAMAS 2006, pp. 392–399. ACM, New York (2006)
6. Fatima, S., Wooldridge, M., Jennings, N.: Multi-issue negotiation with deadlines. J. Artif. Intell. Res. **27**, 381–417 (2006)
7. Lai, G., Li, C., Sycara, K., Giampapa, J.: Literature review on multi-attribute negotiations. Technical report, Robotics Institute, Carnegie Mellon University, Pittsburgh (2004)
8. Garcia, I., Sebastia, L.: A negotiation framework for heterogeneous group recommendation. Expert Syst. Appl. **41**(4,1), 1245–1261 (2014)
9. Garcia, I., Sebastia, L., Onaindia, E.: A negotiation approach for group recommendation. In: Proceedings of the 2009 International Conference on Artificial Intelligence, pp. 919–925 (2009)
10. Keeney, R.L., Raiffa, H.: Decisions with Multiple Objectives: Preferences and Value Tradeoffs. Wiley, New York (1976)
11. Masthoff, J.: Group modeling: selecting a sequence of television items to suit a group of viewers. User Model. User-Adapted Interact. **14**(1), 37–85 (2004)
12. O'Connor, M., Cosley, D., Konstan, J.A., Riedl, J.: Polylens: a recommender system for groups of users. In: Proc. of ECSCW 2001, pp. 199–218. Kluwer Academic Publishers (2001)
13. Raiffa, H.: The Art and Science of Negotiation. Harvard University Press, Cambridge (1982)
14. Rausser, G., Simon, L.: A non-cooperative model of collective decision making: a multilateral bargaining approach. Technical report, Department of Agricultural and Resource Economics. University of California, Berkeley (1992)
15. Ricci, F., Rokach, L., Shapira, B.: Recommender Systems Handbook, 2nd edn. Springer, New York (2015). https://doi.org/10.1007/978-0-387-85820-3

16. Rossi, S., Napoli, C.D., Barile, F., Liguori, L.: Conflict Resolution Profiles and Agent Negotiation for Group Recommendations (2016)
17. Sebastiá, L., Giret, A., García, I.: A Multi Agent Architecture for Single User and Group Recommendation in the Tourism Domain (2011)
18. Felfernig, A., Boratto, L., Stettinger, M., Tkalčič, M.: Evaluating group recommender systems. Group Recommender Systems. SECE, pp. 59–71. Springer, Cham (2018). https://doi.org/10.1007/978-3-319-75067-5_3
19. Villavicencio, C., Schiaffino, S., Diaz-Pace, J., Andres, M.A.: Group recommender systems: a multi-agent solution. Knowl. Based Syst. **164**(15), 436–458 (2019)
20. Wooldridge, M.: An Introduction to MultiAgent Systems, 2nd edn. Wiley, New York (2009)
21. Wooldridge, M., Jennings, N.R.: Agent theories, architectures, and languages: a survey. In: Wooldridge, M.J., Jennings, N.R. (eds.) ATAL 1994. LNCS, vol. 890, pp. 1–39. Springer, Heidelberg (1995). https://doi.org/10.1007/3-540-58855-8_1
22. Wu, M., de Weerdt, M., La Poutre, H., Yadati, C., Zhang, Y., Witteveen, C.: Multi-player multi-issue negotiation with complete information. In: Proceedings of 2nd International Workshop on Agent-based Complex Automated Negotiations, vol. 319, pp. 147–159. Springer, Heidelberg (2009). https://doi.org/10.1007/978-3-642-15612-0_8

Guidance in the Visual Analytics of Cartographic Images in the Decision-Making Process

Stanislav Belyakov[1] (ID), Alexander Bozhenyuk[1](✉) (ID), and Igor Rozenberg[2] (ID)

[1] Southern Federal University, Nekrasovskiy Str., 44, 347928 Taganrog, Russia
`beliacov@yandex.ru`, `avb002@yandex.ru`
[2] Public Corporation "Research and Development Institute of Railway Engineers", 27/1, Nizhego-Rodskaya Str., 109029 Moscow, Russia
`i.yarosh@vniias.ru`

Abstract. This paper considers the task of organizing a rational interaction between a geographic information service (GIS) and a user who analyzes spatial data. The purpose of the analysis is to develop a solution to an applied problem in conditions of incompleteness and uncertainty of information about both the final goal and the solution procedure. The work considers an interactive visual analysis of a space region, where the GIS delivers data from cartographic sources and the user compiles and analyzes the cartographic representation of the workspace in real-time. The task of guiding the analysis process to maintain its intelligent orientation is formulated. The meaning of the analysis process is associated with achieving situation awareness of the user, which will ensure the adoption of higher quality decisions. A control method based on the selection of an adequate context from the set of contexts described in the GIS has proposed. A two-component context model has proposed in the form of a kernel and a set of valid kernel transformations preserving the meaning of the context. The intelligent orientation of the analysis has stabilized using the proposed presentation. The problem of determining the optimal number of GIS contexts has considered which minimizes the complexity of the analysis and relation has obtained for its calculation. The problem of maximizing the utility of cartographic images generated by GIS at the user's request has formulated. A representation of the analysis workspace by skeleton and environment has proposed, which has used to ensure maximum utility. The results of an experimental study of the layout of an intelligent system for managing the analysis are presented too.

Keywords: Analytics process guidance · Intelligent interaction · Geoinformation service

1 Introduction

An interactive study of geographic maps, charts and plans is used to make decisions in various areas of business, production and planning. Cartographic images are rich in information and this allows users with their help to find solutions to difficult difficultly

L. Martínez-Villaseñor et al. (Eds.): MICAI 2020, LNAI 12468, pp. 351–369, 2020.
https://doi.org/10.1007/978-3-030-60884-2_26

formalized problems. A large share of these tasks is associated with the space-time situations and processes of the real world. When solving a problem, the analyst first tries to comprehend the spatial-temporal situation, and then develop a strategy for generating, evaluating, and selecting alternative solutions. Experience and knowledge about how to solve applied tasks that are mapped into a specific area of the real world, form in his mind the mental image of the task and stimulate the figurative thinking of the analyst. The more complex the task, the more likely that he will need to formulate several strategies and re-examine alternatives to solutions in a new meaningful context. Perhaps the analyst will decide on a comparison of previously developed decisions and their adaptation to the prevailing conditions. Such a process may continue indefinitely. The threat of unsuccessful completion of the search becomes quite real. Dialogue with the geographic information system (GIS), which provides cartographic visualization, is an important component. It is able to ensure the timely completion of the overall search and decision-making process. The decisive role in this is played by the nature of the sequence of actions that the analyst performs. To achieve the result, a visual study of the sequence of cartographic images should lead to the gradual accumulation of a certain potential of knowledge by the user-analyst, which will allow him to solve this problem more effectively. Although this knowledge arises and is used in the mind of the user, the impact of the sequence of images on this cognitive process is not in doubt. The information flow from GIS forms situation awareness, that is, the analyst's awareness of the final goal and the way to achieve it in these conditions.

However, if you do not apply special methods and technologies, then to achieve the required level of situation awareness is not easy. In the context of interactive cartographic analysis, this is reflected in the use of intelligent support for the search and selection of space-time and semantic data. It is known that the same space-time region can be visualized in a GIS by large number of ways. Methods differ in the number of objects and relationships, the distribution of their types, the way of visualization. Each method has a different effect on the process of analysis, so its choice is important. Manual selection of the necessary information inevitably reduces the concentration on the main goal, dulls attention to detail. The system analyst-GIS can easily lose the desired reasonable direction of research. To avoid this, measures should be taken to control the analysis process.

The goal of visual analysis management is to create a sequence of cartographic images that will be most useful for finding a solution to the problem. Sequence control does not guarantee the selection of the best solutions of the original problem, but greatly increases the probability of this event due to improved situation awareness of the analyst. The flow of useful images provides the necessary condition for the constructive completion of the search process: either the analyst will find the solution to the problem, or justify the reason for its absence. The management goal is considered achieved if the analyst has received from GIS the maximum useful amount of cartographic information.

In this paper, we consider the implementation of control through the impact on the formation of images in the process of dialogue. Each image on the screen is built by analyst commands through the User Interface (UI), which are converted into calls to the Application Program Interface (API) functions. The result of executing a sequence of commands at any time in a session is the workspace of the analysis, which includes the most important cartographic objects and relations. The flow of UI commands is considered as an external influence that changes the state of the working area and its reasonable content. The controlling effect is to add or remove additional objects in the workspace that maximize utility. We assume that in the execution of UI commands we can include calls to the API of intelligent control functions and thereby make the dialogue "transparent", which does not require additional interaction with the analyst.

The use of intellectual management based on knowledge seems to be the most rational, given the information ambiguity, uncertainty, incompleteness and inconsistency of the purpose and subtasks of the analysis. This paper examines the key problems of implementing the intellectual GIS subsystem for managing the dialogue, namely: a conceptual model of knowledge about the analysis procedure, a knowledge-based management model, a mechanism for automatically extracting this knowledge.

2 Review of Publications on the Topic

Traditional cartographic visualization [1, 2] is the basis of the cartographic analysis of situations for which decisions need to be made. It is based on the creation and reuse of specialized thematic maps. Each thematic map corresponds to a certain class of tasks and is stored in a GIS as an information object consisting of cartographic objects, layers, communication templates and references to external data sources, types and presentation formats [3, 4]. Workspace is a thematic map explicitly chosen by the analyst. The user performs any modifications to the workspace manually. Visualization methods focus on the workspace inspection methods (build angles, views, flying around), which do not take into account its reasonable content.

Image perception control is entirely up to the user. Cartographic images with a high density of objects on the screen are perceived with difficulty. Users scale such images. GIS program tools for visualization allows combining scaling with turning layers on and off [3, 4]. Due to this, the complexity of image manipulation is reduced. However, GIS do not control the content and number of objects and relationships in the image, which significantly affects the perception. Thus, the existing methods of cartographic visualization do not solve the problem of optimizing the dialogue. The analysis process is viewed as following to the analysis pattern, which is implicitly embedded in the thematic map. The control of the user-analyst's reaction to the generated images by the geographic information system is not provided, both parties work independently.

It should be borne in mind that the analysis process in the analyst - GIS system must conform to certain psychological laws, since the result of the joint work is essentially determined by the mental cognitive process in the analyst's mind. Hick's law [5] indicates an increase in decision time as the number and complexity of options increase. The reason is the growth of cognitive load on the user. In the analysis of cartographic images it is reflected in reduced dynamic viewing maps or schemes situation. It is known [6] that changing the scale, panning a cartographic fragment is a fundamental mental process necessary for the analyst to understand the meaning of what he saw. The notion that perception plays a crucial role in the process of interactive visual analysis agrees with modern ideas about the impact of visualization on creative behavior [7]. The results of these works indicate the need to minimize cognitive overload, but do not provide a real solution to the problem.

Important general patterns were revealed in the study of perception and memorization of information. Known is the study of G. Miller of "fragmentation" that affects the perception and memorization of information [8]. Fragmentation means structured presentation for visual analysis of maps, charts and plans. Space-time objects and relations should become elements of such a structure, and relationships should reflect the significance of elements for the analysis task. It is clear that the implementation of "fragmentation" requires additional research.

Note also the works in the field of user experience design (UX, UXD, UED), which are aimed at studying the behavior of the user. In particular, Jacob's law of Internet UX [9] says that professionally oriented user groups have some kind of common intuitive idea of interfaces. Since cartographic images are essentially an interface for obtaining spatial information, this pattern confirms the assumption that there is a general knowledge of the usefulness of images in professionally oriented user groups. The question of the form of their presentation and method of obtaining remains open.

Interactive visual analysis is the subject of intense research at the border of psychology and UX. An example is the work [10], which analyzes the role of visual analysis in the modern sense of "digital creativity" in relation to big data analysis. The authors explore the process of forming the mental image of the problem as a cycle of viewing the image and rethinking the formulation of an applied problem. The search for the technical implementation of the process of targeted formation of a mental image is a continuation of this study.

The main tool for building effective solutions to an applied problem in the analyst-GIS system is situation awareness of the user-analyst [11]. Awareness of the goal, generation of relevant subtasks, finding their solutions through the perception of information about the real world situation, forecasting the development of the situation are components of situation awareness [12]. Achieving maximum situation awareness is a scientific and practical problem that has been solved for many years in engineering, psychology, engineering, and design [13]. Studies of the means of dialogue with technical systems focus on analyzing cognitive processes in resolving difficult situations in which the operator are involved. The purpose of the analysis is the finding the best distribution of cognitive load in human-machine systems with artificial intelligence and cognitive systems [14]. According to this distribution, developers can design an interface. These results should be adapted to the task of guiding the analysis process in the analyst-GIS system.

A special approach to visualization is proposed in neocartography [15]. Neocartography has emerged as a special way of presenting spatial data to geographic information services, which is aimed at increasing the situation awareness of the user. The rejection of cartographic projections and the use of three-dimensional objects on a raster substrate instead of a geographical map can be viewed as a solution to the problem of the complexity of managing dialogue with a GIS. The complexity of the layout of the working area of analysis, the need to make a decision in a tight timeframe has led to the transition to continuous (raster) models of the earth's surface. Analyzing this principle of dialogue interaction, we can conclude that the photorealistic display of the earth's surface really gives the user vivid images of the real world, which are useful in solving many problems. However, the external attractiveness of the interface does not compensate for the lack of numerical and symbolic attributes of objects. The level of abstraction of the visual representation of complex objects remains low, which actually worsens situation awareness. Studies of visualization in neocartography should be viewed as a particular solution to the general problem of the complexity of interactive analysis of geodata.

The possibility of a holistic presentation of cartographic information through the impact on all human senses is investigated by cybercartography [16]. Authors' research focuses mainly on the integration of geospatial data and models for representing heterogeneous knowledge in a cartographic form. The methods of managing the dialogue in the process of using maps for solving complex informal problems remain little studied.

Visualization problems are considered by the research of analytical systems for big data. In particular, the subject of research is the behavior of the user-analyst in the process of image manipulation. So, in work [17], the influence of the method of implementing the image manipulation functions ZOOM IN, ZOOM OUT, PANNED on the efficiency of user-generated content analysis was experimentally investigated. In these studies, user behavior is described in a deterministic way that is, using simplifications that degrade the quality of the results. A separate area of research for interactive analysis of big data is the search for knowledge. In [18], the task of real-time intelligent classification was investigated, and a data-driven and theory-informed approach was proposed for interactive analysis of the state of a modern city. This research direction does not affect the management of the dialogue, focusing on the subjective interpretation of cartographic data in the face of uncertainty.

Recent research in the field of visual analytics has led to a concept of guidance in the human – machine analytics process. An analysis of scientific papers related to decision-making based on visual analytics was carried out in [19]. It emphasizes the idea that visual analysis of difficult situations is no longer an auxiliary decision-making tool. Visual analysis becomes the main component that takes the lead in the process of solving an applied problem [19, 20]. It is especially attractive to realize intelligent guidance, which is focused on achieving a globally set goal of analysis. The generalized guidance systems components are described in [19]. The generalization of the considered approaches does not allow directly implementing the guidance mechanism in the GIS.

So, we can conclude that the well-known approaches to managing the process of interactive analysis of cartographic data for decision-making do not consider the GIS - analyst pair as a system in which the GIS should behave rationally. The intellectual nature of interactive interaction significantly improves the quality of information support for decision-making. This approach has an undoubted advantage, but remains little studied.

3   The Task of Managing the Analysis Process

The analyst-GIS system arises to find a solution to a complex difficult to formalize problem by generating and comparing alternatives [21]. Both processes (generation of alternatives and their comparison) are based on a sequence of useful map data for analysis. The way the analysis of the situation and the assessment of the quality of the decisions made depends on how GIS builds useful images. In order to formulate the task of managing the analysis that the GIS should solve, consider the features of the interactive interaction between the analyst and GIS.

As the practice of solving difficultly formalized problems using GIS has shown, the main user requirement is to obtain the most useful data in terms of intellect. The term "intelligent usefulness" is not unequivocally, so we highlight the following features that determine the usefulness of meaning:

- Amount of visualized data. This indicator depends on the characteristics of the psychophysical perception of images by the user-analyst. It is known that there is a natural limitation of perception, the excess of which makes images useless.
- Correspondence between the content of cartographic images and the goal of the analysis. The degree of correspondence is measured by the proportion of objects and relationships necessary for the analyst to have a holistic mental image of the situation.
- Description of the space-time semantic area within which the analysis retains the chosen sense directionality. Border derangement is seen as a loss of meaning in the imaged images.

Consider an example illustrating the concept of intelligent content. Suppose that a tourist solves the problem of finding accommodation for a stay in a city so that it is located in an ecologically clean and picturesque area, which is located within walking distance from the city's historical and architectural monuments. The complexity of solving this problem lies in the ambiguity and fuzziness of the user's assessment of the place of residence. Assessment depends on location, urban infrastructure and natural landscape in the surrounding area. Suppose that the user solves the problem by visual analysis of the map of the area. In Fig. 1 shows the image of the first possible variant of the analysis area. The image can be estimated as quite acceptable, but a little useful for the analysis. Here there are no important decision-making data on transport infrastructure, mobility on foot or by bicycle, landscape features, etc. In Fig. 2 shows another version of the image of the analysis area, which includes almost all layers of the map used in the GIS.

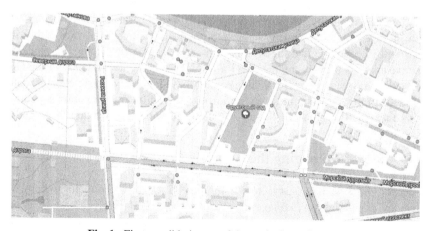

Fig. 1. First possible image of the analysis workspace.

At first glance, it may seem that the second option is rated, higher due to the larger amount of data displayed. However, it is much more difficult to understand. To obtain

Fig. 2. Second possible image of the analysis workspace.

the necessary information, it is necessary to select and scale fragments, combine layers, build special spatial queries. Obviously, visual analysis is complicated. If the previous version was not very useful due to the lack of necessary information, then the one in question is of little use already because of the laboriousness of extracting the necessary information. The map contains a lot of redundant information.

Attempting to obtain information of interest requires the analyst to spend time studying the composition and designation of map layers, turning off insignificant layers, choosing an acceptable level of view scaling, display format. The course of analysis will thus be dictated by the laboriousness of extracting useful data from the map, but not the main purpose of the analysis.

A more appropriate approach to solving this problem is the use of a map on which the most important for the analysis of the entity would be shown. In Fig. 3 depicts the working area after the "intellectual" processing, based on knowledge of the usefulness of cartographic information for solving the problem. Not only practically important objects are shown here. There are also those that indicate some "insignificant" details that help the analyst to understand the situation more deeply. In Fig. 3 these include areas of the map that do not provide actual data, but retain information about the type of landscape. In addition, intra-quarter passage and parking places placed on the image implicitly indicate the possibility of traffic congestion. Perhaps this detail will help the analyst to more reasonably assess the living conditions in the building and make an adequate decision.

To assess the possibilities of "intellectualization", we will consider the formal statement of the problem, which should be solved by an intelligent GIS subsystem designed to manage analysis (intelligent geoinformation system for the analysis guidance, IGSAG).

Let $\Omega = \{\omega_1, \omega_2, \ldots \omega_n\}$ be the set of cartographic objects and relationships stored in a GIS database. To solve an applied problem, the analyst creates a workspace $w \subset \Omega$, $|w| \ll |\Omega|$, into which, using queries via the UI, includes or excludes elements $\omega_i \in \Omega$ that are important for analysis. The sequence of requests $\{q_i\}_{i=0}^{Q}$ in the process of solving a problem generates a sequence of images, each of which has a certain utility

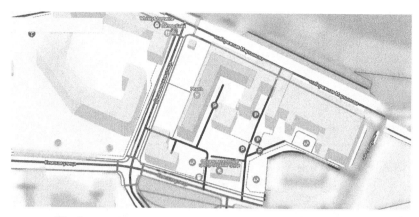

Fig. 3. Image of analysis workspace after "intelligent" processing.

for the analysis process. The utility level of the workspace is estimated by the fitness-function $0 \leq F(w) \leq 1$, where $F(w) = 1$ corresponds to the most useful, $F(w) = 0$ - completely useless image.

We denote by $C = \{C_k\}$ set of contexts, in each of which the intelligent content of images is supported. Working in the context $c_m \in C$ means that when constructing images a limited set of types, instances of cartographic objects are used, and certain rules for visualization of the analysis working area are established. The description of the context is knowledge gained from experts who solved the tasks of the corresponding class.

We represent the set of objects in the working area w in the form of the union of two components:

$$w = B \cup E, B \cup_j q_j, B \subseteq \Omega, B \cap E = \varnothing, E \subset \Omega, \tag{1}$$

here B is the set of map objects selected by query $\{q_i\}_{i=0}^{Q}$.

The set B in expression (1) will be called the skeleton. Objects that are explicitly requested by the user through the UI form the skeleton. Set E in expression (1) is the environment of the skeleton, containing objects that reflect important features of the terrain, influencing the analyst's assessment of the situation. Environment objects are automatically added by IGSAG, which implements the operator:

$$E = K(B, c_m), c_m \in C.$$

This operator assigns to the set of skeleton objects a set of objects of the environment in a given context. Then, in general, IGSDG should solve the following problem:

$$\begin{cases} F(w) \to \max, \\ w = B \cup E, \\ B = \cup_j q_j, \\ E = K(B, c_m), \\ j = 0, 1, 2 \ldots \end{cases} \tag{2}$$

The task is solved every time at the moment of receipt of the next request from the user. By solving problem (2), the IGSDG subsystem contributes to the achievement of the global goal of analysis at a lower cost. This is because any analysis trajectory (classes, instances of objects and relationships used in the session) is an external reflection of the analyst's deep-seated thinking process. Since the goal of analysis is only intuitive to the analyst, repeating such a trajectory in other situations will never bring any benefit. Instead, task (2) always involves constructing a new trajectory, which will be the result of the impact of the generated images on the analyst's mental image. Obviously, informative, meaningful images guide the analysis process so that the result is achieved at the lowest cost.

Analysis management performance is determined by the IGSDG contexts. A change of context allows the analyst to see the work area from a particular perspective. It is impossible to indicate how many intelligent point of view will be used in the session; however, it can be argued that their change is not chaotic. With a high degree of probability, the following context will be in a sense close to the current context. In addition, the closer, the completion of the analysis will be more successful.

The formulated statement of the problem (2) reflects the specifics of the proposed approach. Firstly, guiding the course of analysis from the side of the GIS is to stabilize its intelligent orientation according to the context. The goal of management is to eliminate redundant data that adversely affect the mental image of the situation in the analyst's mind. All redundant objects are localized by environment E.

Secondly, we introduce an indicator of the usefulness of the workspace (w). Usefulness summarizes the intelligent filling of a cartographic image and clearly reflects its influence on the analysis [22, 23].

Thirdly, the usefulness of any sequence of images in the general case depends subjectively on two factors: the correspondence of the intelligent content and the quality of perception of images. Understanding the complexity of assessing the subjective preferences of users [24], we consider the fitness function depending on the composition and number of objects and relationships in the work area. These values integrally characterize its utility.

Fourthly, thanks to the selection of the skeleton and the environment, independent variables (arguments) of the optimization problem are defined. They are subsets of objects included in the skeleton as responses to requests $\{q_i\}_{i=0}^{Q}$. Thus, the course of the analysis is determined by the state of the workspace, to which IGSAG responds. The environment selection operator $K(B, c_m)$ controls its consistency with the context. Thus, the impact on the course of analysis is carried out through the environment of the working area skeleton.

An analysis of the statement of the problem (2) shows that the IGSAG training is to obtain and use knowledge of the contexts and usefulness of the work areas in each of them. Knowledge should take into account the dynamics of changes in the state of the working area and describe the corresponding change of contexts.

Based on (2), the work of the analyst-GIS system is carried out according to the following algorithm:

1. The analyst registers with a GIS session, defining the context for the future analysis.

2. The analyst makes a request to the GIS cartographic database through the UI.
3. The GIS core executes the query and forms the resulting set of objects.
4. IGSAG performs the selection of environmental objects for the resulting set so that the utility of the working area is maximum. For this:

    4.1 Clarifies the context. If the resulting set is substantially beyond the context, the one closest in meaning is determined. Further work goes in a new context. Otherwise, the current context is preserved.

    4.2 While the level of perception of the working area is unsatisfactory, the procedure for changing the complexity that adds or deletes cartographic objects is performed.

5. GIS visualizes the workspace.
6. If the session is not completed, then go to step 2.
7. End the session.

The proposed IGSGA mode of operation uses a context comparison operation. Its implementation significantly affects the quality of control over the analysis. Therefore, a special presentation of contexts is considered below, which makes it possible to evaluate their intelligent proximity.

4 Conceptual Model of Context

As context in the field of research of context-aware systems traditionally understand any information that allows identifying the current situation and taking adequate actions to solve the problem [25]. The conceptual and logical structures of the context depend on the area of application and significantly affect the result of the system. Consider the features of the context for the management of visual analysis in the GIS and introduce a special structure to display the intelligent direction of the analysis.

The term "meaning" used in this paper implies an intuitive awareness of the situation by the analyst in a dialogue with GIS. If the context does not match the meaning, then the interactive interaction between them becomes of little use. It is characteristic that the discrepancy between the context and the meaning of the situation can occur in the process of analysis with a sufficiently high probability. The probability is the greater, the more uncertain the statement of the initial problem and the more noticeable "knowledge gap" in assessing the situation [26]. The key issue of using contexts is to identify the one that most closely matches the meaning of the current situation. For this purpose, various proximity metrics are introduced reflecting the experience of observing the objects under study [27]. Metrics are closely related to the conceptual model of the context itself. The concept of "meaning" we propose to display by a description of the permissible changes in the context within which the intuitively understood essence of the analysis process is preserved. If the boundaries of permissible changes are violated, then the meaning of the analysis in the context used is considered to be lost [28].

We will present the context as follows:

$$c_m = <c_m*, H(c_m)>,$$ (3)

here c_m* is the core of the context, which includes the fundamental knowledge about the objects and relations peculiar to the context of the analysis c_m. In practice, they reflect, for example, a scientifically based pattern or a generally accepted method for analyzing a problem. The context core defines the boundaries of spatial (L_S), temporal (L_t) and semantic (L_a) scope of analysis. If the borders of L_S and L_t are continuous, then the border L_a is a discrete set of types of cartographic objects and software analysis procedures implemented in GIS.

The context core also includes the component necessary for solving the problem (2) - a description of the importance for the analysis of objects and relations. This information is used to implement the procedure for changing the complexity of the workspace. The operation of changing complexity is to purposefully exclude or add elements of the image to achieve the required level of perception by the analyst. If perception is difficult due to an excessive number of objects and connections, then the set of least significant elements is removed. If perception can be improved by adding auxiliary elements, then the most significant are added.

Knowledge concentrated in c_m* is necessary but not sufficient to preserve the intelligent orientation of the analysis for the following two reasons.

First reason: the similarity of nuclei is not the only determining factor of intelligent proximity. For example, in the absence of a GIS context for solving the problem of manual transportation of a consignment, it may seem natural to switch to the context of automobile transportation in the GIS. However, finding a solution in this context can lead to failure due to the lack of a sufficiently short road. At the same time, a context may exist in a GIS that has the "walking path" class of objects as a valid transformation of the semantic boundary. Such a context, for example, may be the context of solving problems of designing urban infrastructure. The transition to this context is not obvious, but it will lead to obtaining useful data on transportation possibilities in a much shorter way. It is also possible that the study of the characteristics of the infrastructure of the city will push the analyst to the original non-standard solution;

The second reason: cores of contexts do not reflect the in-depth knowledge of expert analysts about the transfer of existing experience in analyzing situations. Unlike superficial knowledge, this knowledge operates with "reasonable" (permissible) differences of situations and objects. This allows experts to make reliable decisions in new, previously unexplored conditions. For the task of managing the analysis, the lack of information of the indicated content leads to an incorrect transfer of experience.

In order to increase the reliability of the comparison of the context meanings, (3) introduces a set $H(c_m)$ of permissible transformations of the boundaries of the domain of analysis that preserve the essence of the context c_m. The set $H(c_m)$ includes objects, relations and functions, the presence (or absence) of which in the working area of the analysis indicates that the context has retained its meaning.

Consider an example of using valid transformations. Assume that the map examines the security of a building or structure from man-made or natural influences. Table 1 provides an example of describing the boundaries of the core of the hazard analysis context.

Table 2 lists the permissible transformations of the field of analysis, which, according to experts, do not fundamentally change the essence of the problem being solved. In

Table 1. Description of the boundaries of the context kernel wrappers

Spatial boundary	Semantic border	Temporary border
Buffer area measuring about 200 m, covering the outer perimeter of the building	1) buildings and structures 2) forest, shrubs, grass cover 3) gas pipelines, oil pipelines 4) irrigation systems 5) technical, drinking water supply	For buildings and structures, the date of construction should not be earlier than the last 10 years For grass cover - a period of time when it is more than 4 cm high The forest must be at least 2 years old, shrubs at least 1 year old

particular, the map may display a relief that is not included in the core. The use of this object in the course of visual research is regarded as an attempt to solve a problem using non-standard data that does not contradict the essence of the problem.

Table 2. Description of the valid context boundary conversion

For spatial boundary	For semantic border	For temporary border
1) Buffer zone at a distance of 100 m from a circumscribing circle or polygon 2) Convex hull of a multitude of objects located close to or in the reachable zone of openly propagating fire	Relief Adjacent roads	Time intervals of 1 month preceding the drought and flood season in the last 3 years

In Fig. 4 and Fig. 5 show two variants of the workspace in the same security analysis context, in Fig. 6-in the context of analyzing the state of engineering communications. Difference in the work area in Fig. 5 lies in the fact that it includes the result of executing a query that used the "proximity" relationship for objects of the "Buildings and Structures" and "Roads" types. The images in Fig. 4 and Fig. 5 are constructed according to the mapping rules in the context of security analysis and include the most useful cartographic information. Managing the course of visual analysis is manifested as the stabilization of the intelligent focus. Suppose that the analyst decided to investigate the idea of the location of ground and underground power supply lines and sent the GIS a request to obtain data on the topography and location of the electrical cable with step-down transformers. In this situation, the exact formulation of the research idea is not known, but it can be assumed that the intelligent direction of the analysis is changing fundamentally. For further coordinated work, a decision should be made to move to a different context. This may be the context for analyzing the state of engineering communications. The core of this context is significantly different from the previous one and Fig. 6 illustrates useful map objects obtained by queries in this context. External differences of the visual image are obvious, but the implicit link is the permissible transformation consisting in the display of the relief. Management of the course of visual analysis would allow in this case to choose the best intelligent direction to continue the study.

  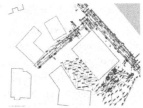

Fig. 4. Image in the context of site security analysis   **Fig. 5.** Image in modified context of site security analysis   **Fig. 6.** Image in the context of engineering communications analysis

The question of how adequately $H(c_m)$ reflects the meaning of the context is decided by the organization of the procedure for obtaining expert knowledge. Note that the valid transformations do not require an analytical description, but represent visualized cartographic objects. The analyst, thus, gets the opportunity in the usual UI to transfer knowledge in a figurative form.

5 Features of Using Contexts with IGSAG

The process of visual analysis can take place in one of two modes:

1. In the mode of explicit indication of the context. This mode assumes that the analyst chooses the context from the list described in the GIS. To do this, he must first examine the properties of the existing contexts. Here, the IGSAG implements the function of providing reference information for selecting a context and stabilizing the intelligent focus within the context chosen by the analyst;
2. In implicit context mode. The mode is that the IGSAG independently determines the most preferred context for the current state of the dialogue. The process of stabilizing the intelligent focus is preceded by the search for the best context.

The task (2) is implemented in both modes. Consider the features of its solution. The first feature is that the level of perception is considered an optimized parameter, and the intelligent orientation is considered as a limitation. The perception level indicator is set out of context individually for each user. Such an indicator is the number of cartographic objects $|w|$ in the working area $w \subseteq \Omega$. The indicator is set in the profile and represents the average number of objects $N*$, which allows it to comfortably perceive the cartographic image of the working area. The value $N*$ does not require high accuracy for its task, since according to the well-known empirical law [29], the change in the intensity of perception logarithmically depends on the number of cartographic elements.

The second feature is the assumption that the fitness function $F(w)$ is unimodal with a maximum at the point $N*$. For example, it can be specified in a piecewise linear form:

$$F(w) = \begin{cases} 1 - (N * - |w|)/N*, & |w| < N*, \\ 1, & |w| = N*, \\ 1 - (|w| - N*)/|w_c|, & |w| > |w_c|. \end{cases}$$

Here $|w_c|$ is the extreme complexity of the image in a given context. It should be noted that not every image consisting of $N*$ objects is a solution to task (2). Of the large number of possible variants are only a few meaningful embodiments. These variants are constructed within the specified context. Therefore, finding a solution to problem (2) is built as a search process, the essence of which is in the construction of a meaningful cartographic image with the number of objects equal to or close to $N*$.

The third feature of solving the problem (2) is the use of the procedure for changing the complexity of the image of the workspace. By complexity is meant the number of cartographic objects from which the workspace is built. Complicating an image is adding objects within the established context. Simplification is to remove insignificant objects or generalize a group of objects with a smaller number of other objects. To implement a complication or simplification, the following preference relation is set in the context:

$$\omega_i \succ \omega_j, i, j = 0, 1 \ldots |w|$$

This relationship is defined on a set of map objects. It allows you to sort the objects of the workspace in order of increasing importance [30]. Accordingly, the first $N*$ elements will always be the most significant for the analysis. The final selection needs to be done, keeping the semantic connections of objects at the border, set by the value $N*$. For this, it is necessary to compare two versions of the image: complicated or simplified to the value $N*$.

The implicit context establishment mode during analysis requires making a decision on the choice of context in the presence of uncertainty about the task being solved by the analyst. If the requested objects and relations can be attributed to valid transformations of one of the known contexts, then the decision about selection this particular context is obvious.

If the requested data does not refer to the valid transformations known for IGSAG, then it is required to find the "most suitable" context from the known ones. Methods of choice may be different. The analysis showed that these methods can be divided into the following three categories.

The first category includes methods based on the analysis of archival data on the sequences (chains) of contexts in the analysis session. This information is accumulated in the form of a sequence of commands formed in the session, from analyst to GIS. We denote by $\{c_{ij}\}, i = \overline{1, m}, j = 1, 2, \ldots$ the set of contexts that were selected in the i-th observation session in the order given by the index j. Having a set of m context chains, one can predict the numbers of neighboring contexts based on any machine learning model [31].

The second category includes methods based on spatial analysis mechanisms in GIS [2]. Assuming that the course of analysis is determined solely by the characteristics of the terrain, it is possible to predict the context of the analysis, using, for example, kriging, topological analysis or time series analysis.

The third category includes methods that use knowledge of the utility of applying contexts in general. In contrast to the two options discussed above, knowledge is the product of the subjective generalization of various experts. Different variants of decision-making methods on choosing the best context can be constructed depending on the conceptual model of knowledge, the way they are presented and the logic of the reasoning.

In this paper, we do not consider the task of constructing an algorithm for choosing the most suitable context. This is the subject of independent research. Now, it is necessary to answer a more important question regarding the joint work of the analyst and IGSAG. Understanding how IGSAG works in each of the modes leads to the question of the limits of applicability of these modes. The feasibility of switching IGSAG from one mode to another is determined by the ratio of the two components of the complexity of the analysis.

The first component (U_1) is determined by the analyst's costs of studying the set of contexts available in the system. Making a reasonable choice of the desired context is impossible without such preliminary work. Obviously, as the number of contexts grows (Q), these costs increase. For small values of Q, growth can be considered linear: $U_1 = u_1 Q$. Here u_1 is the unit cost per context.

The second component of the complexity (U_2) is associated with the study of the working area in the established context. It can be argued that with the increase in the number of contexts, these costs are reduced due to the fact that the analyst receives less redundant data. It can be assumed, that $U_2 = u_2 / Q$, where u_2 is the specific cost of the context. The expression for total costs is: $U_1 + U_2 = u_1 Q + u_2 / Q$.

It is easy to differentiate and find the extremum of this function. Here the minimum cost is achieved when

$$Q* = \sqrt{u_2 / u_1}$$

This expression allows the following conclusions:

1) Regardless of the selected mode of operation, the analyst has the ability to manipulate the workspace with minimal effort;
2) The number of contexts significantly affects the efficiency of the analysis process. There is a certain value $Q*$, which provides a compromise between the increasing complexity of studying the system of contexts itself and the complexity of analyzing the workspace in an established context;
3) With large differences in the ability of users to learn, it is advisable to limit the number of available contexts. The values u_1 and u_2 are individual setting parameters of the user profile.

6 Experimental Study of IGSAG

The purpose of the experimental study IGSAG was to assess the boundaries of the effective application of the method of managing the analysis of cartographic images. The experiment was carried out in a corporate GIS, the information base of which occupies about 2.3 TB and includes a description of approximately 10^6 objects. The system provides geoservice for solving the following groups of applied tasks:

1) accounting and maintenance of process equipment;
2) construction and repair of buildings and structures;
3) engineering communications management;
4) transport logistics in the territory of the enterprise and in the adjacent territory;
5) energy management;
6) provision of surveillance and territorial security;
7) emergency response;
8) transport network design;
9) property management;
10) placement and transportation of hazardous waste.

The following quality indicators turned out to be practically important for geoservice users: the opportunity to formulate an applied problem and designate the direction of the search for a solution (we denote this indicator as A_1); the ability to find a solution to a problem in high-risk conditions (A_2); the ability to find satisfactory solutions with severe restrictions on the time of its search (A_3); the ability to reduce cognitive load caused by the need to perform operations that are not directly related to solving the problem (A_4). The listed indicators are used both independently and in combination. Since in any combination of indicators one of them acts as a criterion, and the rest are limitations, an experimental assessment of the quality of service was carried out for each indicator separately. The evaluation was conducted by a survey of user analysts. It was proposed to use a 10-point satisfaction assessment scale, where 0 corresponds to the absence of influence on the analysis process, 5 - the maximum level of utility for using the service, (-5) - the most negative impact of the service. Here, negative influence means the appearance of data that contradict the logic of the analysis and make it difficult to proceed further.

The survey was conducted among 23 analysts who used geoservice for 1 month. The system described 27 contexts that could be used in solving the problems of the above groups. An example would be the "Warehouses" context, which reflects not only the spatial position of warehouse buildings and premises, but also adjacent transportation, energy communications, video surveillance points and emergency protection facilities. With the number of contexts available, the calculation using formula gives $Q* = 4$, that is, if the context is explicitly selected, the user from 27 possible values is offered to select no more than 4 transition options.

Table 3 shows the results of the survey of service users. The columns correspond to the task groups numbered above, and the lines meet the criteria $A_1 - A_2$.

Table 3. Interview results

	Task group numbers									
	1	2	3	4	5	6	7	8	9	10
A_1	2	3	4	4	2	3	0	1	1	3
A_2	4	3	4	5	1	3	4	3	0	5
A_3	4	4	4	4	5	3	4	5	4	5
A_4	3	1	4	4	−1	3	4	1	0	2

Analysis of the distribution of estimates for individual indicators allowed us to draw the following conclusions:

– The least effect on the indicator A_1 was obtained by analyzing emergencies. This result can be explained by the need for analysts to follow regulated procedures that cover real-world situations. Essentially, emergencies were easily classified. This is evidenced by the practical absence of a change of contexts. A much greater effect on the indicator A_1 was observed when solving problems involving the study of the territory. For example, when solving a group of problems 3, there were on average 5 contexts. It can be assumed that the reason was the uncertainty of the source data.
– The effect of attracting geoservice for making responsible decisions (indicator A_2) turned out to be rather high on average. The possible reason for the deviation by task group 5 can be explained by the low importance of the factors of spatial distribution of energy sources and consumers for decision-making.
– The effect on the indicator A_3 is quite high for all groups of tasks. This can be explained by a decrease in the redundancy of cartographic images and the stabilization of their complexity in the area of the best level of perception.
– As for reducing the level of cognitive load, there is a noticeable scatter in the estimates. For example, for task group 5, satisfaction with this factor is negative, since images have appeared that cause discomfort for analysts. A possible reason for the appearance of such a situation is the absence of the necessary intelligent content in the contexts proposed by the analyst.

7   Conclusion and Future Work

In this paper, an approach to managing the process of interactive analysis of cartographic images based on maximizing their usefulness is proposed and investigated. The usefulness is ensured by the selection of cartographic objects and relations in the established context with a restriction on the level of perception of images by analyst. The decisions made in this case are of higher quality, which is confirmed by the results of the experiment.

A distinctive feature of the management of analysis is the control of its intelligent orientation. For this purpose, it is proposed to present the context by two components - the core and a set of admissible kernel transformations that preserve its meaning. Comparison of online analytics requests with permissible transformations allows not only to detect a change in the meaning of the analysis, but also to select contexts that are close in meaning. A dynamic context change can be viewed as a special method of compensating for uncertainty about the ultimate goal of the analysis that the analyst set himself.

Experimental analysis of the implementation of the proposed control method showed that the greatest positive effect is observed when solving difficultly formalized applied problems in tight time frames.

Further research is supposed to be carried out in the direction of continuous transformation of contexts, which will ensure the continuous stabilization of the analysis process.

Acknowledgments. The reported study was funded by the Russian Foundation for Basic Research according to the research projects N 18-01-00023, N19-07-00074.

References

1. Longley, P., Goodchild, M., Maguire, D., Rhind, D.: Geographic Information Systems and Sciences, 3rd edn. Wiley, New York (2011)
2. Shekhar, S., Xiong, H., Zhou, X. (eds.): Encyclopedia of GIS. Springer, Cham (2017). https://doi.org/10.1007/978-3-319-17885-1
3. https://www.autodesk.com/products/autocad/included-toolsets
4. https://www.esri.com/en-us/arcgis/about-arcgis/overview
5. Hick, W.: On the rate of gain of information. Q. J. Exp. Psychol. **4**(1), 11–26 (1952)
6. Gibson, J.: A theory of direct visual perception. In: Royce, J., Rozenboom, W. (eds.) The Psychology of Knowing. Gordon & Breach, New York (1972)
7. Palmiero, M., Nori, R., Piccardi, L.: Visualizer cognitive style enhances visual creativity. Neurosci. Lett. **615**, 98–101 (2016)
8. Colman, A.: A Dictionary of Psychology, 3nd edn. Oxford University Press, Oxford (2008)
9. Jakob's Law of Internet User Experience. https://www.nngroup.com/videos/jakobs-law-internet-ux/. Accessed 2 July 2020
10. Cybulski, J., Keller, S., Nguyen, L., Saundage, D.: Creative problem solving in digital space using visual analytics. Comput. Hum. Behav. **42**, 20–35 (2015)
11. Endsley, M.: Design and evaluation for situation awareness enhancement. In: Proceedings of the Human Factors Society 32nd Annual Meeting, pp. 97–101. Human Factors Society, Santa Monica (1988)
12. Endsley, M., Bolte, B., Jones, D.: Designing for Situation Awareness: An Approach to Human-Centered Design. Taylor & Francis, London (2003)
13. Ziemke, T., Schaefer, K., Endsley, M.: Situation awareness in human-machine interactive systems. Cogn. Syst. Res. **46**, 1–2 (2017)
14. Nilsson, M., Van Laere, J., Susi, T., Ziemke, T.: Information fusion in practice: a distributed cognition perspective on the active role of users. Inf. Fusion **13**(1), 60–78 (2012)
15. Turner, A.: Introduction to Neogeography. O'Reilly, Sebastopol (2006)
16. Taylor, F., Lauriault, T.: Conclusion and the future of cybercartography. Modern Cartogr. Ser. **5**, 343–350 (2014)
17. Liu, Y., Wang, H., Li, G., Junyang Gao, J., Hua, H., Li, W.: ELAN: an efficient location-aware analytics system. Big Data Res. **5**, 16–21 (2016)

18. McKenzie, G., Janowicz, K., Gao, S., Yang, J., Hu, Y.: POI Pulse: a multi-granular, semantic signature–based information observatory for the interactive visualization of big geosocial data. Cartogr. Int. J. Geogr. Inf. Geovis. **50**(2), 71–85 (2015)
19. Collins, C., et al.: Guidance in the human-machine analytics process. Visual Inform. **2**(3), 166–180 (2018)
20. Andrienko, N., et al.: Viewing visual analytics as model building. Comput. Graph. Forum **37**(6), 275–299 (2018)
21. Goodwin, P., Wright, G.: Decision Analysis for Management Judgment, 3rd edn. Wiley, New York (2004)
22. Andrienko, N., Andrienko, G.: Exploratory Analysis of Spatial and Temporal Data. Springer, Berlin (2006). https://doi.org/10.1007/3-540-31190-4
23. Belyakov, S., Bozhenyuk, A., Belykova, M., Rozenberg, I.: Model of intellectual visualization of geoinformation service. In: Proceedings of the 28th European Conference on Modelling and Simulation ECMS 2014, pp. 326–333 (2014)
24. Ramalho, F., Ekel, P., Pedrycz, W., Pereira, J., Soares, G.: Multicriteria decision making under conditions of uncertainty in application to multiobjective allocation of resources. Inf. Fusion **49**, 249–261 (2019)
25. Dey, A., Abowd, G.: Towards a better understanding of context and context-awareness. In: Proceedings of CHI 2000 Workshop on the What, Who, Where, When, and How of Context-Awareness, pp. 304–307 (2000)
26. Berndtsson, M., Mellin, J.: Active database knowledge model. In: Liu, L., Özsu, M.T. (eds.) Encyclopedia of Database Systems. Springer, Boston (2018). https://doi.org/10.1007/978-0-387-39940-9_508
27. Kotkov, D., Wang, S., Veijalainen, J.: Survey of serendipity in recommender systems. Knowl.-Based Syst. **111**, 180–192 (2016)
28. Belyakov, S., Bozhenyuk, A., Rozenberg, I.: The intuitive cartographic representation in decision-making. In: World Scientific Proceeding Series on Computer Engineering and Information Science, vol. 10, pp. 13–18 (2016)
29. Mackay, D.: Psychophysics of perceived intensity: a theoretical basis for Fechner's and Stevens' laws. Science **139**, 1213–1216 (1963)
30. Sedgewick, R., Wayne, K.: Algorithms, 4th edn. Addison-Wesley Professional, Boston (2011)
31. Bishop, C.: Pattern Recognition and Machine Learning. Springer, New York (2016)

Risk Sensitive Markov Decision Process for Portfolio Management

Eduardo Lopes Pereira Neto[(⊠)] [iD], Valdinei Freire[(⊠)] [iD],
and Karina Valdivia Delgado[(⊠)] [iD]

Universidade de São Paulo, São Paulo, Brazil
dulpneto@ime.usp.br, {valdinei.freire,kvd}@usp.br

Abstract. In the Portfolio Management problem the agent has to decide
how to allocate the resources among a set of stocks in order to maximize
his gains. This decision-making problem is modeled by some researchers
through Markov decision processes (MDPs) and the most widely used
criterion in MDPs is maximizing the expected total reward. However,
this criterion does not take risk into account. To deal with risky issues,
risk sensitive Markov decision processes (RSMDPs) are used. To the best
of our knowledge, RSMDPs and more specifically RSMDPs with exponential utility function have never been applied to handle this problem.
In this paper we introduce a strategy to model the Portfolio Management problem focused on day trade operations in order to enable the
use of dynamic programming. We also introduce a measure based on
Conditional Value-at-Risk (CVaR) to evaluate the risk attitude. The
experiments show that, with our model and with the use of RSMDPs
with exponential utility function, it is possible to change and interpret
the agent risk attitude in a very understandable way.

Keywords: Markov decision process · Risk sensitive Markov decision
process · Planning and scheduling · Portfolio management

1 Introduction

In the Portfolio Management problem [9] the agent has to decide how to allocate
the resources among a set of stocks in order to maximize gains. Stock gains are
stochastic and depend on the behavior of the market which can be calm or
volatile. These characteristics of the problem, the access to real data and the
vast number of assets available have attracted the attention of many researches
and some of them try to tackle the problem modeling it as a Markov Decision
Process [4,5,12].

Markov decision process (MDP) is a mathematical model [13] widely used
in sequential decision-making problems and provides a mathematical framework
to represent the interaction between an agent and an environment through the
definition of a set of states, actions, transitions probabilities and rewards. In
MDPs the agent must find an optimal policy (a mapping from states to actions)

© Springer Nature Switzerland AG 2020
L. Martínez-Villaseñor et al. (Eds.): MICAI 2020, LNAI 12468, pp. 370–382, 2020.
https://doi.org/10.1007/978-3-030-60884-2_27

that maximizes the accumulative discount reward. Many strategies to model the Portfolio Management problem as an MDP can be found in the literature [1,2,4,5,12].

Another aspect studied on the Portfolio Management problem is the risk involving decision making. Some works have applied risk averse models to the Portfolio Management problem [2,12] or have made use of measures with implicit risk aversion criteria [4], however in these models it is impossible to parameterize the agent risk behavior, when it is desired. A risk sensitive Markov decision processes (RSMDPs) [3,6–8,10,11], is an extension of an MDP used to model problems where the attitude of risk needs to be taken into account and to the best of our knowledge, RSMDPs have never been applied to handle this problem. An RSMDP includes a risk factor parameter which allows defining the agent's attitude towards risk. One strategy to handle risk is using the expected utility theory where the main idea is to transform the accumulative discount reward by utility functions [7] and look for optimal policies regarding this utility measure.

In this paper, we propose a strategy to model the Portfolio Management problem focused on day trade operations in order to enable the use of dynamic programming algorithms as Value Iteration to find solutions for this problem. We also introduce a measure based on Conditional Value-at-Risk (CVaR) [14] to evaluate the risk attitude. We run experiments considered two days of real data of Apple and Amazon stocks in order to verify the applicability of the proposed strategy and the measure to evaluate the risk attitude.

2 Markov Decision Process

Markov decision process (MDP) is a mathematical model widely used in decision-making problems that provides a mathematical framework to represent the interaction between an agent and an environment. Formally, an infinite-horizon MDP is defined by a tuple $\langle S, A, R, T, \gamma \rangle$ [13], where: S is a finite set of states; A is a finite set of actions that can be performed by the agent; $R : S \times A \to \mathbb{R}$ is the reward function that defines the reward when an action is taken in a state; $T : S \times A \times S \to [0, 1]$ is the transition function that defines the state transition probability; and $\gamma \in [0.1)$ is the discount factor.

The agent's objective is to find an action for each state, i.e a policy π. The value of a policy π is defined as the expected accumulated discounted reward:

$$V^\pi(s) = E_\pi \left[\sum_{t=0}^{\infty} \gamma^t r_t | s_0 = s \right], \tag{1}$$

where the reward at each decision stage t is represented by r_t. The value of a policy could be computed by solving the following system of equations:

$$V^\pi(s) = R(s, \pi(s)) + \gamma \sum_{s' \in S} T(s, \pi(s), s') V^\pi(s'). \tag{2}$$

The optimal solution for an MDP is an optimal policy π^*. The value function V^* associated to this policy is called optimal value. This optimal value function $V^*(s) = \max_\pi V^\pi(s)$ is the solution of the Bellman equation:

$$V^*(s) = \max_{a \in A} \left\{ \sum_{s' \in S} R(s, a) + \gamma \sum_{s' \in S} T(s, a, s') V^*(s') \right\}. \tag{3}$$

MDPs that maximize the expected reward are considered risk neutral.

3   Risk Sensitive Markov Decision Process

When risk in decision making needs to be taken into account, the environment can be modeled as a Risk Sensitive Markov Decision Process (RSMDP) [7]. An RSMDP is an extension of an MDP that includes a risk factor which allows defining the agent's attitude towards risk. Formally, an RSMDP can be defined as a tuple $\langle S, A, R, T, \gamma, \lambda \rangle$, where S, A, R, T, and γ are defined in the same way as in MDPs and λ is the risk factor.

One strategy to handle risk is using the expected utility theory where the main idea is to transform the accumulative discount reward by utility functions [7] and look for optimal policies regarding this utility measure. Thus, the utility function U is included to transform the accumulative discount reward:

$$V^\pi(s) = E_\pi \left[U \left(\sum_{t=0}^{\infty} \gamma^t r_t \right) | s_0 = s \right]. \tag{4}$$

To define the risk attitude, an RSMDP can use an exponential utility function. This utility function is used because of its mathematical properties that enable the use of Dynamic Programming. The value of a policy π using the exponential utility function for infinite horizon RSMDPs can be defined by [7]:

$$V^\pi(s) = E_\pi \left[-(\lambda) \exp \left(-\lambda \sum_{t=0}^{\infty} \gamma^t r_t \right) | s_0 = s \right]. \tag{5}$$

In this equation, the agent has a risk averse attitude if $\lambda > 0$, a risk prone attitude if $\lambda < 0$ and a risk-neutral attitude when $\lambda \to 0$.

The value of a policy could be computed by solving the following system of equations [7]:

$$V^\pi(s) = -(\lambda) \exp \left(-\lambda R(s, \pi(s)) \right) \gamma \sum_{s' \in S} T(s, \pi(s), s') V^\pi(s'). \tag{6}$$

The optimal value function $V^*(s) = \max_\pi V^\pi(s)$ is the solution of the equation:

$$V^*(s) = \max_{a \in A} \left\{ -(\lambda) \exp \left(-\lambda R(s, a) \right) \gamma \sum_{s' \in S} T(s, a, s') V^*(s') \right\}. \tag{7}$$

Policy Iteration [7] and Value Iteration [7] algorithms can be used to solve RSMDPs. In this paper we use the Risk Sensitive Value Iteration algorithm [7]. This algorithm first initializes V with arbitrary values and at each iteration i the algorithm computes the value of q^i using the following equation:

$$q^i(s, a) = \sum_{s' \in S} T(s, a, s') \left[-sign(\lambda) \exp(-\lambda(R(s, a) + \gamma V^{i-1}(s'))) \right]. \quad (8)$$

To avoid numerical precision errors, we additionally use the log transformation of the value function obtaining:

$$V^i(s) \leftarrow \frac{\ln\left(-sign(\lambda) \max_a \left(q^i(s, a)\right)\right)}{-\lambda}. \quad (9)$$

Given the minimum error ϵ, if $\max_{s \in S}\{V^i(s) - V^{i-1}(s)\} < \epsilon$, the algorithm stops. Finally, the ϵ-optimal policy π^* is obtained through the following equation:

$$\pi^*(s) = \arg\max_{a \in A} \left\{ \sum_{s' \in S} T(s, a, s') \left[-sign(\lambda) \exp(-\lambda(R(s, a) + \gamma V(s'))) \right] \right\}. \quad (10)$$

4   Measure to Evaluate the Risk Attitude in RSMDPs

In the financial market, risk measurement is a very common practice and one measure used for risk analysis is the Conditional Value-at-Risk (CVaR) [14]. CVaR is a pessimistic measure that analyzes a percentile of worst cases. The objective of this measure is to assess, in extreme cases of loss, what is the average of that loss and thereby to evaluate the risk of a given investment.

In addition, a policy that is more prone to risk aims to achieve better accumulative rewards even if for obtaining that the agent has to run the risk of suffering greater losses, as is the case with investments with greater risks in the financial market. This characteristic shows the applicability of the CVaR metric to measure the risk propensity in RSMDPs.

However, the CVaR measure focuses only on the cases where greater losses were obtained and we know that policies that are more prone to risk have also the chance of achieving greater accumulative rewards even if this happens with a small chance. With this in mind, this work proposes an extension of the CVaR measure in order to evaluate the best cases of accumulative reward gain. For this purpose, the average of the $X\%$ worst cases are calculated for $0\% \leq X\% \leq 100\%$ of all the accumulative rewards obtained and the average of the $Y\%$ best cases for $100\% \geq Y\% \geq 0\%$.

Figure 1 shows curves for risk-prone and risk-averse attitudes. The green curve illustrates the typical behavior for the risk-averse case. The risk-averse curve approaches a straight line since for the more risk-averse cases, a smaller variation in the average accumulative reward is expected. The red curve represents the risk-prone case. For the risk-prone agent, it is expected that the worst average accumulative reward will be reached in the worst execution cases and the best average accumulative reward will also be reached in the best execution cases.

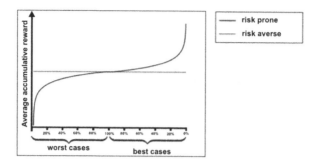

Fig. 1. Average of the accumulative reward of the worst cases and best cases.

5   The Portfolio Management Problem

In the general Portfolio Management problem [9] the agent has a certain amount of money and has to decide the amount of money to be distributed among a set of stocks. The agent has three options: (i) to invest in one selected stock, (ii) to keep the position and do nothing, and (iii) to withdraw from the amount invested.

Many strategies to model the Portfolio Management problem as an MDP can be found in the literature [1,2,4,5,12]. Some of them define the states as a combination of the invested amount and the state of the market [2,12], some works define a relation of current stock open and close prices [5], some works combine cumulative expected return, price variation and invested amount [1] and others works have a state space to represent the invested amount at current time t and a action space to represent the invested amount in each stock at next time $t + 1$ [4]. However, most of them show problems regarding the number of states (solving only small MDPs), or provide a continuous representation of the invested amount [4] making difficult the use of dynamic programming.

In our formulation, first we define the representation for only one stock and then this formulation is extended for multiple stocks.

5.1   Modeling the Portfolio Management Problem with One Stock

In this formulation, one stock is given as an option to investment and keeping the money not invested represents a risk free condition. In this case, the agent has three actions. The first one is to invest $Z\%$ ($0\% < Z\% < 100\%$) of the total of money he has. The second one is to keep the position and do nothing. And the third one is to withdraw $Z\%$ of the total of money from the amount invested. In that way the agent will not be able to invest or withdraw all money in one single action, making actions more tightly dependent on the past decisions. The actions are also deterministic ignoring a possibility of the action to invest or withdraw not to be executed. We also consider no slippage and zero delay in order to simplify the problem. Transaction costs are defined as a percentage of the amount changed at every time t.

In this formulation we introduce a strategy focused on day trade operations in order to enable the use of dynamic programming. Thus, a one day stock trade executed in consecutive times t (where t represents one minute of the day) is represented. The amount of money invested is updated at every moment t according to the stock appreciation or depreciation and rewards are given following this change on the total money invested.

To built the transitions probabilities, a set of data containing the history of trades from a specific stock in a specific day is used. This set of data contains useful information such as the minute of the day and the average price on that given minute t, (avg_price_t). avg_price_t is the average of all prices that the stock was negotiated in that minute of the day.

In each minute t, we compute the return in time t that consists in the percentage of appreciation or depreciation using average price in minute t and average price in minute $t - 1$:

$$return_t = \frac{avg\_price_t - avg\_price_{t-1}}{avg\_price_{t-1}}. \tag{11}$$

With this return we compute the expected return on minute t by computing the mean return over the last N minutes:

$$expected\_return_t = \frac{1}{N}\left(\sum_{i=t-N+1}^{t} return_i\right). \tag{12}$$

After having these expected returns computed for each time t and navigating from the expected return on time t to the expected return on time $t + 1$, transition probabilities are computed. Having defined the actions and expected return, we define the states and rewards as being:

States: A state s is composed by the expected return and the percentage of the total invested money, i.e, $\langle expected\_return_t, invested_{t-1} \pm Z\% \rangle$, such that $0\% \leq invested_{t-1} \pm Z\% \leq 100\%$. As we establish a fixed value for $Z\%$ when defining the actions, the state space S consists of all possible combinations between the expected accumulative returns computed and the invested percentage.

Rewards: The reward is obtained by the amount of gain on time t to time $t-1$ according to the amount invested, i.e:

$$R(s,a) = \frac{avg\_price_t - avg\_price_{t-1}}{avg\_price_{t-1}} \times invested_{t-1},$$

where $s = \langle expected\_return_t, invested_{t-1} \pm Z\% \rangle$ and $a = Z\%$.

To illustrate the computation of transition probabilities, Fig. 2 (left) shows the *return* and *expected_return* computed for the last 4 min from Apple stock (AAPL) on one day. Going from minute 15:56 to minute 15:57 creates an edge from expected return 0.0002 to expected return 0.0002, going from minute 15:57 to minute 15:58 creates an edge from expected return 0.0002 to expected return 0.0001 and finally going from minute 15:58 to minute 15:59 creates an edge from expected return 0.0001 to expected return 0.0. These nodes with the *expected_return* and edges created are shown in Fig. 2 (right). From Fig. 2 (right), for example, we can say that the expected return 0.002 has the probability of 0.5 to go to expected return 0.001 and the probability of 0.5 to stay in the expected return 0.002.

	minute	average	return	expected_return	
					0.0002
386	15:56	191.262	-0.000152	0.0002	
387	15:57	191.279	0.000089	0.0002	0.0001
388	15:58	191.223	-0.000293	0.0001	
389	15:59	191.136	-0.000455	0.0000	0.0

Fig. 2. Expected return of the last 4 min from AAPL stock and the transitions between them represented as a graph. In this graph nodes are expected returns.

In order to create the RSMDP we also need to define the actions. For example, for $Z = 50\%$, if the agent is on a state with 0% invested, he has the option to execute the action to invest 50%. In this case, the agent can go to a states with 50% invested or stay with 0% invested. Notice that the agent can not go from a state with 0% invested directly to a state with 100% and there is no state with negative investment. Figure 3 shows a RSMDP created with transitions between *expected_returns* from Fig. 2 and $Z = 50\%$.

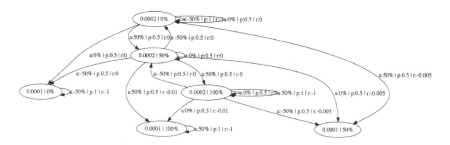

Fig. 3. RSMDP created with transitions between *expected_returns* from Fig. 2 and $Z = 50\%$. In this graph nodes are states of the RSMDP and the edges have the action a, the transition probability p and the reward r.

5.2 Modeling the Portfolio Management Problem with Multiple Stocks

To extend our formulation to a multiple stocks allocation first we define a set of M stocks that are allowed to be used. Then we extend our definition of actions, states and rewards as the following:

Actions: An action a is now a tuple of size M, i.e., $a = \langle Z\_1\%, ..., Z\_M\% \rangle$. We make the restriction that all invested value in all stocks can not be greater than 100%.

States: The state s is now extended to be a tuple of size M:

$$s = \begin{bmatrix} \langle expected\_return\_1_t, invested\_1_{t-1} \pm Z\_1\% \rangle, \\ \langle ... \rangle, \\ \langle expected\_return\_M_t, invested\_M_{t-1} \pm Z\_M\% \rangle \end{bmatrix} \tag{13}$$

Rewards: The reward is obtained by the sum of the difference between expected return on time t and expected return on time $t - 1$:

$$R(s, a) = \sum_{n=1}^{M} \left(\frac{avg\_price\_n_t - avg\_price\_n_{t-1}}{avg\_price\_n_{t-1}} \times invested\_n_{t-1} \right)$$

The transitions probabilities are defined by combining the transitions probabilities obtained for each stock available.

6 Experiments

We run experiments in the Portfolio Management problem considering real data of Apple (AAPL) and Amazon (AMZN) stocks to verify the applicability of Risk Sensitive MDPs for this problem and the proposed measure to evaluate the risk attitude. To build the Portfolio Management environment four parameters must be informed:

- A set of data containing the intraday stock trade history from specific stocks.
- D: the number of decimal places where the expected return will be rounded.
- N: the amount of history data will be used to calculate the expected return for each time t.
- M: the list containing the stocks available to invest.
- $Z\%$: the percentage of the total money that will be invested or withdrawn each time.

These parameters are used to discretize the data and to build the transitions probabilities and the state space. The data analyzed were downloaded from IEX[1] from 2020-03-02 and 2020-03-03 from Apple (AAPL) and Amazon (AMZN)

---

[1] https://iexcloud.io.

stocks. Data from 2020-03-02 were selected since the selected stocks show a tendency of gains and data from 2020-03-03 were selected since the selected stocks show the opposite behavior.

We set M = [AAPL, AMZN] and D = 4 and N = 5. With this configuration we obtained 19 different values of expected return and based on them we built the transitions. We defined $Z\% = 25\%$ what makes actions to be invest 25%, withdrawal 25% and keep the current position in each stocks available. The state space consists of all possible combinations from the expected returns and the 5 possible invested ranges (0%, 25%, 50%, 75%, 100%).

To make a better analysis on agent behavior we combined the data in order to build the following three scenarios:

- **Scenario 1: AAPL with gains and AMZN with gains** that use data from AAPL from 2020-03-02 and AMZN from 2020-03-02.
- **Scenario 2: AAPL with losses and AMZN with gains** that use data from AAPL from 2020-03-03 and AMZN from 2020-03-02.
- **Scenario 3: AAPL with losses and AMZN with losses** that use data from AAPL from 2020-03-03 and AMZN from 2020-03-03.

We evaluate the optimal policies returned for two risk factor values $\lambda = -5$ (risk prone) and $\lambda = 5$ (risk averse). For the experiments we solve an MDP to find the risk neutral policy and use it to compare with the other policies[2].

6.1   Analysis of the Average of Worst and Best Cases

Figures 4a, 5a and 6a show the average of the X% worst cases for $0\% < X\% \le 100\%$. Figure 4b, 5b and 6b show the average of the Y% best cases for $100\% \ge Y\% > 0\%$. As expected, for all scenarios, the risk neutral policy get the highest values when looking at the 100% of accumulative rewards of the worst and best cases.

Additionally, for all scenarios, the curves of the risk averse and the risk prone policies have a similar behavior than the curves of Fig. 1 almost for all the percentages. The exception are the curves of the risk averse that are different than the ideal behavior for less than 20% of the best cases.

First we analyze the behavior of the risk prone policy and then the risk averse policy. The risk prone policy gets worse accumulative rewards than the risk neutral policy for the worst cases and for all scenarios. However, for the best cases, we can see that risk prone policy gets better average rewards than the risk neutral policy when we look at the 25% or less of the best cases. This is a typical behavior on risk prone policies.

For the risk averse policy the average rewards are more stable without greater losses and also without greater gains for all scenarios, that is a typical behavior on risk averse policies. Additionally, the average rewards of worst cases for risk averse policy stays greater than the risk neutral policy for most percentages in

---

[2] https://github.com/dulpneto/rsmdp_portfolio_mngnt.

the first and second scenarios. In the third scenario the risk averse and the risk neutral policies have almost the same average rewards for worst and best cases.

It is also possible to notice that as the scenario changes from Scenario 1 to Scenario 2 and then to Scenario 3 the risk neutral policy gets closer behavior to the risk averse policy and farther from the risk prone policy. This is an expected behavior since the tendency of losses increases as we change the scenarios.

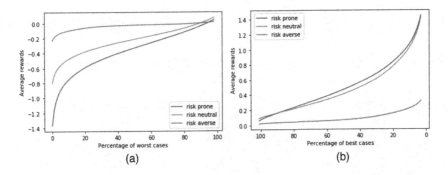

Fig. 4. Average of worst and best cases for AAPL with gains and AMZN with gains

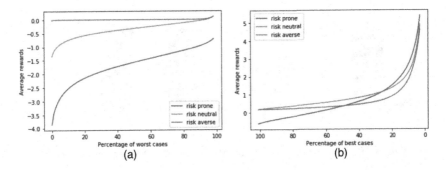

Fig. 5. Average of worst and best cases for AAPL with losses and AMZN with gains

6.2   Analysis of the Total Invested

Figure 7, 8 and 9 show the average of all values invested during execution for the three scenarios. The subplots (a) on Fig. 7, 8 and 9 refer to the risk prone policy average, the subplot (b) to the risk neutral and the subplot (c) to the risk averse policy. The purpose of this analysis is to verify how the agent invests the money available. In all scenarios, it is possible to observe that the more averse the agent is, the lesser is invested. Additionally, for the risk prone case, in all scenarios, the policy prefers investing on AAPL.

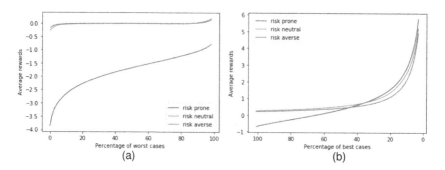

Fig. 6. Average of worst and best cases for AAPL with losses and AMZN with losses

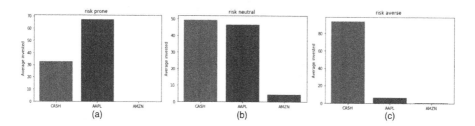

Fig. 7. Total invested running for AAPL with gains and AMZN with gains.

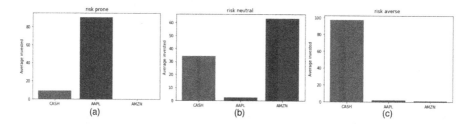

Fig. 8. Total invested for AAPL with losses and AMZN with gains.

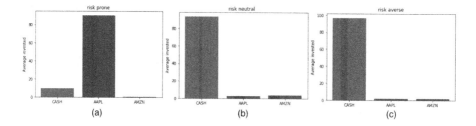

Fig. 9. Total invested for AAPL with losses and AMZN with losses.

In the first scenario where AAPL and AMZN have gains, all the policies invest more in AAPL than in AMZN (Fig. 7). In the second scenario where AAPL has losses, the risk neutral and risk averse policies avoid investing on AAPL while the risk prone policy has the opposite behavior (Fig. 8). In the third scenario where AAPL and AMZN have losses (Fig. 9), the risk neutral and the risk averse policies keep almost the same amount on cash and invest little in AAPL and AMZN. This explains the behavior of the curves on Fig. 6.

7   Conclusion

The first contribution of this paper is the formulation of the Portfolio Management problem that defines the state as being a combination of the expected return from the last N returns and the amount invested for each stock available. Our formulation makes restrictions on the amount invested forbidding the agent to short or long the stock at any time. The objective of these restrictions is to keep markovian states. The expected returns computed from a set of data are also used to build the transitions probabilities and to compute rewards.

The second contribution is the measure based on Conditional Value-at-Risk (CVaR) that is composed by the average of the worst cases of all the accumulative rewards obtained and the average of the best cases of the same accumulative rewards and its main purpose is to define an intuitive way to analyze the risk attitude.

The results show that our model strategy can represent well the data set and the Risk Sensitive Value Iteration is capable of finding policies with different risk attitudes. The results also show the importance of good measures to analyze the risk attitude, such the measure based on CVaR introduced in this paper. This measure shows to be consistent to that type of analysis making possible to verify the risk attitude in a very understandable way.

One weakness of the proposed method is the difficulty to modeling the gain and loss scenarios simultaneously. This may be tackle in future works.

Acknowledgment. Supported by grant #2018/11236-9, São Paulo Research Foundation (FAPESP).

References

1. Bookstaber, D.: Using Markov decision processes to solve a portfolio allocation problem. Undergraduate Thesis, Brown University (2005)
2. Brown, D.B., Smith, J.E.: Dynamic portfolio optimization with transaction costs: heuristics and dual bounds. Manage. Sci. **57**(10), 1752–1770 (2011)
3. Chung, K.J., Sobel, M.J.: Discounted MDP's: distribution functions and exponential utility maximization. SIAM J. Control Optim. **25**(1), 49–62 (1987)
4. Filos, A.: Reinforcement learning for portfolio management. arXiv preprint arXiv:1909.09571 (2019)
5. Gupta, A., Dhingra, B.: Stock market prediction using hidden Markov models. In: 2012 Students Conference on Engineering and Systems, pp. 1–4. IEEE (2012)

6. Heger, M.: Consideration of risk in reinforcement learning. In: Machine Learning Proceedings 1994, pp. 105–111. Elsevier (1994)

7. Howard, R.A., Matheson, J.E.: Risk-sensitive Markov decision processes. Manage. Sci. **18**(7), 356–369 (1972)

8. Littman, M.L., Szepesvári, C.: A generalized reinforcement-learning model: convergence and applications. In: ICML, vol. 96, pp. 310–318 (1996)

9. Lynch, A.W.: Portfolio choice and equity characteristics: characterizing the hedging demands induced by return predictability. J. Financ. Econ. **62**(1), 67–130 (2001)

10. Mihatsch, O., Neuneier, R.: Risk-sensitive reinforcement learning. Mach. Learn. **49**(2–3), 267–290 (2002)

11. Patek, S.D.: On terminating Markov decision processes with a risk-averse objective function. Automatica **37**(9), 1379–1386 (2001)

12. Petrik, M., Subramanian, D.: An approximate solution method for large risk-averse Markov decision processes. In: Proceedings of the Twenty-Eighth Conference on Uncertainty in Artificial Intelligence, Arlington, Virginia, USA, pp. 805–814 (2012)

13. Puterman, M.L.: Markov Decision Processes: Discrete Stochastic Dynamic Programming, 1st edn. Wiley, New York (1994)

14. Uryasev, S., Rockafellar, R.T.: Conditional value-at-risk: optimization approach. In: Uryasev, S., Pardalos, P.M. (eds.) Stochastic Optimization: Algorithms and Applications. Applied Optimization, vol. 54, pp. 411–435. Springer, Boston (2001). https://doi.org/10.1007/978-1-4757-6594-6_17

Risk-Sensitive Piecewise-Linear Policy Iteration for Stochastic Shortest Path Markov Decision Processes

Henrique Dias Pastor[✉], Igor Oliveira Borges, Valdinei Freire,
Karina Valdivia Delgado, and Leliane Nunes de Barros

University of Sao Paulo, Sao Paulo, Brazil
{henrique.pastor,igor.borges,valdinei.freire,kvd,leliane}@usp.br

Abstract. A Markov Decision Process (MDP) is commonly used to
model a sequential decision-making problem where an agent interacts
with an uncertain environment while looking for minimizing the expected
cost accumulated along the process. If the process horizon is infinite, a
discount factor $\gamma \in [0,1]$ is used to indicate the importance the agent
gives to future states. If the agent's mission is to achieve a goal state,
the process becomes a Stochastic Shortest Path MDP (SSP-MDP), the
in fact model used for probabilistic planning in AI. Although several
efficient solutions have been proposed to solve SSP-MDPs, there are little
research carried out when we consider the "risk" in such processes. A
Risk Sensitive MDP (RS-MDP) allows modeling the agent's risk-averse
and risk-prone attitudes, by including a risk and a discount factor in
the MDP definition. The proof of convergence of known solutions based
on dynamic programming adapted for RS-MDPs, such as risk-sensitive
value iteration (VI) and risk-sensitive policy iteration (PI), rely on the
discount factor. However, when solving an SSP-MDP we look for a proper
policy, i.e. a policy that guarantees to reach the goal while minimizing the
accumulated expected cost, which is naturally modeled without discount
factor. Besides, it has been shown that the discount factor can modify
the chosen risk attitude when solving a risk sensitive SSP-MDP. Thus, in
this work we aim to formally proof the convergence of the PI algorithm
for a Risk Sensitive SSP-MDP based on operators that use a piecewise-
linear transformation function, without a discount factor. We also run
experiments in the benchmark River domain showing how the intended
risk attitude, in an interval of extreme risk-averse and extreme risk-
prone, varies with the discount factor γ, i.e. how an optimal policy for
Risk Sensitive SSP-MDP can go from being a risk-prune policy to a
risk-averse one, depending on the discount factor.

1 Introduction

The subarea of automated planning in artificial intelligence studies the problem
of sequential decision making where an agent has to select the best deterministic
action to be taken at each decision step, in order to achieve a desired goal in a

L. Martínez-Villaseñor et al. (Eds.): MICAI 2020, LNAI 12468, pp. 383–395, 2020.
https://doi.org/10.1007/978-3-030-60884-2_28

minimum number of steps. In automated probabilistic planning, the agent has also to deal with the uncertainty over the effects of its actions and guarantee to reach the goal with a minimum expected accumulated cost.

While a Markov Decision Process (MDP) [15], from operational research, is commonly used to model a sequential decision-making agent that interacts with an uncertain environment for a given number of decision-steps (i.e. a finite or infinite horizon), a Stochastic Shortest Path MDP (SSP-MDP) is used to model a probabilistic planning agent where the horizon depends on its distance to the goal (configuring an MDP where the horizon is undefined). Typically, in an infinite horizon MDP, a discount factor γ in $[0, 1]$ is used to indicate the importance the agent gives to future states. On the other hand, in an SSP-MDP, the discount factor should be no necessary. However, for some SSP-MDPs with large distances to the goal, some solutions also include a discount factor [9]. Besides, most of the convergence proofs of the well-known classical dynamic programming algorithms for MDPs, value iteration (VI) and policy iteration (PI) [15], rely on the use of the discount factor. A special proof of the convergence of algorithms for an SSP-MDP without discount factor is given in [1].

An important aspect that has been studied in the field of MDPs is how to include risk in the process. Risk is inherent to decision-making, arising from the uncertainties on future events and the probabilistic nature of the problem itself. In a Risk Sensitive MDP, an agent must choose a risk attitude, through a risk factor k that can vary between an extreme risk-prone and an extreme risk-averse [17]. The traditional MDP agent that minimizes the expected accumulated cost is considered a risk-neutral agent. However, risk is not usually optimized by most of the decision-making criteria, specially when solving an SSP-MDP where most of the solutions make the assumption of a risk-neutral attitude. In fact, the development of risk-sensitive algorithms is a subject little explored in the literature of MDPs and SSP-MDPs [8].

There are different approaches to quantify risk, such as: expected exponential utility [3,10,11,14,16], the use of a piecewise-linear transformation function with a discount factor [12], weighted sum between expectation and variance [5,18] and the estimation of performance in a confidence interval [4]. Such approaches are more difficult to apply to problems and more computationally costly compared to risk-neutral models [8].

An approach to solve an RS-MDP that has optimal stationary policies and known extreme risk factor values, proposes a set of fixed-point operators with contraction properties, based on a piecewise-linear transformation function including risk and discount factors [12]. Based on this approach, in [2] was proposed a Risk Sensitive Value Iteration (RSVI) algorithm for infinite-horizon RS-MDPs. One can easily proof the convergence of this algorithm, and of the infinite-horizon risk sensitive PI version (RSPI) as well, based on the fixed-point operators proposed in [12]. It is also easy to prove the convergence of RS-SSPs using the same approach, considering a discount factor $\gamma < 1$. However, to prove the convergence of RS-SSP MDPs without a discount factor (i.e. $\gamma = 1$), the results of [12] cannot be directly applied.

In this work we formally proof the convergence of the PI algorithm for RS-SSPs using the piecewise-linear transformation function proposed by [12], without discount factor. We also perform experiments in the benchmark River domain showing how the intended risk attitude, in an interval of extreme risk-averse and extreme risk-prone, varies with the discount factor γ, i.e. how an optimal policy for Risk Sensitive SSP-MDP can go from being a risk-prune policy to a risk-averse one, depending on the discount factor.

2 Markov Decision Process

Formally, an infinite-horizon MDP is a tuple: $M = \langle \mathcal{S}, \mathcal{A}, \mathcal{P}, \mathcal{C}, \gamma \rangle$ where: $\mathcal{S}$ is a finite set of states; $\mathcal{A}$ is a finite set of actions; $\mathcal{P} : \mathcal{S} \times \mathcal{A} \times \mathcal{S} \to [0,1]$ is a function that defines the transition probabilities where $\mathcal{P}(s'|s,a)$ represents the probability to transit to state $s' \in S$, given that the agent is in state $s \in \mathcal{S}$ and action $a \in \mathcal{A}$ was chosen; $\mathcal{C} : \mathcal{S} \times \mathcal{A} \times \mathcal{S} \to \mathbb{R}$ is the cost function that defines the cost when action $a \in \mathcal{A}$ is taken in state $s \in \mathcal{S}$ and transits to state $s' \in S$; and $\gamma \in [0,1[$ is the discount factor.

A stochastic shortest path SSP-MDP is a tuple: $\langle \mathcal{S}, \mathcal{A}, \mathcal{P}, \mathcal{C}, S_g \rangle$ where $\mathcal{S}$, $\mathcal{A}$, $\mathcal{P}$ and $\mathcal{C}$ are defined as for infinite-horizon MDP. And $S_g \subseteq S$ is a finite set of goal states. Goal states are absorbent, i.e., $\mathcal{P}(s'|s,a) = 1$ for all $a \in A$, $s \in S_g$ and $s' \in S$.

An SSP-MDP models the interaction between an agent and its environment and the process consists of stages. At each stage, the agent knows the current state s_i and what actions can be taken. These actions have probabilistic effects. The agent then decides to perform an action a_i that has a cost c_i and takes the agent to a future state s_{i+1}. The decision is taken in every stage with the possibility of stopping when the agent reaches a goal state. The solution of a SSP-MDP is a stationary policy π that is a mapping from states to actions (i.e., $\pi : \mathcal{S} \to \mathcal{A}$). The value $V^\pi(s)$ of a policy π is defined by [15]:

$$V^\pi(s) = \lim_{M \leftarrow \infty} \mathrm{E}\left[\sum_{t=0}^{M} c_t \,\middle|\, \pi, s_0 = s \right], \tag{1}$$

where the cost at each decision stage t is represented by c_t.

The value function of a policy π is well defined if a policy π is proper. A policy π is proper if the probability to reach the goal is 1 for every state. In this case, the value function of a policy π could be computed by solving the following system of equations:

$$V^\pi(s) = \begin{cases} 0 & \text{, if } s \in S_g \\ \sum_{s' \in \mathcal{S}} \mathcal{P}(s'|s, \pi(s))[\mathcal{C}(s, \pi(s), s') + V^\pi(s')] & \text{, otherwise.} \end{cases} \tag{2}$$

If there exists at least one proper policy and for every improper policy the corresponding cost is infinite for at least one state, the optimal value function

$V^*(s) = \min_\pi V^\pi(s)$ is the solution of the Bellman equation:

$$V^*(s) = \begin{cases} 0 & \text{, if } s \in S_g \\ \min_{a \in A} \sum_{s' \in S} P(s'|s,a)\left[C(s,a,s') + V^*(s')\right] & \text{, otherwise.} \end{cases} \quad (3)$$

The optimal policy π^* can be obtained based on the optimal value function by:

$$\pi^*(s) = \begin{cases} \text{any } a \in A & \text{, if } s \in S_g \\ \arg\min_{a \in A} \sum_{s' \in S} P(s'|s,a)\left[C(s,a,s') + V^*(s')\right] & \text{, otherwise.} \end{cases} \quad (4)$$

SSP-MDPs that minimize the expected accumulative cost are considered risk neutral.

3   Piecewise-Linear Function Approach for Infinite-Horizon Risk Sensitive Markov Decision Process

One of the most popular approaches to quantify risk, which is based on the utility theory, is the use of exponential utility. In this approach, we need to define a risk factor, but its feasible values depend on the decision problem [14] and the value of the extreme risk averse factor is not known a priori.

Another approach to deal with risk is the one proposed in [12] that is based on a piecewise-linear function and has its extreme risk factor values known a priori. This approach allows to find an optimal stationary policy as a solution, as well as an arbitrary choice for the risk factor. The Mihatsch and Neuneier's approach focuses mainly on Reinforcement Learning (RL) [19] and instead of transforming the accumulated reward (negative cost), as in other approaches, a point-fixed operator is defined [12]. Two risk-like versions of the *Q-Learning* and *Temporal Difference* (TD) algorithms are proposed in [12]. In addition, the authors demonstrate that the proposed algorithms converge and for this, they define different operators.

Following, we describe the Mihatsch and Neuneier's approach that throughout this paper is called infinite-horizon Risk Sensitive Markov Decision Process (RS-MDP). In Subsect. 3.4 and Subsect. 3.5 some of these operators are used to formulate the RSVI and RSPI algorithms, respectively.

Formally, an infinite-horizon RS-MDP [12] is defined by a tuple $\langle M, k \rangle$, where $-1 < k < 1$ is the risk factor and M is an infinite-horizon MDP. The approach proposed in [12] uses the piecewise-linear transformation function $\chi^{(k)}$ which depends on the input x (the temporal difference) be it positive or not and on the risk factor k. This function is defined by:

$$\chi^{(k)}(x) = \begin{cases} (1-k)x & \text{, if } x < 0, \\ (1+k)x & \text{, otherwise.} \end{cases} \quad (5)$$

An important property of $\chi^{(k)}$, that is used in the next section, is given in Lemma 1.

Lemma 1 [12]. *Given* $k \in (-1,1)$, *for each pair of real numbers* a, b *there is* $\xi_{a,b,k} \in [1 - |k|, 1 + |k|]$ *such that:*

$$\chi^{(k)}(a) - \chi^{(k)}(b) = \xi_{a,b,k}(a - b). \tag{6}$$

3.1   Policy Evaluation

Given a stationary policy π, the corresponding value function $V_k^\pi(s)$ can be obtained by solving the following system of equations for all $s \in S$ [12]:

$$\sum_{s' \in S} \mathcal{P}(s'|s, \pi(s)) \chi^{(k)} \Big(\mathcal{C}(s, \pi(s), s') + \gamma V_k^\pi(s') - V_k^\pi(s) \Big) = 0. \tag{7}$$

Note that different from risk neutral MDPs, we do not have a system of linear equations, since $V_k^\pi(s)$ composes the parameter of function $\chi^{(k)}$. If $k > 0$, the agent is risk averse; if $k < 0$ the agent is risk prone; if $k = 0$ the agent is risk neutral and in this case there is equivalence with the classical MDP criterion. At the limit of extreme risk aversion, when $k \to +1$, the objective function solves a problem equivalent to optimization in the worst case scenario. At the limit of extreme risk prone, when $k \to -1$, the agent is very optimistic assuming that for all possible next states, the best case always happens.

3.2   Optimal Policy

Similar to risk-neutral MDPs, there are deterministic stationary optimal policies for infinite-horizon RS-MDPs and the optimal value function is unique.

Theorem 1 *(Optimal policies [12]).* *For each* $k \in (1, -1)$ *there is a unique optimal value function,* $V_k^*(s) = \min_{\pi \in \Pi} V_k^\pi(s), \forall s \in S$, *that satisfies the following equation:*

$$\min_{a \in A} \sum_{s' \in S} \mathcal{P}(s'|s, a) \mathcal{X}^{(k)} \Big(\mathcal{C}(s, a, s') + \gamma V_k^*(s') - V_k^*(s) \Big) = 0, \forall s \in S.$$

A policy π^* *is optimal if and only if:*

$$\pi^*(s) = \arg\min_{a \in A} \sum_{s' \in S} \mathcal{P}(s'|s, a) \mathcal{X}^{(k)} \Big(\mathcal{C}(s, a, s') + \gamma V_k^*(s') - V_k^*(s) \Big).$$

In addition, we can define the optimal function $Q_k^*(s, a)$.

Theorem 2 *(Optimal function Q^* [12]).* *The optimal function* Q_k^* *is the unique solution of the following system of equations:*

$$\sum_{s' \in S} \mathcal{P}(s'|s, a) \mathcal{X}^{(k)} \Big(\mathcal{C}(s, a, s') + \gamma \min_{a' \in A} Q_k^*(s', a') - Q_k^*(s, a) \Big) = 0, \quad \forall s \in \mathcal{S}, u \in A.$$

Furthermore, a policy π^* is optimal if and only if:

$$\pi^*(s) = \arg\min_{a \in A} Q_k^*(s, a).$$

Analogously to classical dynamic programming theory, the proofs of these theorems depend on the contraction property of some operators over the value function and Q function. In [12] different operators were defined. In the next section we describe two of them: the operators $O_{\alpha k}^{\pi}$ and $\mathcal{N}_{\alpha,k}$.

3.3   Operators $O_{\alpha K}^{\pi}$ and $\mathcal{N}_{\alpha,k}$

The operators $O_{\alpha k}^{\pi}$ and $\mathcal{N}_{\alpha,k}$ [12], which will be considered in this work, make use of the function $\mathcal{X}^{(k)}$ and are defined over the space of $V(s)$ and $Q(s, a)$ functions, respectively.

Theorem 3 [12]. *If $k \in (-1, 1)$, $0 \leq \gamma < 1$ and $0 < \alpha \leq (1+|k|)^{-1}$, the operator $O_{\alpha k}^{\pi}[V]$ defined next is a contraction mapping:*

$$O_{\alpha k}^{\pi}[V](s) = V(s) + \alpha \sum_{s' \in S} P(s'|s, \pi(s)) \chi^{(k)}(C(s, \pi(s), s') + \gamma V(s') - V(s)), \quad (8)$$

i.e., for all functions V_1 and V_2, we have: $|O_{\alpha,k}^{\pi}[V_1] - O_{\alpha,k}^{\pi}[V_2]| \leq \rho|V_1 - V_2|$, for some $\rho = (1 - \alpha(1 - |k|)(1 - \gamma)) \in (0, 1) < 1$. The scalar α is a positive step-size.

Theorem 4 [12]. *If $k \in (-1, 1)$, $0 \leq \gamma < 1$ and $0 < \alpha \leq (1+|k|)^{-1}$, the operator $\mathcal{N}_{\alpha,k}$ defined next is a contraction mapping:*

$$\mathcal{N}_{\alpha,k}[Q](s, a) := Q(s, a) + \alpha \sum_{s' \in S} P(s'|s, a) \mathcal{X}^{(k)}\left(C(s, a, s') + \gamma \min_{a' \in A} Q(s', a') - Q(s, a) \right),$$
$$(9)$$

i.e., for all functions Q_1 and Q_2, we have: $|\mathcal{N}_{\alpha,k}[Q_1] - \mathcal{N}_{\alpha,k}[Q_2]| \leq \rho|Q_1 - Q_2|$, where $\rho = (1 - \alpha(1 - |k|)(1 - \gamma)) \in (0, 1) < 1$.

Note that, differently from [12], these theorems state that α can be equal to $(1 + |k|)^{-1}$ if γ is less than 1. Intuitively, the α factor ensures that the V and Q values do not grow much, especially when the discount factor γ is close to 1 and the risk factor k is negative.

3.4   Risk Sensitive Value Iteration Algorithm

In this section we present the Risk Sensitive Value Iteration algorithm based on the operator $\mathcal{N}_{\alpha,k}$ (Eq. 9). The algorithm is called *Risk Sensitive Value Iteration* (RSVI) [2]. Given an infinite-horizon RS-MDP defined by a tuple $\langle M, k \rangle$, where $-1 < k < 1$ and $0 < \alpha \leq (1 + |k|)^{-1}$, the following updating function of Q can be defined based on Eq. 9, which is used in the RSVI algorithm:

$$Q^i(s,a) \leftarrow Q^{i-1}(s,a) + \alpha \sum_{s' \in \mathcal{S}} \mathcal{P}(s'|s,a)\mathcal{X}^{(k)}\left(\mathcal{C}(s,a,s') + \gamma \min_{a' \in \mathcal{A}} Q^{i-1}(s',a') - Q^{i-1}(s,a)\right).$$

In this equation, the scalar function $\mathcal{X}^{(k)}$ is also applied directly to the temporal difference. Given $Q^i(s,a)$, we can obtain the value function at iteration i by:

$$V^i(s) = \min_{a \in \mathcal{A}}\{Q^i(s,a)\}$$

and a greedy policy by:

$$\pi(s) = \arg\min_{a \in \mathcal{A}}\{Q^i(s,a)\}.$$

The stop criterion used in the RSVI algorithm is based on the relative residual: $\text{residual}(s) = \left|\frac{V^i(s) - V^{i-1}(s)}{V^{i-1}(s)}\right|$. Given a minimum error ϵ, if $\max_{s \in \mathcal{S}}\{\text{residual}(s)\} \leq \epsilon$, the algorithm stops. Note that the use of the relative residual is better for the RSVI algorithm than the absolute residual since the magnitudes of values $V^i(s)$ and $V^{i-1}(s)$ depend on the risk factor k and discount factor γ.

3.5   Risk Sensitive Policy Iteration Algorithm

The Risk-Sensitive Policy Iteration algorithm is composed by 2 steps: policy evaluation and policy improvement. Given an infinite-horizon RS-MDP defined by a tuple $\langle M, k \rangle$, where $-1 < k < 1$, $0 < \alpha \leq (1 + |k|)^{-1}$ and a policy π, the policy evaluation step can be executed using the operator $O^\pi_{\alpha k}$ (Eq. 8). The policy improvement step is based on Theorem 5. Given a stationary policy π, using Eq. (10), we obtain an improvement stationary policy π'.

Theorem 5 [12]. *Let $k \in (-1, 1)$. Let π and π' be stationary policies such that:*

$$\pi'(s) = \arg\min_{a \in \mathcal{A}} \sum_{s' \in \mathcal{S}} \mathcal{P}(s'|s,a)\mathcal{X}^{(k)}(\mathcal{C}(s,a,s') + \gamma V^\pi_k(s') - V^\pi_k(s)), \qquad (10)$$

then we have

$$V^{\pi'}_k(s) \leq V^\pi_k(s) \qquad \forall\, s \in \mathcal{S}. \qquad (11)$$

4   Convergence of the Risk Sensitive Policy Iteration for Risk Sensitive SSP-MDPs

In the literature it has been shown that the discount factor γ can modify the chosen risk attitude [6,7,13]. Additionally, probabilistic planning literature usually considers SSP-MDPs where the discount factor is not used. Thus, in this section we demonstrate that the Risk Sensitive Policy Iteration, without discount factor, converges for Risk Sensitive SSP-MDPs.

To prove this convergence, first we demonstrate that the operator $O_{\alpha k}^\pi[V]$ given in Eq. 8 is a contraction mapping even without the discount factor given some conditions over the policy. This operator, that we rename as $T_{\alpha k}^\pi[V]$, is used in the policy evaluation step. Second, we prove that, if π is proper, the policy improvement step works and the next policy is also proper.

We prove contraction by using the weighted sup-norm $||x||_\infty^w = \max_i \frac{|x_i|}{w_i}$. Let A be any matrix and define $||A||_\infty^w = \max_i \frac{1}{w_i} \sum_{j=1}^n [A]_{ij} w_j$, it is known [14] that:

$$||Ax||_\infty^w \leq ||A||_\infty^w ||x||_\infty^w. \tag{12}$$

4.1 Convergence of Values for Proper Policies

Theorem 6. *Let $k \in (-1,1)$, $0 < \alpha < (1+|k|)^{-1}$ and π be a proper policy, the $T_{\alpha k}^\pi[J]$ operator defined next is a contraction mapping:*

$$T_{\alpha k}^\pi[V](s) = V(s) + \alpha \sum_{s' \in S} p_{s,s'}^\pi \chi^{(k)}(c_{ss'}^\pi + V(s') - V(s)) \tag{13}$$

where $p_{s,s'}^\pi$ and $c_{ss'}^\pi$ represent $\mathcal{P}(s'|s,\pi(s))$ and $\mathcal{C}(s,\pi(s),s')$, respectively.

Proof. We divided the proof in two parts. First we construct a new Risk Neutral SSP-MDP, then, we show that the $T_{\alpha k}^\pi[V]$ operator is a contraction mapping for this new Risk Neutral SSP-MDP.

In the first part we use the property of $\chi^{(k)}$ given in Lemma 1. Using this lemma in Eq. 13 we obtain:

$$T_{\alpha k}^\pi[V](s) = \overbrace{\left(1 - \sum_{s' \in S} \alpha p_{s,s'}^\pi \xi(s,s',\pi,V)\right)}^{\widehat{p}_{ss}} V(s) + \sum_{s' \in S} \overbrace{\alpha p_{s,s'}^\pi \xi(s,s',\pi,V)}^{\widetilde{p}_{ss'}} (c_{ss'}^\pi + V(s')).$$

This can be rewritten as:

$$T_{\alpha k}^\pi[V](s) = \widehat{p}_{ss}(0 + V(s)) + \sum_{s' \in S} \widetilde{p}_{ss'}(c_{ss'}^\pi + V(s')), \tag{14}$$

$$T_{\alpha k}^\pi[V](s) = \widehat{p}_{ss}(0 + V(s)) + \widetilde{p}_{ss}(c_{ss}^\pi + V(s)) + \sum_{s' \neq s \in S} \widetilde{p}_{ss'}(c_{ss'}^\pi + V(s')), \tag{15}$$

$$T_{\alpha k}^\pi[V](s) = (\widehat{p}_{ss} + \widetilde{p}_{ss})(V(s)) + \widehat{p}_{ss}0 + \widetilde{p}_{ss}c_{ss}^\pi + \sum_{s' \neq s \in S} \widetilde{p}_{ss'}(c_{ss'}^\pi + V(s')). \tag{16}$$

Considering Eq. 16, let $M = \langle \mathcal{S}, \mathcal{A}, \mathcal{P}, \mathcal{C}, S_g \rangle$ be the original Risk Sensitive SSP-MDP, we define the following modified Risk Neutral SSP-MDP $M_m = \langle \mathcal{S}, \mathcal{A} = \{a\}, \mathcal{P}^{\alpha,\xi,\pi}, \mathcal{C}^{\alpha,\xi,\pi}, S_g \rangle$ where:

$$\mathcal{P}^{\alpha,\xi,\pi}(s'|s,a) = \begin{cases} \widehat{p}_{ss} + \widetilde{p}_{ss} & \text{, if } s = s' \\ \widetilde{p}_{ss'} & \text{, otherwise.} \end{cases} \tag{17}$$

and

$$\mathcal{C}^{\alpha,\xi,\pi}(s,a,s') = \begin{cases} \frac{\widetilde{p}_{ss}c^\pi_{ss}}{\widetilde{p}_{ss}+\widetilde{p}_{ss}} & , \text{if } s = s' \\ c^\pi_{ss'} & , \text{otherwise.} \end{cases} \tag{18}$$

Now, consider matrices: $\mathbf{P}^\pi$, the transition matrix for policy π in SSP-MDP M, $\mathbf{P}^{\alpha,\xi,\pi}$, the transition matrix for the unique policy π in Risk Neutral SSP-MDP M_m, and $\mathbf{I}$, the identity matrix. Let V_1 and V_2 two vectors of size $|S|$, $\xi_{min} = \min\{\xi(s,s',\pi,V)\}$ and ρ^π the spectral ratio of matrix $\mathbf{P}^\pi$. Using this notation, we have:

$$||T^\pi_{\alpha,k}V_1 - T^\pi_{\alpha,k}V_2||^w_\infty = ||\mathbf{P}^{\alpha,\xi,\pi}(V_1 - V_2)||^w_\infty \tag{19}$$

$$\leq ||(\alpha\xi_{min}\mathbf{P}^\pi + (1-\alpha\xi_{min})\mathbf{I})(V_1 - V_2)||^w_\infty \tag{20}$$

$$\leq ||\alpha\xi_{min}\mathbf{P}^\pi(V_1 - V_2)||^w_\infty + ||(1-\alpha\xi_{min})(V_1 - V_2)||^w_\infty \tag{21}$$

$$\leq \alpha\xi_{min}\rho^\pi||V_1 - V_2||^w_\infty + (1-\alpha\xi_{min})||V_1 - V_2||^w_\infty \tag{22}$$

$$= (1 - \alpha\xi_{min} + \alpha\xi_{min}\rho^\pi)||V_1 - V_2||^w_\infty. \tag{23}$$

In Eq. 19, we apply definition of $\mathcal{P}^{\alpha,\xi,\pi}(s'|s,a)$ and added an extra self-transition probability for each state to obtain the superior bound Eq. 20. We use the property of the weighted sup-norm (Eq. 12) in Eq. 20 to obtain Eq. 21. From Eq. 21 to Eq. 22 we make use of the fact that $||\mathbf{P}^\pi V||^w_\infty \leq \rho^\pi||V||^w_\infty$. Note that: (i) $\alpha \leq (1+|k|)^{-1}$; (ii) $\xi_{min} \leq 1 + |k|$; and (iii) $\rho^\pi < 1$ because π is proper [14]. Then:

$$(1 - \alpha\xi_{min} + \alpha\xi_{min}\rho^\pi) < 1,$$

and therefore $T^\pi_{\alpha,k}$ is a contraction.

4.2 Policy Improvement

To guarantee policy improvement, all we need is Theorem 5 with $\gamma = 1$. Instead of proving such a theorem, we refer to the original paper [12] and note that the authors proof does not use the fact that $\gamma < 1$. Therefore the Policy Iteration algorithm converges.

4.3 Notes About Convergence of the Value Iteration Algorithm

We do not have a proof for the convergence of Value Iteration algorithm when $\gamma = 1$, but in our experiments we observe convergence. First, note that policy iteration converges if it starts with a proper policy (Theorems 5 and 6). Second, the value of a non-proper policy diverges, then, after some finite iterations of VI, a proper policy is reached.

5 Empirical Analysis

In this section, we analyze both RSVI and RSPI. The step size α is computed by $(1 + |k|)^{-1}$. The experiments were performed on IntelliJ IDEA2017.1.2 x64 with Intel Core i7-720QM CPU @2.8 GHz, 8 GB RAM memory @1333Mhz.

We run our algorithms in the River domain [7] where a a river is represented by grid with N_x lines and N_y columns; columns 1 and N_y represent the riversides; line 1 contains a bridge and line N_x contains a waterfall. The goal location is always at location (N_x, N_y). The agent's objective is to reach the goal location from any other cell (i.e., river, riverside or bridge cells). The possible actions are: north (↑), south (↓), west (←) and east (→). In this domain the objective of the agent is to reach the goal, starting at any grid cell. Thus there are two ways the agent can reach the goal: (i) walking by the riversides and the bridge in direction to the goal; or (ii) taking a shortcut swimming in the river in the goal direction.

Actions executed on the riversides or bridge have 99% chance of success and 1% chance of failing (i.e., to stay in the same place). Actions executed in the river have 80% chance of being dragged by the flow (towards the south) and 20% chance of success. The cost for each executed action is +1, except in the goal state where the cost is 0. In our tests, in order to have proper policies, the goal state is an absorbing state and if the agent falls into the waterfall, it returns to the initial state. Note that policies for this domain present a clear predicted behavior in terms of risk attitude, as we describe next.

A **risk-averse agent in the River domain** always goes towards the goal walking along the riversides or the bridge. If the agent is in the west (east) riverside he tries to go towards north (south) along the riverside; if he is in the bridge he tries to go east. If the agent is inside the river he always tries to achieve the nearest riverside (or bridge) location, i.e., avoiding the waterfall. A **risk-prone agent in the River domain** always goes towards the goal location as fast as possible. If the agent is in a west riverside cell he jumps in the river towards the goal; and if he is in the east riverside he goes towards the goal along the riverside. If the agent is inside the river he always tries to go toward east i.e., he will seek for the goal even under the risk of falling into the waterfall. Table 1 shows three optimal policies examples generated with $\gamma = 1$. In the policies, "O" indicates the goal location.

Table 1. Some policies obtained with grid 7×10 in the River Domain.

Legend	Extreme Risk-prone	Risk Neutral	Extreme Risk-averse
	$k = -0.9$ and $\gamma = 1$	$k = 0$ and $\gamma = 1$	$k = 0.9$ and $\gamma = 1$

5.1   Risk Factor Versus Discount Factor

In this section we evaluate the optimal policies returned by both RSVI and RSPI with different values of risk factor k and discount factor γ. Table 1 shows the results of running RSVI and RSPI on the 7×10 River instance. Note that equal returned policies have the same color. For $\gamma = 0.90$, and $\gamma = 1$, we observe that the policies returned with extreme risk factor values, i.e., $k = -0.9$ and $k = 0.9$, presented an expected behavior in terms of risk. As predicted by [7], the discount factor γ also influences the risk attitude. The discount factor has the role of attenuating the risk attitudes if γ is small or enhancing the risk attitudes if γ is large. We can see this behavior observing each column individually from top to down. For example for $k = 0.7$, growing values of γ, reinforce the risk-averse attitude.

We also note that the policy of $\gamma = 1$ and $k = 0.4$ appears 10 times in the Table 2. Considering only the value of k this policy would be classified as risk-averse ($k > 0$) for $\gamma = 0.7$ and $\gamma = 0.8$. For $\gamma = 0.9$ the policy would be classified as risk neutral ($k = 0$). Using $\gamma = 1$ we observe that this policy is a slightly more risk-prone than the risk neutral policy ($\gamma = 1$ and $k = 0$). Thus, we can go from being a risk-prune policy to a risk-averse one, depending on the discount factor.

Table 2. Policies returned by RSVI and RSPI algorithms in a 7×10 River instance.

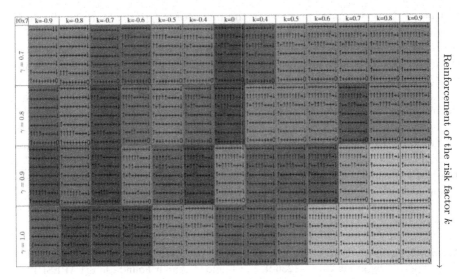

5.2   Convergence Time

Figure 1 shows the CPU time spent by the RSVI (left) and RSPI (right) algorithms in the river domain grid for $\gamma = 1$, varying the size of the grids ($7 \times 10, 10 \times 20, 20 \times 50, 50 \times 20, 50 \times 50$ and 60×60) and also varying the risk factor. The RSPI algorithm has the best execution time for all values of k when the grid is smaller ($7 \times 10, 10 \times 20$ and 20×50). Although the total number of states is the same for 20×50 and 50×20, the execution time of the last one for k equal to $-0.8, -0.9, 0.8$ and 0.9 increased a lot for RSPI, becoming worse than RSVI. For 50×50 and 60×60 the behavior remains as before, but with a sharp increase for $k = 0.8$ and $k = 0.9$.

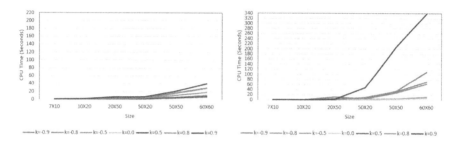

Fig. 1. Time of RSVI (left) and RSPI (right) with varying risk and problem size.

6   Conclusion

In this work we formally prove that the operator $T^{\pi}_{\alpha k}[V]$, where the discount factor is equal to 1, is a contraction mapping for Risk Sensitive SSP-MDPs if π is proper and $0 < \alpha \leq (1 + |k|)^{-1}$. Additionally, if π is proper, we prove that the policy improvement step works and the next policy is also proper. Thus, we prove that RSPI, without a discount factor, converges. Experiments were carried out to compare both RSVI and RSPI algorithms in the River domain to evaluate the influence of the discount factor and the risk factor on the optimal policy and the convergence time.

Summing up, our empirical evaluation has shown that a high discount factor reinforces the chosen risk attitude. Additionally, we observe that for both RSVI and RSPI (i) the convergence time is larger for extreme risk attitudes, both risk-averse and risk-prone; and (ii) policies with risk factor values close to $k = 0$ have a low computational cost. Finally, we observe that RSVI is faster than RSPI for large problems in the River domain.

Acknowledgment. This study was financed in part by CAPES - Finance Code 001 and supported by grant 2018/11236-9, São Paulo Research Foundation (FAPESP).

References

1. Bertsekas, D.P.: Dynamic Programming and Optimal Control, vol. 1. Athena Scientific, Belmont, MA (1995)
2. Borges, I.O., Delgado, K.V., Freire, V.: Análise do algoritmo de iteração de valor sensível a risco. In: XV ENIAC, pp. 365–376 (2018)

3. Denardo, E.V., Rothblum, U.G.: Optimal stopping, exponential utility, and linear programming. Math. Program. **16**(1), 228–244 (1979)
4. Filar, J.A., Krass, D., Ross, K.W., Ross, K.W.: Percentile performance criteria for limiting average Markov decision processes. IEEE Trans. Autom. Control **40**(1), 2–10 (1995)
5. Filar, J.A., Kallenberg, L.C.M., Lee, H.M.: Variance-penalized Markov decision processes. Math. Oper. Res. **14**(1), 147–161 (1989)
6. Freire, V.: The role of discount factor in risk sensitive Markov decision processes. In: 2016 5th Brazilian Conference on Intelligent Systems (BRACIS), pp. 480–485 (Oct 2016)
7. Freire, V., Delgado, K.V.: GUBS: a utility-based semantic for goal-directed Markov decision processes. In: Sixteenth International Conference on Autonomous Agents and Multiagent Systems, pp. 741–749 (2017)
8. García, J., Fernández, F.: A comprehensive survey on safe reinforcement learning. J. Mach. Learn. Res. **16**(1), 1437–1480 (2015)
9. Geffner, H., Bonet, B.: A concise introduction to models and methods for automated planning. Synthesis Lect. Artif. Intell. Mach. Learn. **8**(1), 1–141 (2013)
10. Howard, R.A., Matheson, J.E.: Risk-sensitive Markov decision processes. Manage. Sci. **18**(7), 356–369 (1972)
11. Jaquette, S.C.: A utility criterion for Markov decision processes. Manage. Sci. **23**(1), 43–49 (1976)
12. Mihatsch, O., Neuneier, R.: Risk-sensitive reinforcement learning. Mach. Learn. **49**(2), 267–290 (2002)
13. Minami, R., da Silva, V.F.: Shortest stochastic path with risk sensitive evaluation. In: Batyrshin, I., González Mendoza, M. (eds.) MICAI 2012. LNCS (LNAI), vol. 7629, pp. 371–382. Springer, Heidelberg (2013). https://doi.org/10.1007/978-3-642-37807-2_32
14. Patek, S.D.: On terminating Markov decision processes with a risk-averse objective function. Automatica **37**(9), 1379–1386 (2001)
15. Puterman, M.L.: Markov Decision Processes: Discrete Stochastic Dynamic Programming, 1st edn. Wiley, New York (1994)
16. Rothblum, U.G.: Multiplicative Markov decision chains. Math. Oper. Res. **9**(1), 6–24 (1984)
17. Shen, Y., Tobia, M.J., Sommer, T., Obermayer, K.: Risk-sensitive reinforcement learning. Neural Comput. **26**(7), 1298–1328 (2014)
18. Sobel, M.J.: The variance of discounted Markov decision processes. J. Appl. Probab. **19**(4), 794–802 (1982)
19. Sutton, R., Barto, A.: Reinforcement Learning: An Introduction, vol. 116. Cambridge University Press, Cambridge (1998)

Why Majority Rule Does Not Work in Quantum Computing: A Pedagogical Explanation

Oscar Galindo, Olga Kosheleva⊙, and Vladik Kreinovich⁽✉⁾⊙

University of Texas at El Paso, El Paso, TX 79968, USA
ogalindomo@miners.utep.edu, {olgak,vladik}@utep.edu

Abstract. To increase the reliability of computations result, a natural idea is to use duplication: we let several computers independently perform the same computations, and then, if their results differ, we select the majority's result. Reliability is an important issue for quantum computing as well, since in quantum physics, all the processes are probabilistic, so there is always a probability that the result will be wrong. It thus seems natural to use the same majority rule for quantum computing as well. However, it is known that for general quantum computing, this scheme does not work. In this paper, we provide a simplified explanation of this impossibility.

Keywords: Quantum computing · Reliable computing · Majority rule · Duplication

1 Need for Increasing Reliability of Quantum Computing Results

Quantum computing: a brief introduction. In spite of the tremendous computational speed of modern computers, for many important practical problems, it is still not possible to solve them in reasonable time. For example, in principle, we can use computer simulations to find which biochemical compound can block a virus, but even on the existing high-performance computers, this would take thousands of years.

It is therefore desirable to design faster computers. One of the main obstacles to this design is the speed of light: according to relativity theory, no physical process can be faster than a speed of light, and on a usual 30-cm-size laptop, light takes 1 nanosecond to go from one side to another – the time during which even the cheapest laptop can perform four operations. Thus, the only way to speed up computations is to further shrink computers – and therefore, to shrink their elements.

Already an element of the computer consists of a few hundred or thousand molecules, so if we shrink it even more, we will get to the level of individual

© Springer Nature Switzerland AG 2020
L. Martínez-Villaseñor et al. (Eds.): MICAI 2020, LNAI 12468, pp. 396–401, 2020.
https://doi.org/10.1007/978-3-030-60884-2_29

molecules, the level at which we need to take into account quantum physics – the physics of the micro-world.

Computations on this level are known as *quantum computing*.

Quantum computing: challenges and successes. One of the main features of quantum physics is that:

- in contrast to Newtonian mechanics, where we can, e.g.., predict the motions of celestial bodies hundreds of years ahead,
- in quantum physics, only probabilistic predictions are possible.

This is a major challenge for quantum computing; see, e.g., [1,3].

In spite of this challenge, several algorithms were invented that produce the results with probability close to 1 – and even produce them much faster than all known non-quantum algorithms; see, e.g., [2]. For example:

- Grover's quantum algorithm can find an element in an unsorted n-element array in time proportional to $\sqrt{n}$, while
- the fastest possible non-quantum algorithm needs to look, in the worst case, at all n elements, and thus, requires n computational steps.

An even more impressive speed-up occurs with Shor's algorithm for factoring large numbers:

- this algorithm requires time bounded by a polynomial of the number's length, while
- all known non-quantum algorithms requires exponential time.

This is very important since most existing computer security techniques are based on the difficulty of factoring large numbers.

Still, reliability is a problem for quantum computing. In the ideal case, when all quantum operations are performed exactly, we get correct results with probability practically indistinguishable from 1. In reality, however, operations can only be implemented with some accuracy, as a result of which the probability of an incorrect answer becomes non-negligible.

How can we increase the reliability of quantum computations?

2   Majority Rule – A Usual Way to Increase Reliability of Non-Quantum Computations

Duplication: a natural idea. If there is a probability that a pen will not work when needed, a natural idea is to carry two pens. If there is a probability that a computer on board of a spacecraft will malfunction, a natural idea is to have two computers. If there is a probability that a hardware problem will cause data to be lost, a natural idea is to have a backup – or, better yet, two (or more) backups, to make the probability of losing the data truly negligible.

Similarly, for usual (non-quantum) algorithms, a natural way to increase their reliability is to have several computers performing the same computations.

Then, if the results are different, we select the result of the majority – this way, we increase the probability of having a correct result.

Indeed, suppose, e.g., that we use three computers independently working in parallel, and for each of then, the probability of malfunctioning is some small (but not negligible) value p. Then, since the computers are independent, the probability that all three of them malfunction is equal to p^3, and for each two of them, the probability that these two malfunction and the remaining one perform correctly is equal to $p^2 \cdot (1 - p)$. There are three possible pairs, so the overall probability that this majority scheme will produce a wrong result is equal to $3p^2 \cdot (1 - p) + p^3$, which for small p is much much smaller than the probability p that a single computer will malfunction.

In principle, we can use the same idea for quantum computing. Nothing prevents us from having three independent quantum computers working in parallel: this will similarly decrease the probability of malfunctioning and thus, increase the reliability of the corresponding computations.

But what if the desired computation result is quantum? The majority rule works when the desired result is non-quantum, as in the above-mentioned quantum algorithms. Sometimes, however, the desired result is itself quantum – e.g., in quantum cryptography algorithms; see, e.g., [2]. Will a similar idea work?

What we do in this paper. It is known that for computations with purely quantum results, the majority rule does not work. The usual arguments why it does not work refer to rather complex results.

In this paper, we provide a simple pedagogical explanation for this fact – OK, as simple as it is possible when we talk about quantum computing.

Comment. To provide our explanation, we need to remind the readers the main specifics of quantum physics and quantum computing.

3 Specifics of Quantum Physics and Quantum Computing: A Brief Reminder

Quantum states. One of the specifics of quantum physics is that, in addition to non-quantum states $s_1, \ldots, s_n$, we can also have *superpositions* of these states, i.e., states of the type $a_1 \cdot s_1 + \ldots + a_n \cdot s_n$, where a_i are complex numbers for which $|a_1|^2 + \ldots + |a_n|^2 = 1$; see, e.g., [1,3].

If some physical quantity has value v_i on each state s_i, then, if we measure this quantity in the superposition state, we get each value v_i with probability $|a_i|^2$. These probabilities have to add to 1 – which explains the above constraint on possible values of a_i.

In particular, for a 1-bit system, in addition to the usual states 0 and 1 – which in quantum physics are usually denoted by $|0\rangle$ and $|1\rangle$ – we can also have superpositions $a_0|0\rangle + a_1|1\rangle$, with $|a_0|^2 + |a_1|^2 = 1$.

Similarly, for 2-bit systems, which in non-quantum case can be in four possible states: 00, 01, 10, and 11 – in the quantum case, we can have general superpositions

$$a_{00}|00\rangle + a_{01}|01\rangle + a_{10}|10\rangle + a_{11}|11\rangle,$$

where

$$|a_{00}|^2 + |a_{01}|^2 + |a_{10}|^2 + |a_{11}|^2 = 1.$$

Transitions between quantum states. One of the specifics of quantum physics is that all the transitions preserve superpositions: if the original state s has the form $a_1 \cdot s_1 + \ldots + a_n \cdot s_n$, and then each s_i is transformed into some state s_i', then the state s gets transformed into a similar superposition $a_1 \cdot s_1' + \ldots + a_n \cdot s_n'$.

In other words, transformations are *linear* in terms of the coefficients a_i.

States of several independent particles. Linearity applies also to describing the joint state of several independent particles.

For example, for two 1-bit systems, if the first system is in the state $|0\rangle$ and the second in the state $|0\rangle$, then the 2-bit system is in the state $|00\rangle$.

Similarly, if the first system is in the state $|1\rangle$ and the second system is in the state $|0\rangle$, then the 2-bit system is in the state $|10\rangle$.

Thus, if the first system is in the superposition state $a_0|0\rangle + a_1|1\rangle$ and the second is in the state $|0\rangle$, then the joint state of these two 1-bit systems is the corresponding superposition of the states $|00\rangle$ and $|10\rangle$, i.e., the state

$$a_0|00\rangle + a_1|10\rangle.$$

Similarly, if the first system is in the state $a_0|0\rangle + a_1|1\rangle$ and the second system is in the state $|1\rangle$, then the joint state of these two 1-bit system is the corresponding superposition of the states $|01\rangle$ and $|11\rangle$, i.e., the state

$$a_0|01\rangle + a_1|11\rangle.$$

What if the second system is also in the superposition state $b_0|0\rangle + b_1|1\rangle$? The resulting joint state is the similar superposition of the $a_0|00\rangle + a_1|10\rangle$ and $a_0|01\rangle + a_1|11\rangle$, i.e., the state

$$b_0 \cdot (a_0|00\rangle + a_1|10\rangle) + b_1 \cdot (a_0|01\rangle + a_1|11\rangle).$$

If we open parentheses, we get the state

$$(a_0 \cdot b_0)|00\rangle + (a_0 \cdot b_1)|01\rangle + (a_1 \cdot b_0)|10\rangle + (a_1 \cdot b_1)|11\rangle.$$

This state is called the *tensor product* of the original states $a_0|0\rangle + a_1|1\rangle$ and $b_0|0\rangle + b_1|1\rangle$; it is usually denoted by

$$(a_0|0\rangle + a_1|1\rangle) \otimes (b_0|0\rangle + b_1|1\rangle).$$

What we will do. Let us use these specifics to explain why the majority rule cannot work for quantum computing when the result of the computation is a general quantum state – i.e., a general superposition.

4 Why the Majority Rule Does Not Work: Our Explanation

What would a majority rule mean. Suppose that we have three different systems in states s_1, s_2, and s_3. Based on these three states, we want to come up with the state in which, if two of three original states coincide, the resulting state of the first system will be equal to this coinciding state.

Examples. If we consider three 1-bit systems, then, e.g., the original joint state $|001\rangle$ should convert into a state $|0\ldots\rangle$ in which the first 1-bit system is in the 0 state. Similarly:

- the original states $|000\rangle$, $|010\rangle$, and $|100\rangle$ should convert into states of the type $|0\ldots\rangle$, and
- the original states $|111\rangle$, $|011\rangle$, $|101\rangle$, and $|110\rangle$ should convert into states of the type $|1\ldots\rangle$.

Similarly, if the first two systems are originally both in the same state

$$c|0\rangle + c|1\rangle,$$

where $c \overset{\text{def}}{=} \dfrac{1}{\sqrt{2}}$, and the third system is originally in the state $|1\rangle$, then the resulting state of the first system should be $c|0\rangle + c|1\rangle$.

In this case, if we measure the resulting state of the first system, we will get both 0 and 1 with the same probability $|c|^2 = \dfrac{1}{2}$.

Let us show why all this is impossible. In the last example, the joint state of the three systems is equal to

$$(c|0\rangle + c|1\rangle) \otimes (c|0\rangle + c|1\rangle) \otimes |1\rangle =$$

$$\frac{1}{2}|001\rangle + \frac{1}{2}|011\rangle + \frac{1}{2}|101\rangle + \frac{1}{2}|111\rangle.$$

We know that the state $|001\rangle$ gets converted into a state $|0\ldots\rangle$, and each of the states $|011\rangle$, $|101\rangle$, and $|111\rangle$ gets converted into a state of the type $|1\ldots\rangle$.

Thus, due to linearity, the original state gets transformed into a new state

$$\frac{1}{2}|0\ldots\rangle + \frac{1}{2}|1\ldots\rangle + \frac{1}{2}|1\ldots\rangle + \frac{1}{2}|1\ldots\rangle.$$

So, in the resulting state, the probability that after measuring the first bit, we get 0 is equal to

$$\left|\frac{1}{2}\right|^2 = \frac{1}{4},$$

but, as we have mentioned earlier, the majority rule requires that this probability be equal to $\dfrac{1}{2}$.

Thus, the majority rule cannot be implemented for quantum states.

Discussion. We showed that we cannot have majority rule for *all* possible quantum states, but maybe we can have it for *some* quantum states? A simple modification of the above argument shows that it is not possible.

Indeed, suppose that the majority rule is possible for some quantum state $a_0|0\rangle + a_1|1\rangle$, where $a_0 \neq 0$, $a_1 \neq 0$, and $|a_0|^2 + |a_1|^2 = 1$. Then, if two systems are in this state and the third 1-bit system is in the state $|1\rangle$, the majority rule would mean that in the resulting state, the first system will be in the same state $a_0|0\rangle + a_1|1\rangle$. Thus, the probability that measurement will find the first system in the state 0 is equal to $|a_0|^2$.

On the other hand, here, the original joint state of the three systems has the form

$$(a_0|0\rangle + a_1|1\rangle) \otimes (a_0|0\rangle + a_1|1\rangle) \otimes |1\rangle =$$
$$a_0^2|001\rangle + (a_0 \cdot a_1)|011\rangle + (a_0 \cdot a_1)|101\rangle + a_1^2|111\rangle.$$

Thus, this state gets transformed into

$$a_0^2|0\ldots\rangle + (a_0 \cdot a_1)|1\ldots\rangle + (a_0 \cdot a_1)|1\ldots\rangle + a_1^2|1\ldots\rangle.$$

For this state, the probability that the measurement will find the first system in the state 0 is equal to $\left|a_0^2\right|^2 = |a_0|^4$.

The only case when these two values coincide, i.e., when $|a_0|^2 = |a_0|^4$, is when $|a_0|^2 = 0$ or $|a_0|^2 = 1$.

- In the first case, we have $a_0 = 0$ but we assumed that $a_0 \neq 0$.
- In the second case, due to the general constraint $|a_0|^2 + |a_1|^2 = 1$, we have $|a_1|^2 = 1 - |a_0|^2 = 0$, hence $a_1 = 0$, but we assumed that $a_1 \neq 0$.

So, the majority rule is not possible for *any* properly quantum state – i.e., for any quantum state which is different from the original non-quantum states 0 and 1.

Acknowledgments. This work was supported in part by the US National Science Foundation grants 1623190 (A Model of Change for Preparing a New Generation for Professional Practice in Computer Science) and HRD-1242122 (Cyber-ShARE Center of Excellence).

References

1. Feynman, R., Leighton, R., Sands, M.: The Feynman Lectures on Physics. Addison Wesley, Boston, Massachusetts (2005)
2. Nielsen, M.A., Chuang, I.L.: Quantum Computation and Quantum Information. Cambridge University Press, Cambridge, U.K. (2000)
3. Thorne, K.S., Blandford, R.D.: Modern Classical Physics: Optics, Fluids, Plasmas, Elasticity, Relativity, and Statistical Physics. Princeton University Press, Princeton, New Jersey (2017)

How to Decide Which Cracks Should Be Repaired First: Theoretical Explanation of Empirical Formulas

Edgar Daniel Rodriguez Velasquez[1,2], Olga Kosheleva[2],
and Vladik Kreinovich[2(✉)]

[1] Universidad de Piura in Peru (UDEP), Piura, Peru
edgar.rodriguez@udep.pe
[2] University of Texas at El Paso, El Paso, TX 79968, USA
edrodriguezvelasquez@miners.utep.edu, {olgak,vladik}@utep.edu

Abstract. Due to stress, cracks appear in constructions: cracks appear in buildings, bridges, pavements, among other structures. In the long run, cracks need to be repaired. However, our resources are limited, so we need to decide which cracks are more dangerous. To make this decision, we need to be able to predict how different cracks will grow. There are several empirical formulas describing crack growth. In this paper, we show that by using scale invariance, we can provide a theoretical explanation for these empirical formulas. The existence of such an explanation makes us confident that the existing empirical formulas can (and should) be used in the design of the corresponding automatic decision systems.

Keywords: Decision making · Crack growth · Scale invariance · Empirical formulas

1 Formulation of the Problem

Which cracks should be repaired first? Under stress, cracks appear in constructions. They appear in buildings, they appear in brides, they appear in pavements, they appear in engines, etc. Once a crack appears, it starts growing.

Cracks are potentially dangerous. Cracks in an engine can lead to a catastrophe, cracks in a pavement makes a road more dangerous and prone to accidents, etc. It is therefore desirable to repair the cracks.

In the ideal world, each crack should be repaired as soon as it is noticed. This is indeed done in critical situations – e.g., after each flight, the Space Shuttle was thoroughly studied and all cracks were repaired.

However, in most other (less critical) situations, for example, in pavement engineering, our resources are limited. In such situations, we need to decide which cracks to repair first. A natural idea is to concentrate our efforts on cracks that, if unrepaired, will become most dangerous in the future. For that, we need to be able to predict how each crack will grow, e.g., in the next year.

© Springer Nature Switzerland AG 2020
L. Martínez-Villaseñor et al. (Eds.): MICAI 2020, LNAI 12468, pp. 402–410, 2020.
https://doi.org/10.1007/978-3-030-60884-2_30

Once we are able to predict how the current cracks will grow, we will be able to concentrate our limited repair resources on most potentially harmful cracks.

To make a proper decision, it is desirable to have theoretically justified formulas for crack growth. Crack growth is a very complex problem, it is very difficult to analyze theoretically. So far, first-principle-based computer models have not been very successful in describing crack growth.

Good news is that cracks are ubiquitous. There is a lot of empirical data about the crack growth. Based on this data, researchers have come up with empirical (or sometimes semi-empirical) approximate formulas that describe this available data. In the following text, we will describe the state-of-the-art empirical formulas.

However, purely empirical formulas are not always reliable. There have been many cases when an empirical formula turned out to be true only in limited cases – and false in many others. Even the great Newton naively believed that, since the price of a certain stock was growing exponentially for some time, it will continue growing – so he invested all his money in that stock and lost almost everything when the bubble collapsed.

From this viewpoint, and taking into account that missing a potentially dangerous crack can be catastrophic, it is desirable to have theoretically justified formulas for crack growth. This is what we do in this paper: we provide theoretical explanations for the existing empirical formulas.

With this goal in mind, let us recall the main empirical formulas for crack growth.

How cracks grow: a general description. In most cases, stress comes in cycles: the engine clearly goes through the cycles, the road segment gets stressed when a vehicle passes through it, etc. Thus, the crack growth is usually expressed by describing how the length a of the pavement changes during a stress cycle at which the stress is equal to some value σ. The increase in length is usually denoted by Δa. So, to describe how a crack grows, we need to find out how Δa depends on a and σ:

$$\Delta a = f(a, \sigma), \tag{1}$$

for some function $f(a, \sigma)$.

Case of very short cracks. The first empirical formula – known as Wöhler law – was proposed to describe how cracks appear. In the beginning, the length a is 0 (or very small), so the dependence on a can be ignored, and we have

$$\Delta a = f(\sigma), \tag{2}$$

for some function $f(\sigma)$. Empirical data shows that this dependence is a power law, i.e., that

$$\Delta a = C_0 \cdot \sigma^{m_0}, \tag{3}$$

for some constants C_0 and m_0.

Practical case of reasonable size cracks: Paris law. Very small cracks are extremely important in critical situations: since there, the goal is to prevent the cracks from growing. In most other practical situations, small cracks are usually allowed to grow, so the question is how cracks of reasonable size grow.

Several empirical formulas have been proposed. In 1963, P. C. Paris and F. Erdogan compared all these formulas with empirical data, and came up with a new empirical formula that best fits the data [7]:

$$\Delta a = C \cdot \sigma^m \cdot a^{m'}. \tag{4}$$

This formula – known as *Paris Law* or *Paris-Erdogan Law* – is still in use; see, e.g., [3,6].

Usual case of Paris law. Usually, we have $m' = m/2$, in which case the formula (4) takes the form

$$\Delta a = C \cdot \sigma^m \cdot a^{m/2} = C \cdot (\sigma \cdot \sqrt{a})^m. \tag{5}$$

The formula (4) is empirical, but the dependence $m' = m/2$ has theoretical explanations. One of such explanations is that the stress acts randomly at different parts of the crack. According to statistics, the standard deviation s of the sum of n independent variables each of which has standard deviation s_0 is equal to $s = s_0 \cdot \sqrt{n}$; see, e.g., [10]. So, on average, the effect of n independent factors is proportional to $\sqrt{n}$. Thus, for a crack of length a, consisting of a/δ_a independent parts, the overall effect K of the stress σ is proportional to

$$K = \sigma \cdot \sqrt{n} \sim \sigma \cdot \sqrt{a}. \tag{6}$$

This quantity K is known as *stress intensity*. For the power law

$$\Delta a = C \cdot K^m, \tag{4a}$$

this indeed leads to

$$\Delta a = \text{const} \cdot (\sigma \cdot \sqrt{a})^m = \text{const} \cdot \sigma^m \cdot a^{m/2}, \tag{7}$$

i.e., to $m' = m/2$.

Empirical dependence between C and m. In principle, we can have all possible combinations of C and m. Empirically, however, there is a relation between C and m:

$$C = c_0 \cdot b_0^m; \tag{8}$$

see, e.g., [4,5] and references therein.

Beyond Paris law. As we have mentioned, Paris law is only valid for reasonably large crack lengths a. It cannot be valid for $a = 0$, since for $a = 0$, it implies that $\Delta a = 0$ and thus, that cracks cannot appear by themselves – but they do. To describe the dependence (1) for all possible values a, the paper [2] proposed to use the expression (4) with different values of C, m, and m' for different ranges of a. This worked OK, but not perfectly.

The best empirical fit came from the generalization of Paris law proposed in [8]:

$$\Delta a = C \cdot \sigma^m \cdot \left(a^\alpha + c \cdot \sigma^\beta\right)^\gamma. \qquad (9)$$

Empirically, we have $\alpha \approx 1$.

What we do in this paper. In this paper, we provide a theoretical explanation for the empirical formulas (3), (4), and (8), and (9). Our explanations use the general ideas of scale-invariance, ideas very similar to the ideas used in [4] to explain Paris law.

The existence of theoretical explanations makes us confident that the current empirical formulas can (and should) be used in the design of the corresponding automatic decision systems.

2   Scale Invariance: A Brief Reminder

Scale invariance: main idea. In general, we want to find the dependence $y = f(x)$ of one physical quantity on another one – e.g., for short cracks, the dependence of crack growth on stress. When we analyze the data, we deal with numerical values of these quantities, and numerical values depend on the selection of the measuring unit. For example, if we measure crack length in centimeters, we get numerical values which are 2.54 times larger than if we use inches. In general, if we replace the original measuring unit with a new unit which is λ times smaller, all the numerical values get multiplied by λ: instead of the original value x, we get a new value $x' = \lambda \cdot x$.

In many physical situations, there is no preferred measuring unit. In such situations, it makes sense to require that the dependence $y = f(x)$ remain valid in all possible units. Of course, if we change a unit for x, then we need to appropriately change the unit for y. So the corresponding *scale invariance* requirement takes the following form: for every $\lambda > 0$, there exists a value $\mu(\lambda)$ depending on λ such that, if we have

$$y = f(x), \qquad (10)$$

then in the new units

$$y' = \mu(\lambda) \cdot y \qquad (11)$$

and

$$x' = \lambda \cdot x, \qquad (12)$$

we should have

$$y' = f(x'). \qquad (13)$$

Similarly, for the dependence $y = f(x_1, \ldots, x_v)$ on several quantities $x_1, \ldots, x_v$, we should similarly require that for all possible tuples $(\lambda_1, \ldots, \lambda_v)$, there should exist a value $\mu(\lambda_1, \ldots, \lambda_v)$ such that if we have

$$y = f(x_1, \ldots, x_v), \qquad (14)$$

then in the new units

$$x'_i = \lambda_i \cdot x_i \tag{15}$$

and

$$y' = \mu(\lambda_1, \ldots, \lambda_v) \cdot y, \tag{16}$$

we should have

$$y' = f(x'_1, \ldots, x'_v). \tag{17}$$

Which dependencies are scale invariant. For a single variable, if we plug in the expressions (11) and (12) into the formula (13), we get

$$\mu(\lambda) \cdot y = f(\lambda \cdot x). \tag{18}$$

If we now plug in the expression for y from formula (10) into this formula, we will conclude that

$$\mu(\lambda) \cdot f(x) = f(\lambda \cdot x). \tag{19}$$

It is known (see, e.g., [1]) that every measurable solution to this functional equation has the form

$$y = C \cdot x^m, \tag{20}$$

i.e., the form of a power law.

Similarly, for functions of several variables, if we plug in the expressions (15) and (16) into the formula (17), we get

$$\mu(\lambda_1, \ldots, \lambda_v) \cdot y = f(\lambda_1 \cdot x_1, \ldots, \lambda_v \cdot x_v). \tag{21}$$

If we now plug in the expression for y from formula (14) into this formula, we will conclude that

$$\mu(\lambda_1, \ldots, \lambda_v) \cdot f(x) = f(\lambda_1 \cdot x_1, \ldots, \lambda_v \cdot x_v). \tag{22}$$

It is known (see, e.g., [1]) that every measurable solution to this functional equation has the form

$$y = C \cdot x_1^{m_1} \cdot \ldots \cdot x_n^{m_n}. \tag{23}$$

3   Scale Invariance Explains Wöhler Law and Paris Law

How can we use scale invariance here? It would be nice to apply scale invariance to crack growth. However, we cannot directly use it: indeed, in the above arguments, we assumed that y and x_i are different quantities, measured by different units, but in our case Δa and a are both lengths. What can we do?

To apply scale invariance, we can recall that in all applications, stress is periodic: for an engine, we know how many cycles per minute we have, and for a road, we also know, on average, how many cars pass through the give road segment. In both cases, what we are really interested in is how much the crack will grow during some time interval – e.g., whether the road segment needs repairs right now or it can wait until the next year. Thus, what we are really interested in is not the value Δa, but the value $\dfrac{da}{dt}$ which can be obtained by multiplying Δa and the number of cycles per selected time unit.

Since the quantities $\dfrac{da}{dt}$ and Δa differ by a multiplicative constant, they follow the same laws as Δa – but for $\dfrac{da}{dt}$, we already have different measuring units and thus, we can apply scale invariance.

So, let us apply scale invariance. For the case of one variable, scale invariance leads to the formula (20), which explains Wöhler law.

For the case of several variables we similarly get the formula (23), which explains Paris law (4).

Thus, both Wöhler and Paris laws can indeed be theoretically explained – by scale invariance.

4   Scale Invariance Explains How C Depends on m

Idea. Let us show that scale invariance can also the explain the dependence (8) between the parameters C and m of the Paris law (4a).

Indeed, the fact that the coefficients C and m describing the Paris law are different for different materials means that, to determine how a specific crack will grow, it is not sufficient to know its stress intensity K, there must be some other characteristic z on which Δa depends:

$$\Delta a = f(K, z). \tag{24}$$

Let us apply scale invariance. If we apply scale invariance to the dependence of Δa on K, then we can conclude that this dependence is described by a power law, i.e., that

$$\Delta a(K, z) = C(z) \cdot K^{m(z)}, \tag{25}$$

where, in general, the coefficients $C(z)$ and $m(z)$ may depend on z. It is well known that if we go to log-log scale, i.e., consider the dependence of $\ln(\Delta a)$ on $\ln(K)$, then the dependence becomes linear. Indeed, if we take logarithms of both sides of the equality (25), we conclude that

$$\ln(\Delta a(K, z)) = m(z) \cdot \ln(K) + \ln(C(z)). \tag{26}$$

Similarly, if we apply scale invariance to the dependence of Δa on z, we also get a power law

$$\Delta a(K, z) = C'(K) \cdot z^{m'(K)} \tag{27}$$

for some values $C'(K)$ and $m'(K)$, i.e., in log-log scale,

$$\ln(\Delta a(K, z)) = m'(K) \cdot \ln(z) + \ln(C'(k)). \tag{28}$$

The logarithm $\ln(\Delta a(K, z))$ in linear in $\ln(K)$ and linear in $\ln(z)$, thus it is a bilinear function of $\ln(K)$ and $\ln(z)$. A general bilinear function has the form:

$$\ln(\Delta a(K, z)) = a_0 + a_K \cdot \ln(K) + a_z \cdot \ln(z) + a_{Kz} \cdot \ln(K) \cdot \ln(z), \qquad (29)$$

i.e., the form

$$\ln(\Delta a(K, z)) = (a_0 + a_z \cdot \ln(z)) + (a_K + a_{Kz} \cdot \ln(z)) \cdot \ln(K). \qquad (30)$$

By applying $\exp(t)$ to both sides of the formula (30), we conclude that the dependence of Δa on K has the form

$$\Delta a = C \cdot K^m, \qquad (31)$$

where

$$C = \exp(a_0 + a_z \cdot \ln(z)) \qquad (32)$$

and

$$m = a_K + a_{Kz} \cdot \ln(z). \qquad (33)$$

From (33), we conclude that $\ln(z)$ is a linear function of m, namely, that

$$\ln(z) = \frac{1}{a_{Kz}} \cdot m - \frac{a_K}{a_{Kz}}. \qquad (34)$$

Substituting this expression for $\ln(z)$ into the formula (32), we can conclude that

$$C = \exp\left(\left(a_0 - \frac{a_K \cdot a_z}{a_{Kz}}\right) + \frac{a_z}{a_{Kz}} \cdot m\right), \qquad (35)$$

i.e., the desired formula (8), $C = c_0 \cdot b_0^m$, with

$$c_0 = \exp\left(a_0 - \frac{a_K \cdot a_z}{a_{Kz}}\right) \qquad (36)$$

and

$$b_0 = \exp\left(\frac{a_z}{a_{Kz}}\right). \qquad (37)$$

Thus, the empirical dependence (8) of C on m can also be explained by scale invariance.

5   Scale Invariance Explains Generalized Paris Law

Analysis of the problem. Let us show that scale invariance can also explain the generalized Paris law (9).

So far, we have justified two laws: Wöhler law (3) that describes how cracks appear and start growing, and Paris law (4) that describes how they grow once they reach a certain size. In effect, these two laws describe two different mechanisms for crack growth. To describe the joint effect of these two mechanisms, we need to combine the effects of both mechanisms.

How can we combine the two formulas? If the effect of the first mechanism is denoted by q_1 and the effect of the second one by q_2, then a natural way to combine them is to consider some function

$$q = F(q_1, q_2). \tag{38}$$

What should be the properties of this combination function?

If one the effects is missing, then the overall effect should coincide with the other effect, so we should have $F(0, q_2) = q_2$ and $F(q_1, 0) = q_1$ for all q_1 and q_2.

If we combine two effects, it should not matter in what order we consider them, i.e., we should have

$$F(q_1, q_2) = F(q_2, q_1) \tag{39}$$

for all q_1 and q_2. In mathematical terms, the combination operation $F(q_1, q_2)$ should be *commutative*.

Similarly, if we combine three effects, the result should not depend on the order in which we combine them, i.e., that we should have

$$F(F(q_1, q_1), q_3) = F(q_1, F(q_2, q_3)) \tag{40}$$

for all q_1, q_1, and q_3. In mathematical terms, the combination operation $F(q_1, q_2)$ should be *associative*.

It is also reasonable to require that if we increase one of the effects, then the overall effect will increase, i.e., that the function $F(q_1, q_2)$ should be *strictly monotonic* in each of the variables: if $q_1 < q_1'$, then we should have

$$F(q_1, q_2) < F(q_1', q_2).$$

It is also reasonable to require that small changes to q_i should lead to small changes in the overall effect, i.e., that the function $F(q_1, q_2)$ should be *continuous*.

Finally, it is reasonable to require that the operation $F(q_1, q_2)$ be *scale invariant* in the following sense: if $q = F(q_1, q_2)$, then for every $\lambda > 0$, if we take $q_i' = \lambda \cdot q_i$ and $q' = \lambda \cdot q$, then we should have $q' = F(q_1', q_2')$.

What are the resulting combination functions. It is known – see, e.g., [9] – that every commutative, associative, strictly monotonic, continuous, and scale invariant combination operation for which $F(q_1, 0) = q_1$ has the form

$$F(q_1, q_2) = (q_1^p + q_2^p)^{1/p} \tag{41}$$

for some $p > 0$.

This explains the generalized Paris law. Indeed, if we substitute the expression (3) instead of q_1 and the expression (4) instead of q_2 into the formula (41), we get

$$\Delta a = \left((C_0 \cdot \sigma^{m_0})^p + \left(C \cdot \sigma^m \cdot a^{m'} \right)^p \right)^{1/p} =$$
$$\left(C_0^p \cdot \sigma^{m_0 \cdot p} + C^p \cdot \sigma^{m \cdot p} \cdot a^{m' \cdot p} \right)^{1/p} =$$
$$C \cdot \sigma^m \cdot \left(a^{m' \cdot p} + \left(\frac{C_0}{C} \right)^p \cdot \sigma^{(m - m_0) \cdot p} \right)^{1/p}, \tag{42}$$

i.e., we get the desired formula (9), with $\alpha = m' \cdot p$, $c = \left(\dfrac{C_0}{C} \right)^p$, $\beta = (m - m_0) \cdot p$, and $\gamma = 1/p$.

Thus, the generalized Paris law can also be explained by scale invariance.

Acknowledgments. This work was supported in part by the US National Science Foundation grants 1623190 (A Model of Change for Preparing a New Generation for Professional Practice in Computer Science) and HRD-1242122 (Cyber-ShARE Center of Excellence).

The authors are greatly thankful to Ildar Batyrshin for his encouragement and to the anonymous referees for their useful suggestions.

References

1. Aczel, J., Dhombres, J.: Functional Equations in Several Variables. Cambridge University Press, Cambridge, UK (2008)
2. Bigerelle, M., Iost, A.: Bootstrap analysis of FCGR, application to the Paris relationship and to lifetime prediction. Int. J. Fatigue **21**, 299–307 (1999)
3. Broek, D.: Elementary Engineering Fracture Mechanics. Martinus Lojhoff Publishers, The Hague, The Netherlands (1984)
4. Carpinteri, A., Paggi, M.: Self-similarity and crack growth instability in the correlation between the Paris' constants. Eng. Fract. Mech. **74**, 1041–1053 (2007)
5. Cortie, M.B., Garrett, G.G.: On the correlation between the C and m in the Paris equation for fatigue crack propagation. J. Eng. Fract. Mech. **30**(1), 49–58 (1988)
6. Little, D., Allen, D., Bhasin, A.: Modeling and Design of Flexible Pavements and Materials. Springer, Cham, Switzerland (2018)
7. Paris, P.S., Erdogan, F.: A critical analysis of crack propagation laws. J. Basic Eng. **85**(4), 528–534 (1963)
8. Pugno, N., Ciavarella, M., Cornetti, P., Carpinteri, A.: A generalized Paris' law for fatigue crack growth. J. Mech. Phys. Solids **54**, 1333–1349 (2006)
9. Rodriguez Velasquez, E.D., Kreinovich, V., Kosheleva, O., Hoang Phuong, N.: How to Estimate the Stiffness of the Multi-Layer Road Based on Properties of Layers: Symmetry-Based Explanation for Odemark's Equation, University of Texas at El Paso, Department of Computer Science, Technical Report UTEP-CS-20-49 (2020) http://www.cs.utep.edu/vladik/2020/tr20-49.pdf
10. Sheskin, D.E.: Handbook of Parametric and Non-Parametric Statistical Procedures. Chapman & Hall/CRC, London, UK (2011)

How Powersets of Individual Fuzzy Sets Can Be Defined?

Jiří Močkoř[(⊠)]

Centre of Excellence IT4Innovations, Institute for Research and Applications of Fuzzy
Modeling, University of Ostrava, 30. dubna 22, 701 03 Ostrava 1, Czech Republic
jiri.mockor@osu.cz

Abstract. Zadeh's powerset structure of a crisp set consists of all fuzzy
sets defined in this set. The categorical properties of this powerset structure are generally known, and the related Zadeh extension principle
represents a functor from the category of crisp sets to the category of
complete sup-semilattices, with a wide range of applications. Since the
individual fuzzy set is perceived as a generalization of a crisp set, the
natural question arises as to whether the powerset structure of an individual fuzzy set can be defined, which would be analogous to Zadeh's
powerset structure. In the paper two examples of powerset structures
in the category of individual objects from categorically defined powerset
structures are introduced. These powerset structures generalize classical
Zadeh's powerset structures and functors corresponding these powerset
structures represent generalizations of Zadeh's extension principle for
subobjects of individual fuzzy sets.

Keywords: Powerset structure in a category · Category of individual
fuzzy-type objects · Residuated lattice

1 Introduction

The powerset structures defined for various objects are widely used in many
branches of theoretical mathematics and applications, including algebra, logic,
topology and computer science. Zadeh's extension principle is one of the crucial
tools for application of fuzzy sets in all areas. The classical example of a powerset
structure in a theory of sets is the operator $P(X) = \{A : A \subseteq X\}$ with extensions
of mappings $X \to Y$ to the mappings $P(X) \to P(Y)$, which is used in many
areas of mathematics and computer science. The powerset structure $Z(X)$ for
fuzzy sets in a set X was introduced by Zadeh [12], where the powerset object
was defined as the set of all fuzzy sets in a set X with the extension of mappings
$X \to Y$ to the maps $Z(X) \to Z(Y)$, called the Zadeh's extension maps [12].

Zadeh's extension soon proved to be one of the most widely used tools in
fuzzy sets theory and applications, including computer science, e.g., [1,2,11].

This research was partially supported by the project 18-06915S provided by the Grant
Agency of the Czech Republic.

© Springer Nature Switzerland AG 2020
L. Martínez-Villaseñor et al. (Eds.): MICAI 2020, LNAI 12468, pp. 411–422, 2020.
https://doi.org/10.1007/978-3-030-60884-2_31

Theoretical background of Zadeh's extension was intensively studied by Rod-abaugh in [6], especially the relation between classical powerset extension P and extension Z. Soon the new approach to the powerset structures were investigated in the general environment of the category theory [3–5,10].

However, if we focus in more detail on the relationship between the powerset structure $P(X)$ of a set X and the powerset structure $Z(X)$ of the same set, we must notice that we actually skipped one significant structure when creating these powerset structures. *This structure is individual fuzzy set f in a set X.* Although we can understand individual fuzzy sets in X as a generalization of subsets in a set X, we can also interpret them as basic objects of the theory of "generalized" sets, i.e., analogously as we understand crisp sets. It is then natural to deal with the *powerset structures of individual fuzzy sets*, just as we deal with the powerset structures of crisp sets. Unlike the powerset structures $P(X)$ and $Z(X)$, the powerset structure of an individual fuzzy set is somewhat different. Both structures $P(X)$ and $Z(X)$ are sets based on *crisp relationships* between objects, namely $A \in P(X)$ on the crisp inclusion $A \subseteq X$ and $f \in Z(X)$ on the crisp relation "to be an element" of $[0,1]^X$. If we apply this method of defining a powerset structure to an individual fuzzy set f, we would get the set $\{g \in [0,1]^X : g \leq f\}$ as a powerset structure of f. In that case, however, we ignore the fuzzy character of f and exclude from this powerset structure such fuzzy sets g, which can be understood as subobjects in f with at least a degree $\alpha < 1$.

In this paper, we will focus on two theoretical possibilities of how we can define this powerset structure of individual fuzzy sets. However, in order to use these structures for the widest possible range of objects that have a fuzzy character, we will define this theory not only for L-valued fuzzy sets, but for more general elements $f \in T(X)$, where T is a general powerset structure in category $\mathbf{K}$ and X are objects of $\mathbf{K}$. These structures then include not only classical fuzzy sets, but also crisp sets, sets with similarity relations and extensional fuzzy sets.

2   Preliminaries

In this section we repeat basic definitions of powerset theories and we present principal examples of this theory. By a value structure of fuzzy sets we under-stand a complete residuated lattice $L = (L, \vee, \wedge, \otimes, \rightarrow, 0, 1)$, where $\leftrightarrow$ is the bi-residuum defined by $x \leftrightarrow y = (x \rightarrow y) \wedge (y \rightarrow x)$, and by a similarity relation in a set X we understand an L-valued fuzzy relation $\delta : X \times X \rightarrow L$ which is reflexive, symmetric an transitive with respect to an operation $\otimes$. We use also the category $\mathbf{Set}(L)$ of sets with similarity relations as objects and with morphisms $g : (X, \delta) \rightarrow (Y, \omega)$ defined by a map $g : X \rightarrow Y$ such that $\omega(g(x), g(y)) = \delta(x, y)$ for all $x, y \in X$.

In what follows, by $CSLAT$ we denote the category of complete $\bigvee$-semilattices as objects and with $\bigvee$-preserving maps as morphisms. By $\mathbf{Set}$ we denote the classical category of sets with mappings. Unlike the classical powerset theory defined in [8], we will consider a stronger variant of this theory, which more closely corresponds to powerset structures $P(X)$ and $Z(X)$.

Definition 1. *Let* $\mathbf{K}$ *be a category with a forgetful functor* $\mathbf{K} \to \mathbf{Set}$*. Then* $\mathcal{T} = (T, \eta)$ *is called a* **powerset structure in** $\mathbf{K}$*, if*

1. $T : \mathbf{K} \to CSLAT$ *is a functor,*
2. *For each* $A \in \mathbf{K}$ *there exists a mapping (i.e., a morphism in* $\mathbf{Set}$*)* $\eta_A : A \to T(A)$,
3. *For each* $\mathbf{K}$*-morphism* $f : A \to B$*,* $T(f).\eta_A = \eta_B.f$ *holds, where "." is a composition of* $\mathbf{Set}$*-mappings.*

As examples we consider the following powerset structures. These structures were considered by many authors, e.g., Rodabaugh [6–9], Solovyov [10], Močkoř [3,4].

Example 1. Powerset structure $\mathcal{P} = (P, \eta)$ in the category $\mathbf{Set}$, where

1. $P : \mathbf{Set} \to CSLAT$ is defined by $P(X) = (2^X, \subseteq)$, and for each mapping $f : X \to Y$ in $\mathbf{Set}$, $P(f) : P(X) \to P(Y)$ is defined by $P(S) = f(S)$, $S \in P(X)$,
2. for each $X \in \mathbf{Set}$, $\eta_X : X \to P(X)$ is defined by $\eta_X(x) = \{x\}$.

Example 2. Powerset structure $\mathcal{Z} = (Z, \chi)$ in the category $\mathbf{Set}$, where

1. $Z : \mathbf{Set} \to CSLAT$ is defined by $Z(X) = (L^X, \leq)$, where $\leq$ is a point-wise ordering and for each $f : X \to Y$ in $\mathbf{Set}$, $Z(f) : L^X \to L^Y$ is defined by $Z(f)(s)(y) = \bigvee_{x \in X, f(x) = y} s(x)$,
2. for each $X \in \mathbf{Set}$, $\chi^X : X \to L^X$ is defined by $\chi^X(a) = \chi^X_{\{a\}}$, for $a \in X$.

Example 3. Powerset structure $\mathcal{E} = (E, \rho)$ in the category $\mathbf{Set}(L)$, where

1. $E : \mathbf{Set}(L) \to CSLAT$ is such that $E(X, \delta)$ is the set of all functions $f \in L^X$ extensional with respect to the similarity relation δ, ordered point-wise, and for each morphism $f : (X, \delta) \to (Y, \gamma)$ in $\mathbf{Set}(L)$, $E(f) : E(X, \delta) \to E(Y, \gamma)$ is defined by $E(f)(s)(y) = \bigvee_{x \in X} s(x) \otimes \gamma(f(x), y)$,
2. for each $(X, \delta) \in \mathbf{Set}(L)$, $\rho_{(X,\delta)} : X \to E(X, \delta)$ is defined by $\rho_{(X,\delta)}(a)(x) = \delta(a, x)$, for $a, x \in X$.

3   Powerset Structure of Individual Objects

As we mentioned in the introduction, classical powerset structures in a category $\mathbf{K}$ form complete semilattices of subobjects of a given object X from a category $\mathbf{K}$. This raises the natural question of whether the powerset structure of an individual fuzzy set can also be defined as a complete semi-lattice of "subobjects" of this fuzzy set.

To enable the application of the concept of a powerset structure of a fuzzy set to the largest possible spectrum of objects that have a similar character as fuzzy sets (i.e., classical sets, fuzzy sets in sets with similarity relations or fuzzy sets in soft sets, etc.), the theory of these powerset structures will be defined in a more general environment. For this purpose, instead of L^X, we will use a general powerset structure $\mathcal{T} = (T, \eta)$ in a category $\mathbf{K}$, which will, however, meet some additional properties that are used by default in the L^X structures. For this purpose we introduce the notion of an L-powerset structure in a category.

Definition 2. *Let* **K** *be a category with a forgetful functor* **K** → **Set** *and let* $T = (T, \eta)$ *be a powerset structure in* **K**. *We say that* T *is an L-powerset structure, if*

1. *There exists a* $\bigvee$-*preserving injective natural transformation*

$$T \longrightarrow Z, \quad g \in T(X) \mapsto \overline{g} \in L^X$$

   where Z *is the functor from Example 2,*

2. *For arbitrary* $f \in T(X), x, y \in X$, *the following hold*

$$\overline{f}(x) \leftrightarrow \overline{f}(y) \geq \overline{\eta_X(x)}(y), \quad \overline{\eta_X(x)}(x) = 1_L.$$

It follows that for each object $X \in$ **K** there exists a $\bigvee$-preserving injective mapping $\overline{\{\}} : T(X) \hookrightarrow L^X$ such that for any morphism $u : X \to Y$ in **K**, the following diagram commutes:

$$
\begin{array}{ccc}
T(X) & \xrightarrow{\overline{\{\cdot\}}} & L^X \\
{\scriptstyle T(u)}\downarrow & & \downarrow{\scriptstyle Z(u)} \\
T(Y) & \xrightarrow{\overline{\{\cdot\}}} & L^Y.
\end{array}
\tag{1}
$$

From this diagram it follows that for arbitrary **K**-morphism $u : X \to Y$ and elements $f \in T(X), g \in T(Y)$ we have

$$T(u)(f) = g \Leftrightarrow Z(u)(\overline{f}) = \overline{g}. \tag{2}$$

It is easy to see that powerset structures from Examples 2.1–2.3 are L-powerset structures.

In the following definition we introduce the category $\mathbf{K}_T$ which will be the basic category for powerset structures of individual objects from $T(X)$, where X is an object of **K**. As mentioned in the introduction, the powerset structures that were defined in Definition 2.1, may represent some generalization of classical fuzzy sets, as Examples 2.1–2.3 illustrate. For this reason, it is appropriate to define the powerset structure not only for individual fuzzy sets, but for individual objects from $T(X)$, where (T, η) is a powerset structure in a category **K**.

We use the following notation. Let (T, η) be an L-powerset structure in a category **K** with a forgetful functor **K** → **Set**. For any object $X \in$ **K** and elements $f, g \in T(X)$ we can define an L-valued truth degree $\|g \subseteq f\| \in L$ expressing how true it is that "g is a subobject in f" by

$$\|g \subseteq f\| = \bigwedge_{x \in X} \overline{g}(x) \to \overline{f}(x).$$

Then we obtain the following simple lemma.

Lemma 1. *Let* (T, η) *be an L-powerset structure in a category* **K** *and let* $X \in$ **K**, $f, g \in T(X)$. *Then we have*

$$\|g \subseteq f\| = 1_L \Leftrightarrow g \leq f \text{ in } T(X).$$

Proof. Let $\|g \subseteq f\| = 1_L$. Then $\overline{g}(x) \to \overline{f}(x) = 1_L$ for all $x \in X$ and it follows $\overline{g} \leq \overline{f}$ in L^X. Hence, $\overline{f} = \overline{g} \vee \overline{f} = \overline{g \vee f}$ and for identity **K**-morphism $1_X : X \to X$ we obtain $\overline{g \vee f} = Z(1_X)(\overline{g \vee f}) = \overline{f}$. Therefore, from (2) we receive $g \vee f = T(1_X)(g \vee f) = f$ in $T(X)$ and it follows that $g \leq f$ in $T(X)$. The other implication can be done similarly.

$\square$

Definition 3. *Let* $\mathcal{T} = (T, \eta)$ *be an L-powerset structure in a category* **K** *with a forgetful functor. By* $\mathbf{K}_{\mathcal{T}}$ *we denote the category defined by*

1. *Objects are pairs* (X, f), *where* $f \in T(X)$,
2. *Morphisms* $u : (X, f) \to (Y, g)$ *are* **K**-*morphisms* $u : X \to Y$ *such that* $T(u)(f) = g$ *(or, equivalently,* $\overline{g}.u = \overline{f}$, *as follows from (2))*.
3. *The composition of morphisms in* $\mathbf{K}_{\mathcal{T}}$ *is the same as in the category* **K**.

If $\mathcal{T} = (T, \eta)$ is an L-powerset structure in a category **K**, we define the structure $\mathcal{F} = (F, \xi)$ as follows.

1. For a morphism $u : (X, f) \to (Y, g)$ in $\mathbf{K}_{\mathcal{T}}$, the functor $F : \mathbf{K}_{\mathcal{T}} \to CSLAT$ is defined by

$$F(X, f) = \{w | w : T(X) \to L, w(h) \leq \|h \subseteq f\|, \forall h \in T(X)\},$$
$$F(u) : F(X, f) \to F(Y, g),$$

$$w \in F(X, f), h \in T(Y), \quad F(u)(w)(h) = \bigvee_{t \in T(X), T(u)(t) = h} w(t).$$

2. For $(X, f) \in \mathbf{K}_{\mathcal{T}}$, $\xi_{(X,f)} : X \to F(X, f)$ is defined by

$$t \in T(X), x \in X, \quad \xi_{(X,f)}(x)(t) = \begin{cases} \overline{f}(x), & \text{iff } t = \eta_X(x) \\ 0_L, & \text{otherwise.} \end{cases}$$

We prove that $\mathcal{F}$ is a powerset structure which can be considered as the powerset structure of individual objects from $T(X)$.

Theorem 1. $\mathcal{F} = (F, \xi)$ *is a powerset structure in the category* $\mathbf{K}_{\mathcal{T}}$.

Proof. On the set $F(X, f)$ an ordered relation is defined by $w \leq v$ iff $w(g) \leq v(g)$ for all $g \in T(X)$. Then $F(X, f)$ is a complete $\bigvee$-semilattice. In fact, from $w, v \in F(X, f)$ we obtain $(w \vee v)(h) \leq \|h \subseteq f\|$ for arbitrary $h \in T(X)$ and it follows that $w \vee v \in F(X, f)$.

We prove that $F(u)$ is defined correctly, for arbitrary $\mathbf{K}_{\mathcal{T}}$-morphism $u : (X, f) \to (Y, g)$. Let $w \in F(X, f)$. To prove that $F(u)(w) \in F(Y, g)$, we need to show that $F(u)(w)(h) \leq \|h \subseteq g\|$. Let $t \in T(X)$ be such that $T(u)(t) = h$.

Using the diagram (3) and the properties of a morphism u, we obtain

$$\|h \subseteq g\| = \bigwedge_{y \in Y} \overline{h}(y) \to \overline{g}(y) \geq$$

$$\bigwedge_{y \in Y} \overline{T(u)(t)}(y) \to \overline{g}(y) = \bigwedge_{y \in Y} \overline{Z(u)(\overline{t})} \to \overline{g}(y) =$$

$$\bigwedge_{y \in Y} \overline{(\bigvee_{x \in X, u(x) = y} \overline{t}(x))} \to \overline{g}(y) = \bigwedge_{y \in Y} \bigwedge_{x, u(x) = y} \overline{t}(x) \to \overline{g}.u(x) \geq$$

$$\bigwedge_{x \in X} \overline{t}(x) \to \overline{g}.u(x) = \bigwedge_{x \in X} \overline{t}(x) \to \overline{g}.u(x) =$$

$$\bigwedge_{x \in X} \overline{t}(x) \to \overline{f}(x) = \|t \subseteq f\| \geq w(t).$$

It follows that $F(u)(w)(h) \leq \|h \subseteq g\|$ and $F(u)(w) \in F(Y,g)$. It is easy to see that F is a functor.

Let $(X,f) \in \mathbf{K}_{\mathcal{T}}$. We show first that $\xi_{(X,f)}$ is defined correctly, i.e., $\xi_{(X,f)}(x) \in F(X,f)$. In fact, let $t = \eta_X(x)$. According to the Definition 2.1, from the inequality $\overline{f}(z) \leftrightarrow \overline{f}(x) \geq \overline{\eta_X(x)}(z)$ it follows $\overline{f}(z) \geq \overline{\eta_X(x)}(z) \otimes \overline{f}(x)$, and we obtain

$$\|t \subseteq f\| = \bigwedge_{z \in X} \overline{\eta_X(x)}(z) \to \overline{f}(z) \geq \bigwedge_{z \in X} \overline{\eta_X(x)}(z) \to \overline{\eta_X(x)}(z) \otimes \overline{f}(x) \geq \overline{f}(x).$$

If $t \neq \eta_X(x)$, the proof is trivial.

We prove that for arbitrary morphism $u : (X,f) \to (Y,g)$ in $\mathbf{K}_{\mathcal{T}}$, the diagram

$$
\begin{array}{ccc}
F(X,f) & \xrightarrow{F(u)} & F(Y,g) \\
\xi_{(X,f)} \uparrow & & \uparrow \xi_{(Y,g)} \\
X & \xrightarrow{u} & Y
\end{array}
$$

commutes. In fact, let $x \in X, h \in T(Y)$. Then, we have

$$F(u)(\xi_{(X,f)}(x))(h) = \bigvee_{t \in T(X), T(u)(t) = h} \xi_{(X,f)}(x)(t) =$$

$$\begin{cases} \overline{f}(x), & \text{iff } h = T(u)(\eta_X(x)) \\ 0_L, & \text{otherwise,} \end{cases}$$

$$\xi_{(Y,g)}(u(x))(h) = \begin{cases} \overline{g}(u(x)) = \overline{f}(x), & \text{iff } h = \eta_Y(u(x)) \\ 0_L, & \text{otherwise.} \end{cases}$$

Since $\mathcal{T}$ is an L-powerset structure, we have $T(u).\eta_X(x) = \eta_Y.u(x) = \eta_Y.u(x)$ and the diagram commutes.

Therefore, $\mathcal{F}$ is a powerset structure. □

The powerset structure $F(X,f) \subseteq L^{T(X)}$ represents an analogy of the powerset structure L^X, where elements from $T(X)$ are used instead of X.

Elements from $F(X, f)$ can be interpreted as L-valued fuzzy sets w in a set $T(X)$, whose degrees of membership in elements $g \in T(X)$ do not exceed the value $\|g \subseteq f\|$, describing how much it is true that g is an "subobject" in f.

Let us consider the following illustrative example of objects from powerset structure $F(X, f)$ defined in the category $\mathbf{Set}_{\mathcal{Z}}$.

Example 4. Let L be a Łukasiewicz algebra and let $X \subseteq U \times U$ represent a space of pixels. By an image we then understand a fuzzy set $f : X \to [0, 1]$, where $f(x) \in [0, 1]$ is the grayscale in a pixel $x \in X$ in the image, $f(x) = 0$ represents white color and $f(x) = 1$ represents a black color (simplified).Then $w \in F(X, f)$ is a fuzzy set in a set L^X such that the membership degree $w(g)$ of $g \in L^X$ in w is less or equal than the degree in which g is a sub-fuzzy set in f, i.e., $w(g) \leq \|g \subseteq f\|$. For illustration we present three examples of images (=fuzzy sets in X) f, g and h with different values of sub-fuzzy set degrees (Fig. 1).

It follows that arbitrary powerset object $w \in F(X, f_0)$ has to satisfy the inequalities $w(g_0) \leq 0.6$ and $w(h_0) \leq 1$.

Fig. 1. From left: image $f_0 \in [0, 1]^X$, image $g_0 \in [0, 1]^X$ and image $h_0 \in [0, 1]^X$, where $\|g_0 \subseteq f_0\| = 0.6$ and $\|h_0 \subseteq f_0\| = 1$.

In the previous example, the powerset object $w \in F(X, f)$ is interpreted as one of many possibilities describing truth degrees how the objects from $T(X)$ can be understood as subobjects in f. $F(X, f)$ can therefore be referred to as the so-called local powerset object of f. On the other hand, for any object $f \in T(X)$ we can explicitly determine all possible objects g in $T(X)$ such that for some $\alpha \in L$ we have $\alpha \otimes \overline{g} \leq \overline{f}$. In that case we can say that g is in a powerset of f in a degree at least α. The pairs (f, α) then represent elements of another powerset structure $H(X, f)$ which is in a close relationship with the structure $F(X, f)$. In the next part we show the construction of H.

As in the case of the powerset structure (F, η) we start with an L-powerset structure $\mathcal{T} = (T, \eta)$ in a category $\mathbf{K}$. Let the structure $\mathcal{H} = (H, \mu)$ be defined by

1. The functor $H : \mathbf{K}_{\mathcal{T}} \to CSLAT$ is defined by

$$H(X, f) = \{(g, \alpha) : g \in T(X), 0_L < \alpha \leq \|g \subseteq f\|\} \cup \{\emptyset_X\}.$$

2. If $u : (X, f) \to (Y, g)$ is a morphism in $\mathbf{K}_T$, we put

$$H(u) : H(X, f) \to H(Y, g),$$
$$\emptyset_X \neq (h, \alpha) \in H(X, f), \quad H(u)(h, \alpha) = (T(u)(h), \alpha) \in H(Y, g)$$
$$H(u)(\emptyset_X) = \emptyset_Y.$$

3. For arbitrary $(X, f) \in \mathcal{K}$, we define

$$\mu_{(X,f)} : X \to H(X, f),$$

$$x \in X \quad \mu_{(X,f)}(x) = \begin{cases} (\eta_X(x), \overline{f}(x)) \in H(X, f), & \text{iff } \overline{f}(x) \neq 0_L, \\ \emptyset_X, & \text{otherwise .} \end{cases}$$

Then, we can prove the following theorem.

Theorem 2. *Let* $T = (T, \eta)$ *be an* L-*powerset structure in* $\mathbf{K}$. *Then* $\mathcal{H} = (H, \mu)$ *is a powerset structure in* $\mathbf{K}_T$.

Proof. (1) On the set $H(X, f)$ we define an order relation by

$$(g, \alpha) \preceq (h, \beta) \Leftrightarrow g \leq_X h, \alpha \geq \beta, \quad \emptyset_X \preceq (g, \alpha),$$

where $\leq_X$ is the order relation on $T(X)$ and $\leq$ is the order relation on L. Then $H(X, f)$ is a complete $\vee$-semilattice, where $(g, \alpha) \vee (h, \beta) = (g \vee h, \alpha \wedge \beta) \in H(X, f)$. This definition is correct as follows from

$$\|g \vee h \subseteq f\| = \bigwedge_{x \in V(X)} \overline{g \vee h}(x) \to \overline{f}(x) = \bigwedge_{x \in V(X)} (\overline{g} \vee \overline{h})(x) \to \overline{f}(x) =$$
$$(\bigwedge_{x \in V(X)} \overline{g}(x) \to \overline{f}(x)) \wedge (\bigwedge_{x \in V(X)} \overline{h}(x) \to \overline{f}(x)) \geq \alpha \wedge \beta.$$

(2) Let $u : (X, f) \to (Y, g)$ be a $\mathbf{K}_T$-morphism. We show that the definition of $H(u)$ is correct. Let $(h, \alpha) \in H(X, f)$. We show that $(T(u)(h), \alpha) \in H(Y, g)$. In fact, from the diagram (1) we obtain

$$\|T(u)(h) \subseteq g\| = \bigwedge_{y \in Y} \overline{T(u)(h)}(y) \to \overline{g}(y) = \bigwedge_{y \in Y} Z(u)(\overline{h})(y) \to \overline{g}(y) =$$
$$\bigwedge_{y \in Y} (\bigvee_{x \in X, u(x) = y} \overline{h}(x)) \to \overline{g}(y) = \bigwedge_{y \in Y} \bigwedge_{x \in X, u(x) = y} \overline{h}(x) \to \overline{g}(u(x)) \geq$$
$$\bigwedge_{y \in Y} \bigwedge_{x \in X} \overline{h}(x) \to \overline{g}(u(x)) = \bigwedge_{x \in X} \overline{h}(x) \to \overline{g}(u(x)) = \|h \subseteq g.u\| =$$
$$\bigwedge_{x \in X} \overline{h}(x) \to \overline{f}(x) = \|h \subseteq f\| \geq \alpha.$$

Hence, $H(u)(h, \alpha) \in H(Y, g)$ and the definition is correct. Since $T(u)$ is a morphism in the category $CSLAT$, for arbitrary $h, k \in L^X$, $T(u)(h \vee k) = T(u)(h) \vee T(u)(k)$. It follows that $H(u)$ is also $\vee$-preserving map. Therefore, $H(u)$ is a morphism in the category $CSLAT$.

(3) We show that $\mu_{(X,f)}(x) \in H(X, f)$, for arbitrary $x \in X$. In fact, from the property 2 in Definition 3.1, we obtain

$$\|\eta_X(x) \subseteq f\| = \bigwedge_{z \in X} \overline{\eta_X(x)}(z) \to \overline{f}(z) = \overline{f}(x),$$

and the definition of $\mu_{(X,f)}$ is correct. Then, for arbitrary $\mathbf{K}_T$-morphism $u :$ $(X, f) \to (Y, g)$, the following diagram commutes.

$$
\begin{array}{ccc}
X & \xrightarrow{\;u\;} & Y \\
{\scriptstyle \mu_{(X,f)}}\Big\downarrow & & \Big\downarrow{\scriptstyle \mu_{(Y,g)}} \\
H(X, f) & \xrightarrow[\;H(u)\;]{} & H(Y, g).
\end{array}
$$

In fact, let $x \in X$. If $\overline{f}(x) = \overline{g}(u(x)) \neq 0_L$, we have

$$
\mu_{(Y,g)}(u(x)) = (\eta_Y(u(x)), \overline{g}(u(x))) = (T(u)(\eta_X(x)), \overline{g}(u(x))) =
$$
$$
(T(u)(\eta_X(x)), \overline{f}(x)) = H(u)(\mu_{(X,f)}(x)).
$$

Otherwise, we have

$$
\mu_{(Y,g)}(u(x)) = \emptyset_Y = H(u)(\emptyset_X) = H(u)(\mu_{(X,f)}(x)).
$$

Therefore, H is a powerset structure in the category $\mathbf{K}_T$. $\qquad\square$

We can describe the powerset $H(X, f)$ in more intuitive way.

Proposition 1. *Let (T, η) be an L-powerset structure in a category $\mathbf{K}$. For arbitrary $(X, f) \in \mathbf{K}_T$ we have*

$$
H(X, f) = \{(g, \alpha) : g \in T(X), \alpha \in L, \alpha \otimes \overline{g} \leq \overline{f}\}.
$$

Proof. Let $(g, \alpha) \in H(X, f)$. Because $\alpha \leq \|g \subseteq f\| \leq \overline{g}(x) \to \overline{f}(x)$ for arbitrary $x \in X$, we obtain $\alpha \otimes \overline{g}(x) \leq \overline{f}(x)$ for arbitrary $x \in X$ and it follows that $\alpha \otimes \overline{g} \leq \overline{f}$. On the other hand, if $\alpha \otimes \overline{g}(x) \leq \overline{f}(x)$ for all $x \in X$, we have $\alpha \leq \overline{g}(x) \to \overline{f}(x)$ and we obtain $\|g \subseteq f\| \geq \alpha$. Hence, $(g, \alpha) \in H(X, f)$. $\qquad\square$

The following proposition shows the relationships between both powerset structures F and H in the category $\mathbf{K}_T$.

Proposition 2. *Let $T = (T, \eta)$ be an L-powerset structure in a category $\mathbf{K}$. Then for arbitrary object (X, f) in a category $\mathbf{K}_T$ we have*

$$
H(X, f) = \{(g, w(g)) : g \in T(X), w \in F(X, f)\}.
$$

Proof. If $w \in F(X, f)$, then we have $(g, w(g)) \in H(X, f)$, for arbitrary $g \in T(X)$. Conversely, if $(g, \alpha) \in H(X, f)$, we define a mapping $w : T(X) \to L$ by $w(g) = \alpha$ and $w(h) = \|h \subseteq f\|$ for all $h \in T(X), h \neq g$. Then $w \in F(X, f)$ and $(g, \alpha) = (g, w(g))$. $\qquad\square$

Example 5. Let $\mathcal{P} = (P, \chi)$ be the powerset structure in the category **Set** from Example 2.1. Then $\mathcal{P}$ is an L-powerset structure where the natural transformation $P \to Z$ is defined by the characteristic function

$$A \in P(X) \mapsto \chi_A^X : X \to \{0_L, 1_L\},$$

i.e, instead of subsets A in X we can consider their characteristic mappings $\chi_A^X : X \to \{0_L, 1_L\}$. Because for arbitrary $A, B \subseteq X$, holds

$$\|B \subseteq A\| = \|\chi_B^X \subseteq \chi_A^X\| = \bigvee_{x \in X} \chi_B^X(x) \to \chi_A^X(x) = \begin{cases} 1_L, & B \subseteq A, \\ 0_L, & B \nsubseteq A, \end{cases}$$

we obtain that

$$H(X, A) = \{(B, \alpha) : B \subseteq X, 0_L < \alpha \leq \|\chi_B^X \subseteq \chi_A^X\|\} \cup \{\emptyset_X\} =$$
$$\{(B, 1_L) : B \subseteq X, 1_L = \|\chi_B^X \subseteq \chi_A^X\|\} \cup \{\emptyset_X\} = \{(B, 1_L) : B \subseteq A\} \simeq P(A).$$

If $u : (X, A) \to (Y, B)$ is a morphism in the category $\mathbf{Set}_{\mathcal{P}}$, then $u : X \to Y$ is such that $u(X) \cap B = u(A)$ and $H(u) : H(X, A) \to H(Y, B)$ is such that $H(u)(C, 1_L) = (P(u)(C), 1_L)$. Therefore, the powerset structure $\mathcal{H}$ is identical to the powerset structure $\mathcal{P}$

Example 6. Let $\mathcal{Z} = (Z, \chi)$ be the L-powerset structure in the category **Set** from Example 2.2. Then, according to Proposition 3.1, for arbitrary $X \in \mathbf{Set}, f \in Z(X)$, we have

$$(g, \alpha) \in H(X, f) \Leftrightarrow (g \otimes \alpha, 1_L) \in H(X, f),$$

and we obtain

$$H(X, f) = \{(g, \alpha) : g \in L^X, \alpha \in L, g \otimes \alpha \leq f\}.$$

Therefore, in that case, the powerset structure $H(X, f)$ can be identified with the set

$$\{g \otimes \alpha : g \in L^X, \alpha \in L, g \otimes \alpha \leq f\}.$$

For illustrative example see Fig. 2.

Example 7. Let $\mathcal{E} = (E, \rho)$ be the powerset structure in the category $\mathbf{Set}(L)$ from Example 2.3. $\mathcal{E}$ is an L-powerset structure, i.e., $E \to Z$ defined by inclusion $E(X, \delta) \subseteq L^X$ is a natural transformation. In fact, for arbitrary morphism $u : (X, \delta) \to (Y, \gamma)$ in $\mathbf{Set}(L)$, we prove the commutativity of the diagram (3), i.e.,

$$
\begin{array}{ccc}
E(X, \delta) & \longrightarrow & Z(X) \\
{\scriptstyle E(u)}\downarrow & & \downarrow{\scriptstyle Z(u)} \\
E(Y, \gamma) & \longrightarrow & Z(Y).
\end{array}
$$

Fig. 2. From left: image $f_1 \in [0,1]^X$, image $g_1 \in [0,1]^X$ and image $\alpha \otimes g_1 \in [0,1]^X$, where $\alpha = \|g_1 \subseteq f_1\| = 0.54$. In that case $\alpha \otimes g_1 \in H(X, f_1), g_1 = g_1 \otimes 1 \notin H(X, f_1)$.

For $f \in E(X, \delta), y \in Y$, we have

$$Z(u)(f)(y) = \bigvee_{x, u(x) = y} f(x) = \bigvee_{x, u(x) = y} f(x) \otimes \gamma(u(x), y) \leq$$

$$\bigvee_{z \in X} f(z) \otimes \gamma(u(z), y) = E(u)(f)(y) = \bigvee_{z \in X, u(z) = y} \bigvee_{x \in X} f(x) \otimes \gamma(u(x), u(z)) =$$

$$\bigvee_{z \in X, u(z) = y} \bigvee_{x \in X} f(x) \otimes \delta(x, z) \leq \bigvee_{z \in X, u(z) = y} f(z) = Z(u)(f)(y).$$

For arbitrary $f \in E(X, \delta)$, $f(x) \leftrightarrow f(z) \geq \rho_{(X, \delta)}(x)(y)$ holds for arbitrary $x, z \in X$ and it follows that $\mathcal{E}$ is an L-powerset theory in $\mathbf{Set}(L)$. Let $(X, \delta) \in \mathbf{Set}(L)$ and $f \in E(X, \delta)$. Then, analogously as in Example 3.3, we obtain that the powerset structure $H((X, \delta), f)$ can be identified with the set

$$\{g \otimes \alpha : g \in E(X, \delta), \alpha \in L, \alpha \otimes g \leq f\}.$$

4 Conclusion

In this paper, we show how to define the powerset structure of an individual fuzzy set in a crisp set X, which would have analogous properties to Zadeh's powerset structure L^X of all L-valued fuzzy sets in X. However, because the characteristic properties of Zadeh's powerset structure L^X also have many other powerset structures based on fuzzy sets modifications, such as crisp sets, extensional fuzzy sets or fuzzy soft sets, we chose a general procedure based on the category theory to defined powerset structure for individual objects of general powerset structures in a category.

We introduce the notion of an L-powerset structure in a category $\mathbf{K}$, which represents an analogy of Zadeh's powerset structure in a category $\mathbf{K}$. For arbitrary L-powerset structure $\mathcal{T} = (T, \eta)$ in a category $\mathbf{K}$ we introduced two examples (F, ξ) and (H, μ) of powerset structures in the category $\mathbf{K}_\mathcal{T}$ of individual objects from $T(X)$, where X is an object of a category $\mathbf{K}$. Typical examples of objects from $T(X)$ are subsets of a set X, L-valued fuzzy sets in a set X or extensional fuzzy sets in a set X with a similarity relation. These powerset structures generalize classical powerset structures 2^X or L^X. The functors F and H from these powerset structures can used to define various operations on subobjects of individual elements from $T(X)$ and represent generalizations of Zadeh's extension principle for subobjects of individual fuzzy sets.

References

1. Gerla, G., Scarpati, L.: Extension principles for fuzzy set theory. J. Inf. Sci. **106**, 49–69 (1998)
2. Nguyen, H.T.: A note on the extension principle for fuzzy sets. J. Math. Anal. Appl. **64**, 369–380 (1978)
3. Močkoř, J.: Closure theories of powerset theories. Tatra Mountains Math. Publ. **64**, 101–126 (2015)
4. Močkoř, J.: Powerset operators of extensional fuzzy sets. Iran. J. Fuzzy Syst. (2017). https://doi.org/10.22111/IJFS.2017.3318
5. Močkoř, J.: Fuzzy type powerset operators and F-transforms. In: Torra, V., Narukawa, Y., Aguiló, I., González-Hidalgo, M. (eds.) Modeling Decisions for Artificial Intelligence. MDAI 2018, Lecture Notes in Computer Science, vol. 11144, Springer, Cham. https://doi.org/10.1007/978-3-030-00202-2-15
6. Rodabaugh, S.E.: Powerset operator foundation for POSLAT fuzzy SST theories and topologies. Höhle, U., Rodabaugh, S.E. (Eds.), Mathematics of Fuzzy Sets: Logic, Topology and Measure Theory, The Handbook of Fuzzy Sets Series, vol. 3, pp. 91–116. Kluwer Academic Publishers, Boston (1999)
7. Rodabaugh, S.E.: Powerset operator based foundation for point-set lattice theoretic (POSLAT) fuzzy set theories and topologies. Quaest. Math. **20**(3), 463–530 (1997)
8. Rodabaugh, S.E.: Relationship of algebraic theories to powerset theories and fuzzy topological theories for lattice-valued mathematics. Int. J. Math Math. Sci. **2007**, 1–71 (2007)
9. Rodabaugh, S.E.: Relationship of algebraic theories to powersets over objects in Set and SetxC. Fuzzy Sets Syst. **161**(3), 453–470 (2010)
10. Solovyov, S.A.: Powerset operator foundations for catalog fuzzy set theories. Iran. J. Fuzzy Syst. **8**(2), 1–46 (2001)
11. Yager, R.R.: A characterization of the extension principle. Fuzzy Sets Syst. **18**, 205–217 (1996)
12. Zadeh, L.A.: Fuzzy sets. Inf. Control **8**, 338–353 (1965)

Datacenter Selection in Cloud Framework for Efficient Load Distribution Using a Fuzzy Approach

Mou De[1,2]($\boxtimes$) and Anirban Kundu[1,2]

[1] Netaji Subhash Engineering College, Kolkata 700152, India
[2] Computer Innovative Research Society, Howrah 711103, West Bengal, India
mou.latu@gmail.com, anik76in@gmail.com

Abstract. Cloud architecture delivers fast response to users using multi-tasking in several datacenters. Datacenter executes user query with virtual machine which is configured inside a host. Load balancing in datacenter is depended on utilization of cpu, mips, memory by host, and virtual machine. Prediction of resource utilization with dynamic load improves task scheduling/distribution and load balancing. We propose a cloud architecture to predict load in datacenters using fuzzy reasoning. Fuzzy based datacenter prediction analysis is used to estimate availability of datacenters with dynamic task load execution. Datacenter schedules task load in virtual machines for completing executions. Datacenters and virtual machines load distribution and physical resource utilization have been accomplished using scheduling algorithms.

Keywords: Cloud computing · Fuzzified datacenter · Task load · Datacenter scheduling · Virtual machine scheduling · Efficient load distribution

1 Introduction

Cloud computing [1] deals with virtualized resource sharing among users' queries in static and dynamic situations. On-demand services with time-saving and cost-effective techniques are provided by cloud computing for users. Efficiency of cloud [2] architecture is increased using distributed datacenters with shared physical and virtual resources. Cloud computing provides application, server, and platform-oriented services through internet with minimal maintenance. Datacenters size and location are increases to fulfill user request as the concept of cloud services are accepted progressively.

Network bandwidth is a significant constraint to distribution of datacenter and utilization of virtualized technology. Network configuration and network topology control traffic in cloud datacenters for huge task load distribution and system stability. Several flow scheduling techniques is used for maintaining network [3] routing performance to improve distribution of datacenter location.

Load balancing [4] and job scheduling are crucial constraints to maintain reliability in distributed cloud architecture in real-time job execution. Idle resources are used

© Springer Nature Switzerland AG 2020
L. Martínez-Villaseñor et al. (Eds.): MICAI 2020, LNAI 12468, pp. 423–436, 2020.
https://doi.org/10.1007/978-3-030-60884-2_32

effectively to improve performance of cloud computing. Heuristic scheduling method is applied to improve reliability in distributed cloud computing performance with dynamic task load. In replication method works on dynamic job queue execution with flexible heterogeneous resources within limit.

The major contribution of the proposed framework is to reduce the load in a particular data center and optimal load balancing in different datacenters using a fuzzy decision index. Effective load allocation in virtual machines and hosts accomplish through scheduling algorithms to optimize task waiting time and task execution time.

The main goal of this work is to distribute load efficiently among datacenters to reduce energy consumption using fuzzy-based datacenter selection.

Scope of this work is to reduce uncertainty of datacenter availability during real-time task execution for effective load distribution among datacenters and virtual machines to enhance system performance.

Rest of the paper is organized as follows: Sect. 2 describes related works; Sect. 3 defines efficient load distribution within design framework; fuzzy based datacenter analysis is discussed in Sect. 4; experimental observations have deliberated in Sect. 5; Sect. 6 defines conclusion of the work.

2 Related Works

Datacenter [5] manages massive load using virtual machines using different scheduling algorithms. Cloud datacenter executes enormous task load in real-time which originates enormous energy consumption [6]. Different prediction strategy utilizes to predict the workload of datacenter and physical resource utilization using virtualized technology like a virtual machine. Effective task load management improves datacenter performance and data availability for resource utilization to optimize tasks and reduce energy consumption. Virtual machine aggregation inside datacenter improves task optimization time and reduces energy consumption [7]. Several algorithms are used to schedule virtual machines with datacenter to optimize load dynamically.

Virtual machine migration technique is used in cloud environment to share hardware resources virtually for task optimization. Datacenter migrates virtual machines for completing simultaneous operations in cloud platform. Virtualization [8] of physical resources using different migration approaches in cloud data-center is an important feature where virtual machines are made available in different hosts without affecting the execution of the system. Virtual machine selection [9] depends on several prediction techniques like heuristic search algorithm, particle swarm optimization, min-max [10] algorithm, fuzzy-based approach [11], etc. Virtual machines are embedded with datacenter for executing several tasks for different applications with a similar set of physical resources. Most of the cloud-based architecture enhances their performance by a categorized problem either in virtual machine allocation or in network bandwidth allocation. Overall scrutinization would enhance system performance.

The scheduling algorithm plays a significant role in enhancing resource utilization with fulfilling requirements of tasks during execution. Heterogeneous job requests executed by virtual machines in a data center with limited capacity. Scheduling algorithm [12] manages capacity of resources with enormous task load in real-time for minimizing waiting time and failure. Performance of cloud environment affects by numerous constraints like time complexity, cost, scalability, reliability, security, energy consumption. The prime focus of different scheduling algorithms is to reduce these constraints for improving the performance of cloud environment and fulfill users' requests.

Fuzzy approach is used in complex multi agent system [13, 14] as a problem-solving technique to improve system performance in real-time. Fuzzy set uses universal membership function to predict system performance. Membership values are derived from crisp set ranging from 0 to 1 for forecasting possibilities of particular system elements. Fuzzy based datacenter load [15] prediction optimizes load distribution in real-time to organize load for operating datacenter resources. Crisp input values are used to predict efficient load distribution in datacenters and virtual machines by fuzzy rule base. Different fuzzy expert system is used to forecast efficiency of datacenter load distribution within cloud environment. Fuzzy based algorithms are implemented to increase datacenter response time and to schedule dynamic task load [16] in datacenter and virtual machines. Dynamic fuzzy logic-based task scheduling algorithms are utilized to predict indefinite task in datacenter and virtualization of resources.

3   Design Framework for Efficient Load Distribution

In the proposed framework, several users' requests use to form a cloudlet request. Cloudlet request sends their requirements to cloud broker. Cloud broker forms a similar group of cloudlet requests according to their request type and sent them to the cloud service manager. Cloud service manager passes information to cloud information service where the application manager and hash table module stored information for further processing. Cloud information service transfers cloudlet requests to application manager to categorized request type i.e., web-based application requests passed to a web server. Hash table keeps different datacenters information and their availability. Datacenter process cloudlet request using fuzzified datacenter scheduler which predicts the availability of datacenters. Vmpool selects virtual machines for different datacenters according to the size of tasks using different scheduling algorithms. Vmpool schedules task load in virtual machines. After execution of task, data is stored in the storage cloud. The detailed workflow of proposed system framework is portrayed in Fig. 1.

Algorithm 1: VMpool _scheduling_ VM

Input: VMpool

Output: ith vm selection

Initial Declaration: DC= {DC1, DC2, DC3, ..., DCl};

Vm = {vm1, vm2, vm3, ..., vmm};

H={H1, H2, H3, ..., Hn} ;

T={T1, T2, T3,................., Tk};

$$DC[i] = \sum_{j=0}^{N} Vm_j; Vm \in H;$$

Step 1: Select vm[i] and T [j] for execution

Step 2: if (Task_size[j] <= vm[i]) vm[i]=T[j];

    else

        Call Search_Datacenter(T[j]);

    endif

Step 3: for (int h=0; h<H.length; h++)

        if(H[h].available== False) then   // host not available

          Call Host_Selection(vm[i], task_size[j]);

        else

         H[h] allocate for vm[i];

        endif

    end loop

Step 4: $H = \int(\sum_{k=0}^{N} memory \times \sum_{l=0}^{M} cpu \times \sum_{m=0}^{L} MIPS$);

Step 5: Call Execute_Task (T[j], DC[k])   //Tj is assigned to particular DC[k]

Step 6: for (int i=0, j=0;i<n, j<m;i++, j++)

     Total_Time[i]= vm_bt[i] + vm_wt[i];

       if(Total_Time < Time_quantum) Set priority to task T[j] ;

          Call Execute_Task(T[j]) ;

       else if (Total_Time == Time_quantum) then

         Task_arrive[i]=T[j] + task_arrive[i];

         Call Execute_Task(T[j]) ;

       else if (Total_Time > Time_quantum) then

         T[j]= T[j] + Time_quantum;

         vm_wt[i]=Time_quantum – vm_bt[i];

         if(vm_wt[i]==0) Call Execute_Task(T[j]) ;

         end if

       else

         vm_wt[i]=Total_Time – vm_bt[i];

         Call Search_Datacenter();

        end if

    end loop

Step 7: if (DC[i].available == True)

       if (vm_wt[i] == Null && DC[i]->vm[k]).available == TRUE) then

          DC[i]->vm[k] = T[j];

       else

          Call Search_Datacenter();

       end if

     end if

Step 8: Call Execute_Task(T[j], DC[i]) ;   // Tj is assigned to a new DC[p]

Step 9: Stop

In Algorithm 1, Vmpool is considered as initial input for selecting virtual machines for execution of tasks. The system calculates task size and matches with virtual machines. Virtual machines are assigned with tasks after task size matches with virtual machines otherwise new datacenter searching initiated for further processing. After assigning tasks to a virtual machine, task requirements are coordinated with host configuration to bind physical resources with a virtual machine with task requirements. A new host is searched if the necessities of the task did not fulfill with host capacity. Host physical resources like cpu, memory, and mips are ready as virtual machines to process tasks. Time quantum is calculated for each task to complete execution within a specific period. Total execution time of task is calculated with response time and waiting time of tasks in virtual machine. Tasks are prioritized if total execution time is less than time quantum else task execution takes place as they have arrived in virtual machine. Incase total execution time is bigger than time quantum then waiting time of tasks with particular virtual machines again calculated and time quantum for rest of tasks are also calculated completing task execution. If any virtual machine is available with task requirement then task is assigned to the virtual machine otherwise new datacenter is searched for complete task execution. New datacenter searching process will continue until datacenters and virtual machines are available to fulfill task requirements with zero waiting time.

Algorithm 2: Host_Selection

Input: vm[i], task_size[j]

Output: n^{th} host selection

Step1: Select vm[i]; select H[j] ;   // host selected to bind with vm

Step2 : if (H[j] == 0)   // host not available

      H[j].old_location=H[j].new_location;

      Search(host_new); //Search for new host;

     if (H[j]!=0) Bind(vm[i], H[j]); // Bind host with vm

Step 3: Stop

In Algorithm 2, task size and virtual machine are taken as initial input for selecting host. Physical resources of a host with virtual machines have synchronized with task size to fulfil task requirements for execution. New host is searched if task execution time is bigger or virtual machine is not available with the required task size. New host is ready to process virtual machines available according to task size.

Algorithm 3 is only be executed if and only if new datacenter is searched to relate between vm[i] and T[j].

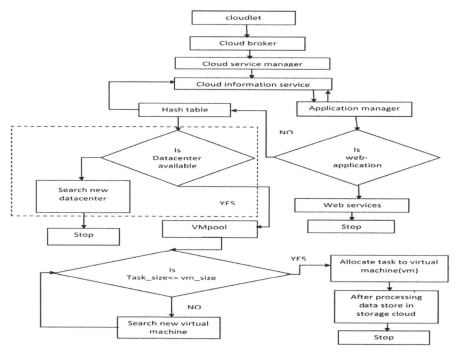

Fig. 1. Proposed system framework

Algorithm 3: Search_Datacenter
Input: task[i]
Output: mth DataCenter Selection
Step 1: if(DC[i].available==False) // Datacentre not available
          search(Datacenter_location_new) // Search new Datacenter location;
    //New host physical resources are virtualized to bind host with virtual machine.
Step 2: DC[i]=DC[i].new_location;
      if(task_size[i]<=vm[i] && vm[i] € DC[i]) vm[i]=T[j];
      else
         for(j=0; j< DC[i].new_location_table; j++)
            vm[j]=T[j]; DC[j]=vm[j];
         end loop
      end if
Step 3: Update (Datacenter_location_table, vm[i], max_size(vm[i]));
Step 4: Stop

In Algorithm 3, initial input is a task that is selected by a datacenter for dynamic accomplishment. Real-time user requests considered as task load which evaluated in a datacenter. Necessities of tasks synchronize with virtual machines inside a particular datacenter before assigning them to a specific datacenter for execution. New datacenters diverse locations are searched until suitable virtual machines are found which encounters requirements of task and balance dynamic task load.

Algorithm 4: Execute_Task
Input : T[i], DC[i]
Output : Complete task execution
   Step 1: if(task_size[i]==vm[j]) then   //task size matched with vm
size

           vm[i]=T[j]; // complete task execution

$$\text{Task}_{\text{execution}} = \sum_{i=0}^{\max\_size} \int(T[i], \text{max\_size}(T[i]));$$

     else

          search (Datacenter_location_new);   //Search new Datacenter loca-
tion;

     end if
   Step 2: for(k=0; k<DC[k].new_location; k++)

          select vm[k];   // vm from new Datacenter is selected

          vm[k]=T[j];   // complete task execution

$$\text{Task}_{\text{execution}} = \sum_{i=0}^{\max\_size} \int(T[i], \text{max\_size}(T[i]));$$

     end loop
   Step 3: Stop

Algorithm 4 describes completion of task execution where tasks and datacenters are used as input. Tasks are assigned to virtual machines after compatibility checking with task size and requirements. Task execution process will continue in virtual machines until all assigned tasks with maximum length of task is completed inside virtual machine.

4 Fuzzy Based Analysis for Datacenter Selection

The fuzzy system works on ambiguous input and output values controlling through fuzzy rule base to predict system accuracy. Fuzzy based datacenter prediction is applied to manage uncertainty of datacenter availability in dynamic load circulation for increasing performance of the proposed system. Fuzzy decision index for datacenter availability increases the proficiency of datacenter and scalable task execution.

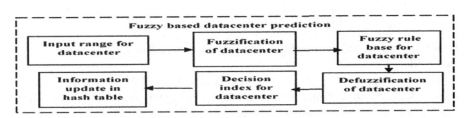

Fig. 2. Fuzzy based analysis for datacenter prediction

Figure 2 describes working flow of fuzzy based analysis to predict datacenter availability. Detailed analysis inside design framework is shown to predict datacenter accesibility for scheduling task load.

Fuzzy logic is applied to check availability of datacenter for task execution. Membership functions and rule functions are used to determine decision index using crisp data set. Datacenter load prediction with tasks in real-time using fuzzy rule functions increases availability of datacenter for task execution.

Table 1. Input range for datacenter selection

Inputs	Specification range
Datacenter availability	0–25 => Full available 20–45 => More than half available 40–65 => Half available 60–85 => Less than half available 80–100 => Not available
Datacenter specification	0.0–0.7 => Existing datacenter 0.6–1.0 => New datacenter

Table 1 shows suggested input ranges of datacenter availability and datacenter specification using fuzzy reasoning for datacenter selection. Incase of dataceneter availability, we have considered five overlapping specification ranges for high succesess rate in prediction. Similarly, incase of datacenter specification we have considered two overlaping specification ranges.

Therefore, we assume crisp value of Datacenter availability is 85. Datacenter specification value is 0.63.

Member function of datacenter availability is shown in Fig. 3. In Fig. 3, five different availability range is depicted as availability of datacenter as per execution load.

$$\therefore \mu\left(\text{datacenter}_{\text{availability}}\right) = \mu(FA), \mu(MHA), \mu(HA), \mu(LHA), \mu(NA)$$

Member function of Datacenter specification range is depicted in Fig. 4. Datacenter specification member function is combination of two different condition i.e. existing datacenter and new datacenter.

$$\therefore \mu\left(\text{datacenter}_{\text{specification}}\right) = \mu(EDC), \mu(NDC)$$

We have considered two condition i) less than half availability of Datacenter and ii) not availability of Datacenter.

After plotting the crisp value of datacenter availability and datacenter specification the member function of datacenter availability μ(datacenter_availability) = {0, 0, 0, 0.85, 0.15} and member function of datacenter specification = {0.3, 0.04}. As a result the rule function of s = {EDC, NDC}.

From Table 2 value we have plotted the graph for availability of existing datacenter and new datacenter (refer Fig. 5).

Table 3 is evaluated after subtraction of membership value of Table 2 using min operation. After Table 3 has been created the rule function is f(0.3, 0.08).

Figure 5 is depicted availability of existing and new datacenter using Table 2 values. Applying maximum method we get existing datacenter availability is higher than new

Table 2. Rule base for datacenter selection

	Full available (FA)	More than half available (MHA)	Half available (HA)	Less than half available (LHA)	Not available (NA)
EDC	Existing	Existing	Existing	Existing	New
NDC	New	New	New	New	New

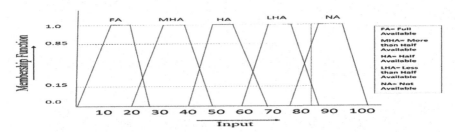

Fig. 3. Membership function applied with datacenter availability

Table 3. Rule base for datacenter selection using membership values

	Full available (FA)	More than half available (MHA)	Half available (HA)	0.85	0.15
0.3	Existing	Existing	Existing	0.3	0.15
0.04	New	New	New	0.04	0.04

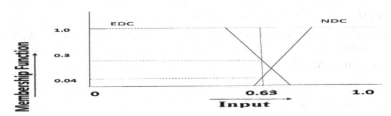

Fig. 4. Membership function applied with datacenter specification

datacenter because fuzzy set of existing datacenter has higher value in respect of new datacenter.

Appling centroid method final decision is considered using formulation of

$$\sum(\mu * D/\sum \mu)$$

$\therefore$ Final decision $= ((0.3 * 0.35) + (0.08 * 0.8))/(0.3 + 0.08) = 0.444$

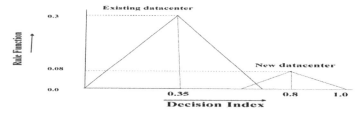

Fig. 5. Fuzzified decision on datacenter availability

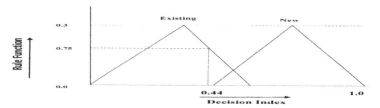

Fig. 6. Fuzzy decision index for datacenter availability

Figure 6 illustrates decision index criteria is 0.75 as existing using the value 0.44 which is applying from centroid method. Therefore, availability of existing datacenter is 75% than from new datacenter availability during load distribution.

5 Experimental Discussions

In experimental section, effectiveness of proposed system work and fuzzy based datacenter prediction are discussed with experimental results. Simulation results of datacenter availability with dynamic task load and task scheduling in virtual machine within datacenter are discussed to achieve our goal. In real-time, datacenter response time with individual tasks and optimization of task load are discussed using graphical representations. Experimental results are discussed on energy usage in datacenter during execution of tasks and virtual machine involvement inside datacenter for processing tasks.

5.1 Experimental Setup

"Windows 10 64 bit" operating system is used for our experimentation with processor "Intel core i3-10110U", cpu speed 2.14 Ghz, Ram 4 GB. "Jdk1.7", "Netbeans", "Microsoft office" and "Cloudsim" software are used to produce results.

5.2 Energy Consumption

Figure 7 shows energy consumption in datacenters during task execution. Expenditure of energy is low but the value is increased due to the increasing load in datacenter. Graph pattern is linear due to synchronization of task with several datacenters.

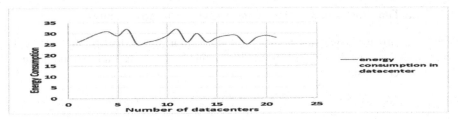

Fig. 7. Energy consumption in datacenter

5.3 Virtual Machine with Task Load

Figure 8 describes execution of real-time tasks load in virtual machines. X-axis represents virtual machines and Y-axis shows quantity of tasks. We have considered 1000 virtual machines. Amount of task execution in virtual machines is decreased where task size (i.e. total execution time for a particular task) is huge. Task load distribution is variant in distinct virtual machines due to task criteria accomplishment.

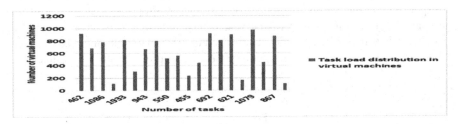

Fig. 8. Virtual machines vs. tasks

Resource utilization of host in virtual machines is depicted in Fig. 9. Virtualization of resources is different with distinct number of virtual machines due to task requirement analysis by "vmpool" scheduling algorithm. Similar task types are scheduled in particular host to improve system performance and to maximize resource utilizations.

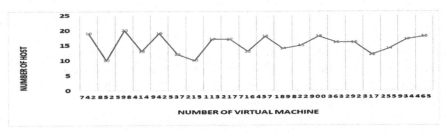

Fig. 9. Host with different virtual machines

5.4   Real-Time Task Load in Datacenter with Comparative Analysis

Number of virtual machines and number of datacenters are mapped in Fig. 10. Accessibility of virtual machines is reduced due to task waiting time calculation for accomplishing large number of tasks.

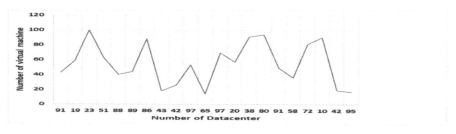

Fig. 10. Number of virtual machines vs. datacenter

Figure 11 depicts availability of datacenter with different task loads having X-axis as response time and Y-axis as number of datacenters. Proposed system maximizes datacenters' response time with real-time task load and minimizes waiting time of tasks. In task load distribution, datacenters are engaged to perform execution of tasks in each second, and response time of datacenter minimization improves system performance.

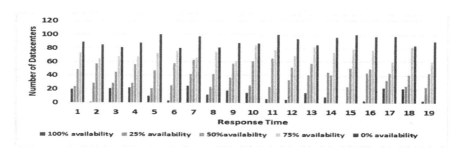

Fig. 11. Comparison between distinct datacenter availabilities with real-time task load

Scheduling tasks in datacenter for execution is depicted in Fig. 12. Waiting time and execution time of tasks are optimized utilizing existing and new datacenters. New datacenter searching time reduces as existing datacenter has executed maximum tasks. Existing datacenter performance graph decreases due to the completion of extremely lengthy tasks which acquires virtual machine inside a datacenter.

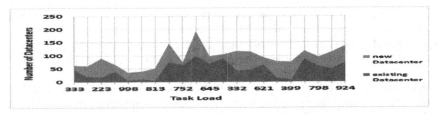

Fig. 12. Comparative study based on execution of tasks in existing and new datacenters

6 Conclusion

Real-time tasks load is efficiently managed in datacenters and virtual machines by proposed scheduling algorithms. Key objective of our approach is effective load distribution among virtual machine and datacenter. Fuzzy based datacenter prediction analysis increases obtainability of datacenters with dynamic task load and improve response time of datacenter during execution. Physical resources of host are virtualized in the form of virtual machine based on task requirements and task size. Task size and number of tasks are scrutinized before assigning them in virtual machines which decreases waiting time of task in virtual machine. Real-time tasks load placement in datacenter and virtual machines are explained to portray system performance. Experimental results are evaluated for efficient system accuracy using optimized energy consumption and to stabilized dynamic load in virtual machines.

Acknowledgment. This research work is funded by Computer Innovative Research Society, West Bengal, India. Award number is "2020/CIRS/R&D/1201-06-15/DSCFELDFA".

References

1. Hussein, S.R., Alkabani, Y., Mohamed, H.K.: Green cloud computing: datacenters power management policies and algorithms. In: 9th International Conference on Computer Engineering & Systems, Cairo, Egypt, pp. 421–426 (2014)
2. Uchiumi, T., Kikuchi, S., Matsumoto, Y.: Misconfiguration detection for cloud datacenters using decision tree analysis. In: 14th Asia-Pacific Network Operations and Management Symposium, Seoul, South Korea, pp. 2–4 (2012)
3. Ferdousi, S., Dikbiyik, F., Habib, M.F., Tornatore, M.: Disaster-aware datacenter placement and dynamic content management in cloud networks. IEEE/OSA J. Opt. Commun. Netw. 7(7), 681–695 (2016)
4. Kundu, A., Xu, G., Liu, R.: Efficient load balancing in cloud: a practical implementation. Int. J. Adv. Comput. Technol. 5(12), 43–54 (2013)
5. Chatterjee, A., Levan, M., Lanham, C., Zerrudo, M.: Job scheduling in cloud datacenters using enhanced particle swarm optimization. In: 2nd International Conference for Convergence in Technology (I2CT), Mumbai, India, pp. 895–900 (2017)
6. Beloglazov, A., Buyya, R.: Optimal online deterministic algorithms and adaptive heuristics for energy and performance efficient dynamic consolidation of virtual machines in cloud data centers. Concurr. Comput. Pract. Exp. (CCPE), 24(13), 1397–1420 (2012)

7. More, R.S., Alone, N.V.: An energy efficient QoS based replication strategy. Int. J. Innov. Res. Comput. Commun. Eng. **3**(6), 5325–5331 (2015)

8. Breitgand, D., et al.: An adaptive utilization accelerator for virtualized environments. In: IEEE International Conference on Cloud Engineering (IC2E), Boston, MA, USA, pp. 165–174 (2014)

9. Masoumzadeh, S., Hlavacs, R.: Integrating VM selection criteria in distributed dynamic vm consolidation using fuzzy q-learning. In: 9th International Conference on Network and Service Management (CNSM) (2013)

10. Li, Y., Zhu, C., Wang, Y.: MIN-Max-Min: a heuristic scheduling algorithm for jobs across geodistributed datacenters. In: IEEE 38th International Conference on Distributed Computing Systems, pp. 1573–1574 (2018)

11. Nivetha, N.K., Vijayakumar, D.: Modeling fuzzy based replication strategy to improve data availabiity in cloud datacenter. In: International Conference on Computing Technologies and Intelligent Data Engineering (ICCTIDE 2016), Kovilpatti, India, pp. 1–6 (2016)

12. Thanavanich, T.: Energy-aware and performance-aware of workflow application with hybrid scheduling algorithm on cloud computing. In: 22nd International Computer Science and Engineering Conference (ICSEC), Chiang Mai, Thailand, Thailand (2018)

13. Das, N., Kundu, A.: Multi-agent based analysis & design of decision support system for real time environment control. Int. J. Green Comput. **9**(1), 1–19 (2018)

14. Kundu, A., et al.: Fuzzy based multi-agent system offering cost effective corporate environment. Open Autom. Control Syst. J. **1**, 65–80 (2008)

15. Jaiganesh, M., Vincent Antony Kumar, A.: Fuzzy-based data center load optimization in cloud computing. Math. Prob. Eng. **2013**, 1–11 (2013)

16. Zulkar Nine, Md.S.Q., Azad, Md.A.K., Abdullah, S., Rahman, R.M.: Fuzzy logic based dynamic load balancing in virtualized data centers. In: IEEE International Conference on Fuzzy Systems, Hyderabad, India (2013)

A Linear Time Algorithm for Counting #2SAT on Series-Parallel Formulas

Marco A. López-Medina[1], J. Raymundo Marcial-Romero[1(✉)],
Guillermo De Ita-Luna[2], and José A. Hernández[1]

[1] Facultad de Ingeniería, UAEMex, Toluca, Mexico
mlopezm158@alumno.uaemex.mx, jrmarcialr@uaemex.mx
[2] Facultad de Ciencias de la Computación, BUAP, Puebla, Mexico
deita@cs.buap.mx

Abstract. An $O(m + n)$ time algorithm is presented for counting the number of models of a two Conjunctive Normal Form Boolean Formula whose constrained graph is represented by a Series-Parallel graph, where n is the number of variables and m is the number of clauses. To the best of our knowledge, no linear time algorithm has been developed for counting in this kind of formulas.

Keywords: #SAT · #2SAT · Complexity theory · Graph theory

1 Introduction

The decision problem $SAT(F)$, where F is a Boolean formula, consists in determining whether F has a model, that is, an assignment to the variables of F such that when evaluated with respect to classical Boolean logic it returns true as a result. If F is in two Conjunctive Normal Form (2-CNF) then $SAT(F)$ can be solved in polynomial time, however if F is in k-CNF, $k > 2$, then $SAT(F)$ is an NP-Complete problem. The counting version consists on determining the number of models of F denoted as $\#SAT(F)$. $\#SAT(F)$ belongs to class #P-Complete even when F is in 2-CNF, the latter denoted as $\#2SAT$ [1].

Although the $\#2SAT$ problem is #P-Complete, there are instances that can be solved in polynomial time [2,3]. For example, if the graph representation of the formula is acyclic, then the number of models can be computed in lineal time. Currently, the algorithms that are used to solve the problem for any formula F in 2-CNF, decompose F into sub-formulas until there are base cases in which it can be counted efficiently. The algorithm with the best time complexity so far was developed by Wahlström [4] which is given by $O(1.2377^n)$ where n represents the number of variables in the formula. The Wahlström algorithm uses the number of times a variable appears in the formula (be it the variable or its negation) as the criterion for choosing it. The two criteria for stopping the algorithm are when $F = \emptyset$ or when $\emptyset \in F$.

On series-parallel graphs the closest work is related to recognizing when a graph is series-parallel and some decision problem as we briefly describe.

© Springer Nature Switzerland AG 2020
L. Martínez-Villaseñor et al. (Eds.): MICAI 2020, LNAI 12468, pp. 437–447, 2020.
https://doi.org/10.1007/978-3-030-60884-2_33

Schoenmakers [5] develops a linear-time algorithm to recognize series-parallel graphs, computing a *source-sink* representation of this graph from a breath-first spanning tree. The complexity of constructing this representation is $O(n\sqrt{n})$. Eppstein [6] gives an algorithm to recognize directed and undirected series-parallel graphs, based on a characterization of their ear decompositions. Takamizawa [7] shows that if a graph is restricted to the series-parallel class, then there exists linear-time algorithms for decision problems and combinatorial problems as: minimum vertex cover, maximum independent vertex set, maximum (induced) line-subgraph, maximum edge (vertex) deletion respect to property "without cycles (or paths) of specified length n or any length $\leq n$", maximum outerplanar (induced) subgraph, minimum feedback vertex set, maximum ladder (induced) subgraph, minimum path cover, maximum matching and maximum disjoint triangle.

In this paper we present an algorithm to count model on a special class of formulas in linear time, the so called, series-parallel formulas [8,9] which to the best of our knowledge has not been tackle previously to count models [10].

2   Preliminaries

2.1   Conjunctive Normal Form

Let $X = \{x_1, ..., x_n\}$ be a set of n Boolean variables (that is, they can only take two possible values 1 or 0). A literal is a variable x_i, denoted in this paper as x_i^1 or the denied variable $\neg x_i$ denoted in this paper as x_i^0. A clause is a disjunction of different literals. A Boolean formula F in conjunctive normal form is a conjunction of clauses.

Let $v(Y)$ be the set of variables involved in the object Y, where Y can be a literal, a clause or a Boolean formula. For example, for the clause $c = \{x_1^1 \vee x_2^0\}$, $v(c) = \{x_1, x_2\}$.

An assignment s in F is a Boolean function $s : v(F) \rightarrow \{0, 1\}$. s is defined as:

$$s(x^0) = 1 \text{ if } s(x^1) = 0, \text{ otherwise } , s(x^0) = 0.$$

The assignment can be extended to conjunctions and disjuntions as follows:

- $s(x \wedge y) = 1$ if $s(x) = s(y) = 1$, otherwise, $s(x \wedge y) = 0$
- $s(x \vee y) = 0$ if $s(x) = s(y) = 0$, otherwise, $s(x \vee y) = 1$

Let F be a Boolean formula in CNF, it is said that s satisfies F, if for each clause c in F, it holds $s(c) = 1$. On the other hand, it is said that F is contradicted by s ($s \not\models F$), if there is at least one clause c of F such that $s(c) = 0$. Thus a model of F is an assignment that satisfies F.

Given a formula F in CNF, SAT is to determine whether F has a model, while $\#SAT$ is to count the number of models that F. On the other hand, $\#2SAT$ denotes $\#SAT$ for formulas in 2-CNF.

2.2 The Restricted Graph of a 2-CNF

There are some graphical representations of a Conjunctive Normal Form, in this case the signed primary graph (restricted graph) [11] will be used.

Let F be a 2-CNF, its restricted graph is denoted by $G_F = (V(F), E(F))$ where the vertices of the graph are the variables $V(F) = v(F)$ and $E(F) = \{\{x_i^\epsilon, x_j^\gamma\} \mid \{x_i^\epsilon \vee x_j^\gamma\} \in F\}$, that is, for each clause $\{x_i^\epsilon \vee x_j^\gamma\} \in F$ there is an edge $\{x_i^\epsilon, x_j^\gamma\} \in E(F)$. For $x \in V(F)$, $\delta(x)$ denotes its degree, that is the number of incident edges in x. Each edge $c = \{x_i^\epsilon, x_j^\gamma\} \in E(F)$ has associated a pair (ϵ, γ), which represent whether the variables x_i or x_j appear negated or not. For example, the clause $(x_1^0 \vee x_2^1)$ has associated the pair $(0, 1)$ meaning that in the clause, x_i appears negated and x_2 not.

2.3 Methods Already Reported to Count in #2SAT

The basic idea considered in related papers to count models on a restricted graph G consists on computing a tuple (α_i, β_i) over each vertex $x_i^{\epsilon_i}$ where α_i represents the number of times that $x_i^{\epsilon_i}$ appears positive in the models of G and β_i the number of times $x_i^{\epsilon_i}$ appears negative in the models of G. For example a clause with a simple vertex $\{x_i^{\epsilon_i}\}$ has associated the tuple $(1, 1)$ Given and edge(clause) $e = \{x_i^{\epsilon_i}, x_j^{\gamma_i}\}$ if the counting begins at $x_i^{\epsilon_i}$ the tuples $(1, 1)$, $(2, 1)$ are associated to $x_i^{\epsilon_i}$ and $x_j^{\gamma_i}$ respectively however if the counting begins at $x_j^{\gamma_i}$ the tuples are associated inversely. The models are the sum of the last two elements of the tuple.

There are reported methods to count models in some graphical representations of a 2-CNF formula F [12], here we stated the methods needed in the paper:

- If the graph represents a path e.g. a formula of the form
  $P_n = \{\{x_1^{\epsilon_1}, x_2^{\gamma_1}\}, \{x_2^{\epsilon_2}, x_3^{\gamma_2}\}, \cdots \{x_{n-1}^{\epsilon_{n-1}}, x_n^{\gamma_{n+1}}\}\}$ of n vertices, the number of models is given by the sum of the elements of the pair (α_n, β_n). where $(\alpha_1, \beta_1) = (1, 1)$ and the tuple for the other vertices is computed according to the next recurrence.

$$(\alpha_i, \beta_i) = \begin{cases} (\alpha_{i-1} + \beta_{i-1}, \alpha_{i-1}) & if \ (\epsilon_{i-1}, \gamma_{i-1}) = (1, 1) \\ (\alpha_{i-1}, \alpha_{i-1} + \beta_{i-1}) & if \ (\epsilon_{i-1}, \gamma_{i-1}) = (1, 0) \\ (\alpha_{i-1} + \beta_{i-1}, \beta_{i-1}) & if \ (\epsilon_{i-1}, \gamma_{i-1}) = (0, 1) \\ (\beta_{i-1}, \alpha_{i-1} + \beta_{i-1}) & if \ (\epsilon_{i-1}, \gamma_{i-1}) = (0, 0) \end{cases} \quad (1)$$

- Let $\{x_i^{\epsilon_1}, x_j^{\gamma_1}\}$ and $\{x_i^{\epsilon_2}, x_j^{\gamma_2}\}$ be two parallel clauses in a formula F, the number of models for this clauses is given by:

$$(\alpha_j, \beta_j) = \begin{cases} (\alpha_i, \alpha_i) & if \ (\epsilon_1, \gamma_1) = (1, 1) \ and \ (\epsilon_2, \gamma_2) = (1, 0) \\ (\alpha_i + \beta_i, 0) & if \ (\epsilon_1, \gamma_1) = (1, 1) \ and \ (\epsilon_2, \gamma_2) = (0, 1) \\ (\beta_i, \alpha_i) & if \ (\epsilon_1, \gamma_1) = (1, 1) \ and \ (\epsilon_2, \gamma_2) = (0, 0) \\ (\alpha_i, \beta_i) & if \ (\epsilon_1, \gamma_1) = (1, 0) \ and \ (\epsilon_2, \gamma_2) = (0, 1) \\ (0, \alpha_i + \beta_i) & if \ (\epsilon_1, \gamma_1) = (1, 0) \ and \ (\epsilon_2, \gamma_2) = (0, 0) \\ (\beta_i, \beta_i) & if \ (\epsilon_1, \gamma_1) = (0, 1) \ and \ (\epsilon_2, \gamma_2) = (0, 0) \end{cases} \quad (2)$$

– Let $\{x_i^{\epsilon_1}, x_j^{\gamma_1}\}$, $\{x_i^{\epsilon_2}, x_j^{\gamma_2}\}$ and $\{x_i^{\epsilon_3}, x_j^{\gamma_3}\}$ be three parallel clauses in a formula F, the number of models for this clauses is given by:

$$
(\alpha_j, \beta_j) = \begin{cases}
(0, \alpha_i) & if \ (\epsilon_1, \gamma_1) = (1,1) \ and \ (\epsilon_2, \gamma_2) = (1,0) \ and \ (\epsilon_3, \gamma_3) = (0,0) \\
(\alpha_i + \beta_i, 0) & if \ (\epsilon_1, \gamma_1) = (1,1) \ and \ (\epsilon_2, \gamma_2) = (1,0) \ and \ (\epsilon_3, \gamma_3) = (0,1) \\
(\beta_i, \alpha_i) & if \ (\epsilon_1, \gamma_1) = (1,1) \ and \ (\epsilon_2, \gamma_2) = (0,1) \ and \ (\epsilon_3, \gamma_3) = (0,0) \\
(\alpha_i, \beta_i) & if \ (\epsilon_1, \gamma_1) = (0,1) \ and \ (\epsilon_2, \gamma_2) = (1,0) \ and \ (\epsilon_3, \gamma_3) = (0,0)
\end{cases}
\tag{3}
$$

3 Counting Separately on Series and Parallel Formulas

In this paper instead of associating a tuple to each vertex, as previously explained, we associate a triple to each edge as described below.

3.1 Directional Element

For a clause $e = \{x_i^{\epsilon_1}, x_j^{\gamma_1}\}$, a triple $Q_e = (x_i, x_j, C_{x_i x_j})$ is associated, where the first two elements are the variables associated to the literals, $C_{x_i x_j}$ is a quadruple which represents the models for the possible assignments of the literals x_i and x_j. Initially, the value of the quadruple for $C_{x_i x_j}$ has three non-zero elements and one zero element which represents the three models that a clause has associated, as represented on Eq. 4.

$$
C_{x_i x_j} = \begin{cases}
(1,1,1,0) & if \ (\epsilon_1, \gamma_1) = (1,1) \\
(1,0,1,1) & if \ (\epsilon_1, \gamma_1) = (1,0) \\
(1,1,0,1) & if \ (\epsilon_1, \gamma_1) = (0,1) \\
(0,1,1,1) & if \ (\epsilon_1, \gamma_1) = (0,0)
\end{cases}
\tag{4}
$$

Each $C_{x_i x_j}$ is called a directional element. For example for a clause $\{x_i^1, x_j^0\}$, $C_{x_i x_j} = (1, 0, 1, 1)$.

3.2 Extended the Counting

Now we present counting methods on clauses of two kinds, paths, which later on will represent series graphs and parallel clauses. Our method consists on contracting edges until a single edge with two vertices is left.

Series counting

Let $e_1 = \{x_i^{\epsilon_i}, x_j^{\gamma_i}\}$ and $e_2 = \{x_j^{\epsilon_j}, x_k^{\gamma_j}\}$ be two clauses such that $i \neq k \neq j$ and whose triples are $Q_{e_1} = \{x_i, x_j, C_{x_i x_j}\}$ and $Q_{e_2} = \{x_j, x_k, C_{x_j x_k}\}$. As can be noticed, these two clauses form a path, since they are joined by x_j. We *contract* e_1 and e_2 into a single clause, lets call it e_{1-2}, its new triple is given by $Q_{e_{1-2}} = \{x_i, x_k, C_{x_i x_k}\}$ where each element of $C_{x_i x_k}$ is computed as:

$$
\pi_1(C_{x_i x_k}) = \pi_1(C_{x_j x_k})\pi_1(C_{x_i x_j}) + \pi_2(C_{x_j x_k})\pi_3(C_{x_i x_j})
\tag{5}
$$

$$\pi_2(C_{x_i x_k}) = \pi_1(C_{x_j x_k})\pi_2(C_{x_i x_j}) + \pi_2(C_{x_j x_k})\pi_4(C_{x_i x_j}) \tag{6}$$

$$\pi_3(C_{x_i x_k}) = \pi_3(C_{x_j x_k})\pi_1(C_{x_i x_j}) + \pi_4(C_{x_j x_k})\pi_3(C_{x_i x_j}) \tag{7}$$

$$\pi_4(C_{x_i x_k}) = \pi_4(C_{x_j x_k})\pi_2(C_{x_i x_j}) + \pi_4(C_{x_j x_k})\pi_4(C_{x_i x_j}) \tag{8}$$

where $\pi_l(C_{x_i x_j})$ is the projection function on l-th element of the quadruple.

Lemma 1. *Let F be a formula representing a restricted path graph $P_n = \{\{x_1^{\epsilon_1}, x_2^{\gamma_1}\}, \{x_2^{\epsilon_2}, x_3^{\gamma_2}\} \cdots \{x_{n-1}^{\epsilon_{n-1}}, x_n^{\gamma_{n-1}}\}\}$, if the contraction rule is applied from $\{x_1^{\epsilon_1}, x_2^{\gamma_1}\}$ to $\{x_{n-1}^{\epsilon_{n-1}}, x_n^{\gamma_{n-1}}\}$ until a triple $(x_1, x_n, C_{x_1 x_n})$ is obtained then*

$$\#2SAT(F) = \pi_1(C_{x_1 x_n}) + \pi_2(C_{x_1 x_n}) + \pi_3(C_{x_1 x_n}) + \pi_4(C_{x_1 x_n})$$

Proof. By induction comparing it with the well known result of Eq. 1. The base case when there is a simple clause $\{x_1^\epsilon, x_2^\gamma\}$, the number of models corresponds with that computed with Eq. 1 as shown in Figs. 1 and 2. In both cases the sum of their tuples is three.

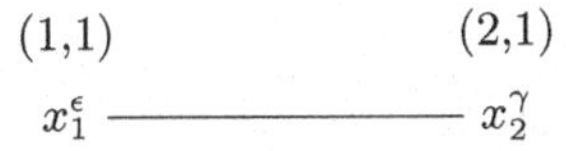

(1,1)   (2,1)

x_1^ϵ —————————— x_2^γ

Fig. 1. Path P_2 using Eq. 1

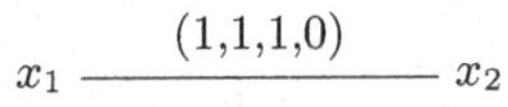

(1,1,1,0)

x_1 —————————— x_2

Fig. 2. Path P_2 using serial counting

On a path P_3, with edges $\{\{x_1^{\epsilon_i}, x_2^{\gamma_i}\}, \{x_2^{\epsilon_j}, x_3^{\gamma_j}\}\}$ the number of models is either 5 if $(\gamma_1 = \epsilon_2)$ or 4 if $(\gamma_1 \neq \epsilon_2)$ (Fig. 3).

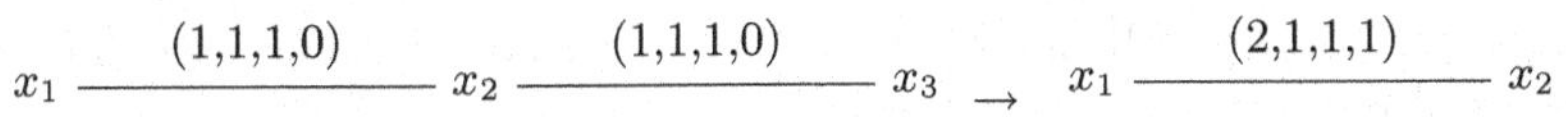

   (1,1,1,0)   (1,1,1,0)   (2,1,1,1)

x_1 ——————— x_2 ——————— x_3 $\rightarrow$ x_1 ——————— x_2

Fig. 3. Path P_2 using serial counting and contraction on x_1

The inductive step is a two case analysis over the values of ϵ and γ.

Example, let $F = \{\{x_1^1, x_2^1\}, \{x_2^1, x_3^0\}, \{x_3^0, x_4^1\}, \{x_4^0, x_5^0\}\}$ be a formula whose restricted graph represents a path. The triples for each clause are: $\{x_1, x_2, (1, 1, 1, 0)\}, \{x_2, x_3, (1, 0, 1, 1)\}, \{x_3, x_4, (1, 1, 0, 1)\}, \{x_4, x_5, (0, 1, 1, 1)\}$.

To make the notation more amenable we use the following representation for the triples.

$$x_1 \;\underset{\text{(1,1,1,0)}}{\rule{2cm}{0.4pt}}\; x_2 \;\underset{\text{(1,0,1,1)}}{\rule{2cm}{0.4pt}}\; x_3 \;\underset{\text{(1,1,0,1)}}{\rule{2cm}{0.4pt}}\; x_4 \;\underset{\text{(0,1,1,1)}}{\rule{2cm}{0.4pt}}\; x_5$$

First we need to contract $\{x_1^1, x_2^1\}$ and $\{x_2, x_3^0\}$ to create a new edge from x_1 to x_3. Using the serial composition equations (6–9) we obtain the new quadruple.

$$x_1 \;\underset{\text{(1,1,2,1)}}{\rule{2cm}{0.4pt}}\; x_3 \;\underset{\text{(1,1,0,1)}}{\rule{2cm}{0.4pt}}\; x_4 \;\underset{\text{(0,1,1,1)}}{\rule{2cm}{0.4pt}}\; x_5$$

Now contracting edges on x_3 we get:

$$x_1 \;\underset{\text{(3,2,2,1)}}{\rule{2cm}{0.4pt}}\; x_4 \;\underset{\text{(0,1,1,1)}}{\rule{2cm}{0.4pt}}\; x_5$$

And finally contracting edges on x_4 we get:

$$x_1 \;\underset{\text{(2,1,5,3)}}{\rule{2cm}{0.4pt}}\; x_5$$

The number of models of the initial formula is obtained by adding the four elements of the quadruple, in this case is 11.

Parallel Counting

Given a clause $\{x_i^{\epsilon_i}, x_j^{\gamma_i}\}$, there are at most four possible parallel clauses of it, including itself: $\{x_i^{\epsilon_i}, x_j^{\gamma_i}\}$, $\{x_i^{\epsilon_i}, x_j^{1-\gamma_i}\}$, $\{x_i^{1-\epsilon_i}, x_j^{\gamma_i}\}$ and the clause $\{x_i^{1-\epsilon_i}, x_j^{1-\gamma_i}\}$. In a formula, at most three of them can be present, otherwise the formula does not have models. In fact, Eqs. 2 and 3 present already known methods for counting models in those classes of parallel clauses.

In this section we extend the contraction method for parallel clauses which again works on clauses instead of vertices. In our method since a clause is represented by a triple $(x_i, x_j, C_{x_i x_j})$, there may be a finite number of parallel clauses of the previous form with different $C_{x_i x_j}$ components, these clauses may come from a serial reduction in a serial-parallel formula.

Let $e_1...e_h$ be parallel clauses on two vertices with triples $Q_{e_l} = (x_i, x_j, C_{x_i y_j}) : 1 \leq l \leq h$. A *merge* of them can be done leaving the result lets say in e_1. The *merge* is accomplished with the following equations:

$$\pi_k(C_{x_i x_j}) = \prod_{l=0}^{h} \pi_k(C_{x_i x_j}) \tag{9}$$

where $k = 1, 2, 3, 4$.

Lemma 2. *Let F be a formula representing a restricted graph of two or three parallel clauses e.g. $F = \{\{x_1^{\epsilon_1}, x_2^{\gamma_1}\}, \{x_1^{\epsilon_2}, x_2^{\gamma_2}\}\}$ or the formula is $F = \{\{x_1^{\epsilon_1}, x_2^{\gamma_1}\}, \{x_1^{\epsilon_2}, x_2^{\gamma_2}\}, \{x_1^{\epsilon_3}, x_2^{\gamma_3}\}\}$, if the merging rule is applied until a single triple is left $(x_1, x_2, C_{x_1 x_2}\}$ then*

$$\#2SAT(F) = \pi_1(C_{x_1 x_2}) + \pi_2(C_{x_1 x_2}) + \pi_3(C_{x_1 x_2}) + \pi_4(C_{x_1 x_2})$$

Proof. A simple case analysis is done comparing the results with the well known results of Eqs. 2 and 3. The result for two parallel clauses is shown in Fig. 4 and their merge in Fig. 5.

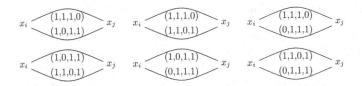

Fig. 4. Parallel cases of two clauses

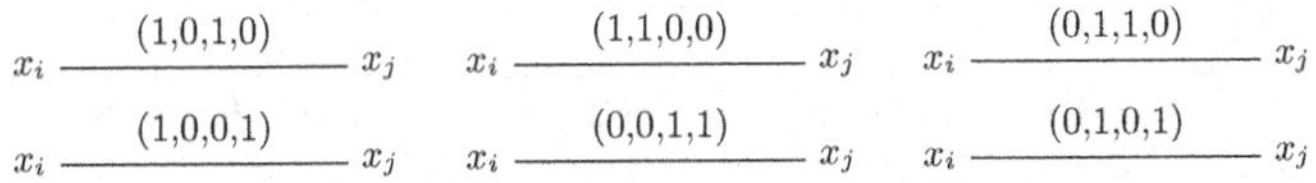

Fig. 5. Applying merging rule on cases of two clauses

From Eq. 2 the pair (α_i, β_i) obtained on cases of two parallel clauses $(x_i^{\epsilon_1}, x_j^{\gamma_1})$ and $(x_i^{\epsilon_2}, x_j^{\gamma_2})$ are $(2,0)$ if $(\epsilon_1, \gamma_1) = (1,1)$ and $(\epsilon_2, \gamma_2) = (0,1)$, it is $(0,2)$ if $(\epsilon_1, \gamma_1) = (1,0) and (\epsilon_2, \gamma_2) = (0,0)$, and $(1,1)$ on the remaining cases. Fot three clauses the analysis is similar.

For example given parallel clauses $e_1 = \{x_i^1, x_j^1\}$, $e_2 = \{x_i^1, x_j^0\}$, with elements $C_{x_i x_j} = (1,1,1,0)$ of e_1 and $C_{x_i x_j} = (1,0,1,1)$ of e_2. They can be merged obtaining the updated element $C_{x_i x_j} = (1,0,1,0)$ as graphically show in Figs. 6 and 7.

$$(1,1,1,0)$$
$$x_i \qquad \qquad x_j$$
$$(1,0,1,1)$$

Fig. 6. Graphical representation of the quadruples for e_1, e_2

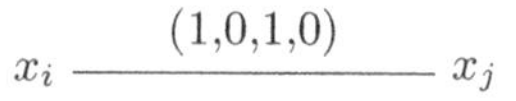

$$x_i \ \underline{\hspace{1cm} (1,0,1,0) \hspace{1cm}} \ x_j$$

Fig. 7. Merging e_1 and e_2

4 Counting on Series-Parallel Formulas

A graph represents a Series-Parallel formula if it can be built from a single edge and the following two operations:

1. Series construction: subdividing an edge in the graph.
2. Parallel construction: duplicating an edge in the graph.

Another characterization of a series-parallel graph is that it do not contain a subdivision of K_4 (complete graph of four vertices). The first characterization implies that a series-parallel graph always has a vertex of degree two and further more given a series-parallel graph we can always deconstruct it using the inverse of the previous described operations. This section presents the algorithm used for counting models on Series-Parallel graphs. Algorithm 1 computes the number of models of a series-parallel formula, it consists of two main steps: serial deconstruction (contraction) and parallel deconstruction (merging).

Algorithm 1. Procedure that computes $\#2SAT(F)$ when F represents a series-parallel graph

---

1: **procedure** $\#2\text{SAT}(F)$
2: Compute the incident matrix of F to get the degree of each vertex
3: **while** $|F > 1|\{$There are more than one clause$\}$ **do**
4:     **for** each vertex x_i of degree 2 **do**
5:         Apply the series contraction rule to the two clauses x_i belongs to
6:     **end for**
7:     **for** each pair of parallel clause **do**
8:         Apply the parallel merging rule to those clauses
9:     **end for**
10: **end while**
11: Let $e = \{x_i, x_j\}$ be the left clause and its triple $Q_e = (x_i, x_j, C_{x_i x_j})$
12: **return** $\pi_1(C_{x_i x_j}) + \pi_2(C_{x_i x_j}) + \pi_3(C_{x_i x_j}) + \pi_4(C_{x_i x_j})$.

Theorem 1. *If F is a series-parallel formula then Algorithm 1 computes $\#2SAT(F)$.*

Proof. A consequence of Lemmas 1 and 2.

4.1 Running Example

We now present an example in order to explain our algorithm, let

$$F = \{\{x_1^1, x_2^1\}, \{x_2^1, x_3^1\}, \{x_3^0, x_{10}^0\}, \{x_1^1, x_4^1\}, \{x_4^1, x_5^0\}, \{x_5^0, x_{10}^1\},$$
$$\{x_1^1, x_6^1\}, \{x_6^0, x_7^1\}, \{x_7^1, x_{10}^0\}, \{x_1^1, x_8^1\}, \{x_8^0, x_9^0\}, \{x_9^1, x_{10}^1\}\}$$

be a formula whose restricted graph represents a series-parallel graph as shown in Fig. 8. The triples for each clause are:

$$x_1, x_2, (1, 1, 1, 0), x_2, x_3, (1, 1, 1, 0), x_3, x_{10}, (0, 1, 1, 1), x_1, x_4, (1, 1, 1, 0),$$
$$x_4, x_5, (1, 0, 1, 1), x_5, x_{10}, (1, 1, 0, 1), x_1, x_6, (1, 1, 1, 0), x_6, x_7, (1, 1, 0, 1),$$
$$x_7, x_{10}, (1, 0, 1, 1), x_1, x_8, (1, 1, 1, 0), x_8, x_9, (0, 1, 1, 1), x_9, x_{10}, (1, 1, 1, 0), .$$

We use the previous graphical representation to make the reductions application clear:

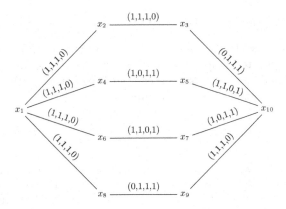

Fig. 8. Representation of a series-parallel formula

First we need to contract on every vertex x_i where $\delta(x_i) = 2$. Then we obtain a new set of edges.

Then we can use the merging of parallel clauses between x_1 and x_{10} (Fig. 10).

The number of models of the initial formula is obtained by adding the four elements of the quadruple, in this case is 38.

5 Complexity Analysis

Although Algorithm1 has a *while* and inside two *for* instructions, in each step either a contraction or a merging operation is applied, hence a clause is removed in each step. So $m - 1$ steps are needed to reduce the graph until a single clause is obtained. Each reduction computes a quadruple so $4(m - 1)$ operations are needed. The computation of the incident matrix takes $m + n$ steps, so in total $5m + n$ operations are required which represents a procedure of order $O(m + n)$ time complexity.

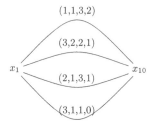

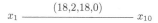

Fig. 9. Result of contracting on x_i where $\delta(x_i) = 2$

$$x_1 \;\underset{\text{(18,2,18,0)}}{\rule{4cm}{0.4pt}}\; x_{10}$$

Fig. 10. Result of merging the parallel clauses of Fig. 9

6 Conclusions

In this paper we present an algorithm to compute the $\#2SAT(F)$ when F is a formula whose restricted graph represents a series-parallel graph. We show that our algorithm is correct and its time complexity is linear with respect to the number of variables and clauses of the input formula.

References

1. Winkler, P., Brifhtwell, G.: Counting linear extensions. Order, **8**(e), 225–242 (1991)
2. López-Medina, M.A., Marcial-Romero, J.R., De Ita Luna, G., Montes-Venegas, H.A., Alejo, R.: A linear time algorithm for solving #2SAT on cactus formulas. CoRR, ams/1702.08581 (2017)
3. López, M.A., Marcial-Romero, J.R., De Ita, G., Moyao, Y.: A linear time algorithm for computing #2SAT for outerplanar 2-CNF formulas. In: Martínez-Trinidad, J.F., Carrasco-Ochoa, J.A., Olvera-López, J.A., Sarkar, S. (eds.) MCPR 2018. LNCS, vol. 10880, pp. 72–81. Springer, Cham (2018). https://doi.org/10.1007/978-3-319-92198-3_8
4. Wahlström, M.: A tighter bound for counting max-weight solutions to 2SAT instances. In: Grohe, M., Niedermeier, R. (eds.) IWPEC 2008. LNCS, vol. 5018, pp. 202–213. Springer, Heidelberg (2008). https://doi.org/10.1007/978-3-540-79723-4_19
5. Schoenmakers, L.A.M.: A new algorithm for the recognition of series parallel graphs. CWI (Centre for Mathematics and Computer Science) (1995)
6. Eppstein, D.: Parallel recognition of series-parallel graphs. Inf. Comput. **98**, 41–55 (1992)
7. Takamizawa, K., Nishizeki, T., Saito, N.: Linear-time computability of combinatorial problems on series-parallel graphs. J. Assoc. Comput. Mach. **29**(3), 623–641 (1982)
8. Gross, J.L., Yellen, J., Zhang, P.: Handbook of Graph Theory. Chapman & Hall/CRC, New York (2013)

9. Dieter, J.: Graphs, Networks and Algorithms., 4th edn. Springer, Heidelberg (2013). https://doi.org/10.1007/978-3-642-32278-5
10. Jakoby, A., Liśkiewicz, M., Reischuk, R.: Space efficient algorithms for directed series-parallel graphs. J. Algorithms **60**(2), 85–114 (2006)
11. Szeider, S.: On fixed-parameter tractable parameterizations of SAT. In: Giunchiglia, E., Tacchella, A. (eds.) SAT 2003. LNCS, vol. 2919, pp. 188–202. Springer, Heidelberg (2004). https://doi.org/10.1007/978-3-540-24605-3_15
12. Marcial-Romero, J.R., De Ita Luna, G., Hernández, J.A., Valdovinos, R.M.: A parametric polynomial deterministic algorithm for #2SAT. In: Sidorov, G., Galicia-Haro, S.N. (eds.) MICAI 2015. LNCS (LNAI), vol. 9413, pp. 202–213. Springer, Cham (2015). https://doi.org/10.1007/978-3-319-27060-9_16

Zone Specific Index Based Model for Data Storage Identification in Search Query Processing

Aditi Bankura[1,2]([⊠]) and Anirban Kundu[1,2]

[1] Netaji Subhash Engineering College, Kolkata 700152, India
aditi.bankura@gmail.com, anik76in@gmail.com
[2] Computer Innovative Research Society, Howrah 711103, India

Abstract. In this paper, zone-specific index based model has been designed to store web pages collected from registered web site and processing of search queries placed at search engine. Identification of relevant web page is accomplished through matching of keywords in search query and web pages. Another key issue of search query processing is response time. It is always desirable that minimum delay in response time to processing of a search query. Response time of search query is dependent on network framework used and indexing mechanism to identify data storage among several available data repository to identify web pages. In proposed model, distribution of web pages among data storage systems is accomplished through matching of keywords presence in each web page to related keywords of zones. Each web page is stored in data storage systems through identification of zones. Search query is processed through zone identification using matching of keywords presence in each search query to related keywords of zones. Presence of specific keywords in web page and search query helps for speedy identification of specific zones as well as identification of data storage systems. Organization of web pages among data storage systems using zone-specific index based mechanism improves response time and accuracy for processing of search queries.

Keywords: Web crawler · Zone-specific keyword · Zone-specific search · Deciding factors · Search query processing

1 Introduction

Today's world is become full of information with improvement in modern technologies. Meaningful information is called as 'data'. Data is now generated exponentially from every aspect of our life via electronic device, sensor device, social networks, business industry, education industry as every instance is stored as a data. Large volume of data is not possible to store and process with traditional database management systems. Big data is introduced to process of large volume of data.

© Springer Nature Switzerland AG 2020
L. Martínez-Villaseñor et al. (Eds.): MICAI 2020, LNAI 12468, pp. 448–458, 2020.
https://doi.org/10.1007/978-3-030-60884-2_34

Volume, variety, velocity, veracity and value are five characteristics of big data. These five characteristics also known as 5Vs. Big data is able to manage big volume of data gathered from variety of sources with rapid generation of data i.e. velocity processing with integrity of data i.e. veracity and data values [1].

Major challenges of gathering of data from heterogeneous sources distributed in network, indexing mechanism to store data, reduction in dimension of data, analysis of data, and discovery of knowledge from data [2]. Indexing of data and reduction in dimension of data reduces processing time of data [3]. Data analysis and knowledge extraction from data is accomplished with applying clustering and classification algorithms based on application area. Hadoop distributed file system (HDFS) is big data analytic tool which works in distributed environment with map-reduce technique in which K-means algorithm is used as a clustering algorithm to perform data analysis and knowledge extraction [4, 5].

Motivation of this research work is to distribute data among data storage systems to provide accuracy in processing of search queries and to improve in query response time for search queries.

Rest of the paper is organized as follows: Sect. 2 represents a brief description on related works; in Sect. 3, design framework for zone-specific searching is discussed; procedure for proposed design framework is introduced in Sect. 4; experimental observations have been depicted in Sect. 5; in Sect. 6, conclusion has been drawn.

2 Related Works

Initially, information is gathered and stored in a temporary repository from various web sites through several crawlers. Fast, effective crawling techniques plays major role for collection of information as web pages [6].

After that, forward indexing mechanism is used in which each web page is parsed to find set of words, occurrence of each word and position of each word and then, the web page is distributed among several storage systems known as barrels by indexer. Here, each web page is mapped to correlated words. Redundant words require more storage space and time as web pages are searched to check presence of words in search queries. Inverted indexing mechanism has been introduced to overcome storage problem and improvements in searching time. Each word is mapped to corresponding web pages. Inverted indexing requires more time to store data among storage systems than forward indexing [7].

Ontology based indexing mechanism is used where words are mapped with context of documents rather than mapping from words to documents. Accuracy in information is enhanced through ontology based indexing [8]. Area related words and statements are used for that purpose. Binary search tree, semantic suffix tree and graph based indexing are a popular clustering index structure for storing ontology information [9–11]. Basic requirement of efficient indexing mechanism is to distribute data among storage systems to search and identify relevant data from repository [12–14].

3 Design Framework for Zone-Specific Searching

We have designed a zone-specific index based system framework to organize web pages collected from registered web sites in Search Engine within available data storage systems, and have retrieved relevant web pages residing in selected data storage systems among all available storage systems for processing of users' search queries. Proposed system performs two major tasks, such as storage of web pages within data storage systems, and identification of search queries related to web pages. The tasks are performed through correlation establishment among keywords with specified zones where each zone is associated with specified set of keywords considered as deciding factors of particular zone.

Each keyword is recognized as a zone-specific keyword (Zspe) through presence of the keyword in specific number of zones. Suppose a word 'Network' is associated with 'Networking', 'Network Security', 'Social Network', 'Cartoon Network' zone etc. 'Cryptography' keyword is associated with 'Network Security' zones. 'Cryptography' is a special keyword through which selection of web pages related with 'Network Security' zone is faster than searching web pages through 'Network' word. Hence, 'Cryptography' is to be considered as zone-specific-keyword (Zspe).

A keyword having less association with number of zones helps to intend the keyword to be 'zone-specific'. Unavailability of keyword in specified number of zones generates 'zone-specific' keyword.

Let, we have set of keywords, $K = \{K_1, K_2, K_3,........, K_m\}$; where 'm' is total number of keywords and, set of zones, $Z = \{Z_1, Z_2, Z_3, ..., Z_n\}$; where 'n' is total number of zones;

Correlation between a keyword and zones is represented as shown in Fig. 1. From Fig. 1, it has been observed that $p_j^{W \to X}$ notation has been used in which p_j represents total number of zones from Z_W to Z_X in which K_i is not available. For example, $p_1^{2 \to 3}$ represents K_i is not available from Z_2 to zone Z_3 and total number of zones from Z_2 to Z_3 is p_1.

∴ K_i is collectively not available in $(p_1 + p_2 + ... + p_t)$ number of zones.

Again, $(p_1 + p_2 + ... + p_t) \neq n$; Because, each keyword is linked with at least one zone. Otherwise, mapping from keyword to zone is not possible.

Let, $p = (p_1 + p_2 + ... + p_t)$;

A keyword is to be considered as 'zone-specific' if and only if the keyword is not available in 'p' number of zones. If a keyword is present in maximum $(n - p)$ number of zones, then keyword is to be considered as 'zone-specific'.

Figure 2 represents proposed design framework. The working procedure of proposed framework is as follows:

Step 1: Generation of keywords from web page or user's search query after elimination of stop-words from content of web page or search query respectively.

Step 2: For each keyword, correlations are established between the keyword to all specified zones.

Step 3: Frequency measurement of each keyword.

Step 4: If frequency of each keyword is less than equal to specified number of zones

Step 4.1: Then, the keyword is identified as 'zone-specific'.

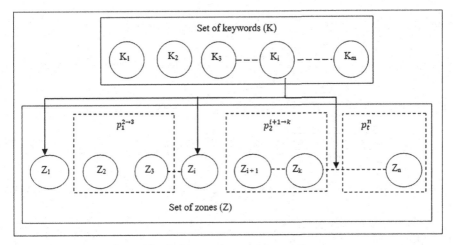

Fig. 1. Keywords to zones mapping

Step 4.2: If web page or search query has 'zone-specific' keyword (s).

Step 4.3: Then, all zone-specific keyword related zones are identified.

Step 4.4: Else, zones are identified for all extracted keywords.

Step 5: All selected zones related databases are identified to store web page or fetch web pages.

Generation of keywords from web pages and search queries is first requirement. Generation of keywords from web pages is performed through crawler module and parser module. Crawler module is a collection of web crawlers where each new web page is fetched from registered web site and downloaded by an available crawler. Then, downloaded web page is stored in repository by that crawler. After that, stored web page is processed by parser module. As a result, set of keywords are generated after elimination of all stop-words from contents of web page. Set of keywords from a web page is an output of parser module. On the other hand, generation of keywords from a particular search query placed by a user is accomplished through elimination of stop-words from search query.

After that, each keyword from list of generated keywords is mapped with zones dependent on prior specified deciding factors of each zone. For example, if a keyword 'K_x' is matched with deciding factors of a particular zone 'Z_j', then association between 'K_x' and 'Z_j' is considered as '1'. If a keyword 'K_x' is not matched with any keyword of a particular zone 'Z_j', then association between 'K_x' and 'Z_j' is considered as '0'.

Next, frequency of each keyword is measured. Presence of each keyword in number of zones is considered as frequency of that keyword. 'F_x' represents that a keyword 'K_x' is present in 'F_x' number of zones.

Then, frequency of each keyword helps to determine a particular keyword is zone-specific. If frequency of a keyword is lies within '1' to '$(n-p)$' where 'n' is total number of zones and 'p' number of zones in which that keyword is not present, then keyword is to be considered as 'zone-specific' keyword. After that, if a web page or search

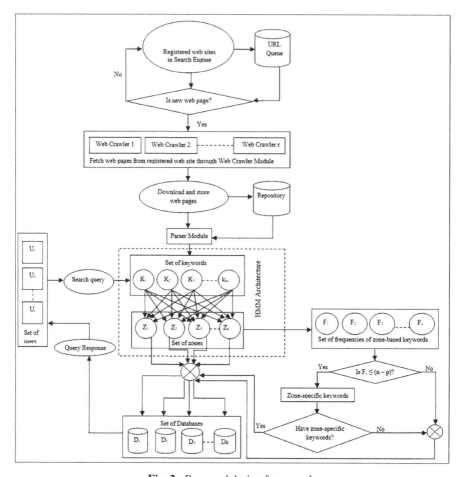

Fig. 2. Proposed design framework

query contains zone-specific keyword(s), then zone-specific keyword(s) based zones are identified. Finally, each identified zone is mapped with specified databases.

4   Procedure for Proposed Design Framework

Zone-specific searching is dependent on presence of keywords in search queries generated by users in search engine and deciding factors of each zone from specified available zones. Each web page and each search query is mapped with a particular zone if and only if at least one keyword in web page or search query is matched with one deciding factor of that zone. Otherwise, mapping from web page or search query to that particular zone is not being possible. Each web page or search query is correlated with specified zones from available zones through matching of keywords in web page or search query and deciding factors of zones before storing of web page in data storage or fetching of relevant web pages from data storage with respect to search query. Searching of relevant web pages from identified data storage systems for user given search queries using zone-specific index based procedure has been explained as follows:

Algorithm 1: Storage_Identification_Using_Zone_Specific_Index ( )

Input i: number of search queries to be processed;

n: total number of zones

p: maximum number of allow zones in which keywords are not to be present

Output URLs of web pages from identified data storage systems

Step 1: For i = 1 to i = number of search queries

Step 2: Extract set of distinct keywords from ith search query

Step 3: For k = 1 to k = number of extract keywords

Step 4: Initialize, KeywordFrequency [k] = 0;

Step 5: End of loop 'k'

Step 6: For k = 1 to k = number of extract keywords

Step 7: For z = 1 to z = number of zones 'n'

Step 8: If k^{th} keyword is matched with deciding factors of zth zone, then

Step 9: Increase KeywordFrequency [k] by 1

Step 10: Add 'z' to list key_zone [k]

Step 11: End of loop 'z'

Step 12: End of loop 'k'

Step 13: Construct ascending ordered list K [{'key', 'value'}], for k = 1 to k= number of extract keywords

Step 14: For j = 1 to j = length of list K [ ]

Step 15: If {'value'}of K [j] ≤ (n − p), then add {'key'} of K[j] to list zone_specific_key [ ]

Step 16: Else, end of loop 'j'

Step 17: End of loop 'j'

Step 18: If length of zone_specific_key [ ] ≠ 0, then

Step 19: For k = 1 to k = length of zone_specific_key [ ]

Step 20: Else, for k = 1 to k = length of K[ ]

Step 21: For z =1 to z = length of key_zone [k]

Step 22: For s = 1 to s = number of databases

Step 23: If z^{th} zone is associated with s^{th} database, then

Step 24: For p = 1 to p = number of web pages in s^{th} database

Step 25: If p^{th} web page is not already fetched, then

Step 26: If k^{th} keyword is matched with p^{th} web page, then

Step 27: Fetch URL of pth web page from s^{th} database

Step 28: Stop

Algorithm 1 describes how multiple search queries are processed, data storage systems are being identified for each query, and relevant web pages are recognized from identified data storage systems through proposed design model. Each search query is processed from Step 2 to Step 27. In step 2, all possible keywords are extracted from a given search query after elimination of all stop-words from it. Then, for each keyword found in Step 2, we have set KeywordFrequency [k] = 0 in Step 4 to ensure that initially each keyword is not linked with existing available zones. After that, each keyword is mapped to zones depending on presence of that keyword in deciding factors of zones using Step 6 to Step 12. If matching of a keyword to a zone is possible, then Keyword-Frequency [k] is incremented by one (refer Step 9) and information of zones is stored to list key_zone [k] (refer Step 10). Suppose, we have $k = 7$, $z = 5$ and KeywordFrequency [7] = 2. Then, we have following information:

- Presently, 7th keyword is comparing with deciding factors of 5th zone.
- Previously, 7th keyword is matched with two zones from 1st zone to 6th zone.
- List key_zone [7] contains information about two zones connected with 7th keyword.

Assume, 7th keyword is matched with any deciding factor of 5th zone, then Keyword-Frequency [7] is incremented by one and set KeywordFrequency [7] = 3 to represent that 7th keyword is matched with three zones from 1st zone to 7th zone (refer Step 9). Due to matching of 5th zone with 7th keyword, list key_zone [7] is modified with adding 5th zone to key_zone [7]. List key_zone [7] contains information about three zones connected with 7th keyword (refer Step 10). Hence, zones are identified from keywords.

After correlation establishment between "keywords & zones" and storing information about correlated zones, an ascending ordered list 'K' is created as key-value pair (i.e.{'key', 'value'}) in Step 13. 'key' and 'value' represent particular keyword and presence of the keyword in number of zones respectively. In list K, 'value' of each 'key' is always greater than zero. Then, 'value' of each 'key' is compared to $(n - p)$ to identify zone-specific keywords from extracted keywords from Step 14 to Step 15. Initially, 'p' is set to maximum number of allow zones in which keywords are not to be present to identify zone-specific keywords, then 'value' of each 'key' should be limited from 1 to maximum $(n - p)$ to become zone-specific keyword. Each 'key' with 'value' limited within 1 to maximum $(n - p)$ is stored in a list zone_specific_key [] which contains all zone-specific keywords from extracted keywords (refer Step 15). List of zone_specific_key [] should be empty if and only if no zone-specific keyword is present in search query. Hence, zone_specific_key[] list which is more accurate over extracted keywords.

Zones are identified through Step 18 to Step 21. If length of zone_specific_key [] list is not equal to zero, then zones are to be identified through zone-specific keywords stored in zone_specific_key [] list. Only zone-specific keywords related zones would be identified where correlated zones are stored in key_zone [] list for each zone-specific keyword in zone_specific_key [] list (refer Step 21). Otherwise, zones are to be identified through K [] list where extracted keywords are stored. Maximum accuracy in zone identification is achieved through identification of zones using zone-specific keywords and all effective keywords are mapped to relevant zones.

Required data storage systems are identified for each zone specified either in zone_specific_key [] list or in K [] list through Step 22 to Step 23. Each effective keyword is mapped to relevant data storage systems through identification of zones using proposed design model.

Each web page in data storage is checked whether previously fetched using Step 24 and Step 25. If a particular web page is not yet fetched, then again it is checked for particular keywords presence in specific web page (refer Step 26). If particular keyword is present in web page, then URL of particular web page is fetched. Each keyword is mapped to required web pages through identification of data storage systems using zone-specific based indexing design model.

5 Experimental Discussions

Search query processing using zone-specific indexing model framework is used for 50 keywords, 10 zones and 10 search queries as a sample study in this section.

Figure 3 shows identification of zone-specific keywords to measure presence of each keyword in number of zones after correlation establishment between keywords and zones. X-axis represent number of keywords and Y-axis represents the presence of each keyword in number of zones $(n-p)$. As per Fig. 3, 10 keywords are correlated with only '1' zone from 10 specified zones. Similarly, 5 more keywords are identified as zone-specific keywords for $(n-p) == 2$ and 4 more keywords are identified as zone-specific keywords for $(n-p) == 3$. Total 15 $(10 + 5)$ keywords are to be considered as total number of zone specific keywords for $(n-p) == 2$ in which 10 keywords and 5 keywords are present in '1' zone and '2' zones respectively. Similarly, total 19 $(10 + 5 + 4)$ are recognized as zone specific keywords where 10 keywords, 5 keywords and 4 keywords are present in '1' zone, '2' zones and '3' zones respectively. Increase of $(n-p)$ value increases number of identified keywords though, more correlation with zones which is not desirable. Hence, $(n-p)$ should be kept minimum for minimum selection of keywords to make web page or search query zone-specific to minimize query response time of search queries.

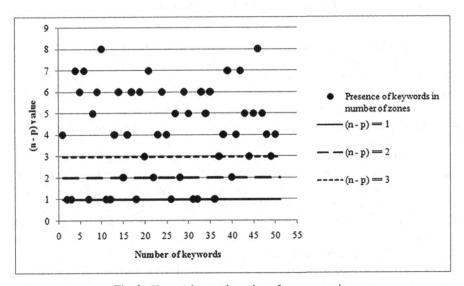

Fig. 3. Keyword to total number of zones mapping

Figure 4 shows number of keywords present in a search query and identifies specific keywords present in the search query. For example, 1st search query, and 2nd search query contains one keyword (3rd keyword), and two keywords (16th and 41th keyword) respectively. Minimum one and maximum three keywords are to be present in each search query as shown in Fig. 4. Therefore, query processing is dependent on presence of keywords in that query.

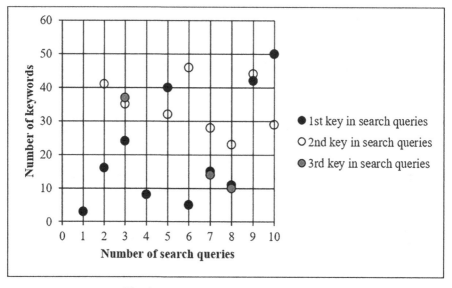

Fig. 4. Search query to keywords mapping

Each search query is identified as zone-specific search query depending on the presence of keywords in that search query in number of zones (refer Fig. 3) as shown in Fig. 5. From Fig. 5 it has been observed that three keywords (24th, 35th and 37th keywords) are present in 3rd search query only 37th keyword is zone-specific keyword for (n–p) ==1among these three keywords (refer Fig. 3). Therefore, 3rd search query is zone-specific search query with respect to (n – p) == 1. Similarly, it has been observed from Fig. 5 that 10th search query is become zone-specific search if and only if (n–p) is set to '3'. Otherwise, 10th search query is not zone-specific search query for (n–p) == 1 and (n–p) == 2 values. Figure 5 depicts that 1st, 3rd, 4th and 5th search queries are zone-specific search query for (n–p) == 1. It has been also found that from Fig. 5, 2nd and 8th search queries are zone-specific search query for (n – p) == 2 and 10th search query are zone-specific search query for (n–p) == 3. 6th, 7th and 9th search queries are not zone-specific for $1 \leq$ (n–p) ≤ 3. There, presence of zone-specific keyword formulates a search query zone-specific search query.

Query response time of proposed system framework is compared with existing system framework such as Google as shown in Fig. 6. Response time of ten search queries has been compared as a sample study. Figure 6 depicts that response time of each search query in proposed design framework is less than existing system. It has been also observed that all search queries are processed at par. Therefore, proposed system

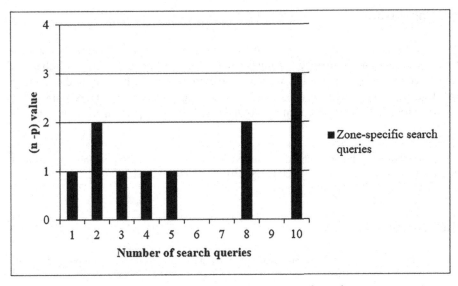

Fig. 5. Identification of zone-specific search queries

framework provides improvement in query response time and performance of the system is not widely varied with respect to query response time.

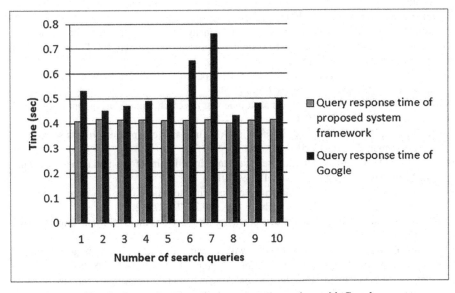

Fig. 6. Comparison based on query response time with Google

6 Conclusion

We have discussed about working procedure of zone-specific index framework and how zone-specific keywords are become important for construction of indexing of web pages and processing of search queries. We have also emphasized mechanism for data storage identification for processing of search queries using zone-specific index framework. Query response time has been improved and consistency in performance of system is achieved.

Acknowledgment. This research work is funded by Computer Innovative Research Society, West Bengal, India. Award number is "2020/CIRS/R&D/2020-07-21/ZSIMDSISQP".

References

1. Lakshmi, C., Kumar, V.V.N.: Survey paper on big data. Int. J. Adv. Res. Comput. Sci. Softw. Eng. **6**, 368–381 (2016)
2. Acharjya, D.P., P, K.A.: A survey on big data analytics: challenges, open research issues and tools. Int. J. Adv. Res. Comput. Sci. Softw. Eng. **7**, 511–518 (2016)
3. Jain, M., Verma, C.: Adapting k-means for clustering in big data. Int. J. Comput. Appl. **101**, 19–24 (2014)
4. Sanse, K., Sharma, M.: Clustering methods for big data analysis. Int. J. Adv. Res. Comput. Eng. Technol. **4**, 642–648 (2015)
5. Sajana, T., Rani, C.M.S., Narayana, K.V.: A survey on clustering techniques for big data mining. Ind. J. Sci. Technol. **9**, 1–12 (2016)
6. Kundu, A., Dutta, R., Dattagupta, R., Mukhopadhyay, D.: Mining the web with hierarchical crawlers - a resource sharing based crawling approach. Int. J. Intell. Inf. Database Syst. **3**, 90–106 (2009)
7. Brin, S., Page, L.: The anatomy of a large-scale hypertextual web search engine. In: Computer network and ISDN systems, pp. 107–117 (1998)
8. Gupta, P., Sharma, A.K.: Context based indexing in search engines using Ontology. Int. J. Comput. Appl. **1**, 49–52 (2010)
9. Kathuri, C., Datta, G., Kaul, V.: Context indexing in search engine using binary search tree. Int. J. Comput. Sci. Eng. **5**, 514–521 (2013)
10. Soe, T.L.: Ontology-based indexing and semantic indexing in information retrieval systems. Int. J. Res. Stud. Comput. Sci. Eng. **1**, 1–9 (2014)
11. Kesavan, V.T., Kumar, B.S.: Graph based indexing techniques for big data analytics: a systematic survey. Int. J. Recent Technol. Eng, pp. 2277–3878 (2019)
12. Mittal, M.: Indexing techniques and challenge in big data. Int. J. Current Eng. Technol, pp. 1225–1228 (2017)
13. Anand, P., Maan, S.: A study on big data with indexing technique for searching and retrieval of data fastly. Int. J. Innovative Res. Comput. Commun. Eng, pp. 505–508 (2018)
14. John, A., Sugumaran, M., Rajesh, R.S.: Indexing and query processing techniques in spatio-temporal data. ICTACT J. Soft Comput. **6**, 1198–1217 (2016)

Exploitation of Deaths Registry in Mexico to Estimate the Total Deaths by Influenza Virus: A Preparation to Estimate the Advancement of COVID-19

Emmanuel Byrd, Miguel González-Mendoza$^{(\boxtimes)}$, and Leonardo Chang

Tecnologico de Monterrey, Escuela de Ingenieria y Ciencias,
Estado de Mexico, Mexico
a01166339@itesm.mx , mgonza@tex.mx, lchang@tec.mx

Abstract. Following the *AH1N1 influenza virus* of 2009, it was suspected that many deaths were being incorrectly registered as caused by *unclassified pneumonia* in Mexico. In light of the current *SARS-CoV-2* (or *COVID-19*) pandemic, it was assumed that a similar phenomenon was occurring. To verify this hypothesis, a machine learning algorithm that can estimate the extent of false negative *AH1N1 influenza virus* registration in Mexico was developed. The INEGI database of deaths in Mexico in 2005 through 2008, and World Health Organization International Classification of Diseases, the deaths by *influenza* and deaths by *unclassified pneumonia* were utilized to train the algorithm in order to differentiate the expected and observed influenza deaths in 2009. By predicting the pattern of *unclassified pneumonia* deaths for the year 2009, it was found that the difference between the expected and observed deaths had a strong correlation with the amount of deaths of *influenza virus*. This reveals that the deaths recorded as *influenza virus* in 2009 are a statistical representation of many deaths registered as *unclassified pneumonia*, but attributable to the same virus. With this, it was possible to estimate the precise ratio of this correlation in 2009. Without the *COVID-19* and *unclassified pneumonia* data for the years 2019 and 2020 available, it is not yet possible to apply the findings of this work to the current global pandemic. However, a generalization method to do so is proposed. This work was made on Python, and the code is available on GitHub (https://github.com/EByrdS/influenza_deaths_mx).

Keywords: COVID-19 · COVID · SARS-CoV-2 · Mexico · Deaths · Machine Learning · Estimation · Prediction · Python · sklearn · INEGI · Influenza

We thank the support of CONACYT, and the doctors *Enrique López Rangel, Pediatric Oncologist, Centro Hospitalario Nuevo Sanatorio Durango*, and *Antonio Berumen, Surgeon, Universidad Panamericana* as their guidance was essential in the development of this project.

L. Martínez-Villaseñor et al. (Eds.): MICAI 2020, LNAI 12468, pp. 459–469, 2020.
https://doi.org/10.1007/978-3-030-60884-2_35

1   Introduction

As this work is being created, the global pandemic of **COVID-19** is causing havoc all around the world. The necessity for analysis of massive amounts of data and information is crucial. The goal of this work is to provide a solid foundation in which we can work immediately when the death databases of Mexico are published, to accurately estimate the actual number of deaths by COVID-19.

Determining the actual number of deaths as a result of the disease can significantly help us understand the advancement of the pandemic and the effect of the safety measures applied to fight it [8]. However, the cause of death of many people who died **infected** by the *SARS-CoV-2* is recorded as **unclassified pneumonia** [6]. Why? Some suspect it may be due to scarcity of tests, their cost, or the lack of an effective treatment for the disease, which make the result of the test invaluable for the individual. More underlying reasons can only be speculated to why not all the *actual* number of deaths of the disease. But there is confidence in that this problem exists, because it has been observed in the past.

Some assumptions regarding one death are useful: the event can only happen once for each individual, it cannot be overlooked. And the processes and institutions that gather this information have not changed much throughout the years.

When a death certificate is produced, its details are stored by the National Institute of Statistics and Geography (INEGI) [3,4]. Each year they publish a new dataset for the deaths recorded. These datasets are formed by individual records containing information like the dates of birth and death, the specific locations of living and death, the sex, cause of death, and other interesting attributes like the profession and level of studies.

The most important attribute on this project is the cause of death, which requires a section of its own. Section 2 explains the International Classification of Diseases, Sect. 3 explains how the raw data was processed before digesting it. Section 4 gives the immediate insights of visualizing the data. Section 5 shows how the data was adjusted for the population growth. Section 6 explains how parts of the population can be used to understand the behavior of the total. Section 7 show the result of adjusting the records of deaths by Influenza. Section 8 shows the conclusions and Sect. 9 presents possible workarounds for the registries of deaths that are still missing and the workarounds to replicate this project without the currently missing databases of deaths.

2   The International Classification of Diseases

The World Health Organization created the 10th version of the International Classification of Diseases, or ICE-10 [5] (CIE-10 [10] in Spanish), which is used in the databases of our interest.

The diseases are classified in Chapters, which are then separated into Groups, and lastly to Diseases and Specifications. Each code is composed by one letter

Table 1. Grouping of selected codes, according to specificity of the microorganism.

Specified microorganism	Unspecified microorganism
J09	J12
J10	J15
J11	J16
J13	J18
J14	

Table 2. Number of records from 17-Dec-2004 to 31-Dec-2018 for each of the used codes.

Code	Percentage	Count
J18	94.072244	203,657
J15	3.479145	7532
J09	1.500762	3249
J11	0.424038	918
J10	0.343203	743
J12	0.131184	284
J13	0.035567	77
J16	0.011548	25
J14	0.002310	5

followed by two numbers. Diseases under the same Chapter start with the same letter, and closely related diseases are closer in their number.

2.1 Codes Used to Identify Influenza and Unclassified Pneumonia

The codes that are used in this work are the following, marked in **bold**:

- Chapter X: Diseases of the respiratory system (J00-J99)
  1. Group J09-J18: Influenza and pneumonia
     (a) **J09** Influenza due to identified zoonotic or pandemic influenza virus
     (b) **J10** Influenza due to identified seasonal influenza virus
     (c) **J11** Influenza, virus not identified
     (d) **J12** Viral pneumonia, not elsewhere classified
     (e) **J13** Pneumonia due to Streptococcus pneumoniae
     (f) **J14** Pneumonia due to Haemophilus influenzae
     (g) **J15** Bacterial pneumonia, not elsewhere classified
     (h) **J16** Pneumonia due to other infectious organisms, not elsewhere classified
     (i) **J18** Pneumonia, organism unspecified

It is speculated that the disease COVID-19 will get a code of its own, and will very likely belong in this same Chapter. While all these codes account for *Influenza and pneumonia*, it can be seen that some codes specify a microorganism and the rest specify that the microorganism is unknown. Thus, the codes were grouped into two categories, shown in Table 1.

From now on, the codes under "Specified microorganism" are referred to as **Influenza**, because that disease composes the vast majority of the selected codes. And the codes under "Unspecified microorganism" are referred to as **Unspecified**. The largest cause of death is **J18: Pneumonia, organism**

unspecified, by a large margin. The number of records for each code are shown in Table 2.

The causes of death in the database are stored with four characters. This means they were recorded with the deepest level of specification of ICD-10, however, only the first three characters were used. This and many other techniques of data cleaning were applied before the machine learning training started.

3 Data Cleaning

All records that had empty values in the selected columns were dropped. And from all the available columns, only the state of home, the age group and the columns that created the date of death were selected.

There were more attributes available that could be useful for the analysis, but they were discarded. Some of them were the district of home (one level of specification deeper on the location of home), the location of death, the date of birth (we are using only the age group, but the exact age at the time of death can be calculated), the level of studies and the profession.

Only the deaths from 5 to 99 years of age were selected, deaths of individuals younger than 5 and older than 99 represent a different case study. 10 age groups were created under the attribute *new_age_group*.

4 The Number of Deaths Cycle with the Seasons

Firstly, an overall visualization of the accumulated deaths over the years was performed.

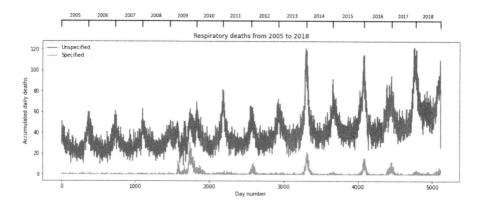

Fig. 1. Blue: codes of unspecified diseases, Orange: Influenza (grouped with other specified diseases) (Color figure online)

It is noticeable that the deaths by respiratory diseases have a cyclic pattern. This cycling follows the seasonality of the years and increase in winter. Their total numbers also increase throughout the years. The highest day of unspecified deaths in late 2005 is almost equal to the lowest of 2018 (Blue line in Fig. 1). With regard to the deaths by Influenza, we can see that the first spike happens approximately in March 2009, matching the first case of AH1N1 in Mexico, registered in 17-March-2009.

The year 2009 has an unexpected fluctuation in the blue line (unspecified deaths), this fluctuation starts almost at the same time as the first case of Influenza, and dissipates when the deaths by Influenza stop. We see that the blue line in Fig. 2 follows a cyclic and very simple pattern, so a Linear Regression model is useful to get its general pattern [11].

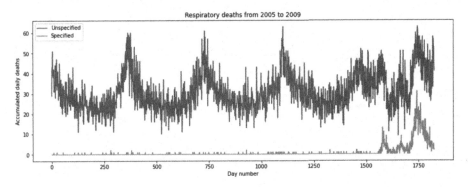

Fig. 2. Closeup of the Influenza and Unspecified deaths from 2005 to 2009

5   Adjusting for the Population Growth

Before producing a model to predict the year 2009, the previous years need to be scaled to compensate for the population growth [7]. To do this, a 28-day period from late June to late August was selected for having low variance. The average of deaths per day on that period is plotted exactly in the middle of that 28-day range, which are the red marks in Fig. 3. The population growth is exponential [2], so an exponential fit to those points was added. To predict the pattern of deaths for 2009, the data of the years 2005

Using the exponential fit Fig. 3, a projected point for this 28-day period on 2009 is generated. Using this projection point, the previous years were scaled to match the population size of 2009.

To combine the data of those years together, a simple mean calculation for each day of the year was performed. This averages are the prediction of the unspecified deaths of 2009, the result is shown in Fig. 4. A linear regression of 12th degree was added to reduce noise.

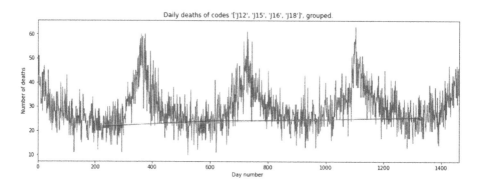

Fig. 3. 2005, 2006, 2007 and 2008. Red: real average of deaths for the selected period each year. Green: Exponential fit of the red line. (Color figure online)

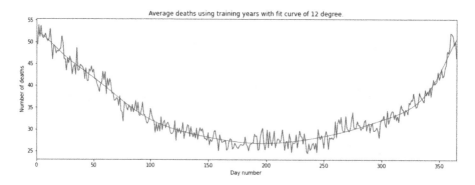

Fig. 4. Blue: Average of deaths between 2005–2008 adjusted to expected growth of 2009. Green: Polynomial fit curve of 12th degree for blue line. (Color figure online)

6   Dividing the Total Population in Groups

Using the previous method, the difference between the observed and the predicted pattern of unspecified deaths for 2009 can be obtained. The same procedure was applied to different groups of the population to reduce generalization errors.

The idea is that by obtaining how much each group of the population differs from their expected behavior, we should obtain a much more specific number for the deviations of the entire population.

This concept is illustrated by separating the population between women and men. The prediction line for each one of them is very similar to Fig. 4. The green line is the prediction for 2009.

Figure 5 shows the **actual** number of deaths for *men* in 2009, with a polynomial fit of 80th degree to reduce noise.

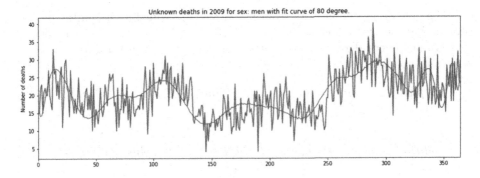

Fig. 5. Blue: Observed number of unspecified deaths of men in 2009. Green: Polynomial fit curve of 80th degree for the blue line. (Color figure online)

The degree of the polynomial fit in Fig. 5 is larger for the actual deaths because they have higher variance. The patterns of the predicted and the observed deaths are now compared in Fig. 6.

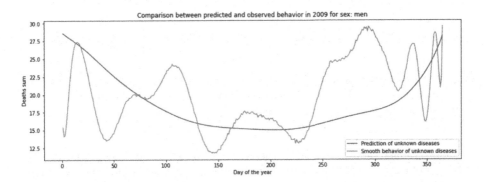

Fig. 6. Unspecified deaths of men in 2009. Blue: predicted behavior. Orange: actual general behavior. (Color figure online)

The same procedure was performed for the group of women, producing a pattern that is clearly different from that of men. The difference between observed and expected number of deaths is calculated in Eq. 1, and for each day, only the different larger than 1 is kept, as in Eq. 6.

$$MenDiff(Time_t) = Men_{observed}(Time_t) - Prediction(Men, Time_t) \quad (1)$$

$$Surplus_{men}(Time_t) = \begin{cases} MenDiff(Time_t) & \text{if } MenDiff(Time_t) > 1 \\ 0 & \text{otherwise} \end{cases}$$

The differences obtained for women and men are added to obtain the deviation of the entire group, as in Eq. 2. This deviation is then added to the predicted pattern of the **total population as a single group**, as in Eq. 3, the result is shown in Fig. 7.

$$Surplus_{total}(Time_t) = Surplus_{women}(Time_t) + Surplus_{men}(Time_t) \quad (2)$$

$$Addition(Time_t) = Prediction(Total, Time_t) + Surplus_{total}(Time_t) \quad (3)$$

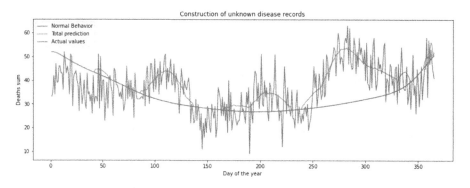

Fig. 7. Unspecified deaths of 2009. Green: Actual daily deaths. Blue: prediction for the entire population. Orange: Addition of the total prediction and the surplus obtained from women and men (Color figure online)

The orange line Fig. 7 matches the green one as expected. But recall that this line was obtained from the surplus of two different groups: women and men. This graph shows that the method of splitting the population in groups is valid. The *surplus* of unspecified deaths obtained in Eq. 2 is compared with the recorded deaths of Influenza.

The graph in Fig. 8 is the most important in this work. The blue line accounts for the registered Influenza deaths across 2009, it might look at first glance as if the orange line was the polynomial fit of the blue but it is not. The orange line is the *surplus* of unspecified pneumonia deaths, obtained by subgroups of the population. They match almost perfectly.

This means that approximately for every death registered as **Influenza**, there is one other death registered as **unspecified pneumonia** that should not be there. The strong similarity between these two lines is not trivial. In other words, this graph shows that from what we could call *actual deaths of Influenza*, only 50% of them were registered as such, while the other 50% were registered as *unspecified pneumonia*. There is an almost 1:1 ratio between registered deaths and miss-classified deaths of the same virus.

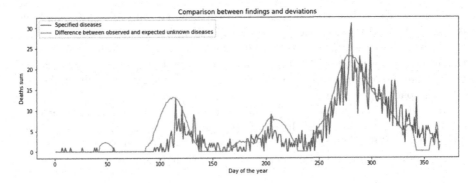

Fig. 8. 2009. Blue: daily deaths of Influenza. Orange: number of unspecified deaths that surpassed our prediction for each sex. (Color figure online)

7   Correcting the Number of Deaths by Influenza

The registered deaths of Influenza are approximately 50% of the actual number. Using this information, their numbers were doubled to visualize how the 100% would look like, and that same amount reduced from the number of deaths by unspecified pneumonia as shown in Eqs. 4 and 5.

$$Actual_{Influenza} = Registered_{Influenza} * 2 \qquad (4)$$

$$Actual_{Unspecified} = Registered_{Unspecified} - Registered_{Influenza} \qquad (5)$$

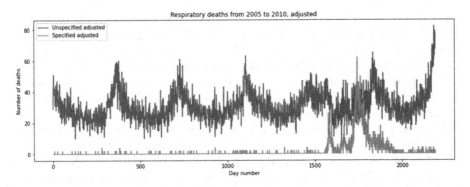

Fig. 9. 2005–2010. Deaths of unspecified pneumonia (blue) and Influenza (orange) after the adjustment. (Color figure online)

Compare the adjustment in Fig. 9 with the original data in Fig. 2. The fluctuations of the blue line in 2009 have almost disappeared. Also note that after this adjustment, there are some days in which the deaths by Influenza surpass the deaths by unspecified pneumonia, knowing that it surpassed the previously biggest cause of death across respiratory diseases (Table 2) should illustrate the actual impact of that pandemic.

Having a mechanized procedure for the previous analysis, the same process can be performed by dividing the population across state of living or age groups. There are 26 different groups when dividing by state of living, and 10 groups when dividing by age. The final results are surprisingly similar.

8   Conclusions

The code produced for the generation of this work has been made publicly available on Github [1]. The registered number of deaths are always a representation of the deaths by the same cause in all the country, with a sufficiently valid correlation. This representation is so precise that it is still valid across different divisions of the entire population. The ratio of this representation for the AH1N1 pandemic of 2009 is **at least 1:1**.

This process can be optimized further to refine the estimation, but we should instead focus those efforts on the currently active COVID-19 pandemic. Each day, INEGI publishes the update of deaths by COVID-19, but the number of deaths by unspecified pneumonia are also needed to replicate the proposed process, for we cannot assume that the records of COVID-19 account for 50% of the actual number as well. When the deaths on 2019 and 2020 are published, the deaths by Influenza should be separated first (for that disease is still causing deaths), and then the process should be repeated for COVID-19.

9   Alternatives for the Missing Information

Some databases of the death registry of Mexico City have been published [1,9], but they do not cover the entire year 2020, nor 2019. They cover only some months. However, we might be able to use that information and stumbly generalize to the entire country by using the following procedure.

It is a safe conclusion that a sample is representative across time, so the number of deaths by unspecified pneumonia for a limited period of time is sufficient. A sample is also representative across different dimensions of the population, which means that it is constant on Mexico City alone. Knowing this, then we would only need to obtain this ratio of representation for COVID-19 on the available information, and generalize to the entire country using the number of registered deaths. This generalization should be valid because the institution and processes that produce all this information are practically the same for Influenza and COVID-19. The problem rests on whether we can dispose of a complete database of deaths by unspecified pneumonia, in a certain region and time where deaths of COVID-19 are also being registered.

---

[1] https://github.com/EByrdS/influenza_deaths_mx.

References

1. Aguilar, S., Arizpe, M.: Las causas de muerte durante la pandemia en la cdmx (2020). https://datos.nexos.com.mx/?p=1435. Accessed 05 June 2020
2. Frey, B.: Growth curve modeling. In: The SAGE Encyclopedia of Educational Research, Measurement and Evaluation, vol. 2, pp. 772–779 (2018)
3. INEGI. Mortalidad (2019). https://www.inegi.org.mx/programas/mortalidad/default.html#Microdatos. Accessed 05 June 2020
4. INEGI. Mortalidad (2019). https://www.inegi.org.mx/programas/mortalidad/default.html#Datos_abiertos. Accessed 05 June 2020
5. W. H. O. Icd-10 version:2016 (2016). https://icd.who.int/browse10/2016/en. Accessed 05 June 2020
6. W.H.O. Pneumonia of unknown cause - China (2020). https://www.who.int/csr/don/05-january-2020-pneumonia-of-unkown-cause-china/en/
7. Patro, S.G.K., Sahu, K.K.: Normalization: a preprocessing stage. CoRR, abs/1503.06462 (2015)
8. Pham, H.: On estimating the number of deaths related to COVID-19. Mathematics **8**, 655 (2020)
9. Romero, M., Despeghel, L.: qué nos dicen las actas de defunción de la cdmx? (2020). https://datos.nexos.com.mx/?p=1388. Accessed 05 June 2020
10. Salud, O.P.D.L., WHO.: Clasificación estadística internacional de enfermedades y problemas relacionados con la salud, décima revisión, volumen 1 (1992). http://ais.paho.org/classifications/Chapters/pdf/Volume1.pdf. Accessed 05 June 2020
11. ScikitLearn. Linear regression (2019). https://scikit-learn.org/stable/modules/generated/sklearn.linear_model.LinearRegression.html. Accessed 05 June 2020

Application of Expert Systems and Simulation Modeling to Calculate Connectivity Between the Nodes of the Graph

Vladimir Mochalov[✉] and Anastasia Mochalova

IKIR FEB RAS, Mirnaya Str. 7., 684034 Paratunka, Kamchatka Region, Russia
{a.mochalova,vmochalov}@ikir.ru
http://www.ikir.ru

Abstract. The problem of accurately calculating the probability of connectivity of graph nodes is not only very important for practical use, but also belongs to the class of NP-hard problems. The paper gives the place of application of expert systems, simulation modeling and other well-known methods in solving the problem of accurately calculating the probability of connectivity of graph nodes. The rule-based expert system Drools was chosen as the basis of our engine. The Monte Carlo method is used as a basis for simulation modeling. The rules of the Drools expert system and examples of the system operation are given.

Keywords: Nodes connectivity · Structural reliability · Expert systems · Drools · Simulation modeling · Monte Carlo

1 Introduction

In paper [1] a mathematical model of the semantic analyzer is proposed, based on the comparison of text with ontosemantic templates. The analyzed text entering the input of the semantic analyzer is gradually reduced: some parts of the text, in accordance with ontosemantic rules, are added to the queue with priority for deletion; sequentially from the analyzed text, the parts of the text corresponding to the element of the queue with the highest priority are removed. The rule-based expert system Drools [2] was chosen as the basis for the implementation of the semantic analyzer. In this paper, the previously obtained results are adapted to the problem of analysis of structural reliability and an approach is implemented for calculating the probability of connectivity between nodes of a given graph, which implies its transformation into a graph of a lower dimension (modified graph) by removing some fragments of the original graph and taking into account the values of the connectivity indicators of the extracted fragments for evaluation connectivity of the modified graph. This allows you to reduce the complexity of the calculations. The graph is modified based on some rules. These rules can be applied simply by a person, which, of course, is not effective. Therefore, to

© Springer Nature Switzerland AG 2020
L. Martínez-Villaseñor et al. (Eds.): MICAI 2020, LNAI 12468, pp. 470–480, 2020.
https://doi.org/10.1007/978-3-030-60884-2_36

perform graph modification based on such rules, it is proposed to use expert systems.

The advantage of using expert systems in the problem under consideration is as follows:

- expert systems do not require expert knowledge in the field of programming and allow him to independently add rules for assessing the connectivity of subgraphs in a high-level language for describing rules;
- in modern expert systems, a fast pattern matching algorithm is implemented, which allows you to significantly speed up the process of searching for patterns in the fact base, especially when it is frequently changed. In the case under consideration, the facts are the nodes and edges of the graph, and when specific subgraphs are found using templates, the graph is modified, i.e. the base of facts is modified;
- modern expert systems have great language capabilities for writing rules.

The problem of accurately calculating the probability of connectivity of graph nodes is not only very important for practical use, but also belongs to the class of NP-hard problems [3]. The paper gives the place of application of expert systems and other well-known methods in solving the problem under consideration.

The paper discusses the use of simulation modeling to calculate the probability of connectivity of nodes of subgraphs, for which the known methods of calculating connectivity cannot be applied.

2 Implementation of Reduction Rules for Graph Size Reduction on the Drools Expert System

The use of reduction rules to reduce the dimension of a graph is considered in various works [4–6] etc. Let us further consider the implementation on the Drools expert system of some rules for reducing the dimension of an undirected graph, in which we need to find the probability of connectivity between two target nodes. All other nodes in the considered graph will be considered transit.

The Drools expert system uses Java objects as facts. To store information about a graph node, the following properties of the implemented Node class were selected:

```
String  type; // node type
String  name; // node name
double probability; // probability of a node's working state
HashMap<Node, Double> hmLinks = new HashMap<Node, Double>();
// Table of probabilities of the working state of edges with
// adjacent nodes
```

Since an adjacent node is used as a unique key in the hmLinks property, a protocol was chosen to calculate the probability of a working state of an edge for parallel connection of edges, according to which, when adding a new edge to

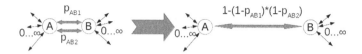

Fig. 1. Calculation of the probability of a working state of the edge for parallel edges

the graph, it is required to call the following Java function addOrParallelRecalcLink, which either initializes the probability of a working edge state (PWES) or calculates a new PWES value according to the formula for calculating PWES for parallel connection of edges (Fig. 1).

```
@Modifies ( "hmLinks" )
public void addOrParallelRecalcLink(Node      node,
                                    Double   probLinkValue,
                                    boolean setForBothNodes)
{
    Double probCur = link(node);
    if(probCur == null) setLinkProbability(node, probLinkValue);
    else{ probLinkValue = 1 - (1 - probCur) * (1 - probLinkValue);
        setLinkProbability(node, probLinkValue); }
    if(setForBothNodes) node.setLinkProbability(this,
                                              probLinkValue);
}
```

Rule 1 (Fig. 2). If the transit node T of the graph has exactly two adjacent nodes (A and B), then: remove the transit node T and its two edges from the graph; add a new edge between nodes A and B and set the probability of its working state to the value $p_{AB} = p_{AT} \cdot p_T \cdot p_{BT}$, where is the probability of the working state of the edge AT, p_{BT} is the probability of the working state of the edge BT and p_T is the probability of the working state of node T.

Fig. 2. Rule 1 reduction of the dimension of an undirected graph

In the language of the Drools expert system, rule 1 can be written as follows:

```
rule "1"
when
$n2 : Node( type == "T", hmLinks.size == 2 )
then
Iterator<Entry<Node, Double>> it =
```

```
$n2.getHmLinks().entrySet().iterator();
Entry<Node, Double> e1 = it.next(); Entry<Node, Double> e2 =
                                                    it.next();
System.out.println("Rule 1 for nodes: " + $n2.getName() + "; " +
    e1.getKey().getName() + "; " + e2.getKey().getName());
e1.getKey().removeLink($n2); e2.getKey().removeLink($n2);
double newLink = e1.getValue() * $n2.prob() * e2.getValue();
e1.getKey().addOrParallelRecalcLink(e2.getKey(), newLink, true);
delete($n2); update(e1.getKey()); update(e2.getKey());
end
```

Rule 2 (Fig. 3). If a transit node T of the graph has exactly one adjacent node (A), then remove the transit node T and its edge from the graph.

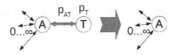

Fig. 3. Rule 2 reduction of the dimension of an undirected graph

In the language of the Drools expert system, rule 2 can be written as follows:

```
rule "2"
when
$n2 : Node( type == "T", hmLinks.size == 1 )
then
System.out.println("Rule 2 for node: " + $n2.getName());
Iterator<Entry<Node, Double>> it =
                $n2.getHmLinks().entrySet().iterator();
Entry<Node, Double> e1 = it.next(); e1.getKey().removeLink($n2);
        update(e1.getKey()); delete($n2);
end
```

Rule 3. If any node of the graph (A) has no adjacent nodes, then remove node A from the graph.

In the language of the Drools expert system, rule 3 can be written as follows:

```
rule "3"
when
$n2 : Node( type != "ALL", hmLinks.size == 0 )
then
System.out.println("Rule 3 for node: " + $n2.getName());
delete($n2);
end
```

Rule 4. If the target node (S_1) has only one adjacent node (S_2), which is also the target, then the final probability of connectivity between the two target nodes is calculated as follows: $p_{ALL} = p_{S1} \cdot p_{S1S2} \cdot p_{S2}$, where p_{S1S2} is the probability of the working state of the edge S_1S_2, p_{S1} is the probability of the working state of S_1 node and p_{S2} is the probability of a working state of S_2 node.

In the language of the Drools expert system, rule 4 can be written as follows:

```
rule "4"
when
$n1 : Node( type == "S", hmLinks.size == 1 )
$n2 : Node( type == "S", hmLinks.size >= 1,
                hmLinks.keySet contains $n1 )
then
System.out.println("Rule 4 for nodes: " + $n1.getName() + "; " +
                                        $n2.getName());
delete($n1); delete($n2); double ret = $n2.link($n1)
                            * $n1.prob() * $n2.prob();
insert(new Node("ALL", ret));
System.out.println("Final connectivity probability: " + ret);
end
```

Rule 5. If the target node (S) has only one adjacent node (T), which is transit, and node T has more than one adjacent node, then: delete node S; make the node T a target, give it the name of the node S and set the probability of the working state of the node T equal to $p_{TNEW} = p_T \cdot p_S \cdot p_{TS}$, where p_{TS} is the probability of the working state of the edge TS, p_T is the probability of the working state of the node T and p_S is the probability of the working state of the node S.

In the language of the Drools expert system, rule 5 can be written as follows:

```
rule "5"
when
$n1 : Node( type == "S", hmLinks.size == 1 )
$n2 : Node( type == "T", hmLinks.size >= 2,
                hmLinks.keySet contains $n1 )
then
System.out.println("Rule 5 for nodes: " + $n1.getName() + "; " +
                                        $n2.getName());
$n2.setProbability( $n2.link($n1) * $n1.prob() * $n2.prob() );
        $n2.removeLink($n1); delete($n1); $n2.setType("S");
$n2.setName($n1.getName()); update($n2);
end
```

Rule 6. The left side of Fig. 4 shows a subgraph (G) with four nodes (A, B, C and D), in which nodes B and D are transit nodes. The dotted line marks the edge AC, which is optional for the subgraph, the presence or absence of which does not affect the logic below for calculating the probability of connectivity

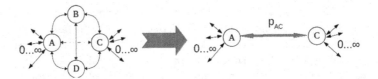

Fig. 4. Rule 6 reduction of the dimension of an undirected graph.

between nodes A and C by using the previously described protocol for accounting for parallel connections of edges (i.e., in the rule below, the possible presence of an edge AC will be taken into account only when calling the *addOrParallelRecalcLinkfunction* on the right side of the rule). If in the graph we meet the subgraph G, then:

- add a new edge between nodes A and C and set the probability of its working state to the value $p_{AC} = p_{DB} \cdot p_1 + (1 - p_{DB}) \cdot p_2$, where p_{DB} is the probability of the working state of the edge DB, p_1 is the probability of connectivity of the node A and C under the condition of the working state of the edge DB and p_2 is the probability of connectivity of the node A and C if the DB edge is not working. We calculate

$$p_1 = p_B \cdot (1 - p_D) \cdot p_{AB} \cdot p_{BC} + p_D \cdot (1 - p_B) \cdot p_{AD} \cdot p_{DC} +$$
$$p_B \cdot p_D \cdot (1 - (1 - p_{AB}) \cdot (1 - p_{AD})) \cdot (1 - (1 - p_{BC}) \cdot (1 - p_{DC})),$$

where p_B, p_D are the probabilities of the working state of nodes B and D, respectively, and p_{AB}, p_{AD}, p_{BC}, p_{DC} are the probabilities of the working state of the edges AB, AD, BC and DC, respectively. Probability $p_2 = 1 - (1 - p_{AB} \cdot p_B \cdot p_{BC}) \cdot (1 - p_{AD} \cdot p_D \cdot p_{DC})$;
- remove nodes B and D;
- remove edges AB, AD, BC and DC.

In the language of the Drools expert system, rule 6 can be written as follows:

```
rule "6"
when
$nA : Node(type != "ALL", hmLinks.size >= 2)
$nB : Node(type == "T"  , hmLinks.size == 3,
                hmLinks.keySet contains $nA)
$nD : Node(type == "T"  , hmLinks.size == 3,
hmLinks.keySet contains $nA && hmLinks.keySet contains $nB)
$nC : Node(type != "ALL", this != $nA, hmLinks.size >= 2,
hmLinks.keySet contains $nB && hmLinks.keySet contains $nD)
then
System.out.println("Rule 6 for nodes: " + $nA.getName() + "; " +
    $nB.getName() + "; " + $nD.getName() + "; " + $nC.getName());
double pDBOK = $nB.prob()*(1-$nD.prob())*$nA.link($nB)*
```

```
        $nB.link($nC)+$nD.prob()*(1-$nB.prob())*$nA.link($nD)*
     $nD.link($nC)+$nB.prob()* $nD.prob()*((1-(1-$nA.link($nB))*
    (1-$nA.link($nD)))*(1-(1-$nB.link($nC))*(1-$nC.link($nD))));
double pDBBad = 1 - (1 - $nA.link($nB) * $nB.prob() *
 $nB.link($nC))*(1 - $nA.link($nD)*$nD.prob()*$nD.link($nC));
double newLinkAllProb = $nD.link($nB)*pDBOK + (1-$nD.link($nB))*
                                                        pDBBad;
$nA.removeLink($nB); $nA.removeLink($nD); $nC.removeLink($nB);
$nC.removeLink($nD); delete($nB); delete($nD);
$nA.addOrParallelRecalcLink($nC, newLinkAllProb, true);
update($nA); update($nC);
end
```

Other rules for the expert system can be written by analogy. Of course, not every graph can be transformed into a final node using only expert rules. If after the operation of the expert system the graph has not transformed into a final node, then an algorithm should be launched to search for subgraphs of the minimum size that can be transformed into a node or an edge of the graph. For each such sub-graph, depending on its size, one of the well-known procedures should be run to calculate the probability of connectivity between its input and output nodes. Examples of such well-known procedures include [7]: direct enumeration method; methods of statistical modeling and Monte Carlo method; method of decomposition of boolean functions; factorization method (branching method, Moore - Shannon method) [3,8,9], etc. After calculating the probability of connectivity between the input and output nodes of each subgraph, the base of facts of the expert system is modified and the inference block is started again based on the rules of the expert system and then the steps are repeated until the final probability is obtained.

After calculating the probability of connectivity between the input and output nodes of each subgraph, the fact base of the expert system is modified as follows:

- if the found subgraph M can be transformed into a node N of the graph (an example is given in rule 5), then: calculate the probability of a working state of the transformed node N; add the transformed node N to the graph (a node becomes target if there is at least one target node in the subgraph, otherwise the node be-comes transitory); delete all nodes of the subgraph M; add link edges to node N with external nodes of the subgraph M; update the fact base of the expert system in accordance with the changes made in the graph; if after deleting the subgraph M in the final graph there is only one target node (this is possible only if there were two target nodes in the subgraph M), then the probability of its operable state (node N) is the final probability of connectivity between two target nodes;
- if the found subgraph M can be transformed into an edge F of the graph (an example is given in rule 6), then: calculate the probability of a working state of the transformed edge F; delete all nodes of the subgraph M except the input

and out-put; remove all link edges with remote nodes from the subgraph M; add a new edge F between the input and output nodes of the graph; update the fact base of the expert system in accordance with the changes made in the graph.

After modifying the fact base of the expert system, the inference block is launched again based on the rules of the expert system, and then the steps are repeated until the final probability of connectivity between the nodes of the graph is obtained.

In addition to the rules for calculating the probability of connectivity between the input and output nodes of a subgraph, other rules for modifying the structure of subgraphs are also of interest.

Figure 5 shows an example of a graph for which it is required to find the probability of connectivity between node 2 and node 17. The probability of working state of each node $p_m = 0.95$, and the probability of working state of each edge $p_{ij} = 0.90$. Only the above 6 rules of the expert system made it possible to accurately calculate the final probability of connectivity between target nodes $p_{ALL} = 0.7213846303144723$.

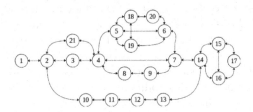

Fig. 5. An example of a graph for which it is required to find the probability of connectivity between node 2 and node 17.

Outputting to the console the sequence of rule triggering:

- Rule 1 for nodes: 21; 4; 2. Rule 1 for nodes: 10; 11; 2.
- Rule 1 for nodes: 20; 18; 6. Rule 1 for nodes: 9; 8; 7.
- Rule 1 for nodes: 8; 4; 7. Rule 1 for nodes 3; 4; 2.
- Rule 1 for nodes: 13; 12; 14. Rule 1 for nodes: 12; 14; 11.
- Rule 1 for nodes: 11; 14; 2. Rule 2 for node: 1.
- Rule 6 for nodes: 14; 15; 16; 17. Rule 5 for nodes: 17; 14.
- Rule 6 for nodes: 5; 18; 19; 6. Rule 1 for nodes: 6; 5; 7.
- Rule 1 for nodes: 5; 4; 7. Rule 1 for nodes: 7; 4; 17.
- Rule 1 for nodes: 4; 17; 2. Rule 4 for nodes: 17; 2.

3 Application of Simulation Modeling to Calculate Connectivity Between the Nodes of the Graph

Figure 6 shows a modified graph from the previous example. For this graph, it is also required to find the probability of connectivity of nodes 2 and 17. The above rules do not allow transformation into an edge a subgraph between node 1 and 14, consisting only of nodes 1, 22, 23, 24, 14 (Fig. 7). To calculate the probability of connectivity between node 1 and 14 of the graph shown in Fig. 7, we apply Monte Carlo simulation. Simulation is performed in N iterations. At each iteration, for each node and edge of the graph, their presence in the simulated graph is determined in proportion to the probability of their working state. In the generated simulated graph, the presence of at least one path between two target nodes is checked using depth-first traversal. If at least one path is found, then the counter of successful simulation attempts M is increased by one. The approximate probability of connectivity is defined as follows $p_e = M/N$. Since we want to transform the subgraph between node 1 and 14 (Fig. 7) into an edge, then to calculate the probability of working state of this edge using simulation, we assume that nodes 1 and 14 do not fail, i.e. the probability of their working state is 1.

On the basis of 10^8 iterations of simulation modeling, the working state of the edge $p_{1\_14} = 0.95314373684210526316$ was calculated, into which the subgraph between nodes 1 and 14 can be transformed (Fig. 7). Figure 8 shows a modified graph, the probability of connectivity between nodes 2 and 17 of which can already be calculated using the rules of the Drools expert system given in the previous section. Thus, the probability of connectivity between target nodes turned out to be $p_{ALL} = 0.8042797443652948$ (Fig. 8).

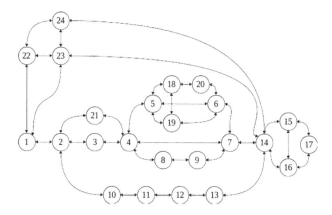

Fig. 6. An example of a graph for which it is required to find the probability of connectivity between node 2 and node 17

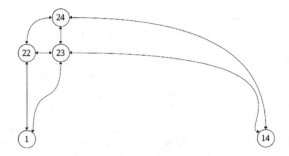

Fig. 7. An example of a subgraph for which it is required to find the probability of connectivity between node 1 and node 14

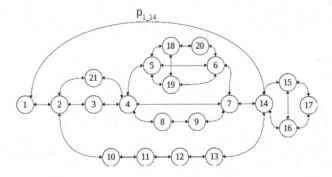

Fig. 8. A modified graph for which the probability of connectivity between nodes 2 and 17 is calculated using the rules of the expert system

4 Conclusions

The paper describes the original approach of using expert systems and simulation modeling to calculate the probability of connectivity between the nodes of the graph. Briefly, the advantage of using expert systems in the problem under consideration is as follows: expert systems do not require expert knowledge in the field of programming; in modern expert systems, a fast pattern matching algorithm is implemented; modern expert systems have great language capabilities for writing rules. Since the manual writing of rules for an expert system is a very laborious work, it is advisable to generate such rules based on the calculated formulas for the probability of connectivity of graphs of small dimension. Thus, in [10], one of the possible ways to obtain such formulas is given, based on an enumeration of options for complete cutting off of each of the graph nodes.

If after the operation of the expert system the graph has not transformed into a final node, then an algorithm should be launched to search for subgraphs of the minimum size that can be transformed into a node or an edge of the graph. For each such subgraph, depending on its size, one of the well-known procedures should be run to calculate the probability of connectivity between its input and output nodes. So, the work provides the application of simulation modeling.

Further areas of work are aimed at: increasing the number of used Drools rules by generating them; estimating the number of all possible rules for subgraphs containing exactly N connected nodes between two target nodes of the graph; estimation of the amount of used RAM of the Drools expert system with a different set of rules; estimation of the accuracy of calculations the connectivity between the nodes of the graph when using simulation modeling; comparison of results with existing benchmarks; integration of the obtained results for the construction of fault-tolerant communication networks (for example, paper [11] shows the place of the evaluation function in the process of constructing a fault-tolerant structure of a sensor network using multi-agent bio-inspired algorithms).

Acknowledgments. The paper was carried out within the framework on the subject Dynamics of physical processes in active zones of near space and geospheres (AAAA-A17-117080110043-4)

References

1. Mochalova, A., Mochalov, V.: Mathematical model of an ontological-semantic analyzer using basic ontological-semantic patterns. In: Sidorov, G., Herrera-Alcántara, O. (eds.) MICAI 2016. LNCS (LNAI), vol. 10061, pp. 53–66. Springer, Cham (2017). https://doi.org/10.1007/978-3-319-62434-1_5
2. Drools - Business Rules Management System. https://www.drools.org/
3. Colbourn, C.J.: The Combinatorics of Network Reliability. Oxford University Press, New York (1987)
4. Lucet, C., Manouvrier, J.-F.: Exact methods to compute network reliability. In: Proceedings of 1st MMR (1997)
5. Rebaiia, M., Ait-Kadi, D.: Network reliability evaluation and optimization: methods, algorithms and software tools. CIRRELT (2013)
6. Shooman, A.M.: Algorithms for network reliability and connection availability analysis. In: Electro 95 International Professional Program Proceedings, pp. 309–333 (1995)
7. Ushakov, I.A.: The Course of the Theory of System Reliability. Drofa, Moscow (2008)
8. Page, L., Perry, J.: A practical implementation of the factoring theorem for network reliability. IEEE Trans. Reliab. **37**(3), 259–267 (1988)
9. Resende, L.: Implementation of a factoring algorithm for reliability evaluation of undirected networks. IEEE Trans. Reliab. **37**(5), 462–468 (1988)
10. Migov, D.A.: Formulas for fast calculation of the probability of connectivity of a subset of vertices in low-dimensional graphs. Probl. Inform. **2**(6), 10–17 (2010)
11. Mochalov, V.A.: Multi-agent bio-inspired algorithms for wireless sensor network design. In: Proceedings of the IEEE 17th ICACT, pp. 34–42 (2015)

Generation of Pseudo-random Numbers Based on Network Traffic

Wilbert Marroquin(iD) and Julio Santisteban$^{(\boxtimes)}$(iD)

Universidad Católica San Pablo, Arequipa, Peru
{wilbert.marroquin,jsantisteban}@ucsp.edu.pe

Abstract. The Pseudo Random Numbers generators can be based on chaotic maps; they are still deterministic functions, so it is possible to predict future results. On the other hand, we have the real random number generators that comply with the mentioned characteristics, this is possible at the cost of high latency and slowness by the use of physical processes. In this article, the use of network traffic in the generation of random sequences is tested. An equation is used to improve the statistical properties of the method. It is verified that network traffic tends to be more chaotic in spaces with a larger number of users. Results show that the method generates very different sequences, but with unequal bit generation. We present a method for the generation of pseudo random numbers based on network traffic, minimizing the repetition of generated sequences.

Keywords: Random numbers · Generation of random numbers · Non-deterministic.

1 Introduction

Currently, there is a great demand for algorithms or processes capable of generating random numbers that meet key characteristics such as unpredictable being both new and previous outputs from a specific result [1]. The demand for high-quality random numbers drives the search and improvement of methods that generate random numbers, this search results in the use of methods that are based on chaotic models or natural physical events, in order to obtain numbers as genuinely random. Within this field, is known as PRN (Pseudo-Random Numbers) which are normally used in cryptographic algorithms. Chaotic systems are commonly proposed to fulfill the role of non-linear systems that are used in this type of method [5].

The generators of PRN have an advantage over other types of generators because of their ease of implementation and speed when generating random bit sequences, despite this the fact remains that their output of random numbers is periodic Even if the short-term evidence is not noticed, this is due to its base in deterministic equations. Even models based on chaotic systems that produce high-quality RN (Random Numbers) are still based on a deterministic equation,

© Springer Nature Switzerland AG 2020
L. Martínez-Villaseñor et al. (Eds.): MICAI 2020, LNAI 12468, pp. 481–493, 2020.
https://doi.org/10.1007/978-3-030-60884-2_37

which suggests that the repetition of a number pattern is inevitable, This leads to being predictable in time.

There are also the calls TRN (True Random Number) or truly random which are generated by events or physical phenomena whose data are collected mostly by sensors, this approach results in a generation of numbers that are nondeterministic and unpredictable given the environment and data that are used for generation.

On the other hand, the TRN generators offer us the independence of each of their data since they do not depend on a periodic function or obtaining previous results to calculate the current output. All this assures us that the numbers of these generators will not be predictable since they are not based on deterministic models. Even with these benefits, these methods tend to have a slow bit-stream generation rate since they do not give us random numbers with good enough statistical properties by themselves, hence post-processing is necessary.

1.1   Motivation

An important point in the studies dealing with random numbers is the difficulty of persisting the entropy index in a generator of PRN as it is stated in [4] a problem like this can be common when it is not taken in considering the total flow of data that are generated by the method, to try to have this factor of being unpredictable these methods can opt for other ways to ensure randomness [10].

We must consider that by itself a TRN generator could not produce random numbers with desirable characteristics, with this we refer or do not have enough entropy index, which leads to post-processing. Given this fact, it makes the PRN generators chosen in most cases and the TRN generators are more suitable for more specific purposes, even becoming seed generators for the methods that generate PRN.

2   Related Works

2.1   Chaotic Systems

Hamdi et al. [5], propose to use a chaotic system defined by the Eq. 1 in conjunction with a *S-Box table*, in order to blur the relationship between the values obtained by the system chaotic and the final response of the process.

$$X_{i+1} = \lambda * X_i(1 - X_i), X_0 \in [0, 1], 0 < \lambda < 4 \tag{1}$$

On the other hand, Hu et al. [6] used Chen's chaotic system for the generation of pseudorandom sequences. It uses three-dimensional vectors to represent the generated chains, in order to avoid a non-linear prediction attack. This vulnerability is present in systems that use a one-dimensional base [17], they propose to build generators with high-dimensional representations.

Both works find that by itself the chaotic system does not provide a uniform distribution, this means that these methods do not ensure a probability of similar appearance in each of its elements. Not having this characteristic generates that the sequence of PRN is predictable by statistical methods.

To solve this in [5] the problem is solved using only a portion of the generated section which has a uniform distribution. On the other hand in [6] the author proposes the use of Eq. 2.

$$
\begin{aligned}
v(3i) &= 3000 * (x(i) + 45) \\
v(3i + 1) &= 3000 * (y(i) + 35) \quad i = 0, 1, 2, ... \\
v(3i + 2) &= 3000 * (z(i) + 45) \\
Kj &= v(j) mod 256 \quad j = 0, 1, 2...,
\end{aligned}
\tag{2}
$$

The first solution is used to give parameters to the author's proposal which is based on the combination of two of these systems with a transformation in blocks. The second solution obtains the random numbers of the combination of the three-dimensional vector that is generated.

The work of Vajargah and Asghari [18] sought to improve LCG (Linear Congruential Generator) by using the Chaotic map of Henon. The LCG is a process that generates random sequences with uniform and statistically independent distribution. The generation method LCG uses the Eq. 3:

$$
\begin{aligned}
X_i &= ax_{i-1} + c \qquad (mod\ m) \\
0 &\le x_i < m \qquad i = 1, 2, ...
\end{aligned}
\tag{3}
$$

The problem of LCG is its small generation period, which is why it is not a good generating method. To solve this, the authors combined this method with Henon's map, since the Henon system is sensitive to its initial values and has a chaotic behavior. The chaotic map of Henon is represented by the Eq. 4 of a two-dimensional state.

$$
\begin{aligned}
x_{k+1} &= -ax_k^2 + y_k + 1 \\
y_{k+1} &= bx_k
\end{aligned}
\tag{4}
$$

Although the results obtained showed a great increase in the period of the sequence, the distribution of this was not uniform, so the generation of numbers was not the most adequate.

In 2016 Vajargah and Asghari in their article [19] modified the CHCG so that it fulfilled the desired statistical properties. For this, he had to apply a control that regulates the distribution of the numbers generated by CHCG. This control consists in dividing the interval in which numbers are generated in sub-intervals and for each iteration of the algorithm a number of a sub-interval that was chosen in a random manner is generated.

2.2   Physical Phenomena

Lo Re et al. in their article [8] they present a model of generation of random numbers using wireless sensors. Seen in this way the model would present a weakness in case the sensor was *hacked* and the outputs of this controlled. To face this, the model is based on the gathering of information that is received by several sensors of a network through an authentication protocol.

Other works such as Myunghwan Park et al. [11] unlike the previous method choose to create their own *hardware* that meet the characteristics of a chaotic system. For this, a Boolean chaotic oscillator was implemented on a circuit. Chaos Boolean is described as a phenomenon that occurred in an autonomous network. Given its high sensitivity to initial conditions shows non-repetitive oscillations. These characteristics make this system ideal for achieving high entropy.

For the tests, the statistical test of NIST (National Institute of Standards and Technology) was used, where a good index of uniform distribution was observed in the data as well as a good frequency in the generation of sequences. This study ended with the production of TRN from a deterministic generator using a chaotic oscillatory system as a data source.

2.3   Parallel Generators

Professor L'Ecuyer et al. [7] show, methods that return a list of random numbers are useful even in a single processor configuration since they reduce function calls, which often take more time to compute. Next random number. Taking this into consideration, several authors propose and implement methods that exploit the power of parallel processing to generate random numbers at a higher speed, mainly to accelerate the generation of a single stream of sequences.

Saito and Matsumoto [14] proposed a 128-bit PRN generator adapting the MT (Mersenne Twister) [9], this method has a period length corresponding to a prime Mersenne number whose value is given by the Eq. 5.

$$M_n = 2^w - 1 \tag{5}$$

To adapt the MT they used a model oriented to SIMD (Single Instruction Multiple Data), seeking to modify the algorithm based on the Eq. 6, which corresponds to MT, so that it is compatible with the new model.

$$X_{k+n} := X_{k+m} \oplus (X_k^u | X_{k+1}^l) A, (k = 0, 1, ...) \tag{6}$$

The results showed an improvement in the sequence generation speed of MT, this was due to the fact that the algorithm did not generate calls to the PRN generator but rather generated chains in a constant way. Years later Saito and Matsumoto improved their proposal by orienting it to environments that use GPU (Graphic Processing Unit) [15], to achieve this the authors took into account the recursive nature of MT describing. The study concluded with a significant improvement in the generation speed of the algorithm compared with other parallel generation methods such as CURAND (CUDA Random Number Generator).

3   Proposal

This proposal seeks to develop a method of generating random numbers using network traffic as a chaotic model to obtain sequences of independent numbers, which are the result of processing packets that circulate through the network.

This model does not ensure that the random sequences have the statistical properties that are desired in the generation of random numbers, to solve this post-processing will be performed on the chains generated by the model, this process will use a variation of the equation described in [5] which will result in a 16-bit sequence with improved their statistical properties. In this case, we will not take into account the generation speed since the proposed model is directly linked to the existing traffic on the network.

3.1   Steps

For the procedure of obtaining random sequences, we must first make sure to obtain all the packets that pass through our network card, for this, it is necessary that our device is in promiscuous mode, in this way our computer will be able to capture all the traffic that circulates through the shared network.

Since the packets are transmitted with the physical address of the computer, the messages are received only by the computer that matches the address, this generates that the computers discard the messages that are not directed to these, the promiscuous mode avoids this comparison between physical addresses, making it possible for our computer to receive messages from the entire network.

The packet capture will be handled with PCAP (Package Capture Library), this library provides a packet capture system with a high-level interface, where each network packet is accessible through this system, this library will allow us to execute a process for each packet that it has been capturing giving us access to the *payload* of each package, being able to limit also the number of packages that we want that they are captured.

The procedure will take into consideration the *checksum* and the TTL (*Time to Life*) of each captured packet generating a 16-bit sequence. The variation of the *checksum* according to the content of the message will guarantee the independence of this with the rest of the packages that circulate through the network, in spite of this it is still possible that we meet again and again with a message that contains the same *payload* so the *checksum* might not be enough. The TTL tells us how many jumps to the destination is allowed a package before disappearing, this number will help us differentiate packages that have the same content but were launched at different times. Both values will be extracted from the IP protocol header.

For the extraction of these elements from the headers, a structure was created that emulated the storage spaces of these. The structures created were IP Header and TCP Header [12].

For the generation of random sequences, each captured packet generates a 16-bit string that represents the number obtained after the process that was applied to the packet, in this case, we will iterate an XOR function through the *payload* of each packet, this procedure will generate a number which will pass through the Eq. 7.

$$BitStream[i] = \quad (Checksum + TTL) * (p(i) + TTL) \quad mod \quad 65536 \qquad (7)$$

This equation was chosen experimentally to improve the statistical properties of the random sequence that we want to create as well as to ensure the size of the bit string. Where $p(i)$ represents the value of the *payload* in the i position. Finally, bitstreams will go through an encoding process in order to balance the amount of 0s and 1s, this process is based on *encoding* techniques used in networks *ethernet* [2], where we will replace bit frames with their equivalents to balance the occurrences of bits as seen in the example in Table 1.

It was approved the methods of *encoding* $4B5B$ and $8B10B$ to see its impact on the entropy of the chains, since each method works with blocks of different sizes, a change in normalization tests is expected.

Table 1. Example encoding table

Data (Binary)	Codes	Data (Binary)	Codes
0000	11100	1000	10010
0001	01001	1001	10011
0010	10100	1010	10110
0011	10101	1011	10111
0100	01010	1100	11010
0101	01011	1101	10011
0110	00110	1110	11100
0111	00111	1111	11001

The final result will be the concatenation of the bit sequences generated by the processing of each captured packet.

4   Test Design

Given that the proposal of a generator dependent on network traffic is linked to the environment in which we find ourselves, that is, under what conditions the process will work, it is that three possible scenarios of use for the algorithm were raised based on the density of packages that circulate in each case.

For the first environment, we propose a common domestic network where the density of data that they travel is not very high, and it depends a lot on the maximum activity peak of the users of this. This test aims to see both the feasibility of the proposed service as well as the quality of the numbers generated in environments with little traffic on the network.

The second test was carried out in the network of the University, where the peak of activity is many times higher given the number of users connected to it. Only the part intended for the use of students will be scanned, not taking into account the teachers' and administrative's network, due to restrictions as well as guarantee the use of the area with the highest level of activity.

Finally, for the last environment, it was chosen to monitor the packets that circulate through a server, in this case, the incidence of packets will depend on the positioning of the server in the middle of the network as well as the process of *routing* that the server chooses as next-hop of the messages.

The messages captured in all these environments Will be that was transported with TCP/IP protocols since the process uses specific properties of this protocol.

5 Tests and Results

Each one of the sequences of bits generated in each test passed through six proposed tests (Frequency, Frequency by Blocks, Binary Matrix, Fourier transform, Approximate Entropy, Linear Complexity). The results before and after the process of *encoding* were evaluated in order to compare the impact of the frequency balance.

In Table 2 to 7 shows the results of each of the environments tested, which show the number of values obtained from the tests by blocks as well as the percentage of chains that obtained a successful result against each of the tests.

Domestic Network. As we can see in Table 2, the domestic network presents a low proportion in the frequency tests, this may be due to the low network traffic that exists in this type of environment, circulating mostly recurrent request packages. If we compare the results after the encoding process in Table 3 we see that there was a negative impact on the pattern test (Fourier Transform) by *encoding* $8B10B$, which can mean a loss of entropy if a sufficiently large chain is generated.

Table 2. Results domestic network

C5	C6	C7	C8	C9	C10	Proportion	Test
117	76	72	64	62	81	0.208	Frequency
149	137	142	152	128	136	0.301	Frequency by Blocks
0	0	4213	0	0	0	1.0	Binary Matrix
1617	0	1788	0	942	1007	0.966	Fourier transform
29	37	60	101	237	9172	0.993	Approximate Entropy
614	0	633	0	1287	4816	0.915	Linear Complexity

Table 3. Results domestic network (*encoding*)

C5	C6	C7	C8	C9	C10	Proportion	Test
0	0	0	0	331	11952	1.0	Frequency
0	0	0	0	0	12283	1.0	Frequency by Blocks
0	0	6949	0	0	0	1.0	Binary Matrix
1382	0	1201	0	484	711	0.87	Fourier transform
27	37	42	77	120	11820	0.995	Approximate Entropy
782	0	735	0	1544	6001	0.914	Linear Complexity

As in the previous case, we can see how post-processing generates a certain drop in the Fourier Transform Test, this may have something to do with the way network is used. We can not rule out that just as in the Domestic Network there is entropy loss with wider chains.

5.1   University Network

Table 4. Results university network

C5	C6	C7	C8	C9	C10	Proportion	Test
658	409	371	368	419	479	0.159	Frequency
807	670	639	524	461	401	0.226	Frequency by Blocks
0	0	17110	0	0	0	1.0	Binary Matrix
12274	0	14024	0	7213	7336	0.947	Fourier transform
1809	2120	2608	3432	5619	53497	0.966	Approximate Entropy
4817	0	4923	0	9683	39147	0.901	Linear Complexity

Table 5. Results university network *encoding*

C5	C6	C7	C8	C9	C10	Proportion	Test
0	0	0	0	3180	96727	1.0	Frequency
0	0	0	0	0	99907	1.0	Frequency by Blocks
0	0	51141	0	0	0	1.0	Binary Matrix
9690	0	8909	0	3434	4895	0.842	Fourier transform
1106	1306	1693	2237	3844	83978	0.985	Approximate Entropy
6313	0	6024	0	12185	48896	0.902	Linear Complexity

5.2   Network Server

As expected, the results in Tables 6 and 7 show us that the ideal environment for our algorithm is the network of a server, due to the diversity of packages that circulate through it. We must bear in mind, that even without encoding, the tests of patterns and entropy have a rate of more than enough, on the other hand, the tests of frequencies are those that in all the tests saw more benefit.

Table 6. Results network server

C5	C6	C7	C8	C9	C10	Proportion	Test
2241	1427	1482	1526	1529	1955	0.384	Frequency
1797	1303	885	604	454	318	0.524	Frequency by Blocks
0	0	41939	0	0	0	1.0	Binary Matrix
1617	0	1788	0	942	1007	0.966	Fourier transform
1740	1674	1760	1976	2741	78340	0.998	Approximate Entropy
5931	0	5899	0	11793	47467	0.919	Linear Complexity

Table 7. Results network server *encoding*

C5	C6	C7	C8	C9	C10	Proportion	Test
0	0	0	0	3203	115774	1.0	Frequency
0	0	0	0	0	118977	1.0	Frequency by Blocks
0	0	63241	0	0	0	1.0	Binary Matrix
12681	0	11757	0	4831	6780	0.875	Fourier transform
596	784	983	1310	2059	111623	0.999	Approximate Entropy
7459	0	7589	0	14868	58638	0.916	Linear Complexity

5.3   Comparison

The proposed method was contrasted with some algorithms implemented within the C ++ STD library such as the *Lehmer random number generator* also known as MinStd [13] , the *Mersenne Twister* [9] and the Ranlux [3], all these processes were examined with the same set of tests with chains of the same size resulting in the Fig. 1, we can observe how the *encoding* processes provide a distribution uniform appearance of bits since normalization tests are highly successful, on the other hand, the fact of carrying out this process negatively affects the entropy of the chains, this tells us that the chains that went through the process $8B10B$ experience a degradation in its randomness factor.

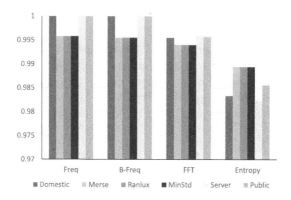

Fig. 1. Comparison with C++ STD library methods

As mentioned before, there may be a degradation in the entropy according to the longer sequences, to check this effectively we generate a point map with the results of each generator where each point will be the combination of two numbers generated by the methods. When carrying out this process and analyzing the results Fig. 2 we can realize that although the process of *encoding* has been used to standardize the chains, it has also given a characteristic pattern to the methods, generating specific groups in which can drop a generated number. On the other hand, the data generated without post-processing show a good result with some accumulations of points in certain sectors that is quite similar to the graphics generated by the methods of the C ++ library.

Although there is such a defined pattern in the generated sequences that went through the $8B10B$ the statistical tests gave us acceptable results, this may mean that even though the chains are uniform, the entire data flow will be affected, so It is expected that tests such as entropy will reduce their value as more data are generated.

Since the degenerative pattern does not occur in the series that were not processed by *encoding*, this would mean that the method itself does not require post-processing, which may be the result of using the equation of the modified LCG.

Given that the best results in both the mapping and the statistical tests were those of the network in a server, it can be said that the most appropriate environment for the method to be executed is that of the last experiment. Taking into account that the numbers are directly linked to the messages of the network, a server with a flow of repetitive messages will not obtain as good results as one that serves as a bridge for different types of messages.

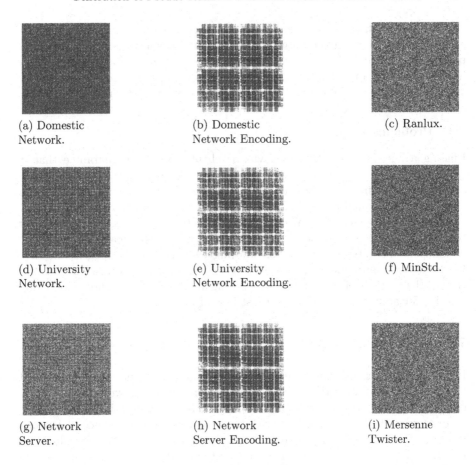

(a) Domestic
Network.

(b) Domestic
Network Encoding.

(c) Ranlux.

(d) University
Network.

(e) University
Network Encoding.

(f) MinStd.

(g) Network
Server.

(h) Network
Server Encoding.

(i) Mersenne
Twister.

Fig. 2. Map of generated points.

6   Discussion

The proposal to use network traffic as a generator of pseudo-random sequences
is viable, given that the generated chains are quite different from each other, this
gives us a high index of independence between results, this being the strong point
of the generator. In spite of this, aspects like the proportion in the frequency
of appearance of bits are not so good, we tried to improve this characteristic
using post-processing, which resulted in a degradation of entropy. The results
are given by this process of *encoding* are more typical of quasi-random systems,
where the spectrum of numbers generated is more controlled.

It has been proven that the network has a chaotic behavior in terms of packet
traffic since the entropy between data without post-processing is quite high, this
does not mean that there is no repetition in the packets, there are many cases
in which a package can be repeated.

The sum of all these cases of multiple shipments and packet repetition generates a chaos factor in the network since it is unknown what will be the next package to go through our generator. As shown in the Tables 6 and 7, even in crowded environments, the percentage of successful sequences in the Fourier Transform test is not 100%, so there are packet emission patterns.

6.1   Problems Found

Finding a data source whose behavior is chaotic does not guarantee that it will provide us with numbers with the statistical properties necessary to be considered random. Checking these characteristics is of great importance, given that the results found can define whether post-processing is required.

When working with such specific objects as network packets, it was necessary to extract certain characteristics that were changing with each issue as well as independent between packets, so working with common aspects of message headers is not recommended. Since the generator works according to network traffic, the generation speed is not a strong point of this method, not being suitable for activities that require a fast flow of numbers.

7   Conclusions

Different methods of random generators were analyzed in order to understand the processes that gave them their statistical properties, as well as to find the category to which this new proposal belongs. The generators based on chaotic systems were the most consistent with the model we proposed since it depends a lot on the type of protocol used in the network as well as the volume of information. These factors can be used as initial conditions so a system Chaotic could be the most correct use.

An algorithm for obtaining random sequences was designed using network traffic as a supply of chains, it was decided to use libraries that would allow us to access the packages' payload. The method proved to have its strong point in the entropy generated by using the network as a data source and failing in string frequency tests, to try to solve this a method of string encoding was used in order to balance the number of bits, which resulted in the creation of patterns that directly affected the chaotic factor of the method.

A comparison of methods used in standard libraries was made to test the effectiveness of the method, the tests carried out showed that the process complies with certain statistical properties of current random generators and failing in others. Part of these tests showed that generators that use chaotic systems tended to have a normalized frequency of occurrence, that is, the repetition of numbers is similar for all chains. Likewise, these chaotic methods do not have entropy along with the frequency tests, which is because the chaotic system remains a deterministic form of calculation.

There are more tests of pseudo-random number generating models that focus on other aspects of the bit string, such as block overlap or asymmetric models

[16]. The next step would be to extend the range of tests of the algorithm. The post-processing designs to stabilize the frequencies.

References

1. Blanchard, P., Guerraoui, R., Stainer, J., Antoniadis, K.: Concurrency as a random number generator technical report. Technical report (2016)
2. Chen, Y., Wang, T.X., Katz, R.H.: Energy efficient ethernet encodings. In: 33rd IEEE Conference on Local Computer Networks, LCN 2008, pp. 122–129. IEEE (2008)
3. Dąbrowska-Boruch, A., Gancarczyk, G., Wiatr, K.: Implementation of a RANLUX based pseudo-random number generator in FPGA using VHDL and impulse C. Comput. Inf. **32**(6), 1272–1292 (2014)
4. Dörre, F., Klebanov, V.: Practical detection of entropy loss in pseudo-random number generators. In: Proceedings of the 2016 ACM SIGSAC Conference on Computer and Communications Security, pp. 678–689. ACM (2016)
5. Hamdi, M., Rhouma, R., Belghith, S.: A very efficient pseudo-random number generator based on chaotic maps and s-box tables. Int. J. Comput. Electron. Autom. Control Inf. Eng. **9**(2), 481–485 (2015)
6. Hu, H., Liu, L., Ding, N.: Pseudorandom sequence generator based on the chen chaotic system. Comput. Phys. Commun. **184**(3), 765–768 (2013)
7. L'Ecuyer, P., Munger, D., Oreshkin, B., Simard, R.: Random numbers for parallel computers: requirements and methods, with emphasis on GPUS. Math. Comput. Simul. **135**, 3–17 (2017)
8. Lo Re, G., Milazzo, F., Ortolani, M.: Secure random number generation in wireless sensor networks. Concurrency Comput. Pract. Experience **27**(15), 3842–3862 (2015)
9. Matsumoto, M., Nishimura, T.: Mersenne twister: a 623-dimensionally equidistributed uniform pseudo-random number generator. ACM Trans. Model. Comput. Simul. (TOMACS) **8**(1), 3–30 (1998)
10. Müller, S.: Linux random number generator-a new approach (2017)
11. Park, M., Rodgers, J.C., Lathrop, D.P.: True random number generation using cmos boolean chaotic oscillator. Microelectron. J. **46**(12), 1364–1370 (2015)
12. Parkhurst, W.R.: Routing first-step. Cisco Press (2004)
13. Payne, W., Rabung, J.R., Bogyo, T.: Coding the lehmer pseudo-random number generator. Commun. ACM **12**(2), 85–86 (1969)
14. Saito, M., Matsumoto, M.: SIMD-oriented fast mersenne twister: a 128-bit pseudorandom number generator. In: Monte Carlo and Quasi-Monte Carlo Methods 2006, pp. 607–622. Springer, Berlin (2008)
15. Saito, M., Matsumoto, M.: Variants of mersenne twister suitable for graphic processors. ACM Trans. Math. Softw. (TOMS) **39**(2), 12 (2013)
16. Santisteban, J., Tejada-Cárcamo, J.: Unilateral jaccard similarity coefficient. In: GSB@ SIGIR, pp. 23–27 (2015)
17. Short, K.M.: Steps toward unmasking secure communications. Int. J. Bifurcat. Chaos **4**(04), 959–977 (1994)
18. Vajargah, B.F., Asghari, R.: A pseudo random number generator based on chaotic henon map (CHCG). IJMEC **5**(15), 2026–37 (2015)
19. Vajargah, B.F., Asghari, R.: A novel pseudo-random number generator for cryptographic applications. Indian J. Sci. Technol. **9**(6), 1–5 (2016)

Author Index

Printed in the United States
By Bookmasters